THE VICTORIA HISTORY
OF THE
COUNTIES OF ENGLAND

—

A HISTORY OF
SHROPSHIRE

VOLUME III

THE VICTORIA HISTORY
OF THE
COUNTIES OF ENGLAND

EDITED BY C. R. ELRINGTON

DIEU ET MON DROIT

THE UNIVERSITY OF LONDON
INSTITUTE OF
HISTORICAL RESEARCH

Oxford University Press, Walton Street, Oxford OX2 6DP

OXFORD LONDON GLASGOW
NEW YORK TORONTO MELBOURNE WELLINGTON
KUALA LUMPUR SINGAPORE JAKARTA HONG KONG TOKYO
DELHI BOMBAY CALCUTTA MADRAS KARACHI
IBADAN NAIROBI DAR ES SALAAM CAPE TOWN

© *University of London 1979*

ISBN 0 19 722730 9

PRINTED IN GREAT BRITAIN BY
ROBERT MACLEHOSE AND CO. LTD
PRINTERS TO THE UNIVERSITY OF GLASGOW

STAFFORDSHIRE
COUNTY
LIBRARY

A -4. OCT. 1979

C 942 . 45

INSCRIBED TO THE

MEMORY OF HER LATE MAJESTY

QUEEN VICTORIA

WHO GRACIOUSLY GAVE THE TITLE TO

AND ACCEPTED THE DEDICATION

OF THIS HISTORY

Thomas Telford (1757–1834)
Shropshire's first county surveyor (1788–1834), with elevations of St. Mary Magdalen's, Bridgnorth (1792), and a bridge

A HISTORY OF

SHROPSHIRE

EDITED BY G. C. BAUGH

VOLUME III

PUBLISHED FOR

THE INSTITUTE OF HISTORICAL RESEARCH

BY

OXFORD UNIVERSITY PRESS

1979

Distributed by Oxford University Press until 1 January 1982
thereafter by Dawsons of Pall Mall

CONTENTS OF VOLUME THREE

LIST OF ILLUSTRATIONS

For permission to reproduce material in their copyright, custody, or possession and for the loan of prints, thanks are offered to Aerofilms Ltd., the Rt. Hon. the Earl of Bradford, the British Library, Mrs. W. H. Butler, Clive House Museum, the Courtauld Institute of Art, the Vicar of Kinlet (the Revd. R. Heywood-Waddington), Sir Michael Leighton, Bt., Mr. Jasper More, M.P., Mrs. Jasper More, the National Trust, the Salop Club, the Chief Executive of the Borough of Shrewsbury and Atcham (Mr. L. C. W. Beesley), the Shrewsbury Public Library, the Shropshire Record Office, the *Shropshire Star*, and Mr. S. R. Turner. The plate facing page 96 is reproduced by permission of the Controller of H.M. Stationery Office (Crown Copyright reserved).

LIST OF MAPS

The maps were drawn by K. J. Wass, of the Department of Geography, University College, London, that on page 40 from a draft by G. C. Baugh, the others from drafts by D. C. Cox.

EDITORIAL NOTE

VOLUME III is the fourth volume of the *Victoria History of Shropshire* to be published, and the third since the revival of the project outlined in the Editorial Note to Volume VIII (1968). The partnership there described between the Salop County Council and the University of London has continued. Major General the Viscount Bridgeman, K.B.E., C.B., D.S.O., M.C., remained Chairman of the sub-committee appointed to superintend those arrangements until 1974. In that year, in consequence of the local-government reorganization which then took effect, local responsibility for the Shropshire *History* passed to the new County Council's Leisure Activities Committee, which devolved supervision on an advisory sub-committee; Mrs. D. I. P. Gask, O.B.E., Chairman of the committee until 1977, was also Chairman of the sub-committee until 1976 when she was succeeded by Mrs. N. B. Hodgson. In 1977 Mr. V. M. E. Holt became Chairman of the Leisure Activities Committee and of a new advisory board which, for the purposes of the *History*, replaced the sub-committee that year. The University would like to express its thanks once more to the County Council for its continued support.

There has been no change in the local editorial staff since the publication of Volume II (1973), Mr. G. C. Baugh remaining County Editor, Dr. D. C. Cox Assistant County Editor. The death in 1974 of Mr. A. T. Gaydon, County Editor from 1961 to 1971, is recorded with great regret.

Many people have helped in the preparation of this volume. Several are acknowledged in the list of illustrations and in the footnotes to the articles on which their help was given. Here, however, special thanks are rendered to the staff of the Shropshire Record Office under Miss M. C. Hill and Mrs. L. B. Halford, successive County Archivists. Generous assistance was given by the staff of the Shropshire County Library, in particular Mr. A. M. Carr and the local-studies staff of the Shrewsbury Public Library. Special thanks are also due to Sir Michael Leighton, Bt., who facilitated the use of his family papers at Loton Park; to the staff of the Department of Manuscripts and Records at the National Library of Wales; and to Mr. J. B. Lawson, Shrewsbury School Librarian.

The *General Introduction* to the *History* (1970) outlines the structure and aims of the series as a whole.

LIST OF CLASSES OF DOCUMENTS
IN THE PUBLIC RECORD OFFICE
USED IN THIS VOLUME
WITH THEIR CLASS NUMBERS

SELECT LIST OF ACCUMULATIONS AND COLLECTIONS IN THE SHROPSHIRE RECORD OFFICE

USED IN THIS VOLUME

NOTE ON ABBREVIATIONS

Among the abbreviations and short titles used the following may require elucidation:

Arch. Camb.	Cambrian Archaeological Association, *Archaeologia Cambrensis*
B.L.	British Library
B.M.	British Museum
Blakeway, *Sheriffs*	J. B. Blakeway, *The Sheriffs of Shropshire* (Shrewsbury, 1831)
Cart. Shrews.	*The Cartulary of Shrewsbury Abbey*, ed. Una Rees (National Library of Wales; 2 vols., Aberystwyth, 1975)
Cranage	D. H. S. Cranage, *An Architectural Account of the Churches of Shropshire* (Wellington; 2 vols., 1901 and 1912, published in 10 parts, 1894–1912). Cited by part.
Dict. Welsh Biog.	*The Dictionary of Welsh Biography down to 1940* (Honourable Society of Cymmrodorion; 1959 edn.)
Eyton	R. W. Eyton, *Antiquities of Shropshire* (12 vols., 1854–60)
Hughes, *Sheriffs*	W. Hughes, *The Sheriffs of Shropshire, 1831 to 1886* (Shrewsbury, 1886)
Huntington Libr.	Huntington Library, San Marino, California
Montg. Coll.	*The Montgomeryshire Collections: Journal of the Powysland Club*
N.L.W.	National Library of Wales, Aberystwyth
Orders of Q. Sess.	*Abstract of the Orders made by the Court of Quarter Sessions for Shropshire*, ed. R. Ll. Kenyon and Sir Offley Wakeman (Shropshire County Records nos. 2–5, 7, 9, 11–17 [Shrewsbury, 1901–16])
Owen and Blakeway, *Hist. Shrews.*	H. Owen and J. B. Blakeway, *A History of Shrewsbury* (2 vols., 1825)
R.O.	Record Office
S.C.C.	Salop County Council
S.C.C. Mins.	*Salop County Council Reports and Minutes*
S.H.C.	Staffordshire Record Society (formerly William Salt Archaeological Society), *Collections for a History of Staffordshire*
S.P.L.	Shrewsbury Public Library
S.P.R.	*Shropshire Parish Registers*
S.R.O.	Shropshire Record Office
Salop. N. & Q.	*Shropshire Notes & Queries*
Salop. Peace Roll, 1400–14	*The Shropshire Peace Roll, 1400–1414*, ed. Elisabeth G. Kimball (Salop County Council, 1959)
T.S.A.S.	*Transactions of the Shropshire Archaeological Society*
Visit. Salop. 1623	*The Visitation of Shropshire, taken in the Year 1623* (Harleian Society, xxviii–xxix, 1889)

COUNTY GOVERNMENT
IN THE EARLY MIDDLE AGES

SHROPSHIRE'S position, facing the hostile Welsh across an ill-defined and shifting frontier, determined the character of its government in the early Middle Ages more strongly than did anything else. In time of peace the universal problem of crime was aggravated in Shropshire by the impossibility of arresting criminals who fled to Wales. The peculiar difficulty was such that the men of Shropshire successfully disclaimed those communal methods of keeping the peace that were enforced by the Crown in most of England, experimenting instead with locally devised alternatives. Until Edward I's conquest of Wales the ever-present threat of war on Shropshire's western border determined the Crown's choice of men to be set over the county as earls, local justiciars, or sheriffs. It determined, too, the degree of privilege allowed to such men as reward and support for their special part in the defence of the kingdom. The privileges accorded to the Norman earls of Shrewsbury were such as to make the earldom itself a danger to the kingdom, and the earldom was accordingly abolished in 1102. Its 'palatine' status was nevertheless recalled in 1307, when the inhabitants claimed privileges said to have been granted to them in the time of the earls.[1]

From the 12th century local administrators everywhere were increasingly made answerable to the Crown, and Shropshire shared in the gradual dispersal of administrative responsibility to the knightly class. The thegns who attended the Shropshire shire court in Edward the Confessor's reign[2] were the same kind of men as Ralph le Botiler and the 'other knights' who sat with the sheriff in the same court in Edward I's reign.[3] The regular shire courts had been for centuries the institutional expression of county society, then called the 'community' (*communitas*)[4] of the county. As with all institutions the busiest and most respected members of the shire court found themselves the spokesmen of that community. In 1341 it was said of three Shropshire knights that they were among the 'wisest and greatest of estate and lordship of the county' and that the 'commons' of the county would not dare oppose them.[5] What happened in the late 12th and 13th centuries was that the Crown tried to increase the efficiency of local administration without allowing more power to accumulate in the sheriff's hands; the Crown created new administrative responsibilities and diffused them among the representatives of the county community, while existing responsibilities were taken from the sheriff and similarly dispersed. Thus the representatives of the county community became also the county's administrative class, the men whom Bracton called *buzones*.[6]

By the end of the 13th century it is possible to discern two local administrative

---

[1] J.I. 1/746 rot. 1(3). This is the earliest example of the term 'palatine' so far noted in connexion with Shropshire.

[2] Florence E. Harmer, 'A Bromfield and a Coventry Writ of King Edw. the Confessor', *The Anglo-Saxons*, ed. P. Clemoes (1959), 90–8, 101–2.

[3] J.I. 1/745 rot. 2.

[4] J.I. 1/746 rot. 1(3).

[5] S.C. 1/28 no. 149 (for the date see *Rot. Parl.* ii. 131). Thanks are due to Dr. J. R. Maddicott for this ref.

[6] G. T. Lapsley, *Crown, Community, and Parliament in the later Middle Ages* (1951), 108.

classes. The higher supplied such officers as keepers of the peace and commissioners of array, from the lower came county coroners and subescheators. Those classes in turn fostered lower classes who supplied their deputies and clerks. There was no strict demarcation between the administrative classes, but a career such as that of Sir John FitzEyre (d. *c.* 1293),[7] who filled nearly every office from subescheator to knight of the shire,[8] was exceptional. The coherence of the higher administrative class in 13th-century Shropshire may be illustrated from the example of the tax commissioners. From at least 1194[9] the occasional assessment and collection of taxes on movables was often entrusted to small *ad hoc* panels of county commissioners. Of 31 known Shropshire tax commissioners between 1225 and 1322,[10] eleven occur in Shropshire at other times as knights of the shire,[11] at least eight as assize or gaol-delivery justices,[12] six as sheriffs,[13] six as keepers of the peace,[14] six or more as commissioners of array,[15] at least three as coroners,[16] and at least two as subescheators.[17] Of the 31 no more than nine are unknown in any of those other capacities, whereas at least thirteen occur in more than one of them.

From Shropshire's creation in the early 10th century until the later Middle Ages the boundaries of the county underwent a succession of important changes. Alterations between the early 10th century and Domesday Book reflected territory won from or lost to the Welsh. Domesday shows the considerable Welsh estates, not hidated, that had been added to Shropshire in that period. It does not, however, show what English, hidated, estates may have been lost to Wales. Along much of the border Offa's Dyke seems to have been the western limit of Shropshire's English territory in 1086. There was, however, some territory in Welsh hands east of the dyke in the district where the Deuddwr and Gorddwr commots met, while in the Montgomery area there was English, hidated, territory west of the dyke.[18] After 1086 and probably before 1102 a large area was transferred to Shropshire on its south-eastern boundary, for tenurial reasons,[19] and for the same reasons part of Halesowen, which lay detached from Shropshire, was transferred to the county from Worcestershire in the same period.[20]

By 1200 most of the Welsh, unhidated, territories of Domesday Shropshire had been lost to Wales.[21] Further losses resulted from the creation during the 12th and 13th centuries of a number of semi-independent lordships from lands on the western limits of Shropshire.[22] After Edward I's conquest of Wales those lordships ceased to be useful to the Crown. On the contrary they then presented an obstacle to the economic and constitutional integration of Wales with England, and were a source of rebellions and a refuge for criminals.[23] The lordships were abolished in Henry VIII's reign and most of those formerly in Shropshire were reunited with it;[24] the lordships of Montgomery and

[7] Eyton, i. 206.

[8] Ibid. i. 205; ix. 314; J.I. 1/739 rot. 47; *Cal. Pat.* 1281–92, 265; *T.S.A.S.* 4th ser. x. 8.

[9] S. K. Mitchell, *Taxation in Medieval Eng.* (1951), 65.

[10] Ibid. 82; *Cal. Pat.* 1232–47, 18, 551; 1266–71, 419; 1292–1301, 104, 299, 612; 1307–13, 23, 185; 1313–17, 50, 324, 474, 530; 1317–21, 348, 380; 1321–4, 224; *Cal. Close,* 1272–9, 251; 1313–18, 188; Eyton, ix. 314.

[11] *T.S.A.S.* 4th ser. x. 8.

[12] *Cal. Pat.* 1225–32, 207, 222–3, 523; 1281–92, 9, 286; *Cal. Close,* 1237–42, 437; 1279–88, 269, 365, 395; Eyton, i. 205.

[13] *List of Sheriffs* (P.R.O. Lists & Indexes, ix; corrected reprint 1963), 117.

[14] *Cal. Pat.* 1281–92, 265; 1292–1301, 517; 1307–13, 31, 54, 204, 328; 1313–17, 108, 123, 482; 1317–21, 289, 460.

[15] Ibid. 1292–1301, 313, 437, 593; 1307–13, 82; 1313–17, 351; *Cal. Close,* 1296–1302, 373, 571.

[16] *Cal. Close,* 1231–4, 66; 1247–51, 69; J.I. 1/739 rot. 47.

[17] *Cal. Close,* 1231–4, 130; *Cal. Fine R.* 1272–1307, 2.

[18] C. Fox, *Offa's Dyke* (1955), pls. XI, XVIII, XXIII; *Dom. Geog. of Midland Eng.* ed. H. C. Darby and I. B. Terrett (1971), 158–61; Wm. Rees, *Hist. Atlas of Wales* (1972), pl. 28; H. C. Darby and G. R. Versey, *Domesday Gazetteer* (1975), maps 40–1; H. C. Darby, *Domesday Eng.* (1977), 329–30. These sources were used for the map on p. 8. Also used were Eyton, *passim*; *V.C.H. Salop.* i–ii, viii; R. Morgan, 'Trewern in Gorddwr: Domesday manor and knight's fief, 1086–1311', *Montg. Coll.* lxiv. 121–32; *Cat. Anct. D.* vi. C 4536 (locates 'Conditre' in Walton).

[19] See p. 43.

[20] *V.C.H. Salop.* i. 348 n.

[21] Rees, *Atlas,* pl. 38.

[22] See pp. 34–42.

[23] Wm. Rees, *Union of Eng. and Wales* (1967), 8–10.

[24] See p. 41.

Wigmore, however, were assigned to Montgomeryshire and Herefordshire respectively.[25] At the same period the uncertain status of Bewdley, on the Worcestershire border, which had afforded another refuge for criminals, was settled when the town was formally assigned to Worcestershire.[26]

There were only slight changes before the 19th century,[27] and few thereafter.[28] The Shropshire part of Halesowen was restored to Worcestershire in 1844.[29] The county magistrates pressed for a great enlargement of Shropshire's area to coincide with the local-government reorganization of 1888–9, but without success.[30] Under the 1972–4 reorganization, in which some counties were divided or amalgamated and others created, Shropshire's boundaries were not affected.

In 1974 its name was fixed for official purposes as Salop.[31] In medieval documents the abbreviated form *Salop'* often stood for the Normanized form of the town's name, *Salopesberia*,[32] which had presumably originated in the difficulty for French speakers of pronouncing the Old English name, 'Scrobbesbyrig'. That *Salop'* could also stand for *Salopescira*, the Normanized form of the county's name,[33] is suggested by the fact that the archdeaconry of *Salop'* in Hereford diocese, so called as early as 1219,[34] excluded Shrewsbury.[35] The Latin form *Salopia*, current by the 16th century,[36] may have been an elegant variation devised by medieval clerks and does not necessarily betoken a contemporary use of Salop in spoken English.[37] It may nevertheless be surmised that during the Middle Ages, as the use of French declined, the form Salop came to be understood by English speakers not as an abbreviation of the obsolescent Normanized forms but as an alternative English name for both county and town.[38]

The Anglo-Saxon Shire

The document known as the County Hidage, to which a 10th-century or early-11th-century date is usually assigned,[39] gives the first complete outline of the shire system of English Mercia: each shire is named after a town and, except for Herefordshire and Staffordshire, has 1,200 hides or a multiple of that number.[40] The system thus described originated in the military arrangements made in the late 9th and early 10th centuries for Mercian operations against the Scandinavian armies in England. Those operations date from the assumption of power in Mercia by the ealdorman Æthelred, King Alfred's ally and son-in-law, who had replaced the Danish nominee, King Ceolwulf, as ruler of Mercia by 883.[41] With his wife Æthelflæd, Æthelred had fortified Worcester by 899.[42] By 902 Æthelred may have been incapacitated by illness. Until his death in 911 Æthelflæd seems to have been the effective ruler of English Mercia. In 907 she restored the defences of Chester, described under 893 as a 'deserted city'.[43] In 911 she became sole ruler of English Mercia, and before her death in 918 had built several burhs, including Stafford (913) and Warwick (914).[44] Of the other three shire towns of

[25] Rees, *Union*, map facing p. 8.
[26] See p. 71.
[27] e.g. Act for uniting whole of Bucknell to Salop., 1554, 1 & 2 Phil. & Mary, c. 19 (Original Act).
[28] See *V.C.H. Salop.* ii. 204.
[29] Ibid. 204, 223.
[30] See p. 166.
[31] Local Govt. Act, 1972, c. 70, sched. 1.
[32] E. Ekwall, *Concise Oxf. Dict. Eng. Place-Names* (1960), 420.
[33] Ibid. 421.
[34] *Cartulary of Shrews. Abbey*, ed. Una Rees (1976), ii, p. 313.
[35] *V.C.H. Salop.* ii. 3.
[36] Leland, *Itin.* ed. Toulmin Smith, ii. 82.

[37] Ex inf. Dr. Margaret Gelling. Thanks are due to Dr. Gelling for advice during preparation of this para.
[38] By a similar, but not identical, process Salisbury acquired by the 13th cent. the spoken and written form Sarum: *V.C.H. Wilts.* vi. 93–4.
[39] C. Hart, *Hidation of Northants.* (Leicester Univ. Dept. of Eng. Local Hist., Occ. Papers, 2nd ser. iii), 14, 45; F. M. Stenton, *Preparatory to Anglo-Saxon Eng.: being the Collected Papers* (1970), 198–9.
[40] F. W. Maitland, *Dom. Bk. and Beyond* (1897), 456.
[41] F. M. Stenton, *A.-S. Eng.* (1971), 259–60.
[42] *Eng. Hist. Doc.* i, ed. Dorothy Whitelock, p. 498.
[43] Ibid. p. 187.
[44] F. T. Wainwright, 'Æthelflæd Lady of the Mercians', *Anglo-Saxons*, ed. Clemoes, 53–69.

English Mercia Hereford had been fortified since at least the 9th century and Gloucester still had its Roman walls;[45] both were described as garrisoned places in 914.[46] Shrewsbury was almost certainly fortified by 901. A charter of that year records a grant made 'in civitate Scrobbensis',[47] which looks like a Latin form of 'Scrobbesbyrig', the form first recorded in 1006.[48] The element *byrig* implies fortifications.[49]

Thus by 914 all the shire towns of English Mercia appear to have been fortified. The Wessex document known as the Burghal Hidage[50] shows, if its provisions are applied to Mercia, that each such town was defended by a fixed number of men drawn from the surrounding shire in direct proportion to the number of hides in the shire. The Burghal Hidage cannot be dated in its surviving form more closely than to the reign of Edward the Elder, 899–924.[51] The burhs in the main part of the document are in Wessex, but an appendix *c.* 915 × *c.* 924[52] includes Warwick (with 2,400 hides) and Worcester (with 1,200). Presumably, therefore, the regular shire system of English Mercia was completed in the early 10th century.

The earliest clear information, that of the County Hidage, suggests that 2,400 hides were deemed necessary for the defence of Shrewsbury.[53] By the 10th century the hide denoted an area of land of recognized value, a hide of good land being smaller in area than one of poor land.[54] The area of Shropshire was thus fixed within fairly narrow limits by the number of hides needed to defend Shrewsbury. The shape of the county was determined by several considerations. On the west the Welsh border fixed the boundary. On the east the eastern boundaries of the ancient border provinces of the Magonsæte and the Wreocensæte were preserved.[55] On the north the southern border of Cheshire, a shire whose 1,200 hides were confined on the west, north, and east by ancient provincial boundaries,[56] fixed Shropshire's limit. Given that Shropshire's north, east, and west boundaries were determined by those of adjoining areas, the line of its southern boundary was determined by the need to mark off the southern limit of 2,400 hides; it is probable that the line was drawn between existing estates or blocks of estates to avoid splitting them between shires.[57] To the south of Shropshire was left the remnant, some 1,500 hides,[58] of the province of the Magonsæte,[59] which became Herefordshire.[60] Because of the practical considerations that dictated Shropshire's original boundary, the hidage that it enclosed could only approximate to the hidage prescribed by the west Mercian scheme. In order to achieve the prescribed hidage it was necessary soon afterwards for persons with local knowledge to adjust the hidage of every estate in the shire.[61] That was presumably done at an assembly representative of all its parts. Thus the existence of a shire court, even if a rudimentary one, may be

[45] *Plans and Topography of Medieval Towns in Eng. and Wales*, ed. M. W. Barley (1975), 20–1, 23–5.

[46] *Eng. Hist. Doc.* i, p. 194.

[47] P. H. Sawyer, *A.-S. Charters* (R. Hist. Soc. 1968), no. 221, and edns. there cited.

[48] Ekwall, *Dict. Eng. P.-N.* 421.

[49] A. H. Smith, *Eng. Place-Name Elements* (E.P.N.S.), i. 58–62.

[50] D. Hill, 'The Burghal Hidage: the Establishment of a Text', *Medieval Arch.* xiii. 84–92.

[51] J. Tait, *Medieval Eng. Borough* (1936), 15–18; Stenton, *A.-S. Eng.* 265.

[52] N. Brooks, 'The Unidentified Forts of the Burghal Hidage', *Medieval Arch.* viii. 88; Stenton, *A.-S. Eng.* 646 n.

[53] Maitland, *Dom. Bk. and Beyond*, 456. Tait suggested an original assessment of 3,200 hides: *V.C.H. Salop.* i. 280–1.

[54] Maitland, op. cit. 464–6; D. C. Cox, 'The Vale Estates of the Church of Evesham', *Vale of Evesham Hist. Soc. Research Papers*, v. 29.

[55] *T.S.A.S.* lvii. 157–9; C. Hart, 'The Tribal Hidage', *Trans. R.H.S.* 5th ser. xxi. 137, 139–41; Wendy E. Davies and H. Vierck, 'Contexts of Tribal Hidage: Social Aggregates and Settlement Patterns', *Frühmittelalterliche Studien*, viii. 230–1.

[56] *Trans. R.H.S.* 5th ser. xxi. 137, 141.

[57] The SE. boundary of Worcs. was so drawn: C. S. Taylor, 'Origin of Mercian Shires', *Glos. Studies*, ed. H. P. R. Finberg (1957), 35–40; *Vale of Evesham Hist. Soc. Res. Papers*, v. 30.

[58] Maitland, *Dom. Bk. and Beyond*, 456.

[59] On the boundaries of the Magonsæte see: *Trans. R.H.S.* 5th ser. xxi. 137, 139–41; H. P. R. Finberg, *Early Charters of W. Midlands* (1972), p. 226; *Frühmittelalterliche Studien*, viii. 231, 238.

[60] On the original boundaries of Herefs. see: *V.C.H. Herefs.* i. 264, 266; *Dom. Geog. of Midland Eng.* 67; Finberg, *Early Charters of W. Midlands*, pp. 226–7; *P.N. Glos.* (E.P.N.S.), iv. 32 n.

[61] There is evidence of systematic apportionment: *V.C.H. Salop.* i. 284–5.

supposed from the beginning. By 1086 Shropshire's hidage assessment had been lowered to some 1,438 hides.[62]

Shropshire, lying within the province of Mercia, might be presumed to have been subject to the ealdormen, later to the earls, of Mercia. In the 11th century, however, earldoms consisting of single shires or small groups of shires were sometimes separated from the greater provinces,[63] and it is possible that Shropshire and Herefordshire formed, or were part of, such an earldom in the Confessor's reign. The only surviving pre-Conquest writ relating to Shropshire, datable to the period between Christmas 1060 and Easter 1061, is addressed to Archbishop Ealdred (who was then administering the see of Hereford), an unidentified Bishop 'Begard', Earl Harold, and all the king's thegns in Herefordshire and Shropshire. It concerns a royal grant of judicial rights to Bromfield minster,[64] which in 1086 lay in Shropshire near the Herefordshire border.[65] It is to be noted that Ælfgar, earl of Mercia from 1057 to at least 1062,[66] is not addressed and presumably exercised no authority in Shropshire at the date of the writ.[67] It thus seems likely that Harold's earldom included both Herefordshire and Shropshire. Harold Godwinson, earl of Wessex, had inherited on Earl Raulf's death in 1057 an earldom that included Herefordshire and Oxfordshire. Raulf's earldom appears to have been created by a partition of the earldom created c. 1050 for Swein Godwinson[68] (d. 1052),[69] which included Somerset, Berkshire, Oxfordshire, Gloucestershire, and Herefordshire,[70] and perhaps Shropshire too. Thus, from at least c. 1050 until Harold's accession as king in 1066, Shropshire may have been included in earldoms separated from that of Mercia. It is possible, indeed, that Shropshire was before that subject to Earl Hrani, who occurs from 1018 to 1041, and whose earldom included Herefordshire.[71] Under 1041 he is described as earl of the Magonsæte,[72] much of whose former province is known to have been in Shropshire.[73]

In the 10th century ealdormen sometimes presided personally over shire courts, as the law required,[74] and even over hundred courts.[75] In the 11th century, however, the earls were more often preoccupied with national politics, and the sheriff, appointed by the king in each shire, became more prominent.[76] No Shropshire sheriff is known by name before 1066, but some of the sheriff's concerns are revealed in the Shropshire folios of Domesday Book. The pre-Conquest sheriff of Shropshire seems to have had greater responsibilities than some. As in Herefordshire, for instance, it was the sheriff who summoned men for expeditions into Wales.[77] In Shropshire it was he, not the earl, who received the 'third penny' of Shrewsbury borough. The Shropshire sheriff was entitled to give the 'king's peace'.[78] On those grounds it has even been suggested that in Shropshire the sheriff had by 1066 superseded the earl as the recognized president of the shire court.[79] That is almost certainly an exaggeration; the Bromfield writ of c. 1061 includes the earl, but not the sheriff, among the addressees.[80] Moreover the earl continued in 1066 to receive the 'third penny' of the hundreds.[81]

The Shropshire sheriff's military duties probably included the maintenance of patrols along the Welsh border; it is recorded that in 1053 many Englishmen 'of the patrols'

[62] Ibid. 281.
[63] Stenton, A.-S. Eng. 415.
[64] Anglo-Saxons, ed. Clemoes, 90–8, 101–2.
[65] V.C.H. Salop. i, map facing p. 309.
[66] Harmer, A.-S. Writs, pp. 546–7.
[67] Ibid. p. 48.
[68] Ibid. pp. 563, 570; F. Barlow, Edw. the Confessor (1970), 103.
[69] Barlow, op. cit. 124.
[70] Stenton, A.-S. Eng. 561.
[71] Ibid. 416.
[72] Eng. Hist. Doc. i, p. 291.

[73] The area of the Magonsæte was that of Heref. dioc.: see above, n. 59.
[74] Harmer, A.-S. Writs, p. 46.
[75] C. Hart, 'Athelstan "Half King" and his fam.', A.-S. Eng. ii. 136.
[76] Stenton, A.-S. Eng. 548–9.
[77] V.C.H. Salop. i. 294; W. A. Morris, Medieval Eng. Sheriff (1927), 27.
[78] V.C.H. Salop. i. 294–5.
[79] Morris, Medieval Eng. Sheriff, 25.
[80] Anglo-Saxons, ed. Clemoes, 102.
[81] V.C.H. Salop. i. 293.

were killed by Welshmen near 'Westbury',[82] which (if the Shropshire Westbury is intended)[83] lay on the principal Roman road from Shropshire into Powys.[84] By the reign of Ethelred *Unræd* it seems likely that the sheriff of Shropshire was in charge of a well organized system for the collection of royal dues. By that time royal estates in Shropshire had been formed into groups, each responsible for providing the whole, or an agreed part, of one day's provisions for the royal household when it came to Shropshire,[85] as happened in 1006 when Ethelred came to Shropshire 'and received there his food-rents in the Christmas season'.[86] Sophisticated arrangements were presumably also needed whenever a geld was collected.

The ordinary criminal court was that of the hundred.[87] The hundred, as a district, was almost certainly more ancient than the shire,[88] and in Shropshire two of the Domesday hundreds, 'Mersete' and 'Ruesset', have names suggesting that they were once the districts occupied by distinct communities of early settlers.[89] It is, however, unlikely that hundred courts, assemblies organized for the administration of the king's justice, existed in Shropshire before the 10th century, nor is it likely that the Shropshire hundred boundaries revealed in Domesday Book were of very ancient origin. It appears that in Worcestershire the hundreds were much altered in Edgar's reign (957–75) to make twelve hundreds of equal size out of the shire's 1,200 hides.[90] That some such reorganization took place in Shropshire, as in other Mercian shires,[91] is suggested by the fact that by 1086 the shire's *c.* 1,438 hides were distributed among fifteen hundreds, ten of which had between 86 and 119 hides.[92] Of the fifteen hundreds ten (apart from Shrewsbury) had a royal estate as their *caput* in 1066, and four of the ten were named after the estate.[93] It has been suggested that such an arrangement may have been older than the shire,[94] but in Shropshire that seems unlikely. Patton ('Patintune') hundred is a particularly instructive example. It had no royal estate in it in 1066 and was attached to the royal estate of Corfham, *caput* of the adjoining hundred of 'Culvestan'.[95] If it may be thought to have once depended on Patton estate (in private hands in 1066),[96] that dependence had probably existed only when Patton estate was in royal hands. In 901 the church of Wenlock, which seems to have owned Patton since the early 8th century,[97] ceded 5 *manentes* there to Ealdorman Æthelred of Mercia and his wife.[98] On Æthelflæd's death in 918 Mercia acknowledged her brother, Edward the Elder, as ruler.[99] Patton estate was thus quasi-royal from 901 and probably royal from *c.* 918. By 1066 it was again in private hands. In other words any relationship of Patton hundred to a royal estate at Patton is hardly likely to have been established before the 10th century. The same may be true of the other nine Shropshire hundreds dependent on royal estates in 1066. Thus the Shropshire hundreds may have been comprehensively altered by royal command, not only in number and size but also in internal organization, in the 10th or early 11th centuries. It is probably no coincidence that the same period witnessed the formalization of the English hundred court as an institution of royal government.[1]

[82] *Eng. Hist. Doc.* ii, ed. D. C. Douglas and G. W. Greenaway, p. 131.

[83] Westbury on Severn (Glos.) is another possible identification: *P.N. Glos.* (E.P.N.S.), iii. 201.

[84] I. D. Margary, *Roman Roads in Brit.* (1973), pp. 344–5.

[85] *V.C.H. Salop.* i. 316; Morris, *Medieval Eng. Sheriff*, 29–30.

[86] *Eng. Hist. Doc.* i, p. 218.

[87] Harmer, *A.-S. Writs*, p. 125.

[88] Stenton, *A.-S. Eng.* 299–301.

[89] *V.C.H. Salop.* i. 283–4.

[90] *Vale of Evesham Hist. Soc. Res. Papers*, v. 35–9.

[91] Maitland, *Dom. Bk. and Beyond*, 459–60.

[92] *V.C.H. Salop.* i. 281, 283.

[93] Ibid. 292–3.

[94] Helen M. Cam, *Liberties and Communities in Medieval Eng.* (1963), 88; Stenton, *A.-S. Eng.* 300–1.

[95] *V.C.H. Salop.* i. 293.

[96] Ibid. 328.

[97] Finberg, *Early Charters of W. Midlands*, pp. 147–8.

[98] Sawyer, *A.-S. Charters*, no. 221, and edns. there cited.

[99] Stenton, *A.-S. Eng.* 329–30.

[1] Ibid. 299; H. R. Loyn, 'The Hundred in Eng. in the 10th and Early 11th Cents.', *Brit. Govt. and Admin.: Studies presented to S. B. Chrimes*, ed. H. Hearder and H. R. Loyn (1974), 1–15.

The Anglo-Norman County

The Norman Conquest brought little immediate change in the government of Shropshire. Earl Edwin of Mercia submitted quietly in 1066 and was allowed to keep the title, if not the full authority, of an earl.[2] By 1069,[3] however, Mercia was under the effective government of Æthelwig, abbot of Evesham 1058–77, an Englishman who had served King Harold and had submitted to the Conqueror. His administrative skill, combined with a reputation for charity and sound judgement, commanded the respect of English and French alike. In Mercia he was perhaps the ideal man to supervise an orderly transfer of land and power into French hands, and to him the Conqueror entrusted virtually the whole government of Worcestershire, Gloucestershire, Oxfordshire, Warwickshire, Herefordshire, Staffordshire, and Shropshire. Æthelwig travelled throughout the territory, hearing pleas (probably 'Crown' pleas)[4] and attending shire courts. The amount of litigation arising from the Norman occupation is attested by the crowds of suitors who followed him, and his counsel was sought by earls, sheriffs, and barons.[5] His contribution to the Norman settlement of the west Midlands can hardly be exaggerated.

Armed resistance to Norman rule in Shropshire was a course favoured only by a disorganized minority. In 1069 a Herefordshire thegn, Edric the wild, attacked Shrewsbury in the company of Welshmen and of men from Chester, with the assistance of some local inhabitants. The rebels scattered before Norman forces could reach the town[6] and a period of guerrilla fighting seems to have ensued. Many fugitives and thieves were living in the woods and they caused much harm.[7] Early in 1070[8] they were ruthlessly crushed; it was impossible to identify the enemy, so the king wreaked indiscriminate devastation on Shropshire and the other disaffected counties.[9] The survivors, mostly old men, women, and children, fled.[10] Their homes and fields were laid waste.[11] At the height of the trouble county government can hardly have been carried on at all. Æthelwig took no part in the destruction and did what he could to care for refugees who poured into Evesham.[12]

In 1071 Earl Edwin was killed by some of his own followers[13] and by 1074 the earldom of Shrewsbury had been granted to Roger of Montgomery,[14] one of the Conqueror's closest friends.[15] Earl Roger probably resumed the functions of the pre-Conquest earls in county government, but his authority was enhanced in several ways. He was made tenant-in-chief of nearly all the land in Shropshire,[16] thus exercising feudal as well as administrative control. Moreover he was enabled to nominate the sheriffs.[17] Like William FitzOsbern, earl of Hereford, he was granted wide authority not only on the Welsh border but also on the south coast of England;[18] it is evident that the exceptional powers of the Shropshire earldom were intended to strengthen national defence.

Operations against the Welsh appear to have dominated the administrative arrangements of the Norman earls of Shrewsbury. Earl Roger died in 1094 and was succeeded

[2] Stenton, A.-S. Eng. 597, 623.
[3] Ibid. 623.
[4] H. A. Cronne, 'The Office of Local Justiciar in Eng. under the Norman Kings', Univ. of Birm. Hist. Jnl. vi. 26, 31.
[5] Chron. Abbatiae de Evesham (Rolls Ser.), 88–90.
[6] Orderic Vitalis, Eccl. Hist. ed. Marjorie Chibnall, ii. 228; Stenton, A.-S. Eng. 603–4.
[7] Chron. Evesham, 90.
[8] Orderic, Eccl. Hist. ii. 234, 236.
[9] Stenton, A.-S. Eng. 605.

[10] Chron. Evesham, 90–1.
[11] Dom. Geog. Midland Eng. 145–7.
[12] Chron. Evesham, 91.
[13] Harmer, A.-S. Writs, p. 560.
[14] J. F. Mason, 'Rog. de Montgomery and his Sons', Trans. R.H.S. 5th ser. xiii. 3–4.
[15] R. Allen Brown, The Normans and the Norman Conquest (1969), 38.
[16] V.C.H. Salop. i. 288.
[17] T.S.A.S. lvi. 247.
[18] Trans. R.H.S. 5th ser. xiii. 3.

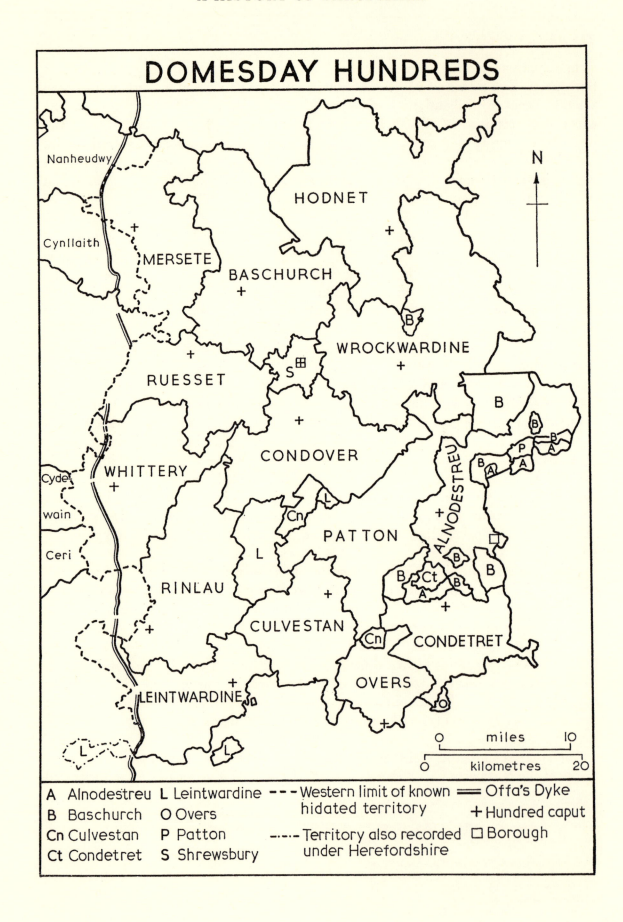

DOMESDAY HUNDREDS

Nanheudwy

Cynllaith

MERSETE

HODNET

BASCHURCH

WROCKWARDINE

B

RUESSET

S ⊞

CONDOVER

B

B

Cyde

WHITTERY

wain

Ceri

Cn

RINLAU

L

PATTON

ALNODESTREU

B

Ct
A

B

B

CULVESTAN

Cn

CONDETRET

L

LEINTWARDINE

OVERS

O

L

L

O   miles   10

O   kilometres   20

A Alnodestreu	**L** Leintwardine	- - - Western limit of known hidated territory	═══ Offa's Dyke
B Baschurch	**O** Overs		**+** Hundred caput
Cn Culvestan	**P** Patton	-·-·- Territory also recorded under Herefordshire	☐ Borough
Ct Condetret	**S** Shrewsbury		

by his sons Hugh of Montgomery, killed in Anglesey by Norwegian invaders in 1098, and Robert of Bellême, who forfeited the earldom in 1102.[19] All three had many interests elsewhere, particularly in Sussex and Normandy,[20] and had presumably to leave the details of Shropshire government to their sheriffs. By 1086 particular estates had been provided in Shropshire by Earl Roger for the support of the successive sheriffs. That

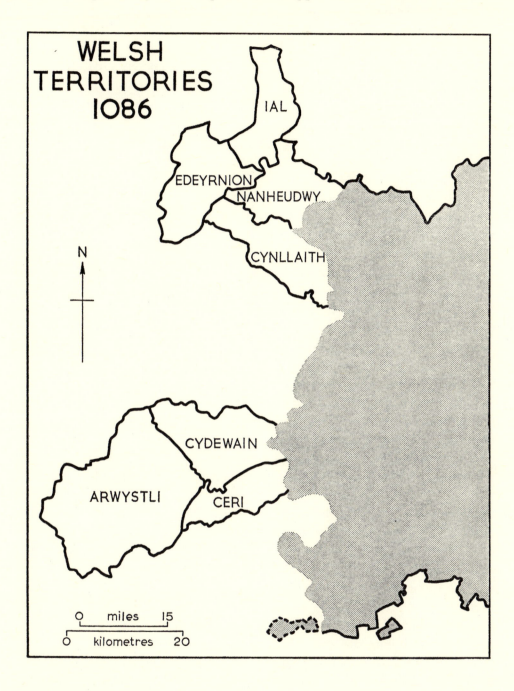

the sheriff was regarded as pre-eminently an agent for defence of the Welsh border is suggested by the fact that part of his estates formed a compact group in 'Mersete' hundred, on the north-west border of the county; only some exceptional purpose would have caused the Normans to depart from their usual practice and allow the formation of a consolidated fief. The career of Earl Roger's first sheriff, Warin the bald (d. c. 1085), leaves no doubt as to the sheriff's peculiar role in Norman Shropshire. Earl Roger gave

[19] *Complete Peerage*, xi. 687–93.   [20] *Trans. R.H.S.* 5th ser. xiii. 1–28.

him his niece in marriage. It was to Warin that Orderic Vitalis gave the credit for suppressing the earl's Welsh and English opponents and for restoring peace to the county, and Warin alone from Shropshire is named in the Welsh history *Hanes Gruffydd ap Cynan* among the leaders of a Norman expedition to the Lleyn peninsula. Warin was succeeded in his estates and office by Reynold of Bailleul, a neighbour of Earl Roger in Normandy. Reynold married Warin's widow.[21] By 1098 Warin's son, Hugh, had replaced his stepfather as sheriff.[22]

The Norman earldom ended suddenly in 1102 when Robert of Bellême, who had supported Duke Robert of Normandy's invasion of England in 1101, was driven by Henry I into open rebellion, was defeated, and was deprived of all his English and Welsh lands and titles.[23] The king was unwilling to revive the earldom, a form of local government in which hereditary feudal and administrative power was vested in one family. Instead, towards the end of 1102,[24] he appointed in Shropshire a local justiciar, Richard of Beaumais (Belmeis), who had the earls' administrative authority but not their dynastic ambitions. Richard, like Sheriff Reynold, had been a neighbour of Earl Roger in Normandy. He had been employed in the household of the earls of Shrewsbury and by 1102 was already familiar with local affairs. He was appointed bishop of London in 1108.[25] His jurisdiction is said to have extended into Staffordshire and perhaps into Herefordshire. He described himself as having the *regimen vicecomitatus* of Shrewsbury[26] and was sometimes styled *vicecomes*,[27] but the word could denote simply someone 'taking the place of an earl';[28] elsewhere he is sometimes styled *dapifer* of the county.[29] It is possible that he combined the functions of earl and sheriff,[30] but it is also possible that the shrievalty passed, as did the shrieval estates, to Alan son of Flaald, a Breton newcomer favoured by Henry I.[31] By 1114 Alan seems to have ranked second in Shropshire to Richard of Beaumais.[32] It was said in 1138–9 that Alan 'honorem vicecomitis Warini post filium eius suscepit'.[33] That might mean simply that he had received the lands of Hugh, son of Warin, but it might also imply that Alan received the office of sheriff, which had thitherto gone with those lands and would do so again in the time of Alan's son and grandson. Alan, dead by 1121,[34] was referred to as *vicecomes* in 1155.[35] Whether the shrievalty was held by Alan or by Richard, the duties of the office were carried out by a deputy; Fulcoius *vicecomes* occurs in Shropshire from 1098 to 1135.[36]

Between 1123 and 1126 Richard of Beaumais was forced by ill-health to resign the justiciarship of Shropshire. He was succeeded by Pain FitzJohn,[37] a royal servant.[38] In 1126 the *comitatus* of Shropshire was granted by Henry I to Queen Adela.[39] It is not clear what the grant implied or how it affected Pain's justiciarship, but it is probable that Pain, like Richard, was virtually free to govern as he wished. He held the lordship (*dominatum*) of both Herefordshire and Shropshire and acted in concert with Miles of Gloucester, later earl of Hereford, who exercised similar authority in Gloucestershire. In Henry I's reign, it was said, 'they had raised their power to such a pitch that from the river Severn to the sea, all along the border between England and Wales, they involved everyone in litigation and oppressed them with forced services'.[40] Pain's daughter

[21] *T.S.A.S.* lvi. 245–6.
[22] *Cart. Shrews. Abbey*, ed. Rees, i, p. 38.
[23] *Complete Peerage*, xi. 692–3.
[24] Eyton, ii. 194.
[25] *D.N.B.*; *T.S.A.S.* lvi. 253–4.
[26] *Cart. Shrews.* ii, p. 318.
[27] *Reg. Regum Anglo-Norm.* ii, no. 900.
[28] Eyton, i. 245.
[29] *Cart. Shrews.* i, p. 1.
[30] Eyton, ii. 194.
[31] *T.S.A.S.* liii. 117.
[32] *Cart. Shrews.* i, pp. 2, 4.
[33] Ibid. ii, pp. 258–9.
[34] *Reg. Regum Anglo-Norm.* ii, no. 1284.
[35] *Cart. Shrews.* i, p. 42.
[36] Ibid. pp. 35, 52; ii, pp. 258, 262–3; *Reg. Regum Anglo-Norm.* ii, no. 618.
[37] *Cart. Shrews.* ii, p. 318.
[38] *Gesta Stephani*, ed. K. R. Potter (2nd edn.), 24 n.; W. E. Wightman, *Lacy Fam. in Eng. and Normandy 1066–1194* (1966), 178.
[39] Wm. of Malmesbury, *Hist. Novella* (Rolls Ser.), 528.
[40] *Gesta Stephani*, 25.

later married Miles's son,[41] and Pain and Miles are mentioned together as having been special confidants ('secretarios et praecipuos consiliarios') of Henry I.[42] They sat as royal justices, not only in their own counties[43] but also in Staffordshire, Northamptonshire, and Pembrokeshire.[44] The 'forced services' that they exacted presumably included the impressment of men for service against the Welsh, and it was in fighting the Welsh that Pain lost his life in 1137.[45] As before, the details of administration were left to the sheriff, and perhaps his deputy; a writ dating from probably 1130 was addressed to Pain FitzJohn and the 'sheriffs' of Shropshire.[46]

The justiciarship of Shropshire was not renewed after Pain's death. Instead control of the county appears to have fallen to William FitzAlan (I), son and heir of Alan son of Flaald and holder of the shrieval estates first granted to Warin the bald.[47] William supported the Empress Maud's claims to the throne and had married a niece of Robert, earl of Gloucester,[48] the empress's half-brother and the effective leader of her party. In 1138 William held Shrewsbury castle against King Stephen but fled when his stand became hopeless; his uncle, and perhaps deputy sheriff,[49] Arnulf of Hesdin refused to surrender and was hanged when the castle fell.[50]

The means by which the county was administered after William FitzAlan's flight are uncertain. In the 1140s Maud continued to acknowledge him as Shropshire's leading man,[51] but he was not actually reinstated until after Stephen's death.[52] Vacant earldoms were normally filled by Stephen or Maud as a means of placing areas of the country under their supporters' control,[53] but neither of them revived the Shrewsbury earldom, perhaps because of the 1126 grant of the *comitatus* to Queen Adela,[54] who lived until 1151. Whatever the reason Shropshire was one of only five counties with no earl in Stephen's reign.[55]

During the 12th century most of the Shropshire hundreds of 1086 were altered both in names and in boundaries. The boundary changes were sometimes great and the *capita* of some hundreds were moved. It has hitherto been assumed that the changes were brought about at roughly the same moment.[56] If so, the reorganization is likely to have occurred between 1138 and 1158 or at latest 1170. By 1170 and perhaps by 1158 Stottesdon, one of the new hundreds, was in existence,[57] and Wrockwardine, a hundred that was altered and renamed, was said in 1189 to have still existed in 1138.[58] The disorders of Stephen's reign may have rendered necessary a general revision of names, *capita*, and boundaries, but it is equally possible that the revisions took place piecemeal. There is, for example, some evidence that the boundaries of the south-eastern hundreds had been altered before 1102.[59] Separate alterations over a long period could have created the same eventual pattern.[60]

[41] *Complete Peerage*, vi. 455.

[42] Gerald of Wales, *Itin. Kambriae* (Rolls Ser.), 34.

[43] H. A. Cronne, *Reign of Stephen* (1970), 273, 293.

[44] *D.N.B. sub* FitzJohn, Pain; Doris M. Stenton, *Eng. Justice between Norman Conquest and Gt. Charter 1066–1215* (1964), 63.

[45] *D.N.B. sub* FitzJohn, Pain.

[46] *Cart. Shrews.* i, p. 53.

[47] Eyton, vii. 232.

[48] *T.S.A.S.* liii. 122–3.

[49] Reynold of Hesdin was under-sheriff to Wm.'s son 1189–90, 1195–6: *List of Sheriffs*, 117.

[50] Orderic, *Hist. Eccl.* ed. A. Le Prevost, v. 113.

[51] *Cart. Shrews.* i, p. 54; *Reg. Regum Anglo-Norm.* iii, nos. 378, 460.

[52] *D.N.B. sub* FitzAlan, Wm.

[53] R. H. C. Davis, *King Stephen* (1967), 129–32.

[54] Cronne, *Reign of Stephen*, 140. Another possible explanation is in Davis, *King Stephen*, 144.

[55] Davis, *King Stephen*, 129.

[56] *V.C.H. Salop.* i. 306.

[57] Stottesdon hund. is mentioned in a writ of Hen. II witnessed by Wm. Beauchamp (d. by 1170: *V.C.H. Worcs.* iii. 341). The king's itinerary led Eyton to suggest the year 1158: Eyton, iv. 242; *Court, Household, and Itin. of K. Hen. II* (1878), 35–6.

[58] Dugdale, *Mon.* v. 359, no. 16. On the date see *V.C.H. Salop.* ii. 50. Eyton, admitting his lack of evidence, favoured Hen. I's reign as the period of the supposed reorganization (Eyton, i. 23; followed by *V.C.H. Salop.* i. 307). That belief forced him to discount (Eyton, vi. 328 n.) the evidence of the Buildwas charter.

[59] See p. 43.

[60] The expression 'beyond Colvestan' to denote the FitzAlan lands in SW. Salop. remained current in 1233: Eyton, iii. 240 n. It was then an archaism if it referred to the hund. of that name, for the Domesday hund. of 'Culvestan' had been superseded by 1203: *Pleas bef. King or his Justices, 1198–1212*, iii (Selden Soc. lxxxiii), pp. 69–86.

The Sheriffs 1154–1345

William FitzAlan was restored in 1155 to the lands and office of sheriff of Shropshire[61] and the shrievalty remained in his family until 1201. William died in 1160 leaving a young son William.[62] Until 1190, when William FitzAlan (II) assumed his father's shrievalty, the office was held for him by men closely connected with his family. Guy Le Strange, keeper of William FitzAlan (II)'s estates and sheriff 1160–4,[63] came from a family that had been intimately associated with the FitzAlans since the 11th century.[64] In 1164 he was replaced as sheriff, but not as keeper of the estates, by Geoffrey de Vere,[65] the earl of Oxford's brother[66] and the young William's stepfather.[67] About Easter 1170, like most other sheriffs, Geoffrey was dismissed as a result of the Inquest of Sheriffs and temporarily replaced by William the clerk,[68] his under-sheriff.[69] Geoffrey was dead by Michaelmas 1170 and Le Strange was restored as sheriff.[70] William FitzAlan (II) was given livery of his estates in 1175 but Guy kept the shrievalty until his death late in 1179 or early 1180.[71] The shrievalty then passed to William's brother-in-law, Hugh Pantulf (d. 1224).[72] In 1190, however, it was granted to William,[73] who remained in office until 1201. In that year King John appointed one of his own court as sheriff, Geoffrey FitzPeter, earl of Essex and chief justiciar,[74] who had been sheriff of Staffordshire since 1198. It has been tentatively suggested that FitzAlan was dismissed for some involvement with the rebel Fulk FitzWarin.[75]

The under-sheriffs between 1190 and 1201 were often manorial lords such as William of Ercall (alias of Hadley), under-sheriff 1190–1, Guy of Shawbury, 1196–7, and Warner of Willey, 1198–1200.[76] Malcolm, under-sheriff 1197–8, was probably Malcolm of Harley, lord of Harley.[77] Others seem to have been relatives or officers of William FitzAlan (II): William of Ercall[78] and Reynold of Hesdin, 1190,[79] were probably his cousins, and Reynold was constable of Oswestry castle in 1212.[80] Rayner of Lea, 1200–1, was a tenant of William FitzAlan (II) and witnessed many of his charters.[81] It thus seems that by the 1190s the Shropshire under-sheriffs were men of substance, to whom much of the administrative burden could be delegated. They are unlikely, however, to have been literate, and it therefore follows that by the 1190s the under-sheriff of Shropshire had a clerk; he certainly did by 1203.[82] By contrast Geoffrey de Vere's literate under-sheriff, William the clerk (1169–70), was one of his household servants[83] and probably handled correspondence personally. Twenty years later the under-sheriff's social standing and administrative role had changed markedly.

Under John and Henry III sheriffs were made more directly responsive to the Crown's financial and military needs.[84] There were experiments in the appointment of sheriffs of low social position, who were easy to discipline and were prepared, in return for an 'allowance', to pay to the Exchequer all their profits in excess of the annual county

[61] D.N.B.
[62] Eyton, vii. 237.
[63] Ibid. iii. 126; vii. 238.
[64] H. Le Strange, Le Strange Records (1916), 9. He had witnessed charters of Wm. FitzAlan (I): Cart. Shrews. i, p. 77; ii, p. 271.
[65] Eyton, iii. 126.
[66] T.S.A.S. liii. 124.
[67] Eyton, iii. 126; vii. 228.
[68] Eng. Hist. Doc. ii, p. 438.
[69] List of Sheriffs, 117.
[70] Eyton, iii. 126.
[71] Ibid. 128; vii. 240.
[72] Ibid. vii. 240; ix. 164, 166.
[73] Ibid. vii. 242.
[74] List of Sheriffs, 117. Unless otherwise stated, sheriffs'

and under-sheriffs' names and dates in the rest of this chapter are taken from this list.
[75] S. Painter, Reign of K. John (1949), 50.
[76] Eyton, ii. 52; vii. 354; viii. 134.
[77] Ibid. vi. 232.
[78] Ibid. vii. 352; T.S.A.S. liii. 122–3.
[79] Eyton, x. 293. Reynold's son was named 'Ernulf' (ibid.) and an Arnulf of Hesdin (d. 1138) was Wm. FitzAlan (II)'s great-uncle (above, p. 11).
[80] Eyton, x. 268.
[81] Ibid. vii. 274.
[82] Pleas bef. King or his Justices, 1198–1212, iii, p. 83.
[83] Eyton, ii. 110 n.
[84] D. A. Carpenter, 'Decline of the Curial Sheriff in Eng. 1194–1258', E.H.R. xci. 1–32.

farm, which for Shropshire had been fixed by 1163 at £265 15s.[85] There remained, however, military and political advantages for the Crown in granting shrievalties to the king's *familiares*, even though such persons were difficult to control and expected to keep most of their profits, paying only a fixed 'increment' above the farm. In Shropshire, a border county, the military desirability of employing such curial sheriffs was sometimes especially compelling until Edward I's conquest of Wales.

In less vulnerable counties the Crown's financial demands upon the sheriffs had by then already made the office unattractive to *curiales*. Moreover the new offices of coroner and escheator, and the regular local sessions of royal justices, had taken away much of the sheriff's former power and profit. Thus the shrievalty had come to be filled by professional administrators or men of purely local standing. After the conquest of Wales such appointments also became usual in Shropshire and Staffordshire. Since the office could no longer be offered to a magnate as a material inducement or reward, the Crown ceased to be much interested in individual appointments, and by Edward II's reign the shrievalty had become more accessible both to the ambition of local men with influential contacts in the administration and to the patronage of courtiers able to dispose of such influence.

The under-sheriff had assumed large responsibilities in the later 12th century. He continued to exercise them in the earlier 13th century except when non-curial sheriffs were appointed. The non-curial sheriffs carried more personal responsibility; for example, they normally rendered their accounts in person.[86] Their deputies held the status and title of mere clerks or receivers.[87] The first non-curial sheriff whose deputy is known to have been called under-sheriff was Robert Corbet of Wattlesborough, 1288–9.[88] By that time local sheriffs like Corbet enjoyed, with their deputies, some of the dignity once reserved for curial sheriffs. Moreover the sheriff was more burdened than before with routine duties and needed a deputy able to share more fully in the responsibility.[89]

In 1204 there was a general dismissal of curial sheriffs, among them Geoffrey FitzPeter.[90] Shropshire and Staffordshire, which had shared Geoffrey as sheriff, were formally combined in a single shrievalty. Geoffrey's Staffordshire under-sheriff, Thomas of Erdington, became sheriff or 'keeper', with Robert de Hawtrey, a clerk,[91] who seems to have been dropped in 1205. Thomas proved to be one of John's most efficient and permanent keepers. Nevertheless, as he rose in royal favour, his effectiveness as a royal revenue collector was eroded by the allowance that he was granted. Few other keepers appear to have received allowances in John's reign. Erdington's exceptional position perhaps owed something both to his personal influence at Court and to his extra responsibilities for the defence of the border.[92] He aspired to link his family with the FitzAlans. In 1214 he bought from the Crown the wardship of the FitzAlan lands for five years, and as part of the bargain married his daughter to William FitzAlan (III), son of the last FitzAlan sheriff. William, however, died childless in 1215 and Erdington's ambition came to nothing.[93]

Baronial opposition to the custodial system later in John's reign brought about its abolition in most counties: curial sheriffs were reintroduced, paying to the Exchequer only the ancient farms and keeping all the profits.[94] In Shropshire and Staffordshire, however, it was John's anxiety to strengthen his military position in the civil war that

[85] G. J. Turner, 'Sheriff's Farm', *Trans. R.H.S.* n.s. xii. 147.

[86] *List of Sheriffs*, 117.

[87] Eyton, iii. 191; vi. 60; ix. 247; A. Harding, 'Salop. Eyre Roll of 1256' (Oxford Univ. B.Litt. thesis, 1957), p. xxxix.

[88] W. A. Morris, *Early Eng. County Ct.* (1926), 151; *Sel. Bills in Eyre* (Selden Soc. xxx), p. 32.

[89] Helen M. Cam, *Hundred and Hundred Rolls* (1963), 6–8.

[90] *E.H.R.* xci. 7.

[91] Eyton, iii. 4; B. E. Harris, 'Eng. Sheriffs in Reign of K. John' (Nottingham Univ. M.A. thesis, 1961), 38, 40 n.

[92] *E.H.R.* xci. 9, 10 n.; Harris, 'Eng. Sheriffs', 38, 40 n.

[93] Eyton, vii. 247–9.

[94] *E.H.R.* xci. 10.

followed Magna Carta that caused him early in 1216 to appoint Ranulph, earl of Chester, as sheriff of Shropshire and Staffordshire, as well as of Lancashire.[95] Later in 1216, as John had promised, Ranulph was relieved of Shropshire and Staffordshire, the shrievalty being given to John Le Strange (II),[96] one of the few Shropshire barons who had remained loyal to the king[97] and nephew of a former sheriff.[98] In 1217, soon after Henry III's accession, Earl Ranulph recovered the shrievalty, which he kept for the next six years. His peacetime conduct of the counties was inefficient and by 1223 he owed large sums at the Exchequer for their farms.[99] He was on crusade from 1218 to 1220[1] and for the whole six years ruled Shropshire and Staffordshire through under-sheriffs: Henry of Audley, 1217–20, and Philip de Kinton, 1220–3. Philip was a former under-sheriff of Warwickshire and Worcestershire.[2] Henry, member of a minor Staffordshire family seated near the Shropshire–Cheshire border, rose through his own abilities and Earl Ranulph's patronage,[3] and during his under-shrievalty was able to build up an important estate.[4] Henry had a deputy under-sheriff[5] to whom the daily administration of Shropshire may have fallen.

In 1223 the king came of age[6] and Earl Ranulph was deprived of his shrievalties. The custodial system was reintroduced throughout England.[7] In Shropshire and Staffordshire the earl was temporarily replaced by Hugh Despenser, by the bishop of Worcester, and then by William Longespee, earl of Salisbury. Salisbury's under-sheriff was John Bonet, who had served him as under-sheriff in Wiltshire 1203–8 and in Lincolnshire 1218–19.[8] In 1224 Bonet succeeded his patron as sheriff, holding office until 1227 and paying all the profits to the Exchequer in return for an allowance. In June 1227 it seems to have been the Welsh threat, leading to war in 1228 and 1231, that caused Bonet to be replaced by the *curialis* Henry of Audley, though Bonet remained as under-sheriff until Michaelmas. Henry held the shrievalty of both counties until 1232, and on increasingly favourable terms probably intended to recompense him for his additional military responsibilities. From 1229 he owed an annual increment of only 40 marks, and in 1230–2 was pardoned even that.[9] Concurrently he acquired more estates.[10]

In 1232 Hubert de Burgh, earl of Kent, was dismissed as justiciar of England and control of the shrievalties passed to Peter des Rivaux,[11] treasurer of the Chamber and the Wardrobe. In 21 counties, including Shropshire and Staffordshire, Peter assumed the shrievalty himself. In Shropshire, Staffordshire, and Sussex he retained the shrievalties after Michaelmas 1232.[12] The duties were carried out by his under-sheriffs;[13] in Shropshire and Staffordshire Robert of Hay. Henry of Audley, however, did not lose local office, for he became royal keeper of Shrewsbury town in 1233[14] and continued to be employed in Anglo-Welsh affairs.[15] In 1234 Robert of Hay was made sheriff, in which office he remained until 1236. He appears to have been a professional administrator with few local connexions.[16] From 1232 to 1236 the shrievalty of Shropshire continued to be held for a very low increment.[17]

The financial administration of the shires was greatly reformed in 1236, to the

[95] Harris, op. cit. 80–1; B. E. Harris, 'Ranulph III, earl of Chester', *Jnl. Chester Arch. Soc.* lviii. 106.
[96] Harris, 'Eng. Sheriffs', 83.
[97] Le Strange, *Le Strange Rec.* 74.
[98] Ibid. 22, 58.
[99] *E.H.R.* xci. 11.
[1] *Jnl. Chester Arch. Soc.* lviii. 107.
[2] G. Templeman, *Sheriffs of Warws. in 13th Cent.* (Dugdale Soc. Occ. Papers, vii), 13.
[3] *D.N.B. sub* Audley, Hen. de.
[4] Eyton, viii. 139; ix. 116, 274.   [5] Ibid. x. 350.
[6] F. M. Powicke, *Thirteenth Cent.* (1962), 19.
[7] *E.H.R.* xci. 10–11.
[8] Harris, 'Eng. Sheriffs', 140–1; *V.C.H. Wilts* v. 9.
[9] *E.H.R.* xci. 12.
[10] Eyton, ix. 116; *V.C.H. Salop.* viii. 228.
[11] Powicke, *13th Cent.* 49.
[12] F. M. Powicke, *K. Hen. III and the Ld. Edw.* (1947), 87.
[13] *E.H.R.* xci. 13–14.
[14] *Cal. Pat. 1232–47*, 35.
[15] Eyton, vii. 185; *D.N.B.*
[16] A man of that name became keeper of Beds. and Bucks. in 1237 (*Cal. Pat. 1232–47*, 207) and was one of the Salop. eyre justices in 1240 (Eyton, ii. 32).
[17] *E.H.R.* xci. 14.

Crown's advantage. Sheriffs were to account for all their profits, and thus lost their former incentive to increase them by extortion. New sheriffs, usually local men without Court connexions, were appointed in seventeen counties.[18] The appointee in Shropshire, however, was John Le Strange (III), son of the sheriff of 1216–17. He held office for twelve years. Although his family had long been prominent in Shropshire, his appointment owed as much to his record of royal service over some twenty years. He was by then constable of Montgomery and was already influential in England's diplomatic relations with the Welsh. His appointment as sheriff of Shropshire and Staffordshire merely reinforced his position. In 1240 his standing in the marches reached its highest point when he was made concurrently justice of Chester. His military and diplomatic activities thereafter could have left him little time for the sheriff's routine business.[19] In Shropshire and Staffordshire he employed under-sheriffs from local families. Robert of Acton, clerk, son of Robert of Leigh, under-sheriff 1227–8,[20] occurs as under-sheriff 1236–7; Nicholas of Willey, son of Warner of Willey, under-sheriff 1198–1200, occurs in 1241.[21] Nicholas married Le Strange's niece.[22] Roger de Puleston occurs in the 1240s; he had been 'clerk of the county' under Nicholas of Willey.[23] In the later 1240s Le Strange lost some of his responsibilities, probably through old age. He ceased to be justice of Chester in 1245, and in 1248 gave up the constableship of Montgomery and the shrievalty of Shropshire and Staffordshire. He continued to be employed in the marches but seems to have retired by the late 1250s.[24]

In Le Strange's time the Exchequer tried to make sheriffs more accountable for their income. In 1241 the former increment system was resumed. Increments, however, were gradually increased, eroding the sheriff's personal profits.[25] Moreover, even sheriffs of Le Strange's standing were required to render their accounts in person, not through their under-sheriffs.[26] Thus, like other sheriffs of the time,[27] Le Strange's successor Thomas Corbet of Caus, 1248–50, was induced to improve his personal income by extortion and oppression.[28] Robert of Grendon, a Warwickshire man,[29] succeeded him until 1255. He had by 1251 a Shropshire connexion through his wife,[30] but seems otherwise to have been an outsider appointed as a peacetime royal servant. The Exchequer continued to exact a high increment[31] and both Grendon and his clerk Remigius were accused of extortion.[32] Hugh of Okeover's shrievalty, 1255–7, was similar. Hugh came of a minor Staffordshire family.[33] He continued to employ Remigius.[34] Sheriffs such as Grendon and Okeover were commonly appointed in the 1250s and were particularly resented; to the leading county families they appeared as tyrannical intruders. The Provisions of Oxford, 1258, embodying the barons' grievances, did not spare such sheriffs. They required them to be local landholders and to render account for their profits in return for an allowance.[35]

In Shropshire and Staffordshire, however, a new Welsh threat had already caused Okeover to be replaced. In 1257 Peter de Montfort, a prominent Warwickshire baron, had been appointed sheriff for military reasons,[36] and it was he who was dismissed under the Provisions. The new sheriff was William Bagot of the Hyde, whose wife may have been a relative of Grendon.[37] Montfort remained, however, as constable of Bridgnorth

[18] Ibid. 16–17.
[19] Le Strange, *Le Strange Rec.* 99–102, 106–19.
[20] Eyton, v. 118–19.
[21] Ibid. ii. 56.
[22] Le Strange, *Le Strange Rec.* 105.
[23] Eyton, viii. 95.
[24] Le Strange, *Le Strange Rec.* 119–21, 124.
[25] *E.H.R.* xci. 21–2.
[26] Ibid. 25 n.; *List of Sheriffs*, 117.
[27] *E.H.R.* xci. 22, 31.
[28] Harding, 'Salop. Eyre Roll', pp. xxxii and n., xli–xlii.
[29] *V.C.H. Warws.* iv. 76.
[30] Eyton, vi. 153.
[31] *E.H.R.* xci. 22.
[32] Harding, 'Salop. Eyre Roll', pp. xxxii and n., xlii.
[33] *S.H.C.* N.S. vii. 16–18.
[34] Harding, 'Salop. Eyre Roll', p. xxxix.
[35] *E.H.R.* xci. 23, 29.
[36] Ibid. 27; *Cal. Pat.* 1247–58, 580.
[37] *S.H.C.* N.S. xi. 136–7; *V.C.H. Warws.* iv. 190.

and Shrewsbury castles.[38] The Provisions allowed Bagot only a year in office[39] and he was succeeded by William of Caverswall. In 1261 the king regained the initiative and appointed the royalist James of Audley,[40] son of the sheriff of 1227–32, son-in-law of the earl of Salisbury (sheriff 1223–4), and brother-in-law of Peter de Montfort[41] whom he had succeeded as constable of Bridgnorth and Shrewsbury in 1260.[42] Caverswall remained as Audley's under-sheriff.[43] The increment system was restored.[44] Except in the county towns and Bridgnorth Audley met much hostility to his appointment as sheriff, and he was ordered by the king to take a firm stand and to prevent fighting.[45] In most counties the barons retaliated in 1261 by appointing anti-sheriffs, but no record of such an appointment in Shropshire and Staffordshire is known.[46] By August 1263 Roger de Somery, baron of Dudley and a member of the baronial party,[47] had gained control of the shrievalty,[48] perhaps in June when Audley had conceded Bridgnorth castle, and probably Shrewsbury castle, to the barons.[49] Audley and Somery had been at law in 1259 over trespasses by Somery's men on Audley's property.[50]

In August 1263 Somery was succeeded by his daughter's brother-in-law, Hamon Le Strange, son of the sheriff of 1236–48[51] and newly appointed constable of Bridgnorth and Shrewsbury castles,[52] who soon afterwards went over to the king's side.[53] After the baronial victory at Lewes in May 1264 Le Strange was not removed, but was faced with a potential rival in Ralph Basset of Drayton, Roger de Somery's son-in-law,[54] who was appointed baronial keeper of the peace of Shropshire and Staffordshire.[55] In the confused period between Lewes and Evesham Basset was authorized to assume the sheriff's military duties and to conduct elections of knights of the shire, presumably leaving the other administrative responsibilities to Le Strange.[56] Le Strange, however, would not co-operate. He refused to give up the castles[57] and in November 1264 led a Shropshire *posse* in a royalist force that attacked Hereford.[58] He was replaced as sheriff in February 1265 by Robert of Grendon, the sheriff of 1250–5 who was required to carry on the financial and legal administration of the county for the barons[59] while Basset was supposed to retain the military command. Le Strange, however, remained the focus of royalist activity in Shropshire.[60]

The earl of Leicester's party was beaten at the battle of Evesham in August 1265 and Ralph Basset killed.[61] By November Grendon had been removed and the shrievalty of Shropshire was held by Thomas Corbet,[62] the sheriff of 1248–50. He had taken little part in the war[63] and may have used Le Strange's preoccupation with the Evesham campaign and its aftermath[64] to gain the shrievalty for himself. Corbet and Le Strange were old enemies[65] and Le Strange's men had used the disordered state of the marches during the war to raid Corbet's property.[66] By August 1267 Le Strange had regained the shrievalty.

With the return of peace it was possible to appoint less distinguished sheriffs. At Michaelmas 1267 Walter of Hopton, a prominent tenant of the FitzAlans and the

[38] *Cal. Pat.* 1258–66, 70.
[39] R. F. Treharne, *Baronial Plan of Reform, 1258–1263* (1932), 208–9.
[40] Ibid. 263.
[41] *D.N.B.*; *Complete Peerage*, i. 337–8.
[42] *Cal. Pat.* 1258–66, 70.
[43] *Cal. Close*, 1261–4, 192.
[44] *Cal. Pat.* 1258–66, 274.
[45] Treharne, *Baronial Plan*, 266.
[46] Ibid. 267 and n.
[47] Eyton, i. 282; x. 276.
[48] *Cal. Pat.* 1258–66, 274.
[49] See p. 32.
[50] *Cal. Pat.* 1258–66, 12.
[51] Le Strange, *Le Strange Rec.* 153–4, 159.

[52] *Cal. Pat.* 1258–66, 266.
[53] Le Strange, *Le Strange Rec.* 128.
[54] Ibid. 159.
[55] *Cal. Pat.* 1258–66, 360.
[56] A. Harding, 'Origins and Early Hist. of Keeper of Peace', *Trans. R.H.S.* 5th ser. x. 92–3.
[57] *Cal. Pat.* 1258–66, 367, 397.
[58] *Cal. Inq. Misc.* i, p. 100.
[59] *Cal. Pat.* 1258–66, 402.
[60] Ibid. 422; *Cal. Close*, 1264–8, 122.
[61] *D.N.B. sub* Basset, Ralph.
[62] *Cal. Pat.* 1258–66, 511.   [63] Eyton, vii. 28.
[64] Le Strange, *Le Strange Rec.* 136–7.
[65] Ibid. 157; Eyton, vii. 27–8.
[66] Eyton, vii. 28–9; *Cal. Close*, 1264–8, 440–1.

Mortimers and a coroner in 1256, became sheriff; distinction as a royal justice was to come later.[67] William of Caverswall, sheriff 1260–1, succeeded him in 1268. At Michaelmas 1269 the shrievalties of Shropshire, Staffordshire, and Herefordshire were granted to Prince Edward,[68] earl of Chester. Edward's under-sheriff in Shropshire and Staffordshire was Urian of St. Pierre,[69] one of his leading Cheshire supporters in the recent war.[70] Urian was the effective sheriff, and his receiver, Ellis de Birkewey (Bercweye), was sometimes called under-sheriff.[71] In May 1270 James of Audley returned as sheriff. After Edward's departure on crusade the shrievalty passed in 1271 to Hugh Mortimer, brother of Roger Mortimer (II) of Wigmore, one of Edward's closest friends. Hugh died c. January 1273 and was succeeded by Ralph, Roger's son.[72] Ralph too died and in 1274 was succeeded briefly by his under-sheriff, Robert of Trelleck. It had been necessary during Edward's absence to appoint trusted and powerful *curiales* as sheriffs.[73] On his return to England the security of Shropshire was entrusted to a royal servant of lower standing. Bevis de Knovill was appointed in October 1274 and remained for four years. During that period he married Hamon Le Strange's widowed sister-in-law and acquired an interest in her valuable estates.[74] His shrievalty was virtually the last in which Shropshire lay in the front line of national defence. In 1277 Edward I began the conquest of Wales, and his rapid success left Shropshire safe from the immediate threat of Welsh hostility.[75]

After 1278 the sheriffs of Shropshire and Staffordshire were usually drawn from the local gentry. Bevis was succeeded by Roger Sprenchose, a Shropshire tenant of the Le Stranges.[76] He served until 1286, a term unequalled in duration since 1248. In 1286 a general reform of peace-keeping in the counties was attempted under the provisions of the Statute of Winchester,[77] and in May Sprenchose was replaced by a royal clerk Leonius of Romsley (*alias* Leonius son of Leonius),[78] a Shropshire man who in the 1260s had been under-sheriff to Hamon Le Strange[79] and was an attorney for him in 1271.[80] Leonius died in 1288,[81] and his successors were likewise local landholders,[82] except perhaps for Ralph of Shirley (1295–8, 1300), a Warwickshire tenant of the king's brother Edmund, earl of Lancaster.[83]

In 1300 the coroners and communities of the counties were allowed for the first time to elect their own sheriffs.[84] Most did not do so. The only known instance of an election, that in Shropshire and Staffordshire, seems to have created an unwholesome clash of local feelings. In 1300 the counties elected Richard of Harley, lord of Kenley and Harley[85] and a grandson of Roger de Puleston, under-sheriff in the 1240s. Harley's administrative ability had already been recognized in local commissions, and his brother was a royal clerk.[86] In 1302, however, on the earl of Arundel's death, he was appointed steward of the heir's estates, under the boy's guardian Amadeus, count of Savoy, the king's cousin.[87] The new post seems to have made Harley particularly disliked by tenants of the FitzAlans. He was rudely chased from the lordship of Oswestry when he tried to hold the earl's court there[88] and he became the object of malicious indictments.[89]

[67] *Welsh Assize Roll 1277–1284*, ed. J. Conway Davies, pp. 100–10.
[68] *Cal. Lib. 1267–72*, p. 128; *List of Sheriffs*, 59. Edw. held other shrievalties between 1266 and 1272: *List of Sheriffs*, 1, 43, 122, 144, 152.
[69] Eyton, vi. 234 n.
[70] G. Ormerod, *Hist of Co. . . . of Chester* (1882), ii. 596.
[71] Eyton, ix. 119; *Cal. Lib. 1267–72*, pp. 126, 143.
[72] Eyton, iii. 44.   [73] *E.H.R.* xci. 31.
[74] Eyton, x. 22–3.   [75] Rees, *Atlas*, pls. 41–5.
[76] *V.C.H. Salop.* viii. 109.   [77] 13 Edw. I.
[78] *Cal. Pat. 1281–92*, 242.   [79] Eyton, iii. 136, 201.
[80] Le Strange, *Le Strange Rec.* 146.
[81] Eyton, iii. 202.

[82] Ibid. i. 94, 97; vii. 104; viii. 25, 56–7.
[83] Burke, *Peerage* (1949), 753.
[84] This para., except where otherwise stated, is based on Morris, *Medieval Eng. Sheriff*, 184–5.
[85] *V.C.H. Salop.* viii. 87, 95.
[86] Eyton, iv. 253; vi. 234–5.
[87] Ibid. iv. 123.
[88] *Cal. Pat. 1301–7*, 288, printing 'Whitchurch' for 'Oswestry'. Both places were called *Album Monasterium* and *Blancminster* (Eyton, ix. 14), hence the mistake.
[89] J.I. 1/745 rot. 1. FitzAlan tenants were among his accusers: Rob. of Bucknell (Eyton, x. 83), Thos. of Rossall (ibid. i. 197; x. 90, 208), and Guy of Glazeley (ibid. x. 114–15).

Complaints about him probably reached the treasurer, Walter Langton. Langton is unlikely to have been sympathetic to Harley, for he had been forced to resign the deanery of Bridgnorth in 1298 in favour of a succession of the king's Savoyard kinsmen.[90] In April 1303 Harley was ordered to be removed and a new election was held. He was, however, re-elected. Two of the Shropshire coroners and some knights of both counties protested that they had not assented to the election. Another election was ordered and Harley was again elected. Several local magnates and prelates were said to have withheld their assent and the Exchequer set aside the election, appointing in Harley's place Walter de Beisin, one of his accusers.[91] By November 1303 Harley was in gaol.[92] Until late January 1304 Beisin ignored royal orders to release him[93] and was himself dismissed in February. Harley evidently emerged from the affair with credit and went on to a busy career on various county commissions, as a knight of the shire, and in the service of local magnates.[94]

The episode shows that the government had grown indifferent to the selection of sheriffs, at least in periods of domestic peace.[95] That indifference made the office more accessible to intriguers and the followers of influential magnates. For example, the sheriff of 1305–7, John de Dene, had become in 1304 the general attorney of the earl of Warwick and had been sheriff of Warwickshire and Leicestershire 1302–4 and 1305.[96] Thus it was that in Edward II's reign, when government again became the object of baronial ambition, appointments to the shrievalty reflected the fortunes of particular magnates and their parties.

In 1311 was appointed Hugh of Audley, the elder,[97] son of the sheriff of 1261–3 and 1270–1, and brother-in-law of Roger Mortimer (III) of Wigmore.[98] Audley and Mortimer supported the king and Gaveston[99] and were thus opponents of the earl of Lancaster's reforming party. Soon after Audley's appointment,[1] however, the reformers were able to impose their Ordinances on the king, and Gaveston was banished.[2] Many sheriffs were dismissed,[3] and Audley was replaced in December 1311 by Hugh of Croft,[4] who had been sheriff 1309–11. The Ordainers' success was short-lived. In January 1312 Gaveston was reinstated, Langton was restored at the Exchequer,[5] and Audley became sheriff again, remaining until 1314. After Bannockburn Lancaster had a new chance to impose reforms. The Ordinances were restored in September 1314 and in the consequent administrative purges nearly all the sheriffs were dismissed.[6] Audley's place was taken by Roger Cheney, a Shropshire officer of the earl of Arundel,[7] an ally of Lancaster.[8] The purge was, however, not wholly effective[9] and in December 1314 Cheney was replaced by William of Maer, an adherent of the Audleys.[10] A further purge early in 1315 removed Langton from the king's council[11] and restored Cheney to the shrievalty. In September 1315 Cheney was again removed, this time in favour of Ralph de Crophull, apparently a royal servant[12] whose appointment may have been intended as a temporary one to secure efficient local preparations for a proposed Scottish expedition.[13] In any case Cheney was restored before August 1316.[14] During 1316 dissatisfaction with

[90] V.C.H. Salop. ii. 125, 128.
[91] J.I. 1/745 rot. 1.   [92] Cal. Close, 1302–7, 113.
[93] Ibid.; Cal. Pat. 1301–7, 207–8.
[94] Eyton, vi. 235; x. 64; Cal. Pat. 1313–17, 611.
[95] E.H.R. xci. 31.
[96] R. C. Palmer, 'County Yr. Bk. Reps.: the Professional Lawyer in the Medieval County Ct.', E.H.R. xci. 779, 782.
[97] Hugh of Croft occurs until Mich. 1311: Recs. of Trial of Wal. Langton (Camd. 4th ser. vi), 168–9. Audley occurs 25 Oct. 1311: Cal. Fine R. 1307–19, 119. That he was the elder Audley is shown by Cal. Pat. 1317–21, 330.
[98] Complete Peerage, i. 347.
[99] J. Conway Davies, Baronial Opposition to Edw. II (1918), 221; J. R. S. Phillips, Aymer de Valence (1972), 12.

[1] Davies, Baronial Opposition, 367.
[2] May McKisack, Fourteenth Cent. (1959), 22.
[3] Davies, Baronial Opposition, 523.
[4] Cal. Fine R. 1307–19, 120.
[5] McKisack, 14th Cent. 23.
[6] Davies, Baronial Opposition, 394–5.
[7] Blakeway, Sheriffs, 10; Eyton, xi. 234.
[8] D.N.B.
[9] J. R. Maddicott, Thos. of Lancaster (1970), 167.
[10] S.H.C. n.s. ix. 255.
[11] Maddicott, Lancaster, 167.
[12] Davies, Baronial Opposition, 454.
[13] Maddicott, Lancaster, 171–2.
[14] Blakeway, Sheriffs, 10.

Lancaster's leadership spread within the reforming party and was supported in the king's household.[15] John, Lord Charlton, chamberlain of the Household,[16] had a private as well as a political grievance against Lancaster and Arundel, for both earls had supported Griffith de la Pole in a violent dispute with Charlton over the lordship of Powys.[17] In July 1316 Charlton's brother[18] Thomas was appointed controller of the Wardrobe and keeper of the privy seal,[19] and in September Cheney was replaced as sheriff by Roger Trumwyn, a Charlton supporter in the Powys dispute[20] and stepfather of Lord Charlton's wife.[21] Trumwyn, who had been sheriff 1307–8, held office for two years, interrupted only by a short-lived attempt in March 1318 to replace him by Peter de Limesey,[22] a Lancaster retainer.[23]

The Parliament of October 1318 marked the beginning of a period in which Lancaster and the marcher lords, recently at odds politically, found themselves drawn together by increasing resentment against the two Despensers. The Despensers came in that period to control the government in the king's interests and to advance their private territorial ambitions at the marchers' expense.[24] Among the few marchers who still supported the Despensers was Edmund, earl of Arundel, whose eldest son married the younger Despenser's daughter.[25] The Despensers were also supported in Shropshire by the family of Edward Burnell (d. 1315) who had married the elder Despenser's sister.[26] Moreover the Burnells and FitzAlans were related to each other by the marriage of Philip Burnell (d. 1294), Edward's father, to the sister of Earl Richard (d. 1302).[27] In November 1318 nearly every sheriff was replaced,[28] including Roger Trumwyn;[29] his friend and relative Lord Charlton had been superseded as chamberlain by the younger Despenser a few months earlier,[30] and at about the same time John's brother had lost the controllership of the Wardrobe.[31] Trumwyn's successor was the Despenser's relative Robert of Grendon, Edward Burnell's cousin and great-grandson of the sheriff of 1250–5 and 1265.[32] Grendon held office for over three years, during which time antagonism to the Despensers' rule increased dangerously. In May 1321 the FitzAlan and Burnell estates in Shropshire were raided by marcher forces[33] and in June the marchers entered into a formal alliance with Lancaster.[34] From December 1321 the king made war upon the marchers. On 1 January 1322, when Edward was at Worcester and preparing to cross the Severn to attack the marchers,[35] Grendon, who had three weeks earlier been appointed a keeper of the peace for Shropshire,[36] was replaced as sheriff by John de Swynnerton of Hilton. Swynnerton was a former Lancaster retainer[37] who had, like his brother Roger,[38] gone over to the king.[39] The leading marchers, Roger Mortimer of Chirk and Roger Mortimer of Wigmore, surrendered later in the month.[40] Lancaster was defeated and executed in March.[41]

In November 1322, with the country at peace, Swynnerton, who was out of sympathy with the Despensers,[42] was replaced by Henry of Bushbury, who remained for over

[15] McKisack, *14th Cent.* 52.
[16] T. F. Tout, *Chapters in Admin. Hist.* vi. 45.
[17] Maddicott, *Lancaster*, 140–1.
[18] *D.N.B. sub* Charlton, Thos.
[19] *Handbk. of Brit. Chron.* 90.
[20] Phillips, *Aymer de Valence*, 54.
[21] *Complete Peerage*, x. 641–2.
[22] *Cal. Fine R.* 1307–19, 354; *Cal. Close*, 1313–18, 531, 541; *S.H.C.* 1917–18, 26.
[23] Maddicott, *Lancaster*, 63.
[24] McKisack, *14th Cent.* 58–63.
[25] *D.N.B.*
[26] *Sir Chris. Hatton's Bk. of Seals*, ed. L. C. Loyd and Doris M. Stenton (1950), p. 245. Edw.'s sis. and heir marr. John de Haudlo (ibid.), one of the elder Despenser's most trusted retainers (Maddicott, *Lancaster*, 267–8).
[27] Eyton, vi. 134.
[28] Maddicott, *Lancaster*, 230.

[29] *Cal. Fine R.* 1307–19, 381.
[30] Phillips, *Aymer de Valence*, 177.
[31] Tout, *Chapters*, vi. 28.
[32] *S.H.C.* xvii. 295–6. He had been sheriff of Glamorgan and Morgannwg under the younger Despenser's bro.-in-law, the earl of Gloucester (d. 1314): *Cal. Ancient Petitions Relating to Wales*, ed. Wm. Rees, p. 299.
[33] Maddicott, *Lancaster*, 267.
[34] McKisack, *14th Cent.* 61–3.
[35] Maddicott, *Lancaster*, 303–5.
[36] *Cal. Pat.* 1321–4, 42.
[37] Maddicott, *Lancaster*, 46.
[38] Ibid. 207; *S.H.C.* 1914, 3.
[39] *S.H.C.* 1917–18, 42.
[40] *Complete Peerage*, viii. 436.
[41] McKisack, *14th Cent.* 66–7.
[42] *S.H.C.* 1917–18, 42.

three years. His subsequent career indicates that, though acceptable to the Despensers, he was not deeply committed to any party. In 1323 Roger Mortimer of Wigmore escaped to France. With Queen Isabel he planned to invade England and seize power. Rumours of invasion were current early in 1326[43] and in January Bushbury was replaced by William of Ercall, another cousin of Edward Burnell[44] and relative of the Despensers; the Despensers presumably looked to him for unreserved local support in the impending crisis. The invasion took place in September and the Despensers' government quickly collapsed. The Despensers were executed. So was Arundel,[45] taken in Shropshire by Lord Charlton.[46] Within days of the accession of Edward III, then a boy under the tutelage of Mortimer and Isabel,[47] Bushbury was restored as sheriff. Like many moderate officials[48] he was not penalized by the new regime. In June 1327, however, his post was given to John of Hinckley, a local officer of Queen Isabel; he had fought with Mortimer in the 1321–2 rebellion.[49] Mortimer by then wielded supreme power and in 1328 secured the title earl of March, but his ambition created fear and hostility.[50] Bushbury was restored in February 1330 but Hinckley was brought back on 20 March, the day after the king's uncle, the earl of Kent, was executed for treason.[51] With the king's connivance Mortimer was arrested in October and executed in November.[52] Hinckley's shrievalty did not long survive Mortimer's fall. In December 1330 Bushbury was again restored, remaining sheriff until 1333.

Bushbury's successor was Richard de Peshall, a relative of the Swynnertons.[53] In 1335 Hinckley returned, perhaps a sign that past conflicts were to be forgotten.[54] There followed a succession of Staffordshire gentlemen[55] until, in 1345, the shrievalties of Shropshire and Staffordshire were separated.

Peace-Keeping Measures 1154–1327

The related laws of frankpledge, mainpast, *murdrum*, englishry, and the hue and cry, which together induced the inhabitants of most English shires to bring wrongdoers to justice without the intervention of paid police officers, hardly existed in Shropshire and the other counties of the Welsh border and in northern England. As far as Shropshire was concerned two related reasons for the exemption were retrospectively advanced by the inhabitants in 1307: the inhabitants were unable to pursue offenders who fled to Wales, to the 'liberties', or to Cheshire, all of which surrounded Shropshire and were 'outside the common law', and they had not the means to pay the penalties that would result if they were held liable for producing such offenders.[56] Exemption from frankpledge was successfully claimed by the inhabitants of Shropshire at least as early as 1221,[57] and the county remained exempt in 1256[58] and 1307.[59] *Murdrum* and englishry had not been required there since at least the late 12th century,[60] and it was alleged in 1307 that the inhabitants had been exempted from englishry by one of the Norman earls.[61] In 1306 the inhabitants claimed that Shropshire had been exempt from the mainpast law ever since the Conquest;[62] in 1221 and 1307, however, they admitted

43 McKisack, *14th Cent.* 81–2.
44 Eyton, vi. 134.
45 McKisack, *14th Cent.* 83–7.
46 *D.N.B.*
47 McKisack, *14th Cent.* 91.
48 Ibid. 93.
49 *S.H.C.* 1917–18, 39; *Cal. Fine R.* 1319–27, 90.
50 McKisack, *14th Cent.* 97–8, 100.
51 *Handbk. of Brit. Chron.* 433.
52 McKisack, *14th Cent.* 100–1.
53 *S.H.C.* N.S. ii, ped. facing p. 98.
54 See McKisack, *14th Cent.* 154.
55 *S.H.C.* 1917–18, 62, 69, 85–7.

56 J.I. 1/746 rot. 1(3).
57 *Rolls of Justices in Eyre, 1221–2* (Selden Soc. lix), p. 533.
58 Harding, 'Salop. Eyre Roll', 233.
59 J.I. 1/746 rot. 1(3). For other counties' exemption see W. A. Morris, *Frankpledge System* (1910), 45.
60 Morris, *Frankpledge*, 51 n.; F. C. Hamil, 'Presentment of Englishry and the Murder Fine', *Speculum*, xii. 290; *Rolls of Justices in Eyre, 1221–2*, p. 533; Harding, 'Salop. Eyre Roll', 233. Hamil refers also to other counties' exemption.
61 'Roger de Betthleem': J.I. 1/746 rot. 1(3).
62 J.I. 1/745 rot. 3.

that in Shropshire a lord was liable if one of his mainpasts, having committed a felony, was received back into the household when the lord knew of his crime.[63] In 1307 the inhabitants asserted that they should not be, and never had been, amerced for failing to raise the hue and cry.[64] That was not true, for there were many earlier instances of such amercement in Shropshire.[65] Even if, as the inhabitants maintained, the hue and cry could not be enforced, it was nevertheless sometimes raised,[66] the injured parties being naturally inclined to pursue a criminal. Nevertheless attempts to enforce regular communal policing were resisted in Shropshire. In 1253, for instance, the Assize of Arms was reissued in England with an unprecedented provision that each vill should pay for a communal store of arms for watches. The gentry of Shropshire then chose to suffer heavy financial penalties rather than accept the obligation.[67] In 1307 the inhabitants claimed exemption from the liability of hundreds for robberies, required in 1285.[68] They alleged that the most that could be required by way of communal peace-keeping was that the townships should twice a year at their hundred or liberty court present the offences committed within their districts.[69] While the 1307 claims were overstated in some respects it remains true that communal policing was virtually unknown in Shropshire in the 13th century, and had probably been so since at least the time of the Norman earls.

There was, however, an ancient service in Shropshire called *stretward*. Its name suggests that it had to do with guarding highways. *Stretward*, according to the 12th-century *Leis Willelme*, had to be performed by the hundred under the supervision of a *guardireve*. One man from every ten hides was to serve between Michaelmas and Martinmas. The duties involved intercepting movements of stolen cattle;[70] hence the brevity of the annual period of service, limited to the season in which cattle were driven in large numbers to market or to new pastures.[71] The *Leis* do not say that *stretward* was peculiar to Shropshire,[72] but it may be inferred that the service was especially appropriate to areas like Shropshire[73] where the cattle trade was important. Exemption from *stretward* was included in royal grants to Lilleshall abbey in 1199[74] and to the canons of Hereford in 1202[75] Estates with fewer than ten hides presumably shared their service with other estates. Those exemptions and anomalies would have made the service difficult to organize and it may easily have fallen into disuse. In Shropshire in 1255 *stretward* was still owed by the hundred to the king[76] but had everywhere been commuted for a money payment, assessed in most hundreds at 4*d.* a year from each hide and in Munslow hundred at 6*d.*[77]

It seems possible that the commutation had been effected in the early 1250s. In 1250 the sheriff of Shropshire and Staffordshire was ordered to proclaim that all men were to keep their own parts of the counties from wrongdoers and disturbers of the king's peace, and that if they should refuse the sheriff should keep those parts at the refusers' expense.[78] In 1251 it was found that the men of Shropshire and Staffordshire had failed to keep the counties and the sheriff was ordered to assess and levy the cost of keeping them upon those who were liable for their keeping.[79] In 1253 four local commissioners

[63] *Rolls of Justices in Eyre, 1221–2*, p. 533; J.I. 1/746 rot. 1(3). The same proviso may have applied in Herefs.: Morris, *Frankpledge*, 84. For other counties' exemption see ibid. 51–3.
[64] J.I. 1/746 rot. 1(3).
[65] e.g. *Trans. R.H.S.* 5th ser. x. 86; J.I. 1/741 rott. 1d.–3.
[66] e.g. Eyton, x. 35; *Cal. Inq. Misc.* i, pp. 596, 609.
[67] Mat. Paris, *Chron. Majora* (Rolls Ser.), v. 410–11; M. R. Powicke, *Military Obligation in Medieval Eng.* (1962), 90–1; and see below, p. 29.
[68] Stat. of Winchester, 13 Edw. I.
[69] J.I. 1/746 rot. 1(3).

[70] *Gesetze der Angelsachsen*, ed. F. Liebermann, i. 512–13.
[71] Ibid. ii(2), 675.
[72] It is possible that the *Leis* were compiled in Coventry Dioc.: F. Pollock and F. W. Maitland, *Hist. of Eng. Law* (1898), i. 104 n. *Stretward* seems to have been known in Ches., at least by name: Du Cange, *Glossarium*, vi (1846), 389.
[73] R. T. Rowley, *Shropshire Landscape* (1972), 241–2.
[74] *Rot. Chart.* (Rec. Com.), 17.   [75] Ibid. 106.
[76] *Rot. Hund.* (Rec. Com.), ii. 71 (Oxenbold).
[77] Ibid. 55–8, 62–3, 70–1, 75–6, 81–3.
[78] *Cal. Close*, 1247–51, 358.   [79] Ibid. 528.

were appointed in each of the two counties to see that the money was levied and paid to the sheriff.[80] The money levied in 1253 may, on the other hand, have been connected with Shropshire's refusal to comply with the police provisions of that year's reissue of the Assize of Arms.[81] It is by no means certain that the money was regarded in Shropshire as a commutation of *stretward*, and in Staffordshire it was presumably regarded otherwise, for *stretward* seems to have been unknown there, at least by that name. Moreover in 1307 *stretward* was stated by the inhabitants of Shropshire to have been commuted time out of mind,[82] a statement that barely permits the commutation to be dated to the 1250s. Whenever it was first commuted, *stretward* was still being paid in 1267[83] and in 1307 the inhabitants claimed unsuccessfully that the payment rendered them exempt from the watch and ward provisions of the Statute of Winchester, 1285.[84] How the sheriff used the money is not known. It was presumably intended to be paid to men for doing local police duties.

Serjeants of the peace, sometimes called 'grithserjeants', were paid county police officers and are known from the 12th to the 13th centuries in those counties that had no communal police system.[85] In Shropshire they originated in the 1180s. Hugh Pantulf, baron of Wem,[86] had private serjeants to guard his barony.[87] Other barons, for example the Mortimers,[88] the Stranges,[89] and the Says,[90] had them too. Those serjeants, like many private officers in Wales and the marches, were paid no salary but instead had the right, called *dofraeth*, of demanding subsistence from their masters' tenants.[91] During Pantulf's shrievalty of Shropshire, *c.* 1179–*c.* 1189, he extended his system of private serjeants to the whole county, granting them *dofraeth* from it.[92] The new county system was perpetuated by his immediate successors in the shrievalty. By 1220, however, the county 'grithserjeants *doverantes*' were a numerous and unwelcome burden upon the inhabitants.[93] In May 1220[94] the king, on a visit to Shrewsbury, ordered twelve to be removed. The under-sheriff immediately tried to profit from the order by agreeing with the county inhabitants to abolish the serjeants for 200 marks. Before he could do so the king forbade the agreement, ordering the twelve serjeants to remain.[95] Eight days later he ordered all the serjeants to be removed.[96] At the Shropshire eyre of 1221, however, Pimhill hundred complained that there were still twelve or more serjeants living off the men of the county, and the knights of the shire added that it would be to the king's advantage to remove them.[97] It seems, however, that only another royal order of 1224[98] succeeded in abolishing them. As county officers they were gone by 1227,[99] but private grithserjeants were still guarding the barony of Wem and living off its tenants in 1292.[1]

County grithserjeants are not known again in Shropshire until the shrievalty of Robert of Grendon, 1250–5, when mention is made of sheriff's bailiffs called 'gritserviauns'.[2] They occur again during the shrievalties of Hamon Le Strange, 1263–5 and *c.* 1267, and Ra¹ph de Mortimer,[3] 1273–4. After the 1220s, however, there is no reference to serjeants having *dofraeth*. It is therefore possible that the revival in Shrop-

[80] Ibid. 1251–3, 479.
[81] Mat. Paris, *Chron. Majora* (Rolls Ser.), v. 410–11; Powicke, *Military Obligation*, 90–1.
[82] J.I. 1/746 rot. 1(3).
[83] *Cal. Close*, 1268–72, 437.
[84] J.I. 1/746 rot. 1(3). Bridgnorth, Ludlow, and Shrews. were amerced in 1307 for failing to keep watch: ibid. rott. 5d.–6.
[85] R. Stewart-Brown, *Serjeants of Peace in Medieval Eng. and Wales* (1936), p. xi.
[86] Eyton, ix. 162.
[87] *Rolls of Justices in Eyre, 1221–2*, p. 536.
[88] B. Penry Evans, 'Fam. of Mortimer' (Wales Univ. Ph.D. thesis, 1934), 418–19.
[89] Eyton, x. 73; xi. 3.

[90] *Cart. Shrews.* i, p. 58.
[91] Ibid.; Eyton, v. 198; Nellie Neilson, *Customary Rents* (Oxf. Studies in Legal and Social Hist. ii (4)), 15.
[92] *Rolls of Justices in Eyre, 1221–2*, p. 536.
[93] *Cal. Pat.* 1216–25, 240.
[94] Owen and Blakeway, *Hist. Shrews.* i. 97.
[95] *Cal. Pat.* 1216–25, 240–1.
[96] *Rot. Litt. Claus.* (Rec. Com.), i. 423.
[97] *Rolls of Justices in Eyre, 1221–2*, p. 536.
[98] *Rot. Litt. Claus.* i. 589.
[99] *Cart. Shrews.* i, pp. 57–8.
[1] Eyton, ix. 134, 171 n.; Stewart-Brown, *Serjeants of Peace*, 136.
[2] Harding, 'Salop. Eyre Roll', 261.
[3] *Rot. Hund.* ii. 107, 110–11.

shire of county serjeants of the peace was associated with a commutation of *stretward* and that the new serjeants were paid out of *stretward* instead of by *dofraeth*. Their function seems often to have been the arrest of suspects.[4] In that, the later serjeants of the peace in Shropshire were hardly different from the bailiffs errant of the later Middle Ages,[5] an impression reinforced by their being termed bailiffs in the 1250s.[6]

The absence of an enforceable system of communal policing in Shropshire was not adequately remedied either by the *stretward* guards, who were few in number and limited in responsibility and had in any case disappeared by 1255, or by the serjeants of the peace, who also suffered from lack of numbers. The lack of adequate means of arrest was aggravated by the fact that, according to the inhabitants in 1307, appeals by 'approvers' had never been allowed in Shropshire.[7] The exemption was probably necessary, for, in counties with frankpledge, membership of a tithing was sufficient defence against an approver's appeal;[8] if such appeals had been allowed in Shropshire, the innocent would have had no such defence.

In 1287 two keepers of the peace were temporarily appointed in each county to take presentments of breaches of the Statute of Winchester, 1285, and generally to preserve the peace.[9] In Shropshire[10] they were John FitzEyre, a former subescheator and a gaol-delivery justice who later occurs as a county coroner and knight of the shire,[11] and William of Hodnet, who later occurs as a county tax commissioner and knight of the shire.[12] The Shropshire trailbaston roll of 1307 reveals the local apathy and inefficiency that were to hamper peace-keeping measures in the Middle Ages: none of the constables elected under the Statute of Winchester had done his duties properly and even the largest towns had failed to maintain watches. Furthermore Shropshire was still trying to preserve its traditional exemption from communal police obligations.[13] Thus the onus of arrest remained as always with the sheriff and his meagre force of serjeants or bailiffs. The keepers of the peace were found to be valuable for dealing with minor offences, but without effective means of arresting felons neither the keepers nor any other body could solve the problem of serious crime. Of ten Shropshire peace commissions between 1300 and 1326,[14] seven were issued between 1314 and 1321. There was presumably some relationship between the frequent commissions and the troubled state of the realm in those seven years. Nevertheless the Shropshire peace commission was affected much less than the shrievalty by contemporary shifts of power. Richard of Harley (d. 1316),[15] sheriff 1300–3, was on all five commissions between 1300 and his death. In all except the first he was accompanied by William of Ludlow (d. 1316), son-in-law of William of Hodnet,[16] a keeper in 1287. William le Botiler (later Lord le Botiller of Wem) was on every Shropshire peace commission from 1308 until his death in 1334[17] and was named first in all of them.[18] The continuity of those men's service, which was paralleled in many other counties,[19] shows that the peace commission was not yet of such importance in county government as to attract royal or baronial interference in its membership.

[4] Ibid.; Harding, 'Salop. Eyre Roll', 261.

[5] See p. 77.

[6] See above. In Norf. bailiffs errant were called 'serjeants errant': Cam, *Hund. and Hund. Rolls*, 135. The similarity of the offices is noted by A. L. Poole, *From Domesday Bk. to Magna Carta* (1955), 391 n.

[7] J.I. 1/746 rot. 1(3).

[8] F. C. Hamil, 'The King's Approvers', *Speculum*, xi. 243–4.

[9] *Trans. R.H.S.* 5th ser. x. 99–100.

[10] *Cal. Pat.* 1281–92, 265.

[11] Eyton, i. 205; J.I. 1/739 rot. 47; *T.S.A.S.* 4th ser. x. 8.

[12] *Cal. Pat.* 1292–1301, 104, 612; *T.S.A.S.* 4th ser. x. 8.

[13] J.I. 1/746.

[14] *Cal. Pat.* 1292–1301, 517; 1307–13, 31, 54; 1313–17, 108, 123, 482; 1317–21, 289, 460; 1321–4, 42, 59.

[15] *V.C.H. Salop.* viii. 87.

[16] Eyton, ix. 334.

[17] Ibid. viii. 21.

[18] See above, n. 14; *Cal. Pat.* 1327–30, 89; 1330–4, 136, 348.

[19] H. Ainsley, 'The Problem Relating to Maintenance of Law and Order in 13th-Cent. Eng.' (Wales Univ. Ph.D. thesis, 1968), 207–8.

Itinerant Justices

The visits of royal justices to the shires to determine the more important civil and criminal business arising there may be said to have begun for Shropshire as early as Abbot Æthelwig's time. The Norman earls of Shrewsbury, however, and their successors the local justiciars administered justice as resident deputies of the king.[20] Under Stephen local courts were left to function without the intervention of royal justices, whether resident or visiting. In Henry II's early years, however, there is evidence that royal justices were occasionally sent out to the shires,[21] and in 1156 or 1157 the chancellor, Thomas Becket, sat in Shropshire with Robert, earl of Leicester.[22]

The effect of the Assize of Clarendon, 1166, was felt less quickly in Shropshire and other counties of the west and north. The justices who travelled the country 1166–7 did not visit them.[23] It is likely, however, that Shropshire was visited in 1168 and 1170,[24] and certain that it was included in 1174, or more probably 1175, when two pairs of justices travelled the counties on two different circuits.[25] In 1176, following the Assize of Northampton, justices were sent out over the whole country in six simultaneous and separate circuits. Shropshire, Worcestershire, Herefordshire, and Gloucestershire formed one circuit.[26] Thereafter such nation-wide visitations, the eyres, became for a while virtually continuous, a new eyre beginning soon after the previous one was completed. Shropshire was visited nine or ten times between 1177 and 1192.[27] The circuits were not always the same and might be altered while the eyre was in progress.[28] Nevertheless Shropshire, Worcestershire, Herefordshire, Gloucestershire, and Staffordshire were almost always in the same circuit.

From 1194 eyres were held less frequently, perhaps because the creation of coroners in that year allowed Crown pleas to be kept efficiently for longer periods.[29] Eyres visited Shropshire in 1194, 1198, 1199, 1203, and 1208.[30] That of 1198 was unusual, being held by the chief justiciar and three colleagues going 'into Wales to deliver David, king of Wales'.[31] Eyres were abandoned from 1208, to be resumed only in 1218 after the civil war.[32] The first post-war Shropshire eyre was in 1221;[33] the others after that were in 1227, 1236, 1240, 1248, 1256, and 1272, and the last was in 1292.[34]

By the early 13th century small panels of local knights, often four in number, were commissioned to conduct gaol deliveries and assizes in their own counties between the eyres.[35] The earliest such assize commission known for Shropshire occurs in 1227[36] and the earliest known gaol-delivery commission in 1232.[37]

There were county and town gaols at Bridgnorth and Shrewsbury, and until the 1260s more than one gaol was sometimes included in a single gaol-delivery commission.

[20] See pp. 7–11. The evidence for activities of visiting royal justices in other cos. *temp.* Hen. I is discussed in W. T. Reedy, 'Origins of General Eyre in Reign of Hen. I', *Speculum*, xli. 688–724.
[21] *Speculum*, xli. 722; *Pleas bef. King or his Justices, 1198–1212*, iii, p. l.
[22] Ibid. p. li.
[23] Stenton, *Eng. Justice*, 72.
[24] *Gesta Regis Henrici Secundi* (Rolls Ser.), ii, p. lxv.
[25] Ibid. p. lxvi; *Pleas bef. King or his Justices, 1198–1212*, iii, p. lvi.
[26] *Pleas bef. King or his Justices, 1198–1212*, iii, p. lvii.
[27] Ibid. pp. lix, lxiv, lxvii, lxix–lxx, lxxii–lxxiii, lxxvi, lxxxiii, xciii.
[28] Ibid. p. lxiv.
[29] *Crown Pleas of Wilts. Eyre, 1249* (Wilts. Arch. and Nat. Hist. Soc. Rec. Branch, xvi), p. 4.
[30] *Pleas bef. King or his Justices, 1198–1212*, iii, pp. c, clviii, ccx, cclxii–cclxiii.

[31] Ibid. p. clviii.
[32] *V.C.H. Wilts.* v. 18.
[33] *Rolls of Justices in Eyre, 1221–2*, p. xii.
[34] *Cur. Reg. R.* xiii, p xvii; *T.S.A.S.* 4th ser. i. 394, 397; iv. 161–2, 164–5, 167–9, 171–2; vi. 169; Eyton, ii. 32; *Roll and Writ File of Berks. Eyre 1248* (Selden Soc. xc), p. xcix; Harding, 'Salop. Eyre Roll', pp. v–vi; J.I. 1/736; D. W. Sutherland, *Quo Warranto Proceedings in Reign of Edw. I* (1963), 220. The eyre of 1261–2, ordered Dec. 1260 to include Salop. (*Cal. Close, 1259–61*, 452), seems not to have done so: in 1272 the last eyre of Salop. was reckoned to have been that of 1256 (J.I. 1/736 rot. 25).
[35] R. B. Pugh, *Itinerant Justices in Eng. Hist.* (Exeter, 1967), 7, 9.
[36] *Cal. Pat. 1225–32*, 207. Assizes were heard at Shrews. in 1226: *Rot. Litt. Claus.* (Rec. Com.), ii. 154.
[37] *Cal. Pat. 1225–32*, 523.

Thereafter, however, separate delivery commissions for each gaol seem to have been normal.[38] Deliveries of Bridgnorth county gaol, which was used for Staffordshire prisoners from the 1240s, seem virtually to have ceased in the 1280s, when the gaol was ruinous.[39] Allowing for the probability that some commissions were not inrolled and that others were not acted upon, it can be said that there was usually a gaol delivery of some kind in Shropshire at least once every two years from the 1230s to the 1250s, and at least once a year from the late 1260s.[40] In the later 13th century, however, deliveries were rarer in the northern and western counties, like Shropshire, than in those of the south-east.[41] Until the 1290s the Shropshire gaol-delivery commissioners were predominantly local men,[42] and in the earlier 13th century the same panels often took the assizes.[43] By the 1280s, however, the assize justices were predominantly justices of the central courts, travelling on circuit. In 1285 Shropshire and Staffordshire, Warwickshire and Leicestershire, and Worcestershire made one assize circuit under the Statute of Westminster II.[44]

To a smaller extent other functions of the eyre were sometimes given to special commissioners in the 13th century. From the 1250s there were occasional commissions, sometimes to royal justices, to inquire into particular homicides,[45] and from the 1280s they were given the additional power of punishing those found guilty.[46] Also from the 1250s there were occasional commissions to royal justices to inquire into royal rights or the conduct of local officials.[47]

Shropshire was visited for the first time in 1293 under the circuit system that had been introduced for criminal business in 1292 and for civil litigation in 1293. The assize and nisi prius justices were commissioned in June,[48] and the gaol-delivery justices arrived in August.[49] The civil circuit consisted of nine other Midland counties besides Shropshire.[50] The same justices visited Shropshire at least seven times between 1293 and 1299.[51] The composition of the circuit was still the same in 1303, when the assize justices, entrusted since 1299 with gaol delivery, visited Shropshire[52] as they did on at least seven other occasions between 1300 and 1304.[53] From 1305 to 1307 trailbaston justices sat in Shropshire as everywhere else. They delivered gaols,[54] but separate gaol deliveries were also held.[55] After 1307 joint gaol deliveries and assizes were discontinued; separate and different circuits were sometimes followed for each.[56] It was probably during this period that Shropshire and six other Midland counties complained that assizes had not been taken there for at least three years; those assigned to take them dared not act because they did not know the law, and the appointment of Sir Henry Spigurnel or a justice of like calibre was requested.[57] In 1310, Shropshire assizes and gaol deliveries seem to have

[38] R. B. Pugh, *Imprisonment in Medieval Eng.* (1968), 256. Coms. including more than one gaol were confined to cos. like Salop. and Staffs. that shared a sheriff.
[39] Ibid. 73–4.
[40] Based on a list of Salop. gaol-del. coms. from the pat. rolls 1233–1300, supplied by Prof. R. B. Pugh.
[41] Pugh, *Imprisonment*, 261.
[42] *Cal. Pat.* 1225–32, 523; 1232–47, 124; 1272–81, 338, 346; 1281–92, 257, 286, 385; Eyton, i. 205, 278–81; viii. 84; *Cal. Close*, 1237–42, 437; 1272–9, 433; 1279–88, 269; 1288–96, 67, 176. The same was true of other cos.: Pugh, *Imprisonment*, 266, 268–9.
[43] Pugh, *Itinerant Justices*, 9; *Crown Pleas of Wilts. Eyre, 1249*, p. 5.
[44] *Cal. Close*, 1279–88, 365.
[45] *Crown Pleas of Wilts. Eyre, 1249*, p. 6. Salop. examples: *Cal. Pat.* 1247–58, 115, 226; 1258–66, 51, 485–6, 664; 1266–71, 134–5, 474.
[46] *Cal. Pat.* 1272–81, 475; 1281–92, 47, 65, 102, 205, 517.
[47] Cam, *Hund. and Hund. Rolls*, 28–9. Salop. examples:

Rot. Hund. ii. 55–113; Eyton, ix. 171. A similar inquiry in 1260 was curtailed before it reached Salop.: Treharne, *Baronial Plan*, 237.
[48] *Cal. Close*, 1288–96, 319–20.
[49] J.I. 3/90.
[50] *Cal. Close*, 1288–96, 319–20.
[51] J.I. 1/742 rott. 1, 3, 6; J.I. 1/743 rott. 1, 2, 6, 8.
[52] *Cal. Close*, 1302–7, 89. Herts. is presumably named in error for Herefs.
[53] J.I. 1/745 rot. 4; J.I. 3/99 rot. 11; J.I. 3/100 rot. 8; J.I. 3/101 rot. 9; J.I. 3/105 rot. 3; *Cal. Close*, 1302–7, 89; *Cal. Chanc. R. Var.* 75, 77.
[54] J.I. 1/744 rot. 11 and d.; J.I. 1/745 rot. 4 and d.; J.I. 1/746 rott. 6, 7d.
[55] Ex inf. Prof. R. B. Pugh (e.g. J.I. 3/105 rot. 3d.).
[56] Pugh, *Itinerant Justices*, 10.
[57] S.C. 8/327 no. E. 832 (ref. supplied by Dr. J. R. Maddicott). Spigurnel's Apr. 1310 com. to take gaol deliveries and assizes in Salop. and 4 other Midland cos. (*Cal. Close*, 1307–13, 337) may have resulted from this petition.

been held jointly in a circuit consisting also of Staffordshire, Worcestershire, Hereford-shire, and Gloucestershire.[58]

It was the Statute of Northampton, 1328, and another statute of 1330 that formally restored the joint sessions.[59] From 1329 Shropshire was part of a circuit consisting also, as in 1310, 1327, and 1328,[60] of Staffordshire, Worcestershire, Herefordshire, and Gloucestershire.[61] Oxfordshire and Berkshire were added to the circuit at some date between 1365 and 1367.[62] Thereafter the Oxford circuit remained unchanged until 1543 when Monmouthshire was added.[63] The boroughs of Shrewsbury (in 1446),[64] Ludlow (1462),[65] and Wenlock (1468)[66] were granted the right to deliver their own gaols, as was the abbot of Shrewsbury in 1466[67] but it is not known how often they did so.[68]

The Statute of Northampton required assizes to be held thrice yearly in each county. In the 1330s they were usually held in Shropshire at least twice a year and sometimes thrice.[69] Under Richard II and Henry IV the average frequency was less, so that only one or two sessions a year were usual in Shropshire;[70] in some of those years, however, as many as four commissions were issued while in others apparently none.[71] In Henry VII's reign one commission a year was commoner than two,[72] but extra deliveries of the county gaol were undertaken by the Council in the Marches of Wales.[73] By the 1580s and 1590s two sessions a year had become normal.[74]

Intermittently from 1329 and permanently from 1389 justices of the peace were empowered to deliver gaols.[75] A few possible instances of their doing so in Shropshire are found in the late 14th and early 15th centuries,[76] and the county gaol was certainly delivered by quarter sessions at Hilary 1597.[77]

In the 1330s four out-of-term seasons may be distinguished at which the assize justices might visit Shropshire: April to early May, July to early August, September, and December to early January.[78] From the 1340s, however, the spring sessions were virtually always held in March.[79] By the 15th century the summer sessions were mostly confined to late July or August,[80] separate autumn sessions were rarely held,[81] and winter sessions virtually never.[82] By the early 16th century the two assize periods of 'Lent' and 'Summer' had become fixed. The Shropshire Lent assizes were always in March.[83] In the 1580s and 1590s the Summer assizes were more often in August than in July.[84]

[58] *Cal. Close*, 1307–13, 337. The same circuit was used for assizes 1327–8: Mary M. Taylor, 'Justices of Assize', *Eng. Govt. at Work*, iii, ed. J. F. Willard, 248–9.

[59] 2 Edw. III, c. 2; 4 Edw. III, c. 2: Pugh, *Imprisonment*, 281.

[60] *Cal. Close*, 1307–13, 337; *Eng. Govt. at Work*, iii. 248–9.

[61] *Eng. Govt. at Work*, iii. 249; J. S. Cockburn, *Hist. Eng. Assizes 1558–1714* (1972), 19.

[62] *Cal. Close*, 1364–8, 191; *Cal. Pat.* 1364–7, 448.

[63] Cockburn, *Assizes*, 23.   [64] *Cal. Pat.* 1441–6, 411.

[65] *Cal. Chart. R.* 1427–1516, 159.

[66] Ibid. 232.   [67] Ibid. 213.

[68] For Shrews. sessions of gaol delivery 1591–1836 see, e.g.: *T.S.A.S.* iii. 319–46; S.R.O. 3365/2429, Apr. 1836. For Ludlow instances 1595–1744 see *T.S.A.S.* 2nd ser. xi. 304–6. For Wenlock see *T.S.A.S.* lix. 290. For Bridgnorth see below, p. 121.

[69] *Eng. Govt. at Work*, iii. 255; J.I. 3/127 rot. 8; J.I. 3/131 rot. 1.

[70] J.I. 3/166 rot. 5; J.I. 3/180 rott. 49, 50–2, 53 and d.; J.I. 1/750 rott. 1 and d., 2d.–4d.; J.I. 3/751 rot. 1.

[71] C. A. F. Meekings, 'Cal. of Assize and Gaol-Del. Coms.', 1377–99 (TS. in P.R.O. Round Room), pp. 1, 6, 22, 24, 31, 37, 39–40, 42, 58, 61. Some coms. may not have been inrolled and others not acted upon.

[72] *Cal. Pat.* 1485–1509, *passim*.

[73] Ibid. 1494–1509, 146, 288, 531; *L. & P. Hen. VIII*, iv(3), p. 2919.

[74] *T.S.A.S.* iii. 311–48, *passim*.

[75] Pugh, *Imprisonment*, 304–5.

[76] Meekings, 'Cal. of Assize Coms.', p. 6; *Cal. Pat.* 1429–36, 474; 1452–61, 255. The last two coms. are to try named individuals.

[77] *T.S.A.S.* iii. 336.

[78] *Eng. Govt. at Work*, iii. 255; J.I. 3/127 rot. 8; J.I. 3/131 rot. 1.

[79] J.I. 1/750 rott. 3, 4d.; J.I. 1/751 rot. 3d.; J.I. 3/131 rott. 10d., 14d., 25d.; J.I. 3/166 rot. 5; J.I. 3/197 rot. 14; S.R.O. 3365/824. A Feb. sitting occurred in 1391 (J.I. 3/180 rot. 49), an Apr. one in 1440 (*Cal. Pat.* 1436–41, 518).

[80] J.I. 1/750 rott. 1 and d., 3, 4; J.I. 1/751 rott. 1, 2d.; J.I. 3/131 rott. 19, 23; J.I. 3/166 rot. 5; J.I. 3/180 rott. 49, 52, 53; *Cal. Pat.* 1436–41, 518; S.R.O. 3365/391, rot. 2. There were Sept. sittings in 1373, 1403, and 1405: J.I. 1/750 rot. 2 and d.; J.I. 3/161 rot. 9d. In 1407 there was a sitting in May (J.I. 1/750 rot. 3d.) besides Mar. and Aug.

[81] One occurred in 1396: J.I. 3/180 rot. 53d.

[82] The last known was in Dec. 1347: J.I. 3/131 rot. 10.

[83] S.R.O. 538/5; 3365/2474; *T.S.A.S.* iii. 312, 317, 338, 340, 343, 346, 348, 350.

[84] *T.S.A.S.* iii. 291, 294, 299, 313, 319, 326, 331, 335, 337, 341, 344, 346, 348. In 1587 Aug. was said to be the normal month for Salop.: ibid. 311. Sessions were held in Sept. then and in 1591: ibid. 322.

In the 1330s it was not necessary for the justices to handle the civil business at the same towns as their gaol deliveries.[85] In August 1331 civil business was heard at Shrewsbury on the first and at Ford on the eighth.[86] In April 1334 civil business was heard at Ludlow on the seventh and the county gaol was delivered at Shrewsbury on the ninth.[87] Wherever the civil business was heard, it appears that the county gaol was invariably delivered at either Shrewsbury[88] or, at least from 1379, Bridgnorth.[89] By Henry IV's reign, presumably in response to recent statutes,[90] the civil business seems usually to have been handled in the same place as the gaol deliveries.[91] Civil hearings at Ludlow occur occasionally in the 16th century,[92] probably because of the presence of the Council in the Marches. The choice of Bridgnorth or Shrewsbury as the place of gaol delivery depended on the justices' convenience. In the 1330s justices travelling between Hereford and Stafford found Shrewsbury more convenient; travelling between Hereford and Wolverhampton they preferred Bridgnorth.[93] Sometimes, at least in the 1330s[94] and in the earlier 16th century,[95] Herefordshire assizes and gaol deliveries were held at Ludford (Herefs.), allowing the justices to hold Shropshire assizes, if not gaol deliveries, across the bridge at Ludlow[96] with the minimum of travelling. By the 1590s, however, assizes and county gaol deliveries at Ludlow were virtually unknown.[97]

The frequent gaol deliveries at Bridgnorth caused the sheriff much inconvenience. Prisoners had to be taken down river from Shrewsbury by boat, the only secure means of carrying them, and they seem to have been kept on the boat at Bridgnorth while awaiting trial.[98] From the 1550s until 1579 Shrewsbury was seldom if ever visited,[99] apparently because Wolverhampton had become the usual town for Staffordshire assizes. In 1579 the queen seems to have personally ordered Staffordshire assizes to be held thenceforth only at Stafford;[1] in 1579 sittings at Shrewsbury were resumed,[2] and those at Bridgnorth seem to have ceased for a few years.[3] They had, however, been resumed by 1590,[4] by which time assizes were again being held at Wolverhampton.[5] In the 1590s the Lent assizes were usually held at Bridgnorth[6] and the Summer ones at Shrewsbury.[7] The justices nevertheless exercised their preferences. Before Lent 1594 the sheriff was told by the chief baron of the Exchequer that if the next Staffordshire assizes were at Stafford the Shropshire ones would be at Shrewsbury, but that if they were at Wolverhampton the Shropshire ones would have to be at Bridgnorth.[8] At Lent 1602 the justices sat at Bridgnorth after a dispute with Shrewsbury corporation about their entertainment.[9] In the 17th century fewer assizes sat at Wolverhampton[10] and so fewer were held at Bridgnorth,[11] where they were last held in 1739.[12] Despite threats to its status as an assize town[13] Shrewsbury remained such until 1971 when assizes were abolished.[14]

[85] Cockburn, *Assizes*, 20.
[86] *Eng. Govt. at Work*, iii. 255.
[87] Ibid.; J.I. 3/127 rot. 7.
[88] J.I. 3/127 rott. 6, 8; J.I. 3/131 rott. 1, 10, 14d., 19, 23, 25d.; J.I. 3/161 rot. 9d.; J.I. 3/166 rot. 5; J.I. 3/180 rott. 49, 50, 51–2, 53 and d.; J.I. 3/189 rot. 23 and d.; J.I. 3/197 rot. 14; *L. & P. Hen. VIII*, iv(3), p. 2921.
[89] J.I. 3/166 rot. 5; J.I. 3/189 rot. 23; *Cal. Pat.* 1436–41, 17; *L. & P. Hen. VIII*, xx(1), p. 320.
[90] 6 Ric. II, c. 5; 11 Ric. II, c. 11: Cockburn, *Assizes*, 20.
[91] Known gaol dels. 1401–9: J.I. 3/189 rot. 23 and d. Corresponding assizes: J.I. 1/750 rott. 1d.–2, 3, 4d.; J.I. 1/751 rot. 1.
[92] S.R.O. 538/5; 3365/2474; *T.S.A.S.* i. 326.
[93] *Eng. Govt. at Work*, iii. 253, 255–6.
[94] Ibid. 255.
[95] *L. & P. Hen. VIII*, iv(3), p. 2921; *T.S.A.S.* xlix. 241.
[96] *Eng. Govt. at Work*, iii. 255.
[97] Summer assizes were held there 1592: *T.S.A.S.* iii. 324.

[98] *Reg. Council in Marches of Wales* (Cymmrodorion Rec. Ser. viii), 172.
[99] *Cal. Pat.* 1554–5, 104; 1563–6, pp. 37, 291; 1569–72, p. 215; *T.S.A.S.* 4th ser. vi. 145.
[1] *V.C.H. Staffs.* vi. 200–1.   [2] *T.S.A.S.* iii. 282.
[3] Ibid. 291, 294, 299, 311–13.
[4] Ibid. 317.   [5] *V.C.H. Staffs.* vi. 201.
[6] *T.S.A.S.* iii. 324, 332, 338, 340, 343, 346. They were at Shrews. 1603: ibid. 350.
[7] Ibid. 319, 322, 326, 331, 335, 337, 339, 341, 344, 346, 348. They were at Ludlow 1592 (ibid. 324), Bridgnorth 1595 (ibid. 332).
[8] *T.S.A.S.* 2nd ser. v. 295.
[9] Blakeway, *Sheriffs*, 98.
[10] *V.C.H. Staffs.* vi. 201.
[11] Cockburn, *Assizes*, 36.
[12] *T.S.A.S.* xlix. 216 n.
[13] e.g. *Shrews. Chron.* 6 Jan. 1888; S.R.O., q. sess. min. bk. 20, p. 226.
[14] Under the Courts Act, 1971, c. 23.

The County Coroners

In 1194 three coroners and a clerk were required to be elected in each county.[15] By 1203 there were at least three county coroners in Shropshire[16] and by 1221 they numbered four.[17] That seems to have been regarded thereafter as their proper number. In 1265, probably because of the disorders of the realm, the number in Shropshire had fallen to three and the election of a fourth was accordingly ordered.[18]

The names of nearly 60 Shropshire county coroners who served between 1194 and 1327 are known.[19] They conform in general to the type of knight or small landowner[20] who normally filled the office in other counties.[21] Five or more were subescheators,[22] at least four were assize or gaol-delivery justices,[23] about three were tax commissioners,[24] and three were knights of the shire.[25] Only one was a keeper of the peace,[26] and one was an under-sheriff.[27] None was a sheriff or, as far as is known, a commissioner of array. Of the known county coroners 47 are not found in any of those other offices. There was, on the contrary, a tendency by the mid 13th century for some of the coroners to be elected from a few families that had become identified with the coronership. Thirteenth-century examples include the Hunalds, William (fl. as coroner *c.* 1247)[28] and his son[29] John (fl. *c.* 1298),[30] and Gilbert of Bucknell (fl. 1248 × 1256)[31] and his heir[32] Walter (fl. 1272 × 1292).[33] Some 13th-century families of coroners continued into the next century: Philip de Clinton (fl. 1261–72)[34] was eventually followed by his heirs[35] Ives (fl. 1292)[36] and John (fl. 1329–c. 1354),[37] and John FitzEyre (fl. 1292)[38] by his son[39] Hugh (fl. *c.* 1307).[40] The tendency continued undiminished in the 14th century: Guy of Glazeley (fl. *c.* 1318)[41] was followed by his son[42] Alan (fl. 1329 × 1333);[43] John de Warenne (fl. *c.* 1325–1336)[44] by his son[45] Griffin (fl. 1353–4).[46]

Evidence of the coroners' activities in 13th-century Shropshire is too fragmentary to show whether each acted in a recognized district. Early-14th-century evidence suggests that he did.[47] Shropshire coroners might act in pairs; a man was tried in 1300 after indictment in Brimstree hundred before two coroners.[48]

The Escheators

When escheators were first appointed, two for each county, in 1232,[49] the choice in Shropshire[50] fell upon Vivian of Rossall, who occurs elsewhere as a knight of the grand assize, a tax commissioner,[51] and a gaol-delivery justice,[52] and Herbert Malvoisin, who

---

[15] R. F. Hunnisett, *Medieval Coroner* (1961), 1–4.
[16] *Pleas bef. King or his Justices, 1198–1212,* iii, p. 74.
[17] *Rolls of Justices in Eyre, 1221–2,* p. 463.
[18] *Cal. Close, 1264–8,* 114.
[19] Ibid. 1231–4, 66, 172, 219; 1237–42, 105; 1247–51, 69; 1251–3, 166, 351; 1272–9, 520; 1296–1318, *passim;* 1323–7, 303; *Pleas bef. King or his Justices, 1198–1212,* iii, p. 74; *Rolls of Justices in Eyre, 1221–2,* pp. 463, 568; Harding, 'Salop. Eyre Roll', 233, 380; J.I. 1/736 rot. 25; J.I. 1/739 rot. 47; Eyton, i. 141; vi. 91.
[20] Most can be identified in Eyton, *passim.*
[21] Hunnisett, *Med. Coroner,* 170–1; Katherine S. Naughton, *Gentry of Beds. in 13th and 14th Cents.* (Leicester Univ. Dept. of Eng. Local Hist. Occ. Papers, 3rd ser. ii), 44.
[22] *Cal. Close, 1307–13,* 316; Eyton, i. 205; iv. 265; *S.H.C.* 1912, 296–7.
[23] Eyton, i. 205; *Cal. Pat. 1272–81,* 346; *Cal. Close, 1279–88,* 269, 365.
[24] *Cal. Close, 1234–7,* 551; Eyton, ix. 314.
[25] *T.S.A.S.* 4th ser. x. 8–9.
[26] *Cal. Pat. 1281–92,* 265.
[27] *Cart. Shrews.* i, p. 25.
[28] *Cal. Close, 1247–51,* 69, 101.
[29] *V.C.H. Salop.* viii. 81.
[30] *Cal. Close, 1296–1302,* 146.
[31] Harding, 'Salop. Eyre Roll', 233.
[32] Eyton, xi. 319–20.
[33] J.I. 1/739 rot. 47.
[34] Eyton, vi. 359; J.I. 1/736 rot. 25.
[35] Eyton, v. 113.
[36] J.I. 1/739 rot. 47.
[37] J.I. 3/214/3 rot. 10d.; *Cal. Close, 1354–60,* 34.
[38] J.I. 1/739 rot. 47.
[39] Eyton, i. 205–6.
[40] *Cal. Close, 1302–7,* 488.
[41] Ibid. 1313–18, 520. [42] Eyton, i. 215.
[43] J.I. 3/214/3 rot. 10; J.I. 3/127 rot. 6.
[44] *Cal. Close, 1323–7,* 303; 1333–7, 599.
[45] Eyton, ix. 209–10, 238.
[46] J.I. 3/131 rot. 19; *Cal. Pat. 1354–8,* 94.
[47] See p. 80. [48] J.I. 3/99 rot. 11.
[49] Powicke, *Hen. III and Ld. Edw.* 106.
[50] *Cal. Close, 1231–4,* 130.
[51] Eyton, x. 88.
[52] *Cal. Pat. 1225–32,* 523.

also occurs as a knight of the grand assize and as a county coroner.[53] When in 1234 the system of two all-England escheatries, north and south of the Trent, was initiated, Shropshire was placed in the southern one. At that stage the escheators worked through the sheriffs.[54] By 1246, however, Shropshire had its own subescheator, independent of the sheriff. He was William Hunald,[55] who also occurs as a county coroner.[56] From about 1272 Shropshire and Staffordshire formed a single subescheatry, and in the period 1272–4 there is evidence that suggests two subescheators, each one acting in both counties.[57] One of the men appears at about the same time acting in Herefordshire.[58] In 1275 the two 'grand' escheatries were temporarily discontinued, the duties of escheator being conferred on the sheriffs, but in 1283 the previous system was resumed. From 1323 to 1327 the grand escheatries were again temporarily discontinued and Shropshire was part of an escheatry consisting also of Gloucestershire, Herefordshire, Worcestershire, Staffordshire, and the 'Welsh marches'.[59]

At least some subescheators were appointed by the Crown.[60] Their periods of office varied unpredictably. William of Ercall served for some four years from 1247,[61] whereas Eudes of Hodnet served only four days in 1252. For some reason the office changed hands four times in Shropshire in that year.[62] The subescheators' standing seems to have resembled that of the county coroners.[63] Of twelve men known to have held the office between 1234 and 1327,[64] at least four were county coroners[65] and at least four were assize or gaol-delivery justices.[66] One occurs as a tax commissioner[67] and the same man alone occurs as a keeper of the peace[68] and a knight of the shire.[69] None was ever a sheriff or, as far as is known, a commissioner of array or under-sheriff. As many as five of the twelve are not known in any of those other offices.

The Militia

In the earlier Middle Ages the feudal summons produced a small but formidable force of cavalry. It has, however, been calculated that by Edward I's reign Shropshire could provide fewer than seventy knights.[70] As campaigns grew in scale it became necessary to support the knights with large bodies of foot soldiers drawn from the county militias. The obligation of able-bodied men to defend their counties was as old as the county itself, but the county militias had been neglected in the earlier 12th century and were first revived by the Assize of Arms of 1181. In theory the militia was available in peace time to assist the sheriff in policing the county and in war time as a source of men for active service. Except in national emergencies, however, the militia seems in practice to have been dormant.[71] As a communal police force it was actively rejected in Shropshire.[72]

Until the 1280s the sheriff was usually responsible for 'arraying' in war time the number of men required from his shrievalty[73] and leading them to a named place of muster. The sheriff had to pay the men's wages from the county boundary to the place of muster, and might attempt to claim the cost at the Exchequer. Roger Sprenchose,

[53] Eyton, vii. 390.
[54] Powicke, *Hen. III and Ld. Edw.* 107.
[55] Eyton, iv. 265.
[56] *Cal. Close,* 1247–51, 69.
[57] *Cal. Fine R.* 1272–1307, 2, 16; *S.H.C.* 1912, 296; Eyton, ix 119.
[58] *Cal. Fine R.* 1272–1307, 48.
[59] *List of Escheators for Eng.* (List & Index Soc. lxxii), 4–5.
[60] *Cal. Close,* 1247–51, 101; 1251–3, 37, 54, 85, 87. Cf. Naughton, *Gentry of Beds.* 39.
[61] *Cal. Close,* 1247–51, 101; 1251–3, 37.
[62] Ibid. 1251–3, 37, 54, 85, 87.
[63] As in Beds.: Naughton, *Gentry of Beds.* 40.

[64] Eyton, iv. 123, 265, 369; *Cal. Close,* 1251–3, 37, 54, 85, 87; 1307–13, 316; *S.H.C.* 1912, 296.
[65] *Cal. Close,* 1247–51, 69; 1307–13, 179, 210; J.I. 1/739 rot. 47.
[66] Eyton, i. 205, 279; *Cal. Pat.* 1272–81, 338, 346.
[67] Eyton, ix. 314.
[68] *Cal. Pat.* 1281–92, 265.
[69] *T.S.A.S.* 4th ser. x. 8.
[70] J. E. Morris, *Welsh Wars of Edw. I* (1901), 36, 41.
[71] Powicke, *Military Obligation,* 28, 46–7, 58–9, 83–90, 118–19.
[72] See p. 21.
[73] Morris, *Welsh Wars,* 92.

sheriff 1278–86, found that difficult and in May 1283 entered into a special contract for the pay of his men. On another occasion, however, the expenses of each Shropshire soldier were borne by his own community.[74]

From the 1280s arraying was usually assigned to special commissioners.[75] Before 1299 Shropshire and Staffordshire were arrayed under the same commission; thereafter Shropshire usually had its own. For the Welsh campaign of 1282–3 both counties were arrayed by a single royal official,[76] and for that of 1294–5 by two royal officials, one of whom led the men to the place of muster.[77] The sheriff, however, arrayed Shropshire and Staffordshire for the campaign of 1287.[78] From the late 1290s the principal campaigns were against Scotland. The Shropshire arrayers for those expeditions were usually knights from the highest ranks of county society. Of fourteen local arrayers commissioned between 1297 and 1327[79] eleven occur at other times as knights of the shire,[80] six as keepers of the peace,[81] and three as sheriffs.[82] Between 1297 and May 1301 each commission named one local man, but in December 1297 he was accompanied by two royal servants as supervisors,[83] and in May 1301 by one royal servant.[84] Thereafter there were usually two local commissioners. A royal servant was attached in December 1301[85] and in March 1316[86] but after 1301 the commissioners usually acted without direct royal supervision. An array commissioner might be appointed to lead the men to the point of muster: Thomas of Rossall took the Shropshire levy to Newcastle upon Tyne in 1298,[87] Walter of Higford was required to lead the men to Carlisle in 1308,[88] and Walter Haket to lead them to Newcastle in May and June 1322.[89] In Edward II's reign different methods of levying militiamen were occasionally ordered over the country generally.[90] The sheriff's ancient power to call out the whole militia, the *posse comitatus*, or any part of it, was revived in Shropshire in 1316 when the sheriff was ordered to summon the *posse* in support of Lord Charlton against Welsh 'rebels'.[91]

On arrival at the place of muster the county levy came, with that of other counties, under the supreme command of a 'captain'.[92] For example in the Welsh campaign of 1277 the forces of Shropshire, Staffordshire, and Herefordshire were placed under Roger Mortimer (II) of Wigmore, based on Montgomery castle.[93] He had a similar command in the 1282 campaign, but died later that year and was succeeded by Roger Le Strange,[94] who also commanded in the next Welsh campaign, that of 1287.[95] Such captains were forerunners of the later lieutenants. So, too, were the county 'keepers of the peace' appointed to military command by both sides in the Barons Wars of the 1260s.[96] Within each county levy there is evidence by the 1280s that every hundred men were placed under a 'centenar'.[97] Stephen of Frankton, the man who killed Llywelyn, prince of Wales, in 1282,[98] occurs as a Shropshire centenar in 1287.[99] It appears that each county levy so organized came under a 'millenar'.[1] In 1295 the Shropshire millenar was Thomas of Rossall,[2] who occurs in 1297 as an array commissioner.[3]

Because of its geographical situation Shropshire was one of eight Midland counties

[74] Powicke, *Military Obligation*, 123–30.
[75] Morris, *Welsh Wars*, 92.
[76] Ibid. 192; *Cal. Chanc. R. Var.* 259.
[77] *Cal. Chanc. R. Var.* 355; Morris, *Welsh Wars*, 254.
[78] *Cal. Chanc. R. Var.* 312.
[79] *Cal. Pat.* 1292–1301, 313, 324, 437, 593; 1307–13, 82; 1313–17, 351, 461; 1321–4, 97, 125, 131, 214; *Cal. Close*, 1296–1302, 571.
[80] *T.S.A.S.* 4th ser. x. 8.
[81] *Cal. Pat.* 1281–92, 265; 1292–1301, 517; 1307–13, 31; 1313–17, 482; 1321–4, 42.
[82] *List of Sheriffs*, 117.
[83] *Cal. Pat.* 1292–1301, 324.
[84] Ibid. 593.
[85] *Cal. Close*, 1296–1302, 571.
[86] *Cal. Pat.* 1313–17, 461.
[87] Morris, *Welsh Wars*, 285.
[88] *Cal. Pat.* 1307–13, 82.
[89] Ibid. 1321–4, 125, 131.
[90] Powicke, *Military Obligation*, 139–56.
[91] *Cal. Pat.* 1313–17, 443.
[92] Powicke, *Military Obligation*, 131–2.
[93] *Cal. Close*, 1272–9, 358; Morris, *Welsh Wars*, 115.
[94] Morris, *Welsh Wars*, 155, 181–2.
[95] Ibid. 207, 209; *Cal. Chanc. R. Var.* 306–7.
[96] *Trans. R.H.S.* 5th ser. x. 96–101.
[97] Morris, *Welsh Wars*, 92.
[98] Powicke, *13th Cent.* 428.
[99] Morris, *Welsh Wars*, 184.
[1] Ibid. 96; Powicke, *Military Obligation*, 121.
[2] Morris, *Welsh Wars*, 96.
[3] *Cal. Pat.* 1292–1301, 324.

from which, almost exclusively, the foot soldiers for Edward I's Welsh campaigns were drawn. As a result the Shropshire levies became skilful and hardened troops, and were much drawn upon for later campaigns against Scotland.[4] Evidence before the 13th century is scanty, but it seems likely, for instance, that Shropshire militiamen accompanied Earl Hugh of Montgomery on the Anglesey expedition in which he died in 1098.[5] In Edward I's Welsh campaigns it was usual for 500–1,000 Shropshire foot to be serving at any one time.[6] In the force that defeated Llywelyn in 1282 the foot were almost entirely from Shropshire.[7] Shropshire levies were more effective in Scotland than those of many another English county.[8] Some 1,700 Shropshire foot were sent for the Falkirk campaign of 1298.[9] Service in Scotland, however, was probably less congenial to Shropshire men than service against the Welsh, and in December 1299 Shropshire men were among the shire levies who deserted.[10] Nevertheless for Edward II's Scottish expeditions large Shropshire contingents continued to be levied.[11]

Royal Castles and County Gaols

There were no royal castles in Shropshire until 1102, when Bridgnorth and Shrewsbury were resumed by the Crown upon Robert of Bellême's forfeiture. Thereafter those castles were usually in the sheriff's custody. Between 1204, however, when sheriffs of modest personal standing began occasionally to be appointed,[12] and the 1270s, when Edward I's conquest of Wales suddenly diminished the strategic importance of the Shropshire castles,[13] military reasons sometimes dictated the appointment of an independent royal keeper for one or both of the castles if a non-curial sheriff was in office.[14]

In May and June 1215, during Thomas of Erdington's shrievalty, Bridgnorth was kept by two royal keepers, Robert de Courtenay and Walter de Verdun.[15] Llywelyn ap Iorwerth had taken advantage of the civil war in England to attack Shropshire, and had captured Shrewsbury.[16] From 1225 to 1227, a period that corresponded closely to the shrievalty of John Bonet, Bridgnorth was kept for the king by Thomas Mauduit,[17] like Bonet a man with strong Wiltshire connexions.[18] During Robert of Hay's shrievalty, 1234–6, Richard of Wrotham occurs as royal keeper there.[19] No independent royal keeper is known to have been appointed for Shrewsbury castle in the earlier 13th century, a fact suggesting that Bridgnorth castle was then reckoned the more important.

The appointment of independent keepers began again in the late 1250s. In May 1257 John de Grey was made captain of the king's army to defend the whole of the Welsh border, and was made keeper of Shrewsbury castle,[20] then in the hands of a non-curial sheriff. In September 1257 a new sheriff, Peter de Montfort, was appointed and was granted custody of both castles.[21] He was allowed to retain them after 1258, when his shrievalty passed to humbler men. In May 1260 the keepership passed from Montfort to his brother-in-law,[22] James of Audley,[23] and Audley kept it when he became sheriff in 1261.[24] In May 1262 Ralph Basset of Drayton occurs as baronial keeper of Shrewsbury castle,[25] but may have been unable to exercise the office; Audley occurs again as

[4] Morris, *Welsh Wars*, 93, 96–7, 296.
[5] Powicke, *Military Obligation*, 41.
[6] Morris, *Welsh Wars*, 96, 128, 156, 182, 192, 208–9, 254, 263–4.
[7] Ibid. 182.
[8] Ibid. 296.
[9] Ibid. 285–6.
[10] Ibid. 98, 298.
[11] *Cal. Pat.* 1307–13, 82; 1321–4, 97, 131; *Cal. Close*, 1318–23, 521, 645.
[12] See p. 13.
[13] R. Allen Brown and others, *Hist. of King's Works*, i. 233.
[14] *E.H.R.* xci. 27.
[15] Eyton, i. 272.
[16] J. E. Lloyd, *Hist. Wales* (2nd edn.), ii. 643.
[17] Eyton, i. 275; *Cal. Pat.* 1225–32, 126.
[18] Emma Mason, 'The Mauduits and their Chamberlainship of the Exchequer', *Bull. Inst. Hist. Res.* xlix. 6–7.
[19] Eyton, i. 278.
[20] *Cal. Pat.* 1247–58, 553–4.
[21] Ibid. 579.
[22] *D.N.B. sub* Audley, Jas. de (d. 1272).
[23] *Cal. Pat.* 1258–66, 70.
[24] Ibid. 163, 200.
[25] Eyton, i. 281.

keeper in July.[26] In June 1263 Bridgnorth surrendered to the barons,[27] and Audley was replaced as keeper of both Bridgnorth and Shrewsbury by Hamon Le Strange.[28] In August Strange became sheriff as well. He soon went over to the king's side, and in 1264 there were unsuccessful baronial efforts to replace him with Ralph Basset.[29] By June 1265 Basset seems to have been in control of at least Shrewsbury castle.[30] After the barons' defeat at Evesham in August 1265 custody of both castles seems to have reverted to the sheriff.

Constables served under the sheriff or keeper.[31] They were usually local men, but of lower rank than the county leaders. Of twelve known constables of Bridgnorth or Shrewsbury between 1209 and 1302,[32] at least two were county coroners[33] and at least two others were hundred bailiffs.[34]

There was a gaol at Bridgnorth by 1203[35] but it is not certain that it was a county gaol. By 1207 there were at least four gaols in Shropshire and Staffordshire repairable by the sheriff. It is therefore likely that both Bridgnorth and Shrewsbury had county gaols by then.[36] It is probable that those gaols were always in the castles, though the earliest evidence comes only from the 13th century.[37] Bridgnorth county gaol was probably abandoned from the mid 1280s, when deliveries of it apparently ceased.[38] The county gaols were in the sheriff's custody, at least when the castles were, and he might be held liable for escapes.[39] On other occasions, however, the gaolers were held responsible.[40] Gaolerships may sometimes have been hereditary: in 1271 William Catchpole was gaoler of Shrewsbury county gaol, having succeeded his father in the post.[41]

[26] *Cal. Lib.* 1260–7, 107.
[27] Treharne, *Baronial Plan*, 303.
[28] *Cal. Pat.* 1258–66, 266, 300.
[29] Ibid. 367, 397.
[30] Ibid. 434.
[31] e.g. *Cal. Lib.* 1260–7, 27.
[32] Ibid.; Eyton, i. 288–9; *Rot. Hund.* ii. 94, 105; *Cal. Close*, 1231–4, 66; *T.S.A.S.* 3rd ser. v. 163.
[33] *Cal. Close*, 1231–4, 66; J.I. 1/736 rot. 25.
[34] Eyton, i. 288–9.
[35] *Pleas bef. King or his Justices, 1198–1212*, iii, p. 80.

[36] Pugh, *Imprisonment*, 73.
[37] Ibid. 74; *Cal. Close*, 1231–4, 94.
[38] Pugh, *Imprisonment*, 74. Coms. to deliver a gaol at Bridgnorth occur until at least 1301 (ibid.), but there is no evidence that it was other than the town gaol (inf. from pat. rolls supplied by Prof. R. B. Pugh).
[39] Harding, 'Salop. Eyre Roll', 248, 291.
[40] *Cal. Close*, 1268–72, 347; J.I. 3/99 rot. 11d. A similar uncertainty attaches to the liability in other cos.: Pugh, *Imprisonment*, 248.
[41] *Cal. Close*, 1268–72, 347.

THE FRANCHISES

The Marcher Lordships and the Border with Wales, p. 34. Private Hundreds, p. 42. Other Franchises and the Development of the Leet, p. 45.

'EVERY lord may summon his man so that he may impose his justice on him in his court.'[1] Thus, baldly, the author of the *Leges Henrici Primi* introduced the subject of feudal jurisdiction, 'the obscurest institution in Anglo-Norman history'.[2] Feudal jurisdiction, which came to be seen as mainly civil in character, could be claimed by a lord only over the tenants who held of his honor, and in this passage the author of the *Leges* was drawing attention to only one of two ways in which great lords might claim other men as belonging to their jurisdiction. For they also had quasi-criminal jurisdiction. Increasingly in the 12th and 13th centuries, as royal government expanded and Crown lawyers developed theoretical defences of the Crown's legal sovereignty, that criminal jurisdiction came to be seen as franchisal; it derived ultimately from the king's delegation or continued toleration of it and carried the right of holding a court in one place which the king's officers held elsewhere. Thence flowed the lord's duty of doing justice, within his liberty, to all sorts and conditions of men, whether they were of his fee or not.

Franchisal jurisdiction was older than feudal jurisdiction: it was known in the Confessor's England no less than the Conqueror's.[3] The franchises also long outlasted the abolition of feudal tenures. To that extent there is historical justification for distinguishing feudal jurisdiction from the liberty of the franchise-holder. Nevertheless undue emphasis of the different origins of feudal and franchisal jurisdictions, hardly appropriate even for a later period,[4] could serve only to falsify discussion of the rights enjoyed in England by the earliest generations of Norman barons whose jurisdiction in criminal matters is adverted to in the last of that obscure collection of rights summarized in the Old English mnemonic, sac and soc, toll and team, and infangthief: the right to hang a thief caught within their liberties. It is moreover from Shropshire that one of the earliest pieces of evidence comes to suggest that the king's barons enjoyed those rights throughout their fees and not in the localized fashion of the later franchises. They seem an inherent element of baronial status, and hence they could be alienated, as when, in 1121 or 1122, William Peverel of Dover granted to Thurstan the steward and his heirs, for the service of ½ knight, Gidding (Hunts.) and Daywall (in Whittington) with sac and soc, toll and team, and infangthief.[5]

Whatever the sources of their different rights and liberties, it seems certain that during the first century after the Conquest neither the king nor his barons were preoccupied by theoretical distinctions between feudal and baronial or franchisal jurisdictions. The jurisdictions influenced each other and combined eventually to define the administrative map of the shire. Nowhere in Shropshire, however, did those jurisdictions combine to such effect as in the lordships which marched with Wales,

[1] *Leges Henrici Primi*, ed. L. J. Downer (Oxford, 1972), 172–3. Cf. ibid. 104–7, 319–20.

[2] F. M. Stenton, *First Cent. of Eng. Feudalism, 1066–1166* (Oxford, 1932), 41.

[3] Salop., e.g., may have had one private hund. before

1066 (see below, p. 43), Herefs. certainly had 5 comital hunds. (*V.C.H. Herefs.* i. 274, 337–8).

[4] N. Denholm-Young, *Seignorial Admin. in Eng.* (1963 edn.), 95.

[5] Stenton, *Eng. Feudalism*, 105, 154–5, 157, 273–4.

and it was there that they did most to modify the limits of the county. It will be convenient first to summarize the development of the liberties in those western marches, and thereafter to deal with the rest of the county.

The Marcher Lordships and the Border with Wales

The five westernmost Domesday hundreds of Shropshire, 'Mersete', 'Ruesset', Whittery ('Witentreu'), 'Rinlau', and Leintwardine,[6] were wholly or partly lost to the county and to England during the Middle Ages, and even Baschurch hundred lost one lordship.[7] The losses of territory were greatest in the north and south. The whole of 'Mersete' and the whole of Leintwardine became marcher lordships. The western portion of 'Rinlau' hundred became the marcher lordship of Clun; the eastern portion became Purslow hundred but, though its lords were also the lords of Clun, Purslow remained in Shropshire. Whittery hundred lost many of its western vills to the welshry of the Upper Gorddwr and many of its southern vills to the marcher lordships of Montgomery and Halcetor. Thus reduced, Chirbury hundred, as it became known, remained in Shropshire though it became dependent on the marcher castle of Montgomery. Least territory was lost from the Domesday hundred of 'Ruesset': Trewern, Roger fitz Corbet's great Domesday manor of 'Alretone',[8] became the welshry of the Nether Gorddwr. The lordship of Caus, however, remained debatable land between England and Wales.[9]

In these parts of the county compact territories were continuously concentrated in few hands from the Conqueror's reign onwards. In the centre lay the block of properties belonging to the Corbets of Caus from the early years of the Conquest until the failure of their male line in the early 14th century.[10] To the north and south respectively were the extensive lands which belonged in 1086 to Reynold of Bailleul and to Picot de Say, all of which passed in the 12th century to the FitzAlans.[11] Further south still, concentrated in Leintwardine hundred, lay the great estates which belonged to the Mortimers of Wigmore and their heirs throughout the Middle Ages.[12] It was on the estates of these families that the western parts of Shropshire were transformed into Welsh marcher lordships, and the continued vigour of the feudal courts over parts at least of the honors of these families seems to have helped such a transformation. That very vigour, however, continuing as it did during a period which elsewhere witnessed the decline of such courts,[13] requires an explanation to be sought in the common circumstances of the Corbets, FitzAlans, and Mortimers.

All three families held compact estates, thereby eluding what was normally one of the greatest obstacles to the development of honorial jurisdiction, the enforcement of suit from widely scattered tenants.[14] Moreover none of the three families was unduly distracted by interests in other parts of the kingdom. The Corbets of Caus indeed were exclusively a marcher family,[15] and the FitzAlans, despite their acquisition of great estates in the south of England in 1243, regarded themselves primarily as a marcher family until the 1330s.[16] The Mortimers had wider interests than the other

---

[6] See map on p. 8.

[7] Ruyton: see pp. 35, 41–2. There were similar losses elsewhere: see e.g. *V.C.H. Glos.* x. 1, 3.

[8] *V.C.H. Salop.* viii. 303.

[9] For this para. and for much of what follows invaluable topographical evidence was provided by Wm. Rees's map, *S. Wales and the Border in the Fourteenth Cent.* (Ordnance Survey, 1932), N.E. sheet, and Prof. Rees's explanatory handbk. of the same title (Western Mail & Echo Ltd., Cardiff, 1933). The administrative boundaries there delineated, however, have not necessarily been accepted. M. Richards, *Welsh Administrative and Terri-*

torial Units (Cardiff, 1969), and Wm. Rees, *Hist. Atlas of Wales* (1972 edn.), were also used.

[10] *V.C.H. Salop.* i. 297; viii. 310–11.

[11] Ibid. i. 296–7.

[12] Ibid. 288–9; *V.C.H. Herefs.* i. 275–6.

[13] Denholm-Young, *Seignorial Admin.* 86 sqq.

[14] Ibid. 98.

[15] A[ugusta] E. C[orbet], *The Fam. of Corbet: its Life and Times* (2 vols. [1915–18]).

[16] *Two Estate Surveys of the FitzAlan Earls of Arundel* (Suss. Rec. Soc. lxvii), pp. xxv–xxvi; *V.C.H. Salop.* ii. 64.

two families, but Wigmore long remained the centre of their power.[17] Thus far the circumstances of the three families coincided, but in two respects the FitzAlans and Mortimers differed from the Corbets. First, unlike the Corbets, both families held the strategic office of sheriff during significant periods, indeed at times which seem to have been crucial to the development of their extensive liberties. Secondly each family long enjoyed uninterrupted royal favour which coincided with, reinforced, and partly explains, their tenure of local office: for the FitzAlans that period was the reign of Henry II, for the Mortimers the years after the battle of Evesham (1265).[18]

The FitzAlans, who acquired the estates of Hugh, son of Warin (Reynold of Bailleul's stepson), probably by 1114,[19] were then recent immigrants from the Côtentin and had probably been in the service of Henry I before he became king.[20] With Hugh's estates they acquired a title, which was to become almost hereditary, to the shrievalty of Shropshire.[21] Prominent among the new men of Henry's reign,[22] they remained unswervingly loyal to his daughter after his death and thus deserved well of Henry II. Early in the new reign, *c.* 1155, the marriage of William FitzAlan (I) to Isabel de Say brought the barony and lordship of Clun to the FitzAlans, though Isabel's long life and two subsequent marriages deferred her son's possession of her inheritance until 1199.[23]

It must have been during this period of their prosperity that the FitzAlans withdrew their lordship of Oswestry from the county.[24] Certainly by 1203 William FitzAlan (II), calling the whole shire court to witness, was claiming that land in his 'hundred' did no suit to the Shropshire county court, that neither the sheriff nor even the king's justices could summon its inhabitants, and that the king's writ did not run there.[25] The FitzAlans' tenure of the shrievalty,[26] and their probable tenure of Oswestry (formerly 'Mersete') hundred,[27] must have assisted their withdrawal of their own lordship's due suit to the county court, and the favour which the family deserved of Henry II may have produced a degree of royal acquiescence. The suits withdrawn from the county by 1203 included not merely those owed for his own lordship but also those owed for the adjacent lordships of Knockin and Ruyton of the Eleven Towns. The lordships were held of FitzAlan's barony by the Le Stranges, another family from the Côtentin who had arrived in England about the same time as the FitzAlans and had probably been connected with them in Henry I's service before 1100. The area thus withdrawn from Shropshire coincided (with the exception of Whittington) with the Domesday hundred of 'Mersete' to which the lordship of Ruyton was attracted from Baschurch (later Pimhill) hundred.[28]

The attraction of the Le Strange lordship of Ruyton from its original hundred into this great liberty[29] suggests that the FitzAlans' hundredal jurisdiction was reinforced by their feudal jurisdiction: they were the Le Stranges' overlords. If the continued vigour of the FitzAlans' feudal and hundredal jurisdictions in association with each

[17] *D.N.B. sub* Mortimer, Ralph de (d. 1104?) and Hugh I de (d. 1181). Ludlow was an important centre of Mortimer power in the later Middle Ages.
[18] See below. [19] See p. 10.
[20] J. H. Round, *Studies in Peerage and Family Hist.* (Westminster, 1901), 120 sqq. The Côtentin was Hen.'s first possession: *D.N.B.*
[21] See pp. 11–12.
[22] Though not one of those who, in Orderic's celebrated phrase (A. L. Poole, *From Dom. Bk. to Magna Carta, 1087–1216* (2nd edn.), 388), were 'raised . . . from the dust'.
[23] Eyton, xi. 228–9; I. J. Sanders, *Eng. Baronies* (1960), 113.
[24] Llinos O. W. Smith, 'The Lordships of Chirk and Oswestry, 1282–1415' (London Univ. Ph.D. thesis, 1970),

90, also suggests the later 12th cent. as the period of withdrawal. Dr. Smith's thesis was seen only after the argument of this para. was written.
[25] *Pleas before the King or his Justices* (Selden Soc. lxxxiii), p. 96. Cf. Eyton, x. 316; xi. 6–7.
[26] See p. 12.
[27] See p. 39. Eyton's suggestion that they acquired the hund. lordship as part of Warin the bald's estates (x. 313) is here discarded: see p. 42.
[28] Eyton, x. 112, 369–71; *T.S.A.S.* 3rd ser. i. 33–8; H. Le Strange, *Le Strange Records* (1916), 1–11, 362–5; W. J. Slack, *Lordship of Oswestry* (Shrews. 1951), 16. For Whittington see below, pp. 38, 41.
[29] Ruyton's absorption of the much greater man. of Wykey (Eyton, xi. 22–3), always in 'Mersete' hund., was presumably coeval.

other can be only surmised in the case of Oswestry and Ruyton, it can be seen more clearly in the case of the lordship and barony of Clun and Purslow hundred. By 1255[30] the FitzAlans were enforcing suits to the court of Purslow hundred and to their honorial court at Clun with equal vigour, though by then Clun no longer formed part of the county. Only the bishop of Hereford's great estate of Lydbury North[31] escaped suit to the hundred court, while all the tenants of the barony of Clun within the hundred (some of whose suits had been drawn there from Leintwardine hundred)[32] also owed suit to John FitzAlan's court at Clun. The close association between the honorial court of Clun and the hundred court of Purslow persisted long after the close of the Middle Ages, and indeed in 1683 it gave an excuse to the lord of More to refuse suit to Purslow hundred, its court (he alleged) being kept improperly as a court of the honor of Clun and Purslow to which More owed no feudal dependence.[33]

The FitzAlans' withdrawal of Clun from the county seems to have occurred later than their withdrawal of Oswestry and its associated lordships. Clun and Obley had formed part of 'Rinlau' hundred in 1086.[34] Subsequently the lordship of both manors[35] and of the hundred passed to the FitzAlans. It is possible that the hundred, known as Purslow by 1183, was originally attached to the manor of Clun,[36] and that the FitzAlans' title to it thus derived from Picot de Say, one of Earl Roger's principal lieutenants in post-Conquest Shropshire.[37] Probably by 1183, certainly by 1255, Purslow was a private hundred of the FitzAlans.[38] Eyton considered that Clun, *caput* of the barony, was withdrawn from Shropshire by the Say family before 1154,[39] but evidence is lacking. If, as seems most likely, it was withdrawn by the FitzAlans, that must have happened in the time of William FitzAlan (III) (1210–15) or in the early years of his successor John FitzAlan (I) (d. 1240).[40] Clun seems to have been summoned to the 1203 eyre, though it evidently did not appear.[41] By 1221, however, the justices in eyre clearly accepted that Clun lay beyond the reach of the king's writ.[42]

The withdrawal of Clun may, as has been surmised in the case of Oswestry, have been countenanced by sheriffs who indulged the FitzAlans' policies. The FitzAlans' quasi-hereditary shrievalty of Shropshire had been ended by King John in 1201. From 1214, however, the sheriffs of Shropshire had special links with the FitzAlan family: in 1214 Thomas of Erdington (sheriff 1204–16) bought the wardship of William FitzAlan (III) and married him to his daughter.[43] William died without issue, probably in 1215, to be succeeded by his brother John, and the new sheriff (1217–23), Earl Ranulph of Chester, was uncle to John FitzAlan's wife.[44]

The Mortimers were settled in England a generation before the FitzAlans; they seem, however, to have fixed the immunities of their marcher lands later than the FitzAlans. Eyton professed to see signs of Ralph de Mortimer's anxiety to free his lands from hundredal jurisdiction as early as 1086[45] but without real evidence; elsewhere he clearly considered a much later date[46] for the Mortimers' establishment of immunities from shire and hundred in the lands which made up the marcher lordship of Wigmore. The early unrecorded disappearance of the Domesday hundred of Leintwardine, perhaps a consequence of its eccentric territorial organization,[47] further

[30] For the rest of this para. see *Rot. Hund.* (Rec. Com.), ii. 76–8.
[31] Eyton, xi. 194; below, pp. 46, 48. Buildwas abbey had withdrawn its suit for Kinnerton in 1254.
[32] *V.C.H. Salop.* i. 306; Eyton, xi. 294–5, 297.
[33] S.R.O. 1037/2, box 4, notes *re* John Walcot's claim for suit of More man. at Purslow hund., Mar. 1683.
[34] *V.C.H. Salop.* i. 287, 306, 335–6.
[35] Eyton, xi. 229, 245–6.
[36] Ibid. xi. 178–9.   [37] Ibid. 227.
[38] *Rot. Hund.* (Rec. Com.), ii. 77. Purslow was in the

centre of FitzAlan territory, and the FitzAlans' tenure of the hund. can thus be reasonably deduced from 1183.
[39] Eyton, xi. 228 (followed by *V.C.H. Salop.* i. 306).
[40] Eyton, vii. 245–6, 249, 252.   [41] Ibid. xi. 229.
[42] Ibid. 247; *Rolls of Justices in Eyre . . . 1221, 1222* (Selden Soc. lix), pp. xlv, 451–2.
[43] Eyton, vii. 247–50.
[44] Ibid. 252; *Complete Peerage*, i. 236–7.
[45] *V.C.H. Salop.* i. 283.
[46] Eyton, xi. 322, 326.
[47] Ibid. 293, 297. Cf. below, p. 43; map on p. 8.

obscures the story. In fact, however, as late as the eyre of 1221 the authority of the king's writ and of the justices in eyre was admitted in these south Shropshire Mortimer territories:[48] whatever their liberties were in the area, they were not yet as high as those established in Oswestry and Clun by the FitzAlans. The records of that same eyre, however, bear witness to the activity of Hugh de Mortimer's feudal court at Wigmore and of the knights who composed it,[49] meting rough, though perhaps adequate, justice to his tenants even in comparatively distant parts of the fee, such as Highley.[50] Within the next 70 years round the *caput* of their honor at Wigmore the Mortimers had succeeded in arrogating to themselves an even greater and more exclusive jurisdiction, withdrawing from the county (and from England) twenty or more vills[51] from which the king's writ and the authority of his justices were thenceforth excluded. After the battle of Evesham Roger Mortimer, who had rendered the royalists such outstanding services in the fighting, began to withdraw the suits of all his vills and manors from the hundreds of Shropshire,[52] and it would be consistent with his position at that time to assume that his privileges in the marcher lordship of Wigmore were established simultaneously. As in the case of the FitzAlans earlier, tenure of the shrievalty may have helped the process, for Roger was one of Edward I's leading councillors before and after his accession and his kinsmen were sheriffs from 1271 to 1274.[53]

The Corbets were ultimately less successful than the FitzAlans and the Mortimers in removing their lands from England. Nevertheless the feudal court of the barony of Caus remained vigorous until the end of the 13th century,[54] and from at least the 1230s Thomas Corbet (d. 1274) and his son Peter (d. 1300) withdrew large parts of their honor from the hundreds of Chirbury and Ford, attracting the suits to their court and liberty of Caus.[55] As with the Mortimers of Wigmore and the FitzAlans of Oswestry the highest franchises were claimed in the land lying around the *caput* of the honor. By 1292 they had long been arrogating to themselves, in the 'liberty of Caus' (Caus, Vennington, and Wallop), all the rights which amounted to the extensive franchise of return of writs: the exclusion of all royal officers, coroner,[56] sheriff, and even the king's justices.[57] Peter Corbet himself, however, had to admit that the liberty lay in Shropshire,[58] and so it remained throughout the Middle Ages; such was the effect of judicial decisions of 1292 and 1539. In the 15th century moreover, among the duke of Buckingham's vast possessions, Caus was the only lordship which could be considered at all Welsh and yet was not visited by the duke's itinerant justices.[59] Whether the Corbets and their heirs retained much of the great administrative liberty they had claimed around Caus in 1292 remains in doubt: in 1292 judgement was reserved.[60] What remained seems to have been a leet jurisdiction, co-ordinate with the sheriff's tourn, over the 'hundred of Caus'.[61] Suits to the court of Caus barony continued to be exacted throughout the Middle Ages; the free tenants, however, rarely attended after the early 14th century, the modest jurisdiction of a leet court perhaps hardly requiring their presence.[62]

[48] *Rolls of Justices in Eyre . . . 1221, 1222*, pp. xlv, 460, 488–9 (pleas *re* property in Trippleton and Leintwardine).
[49] On the *curia militum* see Denholm-Young, *Seignorial Admin.* 92 sqq.
[50] *Rolls of Justices in Eyre . . . 1221, 1222*, pp. xliii–xliv, 459–60, 489, 498–500; Eyton, iv. 261–3.
[51] *Plac. de Quo Warr.* (Rec. Com.), 675, 681; Eyton, xi. 326–7. Their suits were alleged to have been owed to Chirbury and Munslow hunds.
[52] See p. 48.
[53] Eyton, iv. 222; above, p. 17. For evidence that the Mortimers made vigorous use of the Salop. and Herefs. shrievalties see B. P. Evans, 'The Family of Mortimer' (Univ. of Wales Ph.D. thesis, 1934), 366–7.

[54] *V.C.H. Salop.* viii. 325.
[55] *Rot. Hund.* ii. 60, 66; *Plac. de Quo Warr.* 677, 681.
[56] By 1274: *Rot. Hund.* ii. 96.
[57] By 1292: *Plac. de Quo Warr.* 686. Cf. below, pp. 46–7.
[58] *Plac. de Quo Warr.* 686.
[59] T. B. Pugh, *Marcher Lordships of S. Wales, 1415–1536* (Cardiff, 1963), 39.
[60] Eyton, vii. 35; D. W. Sutherland, *Quo Warr. Procs. in Reign of Edw. I, 1278–1294* (1963), 103 sqq.
[61] *V.C.H. Salop.* viii. 325.
[62] *V.C.H. Salop.* viii. 325 (which offers a different explanation of declining attendances). Cf. Denholm-Young, *Seignorial Admin.* 91 sqq.

Some of the Corbets' outlying lands, however, were drawn into welshry. Around 1200 Robert Corbet granted his great western manor of Trewern to Gwenwynwyn, lord of Powys, in marriage with his daughter, and that part of the Corbet barony remained in the welshry of the Nether Gorddwr thereafter.[63] The south-western and northern lands of the barony were also taken into the welshry of the Upper and Nether Gorddwr respectively in the mid 13th century.[64] In the 1250s Thomas Corbet's nephew Gruffydd ap Gwenwynwyn overran many of his uncle's lands,[65] and in 1274 the loss of a third of Corbet's barony to the Welsh was attributed to the military successes in the 1260s of Llywelyn ap Gruffudd, prince of Wales.[66] It is significant, however, that even before those events the Corbets themselves had been taking their lands into welshry.[67] They were only partly successful. The lands of the Upper Gorddwr[68] remained permanently Welsh but those of the Nether Gorddwr lying east of Trewern[69] were adjudged part of Ford hundred in 1292[70] and again in 1539.[71]

The formation of other marcher lordships on the western edge of the county is more obscure. Whittington, originally in 'Mersete' hundred and a royal manor in Henry II's reign,[72] was conferred briefly (c. 1164-6) on William FitzAlan (II)'s stepfather only to be resumed and granted to one of the king's leading servants in north Wales and the marches. In the 13th century it passed to the FitzWarins who seem to have exercised a feudal — baronial or honorial — jurisdiction in their court there. It was unmentioned in the 13th-century inquiries into franchises, and by 1293, in the earl of Arundel's opinion at least, Whittington seems to have been regarded as a marcher lordship, and it was necessary to reunite it to England by the Act of 1536.[73] The lordship of Montgomery, forming part of Earl Roger's great estates in Whittery hundred in 1086, was made the *caput* of an honor bestowed by Henry I on Baldwin de Boullers in marriage with his niece. The heirs male of Baldwin and his wife failed in 1203 and after c. 1215 the Crown treated the honor as an escheat. A new royal castle had been begun there early in John's reign,[74] but from 1208-9 the territory around it was apparently in the hands of native Welsh rulers hostile to the Crown.[75] In 1228-9 Montgomery castle, started on a new site in 1223, passed to its builder Hubert de Burgh, earl of Kent, who a few months earlier had been granted extensive immunities, including quittance of shires and hundreds, throughout his lands.[76] The castelry was finally excluded from the county in 1233 when the Crown specified Offa's Dyke as the boundary between it and the Shropshire hundred of Chirbury.[77] The hundred nevertheless continued to be administered by officials of the lordship of Montgomery.[78]

The great liberties beyond the western boundary of the county became marcher lordships by withdrawal from the English shire system, their lords' privileges thus differing in origin from the more western marcher lands whose lords derived their

[63] R. Morgan, 'Trewern in Gorddwr . . . 1086-1311', *Montg. Coll.* lxiv. 129, 131.
[64] *Plac. de Quo Warr.* 681, 686; Eyton, vii. 34-5; xi. 102.
[65] *V.C.H. Salop.* viii. 178, 180, 202, 325; Eyton, vii. 25; *Welsh Assize Roll, 1277-1284,* ed. J. Conway Davies (1940), 16 sqq.
[66] *Rot. Hund.* ii. 90.
[67] Ibid. 96; Eyton, vii. 114; *V.C.H. Salop.* viii. 325.
[68] *T.S.A.S.* liv. 63-8. A separate ct. was held for them by the 1530s: ibid. 337.
[69] Ibid. 327.
[70] *Plac. de Quo Warr.* 686.
[71] *V.C.H. Salop.* viii. 180, 325.
[72] See p. 49 n. 12.
[73] Eyton, x. 314-15; xi. 29 sqq., 40; below, p. 41. *Cal. Close, 1234-7,* 504, mentions (1237) a judicial combat due to take place in Fulk FitzWarin's ct. *re* an appeal of larceny. Cf. *V.C.H. Wilts.* v. 54.

[74] Eyton, xi. 52, 54-5, 117 sqq., 126, 128, 130; I. J. Sanders, *Eng. Baronies* (Oxford, 1960), 22 (n. 7), 56.
[75] Gwenwynwyn, lord of S. Powys, whose lands were occupied by Llywelyn the Great whenever he supported the king: Eyton, xi. 131, 146; G. T. O. Bridgeman, 'The Princes of Upper Powys', *Collectanea Archaeologica,* i. 84-8, 182-3, 189.
[76] *Cal. Chart. R. 1226-57,* 54, 81, 83. Cf. Denholm-Young, *Seignorial Admin.* 92 n. 4. For an assessment of de Burgh's policies and for his work at Montgomery see R. F. Walker, 'Hubert de Burgh and Wales, 1218-32', *E.H.R.* lxxxvii. 465-94 (esp. p. 492).
[77] *Cal. Pat. 1232-47,* 18. The western part of Brompton, however, continued to extend a small peninsula of Chirbury hund. territory beyond the dyke.
[78] *Rot. Hund.* ii. 61; *Cal. Close, 1333-7,* 224; *Herbert Corresp.* ed. W. J. Smith (1968), p. 63.

privileges from conquest.[79] That historical difference sufficiently accounts for the maintenance of English legal procedure in the courts of Oswestry lordship and doubtless of other withdrawn lordships. In Oswestry normal procedure in pleas of land, for instance, was that of the English sworn inquisition not that of the laws of the march or of Wales,[80] and the lordship's origins as an English hundred[81] were also recalled by the procedure and substantive law of its subordinate borough and manorial courts with their three-weekly hallmoots and twice-yearly tourns or 'hundreds'.[82] The lordship or *patria*, 'Oswestryland',[83] may itself have had a court superior to these courts, though evidence of its activity is slight; feudal suits may have been rendered there.[84]

Whatever their varying origins, during the later Middle Ages the legal status and immunities of the withdrawn and of the conquered lordships in the marches were assimilated to each other and defined by long usage. Edward I had drawn the marcher lordships before his justices of oyer and terminer,[85] but after the marchers' defeat of Edward II royal authority receded from those ill-organized lands between England and the principality of Wales.[86] For over two centuries thereafter there was no regular admixture of royal with seignorial jurisdiction in the marches:[87] the marcher lords possessed full *iura regalia* and their courts were virtually omni-competent.[88] In the lordship of Clun it was claimed in 1319 that the earl of Arundel administered the law and the king's writ ran there only when the earl failed to do justice.[89] A century later the earls of March were said to have held the lordship of Wigmore outside any county and exempt from any other jurisdiction time out of mind, so that the king's writ did not run there.[90] Both the withdrawn and the conquered lordships, moreover, made use of the *dies marchie* and *cydfodau* by which disputes between the inhabitants of different lordships were resolved in the absence of any legal authority superior to their lords'.[91] In 1402 even a charge of aiding Owen Glendower within the lordship of Oswestry lay outside the jurisdiction of King's Bench.[92] Like the palatinate of Chester, these lordships evidently lay outside parliamentary England: their inhabitants could sit in Parliament only after naturalization[93] and they did not contribute to the expenses of the knights of the shire.[94]

The border between Wales and Shropshire c. 1300[95] may best be conceived as the western limits of the running of the king's writ, of the course of the common law, and of the authority of the English royal justices. When such questions were involved

[79] Smith, 'Lordships of Chirk and Oswestry, 1282–1415', 88–90, 99–100.

[80] Ibid. 93–4, 109. See ibid. 103–5 for differing rates of reception of Eng. procedure in Chirk and Denbigh.

[81] Ibid. 51–2, citing examples of the persistence of the term 'hundred' of Oswestry, which, however, was synonymous with lordship of Oswestry in the Middle Ages. See also, e.g., *Cal. Pat.* 1399–1401, 452.

[82] Smith, 'Chirk and Oswestry', 91–3, 96–8.

[83] Sir John Wynn's term: source cited in n. 86, below.

[84] Smith, 'Chirk and Oswestry', 92, 95–6. The holders of Aston and Sandford, and possibly the ld. of Ruyton, owed suit to the ct. at Oswestry in 1301, and the two former may have recognized it as a superior ct.

[85] *Welsh Assize Roll, 1277–1284*, ed. Davies, 86–97.

[86] Sir J. Wynn, *Hist. of the Gwydir Fam.* ed. J. Ballinger (Cardiff, 1927), 41–5; Rees, *Hist. Atlas of Wales*, 40–2, plate 45; above, pp. 19–20. For occasional efforts to assert the authority of the Crown or the prince of Wales in the marches see W. H. Waters, *The Edwardian Settlement of N. Wales in its Administrative and Legal Aspects (1284–1343)* (1935), 95–6, 127; Pugh, *Marcher Lordships of S. Wales*, 29–30, 279–81; R. A. Griffiths, 'Wales and the Marches', *Fifteenth-cent. Eng. 1399–1509*, ed. S. B. Chrimes *et al.* (1974), 145–72.

[87] Smith, 'Chirk and Oswestry', 91. In the principality of N. Wales, by contrast, there were royal cts., sheriffs held the tourn, and there were private franchises: ibid. 101, 105. For the principality sheriffs see R. A. Griffiths, 'Patronage, Politics, and the Principality of Wales, 1413–1461', *Brit. Govt. and Admin.* ed. Hearder and Loyn (1974), p. 70.

[88] Smith, 'Chirk and Oswestry', 87–9, 91, 94–5 (Oswestry), 96–8 (Ruyton), 106–7. Pleas concerning treason (ibid. 87–8) and advowson (ibid. 90, 100 n. 1), however, are said to have been beyond the lords' competence. For the latter see e.g. *Cal. Pat.* 1327–30, 561.

[89] *Yr. Bk.* 12 Edw. II (Selden Soc. lxxxi), 130–2, 158.

[90] *Cal. Close*, 1409–13, 207. But see *Cal. Pat.* 1338–40, 129 (mention of 'Wigmore, co. Salop.').

[91] Smith, 'Chirk and Oswestry', 107–8.

[92] J. E Lloyd, 'Oswestry as a Link between Eng. and Wales', *Arch. Camb.* lxxviii. 206–7.

[93] Ibid. 207 (David Holbache, of Dudleston).

[94] *T.S.A.S.* 4th ser. xi. 29–30 (Clunsland in 1512). This privilege, however, was also enjoyed by Eng. manors of ancient demesne: E. C. Peele and R. S. Clease, *Shropshire Parish Documents* (Shrews. [1903]), 371–2 (Worfield).

[95] See map on p. 40.

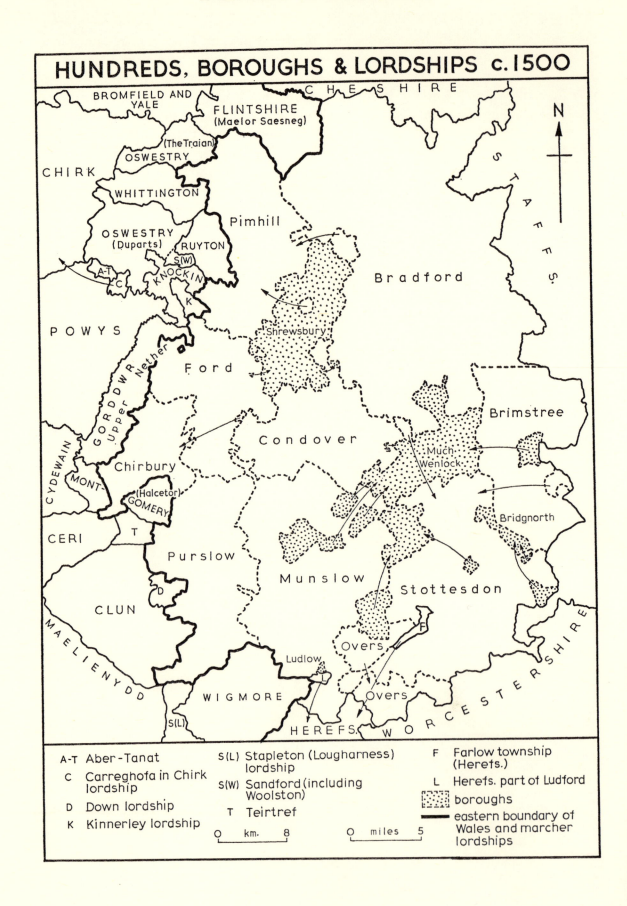

HUNDREDS, BOROUGHS & LORDSHIPS c.1500

CHESHIRE

BROMFIELD AND YALE

FLINTSHIRE (Maelor Saesneg)

(The Traian)

OSWESTRY

CHIRK

WHITTINGTON

Pimhill

STAFFS.

N

OSWESTRY (Duparts)

RUYTON

S(W)

A-T

C

KNOCKIN

K

Bradford

POWYS

Nether

GORDDWR Upper

F o r d

Shrewsbury

Brimstree

CYDEWAIN

MONT-

Chirbury

C o n d o v e r

Much Wenlock

(Halcetor) GOMERY

CERI

T

Bridgnorth

P u r s l o w

M u n s l o w

Stottesdon

CLUN

D

F

MAELIENYDD

Overs

Ludlow

Overs

W I G M O R E

HEREFS.

WORCESTERSHIRE

S(L)

A-T	Aber-Tanat	S(L)	Stapleton (Lougharness) lordship
C	Carreghofa in Chirk lordship	S(W)	Sandford (including Woolston)
D	Down lordship	T	Teirtref
K	Kinnerley lordship		

F Farlow township (Herefs.)

L Herefs. part of Ludford

boroughs

eastern boundary of Wales and marcher lordships

0 km. 8   0 miles 5

in judgements in court that boundary seems to have included such debatable territories as Caus[96] and Ellesmere[97] in England. Contemporaries, however, were more frequently preoccupied with practical administrative matters: the issuing of pardons,[98] the rendering of suits and services, the empanelling of jurors,[99] and the performance of a multitude of duties by the king's officers. To them no such convenient line presented itself, and the complaint of Sheriff Hinckley in 1330, that he should not be charged with the profits of Chirbury, Purslow, and Bradford hundreds or those from half of Overs because they were 'separated' from the county,[1] illustrates the dangers of too legalistic an interpretation of the language of busy officials: it is clear on this occasion that what the sheriff was talking about was the county for which he had to account at the Exchequer. Even in the courts doubts about the border were difficult to resolve. A plaintiff in a suit of 1335 appealed to Domesday Book to demonstrate that Montgomery was within the sheriff of Shropshire's bailiwick. Exchequer and Chancery records of the previous 250 years, however, could resolve nothing about the 'metes and bounds' between Shropshire and Wales. The subject was recommended for discussion in Parliament,[2] and Parliament ascertained that Montgomery, originally in Shropshire, had been drawn into Wales.[3] Two centuries, however, were to elapse before the Anglo-Welsh boundary was defined by statute.

The changes made to the Shropshire border by the great feudatories of the 12th and 13th centuries were largely reversed in Henry VIII's reign, as part of the Crown's policy of introducing a more regular system of law enforcement in the area.[4] By the Act of Union, 1536,[5] the marcher lordships of Oswestry, Knockin, Maesbrook, and Whittington were re-united to Shropshire as the hundred of Oswestry, and Ellesmere was defined as part of Pimhill hundred, Down as part of Chirbury hundred;[6] 'Cawrsland' and the lordship of Clun ('Clunesland' and Tempsiter) were incorporated in the new county of Montgomery.[7] The statute was far from definitive. The lordship of Ruyton of the Eleven Towns, not mentioned in it, was nevertheless part of Oswestry hundred from that time. It was perhaps considered as an under-lordship[8] of Oswestry, though its status in that respect could hardly have differed from the lordships of Knockin and Maesbrook.[9] It is hardly surprising that adjustments to the Act's provisions were necessary within the next few years, Aber-Tanat being transferred from Merionethshire to Shropshire (Oswestry hundred) in 1543[10] and Clun from Montgomeryshire to Shropshire in 1546.[11] The Act of Union's inclusion of 'Cawrsland' in Montgomeryshire is even more obscure. A territory called by that name was certainly part of Shropshire in 1582.[12] It seems unlikely that the 1536 Act intended to include the Shropshire liberty of Caus[13] within Montgomeryshire: the Crown was given the power to rectify inconvenient or inadvertent transfers of territory after the passing of the Act,[14] but no record of any such rectification in this case has been found. The likeliest interpretation of the Act is that, under the name 'Cawrsland', it included

[96] See pp. 37–8.

[97] *Arch. Camb.* lxxviii. 207, where an indictment for acts done at Oteley *c.* 1400 implies that Ellesmere was in Eng.

[98] e.g. to inh. of the hund. of Ellesmere 'in Wales': *Cal. Pat.* 1399–1401, 452.

[99] See e.g. *Cal. Pat.* 1327–30, 561–2, for an empanelling of juries which seems to imply that Caus was not in Salop.

[1] *Cal. Close,* 1330–3, 20.

[2] *Sel. Cases in K.B.* v (Selden Soc. lxxvi), pp. 97–101.

[3] *Cal. Close,* 1337–9, 42. The same conclusion was reached, implausibly, about Chirbury hund.

[4] Wm. Rees, *Union of Eng. and Wales* (1967), 13–16; below, pp. 59, 71.

[5] 27 Hen. VIII, c. 26.

[6] Ibid., s. 11. The map opposite shows Down in the area of Lower Down and Guilden Down. See Rees, *Union of Eng. and Wales,* 63; Eyton, xi. 242–4.

[7] 27 Hen. VIII, c. 26, s. 7.

[8] *T.S.A.S.* 2nd ser. iii. 248. Rees, *Union of Eng. and Wales,* 7–8, discusses sub-lordships and the Act's obscurity.

[9] Eyton, x. 370–1, 377.

[10] Principality of Wales Act, 1543, 34 & 35 Hen. VIII, c. 26, s. 87.

[11] Arundel Jointure Act, 1545, 37 Hen. VIII, c. 32 (Private, not printed): *L. & P. Hen. VIII,* xx(2), p. 414.

[12] Hist. MSS. Com. 9, *Salisbury (Cecil) MSS.* ii, p. 508.

[13] See pp. 37–8.

[14] Townships in Wales Acts, 1536 and 1539, 28 Hen. VIII, c. 3, 31 Hen. VIII, c. 11.

in Montgomeryshire the Upper and part of the Nether Gorddwr, i.e. the welshry of Caus. At first the territory may have formed part of a Montgomeryshire hundred called Ystrad Marchell,[15] though by 1560–1 the hundred of Cawrse, corresponding to the Gorddwr, was in existence.[16]

East of the marcher lordships the medieval sheriffs of Shropshire and the king's other officers administered the shire and its hundreds in much the same way[17] as their contemporaries did elsewhere in England, and it will be convenient first to show the extent to which, at various periods, the Shropshire hundreds were granted to private individuals in fee and secondly to summarize the development of administrative and jurisdictional franchises[18] in the manors of Shropshire.

Private Hundreds

Comparatively few Shropshire hundreds were granted to private lords in fee or tail during the Middle Ages. In this respect the county, with the rest of the counties of the Welsh march, provides a striking contrast to other regions of the kingdom which have been investigated. Two thirds of Wiltshire's hundreds, for example, were in private hands by the end of the 13th century, and the proportions rose even higher in the Wessex counties west of Wiltshire.[19] In Shropshire there were never more than half of the hundreds in private hands during the Middle Ages, and usually there were fewer.

In 1086 10 of the 14[20] Shropshire hundreds belonged to manors held by the earl of Shrewsbury. Two of the hundredal manors were subinfeudated: Maesbury held by Reynold of Bailleul, Alberbury by Roger fitz Corbet. Despite that, however, Earl Roger seems to have retained the ten hundreds: certainly the king's share of their profits is invariably mentioned as a thing of the past, and the readiest explanation[21] of the listing of Alberbury and Maesbury among the earl's demesne manors[22] lies in the assumption that he retained the hundreds belonging to them.

The four hundreds which cannot with confidence be ascribed to Earl Roger in 1086 were 'Condetret', Leintwardine, Overs, and 'Rinlau'; one of them may have been in private hands before the Conquest, but the early tenure of all is obscure. All lay in the south of the county, the only part of Domesday Shropshire where any layman, apart from Earl Roger himself, held in chief.[23] The tenancies probably antedated Roger of Montgomery's acquisition of his Shropshire lands in 1071,[24] and one of the five tenants in chief, Osbern FitzRichard, had inherited his lands from a Norman father settled in Herefordshire by 1052. The other four also held extensive lands in Herefordshire, and they (or their predecessors) had probably been established on their lands by William fitz Osbern, earl of Hereford (d. 1071), whose sphere of influence included south Shropshire as well as Gloucestershire, Worcestershire, and his own county of Hereford.[25] Within that sphere Earl William's position closely resembled that later

[15] Rees, *Hist. Atlas of Wales*, p. 55, plate 57.

[16] N.L.W., Ct. of Gt. Sessions recs. 3 Eliz. I, *nomina ministrorum*; Richards, *Welsh Admin. and Territorial Units*, 301; S. Lewis, *Topog. Dict. Wales* (1834), ii. *sub* Mont.

[17] See pp. 1–32, 54 sqq.

[18] Fiscal immunities, here left out of account, were also of considerable importance: see pp. 45–6.

[19] *V.C.H. Wilts.* v. 71. Cf. Helen M. Cam, *The Hundred and the Hundred Rolls* (1963 edn.), 54–7, 137 sqq., maps facing pp. 208, 296.

[20] Domesday's 15 hundreds (*V.C.H. Salop.* i. 283) include Shrews., here left out of account. See below, p. 49 n. 15.

[21] Which discards Eyton's suppositions (x. 313, 319).

[22] *V.C.H. Salop.* i. 292–3, 315–16.

[23] Ibid. i. 288.

[24] J. F. A. Mason, 'Rog. de Montgomery and his Sons (1067–1102)', *Trans. R.H.S.* 5th ser. xiii. 3–4.

[25] W. E. Wightman, *Lacy Fam. in Eng. and Normandy, 1066–1194* (Oxford, 1966), 120–1. For Osbern's father Ric. son of Scrob (FitzScrob) see F. M. Stenton, *Ang.-Saxon Eng.* (1971), 562 n. 1.

accorded to Roger of Montgomery in Shropshire,[26] though neither that parallel nor any surviving evidence allows the inference that any south Shropshire hundred ever belonged to Earl William. Even in Herefordshire the evidence is incomplete, though it is perhaps significant that there, before the Conquest, the known hundredal manors belonged not to the king but to William fitz Osbern's predecessor as earl,[27] Harold Godwinson.[28]

Osbern FitzRichard may have inherited the lordship of Overs hundred from his father during the Conqueror's reign,[29] and at some date 'Rinlau' was acquired by Picot de Say or his descendants, though whether before 1086, after 1086, or after 1102 must remain in doubt.[30] The history of Leintwardine hundred, however, is utterly obscure after 1086, except for a hint that its territory may have been divided between Munslow and Whittery (Chirbury) hundreds.[31] Only in the south-east of the county does hundredal reorganization, which was there both early and radical,[32] give a clue as to the lordship of 'Condetret' hundred in the time of Earl Roger and his sons.

During his later years Earl Roger's main interests lay in the south-east of the county[33] and there, by 1086, he had begun to consolidate his properties and jurisdictions, a process which was to work changes to the county boundary as well as to the composition of the Shropshire hundreds. Domesday records that his Worcestershire estate of 'Calvestone' was being incorporated in his great demesne manor of Morville, *caput* of 'Alnodestreu' hundred.[34] Later and more permanently his Worcestershire manor of Halesowen followed the same path.[35] The transfer of Earl Roger's, and his younger son's, estates from the Staffordshire hundred of Seisdon must have been substantially complete by 1102.[36] It was no doubt as a consequence of those transfers that the hundreds of 'Alnodestreu' and 'Condetret' were reorganized, and the freedom taken with them suggests that Earl Roger and his sons were lords of both.

With the forfeiture of Earl Robert in 1102 the hundreds which he and his father had held reverted to the Crown. During the following two centuries 'Mersete' (Oswestry) was lost to the county, Purslow passed into private hands probably before 1183 and was reduced from the greater area of 'Rinlau' by the loss of Clun, and Leintwardine disappeared.[37] With those exceptions the Crown suffered no permanent alienation of the Shropshire hundreds. Indeed in the case of Overs hundred the Crown, by agreement with Richard FitzScrob's descendants, actually acquired half of the hundred,[38] perhaps in the 12th century. The Crown's retention of hundreds seems to have been the result of deliberate policy maintained in the marcher shires during the 12th and 13th centuries: in 1274 throughout the region[39] there were only 3½ hundreds in private hands.[40]

By the beginning of Edward III's reign the territorial organization of the Shropshire hundreds was virtually fixed as the Crown sought to define convenient administrative and fiscal divisions of the county.[41] The discrepancies between the Shropshire hundreds

[26] W. E. Wightman, 'The Palatine Earldom of Wm. fitz Osbern in Glos. and Worcs. (1066–1071)', *E.H.R.* lxxvii. 6–8.

[27] Helen M. Cam, *Liberties and Communities in Medieval Eng.* (Cambridge, 1944), 88; above, p. 33 n. 3. Dom. Bk. shows the Ches. hundredal mans. in Earl Hugh's hands.

[28] Stenton, op. cit. 574.

[29] Alleged in a 13th-cent. verdict: *Rot. Hund.* ii. 74.

[30] See p. 36.

[31] See p. 37 n. 51.

[32] *V.C.H. Salop.* i. 306.

[33] *T.S.A.S.* lvi. 252.

[34] *V.C.H. Salop.* i. 315. 'Calvestone' probably represents an estate in Chauson (otherwise held in chief by Wm.

Goizenboded), in Salwarpe (held in chief by Earl Rog.): *V.C.H. Worcs.* i. 262, 309, 317; iii. 208.

[35] *V.C.H. Worcs.* i. 238, 308–9; iii. 141–2.

[36] *V.C.H. Staffs.* iv. 1, 45–6, 48.

[37] See pp. 34–7.

[38] Eyton, iv. 299.

[39] Ches., Salop., Herefs., and Glos. west of the Severn.

[40] i.e. in fee. They were Purslow and ½ Overs (Salop.), Leominster (Herefs.), and Bledisloe (Glos.): Cam, *Hund. and Hund. Rolls*, 262, 266–7, 269, 277, map facing p. 296. Wal. de Pedwardine held Bradford hund. for life only: Eyton, viii. 32.

[41] As the compilation of the 'Nomina Villarum' (*Feudal Aids*, iv. 226–35) perhaps suggests.

of 1327[42] and of 1831[43] are insignificant[44] except for those which resulted from Edward IV's charter to the borough of Much Wenlock in 1468[45] and from the Crown's extensions of the municipal liberties of Shrewsbury in 1495 and 1542.[46] At the same time as the hundred-based divisions were fixed the jurisdiction of the hundred courts was becoming less significant by comparison with the new agencies of law enforcement, notably the keepers and justices of the peace, which were being created by the Crown.[47] The peace-keeping functions of the hundred were by then subordinated to those new authorities while the jurisdiction of the hundred court, convenient for the settlement of small debts and profitable to the lord of the private hundred, was, and perhaps long had been, of little account in the royal hundreds apart from the twice-yearly sheriff's tourn. It was from that period that the tourn began to decline in importance[48] and the Crown began the gradual alienation of the Shropshire hundreds.

Edward II reunited the Crown's half of Overs hundred to the moiety inherited by his kinsmen, the Cornewalls.[49] Chirbury, granted to the Mortimers in effect by Queen Isabel,[50] was but one small part of that family's territorial aggrandisement in the Welsh marches during the period when the queen and Roger Mortimer, the first earl of March, governed the kingdom.[51] Ironically, March's downfall produced another such grant: next year Bradford hundred was granted in tail male to Sir John de Neville of Hornby, who helped to arrest Mortimer in Nottingham castle on 19 October 1330.[52] With one short break[53] Bradford hundred remained in private hands for the rest of the Middle Ages.[54] Meanwhile a new generation of Mortimers had begun to restore the family position in the marches.[55] Chirbury hundred was recovered from the prince of Wales in 1354[56] and in 1358 Munslow hundred was granted to the earl of March in fee.[57] Both hundreds remained part of the earldom,[58] though in 1461 Edward, duke of York and earl of March, became king.[59] Throughout the Middle Ages and beyond the five hundreds of Brimstree, Condover, Ford, Pimhill, and Stottesdon remained in the Crown. Thus private lords held half of the ten Shropshire hundreds 1358–1459 and 1460–1, the highest proportion in private possession at any time before the 17th century. Three of the ten hundreds were private 1459–60 and 1461–1536.[60] After 1536, when Oswestry was reunited to the county, that proportion was 4 out of 11; after 1546, when Clun was returned to Shropshire, it was 5 out of twelve.[61]

---

[42] Used for collecting the twentieth that yr.: *T.S.A.S.* 3rd ser. vii. 375–8, and refs. there cited.

[43] *V.C.H. Salop.* ii. 207–11 (corrections printed below, p. 398).

[44] Upper Ashford, Huntington, and Sheet were in Munslow hund. 1255 (*Rot. Hund.* ii. 70) and 1831 but were taxed in Stottesdon 1327. Ritton and Shelderton, taxed with Chirbury and Munslow hunds. respectively in 1327, were in Purslow hund. by 1831. Shipley, taxed with Stottesdon hund. in 1327, was in Brimstree by 1831. The map on p. 40 shows these places, except for Ritton, in their 1831 hunds. Ritton was still in Chirbury in 1677 (*Herbert Corresp.* ed. Smith, pp. 227 n., 230–1) and is so shown on the map though its precise bounds were not ascertained; for its bounds *c.* 1203 see Eyton, xi. 182.

[45] In 1327 the liberty of M. Wenlock priory was taxed with Munslow hund.

[46] Owen and Blakeway, *Hist. Shrews.* i. 268, 338–9; ii. 139, 142–3; *T.S.A.S.* 2nd ser. ii. 72. The map (for which S.R.O. 3365/773, 996, were also consulted) shows the 1495 changes but not those of 1542. Battlefield coll. was granted ret. of writs in its precincts and in Albright Hussey and Harlescott in 1445 (*Cal. Pat.* 1441–6, 412) but the grant's effect is obscure. The two latter places made suit to the leet ct. of Shrews. libs. in 1518: S.R.O. 3365/996.

[47] See pp. 23, 54.

[48] *V.C.H. Wilts.* v. 64; Cam, *Hund. and Hund. Rolls,* 181–2, 188 sqq.; below, p. 78.

[49] *Cal. Close,* 1333–7, 127.

[50] With the lordship of Montgomery: G. A. Holmes, *Estates of Higher Nobility in Fourteenth-Cent. Eng.* (1957), 13–14.

[51] Ibid.

[52] *Cal. Chart. R.* 1327–41, 231; *Complete Peerage,* viii. 440–1; ix. 489.

[53] i.e. 1335–8 after Neville's death s.p.m.

[54] Those of the Ferrers of Groby fam.: *Cal. Pat.* 1338–40, 5; *Complete Peerage,* v. 345, 356–7. The detailed descents of hunds. are reserved for later vols. of this *Hist.*

[55] Holmes, op. cit. 14 sqq.

[56] Ibid. 15–16; B.L. Add. MS. 30325, f. 118.

[57] *Cal. Pat.* 1358–61, 100.

[58] Which retained a separate administrative identity until 1490: Earldom of March Act, 1489, 4 Hen. VII, c. 14.

[59] In 1459–60, when Ric., duke of York, and his sons were under attainder, they reverted to the Crown: *Cal. Pat.* 1452–61, 552.

[60] E 370/11/13.

[61] See p. 41.

During the 16th and 17th centuries eight[62] Crown hundreds were permanently alienated to private lords. Edward VI granted Chirbury to the Herberts in 1553,[63] James I granted Brimstree and Ford hundreds to the Whitmores in 1612,[64] and Charles I granted Munslow to Gilbert North in 1629.[65] In 1672 the hundreds or reversions of Bradford, Condover, Pimhill, and Stottesdon were granted in fee to Lord Newport,[66] newly appointed treasurer of the Household and the county's greatest landowner.[67] By the early 19th century all twelve hundreds seem to have remained in private hands: Chirbury, Clun, Munslow, Oswestry, and Purslow with the 1st earl of Powis or his heir Lord Clive, heirs of the Clive and Herbert families,[68] Brimstree with the Whitmores,[69] Ford with the heirs of the Owen family,[70] and the Newport family's hundreds with the Vanes, earls of Darlington[71] and later dukes of Cleveland.[72] Overs hundred must be presumed to have passed to the successors of the Cornewalls in the ownership of Burford manor.[73] The only hundreds which then retained any significant jurisdiction in their courts were three of the five which had been longest in private hands: Bradford, Chirbury, and Purslow.[74] Bradford hundred had a debtors' prison in Wellington until 1844[75] and the jurisdiction of Purslow hundred was still sufficient in the 1830s to exclude that of the county court.[76]

No doubt survival of private hundreds' jurisdictions owed much to the fact that their profits contributed significantly to their lords' income — more than did those of the Crown hundreds to the royal revenue. Such seems to have been the case with Chirbury. In 1634 Lord Herbert solicited a grant of return of writs in the hundred;[77] the profits of its jurisdiction were worth increasing by the franchise he desired, and in 1644 Herbert claimed to have lost £40 of the hundred's profits as a result of the Parliamentarians' capture of Montgomery.[78]

Other Franchises and the Development of the Leet

The various rights and privileges which can properly be called franchises were at once extensive and miscellaneous;[79] at the upper end of the scale they included the great liberties of the palatinate county or the private shire, at the lower end free warren and the right to hold a market or fair. Even the hallmoot, the court baron without which an estate could hardly be considered to be a manor, has been suggested as a franchise,[80] though that view is not generally accepted. The franchises in fact included any rights to which the only secure titles were grants by the Crown; on however modest a scale, they were regalities. Analogous to the franchises were the profitable immunities from the multifarious taxes, tallages, dues, tolls, and aids which the Crown

[62] Bradford escheated to the Crown.
[63] B.L. Add. MS. 30325, ff. 51, 94v., 102v.
[64] S.P.L., Deeds 15757.
[65] S.R.O. 3320/25/2. Chas. Baldwyn evid. acquired it within a yr.: Staffs. R.O., D.(W.) 1788, P.34, B.14, lease to Wm. Barker, 1630.
[66] S.P.L., MS. 4071, pp. 189–208.
[67] See p. 254.
[68] C.P. 25(2)/868, 9 Wm. III, Trin. [no. 15]; C.P. 43/895 rot. 9; Walcot Estate Act, 1742, 15 Geo. II, c. 31 (Priv. Act); N.L.W., Powis Cas. Man. Recs. Group II, Chirb. hund. boxes 1–8; T.S.A.S. 2nd ser. vi. 143–4; 3rd ser. iv. 277 n.; 4th ser. iii. 1. Osw. had been bought from the Howards in the 17th cent., Clun and Purslow evidently from the Walcots in 1763 (see below, p. 303).
[69] C.P. 43/883 rot. 263; S.R.O. 1190, box 23, papers re Brimstree hund. (suit and ct. r. 1831–47).
[70] Who had bought it in 1615: V.C.H. Salop. viii. 180.
[71] C.P. 43/889 rot. 466. This carries the descent of Condover hund. (not traced beyond 1672 in V.C.H.

Salop. viii. 2) to 1805.
[72] See pp. 255, 310, 315–16.
[73] The Bowles fam.: V.C.H. Worcs. iii. 366. Cf. S.P.L., MS. 2791, p. 358.
[74] See p. 165. The jurisdictions of Overs and Munslow hunds. had presumably decayed. Clun. hund., though hardly to be counted as a medieval Salop. hund., retained a significant jurisdiction in the 1830s: below, n. 76.
[75] S.R.O., q. sess. Auditing and Finance Cttees. rep. bk. 1837–43, pp. 89–90, 96; Shropshire Conservative, 24 Aug. 1844.
[76] So was that of Clun hund. See Ret. Hund. and Manor Cts. H.C. 338–III, p. 8 (1839), xliii; Ret. Cts. of Requests, Cts. of Conscience, H.C. 619, p. 132 (1840), xli.
[77] Cf. Cal. Pat. 1553–4, 69 (grant of ret. of writs in Purslow hund. to earl of Arundel, 1554).
[78] Herbert Corresp. ed. W. J. Smith (1968), pp. 79–80, 119.
[79] Sutherland, Quo Warr. Procs. 2–3.
[80] Leges Henrici Primi, ed. Downer, 319–20.

could levy on its subjects. All these franchises and immunities were, at least potentially, of great financial account to their owners. That was indeed the primary value of many of them, and markets, fairs, free warren, and their like are interesting chiefly within the context of the growth of towns or the development of estates; such rights are excluded from the present survey. There is, however, another group of franchises whose primary purpose was to devolve, upon certain privileged subjects and their officers and within specified areas, the execution of royal writs and the administration of justice. It is this group that is here considered. Nevertheless, though the subjects dealt with are at the lowest administrative and judicial level, these franchises too were sources of profit to the lord of the liberty and of loss to the Crown: such is the constant preoccupation of the inquiries recorded in the hundred rolls.

No adequate discussion of the antiquity of franchises, however, could be based on Shropshire evidence alone. It is indeed likely that few Shropshire liberties antedated the Conquest.[81] The county did not contain the seat of a bishop, nor was it rich in those great Anglo-Saxon monasteries which elsewhere provide much of the evidence for pre-Conquest privileged jurisdictions and immunities. Nevertheless the bishops of Hereford and of Lichfield probably enjoyed sac and soc on their estates in Shropshire as they did elsewhere;[82] otherwise only the church of Wenlock preserved some dim traditions of a monastic life extinguished before the Conquest and, with them, vestiges of a degree of immunity from secular taxation.[83] The extent of the Shropshire franchises can be judged from the royal inquiries of 1255[84] and 1274[85] and from the *quo warranto* proceedings of 1292–3 based on the latter.[86] Those sources allow an estimate of the extent of the administrative and jurisdictional franchises in the 13th century, and later manorial records, sampled and compared with them, suggest two conclusions: first that, whatever their origins and variety in the early Middle Ages, most liberties which had not acquired any high administrative or jurisdictional franchises by the end of the 13th century retained thereafter little more than the jurisdiction of a court leet; secondly, that the area of the county comprised within the liberties was not greatly extended after the 13th century.

Shropshire, the medieval county reduced by the withdrawal of the marcher lordships, was not a county of great liberties either administrative or jurisdictional. If, in the later 13th century, areas of greater privilege may be distinguished from lesser liberties by their lords' right to execute royal writs in the sheriff's place, an essentially administrative franchise, then few areas of Shropshire can be considered highly privileged. During the earlier 13th century liberties, even if their ancient charters seemed to guarantee quittance from shires and hundreds, had to 'move with changing times'[87] in order to remain immune from the ever-increasing administrative activity of the sheriff and his officers. In the 1250s in particular it was necessary to secure the newly invented franchise of return of writs.[88] The evidence of the 1255 inquiry, however, suggests that in Shropshire that franchise, and hence the significance of Henry III's policies towards the greater liberties, was hardly understood: even the only two claimants to it, the burgesses of Shrewsbury and the abbot of Shrewsbury for his liberty of Foregate, seem hardly to have grasped its implications.[89] By 1274 the position was hardly less confused. The burgesses of Shrewsbury and of Bridgnorth,

[81] For a possible exception see p. 43.
[82] F. E. Harmer, *Ang.-Saxon Writs* (1952), pp. 229, 231; *V.C.H. Staffs.* iv. 37.
[83] *V.C.H. Salop.* i. 282, 291, 312; ii. 38–9.
[84] *Rot. Hund.* (Rec. Com.), ii. 55–86. Cf. Helen M. Cam, 'Studies in the Hundred Rolls', *Oxford Studies in Social and Legal History*, vi(11), 13–14.
[85] *Rot. Hund.* ii. 87–113. Cf. Cam, op. cit. 125, 127.

[86] *Plac. de Quo Warr.* (Rec. Com.), 674–87, 706–9, 718–20; D. W. Sutherland, *Quo Warr. Procs. in Reign of Edw. I, 1278–1294* (Oxford, 1963), 18 sqq.
[87] M. T. Clanchy, 'The Franchise of Return of Writs', *Trans. R.H.S.* 5th ser. xvii. 59, 78; *V.C.H. Wilts.* v. 56–7.
[88] Clanchy, op. cit. 59 sqq., 64 sqq.
[89] Ibid. 67–8; *Rot. Hund.* ii. 67, 78.

it is true, had secured the vital franchise in their charters of 1256.[90] Most Shropshire juries, however, knew nothing of it, and the abbot of Shrewsbury's claim for the Foregate was still inadequately based on prescriptive right since the Conquest.[91] Even Roger Mortimer (II) of Wigmore who, at the height of his influence with the Crown, in 1266, had acquired the right to exclude the sheriff from entering his manors of Cleobury and Chelmarsh to distrain for royal debts and dues, had not had the return of writs expressly granted to him;[92] he nevertheless claimed it in 1274,[93] and the Corbets of Caus also were evidently trying to arrogate a similar franchise to themselves from about that time.[94]

One of the principal jurisdictional franchises, coupled with the administrative privilege of return of writs in the 1274 inquiries, was the right to hold pleas *de vetito namio*. Few matters impinged more directly on the lives of ordinary people than this jurisdiction over unlawful distraint, and it was a franchise enjoyed by few lords.[95] In Shropshire in 1274 only Roger Mortimer in his court of Cleobury and the Templars in the barony of Castle Holdgate claimed it.[96] Eighteen years later even a great lord like the bishop of Coventry and Lichfield was wary of claiming such a franchise on the basis of obsolete words in his charters. In 1299, however, Edward I granted to Bishop Langton, then treasurer of England, and to his successors in the see return of writs and the right to pleas *de vetito namio* throughout their lands. The episcopal manor of Prees thus became, by Shropshire standards, a highly privileged liberty.[97]

By the later 13th century, however, most Shropshire jurisdictional franchises amounted to little more than exemption from the hundred court and the sheriff's twice-yearly tourns in the hundreds: with the exemption went the right, and the duty, to hold a 'great court' twice a year co-ordinate with the sheriff's tourn. The essential features[98] of the franchise were the right to hold 'pleas of the Crown' (the equivalent in Shropshire of the view of frankpledge) and the assizes of bread and of ale and the right to have a gallows. By the time of the Shropshire *quo warranto* proceedings of 1292 lords who could produce charters embellished their claims to the franchise with long recitals of obsolete words; frequent among their incantations, significantly, was the old formula of baronial jurisdiction: sac and soc, toll and team, and infangthief. Few lords can have produced a more sonorous collection of franchises and immunities[99] than the prior of Great Malvern (Worcs.) when impleaded for his claims to jurisdiction in the Shropshire manor of Dowles. What the prior was claiming, however, was simply the jurisdiction later known as a court leet, at once 'the least of the serious franchises, and also the commonest'.[1] The origins and development of the leet, who held it in Shropshire, and how widespread it was are the chief remaining topics.

Returns to the inquiries of 1255 and 1274 survive for seven of the ten Shropshire hundreds, for Bradford and Purslow only those for 1255, for Brimstree none.[2] Predominantly the verdicts recorded in the returns concern questions of suit owed to the shire and hundred courts, and for that reason some caution is necessary in their interpretation: the owing of suit does not always indicate the lack of a liberty.[3] Nevertheless

[90] Owen and Blakeway, *Hist. Shrews.* i. 120; Eyton, i. 308.

[91] *Rot. Hund.* ii. 97. Cf. Clanchy, op. cit. 67.

[92] Eyton, iii. 40; iv. 221–2; *Cal. Chart. R.* 1257–1300, 61.

[93] *Rot. Hund.* ii. 108. [94] See p. 37.

[95] Cf. *V.C.H. Wilts.* v. 57–8; Cam, *Hund. and Hund. Rolls*, 82–5, 115, 210.

[96] *Rot. Hund.* ii. 100, 108. The lord Edw.'s officers of Chirbury hund. were said to hold the plea in 1255 and their predecessors were said always to have done so: ibid. 61.

[97] *V.C.H. Staffs.* iii. 17–18. It was separately represented at the 1305 trailbaston sess.: J.I. 1/744 rot. 1d.

[98] Cf. *V.C.H. Wilts.* v. 58.

[99] Derived from those granted to Westminster abbey in 1235 (*Cal. Chart. R.* 1226–57, 208–9).

[1] Denholm-Young, *Seignorial Admin.* 91–3; *Plac. de Quo Warr.* 675–6; Eyton, iv. 161–2; above, p. 33.

[2] For this and the following paras. see, except where otherwise stated, the sources cited in notes 84–5, above.

[3] e.g. in the cases of Wem, Dodington, and Hinstock, and of Wigwig: see p. 51; *V.C.H. Salop.* viii. 1. Cf. H. R. T. Summerson, 'The Maintenance of Law and Order in Eng. 1227–1263' (Cambridge Univ. Ph.D. thesis, 1976), pp. 39–40, 206–8.

it is clear that exemption from, or the withholding of, suit to the hundred normally shows that a manor came within what may conveniently be called the leet of some private lord.

In 1255, in three of the four southern hundreds, Overs, Purslow, and Stottesdon, the great majority of manors made suit at the hundred courts, while in Munslow at least half did so. In Stottesdon there were few manors in ecclesiastical ownership, though properties belonging to Shrewsbury abbey and Bridgnorth college figured largely among the few which were exempt; among lay lords the Mortimers had as yet withdrawn none of their great holdings, but the barons of Castle Holdgate claimed the suit of one manor for the court of their barony. In Munslow the barons of Castle Holdgate and of Richard's Castle, along with ecclesiastical landowners, accounted for half of the hundredal immunities. In Overs a manor belonging to Bromfield priory, and in Purslow the bishop of Hereford's great liberty, both escaped suit to their respective hundreds; otherwise only Burford, *caput* of Overs, and Clun, *caput* of the honor to which Purslow hundred belonged, were exempt. Both hundreds contained ecclesiastical estates which had not yet established, or were only in the process of establishing, immunities from the hundred.[4] By 1274 the situation had been transformed in three of the southern hundreds by the establishment of immunities on the great estates of Roger Mortimer. Wigmore abbey too had benefited from its patron's prestige[5] by withdrawing a manor from suit of Overs hundred, and in Munslow the new holders of the barony of Castle Holdgate, the Templars,[6] had extended their immunities.[7]

Few liberties developed in central Shropshire during the 13th century. In the hundred of Condover there were some losses of suit to its court after 1255 when the liberties of Castle Holdgate barony were extended and Roger Mortimer established his. Otherwise only a few manors in ecclesiastical ownership, the lands of the barony of Pulverbatch, two manors belonging to, or held of, other families of baronial rank,[8] and the hundred *caput* itself, Condover manor, were exempt.[9] In Ford the hundredal manor again was exempt, but in that hundred and Chirbury the losses to welshry in the west and the development of the Corbets' hundredal exemptions were the most prominent immunities.[10]

The two northern hundreds, Bradford and Pimhill, covered a great area of Shropshire, Bradford being said in 1381 to include one third of the county.[11] In them exemptions were more varied and considerable than in the other hundreds; that was partly owing to the inclusion within their area of six manors formerly of royal demesne, partly owing to the greater number of ecclesiastical estates there, and partly owing to the inclusion of the extensive and well organized barony of Wem almost wholly within Bradford hundred. A closer examination of those three sources of immunity will allow some generalization about the county as a whole and elucidate the development of the Shropshire liberties.

The six manors of former royal demesne within the area of the two northern hundreds form part of a readily identifiable group of fourteen such extensive manors scattered throughout the county and comprising the royal demesnes in Shropshire inherited by Henry II in 1154. Twelve of them represented estates which had been forfeited to the Crown on Robert of Bellême's fall in 1102 and had been preserved

[4] See pp. 50–1.
[5] *Cal. Chart. R.* 1257–1300, 56.
[6] *V.C.H. Salop.* ii. 86.
[7] Eyton, iv. 67; Dugdale, *Mon.* vii. 844.
[8] The FitzAlans (Cound) and Genevilles (Cressage).
[9] *V.C.H. Salop.* viii. 1–2.
[10] For Ford and the Corbets see ibid. 178, 180; above, pp. 37–8.
[11] E 179/242/34 m. 1.

intact by Henry I;[12] of the other two, one had been acquired from Robert of Stafford by Henry I[13] and the other had evidently been regarded as having escheated after the death of William Peverel *c.* 1148.[14]

All 14 manors were separately represented at the Shropshire eyre of 1203,[15] and the separate representation of such manors long after several had been granted in fee by Henry II[16] suggests that already by the mid 12th century their royal status had brought them some immunity from the common burdens and responsibilities[17] falling on the hundred. The extent of those immunities and franchises can only be conjectured. They may indeed have differed even between one royal manor and another, and that was especially likely after their alienation from the Crown. 'The king has soke as well over all lands which are in his demesne', the author of the *Leges Henrici Primi* had written, and when the land was granted away that jurisdiction could be given with it, shared, or withheld.[18] In the following century the evidence of jurors' verdicts is too often imprecise: in 1255 the men of King's Nordley, questioned about the suits owed to the county, to the hundred, or to the courts of manors of the royal demesne, stated that they knew nothing because the manor made no suit except for homicide and the common summons (*pro communi summonicione*).[19] The representatives of other such manors apparently had nothing at all to answer 'because they are not in a hundred nor do they answer with a hundred'.[20] What is certain is that in such royal, or formerly royal, manors exemption from the hundred entailed the holding of a court equivalent to the sheriff's tourn: such, for example, must have been the 'great court' (mentioned in 1274) which the king used to have in Claverley with 'blodwite', the assize of ale, and 'other trespasses'.[21]

Undoubtedly traditional processes of summons to the eyre or appearance at it preserved the identity of most of this group of manors: for a century or more 9 of them continued to make independent appearances before the king's justices.[22] By the mid 13th century, however, many lords of manors had been granted, or were claiming, exemption from suit to the hundred, though only some of them were ever separately represented. The manors of Worthen and Stanton Lacy appeared separately from the 1230s and 1250s respectively, when their lords Thomas Corbet and Geoffrey de Geneville were establishing extensive franchises for themselves;[23] so did Cleobury Mortimer at the 1272 eyre, the first to be held after Roger Mortimer began to claim extensive liberties.[24] Such separate representation, however, was not necessarily a concomitant of such claims. Cleobury Mortimer was not separately represented again, and most manors claiming hundredal jurisdiction never were.

Besides the 14 manors of royal demesne, the extensive liberty of Wenlock priory, containing many manors, was also represented separately at the 1203 eyre, and indeed

[12] Alveley (incl. Nordley: Eyton, iii. 146 n.2),* Claverley,* Condover,* Corfham,* Edgmond,* Ford,* Halesowen,* Gt. Ness, Ch. Stretton,* Wellington, Worfield,* and Wrockwardine. Only 2 other mans. fulfil this criterion: Whittington (possibly outside the county and beyond the jurisdiction of the eyre by 1203: see above, p. 38) and Ditton Priors (granted to Wenlock priory *c.* 1175). For manorial details see Eyton, iii. 64, and i–xii *passim*; *V.C.H. Worcs.* iii. 141–2. For the manors followed by an asterisk (*) see below, n. 22.

[13] Cheswardine. Its transfer from Staffs. to Salop. was presumably coeval. Cf. *V.C.H. Staffs.* iv. 2, 31.

[14] Ellesmere.

[15] *Pleas before the King or his Justices, 1198–1212* (Selden Soc. lxxxiii), pp. 69–70, 73, 76, 83. Boros., not discussed here, were also separately represented.

[16] e.g. Alveley, Cheswardine, Corfham, and Gt. Ness. For a general discussion of Hen.'s policy see J. E. Lally,

'Secular Patronage at Ct. of Hen. II', *Bull. Inst. Hist. Res.* xlix. 159–84, esp. 174 sqq.

[17] See Sir F. Pollock and F. W. Maitland, *Hist. Eng. Law* (2nd edn.), i. 558. Cf. above, pp. 20–1.

[18] Downer, *Leges Henrici Primi*, 122–3, 334, 427–30.

[19] *Rot. Hund.* ii. 73.

[20] Ibid. 63–4, 83–4.

[21] Ibid. 90.

[22] Those marked * in n. 12, above: *Rolls of Justices in Eyre . . . 1221, 1222* (Selden Soc. lix), pp. 534, 541, 546, 554–6, 781, 789; *Rot. Hund.* ii. 60–1, 63–5, 67, 73, 80, 83–4, 87, 90, 93–4, 98, 101, 106, 110, 112; A. Harding 'The Salop. Eyre Roll of 1256' (Oxford Univ. B.Litt. thesis, 1957), pp. 340–5, 351; J.I. 1/736 rot. 24; /739 rot. 46; /744 rott. 5d.–6; /746 rot. 1(1).

[23] Sources in preceding note; Eyton, v. 8–10, 273 sqq.; vii. 19–32; xi. 96 sqq.

[24] J.I. 1/736 rot. 24; above, p. 37.

at all subsequent eyres whose rolls have survived.[25] By 1305 it was known as 'Bourton hundred'[26] from the meeting place of its court.[27] This outstanding liberty may serve to introduce a survey of the franchises enjoyed by ecclesiastical lords of manors. The liberty or franchise of Wenlock itself originated in a charter of Richard I granting the prior *inter alia* hundredal exemption.[28] The priory's estates, deriving from pre-Conquest endowment, were perhaps more compact than those of the other monastic or collegiate churches in the county.[29] The survival of the liberty, however, as a feature of the administrative map of the county as late as the 19th century, owes more to Edward IV's 1468 charter to the priory's borough of Much Wenlock[30] than to the geography or immunities of the priory estates. Thus the peculiar persistence of the liberty should not obscure the fact that in the 12th and 13th centuries, though perhaps slightly more privileged than most,[31] it was only one of many such hundredal liberties developing on manors in ecclesiastical ownership.

Most of the major monastic foundations in the county and its two greatest collegiate churches were situated in central Shropshire: in Shrewsbury or within a few miles of Watling Street.[32] Their estates, and those of Combermere abbey (Ches.), the most considerable Shropshire monastic landowner located outside the county, were more numerous in the two northern hundreds of medieval Shropshire, Bradford and Pimhill, than in the south,[33] and a survey of the development of ecclesiastical liberties in the north suggests conclusions applicable perhaps to the rest of the county.

In Pimhill, by 1255, about sixty per cent of the manors within the hundred were said to have 'liberty' or to owe or render no suit to the hundred and shire courts; in turn just over half of those exempt manors belonged to ecclesiastical lords and overlords: Shrewsbury, Haughmond, and Lilleshall abbeys, and St. Chad's college, Shrewsbury.[34] The same three abbeys, together with those of Buildwas and Combermere and with the bishop of Coventry and Lichfield,[35] were similarly prominent in Bradford. In that hundred almost exactly half of the manors were exempt from, or were failing to do, their suit to the hundred courts; almost forty per cent of the exempt manors belonged to these ecclesiastics,[36] all of whom had some kind of warrant for such immunities. The abbeys had 12th-century charters.[37] The liberties of the bishop may have been older than the Conquest[38] and those of St. Chad's church, whose property was only disentangled from the bishop's during the course of the 12th century,[39] were perhaps derived from them. By contrast with St. Chad's the royal foundation of St. Mary's, Shrewsbury, had no such liberties in 1255.[40]

Though their liberties were grounded on privileges granted in the 12th century, most of the Shropshire monasteries had not effected the freedom from the hundred of all their scattered estates by the earlier 13th century, Wenlock being perhaps an exception. Shrewsbury abbey, for example, was said to have withdrawn its manors' suit of Pimhill hundred only from 1227,[41] and it is clear that other religious houses were doing the same at about the same time: Buildwas probably withdrew the suit of Stirchley from Bradford hundred as soon as the manor was purchased in 1243,[42] but it

[25] Sources in n. 22, above.
[26] J.I. 1/744 rot. 1.
[27] Eyton, iii. 300, 302.
[28] *V.C.H. Salop.* ii. 40.
[29] Ibid. 42–3. Cf. ibid. 21, 31, 73 (Shrews. and Lilleshall abbeys).
[30] Translation in S.R.O. 81/491.
[31] It had, e.g., the unusual franchise of utfangthief (*V.C.H. Salop.* ii. 40) as did Lilleshall abbey (Eyton, viii. 220).
[32] *V.C.H. Salop.* ii. 19, 24–5.
[33] Ibid. 19; *Rot. Hund.* ii. 55–113.

[34] *Rot. Hund.* ii. 74–6.
[35] As ld. of Prees: see p. 47.
[36] *Rot. Hund.* ii. 55–8.
[37] *Shrews. Cart.* ed. Una Rees (Aberystwyth, 1976), i, p. 43; S.P.L., Haughmond Cart. ff. 77, 220v.; *V.C.H. Salop.* ii. 53; Eyton, viii. 220.
[38] See p. 46.
[39] *V.C.H. Staffs.* iii. 20. Cf. Harmer, *Ang.-Saxon Writs*, pp. 228, 415–16.
[40] *Rot. Hund.* ii. 75; Eyton, x. 158, 160.
[41] *Rot. Hund.* ii. 76.
[42] Eyton, viii. 117.

owned the more distant property of Kinnerton for many years before withdrawing its suit from Purslow hundred in 1254.[43] Haughmond abbey's manors in Purslow still did suit to the hundred court in 1255, though in the two northern hundreds, the house's estates were exempt.

Monastic estates were acquired piecemeal and vigilance was evidently necessary to extend hundredal immunities to new properties. That must have been especially true of distant estates or of estates in hundreds like Purslow,[44] whose lords exacted suit with some vigour. Wigmore abbey, for example, acquired Ratlinghope and established a cell there about the beginning of the 13th century[45] but, despite the abbey's privileges,[46] the manor always did suit to Purslow hundred;[47] it was not withdrawn after 1265,[48] as Caynham was from Overs hundred.[49] In fact, of all the ecclesiastical estates in Purslow hundred in 1255, only Buildwas abbey's manor of Kinnerton and the bishop of Hereford's great liberty of Lydbury North escaped the jurisdiction of the hundred.[50] Haughmond abbey's outlying estates on the western slopes of the Long Mynd and Great Malvern priory's distant manor of Stowe never did.[51]

The hundredal immunities of royal demesne manors and of the manors of ecclesiastical lords are relatively easy to trace, the ownership of properties and the wording of charters providing clear reference points. Baronial jurisdiction, however, had obscurer origins, and was only gradually transformed from a personal immunity, rooted in feudal status,[52] to a franchise. Undoubtedly that transformation owed much to the growing sophistication of theories of the Crown's legal supremacy. Though it is not easy to trace in detail, a close examination of the barony of Wem suggests that it was in the earlier 13th century that the barons were transforming their ancient personal immunities into a franchise which amounted to a jurisdiction co-ordinate with the sheriff's tourn in the hundred.

Among the lay lords of liberties in Bradford hundred Ralph le Botiler (d. 1281) was pre-eminent. He held Wem, as a *baro*, for five knights' fees: almost all his barony lay within the hundred where its lord answered for three knights' fees, though parts of the barony were in Pimhill hundred and two other knights' fees were answered for in Pirehill hundred (Staffs.).[53] Botiler's three great demesne manors of Wem, Dodington, and Hinstock were said to do suit to shire and hundred.[54] It seems clear, however, that the suit was made by the steward of Wem who, in those three manors, held courts co-ordinate with the sheriff's tourn for all the members of the barony except Eyton-upon-the-Weald-Moors and Waters Upton.[55]

Apart from the three demesne manors only four manors held of the barony were the subject of separate verdicts in the inquiry of 1255: Eyton-upon-the-Weald-Moors, Dawley Magna, Tibberton, and Waters Upton. All had been subinfeudated by the mid or later 12th century,[56] and there is no evidence to show whether the barons' under-tenants in them owed their own suit to shire and hundred at that time. Probably, however, they did: all escaped suit of shire and hundred by 1255 but such may have been a fairly recent development, for Eyton and Waters Upton had certainly done suit until, *c.* 1245–6, their lords had withdrawn them. Though not alleged in 1255 against

[43] Ibid. xi. 190.
[44] See p. 36.
[45] *V.C.H. Salop.* ii. 80.
[46] See p. 48.
[47] *Rot. Hund.* ii. 77; S.R.O. 552/1/55 (hund. great ct. 1561).
[48] See p. 37. There is no 1274 hund. r. extant for Purslow.
[49] *Rot. Hund.* ii. 103; above, p. 48.
[50] See p. 36 and n. 31.
[51] *Rot. Hund.* ii. 76–7. Stitt, Medlicott, and Stowe were still presenting at the hund. great ct. in 1391: S.R.O.

552, box 46. Cf. S.R.O. 552/1/53, 55, for Stitt and Stowe in the 16th cent. For the Haughmond and Gt. Malvern privileges see above, pp. 47, 50.
[52] See p. 33.
[53] Eyton, ix. 169–72, 174. Almington and Tyrley were the only Staffs. properties kept in demesne: ibid. 192.
[54] *Rot. Hund.* ii. 56, 58. Cf. Eyton, ix. 174.
[55] Eyton, viii. 56. The Wem steward's appearances at the hund. were thus similar to those of the steward of Adderley (*Rot. Hund.* ii. 56).
[56] Eyton, viii. 26–7, 42, 47, 53–4.

Dawley and Tibberton, similar withdrawals had perhaps been achieved there, perhaps rather earlier. Such a supposition is at least consistent with the jurors' occasional unreliability in matters of fact and the lack of any standard form in their verdicts. Thus Dawley, held of the barony by the same lords as Tibberton, was said to have its suit of shire and hundred made for it by the steward of Wem, though no such statement was made of Tibberton; it is, however, clear that Tibberton escaped such suits in a similar way for it paid its *stretward*, normally payable at the hundred,[57] at Wem.[58]

The almost simultaneous withdrawal of the suits of Eyton-upon-the-Weald-Moors and Waters Upton, held as they were by different lords,[59] seems to point to an initiative of their common overlord Ralph le Botiler, the new baron of Wem.[60] Moreover an examination of manorial records over a longer period suggests that the withdrawal of suits was part of a wider policy, proceeding perhaps throughout the 13th century, of rationalizing the manorial organization of the barony.

In the early 16th century Wem and Dodington were the centres of two compact though extensive manors, the one including most of Wem parish with a few outlying members, the other consisting of a continuous stretch of country to the south of Whitchurch;[61] with three or four exceptions[62] their members were held in demesne by the barons, and that seems to have been the case from an early date.[63] By the early 16th century, however, Hinstock manor included within its leet jurisdiction a dozen manors scattered along the eastern side of the hundred;[64] all, apart from Hinstock itself, had been subinfeudated at an early date, mostly to the Eytons of Eyton-upon-the-Weald-Moors and the Pantulfs of Dawley — the former possibly, the latter certainly, cadets of the Pantulfs of Wem.[65] This grouping of subinfeudated manors under the leet court of Hinstock must have proceeded simultaneously with the withdrawal of its members' suits to the sheriff's tourn; there is moreover evidence that this was completed during the 13th century, for in 1310 Dawley and Tibberton both owed suit at Hinstock leet.[66]

Evidence adduced from the barony of Wem and from the estates of the principal ecclesiastical corporations has tended to the same conclusion. Rights and jurisdictions conceded by the Crown during the 12th century could be maintained as working liberties in the 13th century only by efficient administration. The lands of Wenlock priory, welded into a great hundredal liberty more completely than any other monastic estates, seem to provide one example of the success attending the early adoption of a vigorous policy. Another example has been seen in the incorporation of the subinfeudated manors of Wem barony within the leet jurisdiction of Hinstock, a process probably substantially complete by the middle of the 13th century.

By the end of the century the Crown, to judge only from the Shropshire *quo warranto* proceedings,[67] was less concerned to abolish the liberties than to arrest their development at the stages they had reached by the middle years of the century. The ambitions of the Corbets of Caus may have received some check,[68] but by and large the late-13th-century Shropshire hundredal immunities survived as leet courts well beyond the Middle Ages. Once again Bradford hundred provides evidence. Comparison of the manors owing suit to its court in 1255 with those owing suit in 1592 reveals

[57] Eyton, iv. 23.
[58] *Rot. Hund.* ii. 56–8.
[59] Eyton, viii. 30–1, 54–6.
[60] Succ. by 1246: Sanders, *Eng. Baronies*, 95.
[61] S.R.O. 212, boxes 30–1, 61–2, Dodington ct. r.; S.R.O. 167/1 sqq., Wem ct. r.
[62] Steel (in Prees), Harcourt (in Stanton upon Hine Heath), Beslow (in Wroxeter), and Edgeley (in Whit-church).
[63] Eyton, ix. 172, 194–6.
[64] S.R.O. 327, box 4, Hinstock ct. r. 32–6 Hen. VIII.
[65] Eyton, viii. 20–3, 26, 37, 41, 46, 51–2, 125; ix. 179, 370.
[66] Ibid. viii. 43, 47–8.
[67] Cited in n. 86, above.
[68] See pp. 37–8.

almost no differences[69] apart from four manors which had presumably escaped the hundred jurisdiction after their acquisition by privileged monasteries.[70]

In Shropshire the development of the leet was attended by a semantic oddity: in many of the liberties the view of frankpledge, though unknown in the rest of the county,[71] is found at least as a phrase in court records.[72] Whether the actual view of frankpledge was held may be doubted, even where the phrase is used to describe twice-yearly great courts.[73] In general, however, the likeliest explanation of the phrase may lie in the administrative histories of great estates. Their owners were often lords of manorial leets in other counties, where the view of frankpledge was the leading feature of that jurisdiction, and the unconscious or convenient use of uniform legal formulae in the advancement of claims[74] or the administration of courts may easily be conceived.

Under whatever name it was known leet jurisdiction survived the Middle Ages in Shropshire, as it did elsewhere, as a source of profit to the lords who owned it. In effect it amounted to exemption from the hundred jurisdiction, and some of the more considerable manors with leet courts were customarily referred to as 'hundreds'.[75] As the importance of the great hundred or sheriff's tourn dwindled,[76] so the leet's significance as a court diminished *pari passu*. A comparison between the standards of justice meted out by the king's officers and that dispensed by the officers of the franchises cannot be attempted here, though there are ample sources for such an investigation.[77] Even the most casual inspection of the hundred rolls, however, is sufficient to show that the balance was not always in the Crown's favour. The Shropshire rolls bear witness to the misdeeds of the sheriffs and their subordinate officers, and there is no reason to withhold belief in assertions, like those of the jurors of Edgmond and Newport in 1255,[78] that their lord used his liberty well. Other liberties were as certainly abused.[79] No doubt such contrasts and examples could be pointed and multiplied down the ages. One must suffice. About 1500 a petitioner claiming right and title to Edgeley (in Whitchurch) addressed the steward of Sir Gilbert Talbot's court as 'the most worthy and most sufficient steward that ever we knew here'. Forensic flattery must inevitably be suspect, but the petitioner's unusual eloquence carries conviction over the centuries and bears witness on behalf of all those liberties which were well administered, more especially perhaps in his complaint of his adversaries' recourse to 'higher courts': not content with 'your laws here', he alleged, they sued 'at Westminster where men know no more who should have right here than I do know what men do in Rome'. Such courts, when they were well administered, were good because they were local: the justice of the petitioner's case, he claimed, was 'noised in all this lordship' and 'if any man ask what evidence we have, we answer . . . that God and good country through succour of my lord and you and all his good counsel is our evidence . . .' *Vox populi vox Dei*, the petition proclaimed, and *Si Deus nobiscum quis contra nos?*[80] The king himself could ask no higher tribute to his courts.

---

[69] *Rot. Hund.* ii. 55–8; Staffs. R.O., D.593/J/10, ct. r.

[70] Chesthill (Combermere abbey), Nagington and Haughton (Haughmond), and Tern (Lilleshall).

[71] See p. 20.

[72] See e.g. S.R.O. 167/1–30, Wem ct. rec. 16th–19th cents.; S.R.O. 112, box 89, Atcham and Uckington ct. rec. 18th–19th cents.; Staffs. R.O., D.593/J/13 (Lilleshall ct. rec. 17th–19th cents.); Eyton, ii. 156.

[73] Eyton, iii. 263.

[74] Ibid. iii. 176; iv. 273; W. A. Morris, *The Frankpledge System* (1910), 53–5.

[75] See e.g. Eyton, x. 240–2, 381 (Ellesmere); above, p. 37 (Caus).

[76] See p. 44.

[77] Cam, 'Studies in Hund. R.', *Oxf. Studies in Social and Legal Hist.* vi(11), 190. The hist. of the Salop. hunds. suggests that, at least as far as vigour of administration is concerned, the private franchise-holder compared well with the Crown's local officials: above, p. 45.

[78] *Rot. Hund.* ii. 95.

[79] See e.g. *V.C.H. Salop.* i. 489–90.

[80] S.R.O. 3232/13.

COUNTY GOVERNMENT
1327-1603

The Keepers and Justices of the Peace, p. 54. The Sheriff, p. 74. Royal Castles and County Gaols, p. 79. The County Coroners, p. 80. The Escheator and the Feodary, p. 82. The Militia and the Lieutenancy, p. 82. Other Commissions, p. 86.

THE local standing of the *buzones*, those representatives of the county gentry who emerged in the 13th century as the county's administrative class, was also their weakness, for they were unable to subordinate their private interests to those of the Crown or resist the patronage of local magnates. In theory the Crown controlled the membership of local commissions and appointed the sheriffs and escheators; the extent to which it was able freely to exercise that control was the measure of how far royal interests prevailed in county government in the later Middle Ages.

In Shropshire the dynastic misfortunes of the greatest local magnates shaped the eventual triumph of royal over private interests. The FitzAlan interest in Shropshire was permanently weakened by the death without issue of Thomas, earl of Arundel, in 1415. The Talbot interest in the county never recovered from the earl of Shrewsbury's death at the battle of Northampton in 1460; the earldom was held by minors for most of the next thirty years. The eclipse of the Talbots, however, was a prelude to the triumph of Plantagenet, for Edward, duke of York and earl of March, attained the throne in 1461. Thus the most powerful of the surviving baronial interests in the marches was merged in that of the Crown. The Council in the Marches of Wales had its beginning under Edward IV and was seated at Ludlow, *caput* of the earldom of March; it continued (and at the same time surpassed) the tradition of the great baronial councils in offering advancement to its members and servants, the local gentry. Private and royal interests were thus harmonized, and the Council in the Marches became the instrument whereby the perennial lawlessness of the marcher counties was brought within bounds, helping ideals of public service to take root and prosper. From those ideals the county gentry would draw pride and wise governments their local strength.

The Keepers and Justices of the Peace

Keepers of the peace became a permanent part of county government after 1327, when their appointment was first required by statute.[1] Power to determine cases (the power that made them 'justices') was granted to them intermittently from 1329 and continuously from 1368.[2] By the late 14th century membership of the peace commission reflected the influence of the leading local magnates. In late-14th-century Shropshire the FitzAlans, earls of Arundel, predominated; in the 15th power lay with the Talbots (earls of Shrewsbury from 1442) and with the Plantagenet earls of March and dukes of York (kings from 1461). In the late 15th and early 16th centuries the development of the Council in the Marches of Wales (seated at Ludlow, stronghold of the earls

[1] 1 Edw. III, Stat. II, c. 16.
[2] Bertha H. Putnam, *Proceedings before J.P.s in 14th and 15th Cents.* (Ames Foundation, 1938), pp. xxiv–xxv; J. B. Post, 'The Peace Coms. of 1382', *E.H.R.* xci (1976) 98–9.

of March) and the Act of Union, 1536,[3] were stages in the process by which the magnates of the Welsh border were subjected to stricter royal control. From Edward IV's reign the size and composition of the Shropshire peace commission depended much on the Council in the Marches. In the earlier 16th century, when the council was strong and active, members of the council (of whom many were not Shropshire men) were placed in large numbers on the Shropshire commission. In Edward III's reign the average size of the Shropshire commission had been six; in Elizabeth I's it was 46. Growth had been gradual until the late 1530s, when sudden and permanent enlargement took place. As the council's vigour declined, however, the numbers of magistrates fluctuated more sharply and Shropshire residents came to predominate numerically.[4] Moreover the career of Robert, earl of Essex (d. 1601), shows that a great nobleman might yet command a system of patronage embracing local-government appointments in the marcher counties.

In Edward III's reign the Shropshire commission was already subject to sudden changes of size, reflecting the experimental character of the early peace commissions of every county. In 1327 the commission consisted of two local laymen, Sir William Ercall and William, Lord le Botiller of Wem[5] (d. 1334).[6] The first notable increase, in 1339,[7] was perhaps occasioned by the powers of array conferred on magistrates in 1338.[8] In 1351 and 1352, following a further accession of powers,[9] the Shropshire magistracy was transformed by the addition of six non-resident lawyers,[10] most of whom were at some time justices of the 'Oxford' assize circuit.[11] Those lawyers outnumbered the local lay members. In 1361, when magistrates received statutory power to try felons,[12] the lawyers were replaced by local laymen, whose numbers, however, were halved in 1362.[13] In 1364 the magistrates lost their determining powers.[14] When they regained them in 1368 two non-resident lawyers, with Oxford circuit associations,[15] were added to the commission;[16] this time, however, the lawyers were outnumbered by the laymen. Thereafter lawyers connected with Oxford circuit were a regular but small element of the Shropshire commission.

In 1327, and from 1338 to 1344, the magistrates acted under supervisors appointed for a group of counties.[17] In 1338 the earl of Arundel, one of the principal local magnates, whose daughter married Lord le Botiller's son,[18] was among the supervisors for Gloucestershire, Herefordshire, and Shropshire.[19] In 1344, shortly before his appointment as life sheriff of Shropshire,[20] he became a member of the Shropshire commission for the first time,[21] remaining its only magnate until 1362, when the magnates were excluded from all county peace commissions.[22] It was 1380 before another magnate, his son Earl Richard (d. 1397), was appointed in Shropshire.[23] Richard II's reign saw changes in the composition of the peace commission that were at first mainly administrative

[3] 27 Hen. VIII, c. 26.

[4] Commissions 1327–1509 and 1547–64 are in *Cal. Pat.*; those for 1509–47 are in *L. & P. Hen. VIII*. Other lists 1559–1603 are in the sources given in T. G. Barnes and A. Hassell Smith, 'Justices of Peace from 1558 to 1688: Revised List of Sources', *Bull. Inst. Hist. Res.* xxxii. 237–8, 242. Some dates assigned to lists therein are slightly modified in A. Hassell Smith, *County and Court: Govt. and Politics in Norf. 1558–1603* (1974), 344–9. Shropshire lists for 1555, 1582, and 1590 are in: S.P. 11/5 ff. 46–47v.; *Reg. Council in Marches of Wales* (Cymmrodorion Rec. Ser. viii), 216; B.L. Egerton MS. 3788, f. 30 and v.

[5] *Cal. Pat.* 1327–30, 89.

[6] *Complete Peerage*, ii. 232.

[7] *Cal. Pat.* 1338–40, 279.

[8] Putnam, op. cit. p. xxviii.

[9] Ibid. pp. xliii–xliv.

[10] *Cal. Pat.* 1350–4, 91, 284.

[11] Ric. de la Pole, Wm. of Cheltenham (ibid. 1345–8, 182), Rog. Hillary, Wm. Shareshill (Mary M. Taylor, 'Justices of Assize', *Eng. Govt. at Work*, iii, ed. J. F. Willard, 249), Hugh Aston (J.I. 3/131 rot. 19).

[12] Esther Moir, *Justice of Peace* (1969), 18.

[13] *Cal. Pat.* 1361–4, 64, 292.

[14] Putnam, op. cit. pp. xxiv–xxv.

[15] John Mowbray (*Cal. Pat.* 1364–7, 448), David Hanmer (J.I. 3/166 rot. 5).

[16] *Cal. Pat.* 1367–70, 192.

[17] Ibid. 1327–30, 214; 1338–40, 141, 279; 1340–3, 94; Putnam, op. cit. p. lxxxii.

[18] *Complete Peerage*, ii. 232.

[19] *Cal. Pat.* 1338–40, 141.

[20] See p. 74.

[21] *Cal. Pat.* 1343–5, 394.

[22] Putnam, op. cit. p. lxxxii.

[23] *Cal. Pat.* 1377–81, 513. Rog. Mortimer (cr. earl of March 1354) was a member 1351–2, 1353–6: ibid. 1350–4, 91, 449.

but were later increasingly political. The Shropshire commission reflected the fortunes of the earl of Arundel and of his brother, Archbishop Thomas; they were leading opponents of the king[24] and, during their periods as royal councillor and chancellor respectively, were directly involved in selecting magistrates.[25]

Slight revisions of the Shropshire commission occurred in the 1380s, but the most severe took place in all counties in July 1389, shortly after the king had declared himself of age and dismissed Arundel and his brother from the government.[26] Of the eleven Shropshire magistrates of 1388 nine were dropped.[27] Personal reasons may account for the dismissal of Arundel himself and of his kinsmen Richard, Lord Talbot,[28] and John, Lord Strange of Knockin.[29] It is believed, however, that the king acted mainly from a desire to please the Commons, who favoured the removal of all the powerful lords from the peace commissions;[30] for example, Hugh, Lord Burnell, an opponent of Arundel, was also dismissed. Unlike Arundel, Talbot, and Strange, however, he was restored within a year.[31] In December 1390, Arundel having been reconciled with the king and the Commons having petitioned for the restoration of lords to the magistracy, a new commission was issued to all counties.[32] In Shropshire it was politically selective. Arundel, Talbot, and Strange were restored. Burnell, however, was dropped;[33] his first wife had been daughter of Michael de la Pole, earl of Suffolk (d. 1389),[34] Arundel's political enemy.[35]

For several years the character of the Shropshire bench was unchanged. It was suddenly transformed in July 1397 upon Arundel's arrest as leader of a conspiracy against the king. Of the eleven members of the 1396 commission seven were removed, including Arundel (Strange and Talbot were dead). Their replacements included Burnell and, as in all counties, a few of Richard's noble partisans.[36] In Shropshire these were the duke of Surrey and the earls of Rutland and Worcester.[37] It was the first time that magnates with no special interest in Shropshire were appointed to its magistracy.[38] It should be added that some Shropshire magistrates retained their places during the successive changes of Richard II's reign; for example, Sir Robert Charlton and Sir John Hill, royal justices,[39] and Thomas Newport *alias* Gech.

Henry IV's accession did not bring sudden changes in the commission: he allowed Richard's last Shropshire magistrates to remain, except for the absentee dukes of Aumale and Surrey. Henry's most notable addition was that of Thomas, earl of Arundel,[40] who had returned to England from exile.[41] No new commission was issued for Shropshire between 1401 and 1407, and for the rest of the reign the county's magistracy remained stable in size and composition. The extraordinary lawlessness of Shropshire in Henry's reign[42] suggests that it was stability founded not on the Crown's strength but on its weakness. Of the twelve men appointed between 1401 and Henry IV's death, two were Arundel's relatives[43] and two his officers.[44] Three were connexions of Richard, Lord Talbot (d. 1396),[45] one was a Talbot retainer.[46] Influence at Court

[24] *D.N.B.*
[25] Putnam, op. cit. p. lxxvii.
[26] R. L. Storey, 'Liveries and Commissions of Peace 1388–90', *Reign of Ric. II*, ed. F. R. H. Du Boulay and Caroline M. Barron (1971), 136–7.
[27] *Cal. Pat. 1385–9*, 545; *1388–92*, 137.
[28] Marr. Arundel's grand-dau.: *Complete Peerage*, xii(1), 616–17.
[29] Arundel's cos.: ibid. 354.
[30] Storey, op. cit. 138–40.
[31] *Cal. Pat. 1388–92*, 342.
[32] Storey, op. cit. 149–50.
[33] *Cal. Pat. 1388–92*, 344.
[34] *Complete Peerage*, ii. 435.
[35] *D.N.B.*
[36] Storey, op. cit. 152.
[37] *Cal. Pat. 1391–6*, 728; *1396–9*, 229, 235.
[38] Rutland was added to 15 other peace commissions, Surrey to 12: Storey, op. cit. 152 n.
[39] Putnam, op. cit. 401, 423.
[40] *Cal. Pat. 1396–9*, 435; *1399–1401*, 563.
[41] *D.N.B.*
[42] See pp. 70–1.
[43] Ld. Charlton (niece's husband and bro.-in-law's bro.: *Complete Peerage*, iii. 161), Sir Rol. Lenthall (bro.-in-law: *Salop. Peace Roll, 1400–14*, 25).
[44] David Holbache (steward of Oswestry lordship: R. A. Griffiths, *Principality of Wales in Later Middle Ages*, i (1972), 121), Sir John Wele (constable of Oswestry cas.: *Salop. Peace Roll, 1400–14*, 26).
[45] Thos., Ld. Furnivalle (widow's husband), Ld. Talbot (son), John, Ld. Furnivalle (son): *Salop. Peace Roll, 1400–14*, 19–21.
[46] John Winsbury: A. J. Pollard, 'Fam. of Talbot, Lds. Talbot and Earls of Shrews. in the XVth Cent.' (Bristol Univ. Ph.D. thesis, 1968), 269 n.

may partly explain the appointments. Arundel's allies, Henry and Thomas Beaufort,[47] were chancellors 1403–5 and 1410–11 respectively;[48] of the Talbot connexion Thomas, Lord Furnivalle, was treasurer of England 1404–7.[49]

The first important change for many years occurred in February 1416, four months after Arundel had died without issue,[50] and it placed the Talbots in a dominant position. A commission was issued for Shropshire alone. Of the thirteen members of the previous commission (1413) ten were removed,[51] including three Arundel followers.[52] Gilbert, Lord Talbot, and John, Lord Furnivalle, remained, and at least three Talbot followers[53] were among the five men added. Another addition was that of Edmund, earl of March, who had risen in favour since Henry V's accession.[54] In the period 1419–24 the Shropshire commission fluctuated erratically in size and composition,[55] perhaps as a result of members' absence in France; in 1424 only three of the twelve magistrates of November 1416 remained. Ecclesiastics were added for the first time in 1424 soon after Bishop Beaufort became chancellor; Beaufort and Bishop Heyworth of Coventry and Lichfield were appointed in Shropshire.

Changes thereafter were more gradual. The two bishops were dropped in 1432. In the same year Richard, duke of York and earl of March, came of age and was added to the Shropshire commission.[56] John Talbot, Lord Furnivalle (cr. earl of Shrewsbury 1442), and York were the most powerful men in Shropshire during the next twenty years.[57] During the same period Talbot's relatives and followers were much in evidence in the county's stable peace commissions.[58] The commission grew steadily from some thirteen in 1432 to about 25 in 1460.[59] Talbot, though a loyal Lancastrian, was on friendly terms with York but his son, the 2nd earl of Shrewsbury (1453–60), became a firm opponent of the duke.[60] York's emergence as a political force in the 1450s was not of a kind to give him much influence over the Shropshire peace commission, whose predominantly Lancastrian character was not altered until 1460.

Shrewsbury was killed at the Yorkist victory of Northampton (10 July 1460), and the earldom passed to his 11-year-old son.[61] In September the Shropshire magistracy was purged;[62] of the 25 members of the 1458 commission, only ten, presumably Yorkists and the uncommitted, were allowed to remain. Seven new men were put on. Six, perhaps all, of them were active Yorkists[63] and none of the seven had been named in any earlier Shropshire peace commission. After the Yorkists' final victory at Towton (29 March 1461) Edward IV issued commissions for Shropshire[64] that showed a more lenient attitude:[65] four of the surviving magistrates dismissed in 1460[66] were reinstated. There was no further significant change until December 1470, after Henry VI's Readeption. Of the 22 members of the 1469 commission only eight, including John, earl of Shrewsbury (d. 1473), were then allowed to remain. Of the three added, only Sir John Burgh, who had been dismissed in 1460, had been a magistrate before.[67] The small size of the new commission perhaps indicates that little local support could be found for the earl of Warwick's government.[68] The earl of Shrewsbury failed to give him military assistance

[47] D.N.B. sub FitzAlan, Thos.
[48] Handbk. of Brit. Chron. (1961), 85.
[49] Ibid. 102. [50] D.N.B.
[51] Cal. Pat. 1413–16, 422.
[52] Holbache, Lenthall, and Wele.
[53] Hugh Burgh (Pollard, op. cit. 224, 417), Wm. Burley of Broncroft (ibid. 229–30), Edw. Sprenchose (ibid. 24 n.).
[54] D.N.B.
[55] Cal. Pat. 1416–22, 458; 1422–9, 569.
[56] Ibid. 1429–36, 623–4.
[57] Pollard, op. cit. 229.
[58] Ibid. passim.
[59] Cal. Pat. 1429–36, 623–4; 1436–41, 589; 1441–6,

477; 1446–52, 593–4; 1452–61, 675–6.
[60] Pollard, op. cit. 69–87, 228–9, 247.
[61] Complete Peerage, xi. 705–6.
[62] Cal. Pat. 1452–61, 675–6.
[63] Wal. Hopton (ibid. 552), the earls of March and Warwick, Edw. Bourchier (E. F. Jacob, Fifteenth Cent. 516), Rog. Kynaston (Pollard, op. cit. 55 n.), John Lawley (Wedgwood, Hist. Parl. 1439–1509: Biogs. 529).
[64] Cal. Pat. 1461–7, 570.
[65] See Pollard, op. cit. 89, 221.
[66] Thos. Corbet of Leigh, Thos. Horde, Thos. Acton, Ld. Grey of Powis.
[67] Cal. Pat. 1467–77, 627.
[68] See Wedgwood, op. cit. p. xxiii.

in 1471.[69] Edward IV was soon restored and was again lenient:[70] of the surviving magistrates of 1470 only one was removed. Nine of those dropped in 1470 were reinstated and three new men were added.[71]

Until 1483 there were no comparable upheavals in the Shropshire commission. The 1470s, however, saw the beginnings of the Council in the Marches of Wales, which developed from the prince of Wales's council.[72] Between 1473, when the council was enlarged,[73] and 1474 the Shropshire magistracy was twice temporarily swollen by the addition of council members,[74] and some of those added in 1474 gained a permanent place in the peace commission. From about that time the Shropshire magistracy began to include a good proportion of distinguished non-residents who took little direct part in Shropshire affairs.

On the day of his accession (26 June 1483) Richard III issued new peace commissions.[75] Of the Shropshire magistrates of 1480 only six were removed, only two of whom were local men.[76] Of the seven men added three, including the duke of Buckingham, were men with local connexions who had been removed from the Shropshire commission at different dates in the 1470s.[77] Buckingham's fall later in the year, for all his influence in Wales and the marches,[78] had virtually no reflection in the Shropshire commission.[79] In 1485 Richard's defeat and Henry VII's accession brought large changes. Of the eighteen members of Richard's last commission (1483) ten, most of them Shropshire residents, were removed in Henry's first commission; eleven new men, nearly all of them local, were appointed, of whom seven had never served as Shropshire magistrates before.[80] The large proportion of newcomers indicates that Henry found wide local support for his seizure of power. Sir Gilbert Talbot, one of the magistrates reinstated by Henry and uncle of George, earl of Shrewsbury (d. 1538), a minor, had ridden to Bosworth with the whole armed force of the earldom and was the first of those knighted on the battlefield.[81]

In 1493 the prince of Wales's council received judicial powers over Gloucestershire, Herefordshire, Shropshire, and Worcestershire,[82] and a large group of men, most probably members of the council,[83] was added to the peace commission in all four counties.[84] In Shropshire and Herefordshire in 1496 several of those newcomers were replaced on the commission by other council members while several Shropshire residents were dropped from the Shropshire commission.[85] In February 1504, at a time when Henry VII was taking measures to improve justice in the Welsh marches,[86] a number of council members on the Shropshire and Worcestershire commissions were replaced by other councillors.[87] Those, the only notable changes in the Shropshire commission during Henry VII's reign, mainly affected magistrates appointed by virtue of their membership of the prince's council. It should be added that some of those councillors were also Shropshire residents and might have been appointed magistrates for that reason alone, had the council not existed. It nevertheless seems likely that after 1493 the prince's council took a leading part in the appointment of magistrates in

[69] Jacob, op. cit. 567.
[70] Ibid. 600–1.
[71] Cal. Pat. 1467–77, 627.
[72] Penry Williams, Council in Marches of Wales under Eliz. I (1958), 6–8.
[73] Caroline A. J. Skeel, Council in Marches of Wales (1904), 24–5.
[74] Cal. Pat. 1467–77, 627–8.
[75] Ibid. 1476–85, 570–1.
[76] Gilbert Talbot, esq. of the body to Edw. IV (Wedgwood, op. cit. 838), and John Leighton (ibid. 534–5).
[77] Rob. Charlton removed 1471, Buckingham rem. 1473, Sir Rog. Kynaston rem. 1477. Rob. Cressett, also a local man, had been dropped 1475–80. See Cal. Pat. 1467–77, 627; 1476–85, 571.
[78] D.N.B.
[79] Cal. Pat. 1476–85, 570–1.
[80] Ibid. 1485–94, 498.
[81] Wedgwood, op. cit. 838.
[82] Williams, Council in Marches, 9.
[83] The council's composition in 1493 is not fully known. For lists of 1501 and 1502 see ibid. 10.
[84] Cal. Pat. 1485–94, 487–8, 498, 505. They were not added in, e.g., Oxon., Staffs., or Warws.: ibid. 497, 500–1, 503–4.
[85] Ibid. 1494–1509, 641–2, 655–6.
[86] Williams, op. cit. 11.
[87] Cal. Pat. 1494–1509, 655–6, 665–6. Similar changes occurred in Glos. and Herefs. 1505: ibid. 639–42.

Shropshire and the three other English counties.[88] When Prince Henry became king in 1509 the Council in the Marches of Wales continued in existence. Throughout the 16th century the Shropshire commission included many non-resident members of the council. The work of county government, however, fell upon the resident justices; thus the only locally significant changes in the Shropshire peace commission were those affecting them.

Two resident justices were temporarily omitted in the commission of July 1521;[89] it was soon after Buckingham's execution on a charge of treason, but there seems to be no connexion between the events.[90] Otherwise the Shropshire peace commission saw no remarkable change until the 1530s, when the administration of justice in Wales, the marches, and the adjoining English counties was vigorously reformed. Bishop Lee of Coventry and Lichfield, president of the Council in the Marches 1534–43, conducted a vigorous and successful campaign against lawbreakers. A number of statutes, principally the Act of Union, 1536,[91] imposed the English pattern of administration on Wales and the marches;[92] as a result the area of Shropshire was enlarged to include the neighbouring marcher lordships.[93] In 1538 the Shropshire magistracy was permanently enlarged by the addition of equal numbers of resident and non-resident men.[94] The number of resident justices, which was about ten in the earlier part of the reign, then stood at some fifteen.[95] The Shropshire commission was otherwise stable during Henry VIII's reign and many of the resident members enjoyed long uninterrupted periods of office.

Only one Shropshire peace commission appears on Edward VI's patent rolls. Issued in 1547[96] it had 51 members, whereas Henry VIII's last Shropshire commission (1543) had only 41.[97] Both resident and non-resident magistrates were increased in numbers, but there was no noteworthy change in the political character of the residents. From Mary I's reign two complete lists of Shropshire magistrates survive: for 1554 and 1555.[98] By 1555 the total number of justices had not increased, but the proportion of residents had grown to equal that of non-residents. Mary seems to have made no sweeping religious or political change in the Shropshire magistracy: more than half the resident justices of 1554 had been in the 1547 commission, and about half the new men were to keep their places in Elizabeth I's commissions. Among the new names, however, that of Edmund Plowden[99] shows that at least one prominent local Roman Catholic was put on, and there may have been other instances of discrimination: Lewis Jones of Bishop's Castle, though Plowden's brother-in-law,[1] was omitted in 1554 and 1555, and Richard Cornewall had been dropped by 1555; both recur as magistrates in 1559.[2] Sir George Blount, a former adherent of the duke of Northumberland,[3] was dropped by 1555, though his fellow chantry commissioner under Edward VI, Reynold Corbet,[4] remained an active magistrate in October 1556.[5]

In the years following Elizabeth I's accession the Shropshire commission underwent important adjustments that amounted eventually to a purge of the Marian bench. Some thirty resident justices are known to have served under Mary in or after 1555;[6] fourteen

[88] The Act of Union, 1543, 34 & 35 Hen. VIII, c. 26, required the council to nominate the J.P.s of Wales.
[89] Sir Thos. Cornewall, Thos. Scriven: *L. & P. Hen. VIII*, i(2), pp. 1542–3; iii(2), p. 592.
[90] Cornewall was appointed to the Council in the Marches 1521: *T.S.A.S.* 4th ser. xi. 32.
[91] 27 Hen. VIII, c. 26.
[92] Williams, op. cit. 15–35.
[93] See p. 41.
[94] *L. & P. Hen. VIII*, xiii(1), p. 411.
[95] Ibid. i(2), pp. 1542–3; iii(2), pp. 592, 1019; iv(3), p. 2311; v, p. 82.

[96] *Cal. Pat.* 1547–8, 88.
[97] *L. & P. Hen. VIII*, xviii(1), pp. 123–4.
[98] *Cal. Pat.* 1553–4, 23; S.P. 11/5 ff. 46–47v.
[99] R. Somerville, *Hist. of Duchy of Lancaster*, i (1953), 432.
[1] B[arbara] M. P[lowden], *Records of Plowden Fam.* (priv. print. 1887; copy in S.R.O.), 11.
[2] S.P. 12/2 f. 55.
[3] *T.S.A.S.* 3rd ser. viii. 125.
[4] Ibid. 3rd ser. x. 295.
[5] E 372/405 Salop. d.
[6] Ibid.; S.P. 11/5 ff. 46–47v.

of them had been permanently dropped by the end of June 1564.[7] Some of those may have died, others could have been dismissed by Mary. By the end of June 1564 Elizabeth had permanently dismissed probably less than half of the surviving residents who were in the commission at Mary's death.[8] She had, however, dismissed about another quarter whose exclusion proved temporary. In 1561 the government had thought a general reduction in the number of magistrates was desirable; those to be eliminated were naturally those considered unreliable on religious or other grounds.[9] The whole Shropshire commission, 51 men in 1554,[10] was reduced to 29 by the end of 1561;[11] reductions of a similar scale were made, for example, in Norfolk and Sussex.[12] The reduction improved in Shropshire the proportion of resident justices, who thus outnumbered the non-residents by two to one. In June 1564, however, the commission was allowed to rise again to 41 and the non-resident element, though remaining in the minority, gained in relative size.[13]

After the 1564 commission the bishops were asked to return the names of magistrates unfavourable to the established Church. About a quarter of the resident Shropshire justices were so named,[14] all but one of whom[15] is known to have served under Mary. In some counties the bishops' reports had little effect but in Shropshire[16] the men in question were dropped. By 1573[17] one of them was dead[18] and one remained in the commission;[19] the rest[20] had been replaced by men whom the bishops had recommended in 1564. Their recommendations as to removals and appointments were made with the advice of local leaders. The bishop of Coventry and Lichfield's Shropshire advisers were Sir Andrew Corbet and Sir Richard Newport, Shropshire magistrates and first cousins,[21] and George Lee, a bailiff of Shrewsbury.[22] Those Shropshire justices who were added after being named in the bishops' reports were all close relatives of Corbet and Newport.[23]

During the early part of Sir Henry Sidney's presidency of the Council in the Marches (1560–86) the council's authority declined: Sidney rarely attended the council and his vice-presidents were lenient or inactive. In 1576, however, the council, with government encouragement, made many reforms of its procedure, and in 1577 Bishop Whitgift of Worcester, a vigorous and capable administrator, became vice-president.[24] Late in 1577 or early in 1578 council members were added to the Shropshire commission in such a way as suddenly to make the number of non-residents equal to that of the residents again, and the commission grew from 43 members to 57.[25]

By October 1582 the commission had grown gradually to 63 men, the proportions of residents and non-residents remaining equal.[26] In that year the government, again con-

[7] *Cal. Pat.* 1563–6, p. 26.
[8] Higher proportions of dismissals have been calculated for other cos. by including dismissals of non-residents: A. Hassell Smith, 'Personnel of Coms. of Peace, 1554–1564: a Reconsideration', *Huntington Libr. Quarterly*, xxii. 311.
[9] Ibid. 310.
[10] *Cal. Pat.* 1553–4, 23.
[11] B.L. Lansd. MS. 1218, ff. 77v.–78.
[12] Smith, *County and Court*, 82.
[13] *Cal. Pat.* 1563–4, p. 26.
[14] Wm. Charlton of Wombridge, Thos. Eyton (his bro.-in-law: *T.S.A.S.* 4th ser. xi. 40), Thos. Fermour (whose dau. marr. Edm. Plowden's son: Plowden, *Rec. of Plowden Fam.* 16), Wm. Gatacre, Ric. Mytton (his bro.-in-law: *T.S.A.S.* 4th ser. xi. 41), and Wm. Young of Caynton: *Camd. Misc.* ix (Camd. N.S. liii), 15, 45. Reports on Adam Ottley were contradictory: ibid. 15, 44.
[15] Fermour.
[16] As, e.g., in Suss.: Smith, op. cit. 83.

[17] S.P. 12/33, pt. 2, ff. 24v.–25.
[18] Charlton (d. 1567): *T.S.A.S.* 4th ser. xi. 40.
[19] Thos. Eyton.
[20] Mytton d. 1591 (ibid 37), Fermour d. 1580 (ibid. liv. 183), Gatacre d. 1578 (ibid. 2nd ser. ii. 226), Young bur. 1584 (*Visit. Salop. 1623*, ii. 519, MS. addition in S.P.L. copy (MS. 4362)).
[21] *Visit. Salop. 1623*, i. 136, 138. [22] *Camd. Misc.* ix. 44.
[23] Wm. Gratewood (Newport's son-in-law: Blakeway, *Sheriffs*, 91), Rol. Lacon (whose dau. marr. Newport's son: Burke, *Peerage* (1949), 245), Wm. Leighton of Plaish (marr. Corbet's cos.: *Visit. Salop. 1623*, ii. 323), Rob. Needham (Corbet's neph.: ibid. 372), and Thos. Williams of Wollaston (Newport's neph.: ibid. 506–7). Gratewood, Lacon, and Needham were attending q. sess. by Trin. 1568 (E 137/38/6); Williams was a J.P. by 1572 (*T.S.A.S.* lvi. 174).
[24] Williams, *Council in Marches*, 252–65.
[25] S.P. 12/121 ff. 26v.–27; Hatfield Ho., Cecil Papers 223/7, Salop.
[26] *Reg. Council in Marches of Wales*, 216.

cerned at the large size of peace commissions, ordered another general reduction;[27] by the end of 1583 the Shropshire magistracy had been reduced to 51 men.[28] The earl of Leicester, whose influence predominated in north Wales and in the Council in the Marches,[29] complained that justices were dismissed indiscriminately.[30] In Shropshire it was among the resident magistrates that the reduction had been most severe; nine had been removed, four of whom were justices of ten or more years' standing. By 1587 the commission had grown again to contain 62 members,[31] and the government ordered another general reduction;[32] by April 1590 at latest the number of Shropshire justices had fallen to 45.[33] By then it was the non-resident magistrates who had suffered most reduction, and the residents again preponderated.

In the 1590s patronage in Wales and the marcher counties was increasingly dominated by the earl of Essex. Both Sir John Puckering, lord keeper 1592–6, and Sir Thomas Egerton, lord keeper 1596–1603, were friends of Essex and had close connexions with Wales and the marches.[34] It is therefore likely that the composition of the Shropshire peace commissions, under the lord keeper's immediate control, was strongly affected by the Essex interest. The earl of Pembroke, though he attempted to rival Essex's patronage in Wales and the marches, had fewer friends at Court.[35] Between 1590 and 1595 there seems to have been little change in the Shropshire magistracy, though by 1595 the commission was slightly smaller.[36] The government, however, was again anxious to reduce numbers[37] and by July 1595 several Shropshire magistrates had been removed, including about five residents.[38] Two of them, Roland Lacon and Robert Eyton, may have been dropped on grounds of religion.[39] Private interests, however, may explain the removal of Henry Vernon of Stokesay and Sir Walter Leveson, two justices of long standing;[40] they were enemies of Edward Grey, grandson of the last Lord Grey of Powis (d. 1551),[41] and Edward Grey was probably a follower of Essex.[42]

From 1596 until the end of the reign the resident part of the Shropshire magistracy seems to have grown continuously.[43] The whole Shropshire commission grew from 41 members in 1596 to 54 in 1608,[44] and the residents increased their numerical superiority in that period from about two to one to about five to two. At least seven new men were added in 1597;[45] among them was Sir Henry Bromley, who was implicated in 1601 in the Essex rebellion[46] and then dismissed.[47] Aspirants to the peace commission had somehow to bring themselves to the notice of the lord chancellor or lord keeper. For example, in 1598 Francis Wolryche gained a place on the commission[48] on the recommendation of his brother-in-law Roger Puleston,[49] a kinsman of Lord Keeper Egerton.[50]

[27] Smith, *County and Court*, 83.
[28] B.L. Harl. MS. 474, ff. 31v.–33.
[29] Williams, op. cit. 239, 252. [30] Smith, op. cit. 83.
[31] B.L. Lansd. MS. 53, f. 194 (no names given).
[32] Smith, op. cit. 83.
[33] B.L. Egerton MS. 3788, f. 30 and v.
[34] Williams, op. cit. 281–9; Smith, op. cit. 153.
[35] Williams, op. cit. 287–8.
[36] Northants. R.O., Wingfield (Tickencote) Collection, box X.511, Salop.
[37] Smith, op. cit. 78, 85.
[38] S.P. 13, case F, no. 11, ff. 28v.–29v. This list belongs to 1596 (*Bull. Inst. Hist. Res.* xxxii. 238) but later than 24 July, when Reynold Williams was made J.P. (C 231/1 f. 18v.). The removals inferred from the list are not in the Crown Office docquet bk. beginning July 1595 (C 231/1) and were thus presumably made before that, as in Norf. (Smith, op. cit. 85).
[39] Lacon's son was a Roman Catholic and his dau. marr. Thos. Fermour's son; Eyton's father was an opponent of the established Church in 1564: *T.S.A.S.* 3rd ser. viii. 129; above, p. 60 n.
[40] Leveson first occurs as J.P. 1575 (S.P. 12/104 f. 66v.), Vernon 1579 (S.P. 12/145 f. 36v.).

[41] See p. 76.
[42] One of Grey's bros. was baptized 'Devereux': *Visit. Salop. 1623*, i. 106. An Edw. Grey had been dismissed as J.P. between Oct. 1582 and the end of 1583: *Reg. Council in Marches of Wales*, 216; B.L. Harl. MS. 474, ff. 31v.–33.
[43] Between Sept. 1596 and Eliz. I's death at least 22 residents were added and 3 removed: C 231/1 *passim*. Removals for death are not recorded in this source but are unlikely to have brought the number to 22.
[44] S.P. 13, case F, no. 11, ff. 28v.–29v.; S.P. 14/33 ff. 51–52v.
[45] C 231/1 ff. 25v., 28v., 42v.–43.
[46] *T.S.A.S.* 4th ser. xi. 157.
[47] C 231/1 f. 105.
[48] Ibid. f. 50v. He had been added Feb. × Oct. 1595 (Northants. R.O., Wingfield (Tickencote) Collection, box X.511, Salop.; E 137/38/6) but dropped by the end of 1596 (S.P. 13, case F, no. 11, ff. 28v.–29v.).
[49] J. H. Gleason, *Justices of Peace in Eng. 1558 to 1640* (1969), 59–60.
[50] Williams, *Council in Marches*, 304–5; R. B. Manning, 'The Making of a Protestant Aristocracy', *Bull. Inst. Hist. Res.* xlix. 66.

The interests of efficient local government were nevertheless taken into account: one of Puleston's arguments was that another man was needed to assist Sir Edward Bromley, the only justice then resident in the Brimstree and Stottesdon division.[51]

Non-resident magistrates had been in the majority in Shropshire peace commissions of the early 16th century. Since then attempts to reassert the representation of the Council in the Marches on the peace commission had been short-lived. Shropshire residents, supported by influential friends at Court, had come to predominate. Indeed, Shropshire exerted by then a considerable influence upon the Council in the Marches: in Elizabeth I's reign the county furnished more council members than any other, supplied many of its leading officers,[52] and in the early 17th century complained less than the other marcher shires against the council's interference.[53]

The burden of county government was borne by a small proportion of the resident magistrates. By 1399 there were men recognized as the 'chief justices of the peace' in Shropshire;[54] they may be identified from the 14th century by allusions to the bench as consisting of such a person 'and his fellows', and from the 15th by their regular attendance at sessions.[55] From the 14th century the leading keepers and justices of the peace were usually closely related to each other. They usually had connexions, too, with men at Court, either as their local officers or as relatives. Until Elizabeth I's reign many of them were professional lawyers as well, and were thus especially qualified to lead. Such men were likely to be the leaders in all county affairs, for example as members of other commissions[56] or as knights of the shire.[57] Since the tendency of their relatives to succeed to the leading positions was not checked by central government, there flourished among the Shropshire gentry an hereditary governing class enjoying by tradition the acceptance of both government and people.

From the 1350s to the 1370s the recognized leader was Nicholas, Lord Burnell[58] (d. 1383), a second cousin of Richard, earl of Arundel (d. 1376).[59] By 1386 Burnell's son and heir Hugh occupied the same position.[60] With the other local lords, Hugh Burnell was dismissed from the peace commission in 1389[61] and replaced as leader by Sir Robert Charlton,[62] chief justice of Common Pleas and a justice of the Oxford assize circuit.[63] Burnell was restored as leader in 1390,[64] only to be ejected when Arundel gained control of the commission later that year.[65] In the 1390s the names of John, Lord Strange of Knockin,[66] Arundel himself,[67] Thomas Newport,[68] and John Burley[69] occur

---

[51] On the divisions see pp. 74–5.

[52] Williams, op. cit. 144–5, 190–3, 342–61.

[53] Penry Williams, 'The Attack on the Council in the Marches', *Trans. Cymmrodorion Soc. 1961*, pt. 1, p. 13.

[54] *Cal. Pat.* 1396–9, 462.

[55] Some attendances 1390–1603 may be deduced from pipe rolls, where wages (payable under 14 Ric. II, c. 11, to J.P.s below the rank of banneret) were supposed to be recorded. Before the 16th cent., however, they were entered only rarely. The following rolls were searched for this chapter, those marked * having no entry of Salop. wages: E 372/235*, 240*, 245*, 250*, 255*, 260*, 265*, 270*, 292, 297*, 302*, 307*, 312, 317*, 322*, 327*, 331*, 334–5*, 339–40*, 359*, 360, 363*, 370, 375, 391, 396, 401–2*, 405, 406–8*, 409–10, 416*, 418–19*, 421, 423, 426, 428, 433, 435. Justices of the rank of banneret or above were not paid, but other sources show that the rule caused few omissions from the rolls and none of importance.

[56] See pp. 83–4, 86–9.

[57] About half the men mentioned in this section as leaders were M.P.s for Salop. seats, some three quarters of them as kts. of the shire: *T.S.A.S.* 4th ser. xii. 43–7, 269–72; Wedgwood, *Hist. Parl. 1439–1509: Reg.* 671–4.

[58] Burnell 'and fellows' occur 1365, 1371 × 1373, 1376 × 1379, 1377–9: *Cal. Pat.* 1364–7, 149; *Cal. Close,*

1369–74, 590; J.I. 3/161 rot. 9d.; J.I. 3/166 rot. 5. Burnell named first in all Salop. peace coms. 1362–80: *Cal. Pat.* Burnell 'and fellows' occur as justices of labourers 1353 × 1359: *Cart. Shrews.* ii. 434.

[59] *Complete Peerage,* ii. 434–5.

[60] Burnell 'and fellows' occur 1386, 1388–9, 1389 × 1390: *Cal. Close,* 1385–9, 130; *Sel. Cases in K.B.* vii (Selden Soc. lxxxviii), p. 61; J.I. 3/180 rot. 49.

[61] See p. 56.

[62] *Cal. Close,* 1389–92, 40. Charlton 'and fellows' occur 1390 × 1391: J.I. 3/180 rot. 50. Named first in com. 20 Dec. 1389: *Cal. Pat.* 1388–92, 139.

[63] Putnam, *Proceedings,* 401.

[64] Burnell 'and fellows' occur 1390 × 1391: J.I. 3/180 rot. 49 and d. Named first in com. 28 June 1390: *Cal. Pat.* 1388–92, 342. [65] See p. 56.

[66] Strange 'and fellows' occur 1388 × 1391, 1390 × 1391: J.I. 3/180 rott. 49–50d.

[67] Arundel 'and fellows' occur 1391–3: *Cal. Close,* 1389–92, 417; J.I. 3/180 rott. 50, 51d. Named first in all Salop. peace coms. 1390–6: *Cal. Pat.* 1388–92, 344, 524; 1391–6, 441, 728.

[68] Newport 'and fellows' occur 1393 × 1394, 1395, 1395 × 1396: J.I. 3/180 rott. 52, 53 and d.

[69] Burley 'and fellows' occur 1395 × 1396: J.I. 3/180 rot. 53d.

successively as leaders of the bench. Strange,[70] Newport,[71] and Burley[72] all had close affinities with Arundel. Burnell may have resumed the leadership in 1397 upon Arundel's fall,[73] but lost it finally at Henry IV's accession. In Henry's reign Thomas, earl of Arundel, and Burley, one of his officers and a barrister,[74] dominated the Shropshire bench. Arundel was described about 1404 as 'chief justice of the peace' in Shropshire[75] and he sometimes presided at sessions in person.[76] Otherwise Burley seems to have presided alone.[77] He was dropped from the commission in 1413[78] and died, like Arundel, in 1415.[79] Burnell enjoyed the favour of Henry IV and lived until 1420[80] but seems never again to have presided at the Shropshire sessions of the peace. The Arundel interest was against him: in 1413 his property at Pitchford was raided by armed men led by a fellow magistrate, Sir John Wele,[81] who was Arundel's constable at Oswestry castle.[82] In 1413[83] David Holbache, another FitzAlan officer and a lawyer of high reputation in Wales and the marches, occurs as *custos rotulorum* of Shropshire and thus probably replaced Burley as the leading magistrate. Holbache died in 1421.[84]

His successor as *custos* is not known, but by the early 1430s William Burley of Broncroft, another lawyer and son of John, had emerged as leader.[85] He had begun his career in the FitzAlans' service but by 1418 had also become one of the leading officers of Lord Furnivalle (later earl of Shrewsbury). Until his death in 1458 Burley was the most influential member of the Shropshire gentry, not only as a magistrate but also in many other capacities. Later in his career he became an officer and supporter of Richard, duke of York, but remained loyal to the Talbots, who were Lancastrians. Indeed Burley seems to have enjoyed such prestige as to give him some independence of factional interests.[86] During his long career other men were closely associated with him on the Shropshire bench. Hugh Burgh (d. 1430), one of Talbot's closest retainers,[87] was prominent in the 1420s.[88] In the 1430s and 1440s John Winsbury may have been next in importance to Burley,[89] his uncle.[90] Winsbury disappears from the commission between 1449 and 1453.[91]

In the 1450s it seems that Thomas Horde and Thomas Acton, both lawyers,[92] were next in importance to Burley,[93] and in Edward IV's reign they appear to have been the leading Shropshire justices.[94] Horde was perhaps the senior, having been appointed to the bench six years before Acton, in 1448.[95] Their wives were sisters.[96] Both were trusted servants of the earl of Shrewsbury[97] (d. 1460) and were dropped from the

[70] Arundel's cos.: *Complete Peerage*, xii(1), 354.

[71] Steward of Shrews. 13 Ric. II (1389–90), the borough being virtually in Arundel's control: Owen and Blakeway, *Hist. Shrews.* i. 168–9, 539.

[72] Steward of Oswestry lordship by 1392: *T.S.A.S.* lvi. 264. In 1390–1 he had been steward of Blakemere for Ric., Ld. Talbot: Barbara Ross, 'Accts. of the Talbot Household at Blakemere . . . 1394–1425' (Canberra Univ. M.A. thesis, 1970; copy in S.R.O.), i. 121.

[73] See *Cal. Inq. Misc.* vi, p. 89; Owen and Blakeway, *Hist. Shrews.* i. 527 n.; *Cal. Pat.* 1396–9, 509.

[74] *T.S.A.S.* 4th ser. xi. 41.

[75] S.R.O. 567, box 39, petition of Joan Carles (for date see *Salop. Peace Roll, 1400–14*, 70).

[76] *Sel. Cases in K.B.* vii, p. 114; J.I. 3/189 rot. 23; *Salop. Peace Roll, 1400–14*, 18–19, 80.

[77] Burley 'and fellows' occur 1400 × 1401, 1406 × 1407: J.I. 3/189 rot. 23. Burley attended oftener than other J.P.s 1400–12: *Salop. Peace Roll, 1400–14*, 30.

[78] *Cal. Pat.* 1408–13, 484.

[79] *T.S.A.S.* 4th ser. xi. 5.

[80] *Complete Peerage*, ii. 435; *Salop. Peace Roll, 1400–14*, 19.

[81] J.I. 1/753 rot. 4.

[82] *Salop. Peace Roll, 1400–14*, 26.

[83] See p. 67.

[84] Griffiths, *Principality of Wales*, i. 121.

[85] Burley 'and fellows' occur 1442–4, 1446 × 1447: S.R.O. 3365/2473A; E 372/292 Salop. d. Burley heads lists of sitting J.P.s 1433, 1439, 1447, 1456: E 101/584/22 nos. 1–2; E 372/292 Adhuc Res. Salop.; S.P.L., Deeds 6490.

[86] Wedgwood, *Hist. Parl. 1439–1509: Biogs.* 139–40; *T.S.A.S.* lvi. 263–72; Pollard, 'Fam. of Talbot', 229–30.

[87] *T.S.A.S.* 4th ser. xi. 12–13; Pollard, op. cit. 224.

[88] Pollard, op. cit. 219. Heads lists of sitting J.P.s 1421, 1429: C 258/43/11 no. 3; E 101/584/22 no. 3.

[89] Winsbury 'and fellows' occur 1442: S.R.O. 3365/2473A, Mich. 1442. Winsbury attends oftener than other J.P.s 1435–9: E 101/584/22 no. 1. Next to Burley in list of sitting J.P.s 1446–7: E 372/292 Adhuc Res. Salop.

[90] Blakeway, *Sheriffs*, 66; *T.S.A.S.* 4th ser. vi. 231.

[91] *Cal. Pat.* 1446–52, 593–4; 1452–61, 675–6.

[92] *T.S.A.S.* 4th ser. xi. 24; Wedgwood, op. cit. 469.

[93] Next to Burley in list of sitting J.P.s 1456: S.P.L., Deeds 6490.

[94] Horde 'and others' occur 1471–2: E 372/317 Salop. d. Horde and Acton attend oftener than other J.P.s 1465–6: E 372/312 Salop. d.

[95] *Cal. Pat.* 1446–52, 593–4; 1452–61, 675–6.

[96] *T.S.A.S.* 4th ser. v. 222.

[97] Pollard, op. cit. 55, 241 n.

Yorkist commission of 1460,[98] but Edward IV reinstated them after his accession.[99] Horde was made sheriff by the Readeption government of 1470[1] and Acton was included in its peace commission. No harsh reprisals, however, seem to have been inflicted upon them at Edward's restoration and both were allowed to remain in the peace commission.[2] In the 1470s, however, William Burley's son-in-law, Sir Thomas Littleton, the distinguished judge and a trusted supporter of Edward IV,[3] seems sometimes to have presided at the Shropshire sessions.[4] Acton died in 1480.[5]

Horde, whose qualities were evidently recognized by all parties, was made sheriff by Richard III in 1483.[6] During his shrievalty the bench may have been led by John Lawley,[7] a consistent Yorkist who had been appointed Edward IV's attorney general in North Wales in 1461.[8] Robert Cressett, a lawyer,[9] was another Yorkist[10] and a nephew of both Horde and Acton;[11] a man identified with Gloucester's party, he was retained in the peace commission by Richard III[12] and attended sessions frequently during his reign.[13] Edward Hopton, a lawyer and a Yorkist officer,[14] was another leading magistrate under Richard III.[15] Lawley died at about the time of Henry VII's accession.[16] Cressett (d. 1490)[17] and Hopton were omitted from Henry's first Shropshire peace commission[18] and never reinstated. Horde, however, remained a member until his death in 1498[19] and was a leader of sessions to the very end.[20] His long career, whose beginning came as William Burley's was drawing to its end, may have lent some stability to county government in a period of violent political changes.

In the late 1490s some Shropshire quarter sessions were controlled by non-resident members of the Council in the Marches. In 1498, for example, Prince Arthur was present at the Epiphany sessions in Shrewsbury, together with the leaders of the council; other sessions, however, were attended at that period by local men only.[21] Apart from Thomas Horde there were among the local leaders John Horde, perhaps Thomas's son (d. 1499),[22] and Richard Littleton, son of Sir Thomas and a barrister.[23] By the 1500s[24] the leaders included Littleton; Sir Thomas Leighton, a knight of the body to Henry VII;[25] John Salter, grandson of a former clerk of the peace, and later to be justice in North Wales;[26] George Bromley, like Salter a senior member of the Inner Temple;[27] and Thomas Scriven. Salter (d. 1532),[28] Bromley (d. c. 1535),[29] and Scriven (dropped 1529)[30] remained among the leaders well into Henry VIII's reign. They were joined in the early part of the reign by Richard Horde,[31] a lawyer and a grandson of Thomas Horde.[32] Richard Horde and Salter seem to have been the most prominent magistrates in the 1520s and 1530s.[33] Horde had ceased to attend regularly by 1539,[34]

[98] See p. 57.
[99] See p. 57 n.
[1] List of Sheriffs (P.R.O. Lists & Indexes, ix; corrected reprint, 1963), 118.
[2] See p. 58.
[3] D.N.B.
[4] Littleton 'and others' occur 1476–7: E 372/322 Salop. d.
[5] V.C.H. Salop. viii. 109.
[6] List of Sheriffs, 119.
[7] Heads lists of sitting J.P.s 1484: E 137/38/4.
[8] Wedgwood, Hist. Parl. 1439–1509: Biogs. 529.
[9] Ibid. 235.
[10] Pardoned 1459: Cal. Pat. 1452–61, 548.
[11] T.S.A.S. 4th ser. v. 222.
[12] Cal. Pat. 1476–85, 570–1.
[13] E 137/38/4.
[14] Recorder of Ludlow in 1464, 1481: T.S.A.S. 2nd ser. xi. 308.
[15] E 137/38/4.
[16] Wedgwood, op. cit. 529.
[17] T.S.A.S. 4th ser. vi. 215–16.
[18] See p. 58.
[19] Wedgwood, op. cit. 469.
[20] Heads list of sitting J.P.s, East. 1498: E 137/38/4.
[21] Ibid.
[22] Bodl. MS. Blakeway 5, p. 362b; T.S.A.S. liv. 181. Another John Horde, son of Wm. Horde, d. 1498: Wedgwood, op. cit. 468.
[23] T.S.A.S. 2nd ser. vii. 8.

[24] E 137/38/4.
[25] Wedgwood, op. cit. 535.
[26] Griffiths, Principality of Wales, i. 162–3; Blakeway, Sheriffs, 85; S.P.L., MS. 4079, p. 1532.
[27] T.S.A.S. 3rd ser. ii. 314.
[28] Griffiths, op. cit. i. 163.
[29] T.S.A.S. 4th ser. x. 290.
[30] L. & P. Hen. VIII, iv(3), p. 2311. Died c. 1536: T.S.A.S. 4th ser. x. 291.
[31] E 372/360 Res. Salop.; E 137/38/5; E 372/370 Salop. d.; S.R.O. 3365/2474; E 372/375 Adhuc Res. Salop.
[32] T.S.A.S. liv. 181, 207.
[33] Horde heads lists of sitting J.P.s 1519, 1525–6, 1535: E 137/38/5; E 372/370 Salop. d.; S.R.O. 3365/2474, Mich. 1526. Attends oftener than other J.P.s 1535: E 137/38/5. Salter 'and fellows' occur 1527: S.R.O. 3365/2474, Epiph. 1527. Salter heads lists of sitting J.P.s 1526, 1530: ibid. Epiph. and Trin. 1526; E 372/375 Adhuc Res. Salop. Horde and Salter attend oftener than other J.P.s 1526–8, 1530: S.R.O. 3365/2474; E 372/375 Adhuc Res. Salop.
[34] E 101/584/23.

and in the 1540s and 1550s the leading local justice seems to have been Adam (later Sir Adam) Mytton,[35] a barrister.[36] As steward of Caus lordship[37] he served Henry, Lord Stafford (d. 1563), a courtier who supported successively Henry VIII, Somerset, Mary, and Elizabeth I.[38] Also among the leaders were William Charlton of Wombridge,[39] a barrister and another of Thomas Horde's grandsons,[40] and John Corbet of Leigh,[41] another officer of Lord Stafford.[42] They were joined in the 1550s by Richard (later Sir Richard) Newport,[43] son-in-law of the Shropshire *custos* Chief Justice Bromley[44] (d. 1555).[45] None of them was removed by Mary.

Mytton died in 1561[46] and Corbet was removed from the peace commission at some time between 1559 and 1561.[47] Charlton lived until 1567,[48] but may have been dropped by Elizabeth for religious reasons,[49] and Newport until 1570.[50] Until the 1560s Shropshire quarter sessions, in particular those held at Ludlow,[51] were sometimes attended by non-resident members of the Council in the Marches.[52] Indeed, during Bishop Lee's presidency some Shropshire sessions had been deliberately controlled by high-ranking non-residents as part of the drive against crime.[53] By the late 1560s, however, all sessions were held at Shrewsbury and were attended solely by local magistrates[54] — a measure of the council's decline. Newport and Charlton were joined in the 1560s by Humphrey Onslow[55] (d. 1573),[56] *custos rotulorum*,[57] and Sir Andrew Corbet[58] (d. 1578).[59] Onslow's position was probably enhanced by the fact that his nephew,[60] Richard Onslow, was clerk of the council of the Duchy of Lancaster 1561-71, solicitor general 1566-9, and speaker of the House of Commons 1566-7.[61] Corbet, Newport's cousin,[62] was also related to Richard Onslow[63] and to Thomas (later Sir Thomas) Bromley,[64] solicitor general 1569-79 and lord chancellor 1579-87.[65] Apart from those connexions Corbet earned a reputation in the marches for quiet dependability.[66] He was temporary lieutenant of Shropshire in 1569[67] and vice-president of the Council in the Marches 1575-7.[68]

In the 1570s Sir Andrew Corbet was joined as leader by William Fowler[69] (d. 1598),[70] Edward (later Sir Edward) Leighton[71] (d. 1593),[72] and Robert Needham[73] (d. 1603).[74] Fowler was another relative of Humphrey and Richard Onslow;[75] Richard died at Fowler's house at Harnage.[76] Fowler was also a nephew of Bishop Lee.[77] He occurs as

---

[35] Mytton heads lists of sitting J.P.s 1539, 1546, 1551, 1557, and attends oftener than other J.P.s 1539, 1545-6, 1550-1, 1556-7 (with Ric. Newport): ibid.; E 372/391 Salop. d.; E 372/396 Salop. d.; E 372/405 Salop. d.

[36] *T.S.A.S.* 4th ser. xii. 180.

[37] Ibid. 4th ser. xi. 39.   [38] *D.N.B.*

[39] E 372/391 Salop. d.; E 372/410 Salop. d.

[40] *T.S.A.S.* 4th ser. xi. 40.

[41] E 372/370 Salop. d.; E 372/391 Salop. d.; E 372/405 Salop. d.; E 137/38/5.

[42] A. H. Anderson, 'Hen., Ld. Stafford (1501-63) and the Lordship of Caus', *Welsh History Review*, vi. 7-8.

[43] E 372/405 Salop. d.

[44] *T.S.A.S.* 4th ser. xi. 38.   [45] Cranage, vii. 654.

[46] *T.S.A.S.* 4th ser. xii. 181.

[47] S.P. 12/2 f. 55; B.L. Lansd. MS. 1218, ff. 77v.-78.

[48] *T.S.A.S.* 4th ser. xi. 40.   [49] See p. 60 n.

[50] *T.S.A.S.* 4th ser. iv. 55.

[51] E 137/38/4-5; S.R.O. 3365/2474, Trin. 1527, Trin. 1528.

[52] E 372/360 Res. Salop.; E 372/396 Salop. d.; E 372/405 Salop. d.; E 372/409 Salop. d.; E 101/584/23. The practice was confirmed by the 1525 Instructions: Williams, *Council in Marches*, 13.

[53] *L. & P. Hen. VIII*, xiii(1), p. 52.

[54] E 137/38/6.

[55] One of most regular attenders 1563-4: E 372/410 Salop. d. Heads esqs. in lists of sitting J.P.s 1567-8: E 137/38/6.

[56] *T.S.A.S.* 4th ser. iv. 56.   [57] See p. 67.

[58] Heads lists of sitting J.P.s 1563-4, 1567, 1576: E 372/409 Salop. d.; E 372/410 Salop. d.; E 372/421 Salop. d.; E 137/38/6, Mich. 1567. One of most regular attenders 1575-6: E 372/421 Salop. d.

[59] *T.S.A.S.* 4th ser. xi. 42.

[60] *Visit. Salop. 1623*, ii. 378-9.

[61] Somerville, *Hist. Duchy of Lanc.* i. 414.

[62] *Visit. Salop. 1623*, i. 136, 138; ii. 373.

[63] Corbet's sis.-in-law was Onslow's aunt: ibid. i. 136; ii. 379.

[64] Corbet's cos. marr. Bromley's dau.: ibid. i. 136, 138.

[65] *D.N.B.*

[66] Williams, *Council in Marches*, 258-9.

[67] See p. 84.   [68] Williams, op. cit. p. xiv.

[69] One of most regular attenders 1575-6, 1577-8: E 372/421 Salop. d.; E 372/423 Salop. d.

[70] Williams, op. cit. 348.

[71] One of most regular attenders 1580: E 372/426 Salop.

[72] *T.S.A.S.* 4th ser. xi. 40.

[73] Heads list of sitting J.P.s Mich. 1574: S.R.O. 2/262. One of most regular attenders 1575-6, 1577-8: E 372/421 Salop. d.; E 372/423 Salop. d.

[74] *Complete Peerage*, vii. 260.

[75] Fowler's sis. marr. Humph.'s son (Ric.'s cos.): *Visit. Salop. 1623*, i. 190; ii. 378-9.

[76] *D.N.B. sub* Onslow, Ric.

[77] *Visit. Salop. 1623*, i. 190.

clerk of the Oxford assize circuit 1559–97,[78] acting justice of the Anglesey circuit in 1568 and 1570, and prothonotary in North Wales.[79] In 1575 he occurs as *custos rotulorum* of Radnorshire,[80] and in the 1590s he seems to have enjoyed the favour of Lord Keeper Puckering.[81] Leighton too was related to the Onslows;[82] he was also related to Lord Chancellor Bromley.[83] In 1552 he had succeeded Mytton as Lord Stafford's steward of Caus.[84] More important, perhaps, was the fact that Leighton was a cousin of the earl of Leicester (d. 1588)[85] and one of his 'particular friends'.[86] Leighton's brother was uncle of the earl of Essex (d. 1601).[87] Needham, a courtier,[88] was a nephew of Sir Andrew Corbet.[89] He was related to the Onslows[90] and one daughter married a close relative, probably a son, of Thomas Powell of Park.[91]

After the early 1580s Fowler and Leighton seem to have taken a less active part in quarter sessions; indeed Fowler was temporarily dropped from the commission in the early 1580s,[92] perhaps for religious reasons.[93] In the 1580s new leaders emerged, among them Thomas Powell of Park[94] (d. 1588),[95] Rowland Barker of Haughmond[96] (d. c. 1599),[97] and Francis (later Sir Francis) Newport,[98] Sir Richard's son (d. 1623).[99] Powell was an uncle of Sir Andrew Corbet and of Sir Richard Newport.[1] Possessor of an impressive repertoire of Welsh stories, he was nevertheless reckoned a mere 'cipher' at sittings of the Council in the Marches.[2] By the 1580s he was an old man. Barker was related to the Onslows,[3] and his son married Francis Newport's daughter.[4] Newport, probably the richest gentleman in Shropshire,[5] was a grandson of Chief Justice Bromley and a distant cousin of Lord Chancellor Bromley.[6] Barker and Newport were joined in the 1590s by Richard Cressett of Upton[7] (d. 1601);[8] he was a nephew of William Charlton of Wombridge,[9] and was also connected with Sir Andrew Corbet[10] and Francis Newport.[11] Newport, who remained among the leaders until the last years of James I, was joined in Elizabeth I's last years by Francis Newton of Heightley (d. c. 1624),[12] who remained among the leaders for an equal time.[13] He was related locally to Thomas Powell, Sir Andrew Corbet, and the Newports,[14] and at Court to the Bromleys[15] and Sir Christopher Hatton, lord chancellor 1587–91.[16]

[78] J. S. Cockburn, *Hist. Eng. Assizes 1558–1714* (1972), 316, 320, mistakenly suggesting he d. 1577; *Visit. Salop. 1623*, i. 190; *S.P.R.Lich.* ii(5), 1–3.

[79] Williams, op. cit. 349.

[80] *Reg. Council in Marches of Wales*, 145.

[81] Williams, op. cit. 295–6.

[82] Leighton's sis. marr. Humph.'s neph. (Ric's cos.): *Visit. Salop. 1623*, ii. 324, 378–9.

[83] Leighton's dau. marr. Bromley's neph.: ibid. i. 78; ii. 324–5.

[84] *T.S.A.S.* 4th ser. xi. 39.

[85] They were 3rd cousins: *Visit. Salop. 1623*, ii. 324; *Complete Peerage*, iv. 480–1; vii. 549.

[86] Blakeway, *Sheriffs*, 91.

[87] *Visit. Salop. 1623*, ii. 324; *Complete Peerage*, v. 140–1.

[88] T. L. Moir, *Addled Parl. of 1614* (1958), 194.

[89] *Visit. Salop. 1623*, i. 136; ii. 372.

[90] Needham's dau. marr. Humph.'s neph. (Ric.'s cos.): ibid. ii. 372, 378.

[91] Ibid. 372.

[92] *Reg. Council in Marches of Wales*, 216; B.L. Harl. MS. 474, ff. 31v.–33; S.P. 12/190 f. 153.

[93] His bro. was a recusant 1592: S. Shaw, *Hist. and Antiquities of Staffs.* ii (1801), 203; *V.C.H. Staffs.* iii. 101.

[94] One of most regular attenders 1580, 1587–8: E 372/426 Salop.; E 372/433 Salop. d.

[95] Williams, *Council in Marches*, 354.

[96] One of most regular attenders 1587–8, 1589–90, 1594–5: E 372/433 Salop. d.; E 372/435 Salop. d.; E 137/38/6. Named second in lists of sitting J.P.s Epiph.-Trin. 1594: E 137/38/6.

[97] *T.S.A.S.* 4th ser. x. 292.

[98] One of most regular attenders 1594–5, 1602–3,

1611–12, 1620–1: E 137/38/6; E 372/448 Item Salop.; E 372/457 Item Salop. d.; E 372/466 Item Salop. Heads lists of sitting J.P.s Epiph.-Trin. 1594, Mich. 1595, 1596, East.-Trin. 1600: E 137/38/6.

[99] *T.S.A.S.* 4th ser. xi. 155.

[1] *Visit. Salop. 1623*, i. 136, 138; ii. 373.

[2] Williams, op. cit. 261.

[3] Barker's bro. marr. Ric. Onslow's cos.: *Visit. Salop. 1623*, i. 27; ii. 379, 408.

[4] Ibid. i. 27–8; ii. 374.

[5] *T.S.A.S.* 2nd ser. xii. 2.

[6] *Visit. Salop. 1623*, i. 77–8; ii. 373–4.

[7] One of most regular attenders 1594–5, 1600: E 137/38/6.

[8] *T.S.A.S.* 4th ser. vi. 217.

[9] Ibid.; *Visit. Salop. 1623*, i. 101.

[10] Cressett's bro.'s bro.-in-law was Corbet's son-in-law: *T.S.A.S.* 4th ser. vi. 217; *Visit. Salop. 1623*, i. 136–7, 214–15.

[11] Cressett's bro.'s neph. was Newport's son-in-law: *T.S.A.S.* 4th ser. vi. 217; *Visit. Salop. 1623*, i. 214–15; ii. 374.

[12] *T.S.A.S.* 4th ser. x. 296.

[13] One of most regular attenders 1600, 1605–6, 1608–9, 1611–12, 1615–16: E 137/38/6; E 372/454 Item Salop.; E 372/457 Item Salop. d.; E 372/461 Item Salop.

[14] Newton's wife was Powell's niece and cos. of Corbet and Newport: *Visit. Salop. 1623*, i. 136, 138; ii. 373, 375.

[15] Newton's uncle was Ch. Justice Bromley's bro. (ibid. i. 77; ii. 374–5); Newton's bro.-in-law was Chanc. Bromley's son-in-law (ibid. i. 138).

[16] Newton's cos. marr. a distant cos. of Chanc. Hatton: ibid. i. 225–7; ii. 375.

The office of *custos rotulorum* conferred upon the holder the titular leadership of the bench and some real patronage. One Shropshire *custos* is known by name before 1546: David Holbache (occurs 1413).[17] In the 16th century aspirants to the office had to establish or foster a connexion with the lord keeper or lord chancellor, in whom the appointment was vested. In 1546 Thomas (later Sir Thomas) Bromley, a justice of King's Bench, was appointed.[18] He had been a standing counsel to Lord Stafford.[19] Bromley became lord chief justice[20] and died in 1555.[21] Humphrey Onslow first occurs as *custos* in 1562.[22] He died in 1573,[23] and in the same year George (later Sir George) Bromley (d. 1589)[24] first occurs as *custos*.[25] He was a relative of Chief Justice Bromley, the former *custos*, and a brother of Sir Thomas Bromley,[26] solicitor general 1569–79 and lord chancellor 1579–87. George Bromley was a successful lawyer, rising to become chief justice of Chester in 1580,[27] but he held the office of *custos* mainly through his brother's influence; in 1587, a matter of months after Lord Chancellor Bromley's death, Lord Chancellor Hatton replaced Sir George by Edward (later Sir Edward) Leighton.[28] Leighton remained *custos* under Lord Keeper Puckering and died in 1593.[29] Sir George Mainwaring of Ightfield (d. c. 1632)[30] first occurs as *custos* in the summer of 1596.[31] In September, however, a few months after Egerton became lord keeper, Mainwaring was replaced by Sir Richard Leveson,[32] who married a possible niece of the earl of Leicester (d. 1588) and was thus a connexion of the earl of Essex (d. 1601), Leicester's stepson.[33] Leveson died in 1605[34] and in the following year Lord Chancellor Ellesmere appointed his own son, Sir John Egerton[35] (later Viscount Brackley and earl of Bridgwater). The Shropshire *custodes* of the later 16th century, as in Norfolk,[36] were not necessarily regular attenders of sessions or experienced magistrates. Leveson, for example, was a naval commander and diplomat and was often out of the country. Both he and Egerton were only in their twenties when appointed.[37]

After 1545 the office carried with it by statute the appointment of the clerk of the peace.[38] Some earlier clerks seem to have been appointed by the Crown but the appointment had probably fallen more often to the leading magistrates or the *custos*.[39] The clerk perhaps relieved the *custos* of his responsibility, laid down in the peace commission, of safeguarding the records of sessions.[40] The Shropshire clerks, like those of the other counties, were substantial men: two of the 16th-century clerks served as escheators,[41] and one may have been a member of Parliament. None, however, is known to have been a sheriff or coroner as were some clerks elsewhere.[42]

The earliest known Shropshire clerk, Richard Oteley, occurs 1391–1412.[43] John Rodenhurst (d. 1445 × 1448),[44] who occurs 1416–41,[45] had been under-sheriff to John Burley 1408–9,[46] and was therefore perhaps an associate of William Burley of Broncroft,

[17] *Salop. Peace Roll, 1400–14*, 17.
[18] *L. & P. Hen. VIII*, xxi(1), p. 359. Also occurs 1547: *Cal. Pat.* 1547–8, 88.
[19] *T.S.A.S.* liv. 333.
[20] Ibid. 2nd ser. i. 15.
[21] Ibid. 16.
[22] *Cal. Pat.* 1560–3, 442. Also occurs 1564: ibid. 1563–6, p. 26.
[23] See p. 65.
[24] *T.S.A.S.* 4th ser. xi. 47.
[25] S.P. 12/93, pt. 2, f. 24v. Also occurs 1577, 1579, 1583; S.P. 12/121 f. 26v.; S.P. 12/145 f. 36; B.L. Harl. MS. 474, f. 32.
[26] *Visit. Salop. 1623*, i. 77–8.
[27] Somerville, *Hist. Duchy of Lanc.* i. 409.
[28] *Montg. Coll.* ii. 418. Leighton also occurs 1589, 1591, 1593: ibid. v. 429; *Acts of P.C.* 1591–2, 166; Kent Archives Office, U350 03, Salop.
[29] *T.S.A.S.* 4th ser. xi. 40.
[30] Ibid. 4th ser. x. 298; xi. 47–8.

[31] S.P. 13, case F, no. 11, f. 29.
[32] C 231/1 f. 20v.
[33] *D.N.B. sub* Leveson, Ric.; *Complete Peerage*, vii. 550–1. Leveson's wife's aunt may not have been lawfully married to Leicester.
[34] *D.N.B.*
[35] *T.S.A.S.* 4th ser. xi. 159.
[36] Smith, *County and Court*, 90.
[37] *D.N.B. sub* Egerton, John, and Leveson, Ric.
[38] Custos Rotulorum Act, 1545, 37 Hen. VIII, c. 1.
[39] E. Stephens, *Clerks of the Counties 1360–1960* (1961), 30–4.
[40] Putnam, *Proceedings*, pp. xcii–xciii.
[41] Thos. Skrimsher (1523–4), Adam Mytton (1595–6): *List of Escheators for Eng.* (List and Index Soc. lxxii), 134, 136.
[42] Stephens, op. cit. 40.
[43] Ibid. 151.
[44] *T.S.A.S.* ix. 405.
[45] Stephens, op. cit. 151; E 101/584/22 no. 4.
[46] *Sel. Cases in K.B.* vii, p. 189.

one of the leading magistrates. William Bishop was appointed clerk between 1441 and 1446. In 1446, when he was granted the office for life by letters patent, his responsibilities included custody of the magistrates' records, and he was entitled to the 'usual fees and rewards'.[47] He was still alive in 1454.[48] John Salter first occurs in 1462;[49] he recurs until 1490[50] and perhaps continued until his death in 1492.[51] He was styled 'gentleman'.[52] Rowland Gravenor (occurs as clerk 1496–1507)[53] may have been the man of that name who was bailiff of Bridgnorth ten times between 1495 and 1523 and who sat for that borough in the Parliaments of 1487, 1497, and 1504.[54] If so, he may have owed his clerkship to Thomas Horde of Bridgnorth, one of the leading magistrates of the 1490s. In 1507 Thomas Skrimsher was appointed for life by letters patent.[55] He last occurs in 1512.[56] Alan Horde, who occurs 1514–19,[57] was a brother of Richard Horde,[58] one of the leading magistrates. Nicholas Holt, who occurs 1535–46,[59] may have been a relative of Thomas Holt, an active magistrate in the 1530s[60] and councillor of Lord Stafford.[61]

After 1545 newly appointed *custodes* exercised their right to choose a new clerk of the peace. It is to be noted that Nicholas Holt was replaced 1546 × 1550,[62] Thomas Bromley having been made *custos* in 1546. Thomas Salter replaced William Powell 1555 × 1556,[63] Bromley having died in 1555. Salter was replaced by Adam Mytton between c. 1573 and 1575,[64] George Bromley having first occurred as *custos* in 1573; Mytton, who was styled 'esquire',[65] married Bromley's cousin.[66]

It is evident that Mytton was appointed for the duration of Bromley's life, for Mytton was replaced as clerk not at Bromley's dismissal as *custos* in 1587[67] but at his death in 1589; Edward Leighton, Bromley's successor as *custos*, appointed a new clerk before Bromley's corpse was in its grave.[68] Lord Chancellor Hatton had appointed Leighton *custos* on condition that he would, as soon as Bromley died, appoint as clerk Francis Hatton of Shrewsbury, a distant kinsman of the chancellor.[69] Leighton kept the bargain and Hatton was appointed clerk for the duration of Leighton's life.[70] Such appointments were not sanctioned by the 1545 Act, which limited the clerk's term of office to that of the *custos* who appointed him. Lord Chancellor Hatton died in 1591 and Leighton then attempted, contrary to his bargain, to dismiss Francis Hatton from the clerkship. He was successful in spite of protests from the Privy Council,[71] and Thomas Salter, perhaps son of the former clerk of that name,[72] was clerk until Leighton's death in 1593.[73] Thereupon Hatton was reinstated,[74] to be succeeded in 1595[75] by his own brother-in-law, William Wilkes. Wilkes, a Shrewsbury attorney,[76] was under-sheriff of Montgomeryshire 1594–5[77] for his relative Francis Newton,[78] a leading Shropshire magistrate. In 1596, the year of Sir Richard Leveson's appointment as *custos*, Wilkes was replaced

[47] *Cal. Pat.* 1446–52, 28.
[48] Ibid. 1452–61, 169.
[49] Stephens, op. cit. 151.
[50] 1465–6, 1484, 1490: E 372/312 Salop. d.; E 137/38/4; Stephens, op. cit. 151 (who unnecessarily postulates two successive John Salters).
[51] *T.S.A.S.* ix. 124.
[52] Griffiths, *Principality of Wales*, i. 162.
[53] Stephens, op. cit. 151.
[54] Wedgwood, *Hist. Parl. 1439–1509: Biogs.* 389.
[55] *Cal. Pat.* 1494–1509, 535.
[56] Stephens, op. cit. 151.
[57] Ibid.; E 137/38/5.
[58] Bodl. MS. Blakeway 5, p. 362b.
[59] E 137/38/5; E 372/391 Salop. d.
[60] E 137/38/5; *L. & P. Hen. VIII*, xiii(1), p. 52; E 101/584/23 no. 1.
[61] *T.S.A.S.* liv. 333.
[62] Stephens, op. cit. 151.
[63] Ibid.; E 372/405 Salop. d.

[64] Stephens, op. cit. 151; E 372/421 Salop. d.
[65] *List of Escheators*, 136.
[66] *Visit. Salop. 1623*, i. 78; ii. 307, 362.
[67] Mytton occurs as clerk June 1588: E 372/433 Salop. d.
[68] Bromley d. 2 Mar. (*T.S.A.S.* 4th ser. xi. 47); Hatton apptd. 15 Mar. (*Montg. Coll.* v. 429); Bromley bur. 27 Mar. (S.R.O. 1374/1).
[69] *Acts of P.C.* 1591–2, 166.
[70] *Montg. Coll.* v. 429–30.
[71] *Acts of P.C.* 1591–2, 166.
[72] *Visit. Salop. 1623*, ii. 428.
[73] Salter occurs 1591–3: Stephens, op. cit. 151.
[74] Leighton d. 10 Sept. (*T.S.A.S.* 4th ser. xi. 440); Hatton first recurs 2 Oct. (E 137/38/6).
[75] Hatton last occurs 18 June; Wilkes first occurs 2 Oct.: E 137/38/6.
[76] *Visit. Salop. 1623*, i. 226.
[77] *Montg. Coll.* v. 443.
[78] Wilkes's mother-in-law was Newton's cos.: *Visit. Salop. 1623*, i. 226; ii. 375.

by George Holland,[79] perhaps the gentleman of that name who married a niece of Richard Cressett of Upton, a leading magistrate, and died in 1645.[80] Wilkes, however, was reinstated 1597 × 1598 and remained clerk until 1610.[81] He occurs as clerk of Montgomeryshire 1607-9.[82]

When Wilkes left office in Shropshire he passed on no sessions rolls earlier than 1603 and no other records earlier than 1609;[83] it was probably then the practice to keep only current records. Thus by 1610 the records kept by clerks earlier than Wilkes had been lost. Indeed a continuous record of proceedings at Shropshire quarter sessions survives only from 1652.[84]

Not until Henry IV's reign can it be known how faithfully the Shropshire keepers and justices kept to the four statutory seasons for holding their sessions, namely within the quindenes of Michaelmas and Epiphany, in the second week of Lent and between Whitsun and Midsummer.[85] In the period 1400-12 sessions were not held every quarter or always during the statutory periods. In 1400, 1410, and 1412 at least five sessions were held in the year and hardly any fell within the statutory periods; in other years there appear to have been no sessions at all. The record makes no distinction between quarterly and other sessions[86] and it seems likely that no such distinction was conceived in Shropshire at that time. By the late 1420s and early 1430s general sessions were held only twice a year on average and at least sometimes outside the statutory periods.[87] In the period 1435-9 an average of four sessions a year was held.[88] In the 1440s, however, two sessions a year seem to have been normal again, but by then there was a clear preference for holding them in statutory periods and, in particular, on the Tuesdays following Epiphany, the close of Easter, Trinity, and Michaelmas.[89] An Act of 1414,[90] which required the spring sessions to be held in the week after the close of Easter and the summer sessions in the week after the translation of St. Thomas the Martyr, was thus only partly observed in Shropshire; as in some other counties,[91] the summer sessions continued to be held in the period laid down in 1362. In the later 15th century quarterly sessions seem to have been regularly held, often on the preferred Tuesdays, but some sessions still occurred outside the statutory periods.[92] By the end of Henry VII's reign[93] those Tuesdays had become the customary days from which few quarter sessions departed during the rest of the 16th century.[94]

Until the mid 16th century sessions were held in Shrewsbury, Ludlow, Bridgnorth, Newport, and Much Wenlock. Shrewsbury was the place most often used, and the other towns do not appear to have been visited in any regular order.[95] It is likely that the meeting place was chosen by the leading justice or the *custos*, as in Northamptonshire in the early 17th century;[96] it is notable that all the known sittings at Newport occurred between 1498 and 1526,[97] when John Salter of that town was among the leading magistrates, and that Bridgnorth was especially frequented in 1484,[98] during the ascendancy of Thomas Horde of that place. In 1535 quarter sessions were still being held in the various towns.[99] By 1567, however, they had settled permanently at Shrewsbury.[1]

[79] Stephens, op. cit. 151.
[80] *Visit. Salop. 1623*, ii. 344-5; *T.S.A.S.* 4th ser. vi. 217; *S.P.R. Heref.* ii(4), 42, 49.
[81] Stephens, op. cit. 151; S.R.O. 212, box 419, reg. of deeds.
[82] Stephens, op. cit. 135.
[83] S.R.O. 212, box 419, reg. of deeds.
[84] *Orders of Q. Sess.* i, orders 1652-60, 1.
[85] 36 Edw. III, Stat. I, c. 12.
[86] *Salop. Peace Roll, 1400-14*, 28-9, 50-1.
[87] E 101/584/22 no. 3.   [88] Ibid. no. 1.
[89] S.R.O. 3365/2473A.   [90] 2 Hen. V, Stat. I, c. 4.
[91] *Wilts. Co. Rec.* (Wilts. Arch. and Nat. Hist. Soc. Rec. Branch, iv), p. xxi.

[92] E 137/38/4.
[93] Ibid.; S.R.O. 85/6.
[94] Pipe rolls give first day of each period for which J.P.s' wages were paid; the rolls searched for this article are listed on p. 62, n. 55. Dates of other 16th-cent. sessions occur in estreats of fines (S.R.O. 3365/2474; E 137/38/5-6), an indenture for J.P.s' wages 1539 (E 101/584/23), and an indictment 1574 (S.R.O. 2/262).
[95] *Salop. Peace Roll, 1400-14*, 50-1; S.R.O. 3365/2473A, 2474; E 137/38/4-5.
[96] Gleason, *Justices of Peace*, 178.
[97] E 137/38/4-5; S.R.O. 3365/2474.
[98] E 137/38/4.
[99] E 137/38/5.   [1] E 137/38/6.

Throughout the 15th century no ordinary sessions of the peace appears to have lasted more than one day.[2] That of Epiphany 1498 lasted three days[3] but was exceptional.[4] In the early 1500s some sessions of two days began to occur and by the mid 1530s they were normal.[5] One sessions of three days at Ludlow is recorded in 1535,[6] during Bishop Lee's campaign against crime. From the later 1540s until the mid 1570s, however, one-day sittings became common, perhaps normal.[7] Such an indication of reduced activity may reflect the reduced vigour of the Council in the Marches as a supervising body. From the later 1570s until the 1590s two-day sittings were normal again, and three-day sittings became common in the later 1590s.[8]

From Henry IV's reign until the late 1490s attendances of magistrates at sessions[9] averaged three or four.[10] From then until the early 1550s an average of about five men attended.[11] The average rose in the mid 1550s to seven or eight and remained thus until the 1590s[12] when it rose to about ten.[13] In Elizabeth I's last years the average rose to twelve.[14] The increase of *c.* 1500, which accompanied an increase in the duration of sessions, may have been induced by the development of the Council in the Marches and the increased size of the commission. That of the mid 1550s may reflect only the higher proportion of resident magistrates on the commission. That of the 1590s, which coincided with an increase in the length of sessions, is perhaps attributable to increases in the magistrates' duties as well as in the number of resident justices.

As a body for combating crime the Shropshire magistracy was ineffectual, but the gaol-delivery and oyer and terminer commissioners had little more success. The inhibiting influence of the magistrates and others upon criminals must nevertheless be taken into account.

In the 14th and 15th centuries the keepers and justices of the peace were too closely allied with local magnates to act always for the public good. Some magistrates and their families were themselves involved in violent crime;[15] others were guilty of intimidating jurors and corrupting counsel.[16] Such men were perhaps not typical but their activities diminished the authority of their local colleagues. Men sent by the sheriff or the justices to arrest suspects were sometimes set upon by armed mobs and in 1409 were said to be too frightened to act.[17] Henry IV's reign was especially lawless in Shropshire. The Welsh rebels caused widespread and long-lasting destruction in the western parts of the county.[18] Meanwhile those local leaders appointed by the Crown to defend the county had private grievances against each other, and each was jealous of any local advantage that another might gain during the fighting. In 1409 the earl of Arundel's officer Sir John Wele, who was a magistrate, barred the gates of Shrewsbury against John, Lord

[2] *Salop. Peace Roll, 1400–14*, 50–1; S.R.O. 3365/2473A. Pipe rolls give the last day of each period for which J.P.s' wages were paid; it is here assumed that if the last day was one of the customary Tuesdays the last q. sess. of the payment period began and ended on that day. Pipe rolls also give the no. of days attended by the clerk during each payment period; from the late 15th cent. it is safe to divide the clerk's attendances by the no. of quarters in the period to find the average duration of each q. sess.

[3] E 137/38/4.

[4] See p. 64.

[5] E 137/38/4–5; S.R.O. 3365/2474; E 101/584/23 no. 2. Pipe-roll averages (above, n. 2): 1–2 days.

[6] E 137/38/5.

[7] E 137/38/6. Pipe-roll averages: under 1½ day.

[8] E 137/38/6. Pipe-roll averages: 2–3 days. In 1597 3 days were thought usual: *T.S.A.S.* iii. 336.

[9] Pipe rolls (and indentures for J.P.s' wages) give total man-days attended in each payment period; to find the average attendance on each sessions day, that total is divided by the no. of sessions days (indicated by the clerk's attendances) in the payment period.

[10] *Salop. Peace Roll, 1400–14*, 30, 34; E 137/38/4. Pipe-roll and indenture (E 101/584/22) averages: 3–4.

[11] E 137/38/4–5; S.R.O. 3365/2474; *L. & P. Hen. VIII*, xiii(1), p. 52; E 101/584/23 no. 2. Pipe-roll averages: 4–6.

[12] E 137/38/6. Pipe-roll averages: 7–8.

[13] E 137/38/6. Average *c.* 10 in 1589–90: E 372/435 Salop. d. Attendances of 6–12 occur in Wilts. 1563–92: *Wilts. Co. Rec.* p. xxi.

[14] E 137/38/6.

[15] *Cal. Pat.* 1370–4, 310; 1381–5, 444; 1396–9, 161; *Cal. Close*, 1485–1500, 86; *T.S.A.S.* 2nd ser. xi. 19–24; 3rd ser. vi. 217–26; *Sel. Cases in K.B.* vii, pp. 115, 228; Jacob, *15th Cent.* 134; *Salop. Peace Roll, 1400–14*, 11–12; S.P.L., Deeds 2801; C. D. Ross, *Edward IV* (1974), 389.

[16] *Sel. Cases in K.B.* vii, pp. 227–9; Blakeway, *Sheriffs*, 67; C 258/43/11 no. 2.

[17] J.I. 1/753 rot. 15; *Sel. Cases in K.B.* vii, pp. 189–90; *Salop. Peace Roll, 1400–14*, 105.

[18] *Sel. Cases in K.B.* vii, pp. 114–15; Pollard, 'Fam. of Talbot', 15 n.; *T.S.A.S.* 4th ser. xi. 13; *Salop. Peace Roll, 1400–14*, 10.

Furnivalle, another magistrate, who was pursuing Owen Glendower.[19] Furnivalle was an ally of Lord Burnell,[20] constable of Bridgnorth and other castles,[21] who was an old enemy of the FitzAlans.[22] Before the end of the reign Furnivalle and Burnell were to suffer further harassment at the hands of Arundel's men.[23] In 1409 the king required Arundel and his relatives, Lord Strange of Knockin[24] and Lord Charlton, to repudiate their officers who were accused of treating with the Welsh,[25] and Wele and others were accused in 1414 of having aided the Welsh.[26] With its rulers in such disarray it is not surprising that Shropshire became notorious for its lawlessness. In 1414 Parliament prevailed on the king to send the King's Bench into Shropshire to put an end to the troubles.[27] Few wrongdoers were punished as a result of the visitation[28] but it may have discouraged crime for a while.

Little is known of the magistrates' effect on the state of Shropshire in the 15th century. It is certain, however, that violent crime was not effectively controlled until the Council in the Marches brought to the Welsh border a permanent judicial body capable of disregarding private interests and not inhibited from pursuing criminals through different counties and lordships.[29] One of the obstacles to effective justice in Shropshire had been the ability of criminals to find refuge in marcher lordships or in Bewdley, a place that had not been clearly assigned to either Shropshire or Worcestershire.[30] An Act of 1534[31] regulated the Welsh marcher lordships and an Act of 1543 declared Bewdley to be in Worcestershire.[32] Bishop Lee, president of the council 1534–43, struck fear into the criminals by relentlessly hounding and hanging them, acting often through the sessions of the peace. Criminals of social standing, far from enjoying immunity, were marked down by Lee for exemplary punishment.[33] After the Shropshire sessions of Epiphany 1538, attended by magistrates and council members, Lee reported that four gentlemen 'of the best blood of those parts' had been executed, contrary to rumours at Court that no 'gentlemen thieves' were being hanged.[34] Lee pacified Shropshire in a remarkably short time and left it a more governable place.[35]

Quarter sessions were pre-eminently useful in dealing with the common minor offences that disturbed the tenor of daily life.[36] Some 16th-century estreats of fines, though silent as to persons corporally punished or bound over, give the impression of a steady number of offenders coming before the bench. At Easter 1508 three men were fined for trespasses and woundings.[37] At Michaelmas 1535, however, during Bishop Lee's presidency 35 men were fined for riots, forcible entries, and unspecified trespasses.[38] In the period 1567–8 about five people were fined at each sessions for trespasses.[39] Fines in the 16th century varied from 1s. to 4s.; 2s. was particularly common.

The keepers and justices were much employed in regulating local wages, prices, trading, and employment.[40] Unlike ordinary offenders, who often escaped trial because they could not be found,[41] those who broke the economic laws commonly had a fixed place of business; that may partly explain why economic offenders were the only ones punished as a result of the 1414 visitation of King's Bench.[42] There seems to be little record of the Shropshire magistrates' particular share in economic control; there were

[19] Salop. Peace Roll, 1400–14, 26.
[20] He was at one time betrothed to Burnell's grand-dau. and heir: V.C.H. Salop. viii. 7.
[21] Putnam, Proceedings, 340; below, p. 80.
[22] See pp. 56, 62–3.
[23] Salop. Peace Roll, 1400–14, 12; J.I. 1/753 rot. 4.
[24] Arundel's 2nd cos.: Complete Peerage, xii (1), 354–5.
[25] Jacob, op. cit. 65.
[26] Salop. Peace Roll, 1400–14, 26.
[27] Sel. Cases in K.B. vii, p. 227.
[28] Salop. Peace Roll, 1400–14, 41–2.
[29] Williams, Council in Marches, 6–8.

[30] V.C.H. Worcs. iv. 298.
[31] 26 Hen. VIII, c. 6.
[32] 34 & 35 Hen. VIII, c. 26.
[33] Williams, op. cit. 16–19.
[34] L. & P. Hen. VIII, xiii(1), p. 52.
[35] Ibid. p. 194; Williams, op. cit. 33–4.
[36] Putnam, Proceedings, p. cxxviii.
[37] E 137/38/4.
[38] E 137/38/5.
[39] E 137/38/6.
[40] Putnam, op. cit. p. cxxviii.
[41] Salop. Peace Roll, 1400–14, 43.
[42] Ibid. 42.

certainly some persistent offenders who could not be deterred.[43] The magistrates were able not only to fine breakers of the economic statutes but also to make their own local regulations. For example, in or before 1410 they made an order about the measuring of grain at Shrewsbury market.[44] In 1586 the magistrates of every county were required to ensure an adequate supply of corn to the markets and to regulate its price. In Shropshire the magistrates divided themselves, one group being assigned to each market, as required by the Privy Council.[45] It then seems to have been Rowland Barker whose 'careful zeal' brought quantities of rye to Shrewsbury market and sold it to the poor at 5s. a bushel, forcing down the price asked by other traders.[46] In 1597, having received orders from the Privy Council to prevent speculation in food, the Shropshire magistrates resolved to visit the markets weekly. They would ensure fair prices; prevent the conversion of barley into malt for sale; forbid the purchase of grain for re-sale; forbid the purchase of seed corn unless the purchaser offered an equal amount of corn for sale that day; forbid sales of grain except in open market; and execute all previous Privy Council orders on the subject.[47] The last provision suggests that such orders, though enthusiastically received, had had no lasting effect.

Economic regulation was from the 14th century part of the magistrates' contribution to suppressing possible sources of social unrest. Poor-relief, with which the magistrates became intimately involved in the 16th century, had a similar ultimate purpose. That work, too, had begun in the 14th century, when laws were made to punish sturdy beggars, whom the magistrates were to bind over or commit to assizes.[48] The Beggars Act, 1531,[49] required magistrates to punish sturdy beggars directly, and that requirement was reinforced in subsequent Acts. One such, the Poor Relief Act, 1576,[50] had immediate results in Shropshire, where the justices issued orders to parishes for the 'avoiding of vagabonds'.[51] The same Act required the magistrates to provide a house of correction, though none is known to have been established in Shropshire until the requirement was repeated by the Beggars Act, 1597–8.[52] Parish poor-relief was inaugurated by the Beggars Act, 1536,[53] and was regulated by the magistrates. Certain needy persons were relieved directly by the magistrates out of county rates. A regular county rate for the relief of poor prisoners in the county gaol was required by the 1572 Act and was being collected in Shropshire by 1578.[54] A regular rate to provide pensions for injured soldiers was required under an Act of 1593[55] and was being collected in Shropshire by 1594.[56] Under the 1597–8 Poor Relief Act a small contribution was demanded from each county towards the relief of prisoners in the Queen's Bench and Marshalsea prisons; by 1598 it was being collected in Shropshire.[57] In 1591 the magistrates were urged to use their power to license beggars under the 1531 Act to permit the inhabitants of Shifnal to collect money for their town and church devastated by fire.[58] Thus during Elizabeth I's reign poor-relief came to parallel the militia[59] in the extent of the administrative duties that it placed upon the magistrates.

The justices played a minor part in trying to impose religious conformity in Elizabeth

[43] Ibid.; Sel. Cases in K.B. vii, p. 62.
[44] Salop. Peace Roll, 1400–14, 98.
[45] S.P. 12/190 ff. 153, 155.
[46] T.S.A.S. iii. 307. The source names Jas. Barker, but the J.P. of that name was dead (T.S.A.S. 4th ser. x. 292); Rowland Barker, one of the J.P.s assigned to Shrews. market (S.P. 12/190 f. 155), was presumably intended.
[47] N.L.W., Ottley Papers, uncat., Ric. Ottley's letter bk. 1590–7, 27 Aug., 29 Sept. 1597.
[48] Poor-law legislation before 1603 is summarized in J. R. Tanner, Tudor Constitutional Docs. (1930), pp. 469–73.
[49] 22 Hen. VIII, c. 12.
[50] 18 Eliz. I, c. 3.
[51] Peele and Clease, Salop. Par. Docs. 65.
[52] 39 Eliz. I, c. 4; below, p. 105. In Wilts. the 1576 Act led to immediate action: Wilts. Co. Rec. p. xxv.
[53] 27 Hen. VIII, c. 25.
[54] S.R.O. 1374/48, pp. 110–11 (first refs. to the rate in Worfield churchwardens' accts.); first ref. in Condover accts. is in 1582 (S.R.O. 1377/4/1).
[55] 35 Eliz. I, c. 4; below, pp. 100–1.
[56] S.R.O. 1374/48, p. 155; S.R.O. 1377/4/1.
[57] S.R.O. 1374/267.
[58] Hist. MSS. Com. 47, 15th Rep. X, Shrews. Corpn., p. 56.
[59] See pp. 83–6.

I's reign.[60] There were few Puritans on the Welsh border and the real difficulty was that of Roman Catholic recusancy.[61] Except in the period 1582-7 the magistrates had no power to determine recusancy offences[62] and acted rather as agents of the higher courts;[63] the detection and reporting of recusants and priests was often carried out by special commissioners.[64] In 1579 two Shropshire justices arrested a Roman Catholic priest and were required to send him for trial at the Council in the Marches or at the Shropshire assizes.[65] Bishop Whitgift of Worcester, a keen prosecutor of recusants, was vice-president of the Council in the Marches 1577-80; during his term magistrates within the council's area were under unusual pressure to pursue offenders.[66] Sir George Bromley, *custos rotulorum c.* 1573-1587, was zealous in prosecuting recusants,[67] but was not a frequent attender of Shropshire quarter sessions except around the years 1577-8.[68] Except during Whitgift's vice-presidency, and perhaps in the early 1590s, the Council in the Marches provided little such stimulus to the Shropshire magistrates,[69] who are unlikely to have taken the initiative in persecuting harmless Roman Catholics in their midst.[70] During Elizabeth I's reign the number of Roman Catholic recusants seems to have increased in Wales and perhaps in the border counties.[71]

The county magistrates acquired during the 16th century a responsibility for the upkeep of several Shropshire bridges. In 1531 it was enacted that such bridges, with their approach roads, as could not be shown to be anyone else's responsibility were to be maintained by a county rate.[72] By the 17th century the Shropshire magistrates had adopted Atcham, Buildwas, and Tern bridges, the Shropshire half of Tenbury bridge, and the part of Montford bridge outside Shrewsbury liberties.[73] Atcham bridge had been built, and presumably maintained, by the canons of Lilleshall, a house dissolved in 1538.[74] Atcham and Tern bridges were rebuilt in stone by Sir Rowland Hill[75] (d. 1561), lord mayor of London 1549-50 and a generous benefactor of the county.[76] He was a Shropshire magistrate from 1543[77] and it seems likely that his fellow magistrates agreed to adopt those bridges at about the time of rebuilding. Buildwas bridge was maintained by Buildwas abbey[78] until the abbey's suppression in 1536,[79] after which its upkeep presumably fell upon the county. Montford bridge appears to have been maintained in the 14th and early 15th centuries by the earls of Arundel.[80] Half of it lay within Shrewsbury liberties, as extended by the town's charter of 1495.[81]

The later 16th century saw in Shropshire the development of fixed divisions, in which the resident magistrates of each division became accustomed to meeting regularly for certain purposes of local government. By Henry VIII's reign Shropshire magistrates, in their capacity as array commissioners, were commonly assigned to different hundreds,[82] and the Beggars Act, 1531, required magistrates occasionally to divide themselves up in order to license deserving beggars. They were therefore not unused to the idea of divisional administration when, in 1552, the Alehouses Act[83] enabled any two magistrates to license ale-sellers. Ale-sellers naturally applied to the nearest magistrates and thus encouraged the formation of permanent divisions of the county which

[60] Moir, *Justice of Peace*, 43.
[61] Williams, *Council in Marches*, 86.
[62] Smith, *County and Court*, 135.
[63] As in Lancs.: *Lancs. Q. Sess. Recs.* i (Chetham Soc. new ser. lxxvii), p. xvii.
[64] See pp. 88-9. There were also diocesan commissions, which included some J.P.s: see *Bull. Inst. Hist. Res.* xlix. 60-1.
[65] *Acts of P.C.* 1578-80, 293-4.
[66] Williams, op. cit. 91-3.
[67] Ibid. 96.
[68] E 372/423 Salop. d.
[69] Williams, op. cit. 90-1, 94-9.
[70] *V.C.H. Salop.* ii. 8.
[71] Ibid.; Williams, op. cit. 99.

[72] Bridges Act, 1531, 22 Hen. VIII, c. 5.
[73] See p. 101.
[74] *V.C.H. Salop.* ii. 73, 78.
[75] *T.S.A.S.* iii. 259.
[76] *D.N.B.*
[77] *L. & P. Hen. VIII*, xviii(1), p. 123; *Cal. Pat.* 1547-8, 88; S.P. 11/5 f. 46v.; S.P. 12/2 f. 55; B.L. Lansd. MS. 1218, f. 77v.
[78] *Cal. Pat.* 1317-21, 119.
[79] *V.C.H. Salop.* ii. 58.
[80] *T.S.A.S.* 3rd ser. vii. 69-72. On Wele see *Salop. Peace Roll, 1400-14*, 26.
[81] Owen and Blakeway, *Hist. Shrews.* i. 268.
[82] See p. 83.
[83] 5 & 6 Edw. VI, c. 25.

later proved convenient for the transaction of other out-of-sessions business.[84] The divisional boundaries were not at first fixed: in 1575 it was reported from Shropshire that 'the limits and allotments for the justices of peace are not certain, but as by agreement amongst themselves from time to time the same are divided'. By then the divisions were being based on the hundreds. Bradford, the largest hundred, had long been divided into two,[85] Overs and Purslow made one division, and Chirbury and Ford shared two of the three justices assigned to each.[86] By 1590 the divisions used throughout the following century[87] had been fixed: Bradford had north and south divisions, while Brimstree and Stottesdon, Chirbury and Ford, and Clun and Purslow were united in pairs.[88] By 1590 the divisional justices had adopted corporate measures for the dispatch of divisional business. For example the justices of the Condover division were by 1590 licensing numbers of ale-sellers at a single sessions, binding them all to a set of articles previously agreed (and perhaps devised) by the divisional justices among themselves. The articles included provisions as to the opening times of alehouses, the entertaining of undesirables, and the notification of strangers to a constable.[89]

The Sheriff

In 1345 the shrievalties of Shropshire and Staffordshire were made separate;[90] of twenty pairs of shrievalties it was the only one to be divorced before Elizabeth I's reign.[91] In 1345 Richard, earl of Arundel, was appointed sheriff and, though annual appointments had been required by statute since 1340[92] and had been made in Shropshire and Staffordshire until 1345, he retained the office until his death in 1376.[93] In Staffordshire, too, a life shrievalty was granted a few months later to Henry, earl of Derby, Arundel's brother-in-law.[94] The exceptional separation of the counties in 1345 and the life shrievalties then granted suggest that the separate Shropshire and Staffordshire shrievalties were created by Edward III as a personal favour to Arundel, the earlier appointee. By 1376 the commons of Shropshire regarded the life shrievalty as having been to their great 'harm' (*meschief*).[95] Two days after Arundel's death[96] the last of his known under-sheriffs succeeded him and, with minor exceptions, annual appointments were made thereafter. The county was reunited with Staffordshire from 1377 to 1378 but the experiment, if such it was, was not repeated.[97] In the earlier 15th century it does not seem that appointments were dominated by any particular baronial interest; about a third of the Shropshire sheriffs were followers of John Talbot, Lord Furnivalle (later earl of Shrewsbury).[98] In Henry VI's reign Shropshire was one of only three counties in which members of the royal household were not intruded as sheriffs; as in Northumberland and Yorkshire the Crown had no land available in Shropshire on which to establish them.[99] National politics may, however, account for the appointment of Nicholas Eyton, a Yorkist, in 1454; during York's protectorate many shrievalties went to the duke's friends.[1]

Between 1377 and 1643 only six Shropshire sheriffs served a term of more than one year contrary to statute. The explanation of those exceptions is sometimes found in

[84] See pp. 106-7.
[85] It was sometimes divided for militia purposes by 1539: *L. & P. Hen. VIII*, xiv(1), pp. 287-8.
[86] S.P. 12/104 ff. 66-67v.
[87] See p. 106.
[88] *T.S.A.S.* 3rd ser. iii, pp. *iii-iv*.
[89] N.L.W., Ottley Papers, uncat., Ric. Ottley's letter bk. 1590-7, 4 Nov. 1590.
[90] *List of Sheriffs*, 117.
[91] R. B. Pugh, *Imprisonment in Medieval Eng.* (1968), 60.
[92] 14 Edw. III, c. 7.

[93] The source of sheriffs' names and dates in this section is *List of Sheriffs*.
[94] *Complete Peerage*, ii. 244.
[95] S.C. 8/139 no. 6912. Thanks are due to Dr. J. R. Maddicott for this ref.
[96] *Complete Peerage*, ii. 244.
[97] *List of Sheriffs*, 118-21, 127.
[98] Pollard, 'Fam. of Talbot', 243.
[99] R. M. Jeffs, 'The Later Mediaeval Sheriff and the Royal Household' (Oxford Univ. D.Phil. thesis, 1960), 165.
[1] Ibid. 173-4.

national affairs. Most sheriffs appointed in 1397 served until the end of Richard II's reign; the king aimed at controlling the shrievalties by keeping his nominees in office.[2] In Shropshire Sir Adam Peshall, a king's knight,[3] served from 1397 to 1399, his second year being terminated on the day of Henry IV's accession. The first sheriff appointed by Edward IV, Roger Kynaston, served from 1461 to 1463 for reasons of local security, as did many of Edward's first sheriffs,[4] and the same man was appointed at Edward's restoration in 1471. Kynaston had rendered exceptional services to the Yorkist cause before 1461[5] and was especially trusted by Edward. Edward IV's reign is notable for the unusually large proportion of Shropshire sheriffs who served more than once during its course. Edward's Shropshire escheators were likewise often appointed more than once[6] and it may be inferred that Edward IV favoured local government by a limited number of trusted men.[7] Humphrey (later Sir Humphrey) Blount (sheriff 1460–1, 1466–7, 1474–5) was a king's esquire;[8] John Leighton (1467–8, 1473–4, 1481–2) had been steward of Montgomery for the king's father;[9] Roger Eyton (1449–50, 1465–6)[10] and Sir John Harley (1480–1)[11] had also been of special service to the king. The last Shropshire sheriff before 1643 to serve a term of more than one year was Thomas Kynaston (1507–9).[12] Henry VIII's reign, however, saw in Shropshire an even higher proportion of second appointments than did Edward IV's. The same tendency has been noted in Wiltshire[13] and it was presumably the result of royal policy.[14]

Between 1378 and 1603 about three quarters of the Shropshire sheriffs also served at some time as magistrates, though until Henry V's reign the proportion was only a quarter.[15] When the commission of the peace was small it was, of course, impracticable for most sheriffs to serve as keepers or justices. In the 15th century the proportion rose to three quarters and in the 16th century it rose still higher; every one of Elizabeth I's Shropshire sheriffs served on the commission of the peace.[16] The 16th-century escheator declined in standing in comparison with the magistrates;[17] the shrievalty, on the contrary, increased its standing. Whereas in the 15th century about half the men that held the offices of sheriff and magistrate were appointed sheriff first, in the 16th century it became commoner for a man to be appointed magistrate first and sheriff later. In Elizabeth I's time over four fifths of Shropshire sheriffs had been appointed magistrates before their first shrievalty. As the shrievalty came to be regarded as the more senior appointment, competition for it presumably became keener, to the Crown's advantage. Bearing in mind, too, the many re-appointments of Henry VIII's reign, it seems that the Tudors attached at least as much importance to the sheriff as did their predecessors. Indeed, no local-government policy could succeed without an efficient sheriff, for most royal writs and legal processes had to pass through his hands before they took effect.

From Richard II's later years until the early part of Henry VI's reign Shropshire justices were normally put off the peace commission during a term as sheriff.[18] During

[2] T. F. Tout, *Chapters in Admin. Hist. of Medieval Eng.* iv. 43–4.

[3] J. G. Bellamy, 'Parliamentary Representatives of Notts., Derb., and Staffs. in the Reign of Ric. II' (Nottingham Univ. M.A. thesis, 1961), 107.

[4] Jeffs, op. cit. 227–8.

[5] He killed Ld. Audley at the battle of Blore Heath (Staffs.) in 1459, and fought at Ludford: *Complete Peerage,* i. 341; Blakeway, *Sheriffs,* 73.

[6] See p. 82.

[7] See Jacob, *Fifteenth Cent.* 598–600.

[8] Wedgwood, *Hist. Parl. 1439–1509: Biogs.* 83.

[9] Burke, *Peerage* (1949), 1198.

[10] Fought at Ludford (Wedgwood, op. cit. 310); king's serjeant, apptd. constable of Shrews. cas. 1461 (*Cal. Pat.* 1461–7, 57).

[11] Knighted at battle of Tewkesbury, 1471: Blakeway, op. cit. 77.

[12] Appointments in Wilts. were invariably annual after 1463: *V.C.H. Wilts.* v. 20.

[13] Ibid.

[14] Re-appointments of Salop. escheators increased only slightly *temp.* Hen. VIII: *List of Escheators,* 134–5.

[15] Sources of J.P.s' names and dates are given above, p. 55 n.

[16] The proportion in Wilts. was nearly as high: *Wilts. Co. Rec.* p. xii.

[17] See p. 82.

[18] Removals occurred in some other cos. *temp.* Ric. II: Putnam, *Proceedings,* p. lxxxi.

the rest of the 15th century a number of men did hold the offices concurrently, and no removals are known. The practice of removal from the peace commission was revived in Shropshire in the early 16th century. The last Shropshire magistrate known to have acted concurrently as sheriff was George Bromley in 1522, well before removal was required by the Sheriffs Act, 1553.[19]

Such was the influence of the sheriff in the 16th century that private as well as royal interests depended on the appointment. In November 1602 Edward Grey petitioned that Roger Owen should not be appointed sheriff for 1602–3. Lawsuits, to be tried by Shropshire juries, were pending between Grey and Sir Robert and Henry Vernon. According to Grey's petition the Vernons had recently secured Owen's interest by selling estates to him at advantageous prices.[20] The Greys and the Vernons had been at law for half a century about the estates of the last Lord Grey of Powis (d. 1551)[21] and much would depend on the next sheriff's choice of jurors. Whether or not Grey's allegations carried weight, Owen was not appointed that year. As sheriff 1603–4 he interfered by gross intimidation and corruption in the Shrewsbury parliamentary election of 1604.[22]

The appointment of an under-sheriff was a practical necessity. In 1333 more than 2,000 writs are estimated to have reached the sheriff of Bedfordshire in less than a year;[23] a similar number presumably reached other counties at other periods. The sheriff had other public and private responsibilities and could have handled the work only by deputy. During the earl of Arundel's long shrievalty (1345–76) the under-sheriff was virtually sheriff, and was occasionally so styled.[24] Some under-sheriffs belonged to the class of men who regularly filled the minor offices of local government.[25] Richard Bentley (occurs as under-sheriff 1420)[26] was a sheriff's clerk in 1409[27] and a coroner by 1436.[28] Nicholas Gibbons (1585–6)[29] was a Shrewsbury attorney and twice a bailiff of the town.[30] The possibility that some under-sheriffs were attorneys connected with the Inns of Chancery[31] is supported in Shropshire by the example of William Baldwyn (1590–1, 1597–8) of Clement's Inn.[32] It has been observed in several counties that in Elizabeth I's reign some under-sheriffs came from the gentry and were related to the sheriffs who appointed them.[33] In Shropshire Edmund Cornewall (sheriff 1579–80) appointed his grandson Francis Cressett,[34] and Edward Leighton (1587–8) appointed Richard Leighton.[35] Nevertheless the career of Edward Lutwyche (under-sheriff 1577–8), who rose to be an escheator (in 1598)[36] and a magistrate (in 1602),[37] was exceptional.

The extent to which the sheriff delegated his liabilities to the under-sheriff varied from one sheriff to another and thus was probably the subject of private negotiation.[38] In 1491 Thomas Dudley, a former under-sheriff, was imprisoned for having refused several writs,[39] but in 1506 the sheriff himself, Thomas Cornewall, was fined twelve times for not returning writs.[40] William Baldwyn, when appointed under-sheriff in

[19] 1 Mary, Sess. 2, c. 8.
[20] Hist. MSS. Com. 9, *Salisbury*, xii, pp. 496–7.
[21] *T.S.A.S.* 4th ser. xi. 39; *Reg. Council in Marches of Wales*, 172 n.
[22] See p. 241.
[23] Mabel H. Mills, 'The Medieval Shire-House', *Studies Presented to Sir Hilary Jenkinson*, ed. J. Conway Davies (1957), 262.
[24] Blakeway, *Sheriffs*, 11; *Cal. Pat.* 1354–8, 168.
[25] See T. E. Hartley, 'Under-Sheriffs and Bailiffs in Some Eng. Shrievalties, *c.* 1580 to *c.* 1625', *Bull. Inst. Hist. Res.* xlvii. 167–8.
[26] *Cal. Pat.* 1416–22, 297.
[27] *Sel. Cases in K.B.* vii, p. 189.
[28] *Cal. Close*, 1435–41, 74.

[29] S.R.O. 3365/2477, estreat of fines 1586.
[30] *T.S.A.S.* xlvii. 195.
[31] *Bull. Inst. Hist. Res.* xlvii. 167.
[32] Staffs. R.O., D.(W.) 1788/41/15, indentures of appointment 1590, 1597.
[33] Smith, *County and Court*, 143; *Bull. Inst. Hist. Res.* xlvii. 167.
[34] Blakeway, *Sheriffs*, 20; *T.S.A.S.* 4th ser. vi. 218.
[35] S.R.O. 3365/2477, estreat of fines 1588. Ric. was either Edw.'s son or one of the Cotes branch of the fam.: *Visit. Salop. 1623*, ii. 323–5.
[36] *List of Escheators*, 136, For examples from other cos. see *Bull. Inst. Hist. Res.* xlvii. 168.
[37] C 231/1 f. 129v.   [38] *Bull. Inst. Hist. Res.* xlvii. 164.
[39] B.L. Add. MS. 30325, f. 7.   [40] Ibid. f. 7v.

1590, was held liable for the proper custody of the gaol; in 1597, when he was again appointed, that liability was retained by the sheriff. In 1590 Baldwyn was forbidden to handle certain writs without consulting the sheriff; in 1597 no such stipulation was made.[41] In 1598 it was noted as unusual that a Shropshire sheriff had recently impanelled a jury 'without the advice of his under-sheriff'.[42] The under-sheriff needed at least one clerk. In 1391 William Baker, 'clerk of the under-sheriff of Shropshire', was tried at a Shrewsbury gaol delivery for misappropriating a fee and for a wrongful arrest and imprisonment.[43] Such charges imply that the clerk was then held liable for his actions in office. In 1590, however, the under-sheriff was held liable for his deputies' actions.[44]

Bailiffs errant acted under the sheriff in the various parts of the county. In 1409 the sheriff sent his clerk and 'other bailiffs of his' to make an arrest in Ludlow.[45] They seem to have been regarded then as servants of the sheriff, not of the under-sheriff. In 1438 three men described as 'king's bailiffs' were ordered by a leading magistrate to make an arrest.[46] In 1464 four men described as 'king's bailiffs in Shropshire' were ordered by the sheriff to arrest a number of men in the adjacent hundreds of Bradford and Brimstree;[47] one of the four, Reynold Steventon, was in 1466 or 1467 a bailiff errant of Bradford hundred.[48] It seems, therefore, that the Shropshire bailiffs errant, as in Hampshire, Lancashire, and Somerset,[49] were assigned to separate portions of the county.[50] In a document of 1466 or 1467 two men calling themselves bailiffs errant of Bradford hundred formally relinquished their authority in the hundred to three other men,[51] one of whom, Thomas Harris, was among the bailiffs named in 1464; in other words Shropshire bailiffs errant were appointing deputies at that period[52] and may therefore have been men of substance. At least three of the 1464 bailiffs, Harris, Steventon, and Hugh Higford, bore surnames found among the gentry, as did Robert Peshall, one of the bailiffs of 1466 or 1467.[53] In 1566 a bailiff errant of Munslow hundred was appointed for life by the Crown.[54]

In parts of the county the sheriff's authority was curtailed by the existence of franchises, enjoyed by lay lords, ecclesiastics, and municipalities. At one extreme there were on the Welsh border marcher lordships such as Clun and Oswestry, in which the king's writ did not run;[55] they were not joined to Shropshire until Henry VIII's reign.[56] It was not until 1536 that the hundred of Chirbury, which belonged to the lordship of Montgomery, was agreed to be in Shropshire.[57] Within the county proper were liberties, from single manors to whole hundreds, that enjoyed various degrees of exemption at various periods.[58] Their existence and the uncertain nature of some of their exemptions were a source of difficulty for the sheriff, who was not only burdened with the legal and accounting complications created by areas of delegated or exempt jurisdiction within the county but also denied possible sources of fees, profits, and patronage. In 1330 the sheriff of Shropshire and Staffordshire maintained that the hundreds of Bradford, Chirbury, and Purslow, and a moiety of Overs hundred were in private hands and that he was not accountable for them at the Exchequer. The Exchequer had tried to

[41] Staffs. R.O., D.(W.) 1788/41/15, indentures 1590, 1597.

[42] Longleat MSS., Thynne Papers, vol. v, f. 88. Thanks are due to Mrs. Alison Wall for this ref.

[43] J.I. 3/180 rot. 50.

[44] Staffs. R.O., D.(W). 1788/41/15, indenture 1590.

[45] Sel. Cases in K.B. vii, p. 189.

[46] S.P.L., Deeds 2801.

[47] Shrews. Sch., Phillipps Deeds S 14.

[48] Ibid. S 5. Thanks are due Mr. J. B. Lawson, Librarian of Shrews. Sch., for this and the preceding ref.

[49] Helen M. Cam, 'Shire Officials', Eng. Govt. at Work, iii, ed. J. F. Willard, 171–2.

[50] Elsewhere, however, one bailiff seems in the 14th cent. to serve a whole county: ibid. 172–4; V.C.H. Wilts. v. 23.

[51] Shrews. Sch., Phillipps Deeds S 5.

[52] As in Lincs. c. 1400: Cam, op. cit., 174 n.

[53] Cal. Pat. 1396–9, 229, 235; Visit. Salop. 1623, i. 222–4; ii. 444–5.

[54] Cal. Pat. 1563–6, p. 424.

[55] Eyton, x. 316; xi. 228–9; Year Bk. 12 Edw. II (Selden Soc. lxxxi), 130–2.

[56] See p. 41.

[57] Eyton, xi. 53; Cal. Close, 1333–7, 224; 1337–9, 42; Cal. Pat. 1367–70, 204; Sel. Cases in K.B. v (Selden Soc. lxxvi), pp. 97–101; 27 Hen. VIII, c. 26.

[58] See pp. 42–53.

distrain on him for the proceeds of those hundreds,[59] mistakenly assuming that they were subject to an Act of 1328 that required hundreds granted out since the king's accession to be resumed by the sheriff.[60] Acting on royal instructions the sheriff did seize the moiety of Overs hundred but in 1334 was required to restore it to the franchise holder.[61] The private hundreds persisted in the 16th century. At Easter 1544 the sheriff held no tourn in Bradford, Purslow, and Overs hundreds and he did not account for the proceeds of their hundred courts.[62] In 1596 he was not accountable for proceeds from Bradford, Chirbury, Clun, Oswestry, Overs, and Purslow hundreds.[63]

In the royal hundreds (Brimstree, Condover, Ford, Munslow, Pimhill, and Stottesdon) hundred bailiffs were probably appointed by the sheriff until the 16th century, when appointments by the Crown are first recorded.[64] In 1564 the patent appointing a bailiff and collector of Condover hundred stated that his predecessors had been appointed by the sheriff.[65] In 1575 Stottesdon and Pimhill hundreds were subject to a single bailiff,[66] as were Ford and Brimstree in 1589.[67]

At his tourn the sheriff had until 1461 the power to determine indictments and presentments other than pleas of the Crown. After that date, according to statute, they had to be determined by the magistrates.[68] In Shropshire, however, the sheriff's tourn continued to sentence minor offenders, and a formal distinction was maintained between it and the ordinary hundred court held on the same day; the sheriff accounted for their proceeds separately. At the Easter tourns of 1544 a number of fines were imposed for assaults and affrays, some involving bloodshed, and other offences punished included breaches of the assizes of bread and ale, not scouring a highway, and park-breaking; fines from 4d. to 5s. were imposed. Similar offences were punished at the ordinary hundred courts.[69] The business differed little from that which occupied the Wiltshire tourns at Easter 1439.[70] Tourns were not necessarily held in the customary periods, within a month of Easter and Michaelmas. In 1394 the Michaelmas tourn at Stottesdon was held on 10 November.[71] In 1544 Easter fell on 13 April but the Easter tourns were held at dates between 7 April and 12 July. It appears that in 1543–4 there were no Michaelmas tourns in Shropshire[72] and it may be doubted whether tourns were always held twice-yearly at that period. Of procedure at the tourns there is little Shropshire evidence. Violent scenes sometimes occurred: a man was killed in the sheriff's presence at a Stottesdon tourn c. 1340[73] and at Easter 1544 men were fined for assaults committed at the Ford and Munslow tourns.[74]

The Shropshire county court, held by the sheriff, customarily met every four weeks on a Thursday.[75] It seems to have been held at the proper intervals but not necessarily on the customary days. Of eleven county courts between January and November 1544 seven were held on the day after the customary day, one was held on the following Sunday, and another on the following Wednesday.[76] Difficulties arose if a court failed to be held, for the law required an indicted person to be exacted unsuccessfully at four consecutive county courts before he could be outlawed. The sheriff of Shropshire was fined £20 for failing to hold the court in September 1443, thus allowing three men to escape outlawry.[77] In 1576, when plague prevented sittings in Shrewsbury, the court

[59] Cal. Close, 1330–3, 20.
[60] Cam, op. cit. 174–5.
[61] Cal. Close, 1333–7, 221–2.
[62] E 370/11/13.
[63] E 370/13/165.
[64] e.g. V.C.H. Salop. viii. 180; B.L. Add. MS. 30325, f. 78v.
[65] Cal. Pat. 1563–6, p. 244.
[66] Ibid. 1572–5, p. 464.
[67] B.L. Add. MS. 30325, f. 73.
[68] 1 Edw. IV, c. 2.
[69] E 370/11/13.
[70] J. E. Jackson, 'The Sheriff's Turn, Co. Wilts., A.D. 1439', Wilts. Arch. Mag. xiii. 105–18.
[71] J.I. 3/180 rot. 50.
[72] E 370/11/13 (no Mich. tourns recorded).
[73] Cal. Pat. 1340–3, 201.
[74] E 370/11/13.
[75] J. J. Alexander, 'Dates of County Days', Bull. Inst. Hist. Res. iii. 93.
[76] E 370/11/13.
[77] Cal. Pat. 1441–6, 256.

was held at Meole Brace near by.[78] Further evidence of the strict intervals at which the court was kept occurs in 1593. The writ to elect knights of the shire for the next Parliament, beginning on 19 February, reached the sheriff soon after the January county court, and the next county day did not fall until after the Parliament was to assemble. The sheriff, seeking the Privy Council's instructions, was directed nevertheless to await the due county day before holding the election.[79]

The shirehall, at which the county court normally met, was in Shrewsbury castle.[80] In 1485 the knights of the shire were elected at a county court in 'le Shirhousse' at Shrewsbury.[81] County courts were held at the castle in the 1540s,[82] and in the later 16th century, until at least 1601, knights of the shire were elected at the castle.[83] It may therefore be supposed that the shirehall was at the castle from the 15th century, at latest, to the early 17th. Various courts met there: an inquisition post mortem was held at the shirehall c. 1600,[84] and in 1609 it was said that assizes were sometimes held at the castle.[85] Little record of county-court proceedings in Shropshire has survived. In the 16th century the court was sometimes the scene of heated litigation: in 1544 litigants came to blows in at least three separate county courts and there were several fines for 'garrulity', an offence that carried the fixed penalty of 1s.[86]

Royal Castles and County Gaols

Shropshire had three royal castles: Shrewsbury, Bridgnorth, and (from 1461) Ludlow. Shrewsbury castle was entrusted, from 1339 at latest, to constables appointed by the Crown for life and paid out of the issues of the county.[87] It was no longer an important stronghold and by 1400 had decayed so far as to remain virtually useless as a fortress.[88] The constables were undistinguished. Only one became a county justice of the peace.[89] Another was a coroner,[90] and two others served as escheators.[91] Only Roger Eyton[92] (appointed 1461) became sheriff. The constableship was so indifferently regarded by the Crown in 1410 that the holder was allowed to give it to the sheriff's brother-in-law in part exchange for some property in the town.[93] In 1504 the constableship passed by statute to the sheriff.[94] In 1565 the Crown granted the 'late' castle to Richard Onslow[95] and in 1586 conveyed it to Shrewsbury corporation in fee farm.[96] The county gaol was in the castle and the constable was responsible to the Crown for its custody.[97] In 1341 the sheriff's claim to keep the gaol, with free access to the castle and prisoners, was dismissed,[98] to be upheld only by the Gaols Act, 1504.[99] Presumably gaolers were normally appointed by the constables, though in the 14th century, at Shrewsbury and many other gaols, the Crown occasionally appointed gaolers directly and made the nominees responsible to itself.[1] Such instances occur at Shrewsbury in 1335 and 1381.[2]

[78] T.S.A.S. iii. 277; 4th ser. iv. 57.
[79] Acts of P.C. 1592-3, 48.
[80] For parallels in other cos. see Mills, 'Medieval Shire-House', Studies Presented to Sir H. Jenkinson, 255.
[81] Intrationum Excellentissimus Liber (London, 1511; printed by Nic. Pynson), f. 127v.
[82] E 370/11/13.
[83] T.S.A.S. iii. 300, 314, 346. The elections, however, were still held at the castle in the 1830s, long after a shirehall had been provided elsewhere in the town: Life of Thos. Telford, ed. J. Rickman (1838), 22.
[84] Hist. MSS. Com. 9, Salisbury, x, p. 94.
[85] H. M. Colvin and others, Hist. of King's Works, iii(1), 403.
[86] E 370/11/13.
[87] Cal. Pat. 1338-40, 335; 1340-3, 430; 1377-81, 248; 1399-1401, 60; 1401-5, 116; 1405-8, 379; 1408-13, 466; 1436-41, 25, 135; 1452-61, 587; 1461-7, 57; 1485-94, 8.

[88] R. Allen Brown and others, Hist. of King's Works, ii. 836-7.
[89] Cal. Pat. 1388-92, 344.
[90] Cal. Close, 1435-41, 9.
[91] List of Escheators, 132.
[92] M.P. Shrews. 1455-6; Yorkist: Wedgwood, Hist. Parl. 1439-1509: Biogs. 310.
[93] T.S.A.S. liv. 103-4.
[94] 19 Hen. VII, c. 10. The Act affected only constableships of castles with county gaols.
[95] Cal. Pat. 1563-6, p. 274.
[96] T.S.A.S. iii. 307.
[97] Cal. Pat. 1358-61, 259; 1461-7, 57; 1485-94, 8; Cal. Close, 1389-92, 63.
[98] Cal. Close, 1341-3, 188.
[99] 19 Hen. VII, c. 10.
[1] Pugh, Imprisonment, 148-51.
[2] Cal. Pat. 1334-8, 171; 1377-81, 594.

In the 17th century the gaolership was hereditary in the Meriden family[3] and may already have been so by 1557, when Richard Meriden occurs as gaoler.[4]

In the later Middle Ages Bridgnorth castle was in the keeping of constables appointed for life[5] and paid out of the farms of the town and of Pendlestone Mills.[6] Until Henry IV's reign the constables' standing was such as to suggest that Bridgnorth castle was still an important base. Sir John Beauchamp (later Lord Beauchamp of Kidderminster), appointed in 1370, was one of Richard II's ministers; he was impeached in 1388 and beheaded.[7] Hugh, Lord Burnell (appointed 1387), was a justice of the peace in six counties and sat on many local commissions. He was one of Henry IV's council and is credited with a vital part in England's defence against Owen Glendower.[8] During the 15th century, however, the castle was allowed to fall into ruin[9] and the constables declined in importance. One became escheator in 1472[10] but none was a sheriff or county magistrate. In 1605 or 1606 the constableship was granted to two men in survivorship,[11] and the castle was granted away by the Crown c. 1629.[12]

Ludlow castle, which belonged to the earldom of March, became a Crown castle on Edward IV's accession. Keepers, also called porters, were appointed[13] but, with the establishment of Ludlow as seat of the Council in the Marches of Wales, the keeper was subordinated to the president of the council.[14] It was the president, for example, who initiated repairs and alterations to the fabric.[15] The porter was also keeper of the council's gaol.[16] The royal castle at Ludlow, because of its continued usefulness, was one of the very few in England that were kept in repair during the 16th century.[17] In Elizabeth I's reign the keeper was paid out of the fines and amercements imposed by the council;[18] as gaoler he also took fees from the prisoners.[19]

The County Coroners

By the 13th century the number of Shropshire county coroners had been fixed at four.[20] In addition Shrewsbury had two coroners;[21] it remained the only Shropshire borough with coroners until the 1460s when coroners were granted to Ludlow and Much Wenlock.[22] At least three county coroners were active concurrently in the period 1329–33,[23] but by 1366 their number had fallen to two. In that year, following a petition by the commons of Shropshire, the sheriff was ordered to hold elections to restore the number to four.[24]

As in most other counties there were no formal coroners' districts: people simply called out the nearest coroner.[25] A little Shropshire evidence from 1329 suggests that at that time John de Warenne was active in the north-east of the county, Alan of Glazeley in the centre, and John de Clinton in the south-west.[26] In the early 1360s,

[3] See p. 105.
[4] S.R.O. 1/46.
[5] Cal. Pat. 1340–3, 85; 1367–70, 341; 1385–9, 292; 1446–52, 426–7; 1485–94, 21; Cal. Close, 1461–8, 28, 321; B.L. Add. MS. 30325, f. 40; Hist. MSS. Com. 53, Montagu, p. 76.
[6] Cal. Close, 1476–85, 322.
[7] Complete Peerage, ii. 45–6.
[8] Ibid. 435; Putnam, Proceedings, 340; Salop. Peace Roll, 1400–14, 19.
[9] Hist. of King's Works, ii. 577.
[10] Wm. Clerk, M.P. Bridgnorth 1467–8, 1478, M. Wenlock 1472–5; a marshal of king's hall in 1477; attainted 1485, pardoned 1486: Wedgwood, Hist. Parl. 1439–1509: Biogs. 193.
[11] B.L. Add. MS. 30325, f. 87.
[12] T.S.A.S. 4th ser. v. 54.
[13] Cal. Pat. 1452–61, 586–7; 1494–1509, 303; 1557–8, 302; 1563–6, p. 84; 1569–72, p. 420; L. & P. Hen. VIII,

i(1), p. 47; iii(2), p. 999.
[14] Williams, Council in Marches, 167–8.
[15] Skeel, Council in Marches, 69–70, 184–5.
[16] Williams, op. cit. 169.
[17] H. M. Colvin, 'Castles and Govt. in Tudor Eng.', E.H.R. lxxxiii. 233.
[18] Cal. Pat. 1563–6, p. 84; 1569–72, p. 420.
[19] Williams, op. cit. 169–70.
[20] See p. 28; R. F. Hunnisett, Medieval Coroner (1961), 134.
[21] J.I. 2/143 rott. 1–2; J.I. 2/145 rott. 3–11, 13; J.I. 2/146 rot. 1; Cal. Pat. 1555–7, 62.
[22] Hunnisett, op. cit. 94–5, 160.
[23] J.I. 3/127 rott. 6, 8; J.I. 3/131 rot. 1; J.I. 3/214/3 rot. 10 and d.
[24] Cal. Close, 1364–8, 225.
[25] Hunnisett, op. cit. 136. Suss. and Warws. may have had formal districts.
[26] J.I. 3/214/3 rot. 10 and d.

when there were only two coroners, each had to cover a very wide area: Roger Praers held inquests at places as far apart as Market Drayton, Aston Rogers (in Worthen), and Bourton (in Much Wenlock).[27] By the later 14th century four areas may be discerned, though there was much overlapping: the north, the south, the south-east, and the south-west.[28] When a newly elected coroner happened to live in an area already being served by someone else, temporary partition might occur. William Skirmeston, for example, covered north Shropshire in the 1390s. When William Poyner, who came from Wroxeter,[29] was elected he seems to have taken over the eastern part of Skirmeston's territory until Skirmeston's death c. 1403; Poyner then became responsible for the whole northern area.[30] As in most counties, however, when a coronership was vacant a man from the same district as his predecessor was usually elected.[31] The informal districts were thus perpetuated. Another consideration tending to the preservation of the districts was that until 1487[32] coroners had virtually no payment except what they could get by extortion;[33] to them it was a matter of financial interest for the districts to be respected. At least three county coroners were verderers of Morfe Forest during their coronerships: John of Upton[34] (fl. as coroner 1347–c. 1362),[35] Philip Callaughton[36] (fl. 1400–c. 1404),[37] and Roger Drayton[38] (fl. 1405–c. 1419).[39] The two last named are known to have been successive coroners for the south-east.[40] Morfe Forest was evidently outside the coroners' jurisdiction, as were some royal forests in other counties.[41] Possible difficulties were avoided when the offices of verderer and south-east coroner were given to one man. In 1400, however, an inquest in the forest was held jointly by William Worthen, the south-east coroner, and Thomas of Gatacre, a verderer.[42] The highest recorded number of inquests held by one coroner in a year was 25, by Roger Praers in 1367–8.[43]

The coroners of Shropshire, as of all counties,[44] belonged to a somewhat lower class than the county leaders. Of the small proportion of coroners whose names are known, none served as justice of the peace or escheator. William Worthen (fl. 1393–1400)[45] was sheriff 1395–6.[46] Roger Drayton occurs as a sheriff's bailiff in 1404.[47] William Poyner (fl. 1400–15)[48] was a juror at quarter sessions in 1388[49] and during the period 1400–12,[50] and foreman of Bradford hundred jury at the King's Bench visitation of 1414.[51] John Greete (fl. 1419–21)[52] was foreman for Overs hundred on the same occasion.[53] At various times in Henry IV's reign William Worthen, William Skirmeston, John Hodnet (fl. 1401–4),[54] Philip Callaughton, Thomas Bowdler (fl. 1406–9),[55] John Blyke (fl. 1413–14),[56] and Roger Drayton were jurors at quarter sessions.[57] Humphrey Blyke occurs as coroner 1491–3.[58] He was probably a Shrewsbury lawyer, M.P. for Bridgnorth 1491–2, and attorney for Shrewsbury corporation c. 1503.[59] There is no evidence from Shrop-

[27] J.I. 2/142 rott. 3–6.
[28] J.I. 2/144–51.
[29] T.S.A.S. 3rd ser. v. 49.
[30] J.I. 2/147–8; Cal. Close, 1402–5, 30.
[31] Hunnisett, op. cit. 136.
[32] 3 Hen. VII, c. 2.
[33] Hunnisett, op. cit. 121–2.
[34] Cal. Close, 1360–4, 312.
[35] Ibid. 313; J.I. 3/131 rott. 14d., 25d.; Cal. Pat. 1358–61, 98.
[36] Cal. Close, 1405–9, 21.
[37] Ibid. 1402–5, 392; J.I. 2/145 rot. 2 and d.
[38] Cal. Close, 1419–22, 1.
[39] Ibid.; J.I. 2/151.
[40] J.I. 2/145 rot. 2 and d.; J.I. 2/151.
[41] Hunnisett, op. cit. 146–7.
[42] J.I. 2/146 rot. 2.
[43] J.I. 2/142 rott. 1, 2 and d.
[44] Hunnisett, op. cit. 169–71. In Wilts., however, some were kts. of the shire or J.P.s: V.C.H. Wilts. v. 28.

[45] J.I. 2/146.
[46] List of Sheriffs, 118.
[47] B.L. Add. Ch. 66896. Thanks are due to Mr. J. B. Lawson for this ref.
[48] J.I. 2/148; Cal. Close, 1413–19, 237.
[49] Sel. Cases in K.B. vii, p. 62.
[50] Salop. Peace Roll, 1400–14, 132.
[51] J.I. 1/753 rot. 12 (2).
[52] Cal. Inq. Misc. vii, pp. 347–8; Cal. Close, 1419–22, 177.
[53] J.I. 1/753 rot. 18.
[54] J.I. 2/145 rot. 1; Cal. Close, 1402–5, 392.
[55] J.I. 2/149.
[56] J.I. 2/145 rot. 12 and d.
[57] Salop. Peace Roll, 1400–14, 118–20, 122, 126, 135, 139.
[58] T.S.A.S. 2nd ser. xi. 19.
[59] Owen and Blakeway, Hist. Shrews. i. 274; Wedgwood, Hist. Parl. 1439–1509: Biogs. 82–3. A Humph. Blyke of Ludlow, gent. (perhaps the coroner), occurs 1506: S.R.O. 85/6.

shire or, with minor exceptions, elsewhere[60] that coronerships were ever hereditary. The 13th-century tendency of coroners to belong to particular families remained in the 14th century[61] and perhaps beyond; John Blyke and Humphrey Blyke may have been related.

The Escheator and the Feodary

In the years 1327–32 and 1335–40 Shropshire was included in the 'grand' escheatry south of Trent.[62] In the years 1332–5 and 1340–1 the county was part of an escheatry that corresponded in area to the 'Oxford' assize circuit.[63] From 1341 to 1401 Shropshire and Staffordshire formed a single escheatry; thereafter Shropshire had a separate escheator.[64] Before Henry IV's accession escheatorships often lasted two or more years[65] but afterwards annual appointments were normal. In Edward IV's reign an unusually high proportion of Shropshire escheators were re-appointed for separate terms, perhaps revealing a tendency on the Crown's part to prefer the services of a small group of well-tried men. After 1341 about a quarter of the appointees served as sheriffs. Only in the periods 1341–5 and 1389–90 were the offices held concurrently by one man, but it was not uncommon for one man to hold them consecutively. In such instances, in the 14th century, it was usually the shrievalty that was held first; thereafter it was almost always the escheatorship.[66] Thus it seems that the 15th century saw a decline in the relative standing of the escheator.[67] Shropshire escheators in the 15th century were often first appointed before the age of 30.[68] Until Elizabeth I's reign escheators and magistrates had, in Shropshire and elsewhere,[69] roughly comparable standing, the escheator's decline being matched by the widening membership of the peace commission. After 1558, however, such men as held both positions were normally appointed first as escheators and only later as magistrates.[70]

The first Shropshire feodary, who served also for Staffordshire, was appointed in 1513.[71] Most appointees later became Shropshire magistrates.[72] The post was a permanent one and appropriate for a promising young man: Reynold Corbet (occurs 1543)[73] became a justice of Queen's Bench;[74] George Bromley (occurs 1559–60)[75] became chief justice of Chester and a potential speaker of the House of Commons.[76] The feodary enjoyed patronage in his choice of deputy: Bromley appointed his father-in-law.[77] Shropshire feodaries had a distinctly higher social standing than their contemporary escheators.[78]

The Militia and the Lieutenancy

Of the procedures available to the Crown for raising troops in the county, the feudal summons had fallen into disuse by the 14th century.[79] The *posse comitatus*, the able-bodied men of the shire whom the sheriff could summon to help to keep the peace, was of limited military value, though it was summoned in Shropshire in Henry IV's reign

[60] Hunnisett, *Med. Coroner*, 150.
[61] See p. 28.
[62] *List of Escheators*, 5.
[63] Ibid. 52.   [64] Ibid. 130–6.
[65] Contrary to a statute of 1340: 14 Edw. III, c. 8.
[66] *List of Escheators; List of Sheriffs*, 117–19.
[67] H. E. Bell, *Intro. to Hist. and Rec. of Ct. of Wards and Liveries* (1953), 42, notes a decline by the 17th cent.
[68] *List of Escheators*; Wedgwood, op. cit.
[69] Bellamy, 'Parliamentary Representatives', p. ix.
[70] *List of Escheators*, compared with lists of J.P.s noted above, p. 55 n. 4.
[71] *L. & P. Hen. VIII*, i(2), p. 995. He was John Wellys,

probably the Staffs. J.P., escheator, and M.P. of that name (d. 1528): Somerville, *Hist. Duchy of Lanc.* i. 544.
[72] Most feodaries occur in: *L. & P. Hen. VIII; Cal. Pat.* Others occur in: S.R.O. 212, box 369, inqs. p. m., 1578, 1590; Hist. MSS. Com. 9, *Salisbury*, x, p. 94.
[73] *L. & P. Hen. VIII*, xviii(1), p. 446.
[74] *D.N.B.*
[75] *Cal. Pat.* 1558–60, 148, 271.
[76] *T.S.A.S.* 4th ser. xi. 47; liv. 184.
[77] Ibid. 4th ser. xi. 47; *Cal. Pat.* 1560–3, 396.
[78] No known Salop. feodary was ever escheator: *List of Escheators*, 133–6.
[79] *Eng. Historical Doc.* iv, ed. A. R. Myers, p. 951.

to fight the Welsh rebels.[80] In the 14th and 15th centuries the most effective forces were those raised by contracts between the king and his magnates, and between them and lesser men.[81] Lords could also expect customary service from their tenants. By the 16th century, however, social changes rendered the contractual system ineffective; there were fewer magnates able to command large retinues, and tenants were ready to resist their lords' demands. A Shropshire incident of 1542 illustrates the difficulty: eight tenants of Ackleton manor refused to be recruited by their lord, declaring that they did not hold their land by military service and owed obedience only to the county commissioners of array.[82] Thus in the 16th century the county militia, a more ancient force than either the feudal host or the indentured retinues, became the body upon which national defence depended.[83]

The militia, defined by the Statute of Winchester, 1285,[84] as all able-bodied men below the age of sixty, had long been a valued source of men.[85] From 1338 to 1359 the keepers and justices of the peace had power to array the county militia. Before and after that period separate array commissions were issued to groups of local men.[86] Before 1338 the Shropshire commissioners were virtually the same men as the keepers and justices;[87] after 1359 they were apparently somewhat fewer in number than the keepers and justices but were drawn from the same class, with the sheriff added *ex officio*.[88] In the later 14th century the Lords Burnell, Nicholas and Hugh, appear successively to have led the array commissioners[89] as they did the keepers and justices.[90] In Richard II's reign, however, the composition of the array commission seems to have been less affected than that of the peace commission by local interests: Hugh, Lord Burnell, was dismissed from the bench[91] but not from the array commission.[92] In the struggle against Welsh rebels during Henry IV's reign a number of array commissions were issued for Shropshire[93] but thereafter they were renewed only rarely, in Shropshire[94] and everywhere else,[95] until the beginning of the dynastic struggle in the 1450s. Commissions were then renewed frequently, their membership, like that of the peace commissions, reflecting the changes of government. The array commission remained smaller than the peace commission, but all its members were by then magistrates.[96]

For many years after 1485 array commissions were again rarely issued. By Henry VIII's reign it appears that the arrayers and the magistrates had become virtually synonymous; in the Shropshire muster certificates of 1542 the terms are used interchangeably.[97] The commissioners of Henry VIII's time, and probably before that, normally divided themselves up and took musters in the various hundreds.[98] In Elizabeth I's reign the leading array commissioners became, in Shropshire[99] as in Norfolk,[1] a select body of the whole resident magistracy. That magistracy was divided up as before to take musters in the various hundreds and boroughs.[2]

[80] *Cal. Pat.* 1399–1401, 357; *Cal. Close*, 1399–1402, 371; 1402–5, 26.
[81] *Eng. Hist. Doc.* iv, pp. 396, 951–2.
[82] J. J. Goring, 'Social Change and Military Decline in mid-Tudor Eng.', *History*, lx. 188–9.
[83] Ibid. 196.
[84] 13 Edw. I, Stat. II, c. 6.
[85] *Eng. Hist. Doc.* iv, pp. 383–4; *T.S.A.S.* 3rd ser. v. 141–8.
[86] Putnam, *Proceedings*, p. xxviii.
[87] *Cal. Pat.* 1330–4, 419; 1334–8, 138; *Cal. Close*, 1333–7, 470.
[88] *Cal. Pat.* 1358–61, 407; 1364–7, 364, 430; 1374–7, 500; *Cal. Close*, 1360–4, 54.
[89] Nic. named first in array coms. 1377: *Cal. Pat.* 1374–7, 500; 1377–81, 40. Hugh named first 1385, 1392, 1403: ibid. 1381–5, 590; 1391–6, 93; 1401–5, 288. Hugh 'and fellows' occur 1386: *Cal. Close*, 1385–9, 60.
[90] See p. 62.

[91] See p. 56.
[92] *Cal. Pat.* 1391–6, 93.
[93] Ibid. 1401–5, 138, 288, 438; 1405–8, 6, 147.
[94] Ibid. 1416–22, 198; 1429–36, 524.
[95] M. R. Powicke, *Military Obligation in Medieval Eng.* (1962), 220.
[96] *Cal. Pat.* 1452–61, 403, 558, 604; 1461–7, 98; 1467–77, 195, 284, 429; 1476–85, 401, 491.
[97] *L. & P. Hen. VIII*, xvii, pp. 507–9.
[98] Ibid. xiv(1), pp. 287–8.
[99] S.P. 12/54 ff. 21–2; S.P. 12/91 no. 46; *Acts of P.C.* 1578–80, 263; B.L. Harl. MS. 474, f. 84; Staffs. R.O., D.(W.) 1788/V.19, 3 Nov. 1590; N.L.W., Ottley Papers, uncat., Ric. Ottley's letter bk. 1590–7, 18 Nov. 1596.
[1] Smith, *County and Court*, 114.
[2] *T.S.A.S.* 2nd ser. ii. 230–2; S.P. 12/117 no. 18; Staffs. R.O., D.(W.) 1788/V.19, *passim*; N.L.W., Ottley Papers, uncat., Ric. Ottley's letter bk. 1590–7, 18 Sept. 1590; 18 May 1593; 21 Sept., 18 Nov. 1596.

Before 1586 high-ranking men or small groups of such men were appointed in emergencies to take command of the forces of a group of counties, of which Shropshire would be one. Those men, sometimes termed 'lieutenants', acted in co-operation with the contemporary array commissioners.[3] During Henry VIII's reign, as the militia assumed increasing importance, such appointments became commoner and Shropshire was regularly included in the lieutenancy of the 'north'.[4] From Lord Williams's time (1559–60) the president of the Council in the Marches sometimes received array commissions for the counties within its jurisdiction, including Shropshire, and thus acted as lieutenant. He seems often to have delegated the duties to the council as a whole.[5] In 1569 Sir Andrew Corbet, the leading Shropshire array commissioner,[6] was temporarily appointed lieutenant of Shropshire. In 1585 permanent lieutenants began to be appointed throughout the country.[7] Immediately upon Sir Henry Sidney's death in May 1586[8] the counties within the council's jurisdiction were placed under lieutenants,[9] and the earl of Shrewsbury occurs later in the year as lieutenant of Shropshire, Staffordshire, and Derbyshire.[10] In 1587 the new president, the earl of Pembroke, was made lieutenant of all the counties under the council except Gloucestershire. He died in office in 1601 and was replaced as president and lieutenant by Lord Zouche.[11]

Deputy lieutenants first occur in England and Wales in Elizabeth I's reign.[12] Between 1576 and 1590 there were concurrently two deputy lieutenants in Shropshire, Sir Arthur Mainwaring and Edward (later Sir Edward) Leighton.[13] With Corbet they seem to have been a controlling committee within the muster commissioners.[14] In 1590 their number was increased in Shropshire to three.[15] When Leighton died in 1593[16] the number reverted to two until 1597, when it was increased to five.[17] In 1600 two of the deputies died and another had become old and inactive; three new deputies were added, thus keeping the number of active deputies at five while bringing the total to six.[18] As in Wiltshire[19] the 1590s saw notable increases in Shropshire in the number of deputies. Nearly all the deputies were among the leading magistrates.[20]

To maintain the numbers and armament of the militia the county authorities faced administrative tasks of a scale then hardly equalled in other spheres of local government. In 1524 the Shropshire militia numbered some 3,000, of whom about a third were archers and the rest billmen.[21] In 1562 a commission headed by the president of the Council in the Marches was appointed to inquire in Shropshire into the working of the 1558 Militia Act.[22] In 1569, however, the whole Shropshire militia had no more than 1,300 men. Of those only 351 were armed, 116 with firearms, 102 with bows and arrows.[23] Lack of numbers and equipment was a serious problem throughout the country.[24] In Shropshire the muster commissioners reported discontent among the men over subsistence payments during the frequent musters. The commissioners claimed that a

[3] e.g. *Cal. Talbot Papers* (Derb. Arch. Soc. Rec. Ser. iv), 23.

[4] *Cal. Pat.* 1338–40, 134; 1401–5, 138, 216, 294; 1452–61, 606, 647–8, 659; 1461–7, 31, 36, 391; 1467–77, 103, 281, 289; 1476–85, 356, 363; *L. & P. Hen. VIII*, i(1), p. 758; i(2), p. 1243; iii(2), pp. 1027, 1211, 1425; v, p. 632; xx(1), pp. 306, 415; Gladys S. Thomson, *Lords Lieutenants in the 16th Cent.* (1923), 23, 150, 156; *Acts of P.C.* 1547–50, 119; *Cal. Talbot Papers*, 36, 300; *Cal. S.P. Dom.* 1547–80, 349; Addenda 1566–79, 228–9.

[5] *Cal. S.P. Dom.* 1547–80, 139; *Acts of P.C.* 1578–80, 262–4; Williams, *Council in Marches*, 112–13; *Reg. Council in Marches of Wales*, 160–1, 163–5.

[6] Signs first 1569: S.P. 12/54 f. 22.

[7] Hist. MSS. Com. 9, *Salisbury*, i, p. 443; J. C. Sainty, *Lieutenants of Counties, 1585–1642* (Bull. Inst. Hist. Res. Special Suppl. viii), 3.

[8] *D.N.B.*

[9] Thomson, op. cit. 160.

[10] *Cal. S.P. Dom.* 1581–90, 370; Sainty, op. cit. 17.

[11] Sainty, op. cit. 38.

[12] Ibid. 7.

[13] S.P. 12/107 no. 15; Hist. MSS. Com. 41, *15th Rep. V, Foljambe*, p. 26; *T.S.A.S.* 2nd ser. iii. 101.

[14] S.P. 12/117 no. 18; N.L.W., Ottley Papers, uncat., Ric. Ottley's letter Bk. 1590–7, 3 Nov. 1590.

[15] *Acts of P.C.* 1590–1, 23.

[16] *T.S.A.S.* 4th ser. xi. 40.

[17] C 231/1 f. 28v.; N.L.W., MS. 7895 E, 22 Mar. 1600.

[18] *Acts of P.C.* 1599–1600, 399–400. For Kynaston's death: *T.S.A.S.* 4th ser. x. 294.

[19] *V.C.H. Wilts.* v. 82.

[20] See pp. 65–7.

[21] *L. & P. Hen. VIII*, iv(1), p. 425.

[22] *T.S.A.S.* 2nd ser. ii. 221–2.

[23] S.P. 12/54 f. 36.

[24] L. Boynton, *Elizabethan Militia* (1967), 63.

discontented militia, if well organized, might even present a threat to the state: 'when they feel themselves strong we doubt their imaginations'.[25] That might have been a convenient excuse for inactivity. Both then and in 1573 the Shropshire commissioners, like those of other counties,[26] thought it dangerous and expensive to put firearms into the men's hands in peace time.[27] By 1573, however, the government had put repeated pressure on the counties[28] and the total Shropshire militia had risen to 2,040 men, of whom 640 were armed, 200 with firearms. Some additional forces were still provided by noblemen from among their employees, who were thus not held liable for militia duty.[29]

The numbers mustered and armed continued to increase. By 1575 there were 2,440 men, excluding men of Shrewsbury and Ludlow, of whom 1,248 were armed.[30] Selection of the best men for special training had been introduced throughout the country in 1573[31] and by 1577 those 'trained' men numbered 250 in Shropshire, or 300 with Shrewsbury and Ludlow.[32] Until the 1580s the numbers of 'able' men, or the whole militia, and the proportions of armed and trained men, remained about the same.[33] In 1587, however, with growing threats of a Spanish invasion, the number of trained men was increased in Shropshire to 600.[34] Efficient mustering remained difficult Those men of wealth who were charged with supplying horses appear to have been especially negligent. In 1590 the deputy lieutenants felt that they had inadequate powers to deal with those who evaded service. They were dissatisfied, too, with the haphazard customary manner of choosing petty constables, upon whom the militia organization ultimately depended, and recommended that their appointment be vested in the deputies.[35] It appears that by 1595 a muster-master, an experienced soldier directed by the government to be appointed to supervise training, had not been appointed in Shropshire.[36] One had been appointed by 1596 and was paid by a special county rate.[37]

The revival of the militia as a source of active troops dates from 1545, when a Franco-Scottish invasion was feared. Thereafter it was common for members of the militia to be called up for active service.[38] In the second half of Elizabeth's reign Wales and the marcher counties, being near the ports of embarkation, were especially convenient for the recruitment of troops for Ireland.[39] Men for Ireland were called up at an increasing rate from the Shropshire militia,[40] and by 1590 the county militia seems to have included two small contingents maintained in readiness for service in Ireland and in the north respectively.[41] In 1600 and 1602 the quality of Shropshire's Irish levies compared favourably with those of some other counties.[42] Some easy method had to be devised for distributing the burden of active service equally whenever troops were called up. In the 16th century a system of 'allotments' was arranged in Shropshire by dividing up the hundreds and larger boroughs so as to create 100 equal divisions of the county: each such 'allotment' would provide one man in every 100 called up. The system was in use by

[25] S.P. 12/54 ff. 21–2.
[26] Boynton, op. cit. 62.
[27] S.P. 12/54 f. 22; S.P. 12/91 no. 46.
[28] Boynton, op. cit. 63–4.
[29] S.P. 12/91 no. 46. The earl of Shrewsbury's Salop. tenants were separately mustered in 1588: Cal. Shrews. Papers (Derb. Arch. Soc. Rec. Ser. i), 96, 108; Cal. Talbot Papers, 307.
[30] B.L. Lansd. MS. 683, f. 13v.
[31] Boynton, op. cit. 91.
[32] B.L. Lansd. MS. 683, f. 18v.
[33] S.P. 12/117 no. 18i; T.S.A.S. 2nd ser. ii. 252.
[34] Hist. MSS. Com. 41, 15th Rep. V, Foljambe, pp. 20–2.
[35] S.P. 12/203 no. 33.
[36] N.L.W., Ottley Papers, uncat., Ric. Ottley's letter bk. 1590–7, 17 Aug. 1595.

[37] Ibid. 18 Nov. 1596. Northants. had a muster-master by 1586: Northants. Lieutenancy Papers (Northants. Rec. Soc. xxvii), 21.
[38] History, lx. 194.
[39] Williams, Council in Marches, 115–17.
[40] Acts of P.C. 1580–1, 106, 361; 1589–90, 143, 298; 1597, 27; 1598–9, 491, 544, 576; 1599–1600, 416, 798; 1601–4, 82, 226, 242, 476; T.S.A.S. iii. 314, 338, 349; Cal. S.P. Dom. 1581–90, 651; 1591–4, 495; N.L.W., Ottley Papers, uncat., Ric. Ottley's letter bk. 1590–7, 25 July 1591; 5 May 1593; 26 Mar. 1595; 27 Aug. 1596.
[41] Staffs. R.O., D.(W.) 1788/V.19, 4 and 18 Oct. 1590; S.R.O. 1374/323; N.L.W., Ottley Papers, uncat., Ric. Ottley's letter bk. 1590–7, 18 May 1593; 8 Dec. 1595; 4 May 1596.
[42] Hist. MSS. Com. 9, Salisbury, xii, p. 164; xvi, p. 148.

1590[43] and proved equally helpful as a means of assessing local contributions to some kinds of county rates.[44]

Other Commissions

County commissions other than those of the peace and of array were concerned with criminal, financial, economic, and religious matters. They were sometimes more effective in emergencies than the peace and gaol-delivery commissions, having greater powers, but were appointed much less often and did not attain the permanent standing of quarter sessions and assizes.

General and special commissions of oyer and terminer were issued when serious crimes attracted special government attention. Those affecting Shropshire were issued most frequently in the 14th century.[45] Sometimes a commission was stated to have been issued because the magistrates had failed to deal with offenders.[46] Both general and special commissions normally included leaders of the Shropshire magistracy and some non-resident lawyers. Special oyer and terminer commissions, concerned with a particular offender or group of offenders, seem not to have been issued for Shropshire after about 1400.[47] General commissions were usually issued for a group of counties, of which Shropshire would be one. From the later 15th century those general commissions were directed to the Council in the Marches,[48] providing the sanction for the council's criminal jurisdiction.[49] General commissions were especially used to check the misdeeds of local officials,[50] as in 1331[51] and 1340,[52] and to enforce order at periods of exceptional unrest, as in 1381–2[53] (the Great Revolt), 1452[54] (Yorkist risings),[55] and 1459–62, 1468, and 1470[56] (the dynastic struggle).

Little is known of their proceedings. Those commissioners appointed in 1341 sat continuously for three weeks. The general oyer and terminer justices appointed for Shropshire on 6 May 1363 sat at least thirteen times between May 1363 and July 1364, usually at Ludlow or Shrewsbury and at least once at Bridgnorth. The numerous sittings occurred because people indicted at one sitting failed to appear at the next two and were exacted and outlawed in the county court, requiring a fourth sitting of the commissioners to receive formal notification of the outlawry.[57] So many sittings for so little result do not suggest that the commission achieved its object. General and special commissions of inquiry, without determining powers, were issued on similar occasions and to similar people.[58] They were evidently part of the same governmental effort to reinforce the work of the magistrates and the justices of gaol delivery. It is doubtful whether the effort was successful; in the hands of Bishop Lee the general oyer and terminer commission was a formidable weapon against criminals,[59] but in less courageous hands it can have been little more effective than the commission of the peace.

Inquiry commissions were set up from time to time to investigate matters affecting

[43] N.L.W., Ottley Papers, uncat., Ric. Ottley's letter bk. 1590–7, 29 Sept. 1590; 18 May 1593; 18 Nov. 1596; S.R.O., q. sess. order bk. 1, schedule 14 July 1638.
[44] See p. 102.
[45] Besides those cited below, the following are noted: Cal. Pat. 1327–30, 297; 1330–4, 133; 1334–8, 368; 1340–3, 204, 539, 543; 1345–8, 35; 1348–50, 170; 1350–4, 336; 1354–8, 385, 454; 1358–61, 79, 162; 1361–4, 366; 1370–4, 310–11, 487; 1374–5, 55; 1381–5, 496; 1401–5, 195, 426; 1563–6, pp. 41–2, 105; Cal. Close, 1330–3, 425, 537; 1333–7, 88.
[46] Cal. Pat. 1330–4, 445, 573; 1348–50, 318–19.
[47] On a rare 17th-cent. instance see p. 109.
[48] Cal. Pat. 1467–77, 574; 1476–85, 5, 322; 1563–6, p. 180; L. & P. Hen. VIII, i(1), pp. 195, 605–6; i(2), p. 933; iii(2), p. 915; xiii(1), p. 563; xiv(1), pp. 158–9;

C 181/1 ff. 32v.–33.
[49] Williams, Council in Marches, 13, 49–50.
[50] Putnam, Proceedings, p. xxxix.
[51] Cal. Pat. 1330–4, 133, 138. [52] Ibid. 1340–3, 112.
[53] Ibid. 1381–5, 84–5, 138, 141, 247.
[54] Ibid. 1446–52, 580–1.
[55] R. L. Storey, End of Ho. of Lancaster (1966), 99.
[56] Cal. Pat. 1452–61, 557, 564–5; 1461–7, 132–3; 1467–77, 55, 69–70, 249.
[57] J.I. 1/748 rott. 1–2d.; J.I. 1/749 rot. 3.
[58] Cal. Pat. 1354–8, 449, 547–8; 1367–70, 204; 1374–7, 226, 311; 1381–5, 495–6; 1388–92, 142; 1399–1401, 554; 1401–5, 127; 1405–8, 474; 1408–13, 432; 1416–22, 269; 1436–41, 269; 1452–61, 120, 442, 516, 608; 1467–77, 247; 1485–94, 393.
[59] See p. 71.

royal revenues, either in the county or a group of counties generally or in special cases.[60] Vigilance was needed to prevent local frauds, in which there might be attempts to conceal or misappropriate escheats, wardships, temporalities of vacant sees, and other sources of royal income. Leading magistrates were usually among the commissioners, and the sheriff and escheator were sometimes included. Royal taxes required commissioners with local knowledge, to make the assessments and appoint collectors,[61] and the usual county leaders were included. Misappropriation inevitably occurred from time to time.[62] On the other hand collectors took a personal risk, for it was they who had to face the taxpayers. In the early years of Henry V, a time of outstanding lawlessness in Shropshire, two subsidy collectors were assaulted, one of them nearly fatally, in the course of their duties,[63] and were eventually pardoned for arrears that they were unable to collect.[64] Forced loans, which became common in the 15th century,[65] required similar arrangements.[66] Attempts to avoid paying, and the occasional concealment of the proceeds, were likewise inevitable.[67]

Justices of labourers were appointed in each county in the period 1352–9; thereafter the keepers and justices of the peace were normally responsible for regulating wages.[68] Three commissions were issued appointing justices of labourers in Shropshire, in 1354, 1355, and 1357.[69] Of the six men named in the commissions, three occurred in more than one, and those three were the only magistrates among the six. It thus seems likely that the justices of labourers were led by the magistrates among them. From time to time commissions of inquiry into weights and measures were set up for Shropshire and Staffordshire jointly, most often in the 14th century.[70] Usually, however, power to enforce standard weights and measures was vested in the magistrates.[71]

Another commission affecting the economy of Shropshire was that appointed occasionally, under an Act of 1399,[72] to enforce the removal of obstructions, mostly fish weirs, from the county's rivers, especially the Severn.[73] In 1424 there were seven commissioners, in 1427 six. They consisted of the leading magistrates with two professional lawyers; their jurisdiction included all the rivers of Shropshire.[74] In 1473 a commission was appointed to inquire into embanking and draining along the Severn between Worcester bridge and the Breidden. Some of its members were Shropshire magistrates.[75] In the 15th century water bailiffs were appointed by the Crown to search for nuisances on the Severn.[76] In 1575 a commission was set up to inquire by jury into obstructions in the Shropshire part of the Severn. It consisted of thirteen men, nearly all of them county magistrates,[77] headed by the president of the Council in the Marches. They sat at Shrewsbury and made eleven orders. Apart from the alteration or removal of 28 fish weirs, they ordered all trees to be felled within forty feet of the banks to

[60] Cal. Pat. 1327–30, 287–8, 574; 1338–40, 148; 1343–5, 280–1; 1345–8, 181; 1348–50, 456; 1361–4, 546; 1364–7, 202; 1377–81, 417; 1381–5, 567; 1405–8, 154; 1416–22, 207, 269, 390; 1422–9, 361, 467; 1429–36, 275, 426, 526; 1436–41, 449, 539; 1446–52, 140; 1452–61, 169; 1467–77, 407; 1476–85, 393; Cal. Close, 1409–13, 107, 169.

[61] e.g. Cal. Pat. 1327–30, 173; 1330–4, 312, 358; 1334–8, 39; 1338–40, 501; 1358–61, 346; 1408–13, 380; 1429–36, 137; 1436–41, 537; 1476–85, 354, 396; Cal. Close, 1337–9, 439; 1377–81, 425–6; 1409–13, 92, 220–1; L. & P. Hen. VIII, iii(2), p. 1457; iv(1), p. 234.

[62] e.g. Cal. Pat. 1345–8, 395–6.

[63] J.I. 1/753 rott. 13(1), 25(1); T.S.A.S. 3rd ser. vii. 395–6.

[64] Cal. Pat. 1416–22, 28.

[65] Eng. Hist. Doc. iv, pp. 375–6.

[66] Cal. Pat. 1405–8, 200; 1408–13, 204; 1422–9, 354, 481; 1429–36, 50, 126, 354; 1436–41, 249, 505; 1441–6, 430; 1446–52, 299; 1452–61, 53; 1485–94, 355; Hist. MSS. Com. 55, Var. Coll. ii, p. 316; L. & P. Hen. VIII,

iv(1), p. 82; iv(3), p. 2735; xviii(1), p. 478; Acts of P.C. 1556–8, 192; 1590–1, 187; Cal. S.P. Dom. 1581–90, 580; S.R.O. 1060/466, f. 3.

[67] L. & P. Hen. VIII, vi, p. 31; Hist. MSS. Com. 9, Salisbury, i, pp. 272–3.

[68] Putnam, Proceedings, pp. xliv–xlv.

[69] Cal. Pat. 1354–8, 60, 294, 550. Shrews. had separate coms.: ibid. 392–3.

[70] Ibid. 1343–5, 283; 1391–6, 356, 590; Cal. Close, 1396–9, 495; 1405–9, 466.

[71] Putnam, op. cit., p. xxviii. In 1422 the Salop. J.P.s were commissioned (with the sheriff, escheator, and 2 laymen) to inquire into false weights: Cal. Pat. 1416–22, 423.

[72] 1 Hen. IV, c. 12.   [73] e.g. V.C.H. Salop. i. 419.

[74] Cal. Pat. 1422–9, 276, 467.

[75] Ibid. 1467–77, 354.

[76] Ibid. 1446–52, 252; 1485–94, 55.

[77] Ric. Lee was apptd. J.P. after 1579: S.P. 12/145 ff. 35v.–37; Reg. Council in Marches of Wales, 216.

allow the hauling of barges, and all weirs erected in the previous fifty years to be removed.[78] The orders demanded much and suggest that the river had for years been obstructed with impunity.

Inclosure and depopulation were the subject of inquiry commissions appointed for many counties in 1517 and Shropshire was one of six counties under a single commission. The five commissioners included, for Shropshire, Sir Thomas Leighton and Sir Thomas Cornewall; both were county magistrates and both had recently added new inclosures to their parks. They were to inquire what buildings had been demolished since 1488, how much arable converted to pasture, and how much imparked. Shropshire was not among those counties where recent depopulation had been intense; the commissioners' returns, arranged by hundreds, record some 58 houses vacated and 344 persons displaced. Few of the landlords cited in the returns suffered prosecution.[79]

Lay commissioners were concerned in religious matters: to suppress forms of belief that threatened the security of the realm, to regulate the administration of royal foundations,[80] and at the Reformation to assist in the confiscation of church property. In Henry V's time Lollardy was strong in the west Midlands. During the period 1414–17 Sir John Oldcastle, the outlawed Lollard rebel, was allegedly harboured by the abbot of Shrewsbury and the prior of Wenlock.[81] A commission to seek out and imprison Lollards was issued for Shropshire, as for many other counties, in 1414.[82] The Shropshire commission consisted of the leading magistrates,[83] one of whom, Lord Charlton, captured Oldcastle near Welshpool (Mont.) in 1417.[84]

After the Reformation, and especially after 1570 when Roman Catholicism was increasingly associated with treason,[85] county commissioners were appointed from time to time to enforce religious conformity.[86] There were some dangerous elements in Shropshire society: Lawrence Bannister (d. 1588)[87] of Wem, a steward of the duke of Norfolk and well connected in county society,[88] was implicated locally in both the Ridolfi Plot (1571)[89] and the Babington Plot (1586).[90] In 1573 an oyer and terminer commission, headed by the president of the Council in the Marches, was appointed to enforce the Act of Uniformity in Shropshire;[91] it sat at Shrewsbury.[92] In 1581 two Shropshire magistrates, Jerome Corbet and his nephew Robert Corbet,[93] were acting under a commission from the Privy Council and the bishop of Coventry and Lichfield to inquire into Shropshire persons not conformable in religion.[94] In 1584 or 1585, following the Throckmorton Plot and other suspected conspiracies, a commission of six resident magistrates headed by Sir George Bromley, a keen pursuer of Roman Catholics,[95] was appointed to disarm recusants in Shropshire.[96] In 1591 commissions were issued for every county to search out Jesuits and seminary priests,[97] and c. 1597 Sir Edward Kynaston, a Shropshire magistrate, was ordered by the lord chamberlain to search for a priest at Llwynymaen (in Oswestry).[98] In 1600 two Shropshire justices were commissioned to search places in Shropshire and neighbouring counties where priests were harboured, and to examine suspects and commit them for trial.[99] The

[78] Hist. MSS. Com. 13, *10th Rep. IV, Gatacre*, pp. 443–4.
[79] M. Beresford, *Lost Villages of Eng.* (1965), 106–7, 220–1; *T.S.A.S.* 4th ser. xi. 210, 212. Salop. remained quiet during the 1549 inclosure riots: *Cal. Talbot Papers*, 28.
[80] e.g. *V.C.H. Salop.* ii. 107.
[81] Jacob, *15th Cent.* 133.   [82] Ibid. 131.
[83] *Cal. Pat. 1413–16*, 178.
[84] *D.N.B. sub* Oldcastle, Sir John.
[85] G. R. Elton, *Tudor Constitution* (1965), 410–11.
[86] R. B. Manning, 'Elizabethan Recusancy Commissions', *Historical Jnl.* xv. 23–36.
[87] *S.P.R. Lich.* ix. 112.
[88] *Visit. Salop. 1623*, i. 101–2.
[89] C. Hamshere, 'The Ridolfi Plot, 1571', *History Today*, xxvi. 38 (thanks are due to Mr. H. D. G. Foxall for this ref.); Hist. MSS. Com. 9, *Salisbury*, i, p. 521.
[90] *Cal. S.P. Dom. 1581–90*, 370.
[91] *Reg. Council in Marches of Wales*, 104–5.
[92] *T.S.A.S.* iii. 273.
[93] *Visit. Salop. 1623*, i. 136.
[94] S.P.L., Deeds 16137.
[95] Williams, *Council in Marches*, 96.
[96] B.L. Harl. MS. 474, f. 91.
[97] Smith, *County and Court*, 136; *Cal. S.P. Dom. 1591–4*, 179.
[98] *Acts of P.C.* 1596–7, 442–3.
[99] Ibid. 1599–1600, 609.

Corbets and Kynaston are known to have taken active steps to carry out their commissions. Moreover, as sheriff 1598–9, Kynaston was said to have seized 'a horseload of popish books and crucifixes' at Llwynymaen.[1] Nevertheless at the end of Elizabeth I's reign Shropshire seems to have been, like Herefordshire, a Roman Catholic stronghold.[2]

A survey of all ecclesiastical incomes was begun in 1535, to provide the basis for the annual levy of a tenth authorized by an Act of 1534.[3] In each county a commission was appointed consisting of a bishop and a number of laymen. In Shropshire the leading lay commissioner was apparently Sir Thomas Cornewall.[4] The predominantly lay element perhaps suggests that Cromwell attached particular importance to the services of the gentry.[5] Under the Act of Suppression, 1536,[6] six commissioners were appointed in each county to supervise the dissolution of the lesser monasteries. Three of them were professional government agents, the others local gentlemen.[7] The names of the Shropshire commissioners are not known;[8] in most counties, however, the professional commissioners, not the gentlemen, were the effective partners.[9] Under the Chantries Act, 1545,[10] a group of local commissioners was appointed for Staffordshire and Shropshire, to survey the possessions of chantries and other religious corporations.[11] Under the 1547 Chantries Act[12] other local commissioners were appointed for the same area, to dissolve the foundations.[13] Sir George Blount seems then to have been the senior commissioner. He was a Shropshire magistrate and an adherent of the earl of Warwick (later duke of Northumberland).[14] In 1552 commissioners were appointed in every county to take inventories of church goods and to confiscate such valuables as were deemed superfluous to the churches' needs. In Shropshire the active commissioners were county magistrates, including Sir Andrew Corbet, Sir George Blount, and Richard (later Sir Richard) Newport.[15]

[1] *Commons Debates 1621*, ed. W. Notestein and others (1935), v. 127.
[2] *V.C.H. Salop.* ii. 8.
[3] 26 Hen. VIII, c. 3.
[4] Named first in com.: *L. & P. Hen. VIII*, viii, p. 52.
[5] D. Knowles, *Religious Orders in Eng.* iii. 242.
[6] 27 Hen. VIII, c. 10.
[7] Knowles, op. cit. iii. 299–300.
[8] Ibid. 478–9.
[9] Ibid. 305.
[10] 37 Hen. VIII, c. 4.
[11] *L. & P. Hen. VIII*, xxi(1), p. 146.
[12] 1 Edw. VI, c. 14.
[13] *T.S.A.S.* 3rd ser. x. 295.
[14] Ibid. 3rd ser. viii. 125.
[15] Ibid. 2nd ser. xii. 339.

COUNTY GOVERNMENT
1603–1714

The Commission of the Peace, p. 90. Other Commissions, p. 94. Quarter Sessions, p. 94. Divisional Monthly Meetings (Petty Sessions), p. 106. The Lieutenancy and Militia, p. 107. The Sheriff, p. 109. Coroners, Escheators, and Feodaries, p. 111. County Committees 1643–60, p. 111.

THE Tudors had made the country gentry their principal agents of local government as justices of the peace, and that policy was vindicated by the events of the 17th century. Tudor county government derived its strength from the conservatism of provincial communities who accepted the rule of the leading gentry. That strength enabled the Tudor forms of county administration to survive the experiments of those 17th-century governments that sought different distributions of local power. Short-lived attempts were made by governments to replace the traditional county leaders with men of humbler origin and more radical ideas. The county community, however, did not discard its traditional loyalties so easily. The experimental benches and committees created by revolutionary governments found their leaders among those cautious local gentry who had avoided proscription, government by innovating minorities being no more practicable in Shropshire than at Westminster.

Before the Civil Wars detailed supervision of Shropshire administration was exercised by the Privy Council, the assize justices, and to a lesser extent[1] the Council in the Marches of Wales. After the Restoration the administrative controls of Privy Council and assizes were virtually withdrawn,[2] leaving to the counties an unprecedented degree of self-government. Local initiative developed and in Shropshire the late 17th and early 18th centuries saw a number of self-imposed reforms, for example in the procedure of quarter sessions and in the management of county rates.

The Commission of the Peace

The number of magistrates in the working portion[3] of the Shropshire commission varied considerably. There were about 40 in 1608,[4] 53 in 1625,[5] 33 in 1626,[6] 50 in 1642,[7] 28 in 1650,[8] 46 in 1657,[9] 50 in 1660,[10] 55 in 1680,[11] 48 in 1685,[12] 67 in 1700,[13] and 104 in 1712.[14] So far as Shropshire is concerned the figures do not support the conclusion sometimes expressed[15] that there was a marked growth in the size of county commissions throughout the 17th century. Moreover the larger fluctuations in the size of the working portion of the Shropshire commission were not accidental but resulted from political

[1] Penry Williams, *Council in Marches of Wales under Eliz. I* (1958), 196–7.

[2] Esther Moir, *Justice of Peace* (1969), 81; J. S. Cockburn, *Hist. Eng. Assizes 1558–1714* (1972), 186–7.

[3] In all cos. the com. included dignitaries who were expected to play no local part in co. govt. They are named first in the com. and it is usually possible to tell where the names of working J.P.s begin in any list. Dignitaries have been disregarded in this section.

[4] S.P. 14/33 ff. 51v.–52v.

[5] *Orders of Q. Sess.* i, preface, pp. vii–viii; C 231/4 f. 187v.

[6] B.L. Harl. MS. 1622, ff. 64v.–66.

[7] S.R.O. 840, box 29, com. 1642.

[8] C 193/13/3 ff. 53v.–54.

[9] C 193/13/5 ff. 87v.–89v.   [10] C 220/9/4 ff. 71–72v.

[11] C 193/12/4 ff. 98v.–100v.

[12] C 193/12/5 ff. 118–119v. A similar fall occurred in Herefs. and some other cos. 1680–5: L. K. J. Glassey, 'Commission of Peace, 1675–1720' (Oxford Univ. D.Phil. thesis, 1972), 20.

[13] S.R.O., q. sess. rec., box 292, com. 1700. A similar rise occurred in all cos. 1700: Glassey, op. cit. 21.

[14] S.R.O., q. sess. rec., box 292, com. July 1712.

[15] *V.C.H. Wilts.* v. 89; G. C. F. Forster, *E. Riding Justices of Peace in 17th Cent.* (1973), 21.

intervention.[16] Successive governments attached importance to the composition of the commission and, especially at times of crisis, altered its political complexion. The appointment of sympathizers and the dismissal of dissentients were usually symptoms of acute crisis and weak or unpopular government. In contemporary eyes, however, a place on the commission was a criterion of local dignity and in more settled periods the government was given, in its power to bestow or withdraw that dignity, a useful means of political persuasion toward men whose real political weight lay outside the commission of the peace.[17]

As a concession to his anti-Catholic Parliaments of 1625 Charles I purged the county commissions of Roman Catholics and their sympathizers.[18] In Shropshire 22 magistrates were removed between May 1625 and January 1626.[19] They included such known or suspected papists as Sir Charles Foxe,[20] Thomas Ireland,[21] Sir Francis Lacon,[22] and Richard (later Sir Richard) Lee.[23] In 1638, as a confrontation with Parliament became increasingly likely, Charles began to fill up the Shropshire commission with men whom he supposed friendly. Of 33 men added between July 1634 and October 1642, 29 were added after 1637.[24] After June 1641, however, some of the appointments were evidently forced by Parliament,[25] for example those of Sir John Corbet,[26] William Pierrepont,[27] Robert Corbet of Stanwardine,[28] Thomas Mytton,[29] and Humphrey Mackworth.[30]

During the First Civil War appointments fell wholly into the hands of Parliament. The first Parliamentarian commission for Shropshire was probably that of December 1644.[31] Early in 1647 relations between Parliament and the army were becoming strained and in February Parliament added eighteen men to the Shropshire commission.[32] By 1649, however, the army and the Independents had taken control of central government. Following the king's execution came a general purge of commissions of the peace.[33] In Shropshire eleven of the newcomers of 1647 had been removed by April,[34] perhaps through a commission of March 1649.[35] Another fourteen magistrates were removed by February 1650.[36] In October 1653, following the dismissal of the Rump, fourteen moderate justices,[37] roughly half the commission, were removed. They were replaced by ten men whose obscure origins suggest that they held radical views.[38] Everywhere in 1653 such men were appointed to the commissions in large numbers.[39] Under the Protectorate moderates were again appointed,[40] though the radicals of 1653

[16] See J. H. Gleason, *Justices of Peace in Eng. 1558 to 1640* (1969), 68–82.

[17] Glassey, op. cit. 5–6, 392–4.

[18] T. G. Barnes, *Somerset 1625–1640: a County's Govt. during the 'Personal Rule'* (1961), 106.

[19] *Orders of Q. Sess.* i, preface, pp. vii–viii (omits Edw. Jones, appointed May 1625: C 231/4 f. 187v.); B. L. Harl. MS. 1622, ff. 64v.–66.

[20] *T.S.A.S.* 2nd ser. xii. 156; *Cal. S.P. Dom.* 1603–10, 395.

[21] J. Miller, *Popery and Politics in Eng. 1660–1688* (1973), 65.

[22] *T.S.A.S.* 4th ser. v. 52.

[23] Mary F. Keeler, *Long Parliament 1640–1641: a Biog. Study of its Members* (1954), 246.

[24] C 231/5 pp. 156, 196, 213, 281, 287, 314, 325, 337, 374–5, 397, 404, 434, 452, 476, 481, 509, 515, 543. Twenty-three of the appointees were removed by Apr. 1649: *T.S.A.S.* 3rd ser. x. 114. Of those, 8 signed declarations supporting the king in 1642 (ibid. 2nd ser. vii. 242–3, 255); another 5 were restored to the com. soon after the Restoration (C 220/9/4 ff. 71–72v.).

[25] Seven of the appointees 1638–42 were appointed to the co. cttee., Apr. 1643: *Acts & Ords. of Interr.* ed. Firth & Rait, i. 126. Only 1 of the 7 was appointed J.P. before June 1641: C 231/5 p. 281.

[26] Removed from com. 1635 (C 231/5 p. 175), imprisoned for resisting muster-master's fees, released by Commons resolution 1641, supported Parl. in Civil Wars (*D.N.B.*).

[27] A Commons leader in Long Parl.; member Cttee. of Both Kingdoms: *D.N.B.*

[28] Maj.-gen. in Parliamentarian army: *T.S.A.S.* 4th ser. xi. 180–1.

[29] Distinguished commander in Parliamentarian army: *D.N.B.*

[30] Parliamentarian governor of Shrews.; member Council of State (*D.N.B. sub* Mackworth, Thos.), republican (*T.S.A.S.* 3rd ser. x. 109–10).

[31] C 231/6 p. 8. Cf. *Warwick Co. Records*, ii, ed. S. C. Ratcliff and H. C. Johnson, p. xiii.

[32] C 231/6 p. 74.

[33] D. Underdown, *Pride's Purge: Politics in the Puritan Revolution* (1971), 299–300.

[34] *T.S.A.S.* 3rd ser. x. 114.

[35] C 231/6 p. 143. Cf. *Warw. Co. Rec.* ii, p. xiii.

[36] C 193/13/3 ff. 53v.–54.

[37] Most were from traditional magistrate families: see e.g. S.P. 14/33 ff. 51v.–52v.; C 193/13/1 ff. 81–83v.; B.L. Harl. MS. 1622, ff. 64v.–66; C 193/13/2 ff. 56–57v. Seven were restored by Mar. 1657: C 193/13/5 ff. 87v.–89v.

[38] C 231/6 p. 271.

[39] Underdown, op. cit. 312.

[40] C 231/6 p. 343.

were not systematically removed.[41] There was by then a dearth of convinced government supporters capable of discharging local office in Shropshire.[42] Hardly any of the Shropshire justices was sympathetic to the attempted resumption of republican government in 1659.[43]

At the Restoration[44] the justices of the Interregnum were removed and replaced by royalists.[45] One of the conservative justices of the Interregnum, Job (later Sir Job) Charlton,[46] survived the purge. A few others were reinstated before 1670:[47] among them were Thomas Ketelby, Thomas Powys, William Cotton, and Sir Humphrey Briggs.[48] A period of comparative stability seems to have followed in Shropshire as in most counties:[49] no mass removals are recorded between 1660 and 1680.[50] In March 1681, however, in reaction to the Exclusionist agitation of 1678–81, Charles II's government began a general purge of Whigs and dissenters from the commissions of the peace, a policy that was to continue until the end of his reign.[51] Twenty-one Shropshire magistrates were removed from the commission between November 1680 and October 1685, and fourteen were added;[52] the principal purge appears to have been in July 1681.[53]

At James II's accession county benches were dominated by Tories, and most of the gentry in Shropshire, as in other counties, were prepared to support the king loyally.[54] The next few years saw them deeply alienated.[55] In 1687 James remodelled the commissions of the peace to include Roman Catholics; nine were put on in Shropshire.[56] In the summer of 1688 a more extensive reorganization took place, intended to win the support of dissenters in Parliament for the repeal of the penal laws and the Test Act.[57] Of the 45 Shropshire magistrates only nine (seven of whom were Roman Catholics) signified, in reply to the 'three questions', their support for repeal; two others were absent when the questions were put but seem to have indicated support later. Of the remaining 34, 24 signified opposition and 10 were absent. The proportion of opponents was among the highest in England.[58] All 34 were removed. Thirty new men, presumably Whigs or dissenters, were added to the eleven survivors.[59] The new men included some, like Thomas Mackworth,[60] Richard More,[61] Samuel Sandford,[62] and Rowland Hunt the younger,[63] who had held important positions during the Interregnum. Only four of the newcomers, Sir John Trevor,[64] Thomas Burton,[65] Thomas Mackworth,[66] and Richard More,[67] had ever been magistrates before. The inexperience and social inferiority of most of the new justices was resented throughout the English counties.[68] In September 1688, in an attempt to forestall the threatened invasion of William of Orange, James reversed the policy of the previous two years.[69] The magistrates dis-

[41] Five of the 10 remained in Mar. 1657: C 193/13/5 ff. 88v.–89.
[42] J. Berry and S. G. Lee, A Cromwellian Major General (1938), 135, 151, 154.
[43] T.S.A.S. 3rd ser. x. 153.
[44] Probably under a com. of Aug. 1660: C 231/7 p. 27.
[45] C 220/9/4 ff. 71–72v. [46] D.N.B.
[47] Similar nos. of survivors are noted elsewhere: B. Osborne, Justices of Peace 1361–1848 (1960), 127; Forster, E. Riding Justices, 27. More survived in Wilts. (V.C.H. Wilts. v. 109) and Suss. (A. Fletcher, A County Community in Peace and War: Sussex 1600–1660 (1975), 134).
[48] C 231/7 pp. 39, 88, 126, 310.
[49] Forster, op. cit. 27; Glassey, 'Com. of Peace', 46–8.
[50] C 231/7.
[51] Miller, Popery and Politics, 189, 193–4.
[52] S.N., Catalogue of the names of all His Majesty's justices of the peace (1680), 16–17; C 193/12/5 ff. 118–119v.
[53] C 231/8 p. 52. [54] Cal. S.P. Dom. 1685, 108.
[55] Moir, Justice of Peace, 82.
[56] Miller, op. cit. 209, 271. [57] Ibid. 218–19.
[58] Glassey, op. cit. 116 n.
[59] G. Duckett, Penal Laws and Test Act, ii (1883), 179–84, 265–7; C 231/8 p. 194.
[60] Protectorate M.P.: T.S.A.S. 2nd ser. vii. 27–8.
[61] Former member Cttee. for Compounding, etc.: G. E. Aylmer, The State's Servants (1973), 213–14.
[62] Former Surveyor-General Itinerant of the Excise: ibid. 253.
[63] Former member co. cttee.: Acts & Ords. of Interr. ii. 1331, 1377, 1441.
[64] J.P. 1668 (C 231/7 p. 322), removed 1681 × 1685 (E 137/38/8; C 193/12/5 ff. 118–119v.).
[65] J.P. by 1660 (C 220/9/4 f. 72), removed 1681 (C 231/8 p. 44).
[66] J.P. 1653 (C 231/6 p. 255), removed 1659 × 1660 (Orders of Q. Sess. i. 65; C 220/9/4 ff. 71–72v.).
[67] J.P. 1666 (C 231/7 p. 287), removed 1685 × 1688 (C 193/12/5 f. 119v.; Duckett, Penal Laws, ii. 179–82).
[68] Moir, Justice of Peace, 81–2.
[69] Miller, op. cit. 226.

missed in the summer were restored.[70] Public opinion, however, was not placated, and in Shropshire, as elsewhere, there were destructive anti-Catholic riots in December.[7] With the accession of William and Mary stability was eventually restored. Most of the dissenters and Whigs introduced by James were allowed, as in most counties,[72] to remain alongside their Tory predecessors: six of them were attending quarter sessions by Easter 1690, and three more by Epiphany 1692.[73] Shropshire, perhaps because it had a Whig lieutenant, was among the few counties whose commission was effectively purged in 1696 after the abortive plot against the king's life; nine men were dismissed.[74] In 1700 most of them were allowed to return.[75]

Other political upheavals followed, but less frequently.[76] In nearly all counties there was a large-scale reorganization after the Tory victory in the 1710 general election.[77] Eldred Lancelot Lee, an unpopular man who had been excluded from the Shropshire commission since the 1690s,[78] was a relative of the new lord keeper, Sir Simon Harcourt (later Lord Harcourt).[79] Lee was among 39 new men added in Shropshire in February 1711.[80] None was put out on that occasion but a year later Lee secured from Harcourt the dismissal of seven men.[81] Lord Bradford, the Whig lieutenant, was evidently powerless to prevent Lee's action and was in any case replaced as lieutenant in April 1712 by the Tory duke of Shrewsbury.[82] During Harcourt's time as lord keeper (1710–13) and lord chancellor (1713–14) 58 men were added to the Shropshire commission, one of the highest totals in England.[83] There was a sudden reversal of policy after the Whig victory of 1714.[84] Thirty-nine men were added in Shropshire, including all those removed by Harcourt, and fifteen were removed, including Lee and thirteen others appointed by Harcourt.[85] In Shropshire, as in many counties, the changes resulted in an even balance of the parties rather than a Whig predominance.[86]

The titular head of the commission of the peace was the *custos rotulorum*. After 1631 when Lord Bridgwater, who had been *custos* since 1606,[87] became lieutenant[88] the title was usually held in Shropshire by the lieutenant;[89] it was, of course, not so held during the Interregnum, when the lieutenancy was in abeyance. Except for Robert Corbet of Stanwardine[90] (occurs as *custos* 1646 × 1659)[91] and the 2nd earl of Bradford (1708–12, 1714–23)[92] the *custos*, as elsewhere,[93] did not attend quarter sessions regularly. His place was taken by a deputy *custos*; John Lacon, one of the leading justices, occurs as deputy in 1697.[94] The clerkship of the peace was in the gift of the *custos*.[95] The clerk, chief officer of the quarter sessions, had considerable responsibilities[96] and, in men like

[70] C 231/8 pp. 199, 203. Salop. was among the apparently few cos. in which any Rom. Catholics or dissenters were then dismissed: Glassey, 'Com. of Peace', 136–7.

[71] Duckett, *Penal Laws*, ii. 178.

[72] *Warw. Co. Rec.* viii, p. xxi; Glassey, op. cit. 149.

[73] *Orders of Q. Sess.* i. 121–38.

[74] Glassey, op. cit. 182.

[75] Ibid. 204; S.R.O., q. sess. rec., box 292, com. 1700.

[76] In Eng. coms. were issued much less frequently after 1690: Glassey, op. cit. 24. In Salop. (unlike some other cos.) there were no purges 1705–10: ibid. 299.

[77] Ibid. 295–7.

[78] Herts. R.O., Cowper (Panshanger) MSS., D/EP F154. Lee last attended q. sess. in Apr. 1696 (*Orders of Q. Sess.* i. 160) and is not named in the 1700 com. (S.R.O., q. sess. rec., box 292).

[79] Harcourt's stepmother was 1st cousin of Lee's father: Burke, *Peerage* (1949), 938; *T.S.A.S.* 4th ser. xii. 331.

[80] C 234/32 Salop. 15 Feb. 1710/11. Thanks are due to Dr. L. K. J. Glassey for this and subsequent C 234 refs.

[81] C 234/32 Salop. 10 Mar. 1711/12; Herts. R.O., Cowper (Panshanger) MSS., D/EP F159. Beale was restored July 1712: C 234/32 Salop. 22 July 1712.

[82] *T.S.A.S.* 3rd ser. iv. 284; *D.N.B. sub* Talbot, Chas.

[83] Glassey, op. cit. 341. Most, but not all, of the new men were Tories: ibid. 301 n.

[84] Ibid. 351. [85] Ibid. 356–7.

[86] Ibid. 355–7.

[87] *T.S.A.S.* 4th ser. xi. 159.

[88] Ibid. 3rd ser. iii. 341. Ld. Bradford relinquished the lieutenancy in 1704 but remained *custos* until his death: ibid. 3rd ser. iv. 284.

[89] Ibid. 3rd ser. iv. 141, 278, 284–5. In 1714 the *custos* and lieut. were still separate persons in 10 Eng. cos.: Glassey, op. cit. 17 n.

[90] *Orders of Q. Sess.* i, orders 1652–60, 2–63.

[91] Ibid. preface to orders 1652–9, p. v. Wm. Pierrepont ('Lord Pierrepont') was appointed 1659: C 231/6 p. 428.

[92] Attended regularly from 1702 to 1709 but less frequently thereafter: *Orders of Q. Sess.* i. 195–236; S.R.O., q. sess. order bk. 1709–26 (confirmed by estreats of fines, E 362).

[93] e.g. Barnes, *Som.* 70.

[94] *Orders of Q. Sess.* i. 167.

[95] Under the Custos Rotulorum Act, 1545, 37 Hen. VIII, c.1.

[96] E. Stephens, *Clerks of the Counties 1360–1960* (1961), 36–7.

Richard Harries (1631–59)[97] and Richard Jenkins (1676–91),[98] had fairly high social standing. In other counties the clerk's personal influence was impressive,[99] but the surviving Shropshire evidence hardly allows a proper estimate of his importance. In many counties clerks of the peace reorganized their working methods and records in James I's reign, probably as a late response to the additional duties brought upon the clerks by Elizabethan legislation.[1] In Shropshire, deeds of bargain and sale were first inrolled systematically in 1610[2] and the surviving register of badgers', drovers', and ale-sellers' licences was begun in 1613,[3] both during the clerkship of Samuel Bowdler of Arlescott.[4] Quarter sessions orders began to be recorded in special books between 1610 and 1652.[5] A deputy clerk is mentioned in Shropshire in 1657.[6]

Other Commissions

County commissions were occasionally appointed, especially before the Civil Wars, for purposes other than those of the commission of the peace.[7] In Shropshire the most frequent were probably commissions for charitable uses, composed mainly of county magistrates.[8] Some sixteen charitable trusts were investigated by Shropshire commissioners 1603–49, only six in the period 1650–88, and none in the period 1689–1714.[9] After the Restoration other methods of enforcement were preferred.[10] About as frequent were commissions appointed by the Exchequer in matters affecting Crown revenues.[11] Few are recorded after the Restoration. Magistrates were made county commissioners for the taxes voted by Parliament and for most of the non-parliamentary taxes which contributed to local discontent before the Civil Wars.[12] In the early 1660s magistrates were employed as commissioners under the Corporation Act.[13] Special commissions of oyer and terminer, intended to meet extraordinary occurrences of crime,[14] were rarely issued to the Shropshire magistrates; only one is recorded between 1601 and 1673.[15]

Quarter Sessions

The magistrates' principal forum was the quarterly sessions of the peace for the county, which was normally held at Shrewsbury.[16] The number of magistrates attending[17] fluctuated and bore little relationship to the size of the commission. From 1603 to

[97] E. Stephens, *Clerks of the Counties 1360–1960* (1961), 151.
[98] F. A. Hagar, 'Ric. Jenkins and the Residency at Nagpur, 1807–1826' (Univ. of California D.Phil. thesis, 1960; copy in S.R.O. 1071), 1–3.
[99] e.g. T. G. Barnes, *Clerk of Peace in Caroline Somerset* (Leicester Univ. Dept. of Eng. Local Hist. Occ. Papers, xiv); *S.H.C.* 4th ser. vi. 79–80.
[1] *S.H.C.* 4th ser. vi. 84–5. It has been suggested that such a reorganization may have been ordered by the Privy Council: *Wilts. Co. Rec.* (Wilts. Arch. and Nat. Hist. Soc. Rec. Branch, iv), p. xiv.
[2] Under an Act for Inrollment of Bargains and Sales, 1536, 27 Hen. VIII, c. 16: S.R.O. 212, box 419, reg. of deeds.
[3] S.R.O., q. sess. rec., parcel 254.
[4] Appointed 1610 (S.R.O. 212, box 419, reg. of deeds), occurs 1629 (Stephens, *Clerks of Counties*, 151), died 1631 (S.P.L., MS. 4077, p. 121).
[5] See p. 69. Such books were begun in Suss. in 1642: Fletcher, *Co. Community in Peace and War*, 145.
[6] Stephens, op. cit. 153.
[7] Those under the great seal 1601–73, except coms. for charitable uses, are recorded in C 181/1–7.
[8] Commissioners of 21 Nov. 1629, 6 Dec. 1631, and 23 Nov. 1633 are named in C 192/1.
[9] *List of Procs. of Commissioners for Charitable Uses* (P.R.O. Lists & Indexes, x), 91–2.
[10] Gareth Jones, *Hist. of Law of Charity 1532–1827* (1969), 25–6.
[11] *List of Special Commissions and Returns in the Exchequer* (P.R.O. Lists & Indexes, xxxvii), 84–5.
[12] Barnes, *Som.* 161–70.
[13] Owen and Blakeway, *Hist. Shrews.* i. 482; below, p. 284.
[14] Barnes, op. cit. 146 n.
[15] See p. 109.
[16] E 137/38/6–8; S.R.O., q. sess. order bks. 1–9 and 1709–26.
[17] Lists derived from wages entered on the pipe rolls are not always accurate in detail (*V.C.H. Wilts.* v. 90–1) but, as a series, allow generalizations about individuals. The following rolls are used in this chapter: E 372/448, 454, 457, 461, 466, 471, 474, 478, 480, 485, 494. An Act of 1390 (14 Ric. II, c.11) allowed no wages to justices who were peers or bannerets. Baronets appear on the roll: E 372/471 Item Salop. (1625–6) includes Sir Humph. Lee (cr. bt. 1620: Burke, *Ext. & Dorm. Baronetcies* (1844), 305) and either Sir Thos. Harris of Boreatton (cr. bt. 1622: ibid. 245) or Sir Thos. Harries of Tong (cr. bt. 1623: ibid. 246). From 1653 to 1666 and from 1686 to 1709 attendances at most sessions are recorded in *Orders of Q. Sess.* i; some of the gaps can be filled from estreats of fines (E 137/38/7–9; E 362/29/34). Attendances 1709–14 are in S.R.O., q. sess. order bk. 1709–26, pp. 1–58, ff. 59–74v., but estreats of fines sometimes give more names (e.g. E 362/42/33; E 362/43/33).

1642 the average attendance, as in other counties,[18] was about eleven; it fell to about eight in the 1650s, rising to about thirteen in the early 1660s. In the 1670s average attendance was about seventeen; there was another fall, to about nine, in James II's reign, but in the 1690s attendance had returned to about twelve, as in other counties.[19] In 1702 the average attendance rose suddenly to about sixteen and remained at that level until the last years of Anne's reign. In 1713 and 1714 the average was over twenty. There were exceptionally high attendances at Michaelmas 1712, Hilary 1713, and Michaelmas 1714, probably the result of the issue of new commissions.[20] The Michaelmas sessions were, on average, slightly better attended than the others. Some justices, however, never came at all. In 1701 Richard Gough wrote of a Shropshire magistrate: 'I cannot tell whether he knew where the bench was where the sessions was kept, for I never saw him there'.[21] Shropshire resembled other counties[22] in that only a handful of the magistrates present at a sessions were frequent attenders,[23] and the leaders of the magistracy were presumably comprised in that small group.[24] Throughout the period leadership came from the higher social ranks of the magistrates; lawyers and members of Parliament were prominent. Though not uniform in its views the leading group seems always to have excluded extremists; they fell victims, in any case, to government purges without ever attaining a leading position.

In James I's reign the leading group included a few men of radical opinions, like Thomas Edwardes of Meole,[25] Richard Mytton of Halston,[26] and Sir Roger Owen of Condover.[27] They were, however, outnumbered by high-ranking members of the gentry, several of whom owed their social position to the royal prerogative. They included Francis Newton of Heightley, Humphrey (later Sir Humphrey) Lee,[28] Sir Robert Needham (later Viscount Kilmorey),[29] his brother-in-law Sir Robert Vernon,[30] Sir Francis Newport, the greatest landowner in the county,[31] and his son-in-law John Barker of Haughmond.[32]

By 1625 most of the long-established leaders of James I's reign were dead or had ceased to be active, but their conservatism was perpetuated. The new leaders of Charles I's reign included Thomas Ottley, the wealthy Sir Andrew Corbet of Moreton,[33] Sir Richard (later Baron) Newport, son of Sir Francis,[34] Walter Barker, brother of John,[35] John Newton,[36] the learned Thomas (later Sir Thomas) Wolryche,[37] and Timothy (later Sir Timothy) Tourneur.[38] Of those only Walter Barker took the side of Parliament in the Civil Wars.[39] At the outbreak of war the leading gentry of Shropshire, as of most counties,[40] were predominantly royalist.

Sessions were probably not held in 1645 and 1646.[41] They were certainly abandoned

[18] Gleason, *Justices of Peace*, 105.

[19] Moir, *Justice of Peace*, 88.

[20] S.R.O., q. sess. rec., box 292, coms. July and Dec. 1712; Sept. 1714.

[21] *Antiquities and Memoirs of Parish of Myddle* (1875), 98.

[22] Gleason, op. cit. 112.

[23] A frequent attender is here defined as one who attended at least 3 of the 4 sessions in at least 3 (not necessarily consecutive) years.

[24] As in Yorks. E.R.: Forster, *E. Riding Justices*, 32.

[25] *T.S.A.S.* 3rd ser. i. 323–4.

[26] Ibid. 2nd ser. vii. 228–9.

[27] Barrister, M.P., removed from com. for 'seditious' speeches: ibid. 4th ser. xi. 161–2; J. E. Neale, *Eliz. I and her Parliaments 1584–1601* (1957), 408; W. Notestein, *Ho. of Commons 1604–1610* (1971), 333, 384; T. L. Moir, *Addled Parl. of 1614* (1958), 85, 97–8, 115, 124, 147.

[28] Barrister: *T.S.A.S.* 4th ser. ix. 242; Blakeway, *Sheriffs*, 97.

[29] M.P., supporter of king: *T.S.A.S.* 4th ser. xi. 156–7; Moir, *Addled Parl.* 194.

[30] Lawyer, courtier, M.P.: *T.S.A.S.* 4th ser. xi. 163–4; Burke, *Ext. & Dorm. Baronetcies* (1844), 546.

[31] *T.S.A.S.* 2nd ser. xii. 2; 4th ser. xi. 155.

[32] Barrister, M.P.: ibid. 4th ser. xii. 199.

[33] M.P.: ibid. 4th ser. xi. 165–6; Blakeway, *Sheriffs*, 232.

[34] M.P.: *T.S.A.S.* 2nd ser. xii. 2–7.

[35] Blakeway, *Sheriffs*, 107.

[36] Perhaps John Newton of Heightley, sheriff 1634–5: ibid. 21.

[37] M.P.: *T.S.A.S.* 3rd ser. ii. 323–4.

[38] Master in Chancery, ch. just. S. Wales, recorder of Shrews. 1638–45: ibid. 2nd ser. vii. 341 n.; Owen and Blakeway, *Hist. Shrews.* i. 538; C 231/5 p. 257.

[39] *Acts & Ords. of Interr.* i. 94. Sir Ric. Newport withdrew his support from Parl. before war broke out: *T.S.A.S.* li. 14 n., 17.

[40] Underdown, *Pride's Purge*, 27–8.

[41] Stockton constables' acct. 1644–5 mentions expenses at q. sess.: S.R.O. 3067/3/1, p. 58. The 1645–6 pipe roll records no Salop. wages: E 372/490.

in several counties at that time.[42] During the Interregnum the government, however radical, had to rely on the co-operation of moderates, who predominated in the counties.[43] In Shropshire the bench was in the hands of a small group of minor gentry, including Lancelot Lee of Coton,[44] Cresswell Tayleur,[45] Robert Corbet of Stanwardine,[46] Roger Evans of Treflach,[47] Charles Langford, William Jones,[48] Harcourt Leighton of Plaish,[49] Edward Cressett of Cotes,[50] Richard Bagot of Prees,[51] and Thomas Mackworth.[52] It is not surprising that Shropshire[53] was like most counties[54] in that the Interregnum brought little change in the character of quarter-sessions government.

At the Restoration two of the pre-war leaders, Sir Thomas Wolryche and Timothy Tourneur, were joined as leaders by others who had suffered for the king. They included Lord Newport,[55] Sir John Weld the younger,[56] Charles Baldwyn of Elsich,[57] and Arthur Weaver.[58] By the late 1670s, however, the leading group was larger and less harmonious; like Parliament, it included by then a mixture of conservative and radical elements, and others who tried to be neutral. Among its members were Adam (later Sir Adam) Ottley,[59] Sir Humphrey Briggs,[60] Thomas Bawdewin of Diddlebury,[61] Thomas Hill,[62] Richard Scriven,[63] Thomas Burton,[64] Richard More,[65] John Walcot,[66] Sir Vincent Corbet of Moreton,[67] Sir Francis Edwardes of Meole,[68] Edward Whitchcott,[69] Thomas Ottley,[70] Edward Kynaston of Oteley,[71] and Sir Henry Langley.[72]

Throughout the 17th century the leaders in Shropshire, as also for example in Wiltshire,[73] were better able than the general body of magistrates to escape political interference from the government. It remains an open question whether that was due to a realization by governments that the established county leaders, whatever their views, were too important to the effective government of the county to be removed, or whether it happened that only political moderates, unobjectionable to most governments, attained that degree of acceptance by county society which enabled them to become leaders of the bench in the first place. In the anti-Whig purge of 1681 only one of the leaders, Thomas Burton, was removed.[74] James II's attempts at a sweeping reorganization of the commissions of the peace led in Shropshire, as elsewhere,[75] to a breakdown of quarter sessions and its administration. No Trinity sessions was held in 1688, and in 1689 there were no Epiphany or Easter sessions;[76] there was rioting in Shropshire as

[42] *Warw. Co. Rec.* ii, p. xx n.; *S.H.C.* 4th ser. i, p. xlvii; Osborne, *Justices of Peace*, 107; *V.C.H. Wilts.* v. 107; Joyce W. Fowkes, 'Min. Bk. of York Q. Sess. 1638–1662', *Yorks. Arch. Jnl.* xli. 449.
[43] Underdown, op. cit. 302.
[44] *T.S.A.S.* 2nd ser. vii. 357; 4th ser. xii. 331.
[45] Ibid. 2nd ser. ii. 154.
[46] Master in Chancery, M.P. in 1654, *custos rotulorum*: ibid. 4th ser. xi. 180–1; Blakeway, *Sheriffs*, 117.
[47] Blakeway, *Sheriffs*, 141; Gough, *Antiquities of Myddle*, 188.
[48] Barrister, recorder of Shrews. 1645–60, M.P. in Jan. 1659: *T.S.A.S.* 4th ser. xii. 215.
[49] *Orders of Q. Sess.* i, preface to orders 1652–9, p. ix.
[50] *T.S.A.S.* 4th ser. vi. 221–2.
[51] Ibid. 3rd ser. x. 253.
[52] M.P. in 1646, 1656, Jan. 1659: ibid. 2nd ser. vii. 27–8.
[53] *Orders of Q. Sess.* i; J. Hill, 'Study of Poverty and Poor Relief in Shropshire 1550–1685' (Liverpool Univ. M.A. thesis, 1973), 266–7.
[54] Aylmer, *The State's Servants*, 307–11.
[55] M.P. 1640–4, lieut. 1660–87, 1689–1704, *custos rotulorum*, privy councillor: *T.S.A.S.* 2nd ser. xii. 7–13; 3rd ser. iv. 152, 275 n., 278, 284; Keeler, *Long Parl.* 284–5; D. Brunton and D. H. Pennington, *Members of Long Parl.* (1954), 12; C 231/7 p. 27.
[56] M.P. 1679: *T.S.A.S.* 3rd ser. ii. 333.
[57] M.P. 1640–4: Keeler, op. cit. 94.
[58] Lawyer, d. 1688: *T.S.A.S.* liv. 198.
[59] Master in Chancery: ibid. 2nd ser. vii. 366; Shaw, *Knights of Eng.* ii. 255.
[60] M.P. 1646–8 (excluded): *T.S.A.S.* 3rd ser. ii. 330; Brunton and Pennington, op. cit. 228.
[61] Barrister, recorder of Shrews. 1677–85: *T.S.A.S.* 4th ser. ii. 156–7; Owen and Blakeway, *Hist. Shrews.* i. 539.
[62] Perhaps Thos. Hill of Soulton, sheriff 1680–1: Blakeway, *Sheriffs*, 142–3.
[63] M.P. 1679, Court supporter: *T.S.A.S.* 3rd ser. iv. 144 n.; A. Browning, *Thos. Osborne, Earl of Danby*, iii (1951), 45–6, 49.
[64] Barrister, recorder of Shrews. 1690–5: Owen and Blakeway, *Hist. Shrews.* i. 539.
[65] M.P. 1681, 1689, 1695: *T.S.A.S.* 2nd ser. x. 51–3.
[66] M.P. 1681, 1685–7: ibid. 4th ser. xii. 5–6; Duckett, *Penal Laws*, ii. 182 n.
[67] M.P. 1679: *T.S.A.S.* 4th ser. xii. 3.
[68] M.P. 1685, 1689, future Jacobite: ibid. 219; Browning op. cit. iii. 169.
[69] Supported repeal of Test Act: Duckett, *Penal Laws*, ii. 180.
[70] *T.S.A.S.* 4th ser. ii. 339.
[71] M.P. 1685–99, future Jacobite: ibid. 4th ser. xii. 4–5; Browning, op. cit. iii. 206.
[72] Attempted neutrality: Blakeway, *Sheriffs*, 146; Owen and Blakeway, *Hist. Shrews.* ii. 137.
[73] Glassey, 'Com. of Peace', 395–7.   [74] C 231/8 p. 44.
[75] Miller, *Popery and Politics*, 251–2.
[76] *Orders of Q. Sess.* i. 120–1.

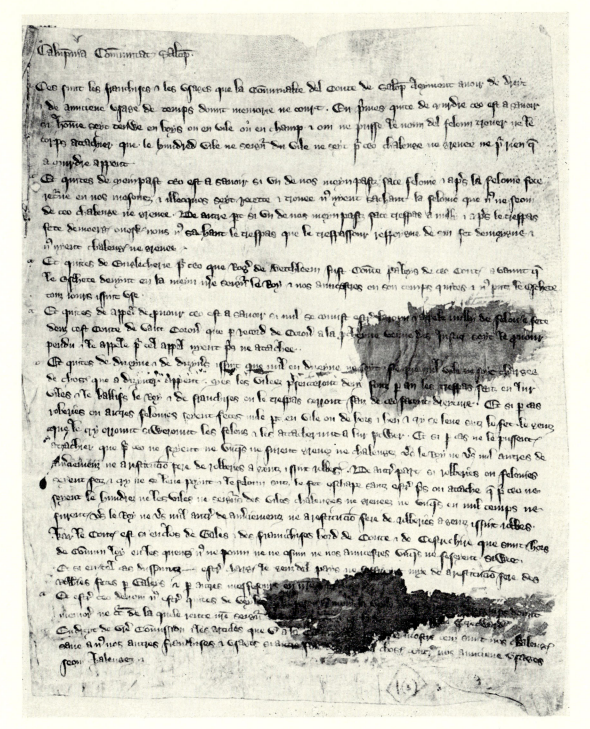

CALUMPNIA COMMUNITATIS SALOP': THE COUNTY COMMUNITY'S CLAIMS TO LEGAL PRIVILEGES, 1307

[see pages 20–3]

THE SQUARE, SHREWSBURY, DURING THE POLL BETWEEN LORD CLIVE AND WILLIAM PULTENEY, 1774
The guildhall buildings are to the right and (concealing High Street) in the centre

late as May.[77] Accounts were not audited,[78] and sessions orders were not enforced.[79] When sessions resumed in 1689 the former leaders were restored but, as in many counties,[80] they were less prominent in the 1690s. Some died, and some of the Jacobites ceased to attend regularly. The new leaders included Robert Cressett of Cound,[81] Rowland Hunt, John Edwardes, Henry Mytton of Shipton, John Kynaston,[82] John Lacon, Arthur Weaver,[83] Robert Clive, and Henry Newton.[84] Leading Jacobites like Edward Kynaston of Oteley, John Kynaston, and George Weld of Willey,[85] were dismissed in 1696[86] but restored in 1700.[87] Lacon and John Kynaston kept their positions beyond 1714 but in the 1700s new leaders emerged to replace their colleagues. They included Richard Corbet of Moreton,[88] Bartholomew Beale,[89] Thomas Jones,[90] Lord Newport (later 2nd earl of Bradford),[91] Thomas Edwardes,[92] William Whitmore,[93] Thomas Hunt, and Sir Robert Corbet.[94] The anti-Whig reorganization after 1710 caused the removal only of Beale[95] and he was restored a few months later.[96] From 1711 to 1714 Eldred Lancelot Lee enjoyed temporary prominence through his connexion with the lord keeper (later lord chancellor), Harcourt.[97]

In James I's reign quarter sessions usually lasted two or three days[98] but from 1625 until the late 1670s they usually took only two days;[99] after the 1670s two, three, or four days might be needed,[1] three days being usual by the late 1690s.[2] By the late 1680s there were also many adjournments to different parts of the county,[3] but they were attended by very few magistrates and were merely a device for dealing with minor matters that could not lawfully be delegated to divisional meetings.[4] Sessions probably continued to meet at Shrewsbury castle until 1712. From about 1662 the castle belonged to the Newports,[5] lieutenants of the county, the owner in 1712 being the Whig Lord Bradford. After the events of 1711 and early 1712[6] he could hardly have tolerated the continued use of his property by quarter sessions, and at Michaelmas 1712 the magistrates began paying to use the guildhall.[7] Quarter sessions gave an opportunity for magistrates, high constables, jurors, and many others of Shropshire's scattered population to transact private, as well as public, business.[8] Private discussions appear to have interfered at times with the conduct of meetings.[9] Procedure was not always as formal as it might have been. Some magistrates arrived late[10] and, as in other counties,[11] people

[77] W. L. Sachse, 'The Mob and the Revolution of 1688', *Jnl. Brit. Studies*, iv (1), 39.

[78] S.R.O., q. sess. rec., parcel 177, co. treasurer's acct. bk. 1666–1764, East. 1690.

[79] *Orders of Q. Sess.* i. 120.

[80] Glassey, op. cit. 153.

[81] *T.S.A.S.* 4th ser. vi. 220.

[82] M.P., Jacobite, 'leader of the Shropshire Tories': ibid. 4th ser. xii. 10–11; Browning, op. cit. iii. 206.

[83] *T.S.A.S.* liv. 198.

[84] Last attended East. 1703: *Orders of Q. Sess.* i. 204. Probably Hen. Newton of Heightley (d. 1703), Tory M.P.: *S.P.R. Heref.* viii(1), 108; below, p. 298.

[85] M.P., d. 1701: *T.S.A.S.* 3rd ser. ii. 335; Browning, op. cit. iii. 169, 206. A list of J.P.s, 1685 (C 193/12/5), distinguishes him from his uncle, Geo. Weld, M.P., d. 1696 (on whom see *T.S.A.S.* 3rd ser. ii. 333).

[86] Glassey, op. cit. 181, 196 n.

[87] Ibid. 204 n.; S.R.O., q. sess. rec., box 292, com. 1700.

[88] M.P., Whig: *T.S.A.S.* 4th ser. xii. 8.

[89] Blakeway, *Sheriffs*, 184.

[90] M.P.: *T.S.A.S.* 4th ser. xii. 224.

[91] See p. 93.

[92] See p. 102.

[93] M.P., Whig: *T.S.A.S.* liv. 196–7.

[94] M.P., Whig: ibid. 4th ser. xii. 9.

[95] C 234/32 Salop. 10 Mar. 1711/12. Clive and Newton were also removed, but had been inactive for some time.

[96] Ibid. 22 July 1712.

[97] See p. 93. In 1712–13 Lee was also one of the 2 treasurers of vagrant money (S.R.O., co. treasurer's acct. bk. 1666–1764, Mids. 1712), the general-purpose co. fund (below, p. 101).

[98] E 137/38/6; E 372/454 Item Salop.; 457 Item Salop. d.; 461 Item Salop.; 466 Item Salop.

[99] E 137/38/7; E 372/471 Item Salop.; 474 Item Salop.; 478 Item Salop.; 480 Item Salop.; 485 Adhuc Item Salop.; 494 Salop. d. For comparable figs. see Forster, *E. Riding Justices*, 30; *V.C.H. Wilts.* v. 88. In Som., however, q. sess. usually took 3–4 days 1625–40: Barnes, *Som.* 68.

[1] E 137/38/8.

[2] E 362/29/34.

[3] *Orders of Q. Sess.* i. 109–221; ii. 11–13; S.R.O., q. sess. order bk. 6, Mich. 1691, Epiph. 1694; bk. 7, Mids. 1694, Mids. 1698; bk. 8, East. 1704.

[4] S.R.O., q. sess. order bk. 6, 12 May, 29 Oct., 14 Nov. 1691, Mich. 1692; bk. 7, 8 Aug. 1696, Mids. 1698; bk. 8, East. 1704; order bk. 1709–26, pp. 47, 51–2.

[5] *T.S.A.S.* 4th ser. vii. 139.

[6] See p. 93.

[7] S.R.O., co. treasurer's acct. bk. 1666–1764, Mich. 1712; 7 Oct. 1729; q. sess. order bk. 1726–41, f. 130; 1741–57, f. 36.

[8] e.g. S.P.L., Deeds 16142.

[9] *Orders of Q. Sess.* i. 88.

[10] Ibid. 129.

[11] e.g. Forster, *E. Riding Justices*, 38.

sometimes left early, seriously weakening the authority of orders made early or late in the sessions. In 1697 it was necessary to order that 'no matter . . . debated by a full court and settled shall afterwards at the latter end of the sessions be controverted'.[12] In 1699 it was ordered that the master of the house of correction could be elected only 'in full and open sessions the second day of the quarter sessions at a full bench and not at the close of a sessions or upon adjournment thereof'.[13]

A 'chief speaker' or 'chairman', sitting 'at cushion',[14] is first mentioned in 1701,[15] but it is not clear whether the position was held continuously by one man.[16] In some counties a chairman is mentioned much earlier than in Shropshire,[17] in others much later.[18] It is possible that in Shropshire the deputy *custos*, mentioned in 1697, performed the same functions.[19] In 1701 the chair was taken by either Arthur Weaver[20] or Henry Newton or, if neither was present, by Robert Clive. In December 1714 Thomas Edwardes is mentioned as the usual chairman. The chairman, in Shropshire as elsewhere,[22] questioned counsel, pronounced on points of law, and recommended to the bench what order to make. A thorough understanding of the law of local administration was evidently needed. The bench normally followed the chairman's lead without discussion; dissentients in a minority seem to have preferred to step off the bench rather than prevent it from making a unanimous order.[23] It was advantageous in time-consuming poor-law hearings, if in no other circumstances, for a 'chief speaker' among the magistrates present to do most of the talking. Moves toward formality at sessions were being made in Shropshire and other counties[24] in the later 17th century; sessions orders of 1691 and 1712 required all motions on matters of dispute between parties to be put by counsel, if any were present.[25] The orders, by introducing greater formality, doubtless helped to simplify and shorten the court's business. In Shropshire counsel had been regularly employed at sessions in poor-law disputes since at least 1668.[26]

The presence of recognized leaders on the bench made it desirable for disputants to secure their favour in advance. It seems to have been a practice by 1700 for parties to show their briefs to the leading justices at their lodgings on the eve of a hearing. A party finding no majority in its support might then withdraw.[27] It can never be known how many disputes were settled in that way, but the practice saved time and expense both for the parties and the court. Alternatively, a party finding that on the day of the hearing the bench was led by unsympathetic magistrates might devise some pretext for claiming an adjournment to the next sessions, hoping that more amenable leaders would then be present.[28]

The commission of the peace did not limit the competence of quarter sessions to determine criminal cases except that the magistrates could determine cases of difficulty only if a justice of one of the benches or of assize was present.[29] By the 1650s, in Shropshire and other counties,[30] the more serious offences were usually dealt with at assizes, the suspect having been committed to gaol by a magistrate out of sessions. Persons suspected of high treason, murder, or serious wounding appeared at quarter

---

[12] *Orders of Q. Sess.* i. 167.
[13] Ibid. 180.
[14] In the 1680s the Norf. chmn. was said to 'have the cushion': Glassey, 'Com. of Peace', 39.
[15] *Orders of Q. Sess.* i. 192; Gough, *Antiquities of Myddle*, 170.
[16] Glassey, op. cit. 38.
[17] Barnes, *Som.* 70–1; *Warw. Co. Rec.* vii, p. li.
[18] *V.C.H. Wilts.* v. 178.
[19] See p. 93.
[20] He seems to have been chmn. in 1706 also: Gough, op. cit. 191.

[21] Herts. R.O., Cowper (Panshanger) MSS., D/EP F154.
[22] e.g. Barnes, op. cit. 72.
[23] Gough, op. cit. 170–1, 173–4, 191.
[24] *Warw. Co. Rec.* vii, p. l.
[25] *Orders of Q. Sess.* i. 136; ii. 13.
[26] Gough, op. cit. 165 (datable from *Orders of Q. Sess.* i. 100–1).
[27] Gough, op. cit. 173–4.
[28] Ibid. 170–1.
[29] Cockburn, *Hist. Eng. Assizes 1558–1714*, 91.
[30] Ibid. 91–3.

sessions only rarely and when they did they were bound over or committed to gaol to await the next assizes.[31]

The offences dealt with at quarter sessions were those endemic in every society, principally trivial larcenies and assaults. For petty larceny the Shropshire magistrates, as everywhere else,[32] usually prescribed a whipping; it was to be administered in Shrewsbury market place, at mid-day or thereabouts, on a market day.[33] Occasionally a private whipping at the gaol was ordered instead of, or as well as, a public one.[34] For assaults and affrays a fine was usual, apparently adjusted, as elsewhere,[35] according to the offence and to the offender's means. Fines varied between 6d. and £5.[36] For assaulting a petty constable and a magistrate a woman was fined £5 in 1693,[37] but in 1697 a man, presumably poor, was fined only 20s. for assaulting another and stealing his gun.[38] In 1695 one offender fined 50s. was given the option of paying 10s. if he would enlist as a soldier.[39] Persons were often bound over to keep the peace; their offences are not recorded but it is likely that they were trivial.

Magistrates in Shropshire, like those of other counties,[40] were not vigorous in applying the recusancy laws. In 1601 a Shropshire magistrate feared that strict enforcement would make the justice's house 'like a quarter sessions' with the number of cases.[41] Occasional prompting from the Privy Council or the assize justices[42] was necessary. In James I's reign the Shropshire magistracy itself included several papists.[43] A notorious recusant, Edward Lloyd of Llwynymaen,[44] had been added to the commission by 1606,[45] presumably through the influence of Lord Chancellor Ellesmere, whose steward he was. Lloyd was not removed until 1621,[46] by which time, to the 'great happiness'[47] of his neighbours, he had been imprisoned for his views. There were sporadic proceedings in Shropshire against recusants between 1606 and 1641[48] though it is not always known whether the magistrates were involved. In 1625 there was severity against recusants in most counties, coinciding with a purge of commissions of the peace.[49] The surviving Shropshire sessions orders rarely mention recusancy except during the Interregnum,[50] though the books are missing for the periods 1673-4 and 1678-81 when magistrates elsewhere were especially strict.[51] In 1665 quarter sessions ordered strict enforcement of the Act of Uniformity[52] but no other general order is recorded.

Closely connected with the problem of suppressing social disorder and religious nonconformity was that of regulating the economy. Fear of unrest arising from poverty underlay Tudor and Stuart economic legislation. Alarming fluctuations in food prices made it necessary to discourage profiteering and hoarding. Under an Act of 1563 two classes of traders, badgers (who bought food, especially grain, for re-sale) and drovers (who dealt in livestock), had to be licensed at quarter sessions.[53] In Shropshire badgers were licensed at any sessions; most drovers, however, were licensed at Easter. In the reigns of James I and Charles I the number of badgers licensed in any year fluctuated between 60 and 150.[54] It is likely that the inconsistencies arose from evasion. Hoarding

[31] *Orders of Q. Sess.* i. 20, 176, 191, 195, 220, 223.
[32] *Warw. Co. Rec.* vi, p. xxxii.
[33] *Orders of Q. Sess.* i. 138, 152, 161, 165, 169, 170, 177, 193, 209, 217; ii. 3.
[34] Ibid. i. 167; S.R.O., q. sess. order bk. 7, Mich. 1697.
[35] Forster, *E. Riding Justices*, 44.
[36] *Orders of Q. Sess.* i. 130, 142, 147, 150, 162, 173.
[37] Ibid. 145. [38] Ibid. 169.
[39] Ibid. 159.
[40] J. L. Miller, 'Catholic Factor in Eng. Politics 1660–1688' (Cambridge Univ. Ph.D. thesis, 1971), 297; Forster, op. cit. 43.
[41] H. Townshend, *Historical Collections, or an Exact Account of the Proceedings of the Four Last Parliaments of Q. Eliz.* (1680), 273.

[42] e.g. Hist. MSS. Com. 13, *10th Rep. IV, Kilmorey*, p. 370.
[43] See p. 91. [44] *Dict. Welsh Biog.* [45] E 137/38/6.
[46] *Commons Debates 1621*, ed. W. Notestein and others (1935), v. 359; C 193/13/1 ff. 80v.-83v.
[47] *Commons Debates 1621*, v. 127.
[48] S.R.O. 1374/278, 287, 289, 297-8; S.R.O. 3067/3/1, pp. 11, 43.
[49] Barnes, *Som.* 14, 106.
[50] *Orders of Q. Sess.* i, orders 1652-60, 3; ibid. i. 55.
[51] Miller, 'Catholic Factor', 294.
[52] 1 Eliz. I, c. 2: *Orders of Q. Sess.* i. 90.
[53] Badgers and Drovers Act, 5 Eliz. I, c. 12.
[54] S.R.O., q. sess. rec., parcel 254, badgers', drovers', and ale-sellers' licensing bk.

and unlicensed trading were easy to conceal and in the 1620s the clerk of the peace, through informers, was trying to track down offenders.[55] Under an Act of 1597 maltsters too had to be licensed in order to conserve grain:[56] a provision which in 1637, on orders from the Privy Council,[57] the magistrates made a special effort to enforce.[58] There is no sign that licensing of traders was rigorously enforced in Shropshire after the Restoration.[59] Sessions orders of 1693, requiring all badgers, drovers, and maltsters to attend and be licensed,[60] suggest that for some time the Elizabethan licensing statutes had been neglected, and licensing of maltsters was abolished by an Act of 1698.[61] No wage assessments made by quarter sessions under the Statute of Artificers, 1563,[62] appear to have survived from Shropshire before 1732.[63] Confirmation of an existing assessment is recorded in 1653 and many times thereafter.[64]

By the 17th century quarter sessions was not only supervising parochial administration but was also beginning to provide public services directly. To pay for them there were four standing rates, and five kinds of occasional rates levied by sessions order as needed.

The principal standing rate[65] was levied to provide the 'maimed soldiers' money', pensions (comparing favourably with poor relief) for soldiers injured in the service of the Crown.[66] Two justices were appointed treasurers each Easter,[67] normally for one year, though double terms were occasionally served.[68] Under-treasurers are mentioned[69] but only a Mr. Garbett, appointed in 1661,[70] is known to have served longer than a year. In Warwickshire a permanent under-treasurer is first mentioned in 1668.[71] Garbett received an annual salary.[72] The Civil Wars, besides disrupting collections,[73] greatly increased the number of applicants for pensions and despite various expedients[74] the fund had a deficit by 1664.[75] By 1668 Garbett was £87 out of pocket[76] and apparently recouping his losses by taking bribes from applicants. In 1668 sessions ordered a reorganization. New pensions would be granted only at a vacancy.[77] Garbett was dismissed.[78] Future under-treasurers were to have no salary;[79] they would apparently be clerks employed by the 'high' treasurers.[80] By Easter 1672 the fund was solvent.[81] The number of applicants gradually fell[82] and by the 1690s a surplus was available which was used for general purposes.[83] By the early 1700s the maimed soldiers' fund had become in Shropshire, as elsewhere,[84] virtually a general-purpose fund.[85] The maimed soldiers' treasurers also administered the 'vagrant money',[86] an occasional rate to

[55] S.R.O., badgers', etc. licensing bk. East. 1623, East. 1625, Trin. 1626, East. and Mich. 1627, East. and Trin. 1628.
[56] Malt Act, 39 Eliz. I, c. 16.
[57] Barnes, op. cit. 194.
[58] Cal. S.P. Dom. 1637, 183.
[59] S.R.O., badgers', etc. licensing bk. (ends 1661, resumes briefly 1714); Orders of Q. Sess. i–ii.
[60] S.R.O., q. sess. order bk. 6, East. and Mids. 1693.
[61] Malt Act, 9 Wm. III, c. 22.   [62] 5 Eliz. I, c. 4.
[63] R. K. Kelsall, Wage Regulation under the Statute of Artificers (1938), 111–19.
[64] Orders of Q. Sess. i, orders 1652–60, 5 sqq.
[65] It yielded some £370 a year by 1666: S.R.O., co. treasurer's acct. bk. 1666–1764, East. 1667.
[66] Under the Soldiers' and Mariners' Relief Act, 1593, 35 Eliz. I, c. 4: Hill, 'Study of Poverty', 262.
[67] As required by the Act. A list of those who served 1653–1714 can be derived from: Orders of Q. Sess. i–ii; S.R.O., co. treasurer's acct. bk. 1666–1764.
[68] i.e. 1654–6, 1656–8, 1672–4, 1674–6, 1684–6, 1688–90.
[69] e.g. S.R.O., co. treasurer's acct. bk. 1666–1764, Epiph. 1671, East. 1701, East. 1709.
[70] Orders of Q. Sess. i. 75.
[71] Warw. Co. Rec. vii, p. lv.
[72] Orders of Q. Sess. i. 101.   [73] S.R.O. 1374/305.
[74] Orders of Q. Sess. i. 40, 55, 74–5, 80.
[75] Ibid. 85.
[76] S.R.O., co. treasurer's acct. bk. 1666–1764, Mich. 1668.
[77] Orders of Q. Sess. i. 101–2.
[78] He had ceased to be under-treasurer by East. 1669; his attachment was ordered later that year: ibid. 105, 107.
[79] S.R.O., q. sess. order bk. 4, East. 1668. In 1686 was begun an ex gratia 'allowance' to the clerks from the fund's surplus: S.R.O., co. treasurer's acct. bk. 1666–1764, Mich. 1686.
[80] Q. sess. order bk. 5, Trin. 1689; bk. 7, Mids. 1695; S.R.O., co. treasurer's acct. bk. 1666–1764, East. 1671, East. 1673, East. 1699, East. 1702–East. 1714.
[81] S.R.O., co. treasurer's acct. bk. 1666–1764, East. 1672.
[82] There were 205 pensioners in 1670, 181 in 1680, and 140 in 1690: ibid. East. 1670, East. 1680, East. 1690.
[83] Ibid. East 1698, East. 1699; Orders of Q. Sess. i. 156–7, 163, 182.
[84] Osborne, Justices of Peace, 174–5.
[85] e.g. S.R.O., co. treasurer's acct. bk. 1666–1764, East. 1701, East. 1702; Orders of Q. Sess. i. 185, 188, 190, 201–2, 204, 226. Some places refused to contribute, claiming that the 1593 Act had expired: Orders of Q. Sess. i. 205, 210, 215, 223–4, 230, 234–5.
[86] S.R.O., co. treasurer's acct. bk. 1666–1764.

reimburse petty constables for conveying vagrants, first levied in 1701.[87] Soon after 1700, when the county became responsible for the cost of conveying vagrants through Shropshire to their place of settlement, most vagrants were being conveyed by the constables of Woodcote and Whitchurch,[88] the two places where one of the principal roads between London and Chester crossed the county boundary.[89] Chester was one of the main ports for Ireland[90] and it seems, therefore, that Irish vagrants caused the county more expense than any others.[91] The magistrates evidently decided to place the whole responsibility on the constables of Woodcote and Whitchurch rather than try to work a system where the constables of every parish along the road would have been separately responsible, and separately eligible for county compensation. The 'vagrant money' became virtually a standing rate. By Easter 1708 its annual yield greatly exceeded that of the maimed soldiers' rate[92] and in 1709 the assets of the maimed soldiers' fund were transferred to the vagrant fund,[93] which thus became the general-purpose county fund.[94]

The other standing rates were small. The 'gaol money', to relieve poor prisoners in the county gaol,[95] and the 'house of correction money', to pay the running expenses and the master's salary,[96] needed no treasurer. By 1697 receipts were paid directly to the gaoler and master, probably through the clerk of the peace, by the high constables and borough officers.[97] The 'King's Bench and Marshalsea money', to relieve prisoners in those gaols,[98] was administered by the maimed soldiers' (later vagrant) treasurers.[99]

Until the vagrant rate was introduced the occasional rate most often levied was 'bridge money' for repair of the county bridges.[1] They were Atcham, Buildwas, and Tern bridges,[2] the part of Montford bridge outside Shrewsbury liberties,[3] and the Shropshire parts of Tenbury[4] and (from 1697) Chirk[5] bridges. Repairs to a bridge or its approach roads were assessed, supervised, and paid for (out of the bridge money) by an *ad hoc* committee of magistrates, appointed by sessions[6] and sometimes assisted by local inhabitants and stone-masons.[7] Bridge rates, when levied, were usually large sums[8] evidently intended not only to cover immediate work but also to create a balance so that urgent repairs would not have to await the delays of rate collection;[9] the practice was usual in most parts of England by the late 17th century.[10] Thus treasurers of bridge money, theoretically appointed to handle the proceeds of only a single levy, became virtually permanent officers in charge of a standing fund.

Except for the vagrant money, the occasional rates — for county gaol[11] or house of correction[12] buildings, for 'suit money' (lawsuits on the county's behalf), and for 'issues lost'[13] (fines on the county for neglect of county bridges) — were levied too

[87] Under the Vagrants Act, 1700, 11 Wm. III, c. 18: *Orders of Q. Sess.* i. 195.

[88] Ibid. 202, 206; S.R.O., co. treasurer's acct. bk. 1666–1764, East. and Mids. 1704.

[89] *V.C.H. Staffs.* ii. 277.

[90] Ibid. 275.

[91] As in 1807: *Orders of Q. Sess.* iii. 137.

[92] S.R.O., co. treasurer's acct. bk. 1666–1764, East. 1708.

[93] Ibid. East. 1709; S.R.O., q. sess. order bk. 1709–26, p. 2.

[94] S.R.O., co. treasurer's acct. bk. 1666–1764; S.R.O., q. sess. order bk. 1709–26, pp. 5, 26, 36.

[95] Under the Poor Relief Act, 1572, 14 Eliz. I, c. 5, s. 37.

[96] Under the Beggars Act, 1610, 7 Jas. I, c. 4.

[97] *Orders of Q. Sess.* i. 165; S.R.O., q. sess. order bk. 9, Epiph. and East. 1706. Wilts. adopted a similar procedure in 1703: *V.C.H. Wilts.* v. 174.

[98] Under the Poor Relief Act, 1597, 39 Eliz. I, c. 3.

[99] *T.S.A.S.* 3rd ser. i. 410; S.R.O., co. treasurer's acct.

bk. 1666–1764.

[1] Under the Bridges Act, 1531, 22 Hen. VIII, c. 5.

[2] S.R.O. 1374/278, *sub* 1610–11; *Orders of Q. Sess.* i–ii; S.R.O., q. sess. order bk. 1709–26, p. 28, f. 62v.

[3] *Orders of Q. Sess.* i, orders 1652–60, 2; ibid. i. 95, 130, 220.

[4] Ibid. i. 110–11, 147, 151, 233.

[5] S.R.O., q. sess. order bk. 1709–26, f. 71v.; below, p. 103.

[6] *Orders of Q. Sess.* i. 21–2, 95, 122, 127, 146, 203; S.R.O., q. sess. order bk. 3, Epiph. 1661, East. 1662.

[7] *Orders of Q. Sess.* i. 172–3.

[8] Ibid. 21, 124, 147, 174, 220, 237; ii. 1; S.R.O., q. sess. order bk. 8, Epiph. 1700; order bk. 1709–26, f. 59.

[9] *Orders of Q. Sess.* i. 116, 138, 146–7, 151, 178, 219–20; ii. 19; S.R.O., q. sess. order bk. 5, East. 1686; bk. 6, Epiph. 1694; order bk. 1709–26, f. 59.

[10] Forster, *E. Riding Justices*, 64.

[11] Under the Gaols Act, 1532, 23 Hen. VIII, c. 2.

[12] Under the Poor Relief Act, 1576, 18 Eliz. I, c. 3.

[13] See *Warw. Co. Rec.* ii, p. xxx.

seldom to acquire the character of standing funds. Their treasurers were often the same as the bridge treasurers.[14] Those treasurers were sometimes magistrates, but not necessarily,[15] and after the Restoration they were usually barristers. Thomas Bawdewin of Diddlebury[16] was bridge treasurer in 1663;[17] Samuel Bowdler from before 1686 to c. 1695;[18] Thomas Edwardes[19] from c. 1697 to 1711 at least.[20] Edwardes was treasurer of all the occasional funds except the vagrant money[21] and during his year as treasurer for maimed soldiers (1707–8) nearly approached the status of 'county treasurer'. His personal standing was perhaps exceptional, for he also served as chairman of quarter sessions.[22]

The occasional rates were assessed by 'allotments' — 100 areas, notionally of equal value, into which the hundreds and liberties were divided. Any sum needed could be divided by 100 to find the amount from each allotment. The system was in use by 1590.[23] By 1638 inequalities were mitigated by rating some areas at more than 1 allotment and others at less, preserving the total of 100.[24] Grievances over ship-money assessments based on allotments led to a controversial adjustment of allotments in 1638[25] which remained in force until 1705.[26] From 1705 and 1706 respectively the vagrant and bridge rates were normally levied at £35 or multiples thereof,[27] so that a fixed proportion of £35 could be assessed once and for all on each parish. The two principal county rates could thenceforth be levied on the parish as multiples of that assessed sum, and the allotment system became obsolete.

By 1714 Shropshire had a simplified rating system and met nearly all expenses from two funds, the vagrant money and the bridge money, the second administered by a permanent treasurer, forerunner of the county treasurer. It was in similar fashion that a permanent county treasurer emerged in most counties in the early 18th century.[28]

As well as repairing county bridges out of county rates,[29] the magistrates had to ensure that places and individuals performed their own prescriptive duties of local bridge maintenance. Presentments or indictments for non-repair took place at quarter sessions. Those indicted were given a reasonable time to put matters right[30] and if they did so were discharged.[31] Enquiries into liabilities and the ordering of repairs following those enquiries were usually delegated by quarter sessions to divisional justices, sometimes subject to confirmation by quarter sessions.[32] Some disputes about liability, however, were decided by quarter sessions alone.[33] It seems that disputants could choose whether to be heard by divisional magistrates;[34] if local justices failed to obtain an agreement, the parties had to appear again at sessions.[35] If a local rate was found necessary, quarter

[14] e.g. Thos. Bawdewin (*Orders of Q. Sess.* i. 81, 97), Sam. Bowdler (S.R.O., q. sess. order bk. 6, Mich. 1692), and Thos. Edwardes (bk. 8, East. 1704; bk. 9, Mich. 1707, Mich. 1708 (loose sheet); *Orders of Q. Sess.* i. 210).

[15] e.g. the non-magistrates Thos. Russell and Ric. Thynne, bridge treasurers 1639 (S.R.O., q. sess. order bk. 1, Epiph. 1639), and Wm. Yopp, bridge treasurer c. 1658–c. 1659 (*Orders of Q. Sess.* i. 56, 67).

[16] Barrister (*T.S.A.S.* 3rd ser. x. 266), steward of Shrews. 1662–76 (Owen and Blakeway, *Hist. Shrews.* i. 540), county J.P. 1663–c. 1690 (C 231/7 p. 211; *Orders of Q. Sess.* i. 123).

[17] *Orders of Q. Sess.* i. 82; S.R.O., q. sess. order bk. 3, East. 1663.

[18] *Orders of Q. Sess.* i. 109, 157. Not a J.P. Styled gentleman: S.R.O., q. sess. order bk. 6, Mich. 1692.

[19] Barrister, town clk. of Shrews. 1681–1720 (Owen and Blakeway, *Hist. Shrews.* i. 544), attended q. sess. until 1721 (S.R.O., q. sess. order bk. 1709–26, f. 149v.).

[20] *Orders of Q. Sess.* i. 167; S.R.O., q. sess. order bk. 1709–26, p. 34.

[21] See above, n. 14.

[22] Herts. R.O., Cowper (Panshanger) MSS., D/EP F154.

[23] N.L.W., Ottley MSS., uncat., Ric. Ottley's letter bk. 1590–7, 4 Nov. 1590 (at end). Yorks. E.R. adopted a comparable system c. 1600: Forster, *E. Riding Justices*, 64–5.

[24] S.R.O., q. sess. order bk. 1, schedule 14 July 1638.

[25] Ibid., sheriff and J.P.s to assize justices [early 1638]; *Orders of Q. Sess.* i, orders 1638–60, 1; *Cal. S.P. Dom.* 1635–6, 256; 1637, 378; 1639, 252; 1640, 173, 180.

[26] *Orders of Q. Sess.* i. 85. A general adjustment made in 1658 was revoked in 1661: ibid. 72.

[27] Ibid. 217, 226, and subsequent refs. A £40 bridge rate ordered 1711 is the only exception: ibid. ii. 9.

[28] Moir, *Justice of Peace*, 117.

[29] See p. 101.

[30] *Orders of Q. Sess.* i. 119, 145.

[31] Ibid. 85.

[32] Ibid. 193; S.R.O., q. sess. order bk. 2, Trin. 1654, Trin. 1659; bk. 3, Epiph. 1662, Trin. 1664; bk. 4, Trin. 1665; bk. 7, Mids. 1697.

[33] *Orders of Q. Sess.* i. 15, 17.

[34] S.R.O., q. sess. order bk. 4, Trin. 1665.

[35] Bk. 2, Trin. 1654.

sessions would impose it.[36] Shropshire was one of those counties that retained certain hundred bridges,[37] including Cynllaith (later Rhydycroesau)[38] and Llanyblodwel bridges (Oswestry hundred),[39] and part of Chirk bridge (Oswestry and Pimhill).[40] It was harder to impose repairs on an unwilling hundred than on a parish[41] and in 1697, after many years of resistance to bridge rates by Oswestry and Pimhill hundreds,[42] quarter sessions adopted the Shropshire half of Chirk bridge as a county bridge.[43]

Until the 1650s the liability of a place for upkeep of its roads was limited to provision by the inhabitants of labour and haulage for six days a year.[44] Defaulting individuals were presented or indicted at quarter sessions and could be fined.[45] Local rates were sometimes imposed by the magistrates in the second half of the century, but statute labour sufficed in most places to meet the magistrates' standards of repair. In 1654 an Ordinance, repealed in 1660, allowed any place needing work in excess of six days to pay for it by a self-imposed rate[46] and some Shropshire parishes did so.[47] A temporary Act of 1662 required parish surveyors to levy rates for highway maintenance,[48] and Shropshire quarter sessions seem to have enforced it.[49] Quarter sessions could fine places indicted for neglect, but did so rarely.[50] Until 1692 such fines had to be paid to the Exchequer, but under an Act of that year[51] they could be used to pay for repairs; on at least one occasion[52] Shropshire seems to have anticipated the Act. Presentment or indictment of a place for non-repair sometimes led to disputes between places over liability. Quarter sessions would refer the dispute to a divisional monthly meeting for report.[53] Upon indictment a place was normally allowed three months to repair its roads; on its producing a certificate of repair from a local justice the indictment would be quashed.[54]

Under the Act of 1692 three highway sessions were held each year by the divisional justices to receive the reports of parish surveyors.[55] Surveyors were enabled by the Act to levy a non-recurring local rate up to 6d. in the pound, subject to the approval of a local justice and confirmation by quarter sessions,[56] and the Shropshire sessions ruled in 1693 that all such rates would be confirmed automatically.[57] After 1692 numerous confirmations were granted in Shropshire[58] and elsewhere.[59] The Act also enabled a local justice to ask quarter sessions to impose a local rate, but that power was seldom used.[60] Most places continued, as they did throughout the country,[61] to rely solely on statute labour.

The parish's most exacting duty, and one of the magistrates' constant concerns, was relief of the poor. The magistrates had to spend much time not only in seeing that relief was given but also in resolving the numerous disputes caused by the Poor Law in a

[36] Bk. 4, Epiph. 1669; bk. 7, Mids. 1697; *Orders of Q. Sess.* i. 58.
[37] S. and B. Webb, *Story of King's Highway* (1913), 107-8.
[38] *Orders of Q. Sess.* i. 58.
[39] S.R.O., q. sess. order bk. 3, Trin. 1664.
[40] Order bk. 1709-26, p. 2.
[41] e.g. *Orders of Q. Sess.* i. 111, 120.
[42] Ibid. 60-1, 67; S.R.O., q. sess. order bk. 1, Trin. 1659; bk. 2, Trin. 1659.
[43] *Orders of Q. Sess.* i. 167.
[44] Under the Highways Act, 1563, 5 Eliz. I, c. 13.
[45] S.R.O., q. sess. order bk. 5, Trin. 1685; *Orders of Q. Sess.* i. 136-7.
[46] *Acts & Ords. of Interr.* ii. 861-9.
[47] *Orders of Q. Sess.* i. 27, 65.
[48] Highways Act, 14 Chas. II, c. 6.
[49] S.R.O., q. sess. order bk. 3, Trin. 1664. Evidence is missing for the effect in Salop. of the temporary Highways and Bridges Act, 1670, 22 Chas. II, c. 12, enabling q. sess. to impose a parish rate.

[50] *Orders of Q. Sess.* i. 103, 112, 114, 214.
[51] Highways and Carriage of Goods Act, 1692, 3 Wm. & Mary, c. 12.
[52] *Orders of Q. Sess.* i. 114.
[53] e.g. S.R.O., q. sess. order bk. 5, Mich. 1686; order bk. 1709-26, pp. 14, 18.
[54] Bk. 8, Mich. 1702, Epiph. 1703; bk. 9, Mich. 1707; order bk. 1709-26, pp. 19-21, 33-4, f. 63r.-v.; *Orders of Q. Sess.* i. 178, 214; ii. 8, 11.
[55] S.R.O. 2253/2.
[56] e.g. S.R.O., q. sess. order bk. 7, Mich. 1695, Mids. and Mich. 1698; bks. 8-9; order bk. 1709-26; *Orders of Q. Sess.* i. 163-4, 178.
[57] *Orders of Q. Sess.* i. 145.
[58] Ibid. i-ii.
[59] Wilts. had a printed form for the purpose by 1719: *V.C.H. Wilts.* v. 171.
[60] *Orders of Q. Sess.* i. 155; S.R.O., q. sess. order bk. 5, Epiph. 1694.
[61] Webb, *Story of King's Highway*, 37-8; *T.S.A.S.* lvi. 320, 322.

litigious age. The principal administrators of the poor-law statutes were the parish overseers, directly supervised by divisional justices. The work was usually done by local consent without quarter sessions' intervention, and has left little trace in sessions records. Other records suggest that, despite a general increase in poverty during the 17th century, the divisional magistrates were reasonably successful in enforcing the Poor Law.[62] Rates were imposed in many Shropshire parishes by the early 17th century and throughout the century endowed charities were of only secondary importance.[63] Parish officers and divisional justices had a financial incentive to punish and remove vagrants for the benefit of the ratepayers, and only an occasional stimulus from quarter sessions or the government was needed.[64] The rarity of general quarter-sessions orders on the poor suggests, in Shropshire as elsewhere,[65] that the magistrates had no clearly defined policy. In practice the crude simplicity of the settlement laws encouraged in most counties,[66] including Shropshire,[67] a legalistic approach to human problems.

In a few instances the divisional magistrates were unable to settle a dispute. Claims from paupers against overseers who refused relief or failed to provide an apprentice-ship or cottage were the most common poor-law matters heard at sessions in the 1650s and 1660s. After the Poor Relief Act, 1662,[68] there was a marked increase in parishes' appeals to sessions against divisional justices' removal orders.[69] Such cases required an investigation, with witnesses, into the pauper's life; a lack of personal records obscured the facts and counsel found ample opportunity for manœuvre.[70] If quarter sessions could reach no decision, it would seek the assize justices' opinion.[71] Once rejected at sessions, however, few appeals were taken to assizes; if the case was too weak to convince sessions, the financial risk of failure at assizes was usually unacceptable. If a sessions removal order was defied, the culprit was liable to imprisonment in the house of correction or, ultimately, prosecution at assizes. Though assizes heard only a small proportion of the total number of Shropshire settlement disputes, such disputes were among the most common of all matters heard at the Shropshire assizes.[72]

Four important matters related to the relief of poverty were of perennial concern to quarter sessions during the 17th century. The provision of pensions to maimed soldiers and the cost of conveying vagrants have been treated elsewhere.[73] The bastardy laws were another concern. Bastard children were among those most likely to become paupers and for their parents the penalties could be severe; fathers went to gaol until they found security for the child's maintenance,[74] mothers to the house of correction for a year.[75] The paternity of a bastard or foundling was sometimes disputed and counsel could be tempted to make false accusations.[76] The court was also concerned with destitution by fire, flood, tempest, or plague, which might befall individuals or even a whole community. Quarter sessions assumed the power to commend to the county or some part of it voluntary collections for the victims. Such collections were common in Shropshire in the late 1650s,[77] but they seem sometimes to have been inadequate[78] and sometimes their funds were mismanaged.[79] After the Restoration sufferers followed a

[62] Hill, 'Study of Poverty', 94, 129, 150–1.
[63] Ibid. 89–90.
[64] Ibid. 242–3; Hist. MSS. Com. 13, 10th Rep. IV, Kilmorey, p. 369; Orders of Q. Sess. i. 78, 133.
[65] Forster, E. Riding Justices, 52; V.C.H. Wilts. v. 182.
[66] Moir, Justice of Peace, 94, 97.
[67] e.g. Orders of Q. Sess. i. 112 (case of Thos. Mason and fam.).
[68] Poor Relief Act, 14 Chas. II, c. 12.
[69] Hill, op. cit. 255–6.
[70] Orders of Q. Sess. i. 141; Gough, Antiquities of Myddle, 165–71 (hearings datable from Orders of Q. Sess.).
[71] Orders of Q. Sess. i. 118, 205; S.R.O., q. sess. order bk. 1709–26, p. 56.

[72] Orders of Q. Sess. i. 113, 166; Hill, op. cit. 261.
[73] See pp. 100–1.
[74] Under the Poor Relief Act, 1576, 18 Eliz. I, c. 3: Orders of Q. Sess. i. 142–3, 150.
[75] Under the Beggars Act, 1610, 7 Jas. I, c. 4: ibid. i. 52, 80, 95, 189; ii. 5; S.R.O., q. sess. order bk. 9, Mids. 1707.
[76] Orders of Q. Sess. i. 214–5, 223, 227, 230, 235; Gough, op. cit. 166.
[77] Orders of Q. Sess. i, orders 1638–60, 4–9; ibid. i. 30–1, 36–7, 42–3, 46, 55.
[78] Ibid. 46, 54, 94, 97; W. A. Bewes, Church Briefs (1896), 280.
[79] Hill, op. cit. 258.

procedure established by Charles I in 1625;[80] they obtained from quarter sessions merely a certificate of loss, which enabled them to petition the lord chancellor for a brief authorizing collections throughout the country or a large part of it.[81] By the end of the 17th century, however, the court occasionally made small payments to petitioners as its maimed soldiers' fund acquired a sufficient annual surplus.[82]

A house of correction, to be erected, owned, and managed by the county, and intended for reform of the undeserving poor, was considered by the government to be a desirable institution for reducing pauperism. The Shropshire quarter sessions decided in 1598 to build a house in Shrewsbury castle and provide a stock of materials to set the inmates on work.[83] A county rate was levied but misappropriated.[84] A house of correction seems to have existed by 1605[85] but in 1619 the assize justices found it unsatisfactory.[86] A new house was established about 1631 in School House Lane (later School Gardens), Shrewsbury,[87] probably in response to Charles I's Book of Orders. By 1641 useful work was provided there[88] but in 1655 the house was also used for the detention and interrogation of royalist conspirators.[89] By 1705, when a new house of correction was provided on the same site,[90] useful work there had ceased, as it had in houses of correction elsewhere.[91] In 1706, instead of selling inmates' work, the master was charging them for lodging. Quarter sessions prevented him, and ordered a new stock of materials.[92] Soon afterwards sentences to hard labour at the house, in the form of hemp-processing,[93] became common.[94] A county house of correction serving Brimstree and Stottesdon hundreds and Much Wenlock liberties was provided at Bridgnorth by local effort c. 1630.[95] By the 1650s it was regulated by quarter sessions,[96] having received since 1633 a portion of the county rate for maintenance.[97] By 1714 the county claimed ownership of the building.[98] The Bridgnorth house contained a school in 1655.[99]

In 1705 a new gaol and house of correction were completed in School House Lane under an Act of 1700.[1] The county built, maintained, and regulated the gaol, but it was the king's prison. By 1629[2] the office of gaoler had fallen to a Shrewsbury resident, Edward Meriden (d. 1654). It passed successively to his son Owen (d. 1659) and grandson Edward (d. 1682). The Meridens seem to have acted in person.[3] The gaoler's income consisted mainly of fees paid by prisoners, including a 'commitment' fee from each new prisoner and rents for lodging. In 1686 the staff included an under-keeper, a porter, and a turnkey, each entitled to fees. Prisoners could not be discharged until their fees were paid.[4] As in other counties,[5] the magistrates had no system of inspection and intervened only when indiscipline or mismanagement became intolerable. In 1685 the prisoners petitioned quarter sessions against the gaoler's exactions, and the fees were

[80] Bewes, op. cit. 17–18, 21–2; W. E. Tate, *The Parish Chest* (1969), 122.

[81] e.g. *Orders of Q. Sess.* i. 75, 94, 97, 98, 100, 106; *T.S.A.S.* 2nd ser. xi. 288–90.

[82] S.R.O., q. sess. rec., parcel 177, co. treasurer's acct. bk. 1666–1764, East. 1699; *Orders of Q. Sess.* i. 185, 188, 199, 226.

[83] Under the Beggars Act, 1597–8, 39 Eliz. I, c. 4: *T.S.A.S.* 3rd ser. i. 410.

[84] Hill, op. cit. 263–4.

[85] *Cal. S.P. Dom.* 1603–10, 234. A petty constable's acct., c. 1601, records payments towards 'erecting the two houses of correction at two several times': S.R.O. 1374/269. There were perhaps two schemes, one abortive the other fruitful.

[86] Hist. MSS. Com. 13, *10th Rep. IV, Kilmorey*, p. 370.

[87] S.R.O., q. sess. order bk. 1, accts. at end; J. L. Hobbs, *Shrews. Street-Names* (1954), 92.

[88] *Orders of Q. Sess.* i, orders 1638–60, 3.

[89] *T.S.A.S.* 3rd ser. x. 143; *Cal. S.P. Dom.* 1665–6, 160.

[90] See below.

[91] S. and B. Webb, *Eng. Prison under Local Govt.* (1922), 16.

[92] S.R.O., q. sess. order bk. 9, Epiph. 1706; *Orders of Q. Sess.* i. 224.

[93] S.R.O., q. sess. order bk. 1709–26, ff. 69v., 72v.

[94] Order bk. 9, Mids. and Mich. 1706, Mids. 1707, Epiph. 1709; order bk. 1709–26, p. 30, ff. 61v., 65.

[95] Hill, 'Study of Poverty', 227–8.

[96] *Orders of Q. Sess.* i. 14, 19, 56–7, 95–6.

[97] Hill, op. cit. 265.

[98] *Orders of Q. Sess.* ii. 17.

[99] Ibid. i. 21.

[1] Gaols Act, 11 Wm. III, c. 19: *Orders of Q. Sess.* i. 212; S.R.O. 503/6.

[2] S.R.O. 1093, box 56, gaoler's indenture of appointment, 1629.

[3] Gough, *Antiquities of Myddle*, 58; *S.P.R. Lich.* xii. 113, 123, 171. By 1685 Thos. Cooper was gaoler: S.R.O. 1093, box 56, gaoler's indenture of appointment, 1685.

[4] *Orders of Q. Sess.* i. 108, 111.

[5] Webb, *Eng. Prisons*, 12.

re-assessed.[6] In 1707[7] and 1716 the gaolers complained of refusals to pay. In 1716 discipline broke down; the gaoler, a woman, could make no profit from the seventy debtors in her custody.[8]

Divisional Monthly Meetings (Petty Sessions)

Divisional meetings of magistrates between sessions have been mentioned in connexion with bridges, roads, and poor-relief. It was during the 17th century that meetings began to be held at monthly intervals and developed into a permanent feature of county government as 'petty sessions', a term found in Shropshire in the 1690s.[9] In James I's reign the justices living in each division or 'limit', comprising a hundred or pair of hundreds, held regular meetings. The pairs of hundreds were Brimstree and Stottesdon, Chirbury and Ford, and Clun and Purslow. Every limit usually had an annual meeting to take ale-sellers' and victuallers' recognizances; in Bradford North the justices met in April or May, in Brimstree and Stottesdon in September or October, in Chirbury and Ford between October and January.[10]

'Tippling' was likely to cause poverty and breaches of the peace, and an Act of 1552 required ale-sellers to be bound before at least two magistrates in an undertaking to keep an orderly house, paying a shilling fee.[11] By 1614 the Shropshire magistrates observed the widespread practice[12] of limiting licences to one year, renewing them at annual divisional meetings.[13] Before the Civil Wars the Privy Council and the assize justices instigated occasional purges of alehouses by Shropshire magistrates,[14] and ordered articles regulating the management of alehouses to be embodied in the bonds,[15] as they were in most counties.[16] In 1656, under the rule of the major-general, James Berry, even stricter limits were imposed by quarter sessions on Shropshire licensees in an effort to suppress 'deboistness and profane practices'.[17]

Bonds were sometimes taken by justices between licensing sessions.[18] Occasionally they were taken by quarter sessions,[19] but the practice led, as in other counties,[20] to persistent conflict between divisional magistrates and the clerk of the peace over the licence fee, which was payable to the clerk if the licence was granted at quarter sessions.[21] Licensees in breach of their bonds could have their licences withdrawn by two justices. An unlicensed ale-seller could be gaoled for three days by two justices; he was released on making a bond not to sell ale, and paid a 20s. fine at quarter sessions. Few such fines, however, occur in surviving Shropshire quarter-sessions records.[22]

In James I's reign the meeting-places of licensing sessions seem to have been traditional, if not fixed. Clun and Purslow met at Purslow, Munslow at Munslow, Brimstree and Stottesdon at Bridgnorth, Condover at Cound.[23] Shortly after Easter there were annual meetings to audit parish officers' accounts.[24] Sometimes licensing and auditing meetings coincided,[25] and sometimes other business was raised as well.[26] Though the

[6] Orders of Q. Sess. i. 108.
[7] Ibid. 229.
[8] Ibid. ii. 26.
[9] S.R.O. 2253/2. The term appears in Orders of Q. Sess. i. 76, without authority from the original.
[10] S.R.O., q. sess. rec., parcel 254, badgers', drovers', and ale-sellers' licensing bk., Trin. 1613–East. 1619.
[11] Alehouses Act, 5 & 6 Edw. VI, c. 25.
[12] S. and B. Webb, Hist. of Liquor Licensing (1903), 9 n.
[13] S.R.O., badgers', etc. licensing bk., Mich. 1614, Epiph. 1616, Mich. 1616, Mich. 1618.
[14] Orders of Q. Sess. i, orders 1638–60, 2–3; T.S.A.S. 3rd ser. iv, p. vi; Hist. MSS. Com. 13, 10th Rep. IV, Kilmorey, p. 370; ibid. 47, 15th Rep. X, Shrews. Corp. p. 61.
[15] S.R.O., badgers', etc. licensing bk., Trin. 1615. Articles are mentioned: ibid. Mich. 1613, East. 1616;

S.R.O. 327, box 64, certificate of recognizances 1638.
[16] Webb, Hist. Liquor Licensing, 11 n.
[17] S. R. Gardiner, Hist. of Commonwealth and Protectorate 1649–1656 (1903), iv. 38–9.
[18] S.R.O., badgers', etc. licensing bk.
[19] Orders of Q. Sess. i. 26, 28, 39, 50, 68, 71, 230.
[20] Stephens, Clerks of Counties, 38.
[21] S.R.O., badgers', etc. licensing bk., Epiph. 1616; S.R.O., q. sess. order bk. 8, Mids. and Mich. 1702; order bk. 1709–26, f. 113v.
[22] S.R.O., badgers', etc. licensing bk., Trin. 1615, Epiph., East., and Trin. 1616, Trin. 1618.
[23] Ibid. passim; S.R.O. 1374/265, 267–8, 274–6; S.R.O. 1977/4/2, sub 1606–7.
[24] S.R.O. 1374/48, p. 253.
[25] Ibid. 1374/268, 275.
[26] Ibid. 1374/267.

meetings had no legal authority beyond that of justices acting together at any time out of sessions,[27] their convenience for clearing routine matters was apparent to magistrates and people alike, and business was inevitably attracted. Petty sessions are believed to have developed in most counties from licensing sessions.[28] In the Bradford North division meetings were being held monthly by 1624.[29]

Only in 1631 did monthly meetings become general,[30] pursuant to the king's Book of Orders of that year. The government was anxious to secure proper administration of the Poor Law, but the new meetings took in every kind of out-of-sessions business.[31] They were not associated with the more unpopular measures of the Personal Rule and continued to be held regularly in Shropshire throughout the 1630s; in Brimstree and Stottesdon they were regularly held as late as 1642.[32] Meetings of some sort continued to be held during the Civil Wars[33] and monthly meetings were resumed in the 1650s.[34] Only in the smaller divisions was there difficulty in the 17th century in holding the meetings when a resident justice died or was unavoidably absent,[35] but the business there was slighter too.

Attendances of magistrates at divisional meetings were small. Licensing sessions in James I's reign were attended by two to four magistrates each.[36] Attendances at monthly meetings after 1631 cannot have been much greater. As the working portion of the commission of the peace rarely exceeded 55 and was often nearer 35, the average attendance in the ten divisions can hardly have exceeded five. Relations between the justices of a division could be affected by conflicting local interests. In the earlier 1690s some of the magistrates of the Brimstree and Stottesdon division found their fellow justice, Eldred Lancelot Lee of Coton, so objectionable that they threatened the lieutenant that they would not act unless he were dismissed from the commission, and he was indeed dismissed.[37] Procedure was informal. A monthly meeting held by two justices at an alehouse in Shawbury in December 1699 was over by two o'clock. A group from Myddle, who had been summoned for that time, found the magistrates enjoying a pipe of tobacco and were invited to join them in a drink. Myddle's business, a dispute over a charity, was discussed at length but the justice who had summoned the Myddle party, having failed to get his way by persuasion, had no alternative but to adjourn the matter to quarter sessions.[38] The episode shows how devoid of authority were the monthly meetings, even after some seventy years. Their usefulness remained that of a clearing house for routine business and a congenial forum where a first attempt could be made to resolve disputes cheaply and quickly.

The Lieutenancy and Militia

The lieutenant was in the 17th century a figure of great personal influence in the county and wielded considerable local military and political power on behalf of the government. Until 1642 the lieutenancy of Shropshire was held, with those of Welsh and other marcher counties, by the presidents of the Council in the Marches of Wales.[39] Parliament dismissed all lieutenants in 1642,[40] appointing in Shropshire Lord Lyttelton,

[27] Barnes, *Som.* 83-4. [28] Moir, *Justice of Peace*, 44.

[29] E. C. Peele and R. S. Clease, *Shropshire Parish Documents* (Shrews. [1903]), 76.

[30] Worfield constables (whose accts. begin in 1590) first record expenses at monthly meetings in 1630-1: S.R.O. 1374/293. Thereafter the item recurs regularly.

[31] Hill, 'Study of Poverty', 236-7, 239-50; Moir, op. cit. 65.

[32] S.R.O. 3067/3/1, pp. 41, 43, 51.

[33] Hill, op. cit. 252.

[34] e.g. S.R.O., q. sess. order bk. 1, Mich. 1657.

[35] Ibid. bk. 8, Mids. 1704; Hill, op. cit. 239.

[36] S.R.O., q. sess. rec., parcel 254, badgers', drovers', and ale-sellers' licensing bk.

[37] Herts. R.O., Cowper (Panshanger) MSS., D/EP F154; and see above, p. 93.

[38] Gough, *Antiquities of Myddle*, 172.

[39] J. C. Sainty, *Lieutenants of Counties, 1585-1642* (*Bull. Inst. Hist. Res.* Special Suppl. viii), 37-8.

[40] Ibid. 10 n.

the lord keeper.[41] He defected soon afterwards to the king[42] and was replaced by the earl of Essex (d. 1646).[43] The king attempted meanwhile to mobilize the militia under commissioners of array.[44] During the Civil Wars the local commanders appointed by each side were hardly comparable in functions with the pre-war lieutenants.[45] During the Interregnum the lieutenancy was in abeyance and the militia was in theory managed by a county committee.[46] At the Restoration the connexion of the lieutenancy with the presidency of the Council in the Marches was not renewed, and the office passed to the leading landowning family, the Newports. At first supporters of the Court, they became Whigs at the time of the Exclusion crisis and were deprived of the office during the years 1687–9 and 1712–14.[47]

The lieutenant was often absent and relied much on deputy lieutenants. From 1595 to 1617 and from 1623 to 1625 they were selected by the Privy Council but otherwise by the lieutenant.[48] Until 1642 the Shropshire deputies numbered up to eight or so;[49] after the Restoration there were generally about eight.[50] As in other counties,[51] they were often among the leading magistrates, and the office, especially before 1642, sometimes passed from father to son.[52] The deputy lieutenants, like the magistrates, were liable to be ejected if their views did not agree with the government's.[53] In most counties there was a chief deputy, through whom the lieutenant's instructions were communicated.[54] In Shropshire Sir Andrew Corbet was chief deputy in Charles I's time,[55] Sir Richard Ottley in Charles II's reign,[56] and John Walcot in that of James II.[57]

The lieutenancy was the government's principal agency of local security. In the early 1660s,[58] on James II's accession,[59] and after the Revolution settlement of 1689[60] Lord Newport, acting on government instructions, employed his deputies to spy upon, disarm, and arrest the disaffected. The most dangerous were interned in Shrewsbury castle;[61] others in the custody of the provost-marshal,[62] the lieutenant's appointee.[63] Searches for arms after the Exclusionist plots of 1683[64] revealed one substantial private armoury.[65] The militia was held in reserve whenever insurrection threatened.[66]

Before the Civil Wars the Shropshire militia numbered 600 trained footmen, selected from some 6,500 'able' men, and 70 horse, selected from some 325. In James I's reign the foot comprised four 'trained bands', each with a captain from the county gentry.[67] The able men formed a reserve; as in most counties,[68] it was from them that men were pressed for foreign service.[69] In Shropshire, as elsewhere,[70] musters and training conflicted with farm work.[71] Equipment was often deficient.[72] In 1605 only 360 of the 600

[41] See p. 359.
[42] D.N.B.
[43] T.S.A.S. 3rd ser. iii. 343–4.
[44] Ibid. 2nd ser. vi. 33–4; ibid. li. 19–23, 39.
[45] See p. 359.
[46] See pp. 113–14.
[47] See pp. 93, 254. Fourteen lieuts. were dismissed 1687: Glassey, 'Com. of Peace', 110 n.
[48] Sainty, op. cit. 8–9, 38; T.S.A.S. 3rd ser. iv. 151.
[49] S.P. 14/28 no. 48; Hist. MSS. Com. 13, 10th Rep. IV, Kilmorey, p. 365; S.P. 16/408 f. 160. The no. was restricted to 4 from Mar. to Nov. 1617 and to 6 from Nov. 1617 to 1623: Sainty, op. cit. 38. There were more deputies in Som. c. 1629: Barnes, Som. 103.
[50] S.P. 29/58 f. 10; Cal. S.P. Dom. 1687–9, 209; 1700–2, 249.
[51] Barnes, op. cit. 104.
[52] Cf. names of leading J.P.s (above, pp. 95–7) with those of deputy lieuts. in: Hist. MSS. Com. 9, Salisbury, v, pp. 304–5; T.S.A.S. 3rd ser. iii, pp. 340, vi; 3rd ser. iv. 176–7; S.P. 16/453 no. 89; and sources cited above, nn. 49–50.
[53] C.J. ii. 759; Duckett, Penal Laws, ii. 183.
[54] Moir, Justice of Peace, 67–8.

[55] Gough, Antiquities of Myddle, 104; T.S.A.S. 3rd ser. iii. 339.
[56] T.S.A.S. 3rd ser. iv. 153, 159–60, 166–70, 175.
[57] Ibid. 182.
[58] Hist. MSS. Com. 4, 5th Rep., Sutherland, p. 150; T.S.A.S. 3rd ser. iv. 156–61, 166, 168–72, 175.
[59] T.S.A.S. 3rd ser. iv. 179.
[60] Ibid. 3rd ser. iii, p. vi; 3rd ser. iv. 279–81.
[61] Ibid. 3rd ser. iv. 160, 166, 169.
[62] Ibid. 169, 175; 3rd ser. iii, p. vi.
[63] Ibid. 3rd ser. iv. 150.   [64] Ibid. 176–7.
[65] L. Boynton, Elizabethan Militia 1558–1638 (1967), 5.
[66] T.S.A.S. 3rd ser. iv. 167–8, 170, 178, 282.
[67] S.P. 14/16 no. 3i; S.P. 14/78 no. 46; Hist. MSS. Com. 53, Montagu, p. 51; ibid. 13, 10th Rep. IV, Kilmorey, p. 365.
[68] e.g. Barnes, Som. 91; W. B. Willcox, Gloucestershire: a Study in Local Govt. 1590–1640 (1940), 91.
[69] e.g. Acts of P.C. 1613–14, 112; 1627, 501; Hist. MSS. Com. 13, 10th Rep. IV, Kilmorey, pp. 368, 370.
[70] Moir, Justice of Peace, 68.
[71] Cal. S.P. Dom. 1603–10, 238.
[72] Ibid.; S.P. 16/41 no. 31; Hist. MSS. Com. 13, 10th Rep. IV, Kilmorey, p. 366.

foot had firearms and, of those, 200 had the old-fashioned caliver.[73] Persons rated for the militia were so often in arrears that it was impossible to punish them all.[74] At times powder was virtually unobtainable.[75] Whatever the difficulties, however, the enthusiasm of the Shropshire gentry for military exercises before the Civil Wars was evident. In 1618 the lieutenant founded a school of horsemanship at Ludlow,[76] and by 1626 one of the Shropshire deputies, Sir Thomas Cornewall, had formed a company of gentlemen volunteers, which trained frequently.[77] Richard Gough wrote in 1701 that before the Civil Wars it was accounted a 'creditable employment' in Shropshire to be a soldier in the county militia;[78] there was less enthusiasm in some other counties.[79] Nevertheless the militia officers, however keen, were amateurs, and a professional muster-master was employed. The sums levied on the county for his salary were resented by the gentry as unnecessary[80] and in Shropshire, as elsewhere,[81] intensified the discontent that preceded the Civil Wars. Sir John Corbet of Stoke was imprisoned in the Fleet for protesting about them at quarter sessions.[82]

Political extremists were principally the lieutenant's concern and rarely came before quarter sessions, at least in the later 17th century.[83] A special commission of oyer and terminer was issued in 1662 to enable the Shropshire sessions to try one case of sedition that could not wait until assizes.[84] During the Civil Wars and Interregnum political suspects were likely to be dealt with by a county committee, the governor of Shrewsbury, or the major-general, James Berry.[85] In that period, however, quarter sessions did make a political scrutiny of high constables and parish 'registers'.[86] After the Revolution settlement of 1689 magistrates everywhere were required by the government to investigate disaffection.[87] An unusual number of political suspects came before the Shropshire bench. Jacobite magistrates tried to intercede for them but with little effect.[88] Some prisoners were discharged on agreeing to take the Oath of Allegiance;[89] the more recalcitrant were gaoled until the assizes.[90]

The Sheriff

The sheriff remained a significant force in county government in the 17th century, particularly in times of crisis, and political considerations affected the government's choice of sheriffs as much as that of magistrates and lieutenants. William Pierrepont (1637–8)[91] and Thomas Nichols (1640–1), one of the leading Shropshire Parliamentarians,[92] were evidently appointed to conciliate opponents of the government at a critical time. Parliament appointed its first Shropshire sheriff, Thomas Mytton, in 1643, but the king made sheriffs concurrently until 1645.[93] The government's long-standing confidence in Edmund Waring (1656–60) is probably attributable to his republicanism.[94] A suitable and willing sheriff was hard to find at that period. The

[73] S.P. 14/16 no. 3i; Hist. MSS. Com. 13, *10th Rep. IV, Kilmorey*, p. 366.
[74] S.P. 16/41 no. 31.
[75] Boynton, *Elizabethan Militia*, 261.
[76] Hist. MSS. Com. 13, *10th Rep. IV, Kilmorey*, pp. 366–7.
[77] S.P. 16/41 no. 31.
[78] *Antiquities of Myddle*, 151.
[79] G. C. F. Forster, 'Eng. Local Community and Local Govt. 1603–1625', *Reign of James VI and I*, ed. A. G. R. Smith (1973), 199.
[80] S.P. 16/41 no. 31; *Acts of P.C. 1627–8*, 216; *Cal. S.P. Dom. 1635*, 304.
[81] A. Hassell Smith, in *Archives*, ix. 217; Forster, 'Eng. Local Community', 200; Fletcher, *Co. Community in Peace and War*, 186.
[82] *D.N.B.*
[83] *Acts of P.C. 1615–16*, 583–4; *Orders of Q. Sess.* i. 89.

[84] Under the Sedition Act, 1661, 13 Chas. II, Stat. I, c. 1: C 181/7 p. 142; *Cal. S.P. Dom. 1661–2*, 295.
[85] *Cal. S.P. Dom. 1649–50*, 549; 1650, 290, 301, 475; *T.S.A.S.* 3rd ser. x. 153, 155.
[86] *Orders of Q. Sess.* i, orders 1652–60, 8; ibid. i. 10, 41–2. 'Registers' were appointed under the Marriages Act, 1653: *Acts & Ords. of Interr.* ii. 715–18.
[87] *Warw. Co. Rec.* ix, p. xiii.
[88] S.R.O., q. sess. order bk. 5, Trin. 1690.
[89] Prescribed by the Oaths of Supremacy and Allegiance Act, 1689, 1 Wm. & Mary, Sess. 1, c. 8.
[90] *Orders of Q. Sess.* i. 122–3, 131.
[91] *D.N.B.*
[92] *T.S.A.S.* 2nd ser. xii. 5; 4th ser. ix. 235; *Acts & Ords. of Interr.* i. 94.
[93] *List of Sheriffs* (P.R.O. Lists & Indexes, ix; corrected reprint, 1963), 120; Blakeway, *Sheriffs*, 22.
[94] *T.S.A.S.* 3rd ser. iv. 174.

office was reckoned too burdensome to be inflicted on the government's friends and too dangerous to be offered to its opponents. In 1655 the major-general, James Berry, considered Thomas Hunt by far the ablest man in Shropshire for the shrievalty, but Hunt was not a wholehearted supporter of the government and was reluctant to serve. Berry tried to find an alternative, but Hunt eventually had to serve for some months in 1656 before Waring's appointment.[95] Jonathan Langley's appointment in November 1688 was an act of conciliation by James II, as were his simultaneous reinstatements of expelled magistrates.

The under-sheriff was appointed by the incoming sheriff, relieving him, in return for the fees, of virtually all ordinary responsibilities except ceremonial ones.[96] As elsewhere,[97] under-sheriffs were mostly local attorneys, like Thomas Dicken,[98] Richard Manning,[99] Moses Reynolds,[1] Andrew Swift,[2] Arthur Tonge,[3] his son Edward,[4] John Wood the elder,[5] and John Wood the younger.[6] No Shropshire under-sheriff is known to have served two years in succession[7] but several acted more than once during their careers.[8]

The sheriff's ancient county court was by the 17th century mainly a small-debts court.[9] In Shropshire it met every four weeks on a Thursday[10] but little is known of its work. Knights of the shire were, in theory, elected by the county court, and the sheriff, as in 1646,[11] had some opportunity to influence results.[12] He had many routine responsibilities in connexion with assizes and quarter sessions, impanelling juries, executing writs and summonses, and carrying out sentences.[13] As keeper of the county gaol he was required by the Shropshire quarter sessions in 1707 to contribute annually to its expenses.[14] The sheriff assumed an unaccustomed authority in 1642 when he became chief agent of the county's commissioners of array;[15] a few months later that authority threatened his personal downfall when Parliament impeached him.[16]

The sheriff's most disagreeable task in the 17th century was probably that of assessing and collecting the notorious 'ship money', first levied in Shropshire in 1635.[17] There was at first no serious local resistance to it.[18] Trouble began during the shrievalty of the unpopular Sir Paul Harris (1636–7).[19] Two Shropshire taxpayers appealed against their assessments to Sir John Bridgeman, chief justice of Chester, who, against Harris's wishes, granted them a reduction. Since the county was liable for a fixed sum, other assessments had to be increased, setting in motion a train of disputes.[20] By the summer of 1638 the sheriff could not cope with the number of refusers;[21] Bridgeman's decision had in any case undermined his authority. New assessments made in 1638[22] failed to retrieve the situation[23] and by 1640 collection had broken down completely.[24] The

[95] Berry and Lee, *Cromwellian Major General*, 136, 147, 151–2.
[96] S.R.O. 1093, box 56, under-sheriffs' indentures of appointment, 1629, 1684; S.R.O. 327, box 268, idem 1700.
[97] Barnes, *Som.* 137.
[98] *S.P.R. Lich.* xvi. 846. Served 1700–1.
[99] Ibid. xii. 893. Served 1694–5.
[1] Ibid. xvi. 810. Served 1687–8, 1692–3.
[2] Ibid. xii. 288. Served 1686–7, 1688–9, 1690–1, 1696–7, 1707–8.
[3] *T.S.A.S.* 4th ser. ii. 121. Served 1677–8, 1689–90, 1691–2, 1712–13.
[4] Ibid. Served 1693–4, 1710–11.
[5] Ibid. 3rd ser. x. 266. Served 1670–1, 1674–5, 1678–9, 1681–2.
[6] Ibid. Served 1683–4.
[7] Cf. C. H. Karraker, *Seventeenth-Cent. Sheriff* (1930), 13.
[8] Blakeway, *Sheriffs*, 21–5.
[9] Karraker, op. cit. 49–50.
[10] J. J. Alexander, 'Dates of County Days', *Bull. Inst. Hist. Res.* iii. 93.
[11] *T.S.A.S.* xlvii. 47.
[12] Karraker, op. cit. 32–4. On the sheriff's part in the 1604 Shrews. election see below, p. 241.
[13] Ibid. 16–20.
[14] *Orders of Q. Sess.* i. 232.
[15] *T.S.A.S.* 2nd ser. vi. 33; ibid. li. 20.
[16] Hist. MSS. Com. 4, *5th Rep., Ho. of Lords*, p. 48; *L.J.* v. 360.
[17] *T.S.A.S.* xlix. 29.
[18] *Cal. S.P. Dom.* 1636–7, 202, 448.
[19] Gough, *Antiquities of Myddle*, 67.
[20] *Cal. S.P. Dom.* 1636–7, 449; 1637, 378–9, 495–6; 1637–8, 199, 311–12.
[21] Ibid. 1637–8, 423.
[22] S.R.O., q. sess. order bk. 1, sheriff and J.P.s to assize justices [early 1638]; ibid. schedule 14 July 1638.
[23] *Orders of Q. Sess.* i, orders 1638–60, 1; *Cal. S.P. Dom.* 1638–9, 392; 1639, 252, 471.
[24] *Cal. S.P. Dom.* 1640, 14.

same pattern of internal disputes and progressive breakdown occurred throughout the country.[25]

Coroners, Escheators, and Feodaries

County coroners were elected by the county court and in Shropshire, as elsewhere,[26] they seem usually to have been attorneys,[27] like the under-sheriffs. Indeed the same men seem occasionally to have served both offices: Michael Stephens, elected c. 1638[28] and mentioned as coroner in 1661,[29] was probably the under-sheriff of 1646–7;[30] Richard Mason, elected c. 1656,[31] may have been the under-sheriff of 1655–6 and 1659–60.[32] Thomas Dicken, however, elected 1707,[33] was probably not the under-sheriff of 1700–1.[34] Mason may also have been the escheator of 1629–30[35] and the clerk of the county committee in 1648.[36]

The escheator held the inquisition post mortem on the death of a tenant in chief and was responsible for taking possession of lands that escheated to the Crown.[37] He was appointed annually, usually, it seems, from young members of the local gentry or from men styled 'gentleman'. No-one above the rank of esquire was appointed escheator for Shropshire in the 17th century.[38] Only a few of the escheators became magistrates, like Walter Acton (escheator 1610–11),[39] John Matthews (1617–18),[40] and probably Francis Forester (1620–1).[41] Some, like Arthur Lewkenor (1634–5),[42] Richard Owen (1639–40),[43] and Francis Burton (1640–1),[44] are known to have acted by deputy, and the Shropshire deputy sometimes acted simultaneously for Montgomeryshire.[45] The same man might be deputy in more than one year, and some deputies, like Isaac Morgan (deputy 1634–5) and Robert Sandford (1639–41), were themselves escheators in other years — Morgan in 1631–2 and 1636–7, Sandford in 1638–9.

Of more influence in the county was the feodary, a permanent official of the Court of Wards and Liveries. His many duties included the valuation of estates taken into Crown wardship.[46] Shropshire and Montgomeryshire came under a single feodary.[47] Both Thomas Lawley (feodary before 1601 until 1617)[48] and Thomas Owen (1617–c. 1625)[49] were esquires, but they were not magistrates during their period of office.[50] John Pay (c. 1625–1645) was styled 'gentleman' only.[51] The feodary was sometimes unpopular locally: in 1638 Pay was one of those feodaries who obtained a royal pardon for previous misdeeds.[52] The offices of escheator and feodary were effectively abolished with tenures in chief in 1646.[53]

County Committees 1643–60

The county committees of the Civil Wars and Interregnum were not an innovation.[54] Special commissions, usually comprising magistrates but charged with duties not

[25] Moir, *Justice of Peace*, 66–7; L. M. Hill, 'Co. Govt. in Caroline Eng.', in *Origins of the Eng. Civil War*, ed. C. Russell (1973), 85–8.

[26] Forster, *E. Riding Justices*, 7.

[27] Some returned election writs survive in C 202. Thanks are due to Dr. R. F. Hunnisett for information on this source.

[28] C 202/20/4.   [29] *Cal. S.P. Dom.* 1661–2, 109.

[30] Blakeway, *Sheriffs*, 22. A man named Stevens (forename not recorded) was under-sheriff in 1650–1 and 1652–3: ibid.

[31] C 202/39/4.

[32] Blakeway, *Sheriffs*, 22–3 (forename not recorded).

[33] C 202/93/2.   [34] See p. 134.

[35] *List of Escheators for Eng.* (List and Index Soc. lxxii), 137.

[36] See p. 113.

[37] H. E. Bell, *Intro. to Hist. and Recs. of Ct. of Wards and Liveries* (1953), 41.

[38] *List of Escheators*, 136–7.   [39] C 231/4 f. 67 (1618).

[40] Ibid. f. 176v. (1625).   [41] C 231/6 p. 74 (1647).

[42] Ward. 9/275 f. 33v.   [43] Ward. 9/276 f. 7.

[44] Ibid. f. 9.   [45] Ibid. ff. 7v., 9.

[46] Bell, op. cit. 39–41.   [47] Ibid. 45 n.

[48] Hist. MSS. Com. 9, *Salisbury*, x, p. 94; Ward. 9/275, 11 Feb. 1617. Probably Thos. Lawley of Spoonhill, M.P. Wenlock 1625–9, cr. bt. 1641: L. G. Pine, *New Extinct Peerage* (1972), 291.

[49] Ward. 9/275, 11 Feb. 1617; 11 July 1625.

[50] Lawley became a J.P. in 1638: C 231/5 p. 287.

[51] Ward. 9/276, 4 Dec. 1645.   [52] Bell, op. cit. 44 n.

[53] Ibid. 159. Abolition confirmed by Tenures Abolition Act, 1660, 12 Chas. II, c. 24.

[54] Aylmer, *The State's Servants*, 11–12.

included in the commission of the peace, were familiar from pre-war days.[55] After 1642 county committees continued to impinge little on the activities of quarter sessions, being concerned with extraordinary matters of finance, military organization, and security. The county committees, however, were so necessary to Parliament's conduct of the war and to the successive governments of the Interregnum that they enjoyed much more power than did pre-war special commissions, and were a focus of local political struggles.[56]

In February 1643 Parliament appointed a committee of its Shropshire supporters, most of them magistrates,[57] to collect the county's 'weekly assessment' for the conduct of the war.[58] In March the same body was also constituted a committee for sequestrations,[59] and it was enlarged in April under an association with Staffordshire and Warwickshire.[60] In September Wem was garrisoned for Parliament and became the committee's headquarters.[61] The rest of Shropshire was then in royalist hands and the committee had little real authority.[62] Its leaders included Thomas Mytton of Halston, Humphrey Mackworth, Thomas Hunt, and Andrew Lloyd of Aston.[63] A rift appeared in the committee over claims to military command. In 1643 the Parliamentarian lieutenant, the earl of Essex, gave Mytton an independent command; the rest of the committee obtained in June 1644 an Ordinance allowing its members, so they said, to assume military rank.[64] Later in the month Mytton was made governor of Oswestry, lately taken by Lord Denbigh for Parliament, and was answerable only to Denbigh.[65] Thereafter bitter enmity, exacerbated by political and religious differences, persisted between the committee and the army commanders,[66] as it did in Staffordshire and Warwickshire.[67] Denbigh called the committee 'Brownists' and 'Anabaptists'[68] and was for his part suspected of royalist leanings.[69] Rival forces under Mytton and William Reinking, a Dutch mercenary employed by the committee,[70] captured Shrewsbury in 1645. Mytton and Reinking disputed the governorship but the committee moved its headquarters to Shrewsbury and made Humphrey Mackworth, a republican,[71] governor.[72] Only the committee's leaders, who included in addition to those already mentioned Samuel More, Robert Charlton, and Leighton Owen, seem to have attended its meetings.[73]

The First Civil War virtually ended in Shropshire with the fall of Ludlow to the Parliamentarians in 1646. In 1647 the committee was reconstituted as a committee for the 'monthly assessment', retaining its former leaders.[74] In the crisis of 1648–9 assessment committees everywhere were purged.[75] Twenty moderates were removed in Shropshire,[76] among them such men as Robert Charlton, one of the leaders, Robert Clive, and Esay Thomas, all three of whom were excluded from Parliament by Pride's Purge,[77] and John Wybunbury, who was to be involved in Sir George Booth's rising in 1659.[78] Ten of those removed were magistrates and, of them, seven were also removed from the commission of the peace.[79] Twenty-three republicans were added to the

[55] See p. 94.
[56] Underdown, *Pride's Purge*, 29–36, 312–15.
[57] S.R.O. 840, box 29, com. 1642; C 231/5 p. 515.
[58] *Acts & Ords. of Interr.* i. 94; *S.H.C.* 4th ser. i, p. xxix.
[59] *Acts & Ords. of Interr.* i. 116.
[60] Ibid. 126. [61] *T.S.A.S.* xlvii. 34; l. 75.
[62] Ibid. 2nd ser. vi. 19; *Acts & Ords. of Interr.* i. 447.
[63] *T.S.A.S.* xlvii. 34; J. R. Phillips, *Memoirs of the Civil War in Wales and the Marches 1642–1649* (1874), ii. 123.
[64] *Acts & Ords. of Interr.* i. 446–50; *T.S.A.S.* xlviii. 57–8.
[65] *T.S.A.S.* xlviii. 49–50.
[66] Ibid. xlvii. 34–47; xlviii. 49–60; *Cal. S.P. Dom.* 1645–7, 276, 470; ibid. 1649–50, 444–5; Hist. MSS. Com. 3, *4th Rep., Denbigh*, p. 271.
[67] *S.H.C.* 4th ser. i, pp. liii–liv, lxxviii.
[68] *Cal. S.P. Dom.* 1649–50, 445.
[69] *S.H.C.* 4th ser. i, p. lxxvi.
[70] *T.S.A.S.* xlvii. 33–4.
[71] Ibid. 3rd ser. x. 109–10.
[72] Ibid. xlvii. 37–43.
[73] Ibid. 36, 38–9, 41 n., 43; xlviii. 55; Owen and Blakeway, *Hist. Shrews.* i. 460 n.; ii. 498, 500.
[74] *Acts & Ords. of Interr.* i. 973.
[75] Underdown, *Pride's Purge*, 314–15.
[76] *Acts & Ords. of Interr.* i. 1090–1; ii. 41, 119–20, 306–7.
[77] Brunton and Pennington, *Members of Long Parl.* 211.
[78] *T.S.A.S.* 3rd ser. x. 154.
[79] S.R.O. 840, box 29, com. 1642; C 231/6 p. 74; *Acts & Ords. of Interr.* ii. 41.

THE FIRST SHIREHALL: THE GREAT HALL OF SHREWSBURY CASTLE

The central entrance (now to the basement) and the windows above are Telford's work; to the right is the original main entrance, restored in the 1920s

JOHN TALBOT, EARL OF SHREWSBURY, K.G., PRESENTING A BOOK TO QUEEN MARGARET, c. 1445

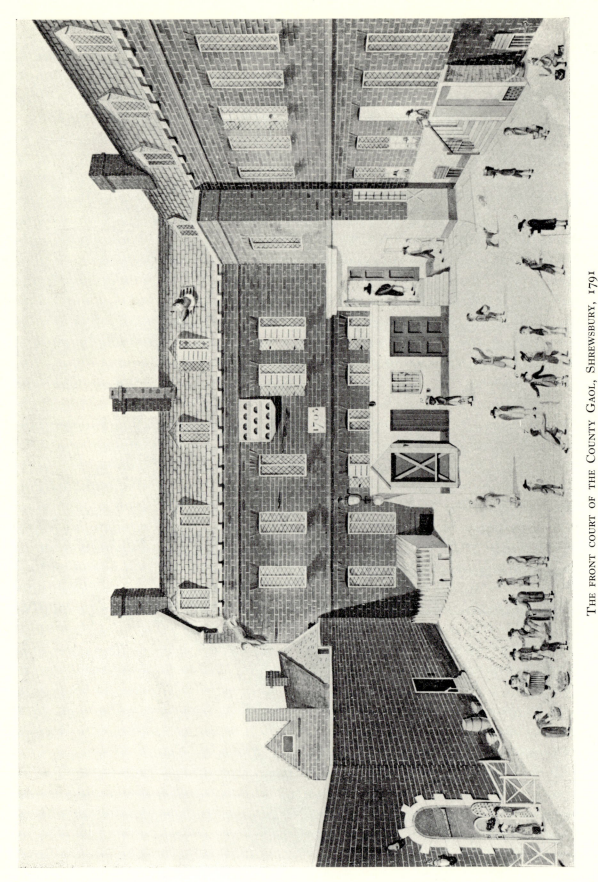

THE FRONT COURT OF THE COUNTY GAOL, SHREWSBURY, 1791

'The noted Cock' escapes through the roof and over an adjoining building; a prisoner stands locked to the post with a loaf stolen from a fellow prisoner; in the foreground provisions are being sold and Amy Butcher cries her vegetables, a highwayman slips a letter to his wife into a woman's pocket, and a pickpocket is at work

committee: they included Humphrey Edwardes, a regicide,[80] and William Brayne, a prosecution witness at the king's trial;[81] eleven of the 23 were to be removed from the committee between 1654 and 1657.[82] Sequestrations were taken out of the hands of county committees in 1650 and entrusted to three commissioners in each county.[83] In Shropshire the three[84] were replaced in 1654 by a single commissioner.[85]

The committee was again reconstituted in 1654[86] and became more conservative.[87] Five of the newcomers between 1654 and 1657 were also added to the commission of the peace.[88] Several committee men, including such moderates as Lancelot Lee, Robert Corbet of Stanwardine (the *custos rotulorum*), Harcourt Leighton, and Edward Cressett of Cotes, were not removed during the political changes of the 1640s and 1650s.[89] They also kept their positions as leaders of quarter sessions throughout the Interregnum[90] and their influence on the county committee, though difficult to assess, may have been as great as that of the transient radicals.[91] Many of the committee's members were magistrates though there was little formal contact between it and quarter sessions.[92] The resumption of republican government in 1659 failed to make the committee into a republican body. It pursued royalists after Booth's abortive rising,[93] but its membership remained predominantly conservative. The assessment committee appointed in January 1660 was intended to be republican,[94] but two-thirds of its members were also appointed to the conservative militia committee of March 1660.[95]

Beside the other committees there was appointed in 1644 a committee for ejecting 'scandalous' ministers and schoolmasters. Its composition was virtually the same as that of the assessment and sequestration committee.[96] The committee began work immediately on appointing new ministers.[97] It was reconstituted with smaller membership in 1654;[98] Thomas Gilbert, rector of Edgmond, became its assistant and earned the nickname 'bishop of Shropshire'.[99]

In 1648 32 Shropshire commissioners for 'settling the militia', drawn from the assessment and sequestration committee,[1] were appointed.[2] Their task, to raise troops for home service, had formerly been carried out by the lieutenant and, at the outbreak of war, by royal commissioners of array associated with the sheriff.[3] The leader of the militia committee appears to have been Humphrey Mackworth the elder,[4] governor of Shrewsbury (d. 1654).[5] Indeed Mackworth seems, through his control of the militia, to have been the unofficial ruler of the county, a figure such as emerged all over England during the Interregnum.[6] In 1648 the committee's clerk was Richard Mason,[7] who became a county coroner and perhaps under-sheriff in the 1650s.[8] In 1650 the militia committee succeeded in raising troops for Ireland[9] but in 1651 was unable to raise troops quickly against the Scottish army in England.[10] After the battle of Worcester most of its activities ceased until 1659.[11]

On Mackworth's death the governorship was inherited by his son Humphrey.[12] In

[80] *T.S.A.S.* 3rd ser. x. 110–11.
[81] Ibid. xlvii. 38 n.
[82] *Acts & Ords. of Interr.* ii. 673, 1078; *Cal. S.P. Dom.* 1653–4, 402–3.
[83] Underdown, op. cit. 301.
[84] *Cal. Cttee. for Compounding*, i. 630.
[85] Ibid. 702–3.
[86] *Cal. S.P. Dom.* 1653–4, 402–3.
[87] *Acts & Ords. of Interr.* ii. 1078.
[88] C 231/6 pp. 305, 315, 343, 361.
[89] *Acts & Ords. of Interr. passim.*
[90] See p. 96.
[91] Underdown, op. cit. 327–31.
[92] e.g. S.R.O., q. sess. order bk. 2, Epiph. 1653; *Orders of Q. Sess.* i, orders 1652–60, 6.
[93] *T.S.A.S.* 3rd ser. x. 153, 155.
[94] *Acts & Ords. of Interr.* ii. 1355.
[95] See below.

[96] *Acts & Ords. of Interr.* i. 449–50.
[97] Hist. MSS. Com. 3, *4th Rep., Denbigh*, p. 268.
[98] *Acts & Ords. of Interr.* ii. 974.
[99] *D.N.B.*
[1] *Acts & Ords. of Interr.* i. 1090–1.
[2] Ibid. 1242–3.
[3] See pp. 84–6, 107–10.
[4] *T.S.A.S.* 3rd ser. x. 119, 128.
[5] *D.N.B. sub* Mackworth, Thos.
[6] Underdown, *Pride's Purge*, 307–9.
[7] Owen and Blakeway, *Hist. Shrews.* i. 464.
[8] See p. 111.
[9] *Cal. S.P. Dom.* 1650, 270.
[10] Ibid. 1651, 333.
[11] The no. of Council of State orders to the cttee. fell markedly: *Cal. S.P. Dom. passim.*
[12] *T.S.A.S.* 4th ser. xi. 179.

1655, however, a new county ruler emerged. In that year Shropshire, with Herefordshire, Worcestershire, and North Wales, was placed under the puritan major-general, James Berry, the former clerk of an ironworks. One of his duties was to raise a standing 'county troop' of militia to suppress disaffection.[13] The Shropshire troop was put under the command of Edmund Waring (later of Humphreston), an Anabaptist.[14] Berry's office was abolished in 1656 but Waring's was not, and in the same year he became sheriff too, holding the position contrary to precedent (and perhaps law)[15] for over three years. From 1656 to 1660 Waring was the most powerful man in Shropshire. In 1657 Thomas Gilbert's assize sermon was dedicated to him with the words: 'You have in your single hand a two-fold *posse*, both civil and military, in this county, an interest in it above both and . . . , for your time, above any gentleman's of your rank in any county of England'.[16]

In 1659, with the resumption of republican government, the militia committee was revived[17] to combat Booth's royalist and conservative rising in Cheshire.[18] Waring was appointed governor of Shrewsbury[19] and in the last months of 1659 tried to round up the many insurgents and royalist plotters said to be 'lurking in holes' in Shropshire.[20] The committee, however, was predominantly conservative. Two-thirds of its members had served on committees during the Protectorate.[21] The army lost control of government early in 1660 and Waring was arrested, to be replaced as governor by Thomas Hunt.[22] As in other counties,[23] a new and even more conservative militia committee was appointed.[24] Only two-fifths of its members had sat on the committee in 1659; half the newcomers had never sat on a county committee before, and another quarter had not done so since 1648.[25] By June, however, the committee had been effectively supplanted by a rival committee[26] appointed by the king from Brussels.[27]

[13] *T.S.A.S.* 3rd ser. x. 146–7; *D.N.B.*
[14] *T.S.A.S.* 3rd ser. iv. 174–5; x. 147–8.
[15] See p. 74.
[16] Blakeway, *Sheriffs*, 131 n.
[17] *Acts & Ords. of Interr.* ii. 1331.
[18] *T.S.A.S.* 3rd ser. x. 149.
[19] Ibid. 150.
[20] Ibid. 153, 155.
[21] *Acts & Ords. of Interr.* ii. 974, 1078, 1247.
[22] *T.S.A.S.* 3rd ser. x. 156–7.
[23] Underdown, *Pride's Purge*, 353.
[24] *Acts & Ords. of Interr.* ii. 1441.
[25] Ibid. i–ii.
[26] *T.S.A.S.* 3rd ser. iv. 147–8.
[27] Ibid. 144–5.

COUNTY GOVERNMENT
1714–1834

The Commission of the Peace, p. 116. Quarter Sessions, p. 116. Petty Sessions, p. 129. The Lieutenancy and the Militia, p. 131. The Sheriff, p. 132. The County Coroners, p. 133.

BETWEEN Anne's death and William IV's accession local government was little affected either by political upheavals of the sort which had characterized the 17th century or by the mass of general legislation which poured forth after 1834. The landed gentry, entrenched in local power by the Revolution of 1689, settled down to rule the counties, and the government of Shropshire seemingly fell into the hands of a Whig clique in the early and mid 18th century. Later in the century, however, the beginnings of an impetus for change and improvement may be detected. The commission of the peace and quarter sessions itself became less socially exclusive in George III's reign than it had been before or was to be later. Reform and rebuilding of the gaol, and an expansion of the magistrates' ambitions to improve transport and travel by adopting and rebuilding many county bridges can be associated with the new men ascending the bench from the 1760s and with the court's greater reliance on professional officers — clerks, treasurers, and surveyors.

Other changes were achieved by means of local Acts of Parliament. The initiative for securing those Acts must invariably have been local, and it was no doubt to its magisterial class, acting as a pressure group on Parliament, that Shropshire owed its turnpike trusts,[1] its statutory courts of requests,[2] and its poor-law incorporations.[3] In Shropshire all these developments,[4] forerunners of the general legislation of the years after 1834, are concentrated in the reign of George III.

Archdeacon Plymley, writing in 1803, argued that the great need in his time was not for new laws but for the due execution of existing ones, so as to restrain straying cattle, abate highway nuisances, and provide work for the poor. Nevertheless he conceded that such things could not be done by magistrates alone, even watchful ones.[5] Accordingly it came to be gradually acknowledged that the law needed to be professionally enforced by clerical officials, inspectors,[6] and police.[7] At the same time in order to achieve contemporary administrative aims a vigorous and intelligent magistracy with deep roots in the county[8] was deemed necessary to give leadership in the last and busiest half-century of the rule of quarter sessions.[9]

[1] The first turnpike Act to affect Salop. passed in 1726 but over 70 per cent of the Salop. Acts passed during the yrs. 1750–79: W. Albert, *Turnpike Road System in Eng. 1663–1840* (1972), 201–23.

[2] At Broseley, Oldbury, and Shrews.: *Ret. of Cts. of Requests*, H.C. 216 (1836), xliii; *Ret. rel. Cts. of Requests*, H.C. 338–I (1839), xliii.

[3] See p. 169.

[4] By the end of the 18th cent., however, the Salop. turnpike roads were evidently among the least improved in the country: E. Pawson, *Transport and Economy: the Turnpike Roads of Eighteenth-Cent. Brit.* (1977), 269–71.

[5] J. Plymley, *General View of Agric. of Salop.* (1803),

348–9.

[6] Weights and measures inspectors were first appointed in Salop. in 1801: *Orders of Q. Sess.* iii, p. xx.

[7] One of Plymley's preoccupations: Plymley, op. cit. 348. From the 1790s the Salop. J.P.s were in the forefront of those pressing for the provision of rural police: *Orders of Q. Sess.* iii, pp. xiv, 41; *T.S.A.S.* 2nd ser. iii. 228–30; below, p. 157.

[8] See e.g. the remarks of Sir Baldwyn Leighton concluding his review of his father's local-govt. work: 'Life of Sir B. Leighton' (TS. in S.R.O. 783, parcel 194), pp. 85–6.

[9] See pp. 135–66.

The Commission of the Peace

The size of the commission of the peace increased greatly during the period. There were 102 working magistrates in 1721, 145 in 1733, and 249 in 1761. During George III's reign numbers, despite some fluctuation, increased even more and there was a more than proportionate increase in the numbers of clerical magistrates. In 1761 there had been 31 clergymen, including 3 bishops, among the 249 magistrates; by 1774 about 50 out of 218 magistrates were clergy. In 1793, however, the working portion of the commission numbered 425, among whom the clergy numbered 114, including 4 bishops. By 1830 total numbers had fallen off, but more noticeably among lay than among clerical magistrates: the strength of the working portion of the commission was then 297, of whom 95 were clergy.[10]

Political alterations to the commission seem to have been restricted entirely to the first few years of the period when the new dynasty was consolidating its position by strengthening its Whig supporters in the counties. The 2nd earl of Bradford was restored as *custos* and lieutenant in October 1714 and, no doubt with his advice, the Shropshire commission was renewed by Lord Chancellor Cowper in December. The result was a transformation of the Tory predominance of Anne's later years into a fairly even balance between the two parties.[11] In 1715, as a result of the Jacobite risings in the autumn, 17 more men were put out of the commission. The dismissals included such prominent Tories as Sir John Astley and Corbet Kynaston and must have resulted in a more decisive Whig majority on the commission. Altogether in 1714–15 31 of the 58 magistrates added by the Tory Lord Chancellor Harcourt (1710–14) were removed. Recognizable Tories like Whitmore Acton and Acton Baldwyn, however, remained, and there had in fact been no drastic purge.[12] Nor were there any thereafter,[13] the large commissions of the later 18th century indicating that political selection was both impracticable and unwanted.

Quarter Sessions

The number of magistrates attending quarter sessions fluctuated, though from about 1775 the average gradually rose to double that characteristic of the beginning of the period. Thus attendance at the court, though it increased over the second half of the period, did not do so in proportion to the growth in the size of the commission of the peace.[14] Despite high attendances in George I's first years,[15] perhaps because of more frequent alterations to the commission,[16] some 14 magistrates attended an average Shropshire quarter sessions during the rest of his reign and the earlier years of his son's.[17] In the second half of George II's reign, however, average numbers fell to 9 and, except for a few years in the mid 1760s when they rose to their former level,[18] they remained at, or even slightly below, 9 until the 1770s.[19] From 1775 average numbers

[10] C 234/32, fiats 2 Jan. 1721, 10 Mar. 1733, 22 Apr. 1761, 29 June 1774, 18 Sept. 1793, 6 Dec. 1830. The fiats list only the working portion of the commission (above, p. 90 n. 3), though sometimes including the law officers of the Crown (here ignored). S.P.L., Deeds 3570, lists 232 J.P.s (5 dead), 1761.

[11] See p. 93.

[12] C 234/32, fiats 7 Dec. 1714, 24 Aug., 26 Dec. 1715; L. K. J. Glassey, 'Commission of Peace, 1675–1720' (Oxford Univ. D.Phil. thesis, 1972), 364–8 (incl. Salop. details), 372–9 (Cowper's general policy).

[13] Ten names struck off the commission in 1731 (C 234/32, fiat 31 July 1731) prove, on examination, to be dead men's.

[14] See above.

[15] Averaging 24 magistrates per sessions 1714–15: E 362/43/33; E 362/44/31.

[16] See above.

[17] i.e. 1714–43: E 362/43/33; E 362/72/36; and intermediate documents.

[18] i.e. 16 1762–6: E 362/92/43; E 362/96/43; and intermediate documents.

[19] i.e. 9 1744–61 (E 362/73/35; E 362/91/43; and intermediate documents), 8 1767–74 (E 362/97/48; E 362/104/51; and intermediate documents).

attending were 15, and by the 1790s that number was showing a tendency to rise,[20] Shropshire's probably being one of the four or five best-attended quarter sessions in the country at that period.[21] Eighteen or so magistrates attended in the early years of the century[22] and by the close of the period that figure had risen to some 30.[23]

Clerical magistrates occasionally attended but not regularly or numerously before George III's reign.[24] Dr. John Fleming[25] and Leonard Hotchkiss,[26] from 1762, seem to have been the first regular attenders, followed by John Holland,[27] occasionally in the 1770s, and Thomas Edwardes (succ. as 7th bt. 1790)[28] regularly from 1775. The number of clerical attenders, however, rarely exceeded one or two before the 1780s when it began to reach 6 or 7, a level regularly maintained from the mid 1780s. By then clerical magistrates often formed a third or more of the bench and it was from that period that some of the leading quarter-sessions magistrates can be identified among the clergy.[29] By the 1790s and in the early 19th century the clergy occasionally formed half the bench[30] and sometimes even outnumbered laymen.[31] By the end of the period, however, they seem to have declined once more to about a quarter of the bench.[32]

Peers hardly ever came, though the lieutenant's son, Lord Newport, attended occasionally in George I's reign[33] and the 9th Viscount Kilmorey occasionally in mid century.[34] Lord Herbert of Chirbury (about to be raised to the earldom of Powis) came to the 1748 Easter sessions[35] but his attendance is not recorded thereafter until October 1761,[36] a few months after his loss of the lieutenancy to Lord Bath.[37] At the next sessions, in January 1762, Bath made his one appearance.[38] From about 1820 Lord Powis and his son Lord Clive began to attend sessions,[39] setting the fashion for the occasional appearances of other peers.[40]

The court was dominated by the squires. Some families played a prominent part in its work through several generations, the Edwardeses providing a notable example in the 18th century. The Whig Cluddes and Pembertons[41] provide another example, obscured by a change of name. William Cludde (d. 1765) of Orleton, after leaving the army, 'acquired those qualifications which rendered him useful and serviceable as a country gentleman', acted as a magistrate over forty years,[42] and attended quarter sessions fairly regularly,[43] as did his son Edward from the 1750s.[44] William's son-in-law Edward Pemberton, long a leading magistrate, was chairman of the court 1785–97, and Pemberton's grandson, Edward Cludde, and his nephew, Thomas Pemberton, both attended in the early 19th century, the latter presiding as chairman 1822–30.[45] Such traditions of involvement in the court's work enabled the landed gentry to retain the leadership at quarter sessions throughout the period, even during George III's reign

[20] i.e. 1775–96: E 362/105/57; E 362/125/88; and intermediate documents.

[21] *Local Govt. in Glos. 1775–1800* (Bristol and Glos. Archaeol. Soc., Records Section, viii), 77, n. 30, stating that the average attendance at Salop. q. sess. in 1795 was 18. The sources cited (E 362/124/86; E 362/125/88), however, show an average of just over 22 for 1795 and almost 20 for 1795–6, placing Salop. above Devon and below Mdx., Surr., and Ess. For 18th-cent. Wilts. figures see *V.C.H. Wilts.* v. 177.

[22] Taking 10 sample yrs. (1797, 1801–3, 1807–9, 1813–15): *Orders of Q. Sess.* iii. 85 sqq.

[23] See p. 137.

[24] Para. based on sources cited for previous para.

[25] Vicar of Acton Scott 1756–80; d. 1780: *Dioc. of Heref. Institutions, etc. (A.D. 1539–1900)*, ed. A. T. Bannister (Heref. 1923), 92, 108, 113; J. Foster, *Al. Oxon. . . . 1715–1886*, ii. 468. He was also vicar of Highley 1756–77.

[26] Formerly (1735–44) head master of Shrews. Sch.; d. 1771: J. and J. A. Venn, *Al. Cantab. . . . to 1751*, ii (1922), 412.

[27] Possibly the elder John Holland, of Ludlow, in Foster, *Al. Oxon. . . . 1715–1886*, ii. 678.

[28] S.P.L., MS. 2789, pp. 47–9.

[29] See p. 119.

[30] See e.g. E 362/122/102 (Jan. 1793); E 362/124/86 (Apr., July 1795).

[31] See e.g. *Orders of Q. Sess.* iii. 86, 190.

[32] See p. 138.

[33] E 362/44/31; E 362/45/36; E 362/49/33; E 362/50/31; E 362/51/33.

[34] E 362/78/38; E 362/79/39; E 362/93/42.

[35] E 362/77/41.

[36] E 362/91/43.

[37] Sir L. Namier, *Structure of Politics at the Accession of Geo. III* (1961), 280–2.

[38] E 362/92/43.

[39] *Orders of Q. Sess.* iii. 210–11, 216–18, 239 sqq.

[40] e.g. Mountnorris, Lyttelton: ibid. 269, 283.

[41] S.P.L., MS. 2793, pp. 219–21; below, p. 261 n. 31.

[42] Memorial in Wrockwardine ch.

[43] E 362/55/34 (1725); E 362/83/40 (1754); and intermediate documents.

[44] E 362/87/45 (1758); E 362/111/66 (1781). He d. 1785.

[45] *Orders of Q. Sess.* iii. 129–316; see below, pp. 118–19, 360.

when numbers of clerical magistrates and Shrewsbury residents began to figure among those most active in county business.

The court was not greatly affected by changes to the political balance of the commission in George I's early years.[46] Of the leading magistrates of Anne's reign only Eldred Lancelot Lee and Thomas Jones were excluded from the commission; in fact, as in earlier periods of political excitement,[47] the leadership of the court was remarkable chiefly for its continuity. John Lacon continued to attend regularly for nearly two years after 1714, John Kynaston for rather longer. Thomas Edwardes's almost unbroken record of attendance until 1721[48] suggests that he remained the usual chairman,[49] his name being most often listed first after the titled magistrates. William Whitmore, another leader of Anne's reign, may have succeeded to that position in the earlier 1720s. Nevertheless much the most regular attender during those years and until 1743 was Thomas Hunt[50] of Boreatton; though he rarely attended the January sessions, he was almost certainly the court's usual chairman.[51]

During the thirty years after Anne's death other new leaders emerged: Sir Charles Lloyd,[52] Thomas Severne, Edward Jorden of Priorslee, and Thomas Langley of Golding.[53] Lloyd's attendance fell off after 1721. From 1727–8 Godolphin Edwards, of Frodesley, and Henry Edwardes (succ. as 5th bt. 1734), of Netley, began to attend regularly. From the earlier 1720s to the earlier 1740s the leading magistrates after Thomas Hunt were Jorden and Langley, with Edwardes and Edwards coming in later. In the 1740s and 1750s Edward Corbett, younger brother of Sir Richard Corbett of Longnor, joined the group of leaders at sessions; before the 1750s were out, however, Langley was dead and Corbett had ceased to attend sessions[54] and, in 1758, Edward Pemberton[55] had begun his long connexion with the court. By that time, of the older generation of the court's leaders, only Sir Henry Edwardes remained, and it seems likely that in the middle years of the century Edwardes acted as the court's chairman. The smaller numbers of magistrates attending in the mid 18th century[56] may reflect the closer management of its business by a small clique[57] of which Edwardes was a leading member. Definite evidence is scarce but, with an unmatched attendance record over the twenty years to 1764, Edwardes must have seemed the natural choice for chairman; besides being the son of a former chairman[58] he belonged to the local Whig oligarchy[59] and busied himself generally on local affairs;[60] he was regularly involved in the work of his petty-sessional divisions,[61] and was foremost among those who audited the county treasurer's accounts.[62]

After Edwardes's retirement[63] Thomas More the younger may have taken first place briefly, but there is no evidence of a regular chairman for the two or so years before 1768 when Charles Baldwyn, of Aqualate (in Forton, Staffs.),[64] evidently began to act. Baldwyn was formally elected chairman in 1773, the first Shropshire magistrate to be

---

[46] This and the following four paras. are based generally on E 362/43–125; *Orders of Q. Sess.* iii. 84 sqq.

[47] See pp. 64, 96–7.

[48] He resigned the Shrews. town clerkship in 1720 (to be succ. by his s. Hen.) and d. 1727: Owen and Blakeway, *Hist. Shrews.* i. 544.

[49] See p. 98.

[50] See p. 97.

[51] See p. 102.

[52] A strong Whig: see p. 300.

[53] All appear in the 1721 commission: C 234/32, fiat 2 Jan. 1720/1.

[54] *T.S.A.S.* 4th ser. iii. 29; iv. 89; viii. 80. Corbett d. 1764: *S.P.R. Lich.* v(6), 60, 63.

[55] See p. 360 and sources there cited.

[56] See p. 116.

[57] See p. 131.

[58] See p. 117.

[59] He was a witness to the 3rd earl of Bradford's will: Prob. 11/669 ff. 25v.–28v. (P.C.C. 4 Ducie); Staffs. R.O., D. 1287/10/46, memorandums relating to execution of will of Hen., earl of Bradford, 27 Apr. 1766.

[60] See e.g. S.R.O. 112, Thos. Hill's letter bk. 1753–9, Hill to Edwardes, 6 May 1755, *re* the sending of a newly printed road Bill and the Cattle Distemper Act, 28 Geo. II, c.18.

[61] i.e. Condover (N.L.W., Castle Hill 2244) and Ford (see e.g. S.R.O., q. sess. rec., parcel 255, reg. of ale-sellers' recognizances 1753–4).

[62] S.R.O., q. sess. rec., parcel 177, co. treasurer's acct. bk. 1666–1764, Jan. 1743, May 1747, Mar. 1755, Jan. 1759.

[63] He d. 1767: Owen and Blakeway, *Hist. Shrews.* i. 544.

[64] *V.C.H. Staffs.* iv. 106.

thus distinguished.[65] Among the new leaders to emerge in George III's first years were Charles Bolas of Shrewsbury[66] and Thomas Harries of Cruckton.[67] In the 1770s the leading members of the court numbered only four or five, as had been the case throughout the previous half century: by the end of the decade Baldwyn, Pemberton, Bolas, and Harries had been joined by the Revd. Thomas Edwardes and the rich Shrewsbury alderman William Smith.[68]

The larger commissions of George III's reign eventually produced better attendances and, by the 1780s, greater numbers of magistrates whose regular attendance marks them out as the court's leading members: these were normally ten or more from the 1780s. While it is unnecessary to single them out by name, it is worthy of note that, as their numbers increased during George III's last forty years, the leading magistrates, like the commission of the peace as a whole, came to be recruited from a wider social range. There were, for example, many more clergy among the leaders. Many of them naturally belonged to the county's landed families, as did Thomas Edwardes (succ. as 7th bt. 1790), Edward Harries (who renounced his orders in 1782),[69] George Scott of Betton Strange,[70] and Archdeacon Plymley (later Corbett).[71] Others, like Edmund Dana, the American-born pluralist,[72] certainly did not.[73] Even more significant, perhaps, was the multiplication of professional and business men and rentiers who became involved in the court's work. William Smith's social pretensions were few, but his long career, from 1775 to the 1820s, as a leading magistrate was eventually rewarded by his appointment as a deputy lieutenant.[74] Dr. Samuel Harwood, who began to attend regularly from 1799, was a retired physician, and Robert Cheney Hart, who began to attend from about the same time, was a son of one of Harwood's former colleagues at the Salop Infirmary.[75]

The formal chairmanship remained a permanent feature of the court from 1773 except for the years 1779–85. Charles Baldwyn ceased to attend in 1779.[76] Indeed his appearance there could only have been a source of embarrassment as his financial difficulties became widely known and his consequent disputes with his son William Childe were well publicized by both parties in a series of pamphlets.[77] The magistrates did not immediately elect a successor. For several years Richard Hill (succ. as 2nd bt. 1783), Edward Pemberton, and the Revd. Thomas Edwardes seem to have presided in turn until, in 1785, Pemberton was formally elected to the chair.[78]

Quarter sessions were held in Shrewsbury throughout the period; before the completion of the new shirehall in 1786 they were held in the guildhall. Sessions opened on Tuesday[79] and normally lasted two or three days, the Epiphany sessions being that most often prolonged to three days in the earlier 18th century. In the later 1740s and in the 1750s sessions did not exceed two days and on one occasion[80] business was finished in one.

The court's criminal jurisdiction was not altered during the period but, as in earlier

[65] See p. 360 and sources there cited.
[66] *T.S.A.S.* 4th ser. iii. 29–30. He was mayor of Shrews. 1765.
[67] *V.C.H. Salop.* viii. 274.
[68] For Smith see *T.S.A.S.* 4th ser. iv. 101–2; S.P.L., MS. 3057, p. 71.
[69] *V.C.H. Salop.* viii. 274.
[70] Burke, *Land. Gent.* (1914), 1677; *T.S.A.S.* 2nd ser. i. 388.
[71] *V.C.H. Salop.* viii. 110.
[72] J. and J. A. Venn, *Al. Cantab. . . . 1752–1900*, ii (1944), 220.
[73] His ecclesiastical preferment shows him to have been a protégé of Wm. Pulteney (*V.C.H. Salop.* viii. 91; *S.P.R. Lich.* xi(1), pp. v–vii; xiii(5), p. v; *T.S.A.S.* 4th ser. vi. 312), the owner of a great American estate (*T.S.A.S.* 4th ser. xii. 239).

[74] For a good character sketch of Smith (d. 1828) see *The Eccentric; or Memoirs of No Common Characters, with Anecdotes . . .* (2nd edn.; London, 1829), 91–4 (copy in S.P.L., accession 3176).
[75] *T.S.A.S.* 4th ser. vii. 207–9.
[76] See p. 119.
[77] S.R.O. 739/4–5; S.P.L., Deeds 19167, Dr. Cheney Hart to Wm. Cheney Hart, 21 Feb. 1780; below, p. 262.
[78] See p. 360.
[79] For this para. see sources cited above, p. 118, n. 46. E 362/72/36 (1743) is the first estreat to specify the guildhall, as against simply Shrews., but see above, p. 97. Q. sess. began on Mon. from Oct. 1817, reverting to Tues. only briefly in 1837–8: *Orders of Q. Sess.* iii. 204, 206; *Salopian Jnl.* 18 and 25 Oct. 1837; 3 and 10 Jan. 1838.
[80] July 1753: E 362/82/39.

and later times,[81] serious offences were reserved for the assizes. Appeals, mainly on the subjects of settlement, bastardy, and the poor rate,[82] formed an increasingly complex branch of the court's business and by 1785, when they took priority of other court business, were far more numerous than trials.[83] During George III's reign the court issued many orders formalizing the procedure for appeals and regulating the appearance of counsel. One reason for the formal election of permanent chairmen from 1773 may have been the need for enhancing the authority of the court over counsel appearing before it.[84]

Miscellaneous duties of inspection, regulation, and licensing were laid on the court during the period, and oversight of madhouses,[85] theatres,[86] friendly societies,[87] printing presses,[88] and savings banks[89] was added to its older responsibilities relating to dissenters' meeting-houses.[90] The first licensed madhouse in the county seems to have been that at Bridgnorth kept by Joseph Proud; it was licensed in 1792.[91] From that date the appointment of committees of Visitors of Licensed Houses was a regular item of quarter sessions' business.[92] It was, however, a great increase in the court's administrative and financial business in the second half of the period which led to the appointment of the first permanent standing committees of the court charged with executive responsibilities. Those committees were the Gaol Visitors[93] and the Auditing Justices. By 1801 the county finances were sufficiently complex to require the annual appointment of a committee of 12 magistrates, 3 for each quarter, to oversee the treasurer's and the gaol accounts. Named to that committee, as was natural, were some of the court's leading members like Sir Corbet Corbet, Archdeacon Plymley, Rowland Hunt, and Edmund Dana; the committee, however, was open to all magistrates who wished to attend and was from the first a general-purposes committee, a forum for the transaction of all public business not usually conducted in open court.[94] The growth of the administrative and financial responsibilities which necessitated the court's appointment of that committee remains to be examined.

One of the few pieces of general legislation affecting local government in the 18th century was the County Rates Act, 1738.[95] Before its passage, for the first 25 years of the period, the old financial system endured: each year at the April sessions two magistrates were elected joint treasurers of the vagrant money, since 1709 virtually a general-purposes fund and levied at £140[96] until that sum was abated by 13s. 6d. in 1724,[97] presumably by the exemption of the borough of Albrighton.[98] Occasionally the same magistrates were continued in office for two, or even three, years, and a two-year term was usual in the 1730s.[99] For the most part the treasurers seem to have been drawn from

[81] See pp. 98–9, 136, 143.

[82] *Orders of Q. Sess.* ii–iii *passim.*

[83] *Salopian Jnl.* 4 Jan. 1843.

[84] *Orders of Q. Sess.* iii. 81–3; above, p. 98. This seems a more adequate explanation for the 1773 change than that suggested in *Orders of Q. Sess.* iii, preface to orders 1783–96, p. v (cf. ibid. iii, pp. xxiii, 31). The 'ungenteel' scene involving counsel at q. sess. 4 Oct. 1774 (S.P.L., MS. 2526, pp. 5, 7) probably occurred at Shrews. q. sess. (cf. S.R.O. 3365/2366, 7 Oct.).

[85] Madhouses Act, 1774, 14 Geo. III, c. 49, ss. 23–4.

[86] Theatrical Representations Act, 1788, 28 Geo. III, c. 30.

[87] Friendly Societies Act, 1793, 33 Geo. III, c. 54, ss. 2–3.

[88] Unlawful Societies Act, 1799, 39 Geo. III, c. 79, s. 23.

[89] Savings Bank Act, 1828, 9 Geo. IV, c. 92, ss. 2–4.

[90] *Orders of Q. Sess.* i, p. xxix; iii, pp. xvi–xvii, xxiv. Protestant meeting hos. had to be registered at q. sess.

1689–1852 (Toleration Act, 1689, 1 Wm. & Mary, Sess. 1, c. 18, s. 19; Protestant Dissenters Act, 1852, 15 & 16 Vic. c. 36), Rom. Cath. meeting places 1791–1855 (Rom. Cath. Relief Act, 1791, 31 Geo. III, c. 32, s. 5; Places of Worship Registration Act, 1855, 18 & 19 Vic. c. 81).

[91] *Orders of Q. Sess.* iii. 57.

[92] See p. 146.

[93] See pp. 125–6.

[94] *Orders of Q. Sess.* iii, preface, p. v; ibid. 103–4, 107, 110, 157, 299–300; *T.S.A.S.* 2nd ser. iii. 216.

[95] 12 Geo. II, c. 29.

[96] £35 multiplied by 4: see *Orders of Q. Sess.* ii. 20 sqq.; above, p. 102.

[97] *Orders of Q. Sess.* ii. 51–2.

[98] The bridge rate of £105 had been abated in Albrighton's favour in 1720: ibid. 37, 39; S.R.O., q. sess. rec., parcel 177, co. treasurer's acct. bk. 1666–1764, note in 1722 receipts. Cf. *T.S.A.S.* 2nd ser. xi. 35–6.

[99] For the rest of this para. see S.R.O., co. treasurer's acct. bk. 1666–1764; *Orders of Q. Sess.* ii. 18–98.

the junior magistrates.[1] The actual work of receipt and payment and of book-keeping was done by the treasurers' clerk or under-treasurer, who received £5 a year out of the rates for the work. The under-treasurer normally changed with the treasurers, who presumably appointed him. Such a supposition seems likelier from the employment of W. Haslewood as under-treasurer while Thomas Acton was one of the treasurers (1716-17): both bore well known Bridgnorth names.[2] The under-treasurer in 1722-3, John Moody, bore a name common in north-west Shropshire[3] where lay the family estates of one of the treasurers, Orlando Bridgeman.[4] Most of the under-treasurers, however, seem to have been prominent Shrewsbury tradesmen like James Millington (1717-19)[5] or John Adams (1719-22, 1724-6).[6] John Rogers, a Shrewsbury bookseller,[7] died in office in 1738 and Robert Baskerville of Shrewsbury, a recent under-sheriff and deputy clerk of the peace,[8] was put in his place.

Baskerville was the last man to deputize for the magistrate-treasurers, for in 1739, in accordance with the Act of 1738, the court appointed the first permanent county treasurer. He was Richard Davis,[9] innkeeper of the Post Office inn[10] and brother of the Shrewsbury postmistress Anne Norgrave.[11] The Post Office may indeed have been a convenient place of deposit for the county accounts between sessions: certainly in January 1724, after Richard Davis and two other men had cast up the county accounts following the death of the under-treasurer, the accounts and vouchers were left with Davis 'the postmaster' to be inspected by the magistrates.[12] Davis's successor Isaac Pritchard (1748-64)[13] was a Shrewsbury mercer and, like many other officers appointed by the court,[14] must have been a nominee of the ruling Whig clique: he had certainly used his power as mayor on behalf of the Whigs during the 1747 election.[15] Pritchard was succeeded (1764-1806) by John Flint (later Corbett), a connexion of the Corbetts of Longnor and the founder of a dynasty of county treasurers which lasted until 1906.[16] Flint was also postmaster of Shrewsbury.[17]

Not only did the 1738 Act provide for the appointment of a permanent county treasurer; it also unified the older county rates.[18] In 1739 the Shropshire divisional magistrates were supplied with copies of the old vagrant, bridge, and gaol rates, and the churchwardens and overseers were summoned before them to produce their rate books and accounts.[19] The new county rate was fixed at £278 13s. 0d., double the old vagrant rate,[20] and, with two minor adjustments in the 1750s, that sum continued to be levied, as need arose, for almost thirty years. The adjustments were occasioned by two boroughs' use of the county house of correction. Bishop's Castle began to send its vagrants and other criminals there in 1750 and was therefore assessed to the county rate; in 1753 Oswestry ceased to pay to the county rate and was accordingly prevented from using the house.[21] Later in the period the cessation of Bridgnorth quarter sessions and gaol delivery (1776), the borough's subsequent resort to the county gaol and sessions, and the inflation of criminal prosecution costs borne by the county rate,[22] led in

[1] To judge from their records of attendance at q. sess.: E 362/43 sqq.

[2] Wm. Haslewood was described as late master of the Bridgnorth ho. of correction in 1741: S.R.O., q. sess. order bk. 1726-41, f. 210v.

[3] S.P.R. St. Asaph, ii(1), iii(1-2), iv-vii; Lich. v(5).

[4] See p. 254.

[5] Owen and Blakeway, Hist. Shrews. i. 582.

[6] Ibid. 536.

[7] Ibid. He had been an under-treasurer in Queen Anne's reign.

[8] Blakeway, Sheriffs, 26; Sir E. Stephens, Clks. of the Counties, 1360-1960 (1961), 153; E 362/71/36.

[9] See p. 361.

[10] S.R.O. 3365/2312. The Old Post Office inn stands near the junction of Wyle Cop and Milk St.

[11] Lichfield Joint R.O., will of Ric. Davis, 4 Nov. 1748; S.P.R. Lich. xvi. 725, 1114; S.R.O., co. treasurer's acct. bk., 21 Sept. 1748; Post Office Records, St. Martin's-le-Grand, list of Shrews. postmasters (showing Anne Norgrave 1721-49).

[12] S.R.O., co. treasurer's acct. bk., 14 Jan. 1724.

[13] See p. 361.

[14] See pp. 125, 129.

[15] C.J. xxv. 426.

[16] See p. 361.

[17] 1753-1806: P.O. Records, list of Shrews. postmasters.

[18] See p. 102.

[19] Orders of Q. Sess. ii. 99.

[20] Ibid. 100.

[21] Ibid. 136, 148.

[22] Cf. V.C.H. Wilts. v. 235.

1824 to Bridgnorth's being assessed — inequitably as some inhabitants complained — to the county rate.[23]

In the 1740s just under two rates a year were levied on average, producing a mean annual income of £474.[24] Quarter sessions had no sources of income other than the county rate, and the figure may be taken to indicate average expenditure. In the 1750s it was higher: an average of just under 3 rates a year produced £753. The increase seems to have been principally due to the increased costs of conveying vagrants, and a new system of payment was accordingly introduced in 1757. At Michaelmas that year the constables of Whitchurch and Woodcote contracted to do their work for annual salaries in lieu of the costs and allowances for which they had previously submitted particular bills.[25] The greatest part of the work of vagrant conveyance, that along the London–Chester road, had long fallen upon these constables,[26] and those at Whitchurch were now to receive 100 gns. a year, those at Woodcote 120 gns.; the duties of the latter also included the conveyance to Shrewsbury of vagrants bound for Oswestry or Montgomeryshire.[27] As a result of the new arrangement costs fell, and in each of the six years 1758–63 only two or, in one year, three county rates were levied; in the early 1760s their average annual product was £626.

During the last seventy or so years of the period expenditure increased greatly. In the 22 years 1768–89 it averaged £2,151 a year, in the 20 years 1790–1809 £5,769, and in the last 25 years 1810–34 £9,631.[28] Inflation[29] may have contributed to these rises, and legislation in the early 19th century increased the burden on the county rate.[30] Broadly speaking, however, the period as a whole saw no conferment of new and permanent duties on the court, and the increase of the county rate must be ascribed principally to the court's more ambitious interpretation of its functions in response to the contemporary administrative revolution.[31] The relative importance of the different objects of expenditure, however, varied greatly during the period, and it is with the changing costs of vagrancy, the county gaol and house of correction, and county bridges, that the story of county administration and finances during the period must be continued.

Vagrancy, in consequence of the Act of 1700,[32] had been the major burden on the county finances in the earlier and mid 18th century. As has been seen, the vagrant money had been the nearest approach to a general-purposes county rate before 1739, and after that date changes in the costs of conveying vagrants had played the major part in determining the levy of the county rate. By the later 1760s, however, vagrancy cost less than the county bridges and the gaol; it averaged some £296 a year throughout the 1770s. Thereafter costs were generally higher, though they rarely rose above £500 and were often much lower.[33] The only exceptional years were 1783–6 and 1816–21 when they averaged £836 and £932 respectively, frequently exceeding £1,000. Those peaks, both in post-war periods, underline, even if they do not fully explain, the connexion of vagrancy with changes in the labour market and in the economy generally.[34] For the

[23] Bridgnorth boro. rec., exclusive jurisdiction papers; *Orders of Q. Sess.* iii. 273.

[24] For this para. see S.R.O., co. treasurer's acct. bk. 1666–1764 (from which the Mar. 1747–Mar. 1748 accts. are missing); *Orders of Q. Sess.* ii. 100–193. Rates evidently levied in Apr. 1751, July 1762, and July 1763 are unrecorded in q. sess. order bks.

[25] See e.g. *Orders of Q. Sess.* ii. 66, 76, 109, 164; S.R.O., q. sess. order bk. 1726–41, f. 69.

[26] See p. 101.

[27] *Orders of Q. Sess.* ii. 93, 165 (printing inaccurate figures); S.R.O., q. sess. order bk. 1726–41, f. 150v.; ibid. 1757–72, ff. 14v.–15, 16. Each sum represented a multiple or multiple and fraction of £35: cf. above, p. 102.

[28] *One Year's Expenses of Co. of Salop.,* . . . *1768*; Co. of Salop., *Acct. of Receipts and Disbursements,* 1769–1834. *Orders of Q. Sess.* are not an accurate guide to the rates levied in these yrs.

[29] T. S. Ashton, *Economic Fluctuations in Eng. 1700–1800* (1959), 67, 103, 151, 181–2, 189.

[30] See p. 149.

[31] See p. 115.

[32] See pp. 100–1.

[33] For the figs. in this para. see sources cited in n. 28, above. For comparable figs. from other cos. see S. and B. Webb, *Eng. Poor Law Hist. Pt. 1: the Old Poor Law* (1927), 385 n. 3.

[34] For the 1780s see Ashton, op. cit. 164–6. 'Straggling seamen' were a general problem: *Orders of Q. Sess.* ii. 258; iii. 24.

magistrates at quarter sessions such social and economic considerations did not exist: their responsibility was for the economical administration of a simple settlement law.

The annual contract between the county and the constables of Whitchurch did not long endure;[35] it was last renewed in 1766. The Woodcote contract was still in force in 1767, when quarter sessions was again troubled by the cost of vagrancy, and in 1769; Wedge, the constable of Woodcote, was contractor in 1775 and 1782.[36] Later other contractors were employed,[37] a fairly common practice of the period,[38] and consideration was given to co-operation with neighbouring counties.[39] Costs were kept at an acceptable level until the years of widespread distress following the end of the wars against Napoléon I. In 1822, however, legislation removed this particular burden from the county rate[40] and not until 1930 was vagrancy again a direct administrative responsibility of the county authority.[41]

The county gaol built in 1705[42] remained in use for almost ninety years until in 1793, as one result of the nationwide movement for prison reform, a new gaol was opened. Reform in this instance did not reduce costs: from 1796 the new gaol, which incorporated the house of correction, cost the county well over £1,000 a year, a figure never before passed and scarcely even approached except in 1784 and 1795. From 1806 in only two years did its costs ever fall below £2,000. The figure was rarely below £3,000 a year from 1816 and in the last twenty years of the period the gaol accounted for much the greatest item of county expenditure.[43]

The internal administrative problems of the gaol in the earlier and mid 18th century sprang from conditions which were widespread and seemingly perennial: cramped and overcrowded premises, ill-rewarded gaolers, extortionate subordinate officers, and the virtually unrestricted association of different classes of prisoner. All are illustrated in a petition submitted to quarter sessions by the debtors in the gaol in July 1739. Thomas Wilding, who had then been gaoler for several years,[44] was an innkeeper.[45] His son, his clerk, and his tapsters oppressed and defrauded the prisoners by condoning or encouraging beatings and the extortion of garnish, by over-indulging certain prisoners on remand, by enlarging the accommodation on the gaoler's side at the expense of the common side, and by forcing debtors to consort with felons.[46] Further objection was lodged against Wilding's conversion of a gaoler's-side lodging room to a store and cheese chamber: well stocked at that time of year, it was 'not only a great nuisance but very infective and . . . will in all probability by the fullness of this gaol cause contagious distempers'.[47] Despite the petition Wilding and, after him, his son Samuel remained gaolers from the 1730s to the 1780s. When the younger Wilding retired in 1784 it was with a reputation for 'humanity' in his care for the prisoners in his charge.[48]

Formal custody of the gaol remained with the sheriff, and the gaolers, though often re-appointed by an incoming sheriff, were not necessarily so.[49] On at least one occasion quarter sessions seems to have been in some doubt about the gaoler's identity.[50] It is, however, clear from the 1739 petition that sessions came to exercise a close supervision over the gaol's administration. Detailed regulations stipulating the gaoler's fees and assigning rooms to the gaoler's and common sides were published over the signature of Thomas Hunt, the court's usual chairman.[51] From the early years of the period the

[35] See Webb, op. cit. 383–5, for the general insufficiency of par. constables.
[36] Orders of Q. Sess. ii. 203, 205, 208, 215, 238, 241, 256.
[37] Ibid. 216; sources cited in n. 28, above.
[38] Webb, op. cit. 383–7.
[39] Orders of Q. Sess. iii. 14, 16, 117, 137.
[40] Webb, op. cit. 391 sqq.   [41] See pp. 146, 216.
[42] See p. 105, and plate facing p. 113.
[43] Sources cited in n. 28, above. For the new gaol see below.

[44] Orders of Q. Sess. ii. 86.
[45] Shrews. Burgess Roll, ed. H. E. Forrest (Shrews. 1924), 305.
[46] Forbidden in 1774: Orders of Q. Sess. ii. 234.
[47] S.R.O., q. sess. files, 1/136.
[48] Orders of Q. Sess. iii. 8.
[49] Ibid. ii. 46, 50; S.R.O. 215/10; 385/2.
[50] Orders of Q. Sess. ii. 56.
[51] S.R.O., q. sess. files, 1/136; above, p. 118.

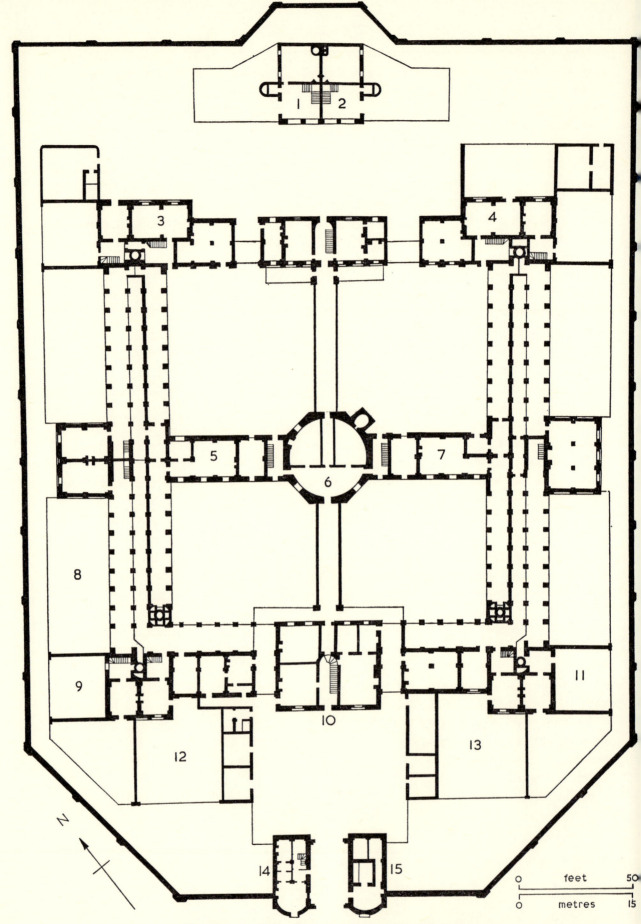

THE COUNTY GAOL, SHREWSBURY: GROUND PLAN, 1797

1, 2 infirmary, male and female; 3 male work room, others on 1st and 2nd floors; 4 female disorderly servants and apprentices, female work rooms on 1st and 2nd floors; 5 capital male accused, male solitary and condemned above; 6 bread room and bakehouse, chapel above; 7 capital male convicts, female solitary and condemned above; 8, 9, 12 male debtors', etc., wards; 10 gaolor's house, committee room; 11, 13 female debtors', etc., wards; 14 porter's lodge, execution drop above; 15 lazarette.

court's control seems to have been exercised through those of its members who lived in Shrewsbury:[52] Alderman William Smith, a leading member of the court from 1775, seems to have been one such magistrate,[53] and the group of Shrewsbury residents seems an anticipation of later, more formal and mandatory arrangements.[54]

Houses of correction may have existed in various Shropshire towns.[55] Their status and history, however, are obscure, and the county bridewell at Bridgnorth is last mentioned in quarter sessions orders in 1741.[56] The Shrewsbury house, adjoining the county gaol though legally distinct from it, was administered by a master elected by quarter sessions;[57] there was also a woman deputy by 1759.[58] The masters changed oftener than the gaolers, some ten holding office in the eighty or so years after Anne's death.[59] In 1749 there were two candidates for the mastership, Price Mucklestone, a Shrewsbury saddler,[60] and one Low, a 'decayed draper' for whom Thomas Hunt, son of a former chairman of the court, made 'great interest'. Hunt and his friends felt sure of a majority among the magistrates but Lord Powis wrote in favour of Mucklestone and Low's friends 'all acquiesced'. 'Lord Powis is more absolute in this part of the world', commented one observer tartly, 'than the king of France is in his capital city'.[61] But deference to a nobleman's wishes in such matters was no doubt common elsewhere[62] and indeed is encountered again in Shropshire.[63]

The beginnings of prison reform in Shropshire may be traced to the 1770s,[64] and John Howard's visits to the county in the years 1774-6 may have given an initial impetus to a change of opinion among the magistrates. The taking of garnish was forbidden in 1774 and the gaol buildings were altered in 1776. By 1780 there was not only an apothecary, but also a surgeon in the gaol, evidence of the consideration and humanity which Howard then noticed as characterizing the Shropshire magistrates' care for the prisoners. Under an Act of 1782 quarter sessions appointed one of its members, William Smith, to inspect the Shropshire houses of correction. Shropshire, not particularly concerned about its gaol in earlier times, had in fact quickly become an outstandingly progressive county[65] in the Howard period.[66] In 1784 the magistrates complained about congestion in the gaol as a result of the end of transportation,[67] and the same year an opportunity for greater changes presented itself with the retirement of Samuel Wilding, the aged gaoler.[68]

At the 1785 Lent assizes the grand jury presented the county gaol as insufficient and a second presentment at the summer assizes, stimulated by quarter sessions, excluded the possibility of rebuilding the gaol even on an enlargement of its existing site.[69] Over the next eight years a new gaol and house of correction was planned and built on Castle Hill to the north of the castle.[70] Within the high containing wall the minutely planned, highly organized buildings allowed a proper classification of prisoners, and new rules, aiming at reformation rather than retribution, harmonized with the building: in the work rooms the prisoners were made to work and allowed to earn, and good conduct

[52] *Orders of Q. Sess.* ii. 28, 30, 64, 71, 96.
[53] Ibid. 227, 258; iii. 57; above, p. 119.
[54] See p. 126.
[55] Bridgnorth, Newport, and perhaps Bp.'s Castle and Oswestry: *Orders of Q. Sess.* ii, pp. iv, 103, 136, 148; above, p. 121.
[56] S.R.O., q. sess. order bk. 1726-41, f. 210v.
[57] *Orders of Q. Sess.* ii. 30.   [58] Ibid. 173-4, 183.
[59] Ibid. 30, 70, 92, 116, 123, 127, 182, 197, 248; iii. 72.
[60] Forrest, *Shrews. Burgess Roll*, 213.
[61] S.R.O. 112, box 20, Thos. Bell to Thos. Hill, 14 Jan. 1748/9.
[62] Sir W. Holdsworth, *Hist. Eng. Law*, x (1938), 239 n. 1.
[63] See pp. 131-2.
[64] Cf. *V.C.H. Wilts.* v. 185 sqq.

[65] *Orders of Q. Sess.* ii. 233-4, 251, 258; iii, pp. ix-x; J. Howard, *State of Prisons in Eng. and Wales* (Warrington, 1780; 2nd edn.), 313-16; T. Phillips, *Hist. and Antiquities of Shrews.* (Shrews. 1779), 143-4; [H. Owen], *Some Acct. of Ancient and Present State of Shrews.* (Shrews. 1808), 429-30; S. and B. Webb, *Eng. Prisons under Local Govt.* (1922), 40.
[66] Reform, rebuilding, etc. of the Salop. co. gaol seem to have been about 2 yrs. behind similar developments in Glos.: J. R. S. Whiting, *Prison Reform in Glos.* (1975), 1-22.
[67] Webb, op. cit. 51.
[68] *Orders of Q. Sess.* iii. 8.
[69] S.R.O. 348/10, ff. 18v.-20v.
[70] Ibid. ff. 20v. sqq.

was rewarded from the funds privately subscribed to the prison charities founded in 1797.[71] An infirmary had separate wings for males and females, and a central chapel allowed the separation of classes during divine service. The building and the men involved in its design seem to symbolize a new spirit of rational, planned improvement hard to detect in any branch of the government of Shropshire before that time.

Like many 18th-century improvements the new gaol was the work of commissioners appointed under a local Act. In effect the leading commissioners were the leading magistrates with an interest in prison administration: William Smith, the Revd. Edmund Dana, and Rowland Hunt. At least one of them, Dana, was also a leading member of the Shrewsbury Streets Act trustees.[72] The gaol, which cost some £30,000, was paid for from the rates which the commissioners levied on the county and boroughs. The commissioners had begun by offering three prizes for plans, and on the basis of those plans J. H. Haycock produced the final design, which owed much to Howard's ideas and to those of his best interpreter, William Blackburn;[73] their advice and criticism were sought from the earliest stages. Haycock was the father of Shropshire's second county surveyor, and the execution of his design for the prison was committed in 1787 to Thomas Telford, whose own employment as Shropshire's first county surveyor may be held to date from 1788, a landmark in the history of the county's government. Before examining Telford's work as surveyor, primarily of county bridges, it will be convenient to summarize developments at the gaol during the rest of the period.

Developments at the gaol during the next forty years owed much to legislation. The 1791 Gaols Act stipulated the quarterly appointment of visiting justices.[74] In Shropshire the members of that committee, though changed quarterly, seem, as before, to have been drawn from the magistrates living in or near Shrewsbury,[75] who could inspect the gaol weekly.[76] New rules were made under the Act, which also conferred on quarter sessions some influence over the appointment of the gaoler.[77] From 1795 the administrations of the gaol and house of correction were unified,[78] but by 1822 the son and successor of the gaoler who had first taken over the bridewell was found to be deranged, and efficient administration had broken down. Continuity of supervision was accordingly improved from 1823 by orders requiring record of the visitors' quarterly reports and quarterly re-appointment of three of the previous quarter's visitors. The 1823 Gaols Act, limiting the fettering of prisoners, necessitated structural alterations to the gaol to improve security.[79]

Expenditure on county bridges was, by its nature, fluctuating. In the earlier 1760s it was little more than 6 per cent (£38) of the court's average annual expenditure (£623).[80] By the later 1760s, however, and until 1782 it was much the greatest item of county expenditure, often exceeding the sum of vagrancy and gaol expenses. That was due to the rebuilding of Atcham (1768–77) and Tern (1778–81) county bridges. Bridge expenditure was low 1783–9 but in 1790 it was again the largest item in the county accounts and it remained high throughout the rest of the period.[81]

The new and more permanent increase in the cost of Shropshire's county bridges from 1790 was due to the great increase in their number, that increase in turn owing

[71] For this para. see Owen, *Ancient and Present State of Shrews.* 430–5; *General Rules . . . of the Gaol and Ho. of Corr. for Co. of Salop.* (Shrews. 1797; copy in S.R.O. 154/1); S.R.O. 348/10. For the hist. of the prison charities see S.R.O., q. sess. rec., box 30, q. sess. cuttings bk. 1877–82, copy letter of J. R. Kenyon to Mr. Secretary Cross, 13 Mar. 1878.

[72] J. L. Hobbs, *Shrews. Street-Names* (Shrews. 1954), 41–2. For Hunt see *Orders of Q. Sess.* iii. 166–7.

[73] For Blackburn and Haycock see H. M. Colvin, *Biog. Dict. Eng. Architects, 1660–1840* (1954), 77–8, 278.

[74] 31 Geo. III, c. 46, s. 5.

[75] *Orders of Q. Sess.* iii, pp. iv, xi, 53, 57.

[76] Ibid. 58.

[77] Ibid. 59; 31 Geo. III, c. 46, ss. 6, 15.

[78] *Orders of Q. Sess.* iii. 72. Cf. ibid. 76, 100; Co. of Salop., *Acct. of Receipts and Disbursements, 1797.*

[79] *Orders of Q. Sess.* iii, pp. xi–xii, 232–4, 238; iv, p. ix.

[80] S.R.O., co. treasurer's acct. bk. 1666–1764, accts. 1759–64.

[81] Sources cited in n. 28, above; S.R.O., dep. plans 6, 182; *Orders of Q. Sess.* ii. 209, 244–5.

much to national developments: changes in the law,[82] increased traffic on the roads,[83] and the improvement of the roads themselves.[84] To the six bridges or parts of bridges which were the county's responsibility at the end of the 17th century[85] two had been added by the later 1760s: Pont-faen bridge partly in Denbighshire and Cornbow bridge in Halesowen.[86] Only from 1788, however, did the number of county bridges begin to increase greatly, so that by 1808 there were 38 and they were expected to increase still more.[87] By 1825, when the county adopted the 1812 Bridges Act,[88] their number had grown to at least 81,[89] and was still increasing: by the end of the period there were 115.[90] Those years coincided with the employment of Thomas Telford as Shropshire's first county surveyor.[91]

Telford was first brought to Shrewsbury in 1787 by William Pulteney, one of the borough's M.P.s,[92] to repair the castle and fit it for his occasional residence.[93] Later that year he was appointed full-time surveyor of the new county gaol,[94] but in 1788 he was also given charge of a county bridge.[95] Soon, in his own words, he became 'regularly employed as the surveyor of an extensive county',[96] and for some years he settled in Shrewsbury, generally residing at the castle.[97] Despite his other employments he remained county surveyor for the rest of his life,[98] though from about 1814 he was largely represented by his able assistant and deputy, Thomas Stanton.[99] Stanton also executed much of the work on the Ellesmere Canal for which Telford was responsible after his appointment as general agent to the canal in 1793,[1] and the canal office at Ellesmere thus became in effect the county surveyor's office in the early years of the 19th century.[2]

Telford's eminence, the fact that he was one of the earliest permanent county surveyors, and the readiness with which quarter sessions undertook the responsibility for a great number of bridges, has reflected credit on the Shropshire magistrates.[3] His first two years and more in Shrewsbury, however, were 'one continual scene of contention' in which he was 'always the prominent feature'. In part his problems may have been political, for Telford had to contend with Lord Clive, one of the county's greatest landowners, head of its magistracy, and a 'natural opponent' of Telford's patron Pulteney. There are, however, hints of other difficulties, arising no doubt from the professional man's zeal for improvements and the extension of his own employment. His recommendations were occasionally resisted and in 1789 he was 'very busy' bullying the magistrates at the Michaelmas sessions, though successfully. He found some of them 'ignorant and obstinate', though on the whole they formed 'a very respectable bench' and 'with the sensible part', he added, 'I believe I am on good terms'.[4] Certainly his reputation rapidly increased among the magistrates[5] and his ideas were taken up and publicized by leading members of the court like Archdeacon Plymley,[6] with whose family Telford was on friendly terms by 1793.[7]

[82] S. and B. Webb, *Story of the King's Highway* (1913), 96–100, 109–10.
[83] Ibid. 102 sqq.
[84] But see p. 115, n. 4.
[85] See p. 101.
[86] S.R.O., q. sess. bridge bk. 1741–1827, ff. 7, 9. Cf. *V.C.H. Worcs.* iii. 143.
[87] S.R.O., q. sess. files 8/138.
[88] 52 Geo. III, c. 110. See S.R.O., q. sess. bridge bk. 1741–1827, f. 120; *Orders of Q. Sess.* iii. 250.
[89] S.R.O., q. sess. order bk. 1819–27, ff. 252–3. This, the first co. bridge list, does not list all the bridges which had been repaired out of the co. rate in the previous 40 or so yrs. Ref. to q. sess. bridge bk. 1741–1827, might add half a dozen.
[90] See p. 153.
[91] See p. 361.
[92] See p. 361.
[93] *Life of T. Telford*, ed. J. Rickman (1838), 20.
[94] See p. 126.
[95] S.R.O., q. sess. bridge bk. 1741–1827, f. 45.
[96] Rickman, op. cit. 27.
[97] S.R.O. 1066/20, 5 Nov. 1793.
[98] See p. 361.
[99] Sir A. Gibb, *The Story of Telford* (1935), 23.
[1] Ibid. 27–9, 280.
[2] Corresp. in S.R.O., dep. plans and q. sess. files.
[3] Esther Moir, *Justice of the Peace* (1969), 118; Webb, *King's Highway*, 103.
[4] Gibb, op. cit. 13–20. For Clive and Pulteney see below, pp. 269 sqq.
[5] Gibb, op. cit. 27–9.
[6] Ibid. 23–4; J. Plymley, *General View of Agric. of Salop.* (1803), 273 sqq.; above, p. 119.
[7] S.R.O. 1066/20, 5 Nov. 1793.

Telford's responsibilities increased, and by 1808 his work for quarter sessions comprised the surveyorship of county bridges and of all other county buildings and works. His public work was paid sometimes by a percentage of expenditure, sometimes by bills of expenses, and his numerous employments made it necessary for him to have clerks under him at Shrewsbury and other places.[8] Apart from repairs and alterations at the gaol[9] and the construction of lock-ups,[10] Telford acquired responsibility for the shire-hall which had been built in 1784–6;[11] one of his last official duties for the county was the compilation with Sir Robert Smirke of a report on its condition before Smirke's rebuilding of 1833–7.[12] It is nevertheless principally for his work on county bridges that Telford's surveyorship has been remembered.

Most of the 42 Shropshire bridges which were built under his direction[13] were county bridges.[14] Some, like Montford and Buildwas bridges, were considerable works. 'The rebuilding of a Severn bridge', wrote Telford, was 'an important and expensive undertaking', and Buildwas bridge placed the county in the forefront of bridge design: the first of the Shropshire county bridges to be built of cast iron, it owed much to the impression made on Telford by T. F. Pritchard's design for the Iron Bridge. Five more iron county bridges were to follow during Telford's surveyorship, three of them to Telford's own designs.[15] Perhaps more significant than such technical innovations, however, was the great number of modest structures thrown over little streams. They contributed as much as the larger works to the amenities of travel, but also symbolized, by their very number, quarter sessions' new commitment to the regular, planned improvement of local life undertaken with the stimulus of professional advice.

Senior to the county treasurer and surveyor, incumbents of relatively new offices, and chief of those who served the magistrates and the court of quarter sessions, was the clerk of the peace. In earlier periods the clerkship had been filled and vacated at the pleasure of the *custos*, in whose gift it lay;[16] the attempted dismissal of John Lacon in 1712[17] was perhaps a last instance of this practice.[18] During the 125 years after Anne's death, however, there was greater continuity in the tenure of the office of *custos*[19] and that seems to be reflected in a similarly enhanced continuity in the clerkship of the peace. Indeed it was during this period that the clerkship, like the county treasurership,[20] became virtually the prerogative of a dynasty of relatives and business connexions, all of them leading Shrewsbury attorneys. The dynastic character of the clerkship is probably also evidence of the growing complexity of county business: the administration of that business, too important to be conferred at whim, was left to those for whom the administrative routine of the clerkship were family and business traditions.[21]

The first clerk appointed during the period, John Skrymsher (1718–37), was a Staffordshire man,[22] but he settled in Shrewsbury where he was clerk of the county court in the 1690s.[23] His successor Richard Baldwyn (1737–79) may have been a family connexion, for Skrymsher's second cousin Mary Skrymsher had brought Aqualate (in

[8] S.R.O., q. sess. files 8/138, J. Loxdale to Devon clk. of peace who had requested inf. on Telford's position (ibid. /137).

[9] *Orders of Q. Sess.* iii. 129, 137.

[10] Ibid. 129, 135. The ct. had begun to authorize lock-ups in 1776: ibid. ii, preface to orders 1772–82, p. iii; ibid. 241.

[11] S.R.O. 348/10, f. 13r.–v.

[12] S.R.O. 348/15, 19; Mary C. Hill, *Hist. of Shropshire's Many Shirehalls* (Shrews. 1963), 2 sqq.

[13] Rickman, *Telford*, 30.

[14] Gibb, *Telford*, 302–7, lists some that were not.

[15] Rickman, op. cit. 27–30; *Atlas to Life of Telford* (1838), plates 5–6; *T.S.A.S.* lvi. 104–15.

[16] See p. 68.

[17] *Orders of Q. Sess.* ii. 12, 14. Lacon was a distant relative of John Lacon, leading J.P. and deputy *custos* (above, p. 93), and therefore *persona grata* with the Newports.

[18] The articles against Lacon were drawn up shortly after the duke of Shrews. became *custos* (below, p. 359), the last such political change in that office (apart from the Newport restoration in 1714) before 1760 or 1839.

[19] See pp. 359–60. [20] See pp. 121, 361.

[21] The clks.' and deputy clks.' names, dates, etc., in the following para. are taken from Sir E. Stephens, *Clks. of the Counties, 1360–1960* (1961), 152–3.

[22] *S.H.C.* ii(2), 95–7.

[23] S.R.O. 3365/2716. He lodged next door to the Plough in the Square, perhaps at 'Mrs. Wingfield's' house.

Forton, Staffs.) to the Baldwyn family.[24] On Baldwyn's death Lord Clive appointed Thomas Wingfield, one of his principal political agents and allies in Shrewsbury,[25] but for much of Wingfield's term of office the duties were performed by his deputy Joseph Loxdale.[26] The Loxdales, whose origins lay in Forton (Staffs.)[27] and thus suggest a connexion with the Skrymshers, had in fact been connected with the county business for many years before Wingfield's appointment, Thomas Loxdale occurring as deputy clerk of the peace as early as 1747. Joseph Loxdale succeeded Wingfield as clerk in 1802 and was succeeded by his own son John in 1833. By the close of the period the Peeles were already a family of consequence among the county officials,[28] but their connexions had been with the Newport estate and the Pulteney family;[29] when at last they gained a toe-hold in the clerk of the peace's office it was owing to their business connexions with the Loxdales.[30]

For almost the whole period the clerks were remunerated with fees authorized by quarter sessions in 1700 or by later Acts of Parliament. During the years 1792-1823 their annual income averaged £423. About three quarters of that income, however, was received in allowances for special duties. A committee of magistrates which investigated the clerk's remuneration in 1827-9 found it 'highly gratifying' that county expenditure on the clerkship was below that of several neighbouring counties and that the clerk's charges were invariably warranted by custom or statute.[31]

Petty Sessions

The work of the justices out of sessions was done either in the regular monthly meetings of magistrates acting within the various hundreds (petty sessions) or in the 'justice rooms' of their own houses. The monthly meetings were dominated by poor-law business, notice of the Condover meetings invariably including a summons to 'all paupers and other persons . . . that have business'.[32] By the mid 18th century the divisional meetings, if those in Condover hundred may be taken as typical,[33] were well organized. Three times a year in addition to their monthly meetings the Condover magistrates held 'special' or 'general'[34] meetings. In January the previous year's high-way surveyors were summoned to give an account of their office and the new surveyors were appointed; after Easter it was the turn of the overseers of the poor; and at Michaelmas the magistrates held their licensing sessions for innkeepers and alehouse keepers. The January, Easter, and Michaelmas meetings also formed the thrice-yearly special highway sessions prescribed by statute. From 1767[35] the highway surveyors were appointed at a special sessions in October.[36] Tax commissioners were more numer-

[24] V.C.H. Salop. iv. 104; Staffs. R.O., introduction (incl. pedigrees) to list of D.(W.) 1788.

[25] See p. 269. Earlier the Wingfields had been connected with Ld. Powis's private and political affairs. See S.R.O. 112, Thos. Hill's letter bk. 1753-9, Hill to Powis, 12 Feb. 1757, for Powis's appt. of Thos. Wingfield, jnr., as steward to Ld. Montfort. Wingfield's mayoralty in the election yr. 1767-8 (Owen and Blakeway, Hist. Shrews. i. 536) is also significant.

[26] Orders of Q. Sess. iii, preface to orders 1783-9, p. v.

[27] Introduction to list of N.L.W., Castle Hill.

[28] For their connexion with the co. treasurership (and the Corbetts of Longnor) see p. 361; Shrews. Chron. 25 Aug. 1911 (obit. of E. C. Peele).

[29] In 1742 Joshua Peele was a witness to Mrs. Anne Smyth's will: Prob. 11/722 (P.C.C. 337 Trenley); below, p. 254. In 1758 he was still involved in the admin. of John Newport's estate under Ld. Bath: S.R.O. 112, Thos. Hill's letter bk. 1753-9, Hill to Bath (26 June 1758) and Peele (28 June 1758). See also S.P.L., Deeds 19167,

Dr. Cheney Hart to Wm. Cheney Hart, 7 Dec. 1778.

[30] T.S.A.S. 2nd ser. iii. 220; below, pp. 146-7. The Peeles' connexion John Flint (later Corbett) was elected co. treasurer during Bath's lieutenancy: below, pp. 359, 361.

[31] T.S.A.S. 2nd ser. iii. 218-21; S.R.O., q. sess. rec., box 304, bk. of procs. of cttee. for settling clk. of peace's fees.

[32] N.L.W., Castle Hill 2244. See e.g. Stapleton par. rec. (S.R.O. 883) which contain many bastardy and settlement depositions, consents to pauper apprenticings, etc., for the period.

[33] Nevertheless Sir Hen. Edwardes, a leading q. sess. J.P. (above, p. 118), figured prominently on the divisional bench, and the presence of the meetings bk. in the Castle Hill collection suggests that Thos. Loxdale, dep. clk. of the peace (see above), was the divisional justices' clk.

[34] The terms seem to be synonymous.

[35] In accordance with the Highways Act, 7 Geo. III, c. 42, s. 1.

[36] See e.g. N.L.W., Castle Hill 2244.

ous than the magistrates, but the two bodies of men overlapped and the assessment of the land and window taxes seems to have been engrossed by the divisional magistrates; they dealt with it at a midsummer meeting when they sat as commissioners.[37]

The special meetings, and doubtless the ordinary monthly meetings too, were evidently held in some convenient alehouse. In 1753 the Condover magistrates, for example, met at Mary Gwynn's house in Condover in January and at Thomas Gower's, Longnor, in September; both were licensed ale-sellers.[38] Attendance at the Condover special meetings averaged just under 4 in the 1740s and 1750s, just under 3 in the 1760s and earlier 1770s. Attendances at the ordinary monthly meetings are hardly likely to have been greater.

Much of a magistrate's work was done in his own house, and by the later 18th century that work was felt to include the moral supervision of his neighbourhood. By 1790 the magistrates were at last trying to carry into effect the long-established royal proclamation (regularly repeated at quarter sessions) against vice and immorality,[39] and by the turn of the century Archdeacon Plymley argued that the magistrate, in addition to administering the law[40]

should be the adviser and peace-maker of his district; he should co-operate in the improvement of rural arts; he should be the pattern of improved husbandry; he should set an example of scrupulous obedience to the laws in his own person, and endeavour to sustain the tone of Christian morality throughout his neighbourhood.

Attempts to give effect to such high ideals were not always rewarded with the gratitude even of a neighbouring magistrate. In 1768 Richard Hill's attempts to put down the Shawbury wakes, then the scene of 'much more rioting and rabble . . . than usual', evoked the sarcastic thanks of Andrew Corbet, the resident magistrate, 'for taking the trouble to inform him in the nature of the laws and how to treat his own tenants':

when he . . . shall stand in need of Mr. Hill's assistance to regulate the diversions of his tenants, he shall then be obliged to him for the favour of it; and whenever Mr. Hill shall desire Mr. Corbet's assistance in Hodnet parish will readily return the compliment, but would not presume to intermeddle unasked or unrequested.

Hill nevertheless returned to the attack two years later.[41]

Corbet's aversion to Hill's Evangelical zeal was by no means peculiar to himself,[42] but his jealous interest in his neighbourhood, in his own tenantry and his fellow parishioners, was probably even more typical of the attitude of the contemporary magistrates. That attitude, at its best, was founded in the magistrate's thorough acquaintance with the habits and weaknesses of his neighbours and in the application of common sense to the resolution of the problems they created. One magistrate who has left a record of such work over almost forty years was Thomas Netherton Parker of Sweeney. Arbitrating in little disputes over rent and debts, arranging for the custody of unprotected children, resolving boundary disputes and quarrels over wills, reconciling relatives or neighbours at variance with each other and servants and apprentices with their masters,[43] Parker, like his numberless colleagues in provincial England, was providing for the needs of classes whose secular affairs were too small in scale to be worth any official care and attention but that of the resident magistrate.

[37] Ibid.; below, p. 260 and notes 21–2. Cf. W. R. Ward, *Eng. Land Tax in Eighteenth Cent.* (1953), 4.

[38] S.R.O., q. sess. rec., parcel 255, reg. of ale-sellers' recognizances 1753–4.

[39] By pressing for rural police: *Orders of Q. Sess.* i, pp. xxix–xxx, 207–8; iii. 41, 46; above, p. 115, n. 7.

[40] J. Plymley, *General View of the Agriculture of Salop.* (1803), 349–50.

[41] S.R.O. 322, box 71, And. Corbet to Ric. Hill [Aug. 1768]; Hill to Corbet, 7 Aug. 1768; Hill to [?Cotes],

10 Aug. 1770; Hill to Corbet, 16 Aug. 1770; Mary C. Hill, *Guide to Salop. Recs.* (1952), 76; *Salop. N. & Q.* n.s. viii. 94. For the wakes see *V.C.H. Salop.* ii. 177, 180.

[42] e.g. the pamphlets (1782) in S.P.L., accession 2556, suggest that Hill's introduction of biblical and religious sentiment and language into Parliament and politics was deplored in some circles. Cf. below, p. 271 n. 93.

[43] See his justice bks. 1803–43: S.R.O. 1060/168, 171.

The Lieutenancy and the Militia

For the first twenty years of the period the earls of Bradford retained the offices of lieutenant and *custos* restored to them on George I's accession and earned by their staunch Whiggery in the previous reign. The succession of an imbecile earl in 1734, however, ended the Newports' primacy and inaugurated that of the Herberts. In 1735 the lieutenancy was conferred on H. A. Herbert of Oakly Park, created Lord Herbert of Chirbury in 1743 and earl of Powis in 1748. With one short break (1761–4) it remained with the Herbert and Clive families for the rest of the period; they were allied in politics from 1763 and connected by marriage from 1784. The death of the 2nd Lord Powis in 1801 joined his father's inheritance to the great estates accumulated by Clive of India. Thus for almost the whole period the power of the lieutenancy was united to the influence of the principal resident landowner, as had usually been the case since 1660. The Clives and Herberts co-operated to keep the lieutenancy in their united families when the 2nd Lord Clive went to India in 1798, for Clive's brother-in-law Powis then became lieutenant. He died before Clive's return[44] and Lord Berwick was anxious to secure the appointment for himself. The managers of Clive's affairs, however, arranged for the lieutenancy to be placed in commission. Early in 1801, less than three weeks after Powis's death, William Clive wrote to his nephew of his hopes that 'your concerns in this part of the world will suffer as little as possible': neighbouring landowners were being helpful over the lieutenancy, and the king himself had agreed to its being put in commission. The choice of commissioners — Lord Berwick, John Cotes, and William Clive[45] — seems to have owed something to the advice of Lord Chancellor Loughborough, who must certainly have been thoroughly conversant with Clive's affairs.[46]

The lieutenants wielded great political influence but rarely needed to intervene in the detailed government of the county as local affairs became divorced from national politics. Lord Powis's intervention in the election of a master of the county house of correction in 1749, though successful, can hardly have been undertaken without regard to the feelings of the country gentlemen at quarter sessions.[47] A year earlier, during the previous vacancy in the mastership, he had been reluctant to intervene but had recommended that the Whig magistrates should meet on the evening before the selection to agree upon a candidate lest a Tory protégé succeed by a split Whig vote.[48] Such private operations of a Whig caucus had evidently long been a feature of quarter sessions.[49]

The lieutenants and their aristocratic connexions, if they risked offending the country gentlemen by intervening in the detail of county government, could also rely on a general feeling of deference to their position in the county. In 1779 the 2nd Lord Powis, presumably with the help of the lieutenant, his political ally and future brother-in-law Lord Clive, repeated his father's success of 1749 during another vacancy in the mastership of the house of correction. Attendance at the January sessions was swollen to thrice the normal figure; lay and clerical magistrates attended from south Shropshire and the

---

[44] See pp. 256, 359–60. For what follows see N.L.W., Clive Corresp. 2180; S.R.O. 112/mil./9 sqq.

[45] See e.g. S.R.O. 190/23; S.R.O. 1060/161. There was some difficulty over Berwick's wish to command the militia, in which he was 'universally disliked'.

[46] As Alex. Wedderburn he had been a Clive M.P. for Bp.'s Cas.: below, p. 305.

[47] See p. 125. Some offence, however, was given, to judge from Thos. Bell's remarks.

[48] S.R.O. 567, box 47, Sir Ric. Corbett to his bro. 17

Mar. 1747/8. Ibid., same to same (n.d. but probably on same occasion), says that Powis is coming secretly to Shrews. and will do his best for Price Mucklestone. If so, Powis failed, for Mucklestone was elected only on the next vacancy in 1749: *Orders of Q. Sess.* ii. 123, 127.

[49] The implication of what Sir Ric. was told by Mr. Edwards (presumably Godolphin Edwards) probably about the previous election: S.R.O. 567, box 47, Corbett to his bro. 17 Mar. 1747/8; E 362/74/35; *Orders of Q. Sess.* ii. 116.

Ludlow area, most of them rarely seen in court.[50] Dr. Cheney Hart of Shrewsbury, an avowed opponent of the Powis–Clive political interest,[51] even arranged to qualify himself as an acting magistrate simply to attend quarter sessions and oblige Powis by voting for his candidate, John Baugh, on this occasion.[52]

The most notable piece of preferment in the gift of the *custos* was the clerkship of the peace, and some of the clerks appointed during the period were involved in the political affairs of the lieutenants as well as in the public business of the magistracy.[53] That was inevitable, for by the middle of the 18th century the real importance of the lieutenant's office was to provide a focus of loyalty to the Crown and its ministers and a channel of patronage. That role the 1st earl of Powis (d. 1772) filled with remarkable success.[54] More formally, however, the lieutenant's principal duty was to command the county militia.

During the earlier years of the period the county militias continued to be governed under the 1662 Act,[55] but under an Act of 1757 they were reorganized. Liability to supply a quota of private soldiers was laid on the county, and lieutenancy meetings in the different divisions of the county were to assign proportions of that quota to each parish. The Act provided for the choice of men by ballot from the number liable for duty in each place. Shropshire's quota was 640.[56] The Act, however, was unpopular[57] and the Shropshire militia was not embodied until 1762, the year after failure to raise the militia was made punishable by a fine on the defaulting county. Late that year it was embodied under the command of Lord Bath, the lieutenant.[58]

The 1757 Act somewhat reduced the powers of the Crown over the militias and, by fixing a property qualification for deputy lieutenants[59] and militia officers, enhanced the forces' connexions with the landowning class.[60] After 1757, however, the activities of the militias are merely a reflection of the successive military necessities of the nation. After 1762 the Shropshire militia was embodied only three times during the period: 1778–83 during the war of American Independence; 1793–1802 and 1803–15 during the French wars.[61] During the latter two periods neither the great amount of work which the organization of the augmented militia brought on the lieutenants, the lieutenancy commissioners (1801–4),[62] the clerk of the lieutenancy (also clerk of the peace), and the deputy lieutenants,[63] nor the increased local expenditure on allowances to militia men's families[64] endow the story of the Shropshire militia with any local significance. After 1815 in Shropshire, as everywhere, the militia fell into abeyance.

The Sheriff

During the 18th century the responsibilities of the sheriff's office consisted of routine legal duties, normally performed by his under-sheriff, and attendance at quarter

[50] *Orders of Q. Sess.* ii. 248; E 362/109/59.
[51] S.P.L., Deeds 19167, Hart to Wm. Cheney Hart, 23 Nov. 1774. With Ld. Pigot (whose adviser his son became: Bridgnorth boro. rec., papers in *Rex v. Hart*) he came out in support of Sir H. Bridgeman in opposition to Ld. Powis in 1766: Staffs. R.O., D. 1287/10/4b; below, p. 261.
[52] S.P.L., Deeds 19167, Hart to Hart, 7 and 18 Dec. 1778; *Orders of Q. Sess.* ii. 248. Baugh, who was successful, may be the Ellesmere coroner (fl. 1772) of that name (Co. of Salop., *Acct. of Receipts and Disbursements, 1772*).
[53] See pp. 128–9.
[54] See p. 255.
[55] Militia Act, 1662, 14 Chas. II, c. 3.
[56] Militia Act, 1757, 30 Geo. II, c. 25.
[57] J. R. Western, *Eng. Militia in the 18th Cent. . . . 1660–1802* (1965), pp. 140–1, 290 sqq.
[58] G. A. Parfitt, *Salop. Militia and Volunteers (Hist. of*

Corps of King's Salop. Light Inf. iv [1970]), 9, 164.
[59] See S.R.O., q. sess. rec., box 302, file of dep. lieuts.' qualifications 1760–95.
[60] Parfitt, op. cit. 11.
[61] Ibid. 164–8. Cf. C. M. Clode, *Military Forces of the Crown* (1869), i. 48. For increases in Salop.'s quota during the wars against France see Western, op. cit. 449.
[62] See e.g. S.R.O. 190; S.R.O. 1310/1–72.
[63] Reflected in S.R.O., q. sess. rec., box 304, lieutenancy general meetings order bk. 1804–32.
[64] Experienced everywhere else: see e.g. *V.C.H. Wilts.* v. 192. The figures of q. sess. expenditure given above (p. 122), being based on rates levied, do not include the considerable sums reimbursed to the ct. from 1796 (Co. of Salop., *Acct. of Receipts and Disbursements, 1796*, sqq.) for the relief of militia men's families. Cf. Western, op. cit. 287–90; *Orders of Q. Sess.* iii. 64.

sessions[65] and assizes. The legal routine is described in Ralph Leeke's appointment of a deputy sheriff during the absence of his under-sheriff in 1796: the deputy was to execute, and return inquisitions upon, writs of inquiry and damages, to take inquisitions in the county court, and to try all causes in that 'my said court',[66] and doubtless to levy the fines imposed at assizes and other sums of money due to the Crown.[67]

Attendance on the assize justices involved some trouble and expense which had long been considered burdensome. Some hint of that is evident in 1755 when Thomas Hill offered to lend F. T. Blithe a javelin man.[68] Certainly the assize justices could be exacting in their requirements, as in 1735 when the sheriff's bailiff was fined 40s. for not attending them from Shrewsbury to the confines of the county.[69] Some relief, however, was given to the sheriff by the Treasury, and after quarter sessions had purchased a house in Shrewsbury for a judges' lodging in 1821 the sheriff paid his Treasury allowance for the judges' accommodation to quarter sessions.[70] In 1802 the Privy Council discovered that the man pricked sheriff of Shropshire was dead and the two others on the list were ineligible;[71] they asked the lieutenancy commissioners[72] to find a new sheriff. Richard Topp of Whitton was asked to serve, but he successfully excused himself on the ground that his 'very small' estate had borne the burden twice before. Loxdale, clerk of the lieutenancy, awaiting the commissioners' instructions, asked every gentleman liable whom he met, who was not too poor, to take the office.

The 18th- and early-19th-century sheriffs are readily identifiable country gentlemen almost without exception. Thomas Clarke of Peplow, however, was a newcomer to the county and the only sheriff (1801–2) of the period without armorial bearings: a rich Liverpool merchant, he used a cipher on his seal and a sailing ship on his banners.[73]

The under-sheriffs of the period were normally local attorneys from the market town nearest to the sheriff's residence. Many of their surnames recur regularly throughout the period.[74] Occasionally a sheriff might appoint his son or brother as his under-sheriff.

On one occasion the resolute action of an under-sheriff saved the lives of ten men.[75] In 1757 Thomas Leeke of Wellington, under-sheriff to St. John Charlton of Apley, delayed the execution of ten colliers who had been sentenced to death for rioting. He acted without authority and against the advice of neighbouring magistrates. In the end, however, the men were reprieved; Leeke received due praise for his undutiful, though humane, conduct from the severe Chief Justice Willes,[76] and the king's pleasure at what had been done was made known.

The County Coroners

The four county coroners[77] in the 18th century and later seem to have operated within recognized, if informal, divisions of the county, and certain areas became

[65] *Orders of Q. Sess.* ii. 198.

[66] S.R.O. 81/556. Cf. S.R.O. 796/274.

[67] See T. Tidmas, 'Forms, Precedents, and Directions for Executing the Office of Under Sheriff, 1794', in Warws. R.O., CR 556/432 (esp. pp. 215–21); below, p. 228. Tidmas's acct. would apply in other cos.

[68] S.R.O. 112, Thos. Hill's letter bk. 1753–9, Hill to Blithe, 4 Feb. 1755; cf. *T.S.A.S.* lix. 59. The 'javelin men' were abolished in 1859: S.R.O., q. sess. Const. Cttee. rep. bk. 1854–65, p 117.

[69] E 362/64/36.

[70] Under a local Act of that yr.: *Orders of Q. Sess.* iv, pp. xx–xxi.

[71] For what follows see S.R.O. 3003/4, Loxdale to Wm. Clive, July 1802. The unsatisfactory list furnished to the Privy Council was symptomatic of the difficulties experi-

enced locally when it was drawn up: *Orders of Q. Sess.* iii. 110.

[72] See p. 360.

[73] For this and the following para. see Blakeway, *Sheriffs*, 25–9, 168–245; Hughes, *Sheriffs*, pp. v, 5–12.

[74] e.g. Ashby, Chambre, Elisha, Jeffreys, Langley, Leeke, Pemberton, Stubbs, Windsor.

[75] For what follows see S.R.O. 81/548–55.

[76] *D.N.B.* Willes was evidently acting as senior commissioner of the great seal.

[77] The source cited in the following note occasionally mentions more than four coroners in one yr., but some of those may have been liberty coroners such as seem to have existed e.g. at Ellesmere. See *T.S.A.S.* lix. 64 n. 6; below, p. 163, n. 92.

traditional places of residence for them. One succession of coroners worked in south-west Shropshire: William Harris of Bishop's Castle, coroner there by the 1770s,[78] was followed by two successive members of the Wollaston family until 1833 when the office was briefly (1833–4) occupied by Samuel Heighway[79] of Pontesford, a minor land-owner.[80] Heighway's successor was a Ludlow attorney.[81] In south-east Shropshire the coroners normally lived at Cleobury Mortimer by the later 18th century.[82] A third succession of coroners served the north-west and seem to have lived in or near Oswestry or Ellesmere.[83] In the north-east the coronership was held by the Dicken family of Wollerton throughout the century and beyond.

The coroners were no doubt normally of the attorney class, shading off into minor landowners. Such seems to have been the status of the Dickens.[84] Thomas Dicken, elected a coroner in 1707,[85] is probably to be identified with the man of that name who died in 1738. His eldest son John was a land steward to Richard Hill of Hawkstone,[86] his second son Thomas died as coroner in 1770.[87] When Thomas's son Rowland died in 1808 he had been coroner for over thirty years, though he had recently resigned in favour of his son;[88] the family retained the coronership for almost a further half-century.[89] Several of the coroners, however, were medically qualified rather than lawyers. At Cleobury Mortimer the coroners were apothecaries or surgeons until 1824,[90] and John Wollaston of Bishop's Castle, elected a coroner in 1818,[91] was also a surgeon.[92]

[78] Co. of Salop., *Acct. of Receipts and Disbursements of the Co. Rate, 1770,* sqq.
[79] C 202/180/13; C 202/206/19; C 202/222/20.
[80] *V.C.H. Salop.* viii. 254, 275.
[81] Wm. Downes: see p. 163.
[82] *Salopian Jnl.* 4 Feb. 1824.
[83] Cf. the names in the source cited above, n. 78, with those in C 202/160/7; C 202/186/10; C 202/231/23.
[84] For genealogical details see S.P.L., MS. 4360, p. 138; MS. 2793, p. 369.
[85] See p. 111.
[86] *T.S.A.S.* lvi. 34 sqq.
[87] *S.P.R. Lich.* xi(2), 212; C 202/158/11.
[88] *S.P.R. Lich.* xi(2), 170, 299; C 202/194/17. In 1762 he was an excise officer.
[89] See p. 164.
[90] C 202/170/12; C 202/206/18; C 202/213/24; *T.S.A.S.* 4th ser. vii. 215–16; *Salopian Jnl.* 4 Feb., 31 Mar., 7 Apr., 5 May, 1 Sept. 1824 (giving details of contest between Jones and Southam).
[91] C 202/206/19.
[92] *T.S.A.S.* 4th ser. vii. 214–15.

COUNTY GOVERNMENT
1834-89

The Commission of the Peace, p. 136. Petty Sessions, p. 136. Quarter Sessions, p. 137 (Attendance and Leadership, p. 137; Procedure, p. 143; Finance, p. 148; Bridges and Roads, p. 152; County Gaol and House of Correction, p. 154; Police, p. 157; Pauper Lunatic Asylum, p. 160; Executive Committee, p. 162). County Coroners, p. 163. Constitutional and Legal Changes: the Militia, the County Courts, and the Sheriff, p. 164.

T HE Whig statesmen and administrators of the 1830s reasserted central authority over local government to a degree unprecedented in almost two centuries and in the interests of efficiency conceived as strict economy. At the same time wishing to introduce local accountability, the devisers of the 1834 Poor Law Amendment Act[1] laid the management of the most important branch of local expenditure on the ratepayers' elected representatives. Edwin Chadwick, however, the great bureaucrat largely responsible for the Act, both hoped and believed that the ratepayers' representatives would have no significant power;[2] for him 'local self-government' was a 'mischievous fallacy'.[3] Even more than the Acts of 1888 or 1929 the 1834 Act thus marks an epoch, for it introduced two divergent tendencies which persisted into the 20th century, when local government, regulated in ever greater detail by the state, yet seemed to remain answerable also to local electors.

More obvious than the Act's historic significance in the early years were the contrasts[4] between the anomalies of the historic county boundaries and the utilitarian areas of the new poor-law unions, each designed to centre on a convenient market town. In contrast to the magistrates, appointed from the landowning gentry, the poor-law guardians derived a more modern authority from election by the ratepayers. Changes seemingly presaged by such contrasts[5] did not follow. The magistrates' rule of the counties, cheap and incorrupt, survived for over half a century, and county boundaries generally were not seriously modified for almost a century and a half. When representative county government was at last introduced, by the Conservatives, in 1888-9 there was no disposition in Parliament to abolish the historic counties. Had the Shropshire magistrates had their way the story might have been different. In 1887-8 they displayed little sentiment for the county they had ruled for centuries, wishing to see it altered, and enlarged, to coincide with the 'registration county', that bundle of poor-law unions which had co-existed with historic Shropshire since the 1830s.[6] It was in fact the union, rather than the county, boundary which preoccupied them, for the preponderantly Tory country gentlemen who dominated the bench had taken over the administrative machinery of the new Poor Law with zeal and conviction. The rulers of the county had become the rulers of the unions.[7]

[1] 4 & 5 Wm. IV, c. 76.
[2] Ursula Henriques, 'Jeremy Bentham and the Machinery of Social Reform', *Brit. Govt. and Admin.* ed. H. Hearder and H. R. Loyn (1974), 179-86.
[3] *Nineteenth-Cent. Constitution, 1815-1914*, ed. H. J. Hanham (1969), 383.

[4] More apparent than real: see pp. 169-71.
[5] *V.C.H. Wilts.* v. 231.
[6] See map on p. 170. The registration counties are mapped in *Census, 1891.*
[7] See pp. 167, 172.

The Commission of the Peace

The size of the acting portion of the Shropshire commission of the peace increased slightly over the first forty or so years of the period: at the beginning there were about 140 acting magistrates,[8] by 1871 154.[9] Over the next fifteen years, however, there was a great increase, and there were 207 acting magistrates by 1885,[10] after which numbers stabilized again.[11]

Petty Sessions

Much of the magistrates' routine work had long been done out of sessions — in their own houses and on the divisional benches. In 1828 and 1877 there were 18 petty-sessional divisions, based on the hundreds, the magistrates of Clun and Purslow and those of Munslow (Lower Division) and Overs meeting as single bodies.[12] The divisions were altered occasionally, notably in 1836, and new divisions cutting across hundred boundaries were formed.[13]

Unlike their criminal jurisdiction the local benches' few administrative duties did not increase. Sparse evidence from the 1860s and 1870s indeed suggests that the local magistrates were indolent and inefficient in administration. In 1865–6 successful cattle-plague controls were introduced only after the local benches' powers had passed to a quarter-sessions committee.[14] Even the financial accountability of justices' clerks was improved only as the court extended its supervision over them.[15]

One of the oldest duties of the local benches, the licensing of beer sellers,[16] was greatly curtailed during the earlier *laissez-faire* years of the period. When controls were reintroduced,[17] however, the local justices' exercise of their revived powers was soon subjected[18] to the confirmation of a statutory quarter-sessions Licensing Committee: its authority, wider-ranging than any local bench's, could be used to develop a licensing policy for the whole county.[19]

Indications of the quality of justice dispensed out of sessions, the lowest level of the judicial hierarchy, are few. Such as there are, however, suggest reasonable conscientiousness and competence. For the beginning of the period T. N. Parker's 'justice book' survives to modify the lurid stereotypes of ignorance and rural tyranny encountered in 18th-century literature.[20] The divisional benches have left few similarly revealing records of their work, but as the 19th century wore on their jurisdiction, increased at the expense of quarter sessions, was more closely regulated by statute.[21] From about 1853 evidence of greater efficiency may be seen in the striking diminution of the number of bills ignored by Shropshire grand juries.[22]

On one occasion a Shropshire petty-sessional bench attracted national attention.[23]

[8] S.R.O., q. sess. Finance Cttee. min. bk. 1, loose printed lists, 1838 and 1844, give 138 and 141.

[9] Edw. Cassey & Co. *Dir. Salop.* (1871), 20-2.

[10] *Kelly's Dir. Salop.* (1885), 787-8.

[11] Ibid. (1891), 251-2, also giving 207; (1905), 10-12, giving 226.

[12] S.R.O., q. sess. order bk. 1828-33, ff. 59-60; q. sess. recs., box 299, printed list of acting J.P.s, 1877.

[13] *V.C.H. Salop.* ii. 207-11; *Orders of Q. Sess.* iv. 71.

[14] See pp. 162-3. Cf. *Copy of a Complaint . . . to the Sec. of State by certain J.P.s for Salop.*, H.C. 382 (1866), lix.

[15] S.R.O., q. sess. Auditing Cttee. and Finance Cttee. rep. bk. 1837-43, pp. 103-4; *Shrews. Chron.* 8 Jan. 1869; *Eddowes's Jnl.* 20 Oct. 1869.

[16] See pp. 73-4.

[17] In 1869: S. and B. Webb, *Hist. Liquor Licensing* (1903), 142. Cf. ibid. 123-34; *Orders of Q. Sess.* iii. 280, 286.

[18] Under the Licensing Act, 1872, 35 & 36 Vic. c. 94, s. 37: *Eddowes's Jnl.* 16 Oct. 1872; 1 Jan. 1873.

[19] See e.g. ibid. 30 Sept. 1874.

[20] See p. 130.

[21] Notably the Indictable Offences and Summary Jurisdiction Acts, 1848, 11 & 12 Vic. cc. 42-3; the Larceny Act, 1861, 24 & 25 Vic. c. 96; and the Summary Jurisdiction Act, 1879, 42 & 43 Vic. c. 49.

[22] *Orders of Q. Sess.* iv, p. v.

[23] For what follows see *T.S.A.S.* lix. 155-7; Loton Hall MSS., Sir B. Leighton's diary, 27 Aug. 1867; B. Semmel, *The Governor Eyre Controversy* (1962); G. Dutton, *The Hero as Murderer: The life of Edw. John Eyre . . .* (1967); *Eddowes's Jnl.* 27 Mar., 3 Apr. 1867.

E. J. Eyre, the former governor of Jamaica living at Adderley Hall, was prosecuted at Market Drayton as accessary to the alleged murder of G. W. Gordon, tried and executed during the 1865 disturbances in the colony. Radical opinion regarded Eyre's prosecution as one of the most important constitutional battles of the day. Briefly, therefore, the capacities and objectivity of a group of Shropshire magistrates were thrown into high light. The chairman of quarter sessions, Sir Baldwin Leighton, temporarily chaired the local bench, and his diary does much to modify accounts of the Tory magistrates' 'obvious sympathies' for Eyre. Unawed by the formidable talents of counsel[24] Leighton kept a firm grip on proceedings. Though without formal legal training,[25] he surprised the lawyers and readily apprehended the crucial legal issue, the legality of Gordon's court martial. The prosecution, however, did not try to prove the court martial's illegality and, in Leighton's view, the case against Eyre therefore 'fell to the ground', there being no reasonable presumption that the evidence produced against Eyre could secure conviction by a trial jury. During later proceedings against Eyre in Queen's Bench the learned Justice Blackburn[26] in effect confirmed the correctness of the principles Leighton had acted upon.[27]

Quarter Sessions: Attendance and Leadership

In the early years of the period, as in the later, over a fifth of the county's acting magistrates attended quarter sessions; in the middle years, when fewer clerical magistrates attended,[28] that proportion was lower.[29] Thus only a few acting magistrates came to quarter sessions. As its criminal jurisdiction was reduced the court was more concerned with the county's finances and administration and became more particularly the resort of those magistrates who felt qualified for that business. The court's judicial work also became more specialized and attracted fewer magistrates.[30]

The numbers of magistrates at quarter sessions rose over the period as a whole. At the outset about 30 magistrates attended. From 1842, perhaps in consequence of the fall in the number of clergy, that figure declined, and over the next twenty years attendance averaged some 23, though by the late 1850s it had probably grown to about 27.[31] From about 1862 to the end of the period some 40 magistrates assembled for an average sessions.[32] Best attended were the Epiphany sessions, when most of the committees were re-elected[33] and, from 1853 to 1880, the previous year's accounts were presented,[34] and the October sessions; worst were the Midsummer sessions. Midsummer and March sessions in 1855 and 1871 were unusually crowded for the election of a new chairman of the court. Easter sessions were unusually well attended on four occasions when difficult or contentious business[35] was before the court.

Quarter sessions was the squires' preserve, and few of the leading families[36] stood aside completely from attendance throughout these years. Though the bench was not

[24] H. S. Giffard (a future ld. chancellor) and J. FitzJames Stephen (a future high-ct. justice).
[25] Sir Baldwyn Leighton, 'Short Acct. of Life of Sir Baldwin Leighton' (TS. in S.R.O. 783, parcel 194), p. 73.
[26] D.N.B. Suppl.
[27] The Law Reports: Ct. of Queen's Bench, iii (1868), 491.
[28] See p. 138.
[29] See figs. cited below, and above, p. 136.
[30] See pp. 143 sqq.
[31] Orders of Q. Sess. iii. 309, 313-23; iv. 1-143; S.R.O., q. sess. recs., box 30, cuttings bk. 1857-71; below, p. 138. Attendances recorded in the order bks. before Oct. 1837 (Orders of Q. Sess. iii. 298-312) are clearly incomplete, except for that of Oct. 1836 (ibid. 309).

[32] Orders of Q. Sess. iv. 144-289; S.R.O., q. sess. recs., box 30, cuttings bks. 1857-89. For each session between 1857 and 1874 (see Orders of Q. Sess. iv. p. ii) 4 or more names not in the order bks. are in the newspaper reps., though occasionally in the mid 1860s and in 1870-1 those reps. add many more; similarly 1 or more names not in the newspaper reps. are in the order bks.
[33] See p. 145.
[34] S.R.O., q. sess. Finance Cttee. rep. bk. 1851-7, pp. 65-6; Co. of Salop., Acct. of Receipts and Expenditure of Public Stock, 1878-9.
[35] Petitions to Parl. in 1847 and 1861, police business in 1859 and 1872.
[36] See p. 311, nn. 56-8. This para. is based on the sources cited in nn. 31-2, above.

politically homogeneous,[37] it was socially exclusive for virtually the whole period and to a greater extent than in George III's reign:[38] outside the ranks of the gentry even leading agriculturists were not made magistrates.[39] Nevertheless the bonds of rural society were stronger perhaps in this period than in any other,[40] and the popularity earned by the gentry on the turf,[41] in the hunting field,[42] and even on the roads,[43] gave an unprecedented mandate to their rule of the county. At the same time the higher standard of morality prevailing in the landed classes[44] was a source of authority and self-confidence.

At the beginning of the period seven or eight clergymen attended an average quarter sessions forming about a quarter of the magistrates present,[45] probably a proportionate representation of their strength on the commission.[46] After 1842 numbers fell sharply and there were rarely more than two or three present. At first the influence of a Whig lieutenant, the duke of Sutherland, may have been responsible,[47] but his Conservative successor, Lord Hill, disapproved of clergymen, especially those with parochial duties, acting as magistrates,[48] and numbers remained low for twenty years after his appointment.[49] With but one exception the clergy who attended during those years[50] were closely related to leading landowners. The exception, Daniel Nihill, rector of Fitz[51] and an assiduous magistrate, held that there was 'a strict concurrence' between the magistrate's and the clergyman's objects,[52] a view he had put into practice as governor of the Millbank Penitentiary 1837–43.[53]

In the mid and later 1860s numbers increased slightly. Five clergymen might be found at an average sessions, but they were then a smaller proportion of the magistrates present than at the beginning of the period. The new clerical recruits to the quarter-sessions bench were for the most part either substantial landowners in their own right[54] or near relatives of county landowners.[55] Again there seems to have been only one exception, H. O. Wilson, rector of Church Stretton and chairman (1857–79) of the Church Stretton guardians.[56]

With few, though noteworthy, exceptions, the peers, some half-dozen of whom were the county's greatest landowners,[57] did not come to quarter sessions. Nor, it seems, did other members of their families, though in the 1850s Lord Combermere's cousin, the Revd. H. C. Cotton, provides an exception, as does the 1st Earl Brownlow's nephew, Capt. H. F. Cust (later Cockayne-Cust),[58] from 1855 when he came to Ellesmere as resident agent to the 2nd earl.[59] The 4th and 6th Lords Berwick attended regularly both before and after inheriting the title.[60] Except for the earls of Powis and the Her-

[37] See pp. 138, 141, 155. [38] See p. 119. [39] See p. 163.
[40] F. M. L. Thompson, *Eng. Landed Soc. in Nineteenth Cent.* (1963), 133–50, 287–91.
[41] *V.C.H. Salop.* ii. 181–2. [42] Ibid. 165–6, 181.
[43] As gentlemen coachmen: *T.S.A.S.* ii. 141–3, 156–60, 163–4; *Shrews. Chron.* 20 Feb. 1925; E. W. Bovill, *The Eng. of Nimrod and Surtees* (1959), 139.
[44] *T.S.A.S.* lix. 143–4.
[45] For this para. and the next see sources cited in nn. 31–2, above.
[46] E. J. Evans, 'Growth of Eng. Rural Anti-Clericalism c. 1750–c. 1830', *Past & Present*, lxvi. 101.
[47] As happened in Warws.: R. Quinault, 'The Warws. County Magistracy and Public Order c. 1830–1870', *Popular Protest and Public Order*, ed. R. Quinault and J. Stevenson (1974), 188–9.
[48] *Eddowes's Jnl.* 17 Oct. 1855. Hill's views were shared by Ld. Chancellor Cranworth and perhaps some of his successors: ibid.; Thompson, op. cit. 288.
[49] Cf. *Orders of Q. Sess.* iv. p. ii.
[50] The Hon. Ric. Noel-Hill (4th Ld. Berwick 1842), Hen. Burton, H. C. Cotton (see below), J. O. Hopkins (Burke, *Land. Gent.* (1952), 324, 1505), and Dan. Nihill (see below).

[51] J. and J. A. Venn, *Al. Cantab. . . . 1752 to 1900*, iv (1951), 552.
[52] *Eddowes's Jnl.* 17 Oct. 1855.
[53] A. Griffiths, *Memorials of Millbank, and Chapters in Prison Hist.* (1875), i. 194 sqq.
[54] W. B. Garnett-Botfield of Decker Hill, W. C. E. Kynaston of Hardwick, F. H. Wolryche-Whitmore of Dudmaston. Cf. below, p. 311.
[55] R. G. Benson, E. G. Childe, C. O. Kenyon, Edw. Warter, and Geo. Whitmore: Burke, *Peerage* (1949), 1114; Burke, *Land. Gent.* (1952), 160, 430, 2650, 2707.
[56] *S.P.R. Heref.* viii (2), pp. iv, vi; S.R.O. 19/2/5, p. 292; S.R.O. 456/1, f. 9.
[57] See pp. 310–11.
[58] Burke, *Peerage* (1949), 277, 454–5; *Orders of Q. Sess.* iv. 12–79, 105–256; *S.P.R. Lich.* xx (1), p. vii. Cotton's dau. had marr. a son of the chmn. of q. sess. in 1844: Loton Hall MSS., Sir B. Leighton's diary, 15 Aug. 1844.
[59] S.R.O. 212, parcel 282, Salop. and Chester rentals 1854–5, pp. 1–2.
[60] *Orders of Q. Sess.* iii. 311 sqq.; iv. 80 sqq. The 5th baron was a recluse: Loton Hall MSS., Sir B. Leighton's diary, 18 May 1861.

bert and Clive families,[61] however, the only other peers regularly attending were the three who headed the county magistracy: the 2nd duke of Sutherland (1839–45), the 2nd Viscount Hill (1845–75), and the 3rd earl of Bradford (1875–96).

Sutherland did not live in the county.[62] Melbourne had had to seek a Whig lieutenant among the county's non-resident aristocratic landowners.[63] The duke attended once or twice a year during his first three years,[64] and in 1843 he assured the magistrates that he would be 'happy to attend upon all occasions'.[65] Thereafter, however, he came only twice during his last three years of office.[66]

By contrast Lord Hill attended the court regularly for all but his last two years as lieutenant[67] though he had not done so during his previous 14 years as a magistrate.[68] He was supported by a tribe of relatives,[69] and in the mid century the Hills, their kinsmen, and their friends were the most numerous and influential group regularly attending the court. The Hills had long dominated the Northern parliamentary division,[70] and their political importance was reinforced socially by the prominence of the owner of Hawkstone in the hunting field[71] and as a patron of the local turf.[72] The family's military traditions[73] also conferred social distinction: three generations had monopolized command of the North Shropshire Yeomanry Cavalry[74] and when Lord Hill became lieutenant he immediately began to promote his relatives and friends to a similar eminence in the moribund county militia.[75]

The Hills' weightiest connexions in county affairs were with the Kenyons of Pradoe: in 1833 Lord Hill's brother John had married the Hon. Thomas Kenyon's only daughter.[76] Kenyon and his close friend[77] J. A. LLoyd, of Leaton Knolls, were the most influential magistrates at quarter sessions: Kenyon chaired the court from 1830 to 1850 and nominated LLoyd its first deputy chairman in 1845.[78] Between them Kenyon and LLoyd almost monopolized the chairmanships of the court's four main committees during the 1830s and 1840s,[79] and LLoyd was chairman of the Police Committee when a connexion of Lord Hill was made chief constable in 1840,[80] not without allegations of undue influence.[81] Few magistrates outside this circle of relatives and friends chaired a major committee before 1855, with the notable exceptions of J. T. Smitheman Edwardes and Sir Baldwin Leighton. When LLoyd retired in 1848[82] Kenyon nominated Panton Corbett as deputy chairman with Lord Hill's help and to Leighton's displeasure.[83] Corbett's son Edward later succeeded to the chair of the Asylum Justices' Committee as a result of Smitheman Edwardes's death in 1851. Four years later, when Panton Corbett resigned the chair of quarter sessions, the Hills spitefully, though unsuccessfully, put forward his nephew Uvedale Corbett in opposition to Leighton, then deputy chairman.[84]

Few of the Hills or their relatives seem to have attended quarter sessions regularly

[61] See pp. 117, 256, 315 n. 19.
[62] *Salopian Jnl.* 4 Jan. 1843.
[63] See p. 310.
[64] *Orders of Q. Sess.* iii. 322; iv. 9–20.
[65] *Salopian Jnl.* 4 Jan. 1843.
[66] *Orders of Q. Sess.* iv. 30, 33, 51.
[67] Ibid., p. ii.
[68] Ibid. iii. 284 sqq.
[69] Cf. Burke, *Peerage* (1949), 185, 471–2, 1011–12; *Orders of Q. Sess.* iv, *passim.* For Sir A. V. Corbet, however, see *Eddowes's Jnl.* 19 Sept. 1855; Loton Hall MSS., Sir B. Leighton's diary, 24 Sept. 1855. The most notable friends were the Corbetts of Longnor.
[70] See p. 319.
[71] *V.C.H. Salop.* ii. 169–70, 176.
[72] Ibid. 179, 182.
[73] E. Sidney, *Life of Ld. Hill, G.C.B.* (1845), 3.
[74] C. Wingfield, *Hist. Record of Shropshire Yeomanry Cav.* (Shrews. 1888), 12–13.

[75] S.R.O., q. sess. recs., box 302, reg. of coms. in militia 1834–72; below, p. 164.
[76] Katharine M. R. Kenyon, *A House That Was Loved* (1941), 153, 179–80, 189–96, 200, 202–5.
[77] *Eddowes's Jnl.* 29 June 1864. Cf. Hughes, *Sheriffs,* 60–1; below, p. 320.
[78] *Orders of Q. Sess.* iv, pp. iii, 45.
[79] Dates, etc. of chmnships are based on the sources cited below, pp. 148 sqq. Cttee. min. bks. often record elections and resignations of chmn., the signatures in cttee. rep. bks. confirming and amplifying the min. bks.' evidence.
[80] See p. 157.
[81] S.R.O., q. sess. min. bk. 1, 25 Jan. 1840.
[82] *Eddowes's Jnl.* 18 Oct. 1848.
[83] *T.S.A.S.* lix. 157. Leighton had been named as LLoyd's associate when LLoyd was made dep. chmn. in 1845: S.R.O., q. sess. Finance Cttee. rep. bk. 1843–50, p. 51.
[84] *T.S.A.S.* lix. 158–9.

before 1845;[85] after 1875 only John Hill, who long continued active as a local magistrate, made even occasional appearances.[86] Old age and death removed Lord Hill's generation,[87] disinclination, ill-health, and pressure of debt his heir.[88] During the earlier years of Hill's lieutenancy, however, the group seems to have been given a coherence it might not otherwise have had by the repeated attacks on its pervasive influence made by one of the county's most ambitious squires, Sir Baldwin Leighton.

In 1825 Leighton went down from Oxford to restore the prosperity of the dilapidated family property. Thereafter he lived on his estate, conveyed to him by his father in 1827, improving it by judicious investment and regulating its economy with the same meticulous attention to detail which he also applied to public affairs.[89] In 1833, the year after his marriage, he began to act as a Shropshire magistrate.[90] Unfitted for field sports[91] and with a weakly constitution[92] yet an evident ambition to figure in public life, Leighton applied himself unremittingly to the grind of county business and eventually to a parliamentary career also. He attended Shropshire quarter sessions with such regularity that when he died in 1871 he had missed only three sessions.[93] He was effectively chairman of Montgomeryshire quarter sessions from 1844 until 1855 when he resigned, arranging for Lord Powis to succeed him,[94] to become chairman of the Shropshire court, a position he retained until death. From 1836 until he died Leighton was chairman of the Atcham guardians,[95] and it was under his energetic rule that Atcham set the standard of poor-law administration in the county and endowed him with a more than local reputation long before he entered Parliament in 1859.[96]

Leighton worked more easily with subordinates than equals: it was a trait which, as he noticed in others,[97] left him imperfectly equipped for the magistrates' transaction of county business by debate and compromise. 'Reserved, taciturn, and inexplicit', Leighton developed principles of administration during his public life, but those very principles he 'could hardly explain'.[98] At the Atcham board explanation was not called for. Leighton himself mastered the details of individual cases and the officials could have had little scope for an independent role; the other guardians gave him loyal support.[99] County affairs, however, were more complex. At quarter sessions each magistrate could claim an equal voice and the professionalism of the court's principal officers was deferred to, occasionally in a degree which Leighton found excessive.[1] The entrenched influence of the Kenyons and Hills might have counselled a conciliatory approach. Leighton, however, insensitive and direct to the point of bluntness,[2] liked 'straightforward'[3] behaviour in others and was thoroughly opposed to the family[4] and political[5] jobbery and intrigue which seemed to characterize the conduct of county affairs during the earlier part of the period. With scant regard for tact and with motives that were perhaps occasionally calculated Leighton repeatedly antagonized the formid-

[85] Except Sir Rob.: *Orders of Q. Sess.* iii. 248 sqq.; Sidney, *Life of Ld. Hill*, 393.

[86] *Orders of Q. Sess.* iv. 226, 252–3, 259, 267, 275, 285; *Shrews. Chron.* 10 July 1925.

[87] Burke, *Peerage* (1949), 1011–12.

[88] *Shrews. Chron.* 20 July, 31 Aug. 1894; 5 Apr. 1895; below, p. 319. He last attended q. sess. July 1866: *Orders of Q. Sess.* iv. 169.

[89] See *T.S.A.S.* lix. 127–69, and (for further details) the sources cited ibid. 134 n. 11.

[90] *Orders of Q. Sess.* iii. 294.

[91] Loton Hall MSS., Sir B. Leighton's diary, 12 Dec. 1863.

[92] Leighton, 'Life of Sir B. Leighton' (TS. in S.R.O. 783, parcel 194), p. 82.

[93] *Orders of Q. Sess.* iv. 178–9; Loton Hall MSS., Sir B. Leighton's diary, 30 Dec. 1867. During his shrievalty (1835–6) he was disqualified as a J.P.

[94] Loton Hall MSS., Sir B. Leighton's diary, 4 Jan. 1855. Cf. *T.S.A.S.* lix. 158.

[95] See p. 171.

[96] *T.S.A.S.* lix. 150.

[97] e.g. E. W. Smythe Owen: Loton Hall MSS., Sir B. Leighton's diary, 17 Apr. 1863.

[98] Leighton, 'Life of Sir B. Leighton', p. 58.

[99] *T.S.A.S.* lix. 167–8; J. Bowen-Jones, *Rep. on Progress of Atcham Union . . .* (Shrews. [1890]), 19–20.

[1] See pp. 147 (sources cited in n. 24), 158, 160.

[2] *Extracts from Letters & Speeches, &c., of Sir B. Leighton, Bt.*, ed. F.C. Childe (Shrews. priv. print. 1875), 4.

[3] A word he applied approvingly to J. T. Smitheman Edwardes and J. M. Severne: diary, 29 Oct. 1851; 8 July 1855.

[4] See p. 139, but cf. p. 142.

[5] *Salopian Jnl.* 10 Jan. 1838 (remarks on political canvassing for post of gaol surgeon); Loton Hall MSS., Sir B. Leighton's diary, Apr. 1852 (on patronage of ld. lieuts.).

able Hill clan, forcefully opposing their policies and interests, notably over the affairs of the county police[6] and militia[7] and over county officers' salaries.[8] He did so often enough with the help of the 3rd Lord Powis to give their connexion sometimes the appearance of an alliance.

The rivalry of Hill and Leighton in the 1840s and 1850s was thus the nearest thing to politics[9] to disturb the court during the period. It did not long outlast the 1850s. Leighton's election as chairman of quarter sessions in 1855 and his return to Parliament in 1859[10] freed him to try to realize his aspirations in public life, and he was on good terms with Hill by 1865.[11] In 1867 Hill helped to dissuade him from resigning the chair of quarter sessions.[12]

Leighton died in 1871. Hill, almost his exact contemporary, virtually ceased to attend the court little more than fourteen months later.[13] Their successors were not personal rivals. The new lieutenant, Lord Bradford, did not so obviously aspire to advance his family and friends.[14] That was perhaps partly due to a more retiring disposition,[15] though it is also true that the lieutenants' patronage, in the military sphere at least, had been diminished in 1871 when they lost the power to grant militia commissions.[16] Even more inhibiting perhaps was the changed political and social atmosphere in which Leighton's successors and Bradford worked.

From the 1860s on, as has been seen,[17] greater numbers of magistrates attended the court, and by the late 1870s there were a dozen or so who seem to have been neither landowners nor clergy,[18] but industrialists,[19] professional,[20] or retired[21] men, types who were later to play a greater part in the county council.[22] Yet others seem to have come from the class of tenant gentry[23] or from the lesser landowners.[24] In Shropshire, as in the country generally,[25] the increased volume and complexity of local government stimulated interest in the rates. By 1876 the Shropshire tenant farmers were showing an interest in the proposed county boards on which ratepayers as such would be represented,[26] and within a few years even the lieutenant's son, Lord Newport, though too indolent to make any regular contribution to public life, was known to favour the new boards.[27]

It was Newport's indolence, more than his support for the new boards, which typified a changed outlook among the traditional rulers of the county.[28] As early as 1868 Leighton had deplored 'a sad want of aptitude for business' among the Shropshire 'country gentlemen'. In his absence from the March sessions of that year he noted that two lawyers, 'neither of them country squires', had presided over the courts, and the Finance Committee had been chaired by Layton Lowndes, 'only a tenant'. He feared for the country gentlemen 'losing their influence' in the next half-century, believing that they could hold their own with the 'manufacturing and commercial classes' only

[6] See p. 158. [7] *Eddowes's Jnl.* 3 Jan. 1855.
[8] See p. 147 n. 24 and sources there cited.
[9] Leighton and Ld. Hill were both Conservatives, but Hill helped to keep him out of Parl. in Apr. 1859: see p. 321.
[10] See p. 315.
[11] *T.S.A.S.* lix. 134.
[12] *Eddowes's Jnl.* 3 July, 16 Oct. 1867.
[13] *Orders of Q. Sess.* iv. 196, 204-18.
[14] A protégé was, however, made gaol chaplain in 1875: *Orders of Q. Sess.* iv. 220, 226; *S.P.R. St. Asaph*, iii (1), pp. v, xi. Cf. below, p. 318.
[15] He was oftener absent from, than present at, q. sess.: *Orders of Q. Sess.* iv. 220-90. See also below, p. 342.
[16] By the Regulation of the Forces Act, 1871, 34 & 35 Vic. c. 86, s. 6.
[17] See p. 137.
[18] For those named in nn. 19-24 see *Illustrated Official*

Handbk. to Co. Council of Salop (Shrews. 1890); *P.O. Dir. Salop.* (1879); *Kelly's Dir. Salop.* (1885).
[19] e.g. J. A. Anstice and C. C. Walker.
[20] e.g. E. Burke Wood.
[21] e.g. R. G. Venables: Oswestry Adv. *Unconventional Portraits* (1910), 19.
[22] See p. 184. Anstice and Venables were elected to the first co. council.
[23] e.g. Maj. W. E. Stuart. W. Layton Lowndes too might be included in the class: see below.
[24] e.g. Heighway Jones of Earlsdale, T. J. Provis, and J. Loxdale Warren.
[25] *V.C.H. Wilts.* v. 261-4.
[26] *T.S.A.S.* lix. 172 n. 6, 181.
[27] *Wellington Jnl.* 26 Apr. 1884.
[28] Cf. (for Ches.) J. M. Lee, *Social Leaders and Public Persons: A Study of Co. Govt. in Ches. since 1888* (1963), 42-3.

'by equal if not superior cleverness and knowledge in managing our county affairs'.[29] Nearly three years later, intending to resign the chair of quarter sessions, he discreetly, though unsuccessfully, sought to smooth the way to the deputy chairmanship for his younger son Stanley.[30] It seems an odd close to a public life throughout which Leighton had consistently opposed any hint of family jobbery, but he had a genuine regard for his son's abilities,[31] and saw the economy and integrity of local government as founded upon the landed gentry's due exercise of their privileges and responsibilities.

Leighton was unduly gloomy about the immediate prospect: the two lawyers who presided over the courts during his absence in 1868 were, after all, J. R. Kenyon and Uvedale Corbett,[32] while Lowndes, though not a Shropshire landowner, belonged to a family which had long served the state with distinction.[33] Moreover the leaders of the court continued to be drawn from the established landed families until the end of the period. After 1855, it is true, Leighton's success in challenging the power of the Hills had helped to disperse the clique of friends and relatives which had dominated the court, and the important committees came to be chaired by representatives of a less restricted group of families: Robert Burton,[34] A. C. Heber-Percy,[35] John Bather,[36] and M. G. Benson.[37] The Bathers[38] and Bensons[39] were relative newcomers to landed society, but the Burtons had been seated at Longner since the 16th century[40] and Heber-Percy's wife's ancestors had inherited Hodnet in 1752.[41] Moreover a Herbert was to chair the Police Committee for 22 years[42] and the Kenyons of Pradoe continued to influence the court's policies.

J. R. Kenyon, deputy chairman (1855–71) and chairman (1871–80) of quarter sessions and the last chairman of the Gaol Justices (1871–8), was the second generation of his family to preside over the court. When he died in 1880 his younger brother, Lt.-Col. William Kenyon-Slaney, a former chairman of the Police Committee (1861–4), was elected deputy chairman. Col. Edward Corbett, son of a former chairman of the court and with over half a century's experience of its work, could truly claim, in seconding Kenyon-Slaney's election, that he never recollected the time 'when there was not a Kenyon doing active work for the county'.[43] Kenyon-Slaney's election was a tribute to his brother's and his father's services;[44] to any who apprehended the erosion of the landed gentry's control of county affairs, however, it was perhaps equally welcome as a sign of continuity. The existence of such fears is suggested by Lord Bradford's almost apologetic proposal of W. Layton Lowndes as chairman. 'Other names', he admitted, 'had, of course, been mentioned', hastening to reassure the court that Lord Powis had 'fully concurred' in the propriety of choosing Lowndes.[45]

Lowndes's chairmanship was brief. He resigned suddenly at the end of 1882[46] leaving the county soon after.[47] Kenyon-Slaney, in failing health, retired simultaneously.[48] The new chairman, Alfred Salwey, came from an old landed family,[49] and

[29] Loton Hall MSS., Sir B. Leighton's diary, 16 Mar. 1868.
[30] Ibid. 3 Jan. 1871.
[31] Ibid. 1 May, 18 Dec. 1858; [Feb.], 8 July 1862; 11 Aug. 1869.
[32] Ibid. 16 Mar. 1868.
[33] G. Lipscomb, *Hist. of Co. of Buckingham* (1847), iii. 544; Burke, *Land. Gent.* (1952), 1907–8; J. Foster, *Al. Oxon. . . . 1715–1886*, iii. 877.
[34] Chmn. of Finance Cttee. 1856–60.
[35] Chmn. of Police Cttee. 1864–6.
[36] Chmn. of Visiting Justices of Asylum, 1855–77.
[37] Chmn. of Judges' Ho. Cttee. 1855–9, Police Cttee. 1858–61.
[38] Bather's gt. grandfather bought the man. and advowson of Meole Brace in 1779: *S.P.R. Heref.* xviii (3), pp. iv, vi–vii.

[39] Benson's grandfather, a Liverpool W. India merchant, bought Lutwyche about the time the Bathers acquired Meole Brace: Burke, *Land. Gent.* (18th edn.), ii (1969), 40–2; *S.H.C.* 1950–1, 281; S.R.O. 1119/6, Lutwyche; F. Leach, *Co. Seats of Salop.* (Shrews. 1891), 395.
[40] *S.P.R. Lich.* xiv (2), pp. iv–vi, viii.
[41] Ibid. xi (2), p. iv; Blakeway, *Sheriffs*, 242; Hughes, *Sheriffs*, 46–7.
[42] Ld. Powis's bro., the Hon. R. C. Herbert, chmn. 1867–89.
[43] *Shrews. Chron.* 2 July 1880; above, p. 139; below, pp. 157, 360.
[44] Hughes, *Sheriffs*, 65.
[45] *Shrews. Chron.* 2 July 1880. [46] Ibid. 5 Jan. 1883.
[47] *Kelly's Dir. Salop.* (1891), 252.
[48] *Shrews. Chron.* 5 Jan. 1883.
[49] Burke, *Land. Gent.* (1952), 2238–9; below, p. 337.

his deputy Sir Offley Wakeman, an active Shropshire magistrate of some ten years' standing,[50] came from a family which, though newcomers to the county,[51] had been Shropshire landowners for over 60 years.[52]

Quarter Sessions: Procedure

Throughout the 55 years from 1834 quarter sessions were held in Shrewsbury, normally in the shirehall. The court's policies were thus free from the rivalries and administrative discontinuities experienced in counties whose quarter sessions itinerated round the principal or historic towns.[53]

Sessions, normally lasting two or three days, opened with legal business at the beginning of the period but financial and administrative business soon took precedence. Appeals, the most complex branch of the court's legal business, were always heard before trials began; that suited the convenience of the bar and of the magistrates. Appeals and trials, however, both declined in volume, the former in consequence of the new Poor Law,[54] the latter owing to changes in the criminal jurisdiction of quarter sessions. In 1842 the court lost the power to try capital offences, the more serious felonies, and other specified offences.[55] In practice, however, such matters had normally been sent to assizes,[56] and it was in fact the later enlargement of the criminal jurisdiction of petty sessions which reduced the number of trials at quarter sessions; they fell from 270 in 1844 to 125 in 1864 and 73 in 1884.[57]

After the 1840s, as the volume of its legal business declined, the court's administrative work grew in importance and attracted greater publicity. From 1834 the magistrates had to conduct the county-rate business in open court,[58] and the county newspapers gave more space to it as time went on. From 1857 the papers printed the committee and officers' reports in full,[59] those reports and the magistrates' discussion of them thus being made available to the county ratepayers.[60] The magistrates were not averse to such developments for increasing prestige attached to a prominent role in the efficient transaction of county business, and in 1852 Sir Baldwin Leighton, ambitious to get into Parliament and with hopes of becoming chairman of quarter sessions, was gratified to receive an address signed by 150 farmers thanking him for his efforts to reduce county expenditure.[61]

The court adapted its procedure to these changes. From 1838 sessions began with the county-rate business on Monday afternoon[62] in the statutory quarter-sessions weeks,[63] legal business being reserved to Tuesday morning. The change 'brought the magistrates more together at an earlier period of the sessions';[64] it served well for the rest of the period, mainly perhaps because it allowed ample time for private discussion of county business on the first day.[65] Confidential matters of county administration

[50] *Orders of Q. Sess.* iv. 213.
[51] *V.C.H. Worcs.* iii. 303, 306-7.
[52] *V.C.H. Salop.* viii. 230, 275; *S.P.R. Heref.* viii (1), pp. v, ix; *T.S.A.S.* 4th ser. xii. 326-7.
[53] e.g. Mont., Wilts.: Loton Hall MSS., Sir B. Leighton's diary, 17 Oct. 1850; *V.C.H. Wilts.* v. 232.
[54] *Salopian Jnl.* 4 Jan. 1843; S.R.O., q. sess. recs., box 30, cuttings bk. 1883-9, 2 July, 15 Oct. 1883; *Orders of Q. Sess.* iv, p. ix.
[55] Q. Sess. Act, 1842, 5 & 6 Vic. c. 38.
[56] Only 2 such offences (bigamy and concealment of birth) had been tried at q. sess. in the 1820s: *Abstr. of Q. Sess. Rolls, 1820-1830,* ed. Mary C. Hill (Shrews. 1974), 301/61-6, 99; 319/4-6, 13, 15.
[57] *Orders of Q. Sess.* iv, p. v.
[58] Under the County Rates Act, 1834, 4 & 5 Wm. IV, c.

48: *Salopian Jnl.* 17 Sept., 22 Oct. 1834.
[59] S.R.O., q. sess. Finance Cttee. rep. bk. 1851-7, p. 199.
[60] S.R.O., q. sess. recs., box 30, cuttings bks. 1857-89. Many of the newspaper citations in this article are from these bks.
[61] Loton Hall MSS., Sir B. Leighton's diary, Apr. 1852; above, pp. 140-1; below, p. 320.
[62] When new rules of ct. were published: *Salopian Jnl.* 14 Mar., 4 Apr. 1838.
[63] Defined in the Law Terms Act, 1830, 11 Geo. IV & 1 Wm. IV, c. 70, s. 35, and in the Apr. Q. Sess. Act, 1834, 4 & 5 Wm. IV, c. 47.
[64] As in Staffs. and Worcs.: *Salopian Jnl.* 10 Jan. 1838.
[65] Ibid. 4 Jan. 1843; *Shrews. Jnl.* 4 July 1883; S.R.O., q. sess. recs., box 53, agendas 1873-89.

were also transacted at the magistrates' dinner after the first day's public business.[66]

By the 1850s the order of business was beginning to affect the court's legal and judicial business adversely. A rota of magistrates to help the chairman and deputy chairman of sessions in their courts had to be made in 1851–2[67] but it soon ceased to work. Magistrates attended primarily for the administrative business and in 1856, after judicial business had been delayed for a month by the magistrates' withdrawal when that business was finished, the court had to be guaranteed the services of magistrates living near Shrewsbury for the duration of each sessions.[68]

The court's administrative work was devolved on four principal standing committees. The Visiting Justices of the Gaol had been established in 1791,[69] but it was during the years 1839–41 that the other three main standing committees were constituted. In January 1839 the Auditing Justices' Committee was replaced by a larger Finance Committee with a more comprehensive commission.[70] In December 1839 the Constabulary Committee was set up and next year it was given the statutory duty of levying the police rate.[71] After over two years' discussions by temporary committees the committee of Visiting Justices of the Asylum was formed in 1841, charged with the planning and administration of a county asylum for pauper lunatics.[72] The establishment of the four committees, whose detailed work is discussed below,[73] within two or three years is indicative of an increased vigour imparted to the government of the county. There were, however, many differences between the committees' respective powers and memberships.

From 1861 the Finance Committee, which gradually became a general-purpose committee too, was normally chaired by the court's chairman. Its large membership was intended to represent all parts of the county. Any magistrate wishing to share in county administration was put on it,[74] and about a week before quarter sessions every magistrate was notified of the committee's meeting. The Police Committee too was intended to represent the whole county. Indeed from 1857 to 1863 the membership of the two committees, both of whom imposed rates on the county, was normally identical[75] and they met on the same days. The Police Committee, however, was reconstituted in 1863. Its chairman, alleging that it was too large, narrowly carried a motion reducing it to eleven: five *ex officio* members[76] and six members elected in court by ballot. The experiment failed. Next year, under a new chairman, the committee resumed a representative character: to the six members elected in court and four *ex officio* members[77] was added a member of each petty-sessional bench.[78] The membership of the Finance and Police committees did not coincide thereafter.[79]

The Visiting Justices of the Gaol and of the Asylum had fewer members than the Finance and Police committees, their 'constant attendance' at the institutions they administered being 'very desirable'.[80] Unless building expenditure was involved, the asylum visitors were independent of the court. They fixed the weekly maintenance for

[66] *Salopian Jnl.* 4 Jan. 1843; and see e.g. S.R.O., q. sess. min. bk. 1, 18 Oct. 1841. At the beginning of the period the magistrates dined on the 2nd evening of sess. (Tues.): *Orders of Q. Sess.* iii. 300.

[67] S.R.O., q. sess. Finance Cttee. rep. bk. 1851–7, pp. 24, 35–6.

[68] S.R.O., q. sess. min. bk. 6, 31 Dec. 1855; 1–2 Jan., 10 Mar. 1856; q. sess. Finance Cttee. rep. bk. 1851–7, p. 163; *Orders of Q. Sess.* iv. 110.

[69] See p. 126.   [70] See p. 148.

[71] Under the County Police Act, 1840, 3 & 4 Vic. c. 88.

[72] See p. 160.   [73] See pp. 148–62.

[74] Much of what follows is based on R. H. Spearman, *The Co. Councillor's Manual* (1889), 1–6 (Introductory Chap. 'On the Former Procedure of Cts. of Q. Sess. in Co.

Business' by Spearman's bro.-in-law W. L. Lowndes: Burke, *Peerage* (1967), 2344).

[75] S.R.O., q. sess. Finance Cttee. rep. bk. 1851–7, p. 196; 1857–63, p. 210; Const. Cttee. rep. bk. 1854–65, pp. 51, 155.

[76] Chmn. and dep. chmn. of q. sess. and chmn. of the 3 other main cttees.

[77] H.M. Lieut., chmn. and dep. chmn. of q. sess., and chmn. of Visiting Justices of Asylum.

[78] *Eddowes's Jnl.* 7 Jan. 1863; 6 Jan. 1864; S.R.O., q. sess. Const. Cttee. rep. bk. 1854–65, pp. 176, 208.

[79] S.R.O., q. sess. Const. Cttee. rep. bk. 1854–65, p. 208; Finance Cttee. rep. bk. 1863–7, p. 61; Co. of Salop., *Acct. of Receipts and Pmnts. of Treasurer of Co. of Salop.*, 1883–9.

[80] Ld. Powis's view: *Eddowes's Jnl.* 7 Jan. 1863.

the patients and issued precepts to the poor-law unions. They also appointed their own clerk, surveyor, and other officers.[81]

Three of the four committees were appointed annually at the Epiphany sessions.[82] The prison visiting justices were appointed quarterly until 1878[83] when the court began to appoint five magistrates annually at the Epiphany sessions to serve on the new Visiting Committee of the Prison.[84] Both visitors' committees became joint committees as the asylum and the gaol came to serve areas outside the Shropshire court's jurisdiction.[85]

The leading quarter-sessions magistrates were the chairmen of the court's four main standing committees. In 1888 George Butler Lloyd told the court that his 'rule' was 'never, if possible, to oppose a report sent in by a committee'.[86] That, as he must have known from his family and business connexions with some of the leading magistrates and the court's officers,[87] had been the magistrates' principle for over half a century, and on occasion the court was even prepared to accept a committee report in defiance of its own rules of procedure.[88] Committee members spent much 'time and attention' on their duties,[89] and in 1888 Stanley Leighton, reviewing half a century of the court's work, attributed the success of its financial administration primarily to the magistrates' invariable trust of their chairman:

They had placed the responsibility of conducting the work of the court upon a few men in whom they had showed their confidence. They had not made the court a place in which to make long and excited speeches. There was no place that he knew of . . . where more business was done with fewer words than had been the case in that court during the last 50 years.

Leighton had been a mere onlooker for ten or twelve years, absorbed in 'political business' to the exclusion of 'local business'.[90] About the same time, however, W. Layton Lowndes made the same point, drawing on his continuous involvement in the court's work since 1851: the 'greater part' of that work, he averred, fell on the committee chairmen and 'the few members' who helped them to prepare it;[91] he himself had been pre-eminent among the latter during Sir Baldwin Leighton's later years.[92]

Besides the court's main standing committees, *ad hoc*, temporary, and other special committees were occasionally appointed. Though general oversight of county bridges, for example, was the Finance Committee's responsibility,[93] *ad hoc* committees of local magistrates were set up to consider the rebuilding or repair of particular bridges.[94] Notable among the temporary committees were those appointed periodically to revise the county's rateable value.[95] Special committees often considered new legislation. Such were the Highways Committees set up in 1862 and 1876[96] and the committees established in 1887–8 to prepare for the advent of the county council.[97]

[81] Lowndes, 'Procedure of Q. Sess.', 3; below, pp. 147–8, 160–2.

[82] S.R.O., q. sess. cttee. rep. bks.; q. sess. recs., box 53, agendas 1873–89.

[83] Under the Gaols Act, 1823, 4 Geo. IV, c. 64, s. 16, and the Prison Act, 1865, 28 & 29 Vic. c. 126, ss. 53–5: see e.g. S.R.O., q. sess. Visiting Justices of Prison rep. bk. 1823–38, p. 118; q. sess. recs., box 53, agendas 1873–8.

[84] Under the Prison Act, 1877, 40 & 41 Vic. c. 21, s. 13: S.R.O., q. sess. Visiting Justices of Prison rep. bk. 1872–8, pp. 76–7; q. sess. recs., box 53, agendas 1878–89.

[85] S.R.O. 183/3/3, 8 Apr. 1844; *Rep. Medical Supt. of Lun. Asylum*, 1872–88; S.R.O., q. sess. Visiting Justices of Prison rep. bk. 1872–8, p. 76.

[86] *Shrews. Chron.* 19 Oct. 1888.

[87] His father W. Butler Lloyd had attended q. sess. 1852–74 (*Orders of Q. Sess.* iv. 88–213) and had been a banking partner (in Burton, Lloyd, Salt & How) of Rob. Burton, chmn. of the Finance Cttee. (*Shrews. Chron.* 21 Sept. 1860; below, pp. 147–8). G. Butler Lloyd was a partner in the Salop Old Bank with E. C. Peele, successively co. treasurer

and clk. of the peace, and G. M. Salt, co. treasurer: S.R.O. 2620, box 25, arts. of partnership 1884 (copy).

[88] For the 'extraordinary scene' (M. G. Benson's phrase: *Shrews. Chron.* 22 Mar. 1867) it provoked, see *Eddowes's Jnl.* 2 Jan. 1867. The rule was later revised: ibid: 20 Mar., 3 July, 16 Oct. 1867; 1 Jan. 1868.

[89] *Eddowes's Jnl.* 2 Jan. 1867.

[90] *Shrews. Chron.* 19 Oct. 1888.

[91] Lowndes, 'Procedure of Q. Sess.', 4.

[92] *Shrews. Chron.* 2 July 1880; 5 Jan. 1883; above, p. 141.

[93] Unlike e.g. Devon which had a co. bridge cttee. from 1822: D. R. Tucker, 'Development of Q. Sess. Govt. in Devon in Nineteenth Cent.' (London Univ. M.A. thesis, 1948), 72 sqq., 92–3.

[94] See e.g. *Eddowes's Jnl.* 2 July 1873; 28 June 1876.

[95] See S.R.O., q. sess. recs., box 30, cuttings bks. 1857–89; below, p. 152 (Table III).

[96] See p. 178.

[97] e.g. the Boundaries and Electoral Divisions cttees. and the cttee. of the whole ct. on the Local Govt. Bill: S.R.O. 68/6; below, p. 166.

Two classes for whom the court had no direct administrative responsibility never-theless came within its purview: they were non-pauper lunatics[98] and vagrants. The inspection of private (licensed) lunatic asylums, a statutory duty of the court through-out the period,[99] was carried out by a small committee of Visitors of Licensed Houses appointed each Michaelmas sessions.[1] Its clerk was the clerk of the peace until 1886 when one of his clerks, William Baxter who had performed the duties of the office, was appointed.[2] The inadequacies of the licensed houses prompted the formation of an unofficial committee in 1865 under quarter sessions' auspices to invite subscriptions for the establishment of a middle-class asylum,[3] but it evidently failed.

The unofficial Vagrancy Committee (1883–6) is noteworthy as the last of a centuries-long series of administrative efforts[4] by the county magistrates to deal with the prob-lems caused by vagrancy. Those problems, especially acute in periods of unemploy-ment, the magistrates had little alternative but to treat as problems of law and order.[5] In 1883, however, after receiving a report by Sir Baldwyn Leighton, the court set up a Vagrancy Committee to administer a privately subscribed system of bread relief,[6] the 'Berkshire' or 'way-ticket' system intended to dispense poor bona fide travellers in search of work from the rigours of the Casual Poor Act, 1882.[7] The committee, how-ever, spent more on incidental expenses, notably gratuities to policemen's wives who gave out the bread relief, than on bread. By 1885 subscriptions were falling off and, having manifestly failed in its purpose, the committee was ended in 1886. It blamed the unions' lax administration of the 1882 Act and the continuance of private charity which made begging more lucrative than the bread dole.[8] The committee's failure, however, must be seen in the perspective of the sixty or so years that vagrancy re-mained a problem in Shropshire, for no administrative solution was ever found, even after 1930, when the relief of vagrants became the direct responsibility of the county authority.[9]

Three principal officers served the court generally, though there were three or four other salaried ones who served particular committees only.[10] The three principals were the clerk of the peace, the county treasurer, and the county surveyor. All were part-timers; thus they often had private and professional connexions with magistrates[11] and their official posts evidently assisted the extension of their private practices.[12] Occasional embarrassment or inconvenience was caused, but such informal con-nexions[13] doubtless facilitated the magistrates' appointment of acceptable men.[14]

Until 1889 the *custos rotulorum* appointed the clerk of the peace,[15] but no *custos* ventured to disturb the legal dynasty which held the clerkship throughout the period and beyond.[16] The Loxdales and Peeles were in partnership as Shrewsbury solicitors

[98] For the pauper asylum see pp. 160–2.
[99] See p. 120.
[1] From 1845 under the Lunatics Act, 1845, 8 & 9 Vic. c. 100, s. 17.
[2] S.R.O., q. sess. Finance Cttee. rep. bk. 1871–4, p. 84; S.R.O. 324, box 125, Baxter to A. Salwey, 5 Dec. 1885; *Shrews. Chron.* 8 Jan. 1886.
[3] *T.S.A.S.* lix. 154; *Eddowes's Jnl.* 18 Oct. 1865; *Shrews. Chron.* 20 Oct. 1865.
[4] See pp. 72, 101, 104, 122–3.
[5] *T.S.A.S.* ii. 154–6; *Orders of Q. Sess.* iii. 284; S.R.O., q. sess. Auditing Cttee. rep. bk. 1824–37, p. 104; q. sess. Const. Cttee. rep. bk. 1839–53, pp. 202–4; *Shrews. Chron.* 3 Jan. 1851; *Eddowes's Jnl.* 20 Oct. 1858.
[6] S.R.O., q. sess. recs., box 30, cuttings bk. 1877–82, 26 June, 16 Oct. 1882; *Shrews. Chron.* 6 Apr. 1883.
[7] 45 & 46 Vic. c. 36. See S. and B. Webb, *Eng. Poor Law Hist.: the Last Hundred Years* (1929), i. 412–13.
[8] *Shrews. Chron.* 3 July, 23 and 30 Oct. 1885; 8 Jan.,

9 Apr. 1886.
[9] See pp. 216–17.
[10] i.e. the gaol governor and chaplain, the ch. const., and the asylum supt., all full-time. See *Shrews. Chron.* 9 Jan. 1852.
[11] For the surveyors see: *Shropshire Mag.* Feb. 1960, pp. 17–18; *Shrews. Chron.* 21 Sept. 1860 (Rob. Burton's employment of Thos. Groves as a builder).
[12] *Eddowes's Jnl.* 17 Mar., 30 June 1875 (remarks of Stan. Leighton).
[13] S.R.O., q. sess. Finance Cttee. rep. bk. 1843–50, p. 127. Cf. *Eddowes's Jnl.* 8 Apr. 1885 (Ld. Bradford's re-marks on J. Loxdale's death).
[14] Suggested by the warm opposition to Leighton over the ch. constableship: *Shrews. Chron.* 7 Jan. 1859; *Eddowes's Jnl.* 19 Oct. 1864; S.R.O., q. sess. Const. Cttee. rep. bk. 1854–65, p. 221.
[15] *Orders of Q. Sess.* iii, p. xxv; below, p. 188.
[16] See pp. 188–9.

in the 1830s[17] and had long been colleagues in the county administration. J. J. Peele (county treasurer 1829-73) was deputy clerk of the peace under John Loxdale from 1843,[18] and the Loxdales had then been associated with the clerk's office for almost a century while the Peeles and their ancestor, John Flint (later Corbett), had held the county treasurership for almost eighty years. With John Loxdale's retirement in 1872 after 56 years in the clerk of the peace's office, 38 of them as clerk, the clerkship passed to the Peeles who were to hold it for almost 40 years thereafter.[19] To the 3rd Lord Powis families like the Loxdales, connected for so long with the county business, recalled the *noblesse de robe* of the French *ancien régime*.[20] Such dynastic continuity in the offices of clerk of the peace[21] and county treasurer[22] was by no means unknown in other counties, but in Shropshire the intimate personal connexions between the two offices over so long a period are as notable as the absence of any financial scandal, often the concomitant of such arrangements.[23]

The clerk was paid by fees until 1853 when the court voted him a salary with expenses. The salary was based on the fees formerly taken[24] and occasional extra duties had therefore to be remunerated by gratuities.[25] The clerk was normally also clerk to the court's committees, but he had no enforceable right to such appointments[26] and at least one prominent magistrate considered the practice an unnecessary expense.[27]

Like the clerks the county treasurers were solicitors and bankers in Shrewsbury. J. J. Peele, the county treasurer, was a partner in Loxdale & Sons (later Loxdale & Peele), solicitors, by about 1830 and later became a partner in the bankers Rocke, Eyton & Co.[28] The firm had been bankers to the county since at least 1816[29] when the Loxdales had become principal partners.[30] In 1885, when Rocke, Eyton & Co. merged with Burton, Lloyd & Co. to form the Salop Old Bank, E. C. Peele, county treasurer since 1873, became a partner.[31] It was indeed primarily as bankers that the county treasurers served quarter sessions, for the magistrates, striving to minimize the court's expenditure and abolish its debt, were the architects of their own financial policy.[32]

The county surveyor also served part-time.[33] Like the clerk, he was originally paid separately for each piece of county work, but from 1849 he was salaried.[34] Telford's successors, Edward Haycock[35] and Thomas Groves,[36] were architects. The great period of bridge building in the county was over by the time of Telford's death in 1834[37] and his successors' main duties came to be the oversight of the county's buildings: the shirehall, judges' lodgings, county gaol, county police headquarters, and militia depot in Shrewsbury and the local police stations and lock-ups elsewhere. By separate appointments of the Asylum Justices they were also surveyors of the asylum

[17] See e.g. S.R.O. 348/19, p. 3; *Eddowes's Jnl.* 16 July 1873 (obit. of J. J. Peele); *Orders of Q. Sess.* iii, p. xxvi.

[18] E. Stephens, *Clerks of the Counties 1360-1960* (1961), 152-3.

[19] *Orders of Q. Sess.* iv. 205, 269; below, p. 361.

[20] *Shrews. Chron.* 10 Apr. 1885.

[21] See e.g. for Ches. and Staffs.: Lee, *Social Leaders*, 67-8; S. A. H. Burne, *A Legal Bi-Centenary, 1760-1960* (Stafford, priv. print. 1960).

[22] e.g. the Hultons in Lancs. 1818-50, the Payns in Berks. 1779-1840, the Smiths in Warws. 1866-87, the firm of solicitors founded by Chas. Gilbert in E. Suss. 1761-1875, and the Woods in Glam. 1786-1824: *Local Govt. Finance*, lvi. 154-5; lviii. 89; lix. 39, 97, 268; lxi. 261, 264.

[23] Ibid. lvi. 154-5, 278-9; lix. 97; lxi. 261-2.

[24] Loton Hall MSS., Sir B. Leighton's diary, Jan. and Apr. 1852; *Shrews. Chron.* 17 Oct. 1851; 9 Jan., 9 Apr. 1852; S.R.O., q. sess. min. bk. 5, pp. 10, 14-15, 18, 27-8, 31, 44, 50-1; Finance Cttee. rep. bk. 1851-7, pp. 24, 30-4, 47-8, 59-60, 78; *Orders of Q. Sess.* iv. 94.

[25] *Shrews. Chron.* 5 Jan. 1883; 2 July 1886; *Orders of Q.

Sess.* iv. 290.

[26] *Orders of Q. Sess.* iv, p. xxii; Stephens, *Clerks of Counties*, 152.

[27] *Shrews. Chron.* 17 Oct. 1851.

[28] *Eddowes's Jnl.* 16 July 1873 (obit.); ex inf. Mr. M. C. de C. Peele (1976).

[29] *Shrews. Chron.* 11 May 1906 (stating that the Salop Old Bank had been bankers to the county for 100 years).

[30] S.R.O. 665/1/447.

[31] S.R.O. 2620, box 25, arts. of partnership 1884 (copy); below, p. 361.

[32] See pp. 148 sqq.

[33] *Eddowes's Jnl.* 17 Mar., 30 June 1875.

[34] S.R.O., q. sess. Finance Cttee. rep. bk. 1843-50, pp. 130, 141-2; q. sess. Const. Cttee. rep. bk. 1839-53, p. 374.

[35] H. M. Colvin, *Biog. Dict. Eng. Architects, 1660-1840* (1954), 278.

[36] *P.O. Dir. Salop.* (1879), 409, 469; *Shrews. Burgess Roll*, ed. H. E. Forrest (Shrews. 1924), 126; above, n. 11.

[37] *T.S.A.S.* lvi. 115; S. and B. Webb, *Story of the King's Highway* (1913), 103.

buildings.[38] From the 1830s until the 1870s the work of supervising county bridges declined and the salary for it was reduced.[39] In 1875, however, in anticipation of a great increase of county bridges as disturnpiking progressed, the salary was restored almost to its former level,[40] and Groves's successor, appointed in 1887, was a civil engineer with much relevant experience.[41]

The surveyor worked mainly with the Finance Committee which controlled work on all county buildings and bridges, receiving the surveyor's reports as well as those of the small committees which had charge of particular county buildings.[42] In 1887 the Finance Committee charged the surveyor with reporting on all parliamentary Bills affecting county property.[43]

Besides the three principal officers, their clerks, and the gaol and asylum staffs and police force, the court employed few other officers. A county inspector of weights and measures was employed until 1886, though from 1850 to 1875 separate northern and southern districts each had an inspector. They received salaries as well as allowances and fees from 1849. In 1887, however, inspection of weights and measures became a police duty.[44] A county analyst, first appointed in 1870,[45] was paid by fees.[46]

Other officers employed on county business had their remuneration controlled by quarter sessions, though the court neither appointed nor employed them. Justices' clerks were appointed by the divisional magistrates they served,[47] but their fees,[48] and the salaries which replaced the fees from 1878,[49] were fixed and periodically reviewed by the court,[50] as were coroners' expenses from 1837[51] and the salaries in lieu from 1861.[52]

Quarter Sessions: Finance

During the years 1834–89 the court's finances were at first overseen by the Auditing Justices' Committee and, from 1839, by the Finance Committee which took over the Auditing Justices' responsibilities with a more comprehensive commission.[53] In April 1840 the new committee reviewed the court's finances and made comprehensive recommendations for economies and the planning of expenditure.[54] Thus began the strict financial control which the committee was to maintain for the court. For almost forty years three men, all of great influence in county affairs,[55] presided over those committees: J. A. LLoyd until 1849, Sir Baldwin Leighton 1850–5 and 1861–71, and Robert Burton 1856–60. In 1861 and thereafter the court's chairman was elected each year to preside over the Finance Committee.[56]

The chairmanships coincide with a period in which the income from the county and police rates rarely varied much from a yearly average of £13,400 (Table I).[57] By 1872–3,

[38] S.R.O., q. sess. Finance Cttee. rep. bk. 1843–50, pp. 141–2; Visiting Justices of Asylum rep. bk. 1847–67, pp. 285, 288. Cf. *Orders of Q. Sess.* iv. 68.

[39] *Eddowes's Jnl.* 17 Oct. 1866; 2 Jan. 1867; below, p. 152.

[40] *Eddowes's Jnl.* 17 Mar., 30 June 1875; below, p. 153.

[41] See p. 361 and sources there cited.

[42] i.e. the shirehall, judges' lodgings, militia depot: see e.g. S.R.O., q. sess. Finance Cttee. rep. bk. 1851–7, pp. 135, 142–7, 154–5; 1857–63, pp. 23, 47, 65, 160; *Shrews. Chron.* 21 Oct. 1887.

[43] *Shrews. Chron.* 21 Oct. 1887.

[44] S.R.O., q. sess. Auditing Cttee. and Finance Cttee. rep. bks. 1824–57; q. sess. recs., box 30, cuttings bk. 1872–7, 15 Mar., 28 June 1875 (incl. loose papers); *Shrews. Chron.* 2 July, 22 Oct. 1886; below, p. 159.

[45] *Eddowes's Jnl.* 17 Mar. 1869; 5 Jan. 1870.

[46] Ibid. 9 Mar. 1870; 4 Jan. 1871.

[47] S.R.O., q. sess. min. bk. 6, 10 Mar. 1856; *Orders of Q. Sess.* iv, p. xxii.

[48] Summary Jurisdiction Act, 1848, 11 & 12 Vic. c. 43, s. 30; *Eddowes's Jnl.* 28 June, 18 Oct. 1871; 20 Mar. 1872; S.R.O., q. sess. recs., box 30, cuttings bk. 1872–7, 1–10 July 1872.

[49] Under the Justices Clerks Act, 1877, 40 & 41 Vic. c. 43: *Eddowes's Jnl.* 1 Jan. 1879.

[50] See e.g. *Shrews. Chron.* 6 July 1888.

[51] Under the Coroners Inquests Act, 1837, 7 Wm. IV & 1 Vic. c. 68: S.R.O., q. sess. Auditing Cttee. and Finance Cttee. rep. bk. 1837–43, pp. 175–6, 183.

[52] *Eddowes's Jnl.* 2 Jan., 20 Mar., 3 July 1861; 17 Oct. 1866; *Shrews. Chron.* 8 Jan., 9 Apr. 1886.

[53] S.R.O., q. sess. Auditing Cttee. and Finance Cttee. rep. bk. 1837–43, pp. 60–3.

[54] Ibid. pp. 97–105.   [55] See pp. 139 sqq., 328.

[56] S.R.O., q. sess. Auditing Cttee. and Finance Cttee. rep. bks. and Finance Cttee. min. bks.

[57] For all such figs. in this section see the sources for Table I.

the year after Leighton's death, the income from them (£9,990) was lower than in any year but one since 1837 and had fallen for the fourth successive year, as had the court's gross income also. Nevertheless the court's gross income, a truer indication of expenditure,[58] tended to rise over the same forty years. That was undoubtedly due to the growth of government grants in aid of county expenditure (Table I), of all the developments begun during the period the one heaviest with consequences for the future.

TABLE I

Court of Quarter Sessions: Income 1835–89

Period[a]	Total receipts[b]	From rates	% of total	From govt.[c]	% of total
1835–45	£185,092	£153,584[d]	83·0	£17,702	9·6
Average p.a.	£16,830	£13,960		£1,609	
1846–57[e]	£189,196	£139,318	73·6	£27,291	14·4
Average p.a.	£17,200	£12,660		£2,480	
1857–74	£326,332	£230,716[f]	70·7	£59,074	18·1
Average p.a.	£19,200	£13,570		£3,475	
1874–87[g]	£371,996	£237,997	64·0	£84,737	22·8
Average p.a.	£29,750	£19,040		£6,780	
1887–9	£75,882	£48,918	64·5	£21,007	27·7
Average p.a.	£37,941	£24,459		£10,503	

Based on Co. of Salop., *Acct. of Receipts and Disbursements of Co. Rates*, 1835–7; idem, *Acct. of Receipts and Expenditure of County Stock*, 1838–83; idem, *Acct. of Receipts and Payments of Treasurer of Co. of Salop.*, 1883–9.

[a] Coinciding with changes in the major govt. grants.
[b] Excluding loans: see p. 150.
[c] Also including various small pmnts.: sheriff's allowances for judges' lodging (see p. 133), ct.'s allowance for militia staff's accommodation 1861–81, rent (1862–80) and allowance (1880–9) for Cleobury Mortimer ct. ho., and in 1886–7 a grant for registering parl. electors.
[d] No record of police-rate receipts 1840–1 has been found; the sums ordered to be levied (*Orders of Q. Sess.* iv.

8–15) are included instead.
[e] Omitting receipts Jan.–Sept. 1852 because of the change of accounting yr. in 1852.
[f] Omitting the £29,228 received from a cattle-plague rate (just over 6½d. in the £) in 1866–7. See p. 163.
[g] The accounting yr. was changed in 1879 and receipts Mich. 1878–Lady Day 1879 are supplied from S.R.O., q. sess. public stock bk. 1874–85; q. sess. constabulary cash bk. 1876–80.

The first government grants, made in 1835,[59] were for half the cost of criminal prosecutions and the whole cost of conveying 'transports', both of which had been greatly inflated by legislation.[60] From 1846[61] the government bore the full cost of prosecutions and also the maintenance of felons and misdemeanants. In 1857 the government began to reimburse the court a quarter of police costs, and the establishment of county police forces became simultaneously obligatory.[62] Much more than the earlier government grants the police grant was a significant step towards stimulating the provision of local-government services to a national standard. The gaol and asylum had long been subject to inspection[63] but the prison inspectors and lunacy commissioners could in the main only advise and persuade. In 1857, for the first time, an inspectorate was created whose reports were backed by immediate financial sanctions, for the Treasury police grant was dependent on the inspector's annual report. Ultimately the government was thus able to insist on standards of efficiency beyond the magistrates' ambitions, and Shropshire police costs doubled between 1857 and 1875.[64]

[58] Esp. in view of the practice of leaving the treasurer only small balances: see p. 150.
[59] Under the Appropriation of Supply Act, 1835, 5 & 6 Wm. IV, c. 80, s. 17. For other small regular govt. pmnts. see note c to Table I.
[60] i.e. the Highway Robbery and Felony Act, 1818, 58

Geo. III, c. 70, and the Criminal Law Act, 1826, 7 Geo. IV, c. 64. Cf. *V.C.H. Wilts.* v. 235.
[61] In that year under the Appropriation of Supply Act, 1846, 9 & 10 Vic. c. 116, s. 18.
[62] See p. 158.
[63] See pp. 154, 160.
[64] See pp. 158–9.

In 1842 quarter sessions, appreciating the implications of a police grant, had refused to petition the government for one.[65] By 1868, however, under Leighton's influence and anxious above all to keep down the rates, the court, like those of other counties, began to petition for more government aid.[66] It was eventually forthcoming[67] but not before, in Shropshire at least, the government's correspondingly increased power was felt and resented: already in the early 1870s debates on the asylum and the police began to be embittered.[68]

In 1868 only the incorrigibly old-fashioned John Bather had been sufficiently far-sighted to have misgivings about the consequences of soliciting government aid.[69] By then it was too late for such doubts: in the government's view the magistrates controlled little more than a quarter[70] of the court's expenditure, the rest being expended 'by statute'.[71]

The stability of the county's finances during the forty or so years up to 1873 is nevertheless remarkable, for those years witnessed the rebuilding of the shirehall

TABLE II

County Debt 1821–69

Purpose	Loans	Raised	Repaid
Judges' Lodging	£4,000	1821	1848–69
Shirehall	£14,500	1834–8	1835–49
Pauper Asylum	£16,501 £3,850	1841–9 1855–6	1846–68
Armoury	£3,250	1854	1856–68
TOTAL	£42,101	1821–56	1835–69

Based generally on Co. of Salop., *Acct. of Receipts and Disbursements of Co. Rates,* 1835–7; idem, *Acct. of Receipts and Expenditure of Public Stock,* 1838–69; S.R.O., q. sess. Finance Cttee. rep. bks.; S.R.O., q. sess. public stock bks. 1837–89. For particular points see 'Acct. of Receipts and Disbursements of Co. Rates, 1823' (MS. in 'Co. of Salop. Accts. 1768–1883', vol. of mainly printed accts. *penes* co. treasurer, 1974); *Orders of Q. Sess.* iv. 188; S.R.O. 348/15, pp. 51–2; ibid. /19, p. 79; S.R.O., q. sess. recs., parcel 227, lun. asylum accts.

(1833–7), the creation of the county police (1839–40), the building of the pauper asylum (1843–5) and its subsequent enlargement, the provision of separate cells in the gaol, and the purchase (1854) and enlargement of the militia armoury.[72] The heavy expenditure incurred on public works amounted to some £70,000.[73] The greater part, as capital expenditure, was financed initially from loans, amounting during the period to £42,101 (Table II). When the last instalment was repaid in 1869 the magistrates, in a self-congratulatory mood, asserted that Shropshire was almost the only English county out of debt.[74]

Much of that achievement was acknowledged to be owed to Sir Baldwin Leighton and to the 'excellent system' which he developed in the Finance Committee, that of borrowing seldom, repaying loans by small annual sums, and avoiding large balances in the treasurer's hands.[75] Autocratic in committee,[76] standing in no awe of government

[65] See p. 157, source cited in n. 85.
[66] *Shrews. Chron.* 20 Mar. 1868; *Eddowes's Jnl.* 1 July 1868; 19 Oct. 1870; 4 Jan., 15 Mar. 1871.
[67] See p. 151.
[68] See pp. 158, 162.
[69] *Shrews. Chron.* 20 Mar. 1868.
[70] i.e. £5,675 spent on bridges, salaries, printing etc., and misc. costs.
[71] *Ret. of Sums expended in various Cos. . . . levied on the Co. Rate, . . . 1867,* H.C. 156, p. 3 (1868–9), lii.
[72] See above, p. 128; below, pp. 154–7, 160–1; *Orders of Q. Sess.* iv, p. xxi.
[73] *Eddowes's Jnl.* 6 Jan. 1869.
[74] Ibid.
[75] Ibid. 21 Oct. 1868. Cf. ibid. 4 Jan. 1865.
[76] *Shrews. Chron.* 17 Mar. 1893.

inspectors or county officials,[77] Leighton paid meticulous attention to the detail of county accounts.[78] Symptomatic of his policies was his persistence over several years to save the county £20 a year in statutory contributions to the relief of prisoners in the Queen's Prison,[79] rewarded in 1861 by their abolition.[80] By no means apologetic about cheeseparing, he told the court in 1852 that, if savings were to be rejected merely as 'paltry', the Finance Committee might as well be dismissed.[81]

The twenty or so years during which Leighton influenced quarter sessions and its financial policies were perhaps almost the last during which such mastery was possible, for the court's income and expenditure were still comparable with those of a private gentleman. Leighton, for example, was not among the greatest of the county's landowners[82] but in 1855 his own gross income was almost 40 per cent of that of quarter sessions;[83] by about 1880, however, the income of his successor at Loton was barely 16 per cent of the court's.[84] Nor was it simply a matter of amount: as government subventions increased and quarter sessions itself began to reimburse part of other local authorities' expenditure, the county accounts became more complex.[85] Leighton, never robust,[86] had succeeded in mastering the county accounts of his day. For succeeding chairmen the task was harder, and by 1888 Alfred Salwey acknowledged Leighton's 'exploits' as 'financial deeds to which he never could aspire'.[87]

From 1874 to 1889 the court's gross revenue averaged £30,880 a year (Table I). Expenditure was growing rapidly from the mid 1870s: more bridges began to come on the county rate in the 1870s, that rate had to contribute to the cost of main roads from 1878, and increased expenditure on the asylum and police were ultimately forced on the county. Such were the effects of legislation and government pressures, and increased calls were naturally made on the county rates: average annual revenue from them, at £19,780 (Table I), was almost 50 per cent higher than during the previous forty years or so and it grew even more sharply during the last two years of quarter sessions' rule. Only in part, however, were those increased calls on the rates due to legislation or government pressures. Indeed the government became responsible for the gaol in 1878 and the militia's accommodation in 1888 and increased its contribution to expenditure on police (from 1874), lunatic paupers (from 1875), animal-slaughter compensation (from 1878), and main roads (from 1887). Accident and delay in fact played large parts in the rate increases of the 1880s: rebuilding after the shirehall fire of 1880 and the enlargement of the asylum (1882–5) after the long delay produced by the visitors' search for an alternative policy necessitated the raising of almost £65,400 in loans in 1882–5.[88] The county debt was never liquidated thereafter.[89] In 1886 floods damaged many county bridges, and at the same time a bad outbreak of swine fever placed unforeseeable burdens on the rates in 1886–7.[90]

In 1887 Alfred Salwey recalled to quarter sessions that in the 1860s and 1870s the annual levy of county rates had been little more than 1d. or 1¼d.; by 1887, however, it was difficult to keep the levy down to 3d. The new county debt cost about £4,500 a year (just over a ¾d. rate) in repayments and interest, the main roads some £8,000 a

[77] See e.g. below, p. 158.   [78] Shrews. Chron. 8 Jan. 1869.
[79] S.R.O., q. sess. Finance Cttee. rep. bk. 1843–50, p. 88; 1851–7, pp. 55–6, 70, 105; Eddowes's Jnl. 2 Jan., 20 Mar. 1861.
[80] Act for Abolition of certain co. contributions, 1861, 24 & 25 Vic. c. 12; Loton Hall MSS., Sir B. Leighton's diary, 23 July 1861; above, p. 72.
[81] S.R.O., q. sess. min. bk. 5, p. 18. Cf. Shrews. Chron. 17 Oct. 1851; Eddowes's Jnl. 20 Oct. 1869.
[82] See p. 311.
[83] i.e. £6,740 (Loton Hall MSS., Sir B. Leighton's diary [Jan.] 1856) compared with £17,415.

[84] i.e. £5,421 (J. Bateman, Great Landowners of Gt. Brit. and Ireland (1883), 265) compared with (1879–80) £34,623.
[85] They were printed in a new form from 1883–4.
[86] See p. 140.
[87] Shrews. Chron. 19 Oct. 1888.
[88] See below, p. 162; Co. of Salop., Acct. of Receipts and Expenditure of Public Stock, 1874–5, 1882–3; idem, Acct. of Receipts and Pmnts. of Treasurer of Co. of Salop. 1884–6; S.R.O., q. sess. recs., box 30, cuttings bk. 1877–82, 3 Jan., 27 June 1881; Shrews. Chron. 4 Jan. 1884.
[89] Orders of Q. Sess. iv, p. xvi.
[90] Shrews. Chron. 8 Apr. 1887.

year (just over a $1\frac{3}{8}d$. rate).[91] The increases were felt the more keenly owing to the agricultural and commercial depression and the consequent reduction of the county rate basis in 1886, after which every $1d$. rate produced £325 less than it had during the previous eight years (Table III). In 1888–9 there was talk of an eventual easing of

TABLE III

County Rateable Value 1837–89

Year of Assessment	County Rate		Police Rate	
	Rateable value	1d.-rate product	Additional rateable value[a]	1d.-rate product
1837	£1,064,616[b]	£4,431	—	—
1857	£1,068,904[c]	£4,454	£58,800	£4,699
1869	£1,277,158	£5,321	£67,991	£5,605
1878	£1,449,844	£6,041	£73,265	£6,346
1886	£1,377,445	£5,726	£70,531	£6,020

Based in general on S.R.O., q. sess. order bks. 1833–74; q. sess. co. rate accts. 1841–87; q. sess. police rate accts. 1852–87; S.R.O. 119/118; *Orders of Q. Sess.* iv. For the 1878 fig. see also S.R.O., q. sess. Finance Cttee. rep. bk. 1878–80, p. 79. For assessment before 1837 see above, pp. 121–2.

[a] i.e. the mun. boro. of M. Wenlock assessed for the co.-police rate. See below.
[b] Deducting the assessments of Dowles (£1,121) and Halston (£2,000) from the rates levied on them.

[c] In 1842 the mun. boros. of Oswestry (assessed at £14,244 in 1837) and M. Wenlock (£43,920), and in 1844 the thitherto Salop. parts of Halesowen (£35,927), had ceased to be assessed to the co. rate.

pressure on the rates as the debt and its interest rate were reduced and the new government main-roads contribution came in. By 1888, however, as the end of its responsibility for county finances drew on, the court became more complacent, more disposed to congratulate itself on half a century of economical administration. Salwey pointed out that the county rates, though only $1d$. for many years, had averaged $2d$. a year over the past fifty years. Stanley Leighton, listing the great improvements which had been made, pointed out that fifty years before the county rate had been the same as it was then. It was $3d$. in the £,[92] and within a few years Salwey, as chairman of the county council, had come to regard it as the 'normal' annual rate.[93]

Quarter Sessions: Bridges and Roads

Through the Finance Committee and the county surveyor the court continued until 1889 to execute the county's responsibility to maintain certain bridges and their approach roads.[94] Expenditure, though it varied greatly from year to year,[95] decreased over the thirty years after 1835. In the later 1830s it averaged £1,510 a year or about 12·3 per cent of quarter sessions' expenditure. Thereafter it averaged £1,030 a year in the 1840s, £630 in the 1850s, and £490 in the 1860s. In the 1870s it averaged £740 a year but most of the increase was caused by the rebuilding of three bridges in 1877–8 at a cost of £1,435; without that expense costs would have averaged only £600 a year in the 1870s.[96] The decline in the court's expenditure on bridges, paralleled by a reduc-

[91] *Shrews. Chron.* 8 Apr. 1887.
[92] Ibid. 19 Oct. 1888; 4 Jan. 1889.
[93] See p. 190.
[94] See p. 73.

[95] *Shrews. Chron.* 6 July 1888.
[96] Co. of Salop., *Acct. of Receipts and Disbursements of Co. Rates,* 1835–7; idem, *Acct. of Receipts and Expenditure of Public Stock,* 1838–79; *Eddowes's Jnl.* 1 Jan. 1879.

tion in the turnpike trusts' expenditure on their roads, was attributed in 1860 to the spread of the railways.[97]

In the middle of the century the repair of approach roads to county bridges cost much more than the bridges themselves — over twice as much in the 1850s and three times as much in the 1860s.[98] The Finance Committee accordingly devoted much attention to the approach roads, which were normally repaired under contract. Prompt submission of contractors' accounts was insisted on,[99] and from the later 1840s the court began to check the amount per mile spent by the turnpike trusts and to invite them to maintain the furlong of approaches to each county bridge at the same rate.[1]

The Holyhead Road commissioners and the turnpike trusts often contracted for the approach roads of bridges in their districts, while other local contractors and farmers also undertook them in their neighbourhoods.[2] The same contractors were normally continued year after year.[3] In 1835 34 of the 115 approach roads were contracted for by the road commissioners or turnpike trusts and 23 by other contractors, while 33 were repaired under the direction of magistrates living near by. The magistrates, however, dropped out of the work, and W. Lacon Childe of Kinlet Park[4] was for long the only magistrate undertaking it, though he continued to direct the repair of the 7 bridge approach roads between Bridgnorth and Cleobury Mortimer almost to the end of the period.[5] In the 1860s and 1870s highway boards replaced turnpike trusts as contractors.[6]

In the 1880s the average annual cost of county bridges was £1,730.[7] The steep rise was due partly to the 1886 floods which damaged many bridges.[8] More significant, however, was the growing number of county bridges. From 1870 bridges repairable by the turnpike trustees became county bridges as the trusts were terminated.[9] Disturnpiking proceeded at an accelerating pace during the 1870s[10] and the first Shropshire turnpike-trust bridges were thrown on the county rate in 1877.[11] Between 1878 and 1886 county bridges increased from 169 to 269.[12]

Quarter sessions was responsible for compelling the repairers of non-county bridges to act. Oswestry hundred, for example, was indicted by the county surveyor in 1855 and by the grand jury in 1886 for not repairing Llanyblodwel bridge.[13]

From 1878 the court had to repay the highway authorities half their expenditure on 'main' roads, i.e. roads disturnpiked after 1870 or declared main by the court.[14] The change was intended to distribute the expense of main roads more equitably over a wider area. Almost 620 miles of Shropshire roads had been disturnpiked in 1871-8, and by 1878 they were costing the highway authorities some £9,100 a year. A further 84 miles, costing £1,050, were to be disturnpiked during the years 1878-83.[15] A large item was thus immediately added to the county rate: from 1878 to 1889 quarter

[97] S.R.O., q. sess. Finance Cttee. rep. bk. 1857-63, pp. 138-9.
[98] *Acct. of Receipts and Expenditure of Public Stock*, 1850-69.
[99] S.R.O., q. sess. Finance Cttee. rep. bk. 1843-50, pp. 14-15, 69-70, 81-2.
[1] Ibid., pp. 99-100, 104-5, 170-1, 182-3; ibid. 1851-7, p. 81; 1857-63, pp. 70, 138-9.
[2] S.R.O. 119/33.
[3] Ibid.; S.R.O., q. sess. Finance Cttee. rep. bk. 1857-63, p. 96; ibid. 1875-8, p. 210.
[4] S.R.O. 119/33, bridge lists for 1835 and 1856; S.R.O., q. sess. Finance Cttee. rep. bk. 1843-50, pp. 170-1; above, p. 127.
[5] S.R.O. 187/1.
[6] S.R.O. 119/33; q. sess. Finance Cttee. rep. bk. 1863-7, pp. 99, 110-11, 124.
[7] Co. of Salop., *Acct. of Receipts and Expenditure of*

Public Stock, 1880-3; idem, *Acct. of Receipts and Pmnts. of Treasurer of Co. of Salop.*, 1883-9.
[8] *Shrews. Chron.* 2 July 1886; 1 July 1887.
[9] Under the Annual Turnpike Acts Continuance Act, 1870, 33 & 34 Vic. c. 73, s. 12.
[10] S. and B. Webb, *Story of the King's Highway* (1913), 222.
[11] S.R.O., q. sess. Finance Cttee. rep. bk. 1875-8, pp. 156, 190-1; above, p. 151.
[12] S.R.O. 187/1; 119/33, bridge list for 1886.
[13] *Orders of Q. Sess.* iv, pp. xvii, 107; *Shrews. Chron.* 8 Jan. 1886; Webb, op. cit. 107.
[14] 41 & 42 Vic. c. 77, s. 13.
[15] *Ret. of Turnpike Roads Disturnpiked between 31st Dec. 1870 and 31st Dec. 1878*, H.C. 335, p. 5 (1878), lxvi; *Ret. of Turnpike Roads Disturnpiked between 31st Dec. 1870 and 30th June 1878*, H.C. 353, pp. 7, 15 (1878), lvi.

sessions repaid the highway authorities an average of just over £8,000 a year.[16] At the end of the period, when there were just over 700 miles of main road,[17] some relief was in turn afforded to the county rate when the government began to repay the court half its reimbursement of the highway authorities.[18]

Quarter sessions acquired no executive responsibility for roads under the 1878 Act, but its new financial responsibility required the inspection of the main roads on its behalf; the duty was laid on the police superintendents.[19] The court also had quasi-judicial powers of supervising the maintenance of roads, and under the 1878 Act the county surveyor could be required to act as a road inspector in the case of complaint against a highway authority.[20]

Quarter Sessions: the County Gaol and House of Correction

In 1835, when the Prisons Act[21] was passed, the county gaol and house of correction at Shrewsbury accounted for about 30 per cent (some £3,200) of quarter sessions' expenditure (£10,385).[22] It remained the largest item until about 1841 when the county police was brought up to full strength.[23] During the last 44 years that the gaol was administered locally (1835–78) its cost varied little, averaging some £3,700 a year.[24] As the court's expenditure increased, therefore, the gaol became a less significant item.

The Gaol Justices continued to administer the county gaol and house of correction under the 1823 Act,[25] but the gaol remained the king's prison theoretically kept, in Shropshire as elsewhere, by the sheriff and his nominee, the gaoler.[26] There was thus a certain appropriateness when, as a result of the 1835 Act, prisons were the first branch of quarter sessions' administration to come under the regular oversight of government inspectors.[27]

The Shropshire magistrates tried to administer the gaol according to the most progressive ideas, as then conceived. The rival 'separate' and 'silent' systems aimed to make sentences reformatory yet so unpleasant that no discharged prisoner would risk incurring a second term. Rigorous enforcement of the silent system[28] aimed at each prisoner's intellectual isolation, but in practice it was less successful than the separate system[29] which isolated each prisoner in a cell. On his first visit to the county gaol the inspector found that the silent system had been partly enforced for some years, prisoner monitors maintaining silence in the wards, the taskmaster at work. The prisoners were classified, and at night each slept in a separate cell. There were plans to bring the silent system into complete operation but the inspector foresaw that more officers than the staff of eleven would be needed to enforce more than nominal silence.[30]

By 1836 the Gaol Justices were considering the rival, ultimately prevalent, system of separate confinement.[31] In 1837, after a small-scale experiment and with government encouragement, they decided to extend the practice and next year 37 separate cells

[16] Co. of Salop., *Acct. of Receipts and Expenditure of Public Stock*, 1878–83; idem, *Acct. of Receipts and Pmnts. of Treasurer of Co. of Salop.*, 1883–9; S.R.O., q. sess. public stock bk. 1874–85, Oct. 1879–Apr. 1880. Some £89,600 (£8,530 a year) was due from the county to the highway authorities for 1878–89, but some £5,000 was paid only in 1889–91: S.R.O. 62/1; S.C.C. *Abstr. of Accts.* 1889–91.

[17] S.R.O. 62/1.

[18] In 1888–9 the co. received £8,295 for the years 1886–8: *Acct. of Receipts and Pmnts. of Treasurer of Co. of Salop.*, 1888–9. Cf. *Shrews. Chron.* 19 Oct. 1888; 4 Jan. 1889.

[19] See p. 159.

[20] 41 & 42 Vic. c. 77, s. 10.

[21] 5 & 6 Wm. IV, c. 38.

[22] Co. of Salop., *Acct. of Receipts and Disbursements of Co. Rates, 1835*.

[23] S.R.O., q. sess. Auditing Cttee. and Finance Cttee. rep. bk. 1837–43, pp. 98–9, 102; below, p. 157.

[24] Sources cited above, p. 152, n. 96.

[25] See p. 126.

[26] S. and B. Webb, *Eng. Prisons under Local Govt.* (1922), 3–4, 17, 34, 108–9; *Orders of Q. Sess.* iv, pp. ix–x.

[27] 5 & 6 Wm. IV, c. 38, s. 7. The inspectorate was to some extent modelled on the new poor-law inspectorate: *Past & Present*, liv. 76.

[28] Most notably at Mdx. Ho. of Corr., Coldbath Fields: Webb, op. cit. 95–6, 122–5.

[29] Enforced at Millbank Penitentiary: ibid. 117.

[30] *1st Rep. Prison Inspectors, S. and W. Dist.* H.C. 117, pp. 56–61 (1836), xxxv.

[31] S.R.O., q. sess. Visiting Justices of Gaol rep. bk. 1823–38, p. 131.

were provided, enough for the confinement of all those committed summarily.[32] Shropshire was thus one of the first counties to begin to introduce the system[33] before it was regularized by the Prisons Act, 1839.[34] By 1840 every prisoner summarily committed spent his full sentence in separate confinement and, whenever cells were available, felons and misdemeanants finished their sentences in them. Prisoners from every class had been in the cells by September 1840, though only one had spent as long as six months there.[35]

Though party politics played no part in quarter sessions' debates[36] the separate system was one of the few policies to have been opposed by groups identifiable in party terms. Supported by most of the court, it was opposed on humanitarian grounds from the early 1840s by R. A. Slaney[37] and some other Liberal magistrates.[38] The *Salopian Telegraph*, a radical organ, attacked the system;[39] so did the extreme Tory *Shropshire Conservative* which shrank neither from support of its political opponents on the issue[40] nor from strong attacks on the Gaol Justices,[41] among them leading Conservative magistrates like J. A. LLoyd and Sir Baldwin Leighton.[42]

Despite staff increases and the provision in 1843-4 of more cells, however, discipline remained mixed, separation, association, and the professed observance of silence all being in use.[43] The survival of several types of discipline was due to no unwillingness on the magistrates' part to provide the necessary cells. They were indeed anxious to impose the separate system.[44] More cells were made in the 1860s as the number of prisoners increased,[45] and by 1866, when the Home Secretary was able to enforce the system in all local prisons,[46] there were enough for all prisoners.[47]

At first the inadequacies of successive gaolers inhibited the working of the separate system[48] and the efficient running of the gaol.[49] Early in 1846, however, John Shepherd, a former naval officer, was appointed governor and during his twenty years[50] there were great improvements in administration. Thereafter the most enduring obstacle to a uniform discipline was the heterogeneous character of the prisoners. In the 1840s and 1850s, as well as adult criminals and prisoners awaiting trial, the gaol contained juvenile offenders, nursing mothers, and debtors. To them the harsh discipline of separate confinement could not with justice be applied,[51] and a uniform system of discipline was achieved only as alternatives to the committal of such classes were devised.

The removal of young offenders was urged on the magistrates by the government inspector during Shepherd's governorship,[52] and there were Shropshire magistrates[53] who had been eager to support the reformatory-school movement from its beginnings about 1851.[54] Eventually, after the passing of the 1857 Reformatory Schools Act,[55] the

[32] Ibid., pp. 139-40, 146-50; S.R.O. 154/60.
[33] *28th Rep. Prison Inspectors, S. Dist.* [3215], p. 67, H.C. (1863), xxiii; Webb, op, cit. 132.
[34] 2 & 3 Vic. c. 56.
[35] *6th Rep. Prison Inspectors, S. and W. Dist.* [335], pp. 224, 228-9, 231, H.C. (1841 Sess. 2), v.
[36] See e.g. *Shrews. Chron.* 17 Oct. 1851.
[37] See e.g. ibid. 6 Jan. 1860 and sources in following notes.
[38] e.g. E. W. Smythe Owen and John Cotes: *Salopian Jnl.* 4 Jan. 1843; *Eddowes's Jnl.* 28 June, 18 Oct. 1843.
[39] *Salopian Telegraph*, 30 Apr. 1842; below, p. 313.
[40] e.g. *Shropshire Conservative*, Oct.–Dec. 1843.
[41] Ibid. 19 Oct. 1844.
[42] Ibid. 5 July, 18 Oct. 1845; 3 and 10 Jan. 1846.
[43] *9th Rep. Prison Insp. S. and W. Dist.* [542], p. 376, H.C. (1844), xxix; *10th Rep. S. and W. Dist.* [676], pp. 1, 5, 8, H.C. (1845), xxiv; S.R.O. 154/60; Co. of Salop., *Acct. of Receipts and Expenditure of Public Stock*, 1840-9.
[44] See e.g. S.R.O., q. sess. Visiting Justices of Gaol rep. bk. 1838-45, p. 110.

[45] *27th Rep. Prison Insp. Midl. Dist.* [2991], p. 102, H.C. (1862), xxv.
[46] Webb, *Eng. Prisons*, 189-91; below, p. 156.
[47] *31st Rep. Prison Insp. S. Dist.* [3671], p. 172, H.C. (1866), xxxvii.
[48] *6th Rep.* [335], 228.
[49] *10th Rep.* [676], 7-8; *Orders of Q. Sess.* iv, pp. ix, 1, 49, 51; S.R.O. 362/2; q. sess. Visiting Justices of Gaol rep. bk. 1823-38, pp. 154-5, 160-5; 1838-45, pp. 1-6, 35; 1845-57, pp. 9-11; q. sess. min. bk. 1840-2, 1 Feb. 1840.
[50] *Orders of Q. Sess.* iv, pp. x, 53, 170.
[51] *21st Rep. Prison Insp. S. and W. Dist.* [2133], p. 61, H.C. (1856), xxxiii; S.R.O., q. sess. Visiting Justices of Gaol rep. bk. 1845-57, pp. 109-10.
[52] *21st Rep.* [2133], 61.
[53] Notably Sir B. Leighton, W. Wolryche Whitmore, the Revd. D. Nihill, and T. W. Wylde Browne: S.R.O., q. sess. Visiting Justices of Gaol rep. bk. 1845-57.
[54] *Shrews. Chron.* 3 Jan. 1851; *D.N.B. sub* Carpenter, Mary (1807-77).
[55] 20 & 21 Vic. c. 55.

court's efforts culminated[56] in the appointment of a committee[57] under its chairman, Leighton, and in 1858 agreement was quickly reached with the Philanthropic Society to board young offenders at its farm school at Redhill (Surr.).[58]

If the inspector's suggestions about reformatories were well received, the elimination of other unconformable classes of prisoner was achieved more slowly and only with the progress of legislation. The committal of nursing mothers hindered the achievement of a uniform diet and discipline[59] until they became statutorily harsher and more punitive,[60] but when imprisonment for debt was abolished in 1869, the gaol came to be inhabited almost exclusively by adult criminals to whom a uniformly severe, deterrent discipline could be applied.[61]

Apart from the slowness with which the separate system came to be applied to all prisoners the inspector rarely commented adversely during Shepherd's governorship. In his 1852 report indeed the well conducted county gaol contrasts strongly with the Bridgnorth and Ludlow borough gaols: the administration of Ludlow gaol was said to amount to 'an habitual violation of the law', and the inspector's comments secured the closure of the last two borough gaols in Shropshire.[62] Despite fourteen deaths in the gaol during the 1849 cholera epidemic, prisoners' health was good and the scrubbing of their clothes produced an unusual 'purity of atmosphere' in the cells.[63] The gaol surgeon's resignation in 1857, however, may have owed something to the inspector's criticisms.[64] Several years' comment on the chapel was necessary before it was enlarged in 1857–8 to accommodate all prisoners.[65]

From 1866 the government enforced the separate system rigorously in all local prisons. Variations in discipline and diet were in theory abolished,[66] and Captain W. H. Fenwick, R.N., governor 1867–78,[67] ran the gaol with great efficiency within the narrow limits of statutory and Home Office rules. The new cells completed in 1866[68] allowed the immediate and full enforcement of the separate system. Shot drill, crank labour, and a Home Office dietary were introduced, and in 1867–8 a covered treadwheel was built.[69] Fenwick's previous experience facilitated the placing of young offenders in reformatories,[70] and year by year the gaol contained fewer prisoners unconformable to the harsh new statutory regime.[71] Costs were reduced. In 1871 the court raised the governor's salary in recognition of his strict economy; despite rising prices, the introduction of staff superannuation, and an increase of prisoners, gaol expenses were no greater than they had been ten years earlier. In 1871–2 costs per prisoner were lower than in many comparable gaols.[72] The gaol's annual cost continued to fall and in 1873–4 was almost £1,000 less than in 1867–8.[73]

[56] For earlier efforts see S.R.O., q. sess. Visiting Justices of Gaol rep. bk. 1845–57, pp. 108–13, 165, 171–3, 176, 178, 189–90, 200, 204–6.

[57] *Orders of Q. Sess.* iv. 124.

[58] S.R.O., q. sess. min. bk. 1858–62, 26 June 1858; q. sess. Visiting Justices of Gaol rep. bk. 1857–71, p. 27. See also *V.C.H. Surr.* iii. 233.

[59] S.R.O., q. sess. Visiting Justices of Gaol rep. bk. 1857–71, p. 145.

[60] Under the Prison Act, 1865, 28 & 29 Vic. c. 126, on which see Webb, *Eng. Prisons*, 187–91.

[61] Webb, op. cit. 195.

[62] *17th Rep. Prison Insp. S. and W. Dist.* [1495], pp. 46–57, H.C. (1852), xxiv; *19th Rep.* [1853], p. 89, H.C. (1854), xxxiv.

[63] *17th Rep.* [1495], 46–8.

[64] *21st Rep.* [2133], 62–3; *Orders of Q. Sess.* iv. 118.

[65] *17th Rep.* [1495], 48; *19th Rep.* [1853], 89–90; *21st Rep.* [2133], 58; *24th Rep. Midl. Dist.* [2595], p. 108, H.C. (1860), xxxv; S.R.O., q. sess. Visiting Justices of Gaol rep. bk. 1857–71, pp. 3–5, 17.

[66] Under the Prison Act, 1865, on which see Webb, op. cit. 189–92.

[67] *Orders of Q. Sess.* iv. 173, 233; *Eddowes's Jnl.* 27 Mar. 1878. In 1878 he became an insp. of prisons.

[68] See p. 155.

[69] S.R.O., q. sess. Visiting Justices of Gaol rep. bk. 1857–71, pp. 154–5, 175, 180–1, 186, 200, 214–15.

[70] *Eddowes's Jnl.* 18 Oct. 1871. He had been supt. of the *Akbar* reformatory ship at Liverpool 1856–61: ibid. 2 Jan. 1867.

[71] Rules for those that remained were made in 1873: S.R.O., q. sess. Visiting Justices of Gaol rep. bk. 1872–8, pp. 18–19.

[72] S.R.O., q. sess. cuttings bk. 1872–7, loose paper between reps. of Oct. 1873 and Jan. 1874 endorsed by J. R. Kenyon 'Cost of maintenance of Prisoners in Salop. & other gaols'. The average ann. cost per prisoner in 10 co. gaols (incl. Salop.) was almost £35; in Salop. it was just over £29.

[73] *Eddowes's Jnl.* 18 Oct. 1871; 1 July 1874.

Responsibility for the gaol passed to the government in 1878,[74] though the sheriff remained responsible for carrying out sentences of death. Each year the Epiphany quarter sessions had to appoint five magistrates to a local committee of visitors, and thenceforth Montgomeryshire was represented on it, the Montgomeryshire gaol closing in 1878. From 1878, however, the visitors served mainly as a body of local inspectors for the Home Secretary, and their executive powers ceased.[75] It remained only for quarter sessions to secure for the county the statutory compensation for the gaol,[76] finally settled, after prolonged and acrimonious negotiations with the government, at £4,000.[77]

Quarter Sessions: Police

In December 1839 quarter sessions adopted the new County Police Act. A year earlier the court had expressed a wish for such legislation and its views had been circulated round the other English and Welsh courts by the Home Office. Some opposition was manifested at the unusually crowded December sessions, but on the chairman's motion a substantial majority of the court voted to establish a county constabulary of 6 superintendents and 43 'petty constables' under a chief constable.[78] A committee was formed to supervise the force, and Commander Dawson Mayne, a former coastguard inspector and a younger brother of a metropolitan police commissioner, was appointed chief constable in January 1840; shortly afterwards he married a cousin of Sir Rowland Hill, a magistrate and deputy lieutenant and later, as the 2nd Lord Hill, to become lieutenant.[79]

The force remained small. Seven constables were added in 1841, partly owing to the union of Much Wenlock with the force, and another constable in 1856 at Wenlock's request.[80] There was no pay increase in the early years[81] and the cost of the force, just over £4,000 a year,[82] was virtually unchanged until 1857, the annual police rate[83] averaging just under 1d. 1840-57.[84] From the beginning the court valued its independence as a safeguard of the economy which was practised.[85]

The most serious difficulty in the early years was the recruitment and retention of suitable men. In the first 17 years there were 76 resignations and 48 dismissals from the 57- or 58-strong force, an average loss of over 8 men a year.[86] Dismissals probably resulted as often from inefficiency as from wrongdoing, but they must have lowered morale in an undermanned, poorly paid force. The occasional scandal could have more lasting consequences. In 1850 a Police Committee report, evoked by a superintendent's malversations, was highly critical of the chief constable,[87] and Mayne was probably

[74] Under the Prison Act, 1877, 40 & 41 Vic. c. 21.

[75] *Eddowes's Jnl.* 27 Mar., 17 Apr. 1878; S.R.O., q. sess. cuttings bk. 1877–82, notes of J. R. Kenyon, 15 Apr. 1878; *Copy of Orders for Discontinuance of certain Prisons*, H.C. 128, pp. 3–4 (1878), lxiii.

[76] Webb, *Eng. Prisons*, 200 n. 1.

[77] *Shrews. Chron.* 18 Oct. 1878; *Eddowes's Jnl.* 9 Apr., 15 Oct. 1879; 7 Jan., 7 Apr., 20 Oct. 1880; *Orders of Q. Sess.* iv, pp. ix, 236, 248; S.R.O. 154/60.

[78] 2 & 3 Vic. c. 93; L. Radzinowicz, *Hist. of Eng. Criminal Law and its Admin. from 1750*, iv (1968), 259–60; *T.S.A.S.* 2nd ser. iii. 231–3; *Orders of Q. Sess.* iii. 322–3.

[79] *T.S.A.S.* 2nd ser. iii. 233; *Orders of Q. Sess.* iv. 1. For Mayne see W. R. O'Byrne, *Naval Biog. Dict.* (1849), 751; Burke, *Peerage* (1949), 1011–12; Burke, *Land. Gent.* (1952), 532. For his bro. Ric. see *D.N.B.* For Hill see S.R.O., lieutenancy reg.; above, pp. 139, 141.

[80] *Orders of Q. Sess.* iv. 9, 12, 15; S.R.O. 1912/1–2; S.R.O., q. sess. Const. Cttee. rep. bk. 1854–65, pp. 20, 24–5, 32. 36. Bridgnorth's union with the co. police 1850–5 temporarily added a const.: *Orders of Q. Sess.* iv. 78–9, 83,

105; *T.S.A.S.* 2nd ser. iii. 233–5; S.R.O. 1912/3.

[81] S.R.O., q. sess. Const. Cttee. rep. bk. 1839–53, pp. 460, 508–9.

[82] Average based on 1840–52 figs. in *Abstr. of Ret. of Several Cos. of Eng. and Wales, their Pop., the No. of Rural Police . . . the Total Cost annually . . .*, H.C. 211, p. 6 (1854), liii, which are exceeded by £770 in an average yr. by the figs. in Co. of Salop., *Acct. of Receipts and Expenditure of Public Stock, 1847–51*.

[83] Levied by the cttee., separately from the co. rate, under the Co. Police Act, 1840, 3 & 4 Vic. c. 88.

[84] As forecast by the Finance Cttee. in 1840. See S.R.O., q. sess. Auditing Cttee. and Finance Cttee. rep. bk. 1837–43, p. 102; *Orders of Q. Sess.* iv. 8–118.

[85] S.R.O., q. sess. order bk. 1840–3, p. 162.

[86] S.R.O., q. sess. Const. Cttee. rep. bk. 1839–53, pp. 246, 295, 384, 493, 516, 537; 1854–65, pp. 47, 65. The force numbered 58, 1850–5: see above, and above, n. 80.

[87] *Shrews. Chron.* 22 and 29 Mar. 1850; S.R.O., q. sess. Const. Cttee. rep. bk. 1839–53, pp. 415–19.

saved from more serious consequences only by his wife's connexions. The affair, delaying the Hon. Thomas Kenyon's resignation of the chair of quarter sessions, was thereby doubly unfortunate for Mayne as it temporarily frustrated the ambitions of Sir Baldwin Leighton,[88] an early critic of the force's command and administration.[89] He became convinced that no chief constable ought to have personal connexions with the magistracy,[90] and in 1858, when he had become chairman of the court, he was able to make Mayne's position untenable.[91]

Under the County and Borough Police Act, 1856,[92] police forces came under the oversight of government inspectors, and the government was given financial sanctions to achieve minimum standards of efficiency. In 1857 the inspector induced quarter sessions to increase the establishment from 58 to 84 with new ranks and grades. The prospect of the government grant helped to reconcile the court to the increase,[93] but in the event the county lost the grant for 1856–7, the inspector having reported the force inefficient in numbers.[94]

The 1860s and early 1870s produced growing strain between the magistrates on the one hand and the government inspectors and chief constables on the other. Some of the inspector's suggestions to improve efficiency were rejected year after year by the magistrates.[95] Increases of establishment were generally secured, but only at the inspector's insistent behest as the magistrates strove to keep down expenditure. Four men were added when the Oswestry police joined the county force in 1861.[96] Even so the 88-strong establishment was inadequate: a constable to every 2,252 of the population was a far worse ratio than that of any other county force,[97] and the detection rate was one of the lowest.[98] Shropshire's was the only county police rate less than $1d.$ in 1861.[99] Increases in 1862, 1865, and 1867 added 34 men[1] but left the force still one of the weakest in the Midlands,[2] and, after discussions with the inspector, 14 men were added in 1872.[3] Many magistrates were by then openly hostile to increases forced on them through fear that a refusal would jeopardise the government grant. Notably outspoken were John Bather and M. G. Benson, a former chairman of the Police Committee (1858–61).[4] In 1867 Leighton, supporting Benson, asked the court to fix a final figure for the force and to 'stick to it' in spite of the inspector and the chief constable. By the winter of 1871–2 many magistrates, including the Police Committee's chairman, the Hon. R. C. Herbert (1867–89), felt that the inspector was assessing the force's efficiency unfairly. In 1872 Bather mordantly expressed the mood of the well attended Easter sessions, declaring that it was beneath the dignity of gentlemen to meet and have the management of the police and 'to be bribed over by a government inspector . . . to go beyond our right judgement'.

[88] Loton Hall MSS., Sir B. Leighton's diary, 11 Apr. 1850; above, pp. 139–41.

[89] S.R.O., q. sess. Const. Cttee. rep. bk. 1839–53, pp. 167, 169–75.

[90] Ibid. 1854–65, p. 221; *Eddowes's Jnl.* 19 Oct. 1864.

[91] S.R.O., q. sess. Const. Cttee. rep. bk. 1854–65, pp. 77, 89, 98; q. sess. min. bk. 7, 23 Mar.–3 Apr. 1858; q. sess. Const. Cttee. min. bk. 1858–68, 27 Nov.–18 Dec. 1858; *Shrews. Chron.* 7 Jan. 1859.

[92] 19 & 20 Vic. c. 69.

[93] *Orders of Q. Sess.* iv. 120; *Eddowes's Jnl.* 1 July 1857; *Shrews. Chron.* 23 Oct. 1857; S.R.O., q. sess. Const. Cttee. rep. bk. 1854–65, pp. 56–7, 62–3.

[94] *Rep. Insp. of Constabulary,* H.C. 20, p. 18 (1857–8), xlvii.

[95] e.g. provision of supts.' carts: *Rep. Insp. Const.* H.C. 67, pp. 29–30 (1861), lii; ibid. H.C. 27, p. 26 (1870), xxxvi.

[96] *Orders of Q. Sess.* iv. 140–1; *Shrews. Chron.* 14 Mar.

1862; S.R.O. 1912/4–6.

[97] *Ret. of Cos. (in Eng.) shewing the strength of their Const., and amount of Police Rate* (1862; in S.R.O., q. sess. recs., box 107).

[98] *Eddowes's Jnl.* 16 Oct. 1861; 1 Jan. 1862; *Shrews. Chron.* 14 Mar. 1862; *Rep. Insp. Const.* H.C. 67, pp. 29–30 (1861), lii.

[99] *Ret. of Cos. (in Eng.) shewing the strength of their Const., and amount of Police Rate* (1862).

[1] *Orders of Q. Sess.* iv. 147, 166 (where 'Eleven' should read 'Seven'), 179.

[2] *Rep. Insp. Const.* H.C. 54, pp. 50–1 (1866), xxxiv; ibid. H.C. 132, p. 40 (1867–8), xxxvi.

[3] *Orders of Q. Sess.* iv. 203. The insp. had wanted 17: *Eddowes's Jnl.* 20 Mar. 1872.

[4] For the rest of this para. see *Shrews. Chron.* 14 Mar. 1862; *Eddowes's Jnl.* 18 Oct. 1865; 16 Oct. 1867; 18 Oct. 1871; 3 Jan., 20 Mar. 1872; S.R.O., q. sess. Const. Cttee. min. bk. 1858–68, 27 Apr. 1858–27 June 1861.

The chronic recruiting difficulty remained, and the retention of unsuitable men in the force led to the court's loss of confidence in the chief constable in 1863 and to his resignation next year.[5] Turnover, however, remained high[6] and was not abated by increases in pay[7] and allowances,[8] by long-service and good-conduct increments,[9] or by the introduction of a bounty system in 1874.[10] The 1872 increase was not recruited until April 1875, and accordingly in 1874 the inspector again reported the force inefficient in numbers; only in 1875 did the court persuade the Home Secretary[11] to authorize the government grant for 1873–4.[12] The difficulties of the undermanned force in the 1860s and early 1870s were exacerbated by the increasing number of extra duties laid on the police by quarter sessions[13] and the government,[14] though the Home Office kept a check on these[15] and sometimes stopped them.[16]

After about 1875 the main difficulty, the recruiting problem, seems to have eased. In 1862 the inspector had noted that men drawn from agricultural employment were the 'best class' for 'permanent policemen',[17] and the trade and agricultural depression of the later 1870s[18] coupled with the numerous increases in the force's pay and allowances in the 1860s and early 1870s[19] evidently increased the eligibility of police employment.[20] The superannuation fund eventually began to show the effects of more stable manning: by 1888 expenditure was exceeding income and it seemed possible that the fund would be exhausted within a few years. That, however, was a general problem.[21]

The addition of a constable for Oswestry in 1877[22] and two superintendents in 1887[23] brought the force up to 139. Quarter sessions had appointed the superintendents as main-roads inspectors in 1879[24] but in 1887 the Home Secretary allowed them to be made inspectors of weights and measures only when they were increased to eight.[25]

The force thus remained small by the standards of county forces. Over the 18 difficult years 1857–75 its cost had been doubled by increases of establishment and the numerous increases of pay and allowances necessary to keep it fully recruited.[26] Between 1875 and 1889, however, its cost increased by only $9\frac{1}{2}$ per cent.[27] The average annual police rate levied 1857–89 was only fractionally over 1d.[28] In part that was due to a new rate basis introduced in 1869,[29] in part to the raising in 1875 of the government share of police costs to a half.[30] It was, however, also due to the magistrates'

[5] Eddowes's Jnl. 1 July, 21 Oct. 1863; Rep. Insp. Const. H.C. 26, p. 44 (1864), xlviii; S.R.O., q. sess. Const. Cttee. rep. bk. 1854–65, pp. 183–4, 195–206; Const. Cttee. min. bk. 1858–68, 12 July–22 Aug. 1863. Cf. Eddowes's Jnl. 29 June 1859.

[6] Rep. Insp. Const. H.C. 14, p. 38 (1867), xxxvi.

[7] In 1859, 1866, 1872 (twice), and 1873: S.R.O., q. sess. Const. Cttee. rep. bk. 1854–65, p. 95; 1866–75, pp. 11, 148–50, 164–5, 189.

[8] In 1858, 1873, 1874, and 1875: ibid. 1854–65, p. 89 (boot money); 1866–75, pp. 188 (extra-duty pay), 198–9 (supts.' horse allce.), 219–20 (rent allces.).

[9] In 1871, 1872, and 1874 (ibid. 1866–75, pp. 115–16, 198–200) after the insp.'s observations (Rep. Insp. Const. H.C. 27, p. 26 (1870), xxxvi).

[10] Orders of Q. Sess. iv. 214; Rep. Insp. Const. H.C. 23, pp. 58–60 (1877), xlii; S.R.O. 1968/3.

[11] R. A. Cross, chmn. of Lancs. q. sess. 1866–74.

[12] Rep. Insp. Const. H.C. 18, pp. 5, 59–60 (1875), xxxvi; ibid. H.C. 30, pp. 59–60 (1876), xxxiv; Eddowes's Jnl. 21 Oct. 1874; 17 Mar., 30 June 1875; Shrews. Chron. 19 Mar. 1875; S.R.O., q. sess. cuttings bk. 1872–7, 15 Mar.–28 June 1875.

[13] S.R.O., q. sess. Const. Cttee. rep. bk. 1839–53, pp. 367–8; 1854–65, pp. 89–90, 151, 223–4; 1866–75, p. 200; Rep. Insp. Const. H.C. 23, pp. 58–60 (1877), xlii; below, pp. 163, 165 (and n. 37).

[14] S.R.O., q. sess. Const. Cttee. rep. bk. 1854–65, p. 90; Orders of Q. Sess. iv, p. viii; Eddowes's Jnl. 19 Oct. 1870;

4 Jan., 15 Mar. 1871; 30 June 1875; 2 July 1879; Shrews. Chron. 3 July 1885.

[15] Reported yearly in Rep. Insp. Const. See S.R.O., q. sess. Const. Cttee. rep. bk. 1866–75, pp. 116–17, 122–3.

[16] See e.g. Const. Cttee. rep. bk. 1866–75, p. 200.

[17] Eddowes's Jnl. 15 Oct. 1862.

[18] R. C. K. Ensor, Eng. 1870–1914 (Oxford, 1936), 111, 115–18; M. Flamant and Jeanne Singer-Kerel, Crises et Récessions Économiques (Paris, 1968), 37.

[19] See above.

[20] Rep. Insp. Const. H.C. 30, p. 6 (1876), xxxiv; H.C. 23, pp. 6, 58–60 (1877), xlii; H.C. 33, pp. 7, 60–1 (1878), xl; H.C. 41, pp. 6, 62–3 (1878–9), xxxiii.

[21] Shrews. Chron. 4 Jan. 1889.

[22] S.R.O., q. sess. Const. Cttee. rep. bk. 1875–84, pp. 42, 47–8; S.R.O. 1912/7–10.

[23] Orders of Q. Sess. iv. 280.

[24] Ibid. 241.

[25] Shrews. Chron. 22 Oct. 1886; 7 and 21 Jan., 8 Apr. 1887.

[26] From £5,515 in 1857–8 to £11,031 in 1874–5: Co. of Salop., Acct. of Receipts and Expenditure of Public Stock, 1857–75.

[27] From £11,512 (1875–6) to £12,603 (1888–9): ibid. 1875–83; Co. of Salop., Acct. of Receipts and Pmnts. of Treasurer of Co. of Salop., 1883–9.

[28] Orders of Q. Sess. iv. 120–290.

[29] See p. 152.

[30] Police (Expenses) Act, 1875, 38 & 39 Vic. c. 48.

preoccupation with the minimizing of expenditure. Even in 1873–4, the year for which the force was reported inefficient in numbers, the chairman of quarter sessions felt it an appropriate boast that the police rate was only 1*d.* when the national average was 2¼*d.* and that therefore the county had 'nothing to grumble at'.[31]

Quarter Sessions: Pauper Lunatic Asylum

Shropshire had no public institution for pauper lunatics until the opening of the asylum at Shelton in 1845.[32] Discussions leading to its construction, however, had begun in December 1838 on the motion of Sir Baldwin Leighton and his neighbour J. M. Severne.[33] Leighton chaired a committee appointed by the court in 1839 and, from 1841 to 1846, its successor the Asylum Visiting Justices' Committee; he thus had great influence on the asylum's planning and building and was largely responsible for Montgomeryshire's joining the asylum partnership between Shropshire and Much Wenlock in 1846[34] after the provision of pauper asylums had become statutory.[35]

Leighton's committee found that nearly 300 idiots and lunatics (including criminals) were maintained at public expense in various places.[36] Classification and treatment were impossible. The guardians gave average of 2*s.* a week out-relief to about half of them, most of whom lived in labouring or pauper families. Some 75 were in workhouses. Just over 50 were kept in two asylums, simply places of safe custody: most in James Jacob's private asylum at Kingsland,[37] the rest in Morda House, the Oswestry incorporation's workhouse. At Kingsland the bad cases were kept in damp dark cells; accommodation at Morda House was better but there was no adequate staff. Condemning the established practice of confining these defenceless paupers to proprietary asylums whose 'principal object' was profit, the committee recommended in 1839 the provision of a county asylum.

Built and furnished for £18,500 in 1843–5 the asylum opened to accommodate 120 patients, some of the first to be received coming from the asylum at Kingsland.[38] Badly designed according to its first medical superintendent, the asylum was enlarged and improved in the 1840s and 1850s.[39] Shrewsbury and Oswestry joined it in 1850 and 1851, each paying a rent representing an interest charge on part of its capital cost.[40]

Dr. Richard Oliver, a general practitioner with some years' interest in the provision of public asylums, was appointed medical superintendent in 1844.[41] Leighton opposed the appointment. Deeming him 'very ignorant' and inefficient and 'not the sort of person I could act with, with any pleasure to myself', he twice strove for his dismissal. Finally, in 1846, Leighton stood down from the committee, privately recording great annoyance at leaving an establishment 'erected and opened I may say almost entirely through my exertions'.[42] From 1844 to 1863, however, Oliver ran the asylum to the entire satisfaction of the visitors and lunacy commissioners.[43]

[31] *Eddowes's Jnl.* 7 Jan. 1874.
[32] *Reps. Medical Offr. of Lun. Asylum, 1846–7,* 3 (copy in S.R.O.).
[33] Loton Hall MSS., 'Some Intimate Details Concerning Several Salop. Families by Sir Baldwin Leighton & His Daughter', transcript of Lady Leighton's diary, 31 Dec. 1838; S.R.O. 183/1.
[34] S.R.O. 183/1–4; *Orders of Q. Sess.* iv. 37, 58; *Eddowes's Jnl.* 15 Mar. 1871.
[35] Lunatic Asylums Act, 1845, 8 & 9 Vic. c. 126.
[36] For this para. see S.R.O. 183/1; S.R.O. 324, box 122, returns of lunatics, 1839.
[37] i.e. in that part of the Shrews. Ho. of Ind. let to Jacob (contractor for the poor) as an asylum since 1832: S.R.O. 83/3, pp. 165–7, 181–3, 185–6, 191–2. Cf. *V.C.H. Salop.*

ii. 157.
[38] *Orders of Q. Sess.* iv. 30, 47; *Rep. Medical Supt. of Lun. Asylum, 1848,* Abstr. of Acct. following Suppl.; ibid. *1851,* 6.
[39] *Rep. Medical Supt. 1848,* Suppl.; *1853,* 5–6; *1859,* 6–7.
[40] S.R.O., q. sess. Visiting Justices of Asylum rep. bk. 1847–67, pp. 49–50, 66; *Orders of Q. Sess.* iv, p. xix.
[41] R. Oliver, *Suggestions as to the expediency of erecting a Public Asylum for the Insane belonging to the Cos. of Cumb. and Westmld.* (Carlisle [1842]); S.R.O. 183/4.
[42] S.R.O. 183/4; Loton Hall MSS., Sir B. Leighton's diary, 5 Jan. 1846.
[43] *Orders of Q. Sess.* iv. 152; *Rep. Medical Supt. 1846–63* (containing, from 1850, the lun. comrs.' reps. on the asylum and, from 1859, the visitors' ann. reps.).

'Distress being too generally the disease, how simple it seems to make comfort the remedy.' Thus, about 1851, a casual visitor summed up his conception of Oliver's humane and practical methods.[44] According to Oliver most patients, already paupers or pauperized by insanity, were disordered by the 'ceaseless labours and anxieties of the lowest rank of labouring independence'; many had few mental or physical reserves to deal with the catastrophes of life at that level. Adequate nourishment, with rest and useful recreation, were therefore the foundations of his treatment; success was likeliest, he argued, if patients were sent to the asylum as soon as symptoms showed.[45]

From the 1860s the asylum was an increasingly contentious subject at quarter sessions.[46] As early as 1855 Oliver had forecast that the 1853 Lunatic Asylums Act[47] would cause relieving officers and overseers to send greater numbers of patients to the asylum.[48] Such proved the case, though it was over ten years later that the Act's full effects began to be felt. The Visiting Justices, though overseeing the asylum's administration, had no control over admissions. They could discharge patients, and discharges were notably higher in the 1870s and early 1880s when the asylum was over-crowded;[49] in general, however, they seem to have done so only sparingly and on the medical superintendent's certificate.[50] Ever costlier enlargements were thus forced on an increasingly reluctant committee, and its resentment at having to plan for the consequences of policies it did not initiate was powerfully expressed by its formidably outspoken chairman John Bather.

Bather had a clear conception of the asylum's role from the early years of his long chairmanship (1855-77). In 1858, asserting that only curable or dangerous patients should be admitted, he protested against the asylum's becoming 'a sort of opaque vivarium'[51] for harmless imbeciles. His views were unchanged when he resigned the chair, unable any longer to recommend to the court policies which were unacceptable to him but which he probably then realized to be inevitable.[52] The guardians, however, following the lead of the Atcham board and with the lunacy commissioners' encouragement, sent increasing numbers of chronic imbeciles to the asylum to segregate them from the community,[53] and Bather's opposition to that policy, though influential, did not prevail. The shared responsibility with the guardians and the partnership with Montgomeryshire kept both committee and court divided over fundamental policies. In 1863 Bather, troubled by the asylum's overcrowding and the cost of enlargement, proposed that the guardians be urged to make workhouse wards for harmless patients,[54] but he was vigorously opposed by magistrates who were, or had been, leading guardians.[55] Next year, after Montgomeryshire had refused assent to an enlargement of the asylum, Bather began to urge the dissolution of the partnership with that county,[56] but Montgomeryshire had an influential advocate on the Shropshire bench in the 3rd Lord Powis.[57]

Despite Montgomeryshire's opposition accommodation was increased in the 1860s, though places barely kept up with the rising numbers of patients sent there, and in

[44] *Rep. Medical Supt. 1851*, 5.
[45] Ibid. *1854*, 9-10; *1856*, 6-9.
[46] This para. is generally based on S.R.O., q. sess. recs., box 30, cuttings bks. 1857-89.
[47] 16 & 17 Vic. c. 97.
[48] *Rep. Medical Supt. 1854*, 8.
[49] In the years 1845-88 380 patients were discharged 'not improved', 281 of them in the years 1871-84: ibid. *1888*, 20. Cf. *Eddowes's Jnl.* 3 Jan. 1877.
[50] *Eddowes's Jnl.* 17 Oct. 1860; 21 Oct. 1863.
[51] Ibid. 6 Jan. 1858.
[52] Ibid. 30 June, 20 Oct. 1875; 18 Oct. 1876; 4 Apr. 1877.
[53] For the Atcham union's policy see J Bowen-Jones, *Rep. of Progress of Atcham Union from its formation to . . .*

1890 (Shrews. [1890]), 35. For Bather's criticism of it and its influence in other unions see *Eddowes's Jnl.* 18 Oct. 1876, for the lun. comrs.' views ibid. 20 Oct. 1875.
[54] Under the Lunacy Acts Amendment Act, 1862, 25 & 26 Vic. c. 111, s. 8: *Eddowes's Jnl.* 7 Jan. 1863.
[55] Sir B. Leighton (pp. 140, 171), M. G. Benson (S.R.O. 19/2/3, f. 107; 19/2/4, f. 4), and Lt.-Col. T. H. Lovett (S.R.O. 122/4, p. 258; 122/5, pp. 257-8).
[56] *Eddowes's Jnl.* 29 June 1864.
[57] See e.g. ibid. 21 Oct. 1863; 19 Oct. 1864; 15 Mar. 1871; 1 Jan. 1873; 2 Jan. 1878; *Shrews. Chron.* 18 Oct. 1878. In Mont. Powis was chmn. of q. sess. 1855-91 and lieut. 1877-91: N.L.W., Mont. q. sess. order bks.; *Complete Peerage*, x. 654.

1866 and 1869 Bridgnorth and Ludlow joined the asylum.[58] The lunacy commissioners' reports first became critical in the mid 1870s. Overcrowding was putting the patients' health at risk and low wages made it difficult to keep an efficient staff.[59] By 1872 the Shropshire magistrates were arguing that the limit had been reached and that enlargement would be unwise, and the alternatives to enlargement, outlined by Bather,[60] were sufficiently plausible to produce many years' fruitless discussion.

Boarding in other asylums offered one solution to overcrowding; first tried in 1864–5, when Montgomeryshire resisted enlargement,[61] it became increasingly useful in the 1870s and 1880s,[62] but by 1876 it was clear that the lunacy commissioners would allow it only as a temporary expedient.[63] Thrice in the 1870s the visitors voted to dissolve the partnership with Montgomeryshire, hoping to avoid enlargement by the purchase of its share in the asylum. Montgomeryshire, however, resisted and the Home Secretary vetoed any dissolution not agreed by Montgomeryshire.[64] Retention of harmless imbeciles in proposed workhouse lunacy wards seemed another alternative to enlargement, but a committee (1879–80) chaired by Sir Baldwyn Leighton, dealt it a final blow; in neither county could any workhouse provide the asylum standards of care long insisted on by the commissioners,[65] nor was there a building suitable for a joint imbecile asylum.[66]

Meanwhile Alfred Salwey had become the visitors' chairman (1877–85). The court approved enlargement in 1880[67] and, despite continued opposition,[68] work began in 1882.[69] When it was finished in 1885, some thirteen years after overcrowding had been acknowledged as a serious problem, the asylum had 800 places.[70]

Early in 1885, as the building neared completion, the lunacy commissioners circulated their view that a proportion of pauper lunatics might properly be accommodated in workhouses.[71] Numbers of patients continued to increase, and within a few years the Visitors' Committee had to adopt the policy so long urged by Bather.[72] Meanwhile, in the later 1880s, the asylum's water supply, sewerage, and drainage were matters of contention,[73] and in 1888 one influential magistrate, W. C. P. Purton,[74] asserted that of the various responsibilities about to pass from the court to the county council none would be more difficult than the asylum.[75]

Quarter Sessions: Executive Committee

An outbreak of cattle plague in 1865, especially severe in north Shropshire,[76] led to legislation next year[77] under which quarter sessions became a local authority empowered to slaughter animals and pay compensation out of the county rate. Weekly adjourned sessions, at first under the authority of an Order in Council, developed into

[58] S.R.O., q. sess. Visiting Justices of Asylum Cttee. rep. bk. 1847–67, p. 245; *Eddowes's Jnl.* 19 Oct. 1864; 4 July 1866; *Rep. Medical Supt.* 1865–9; S.R.O., Lun. Asylum min. bk. 1884–91, p. 64.

[59] *Eddowes's Jnl.* 1 July 1874. Low wages and too frequent staff changes had caused comment earlier: ibid. 19 Oct. 1870.

[60] Ibid. 16 Oct. 1872; 1 Jan. 1873.

[61] S.R.O., q. sess. Visiting Justices of Asylum Cttee. rep. bk. 1847–67, pp. 236, 252; *Rep. Medical Supt.* 1865, 4.

[62] *Rep. Medical Supt.* 1874–85.

[63] Ibid. *1876*, 5–6; *Eddowes's Jnl.* 3 Jan. 1877.

[64] *Eddowes's Jnl.* 1 Jan., 12 Mar., 2 July 1873; 17 Oct. 1877; 2 and 23 Jan., 3 July, 14 Aug. 1878; *Shrews. Chron.* 23 Aug., 18 Oct., 1 Nov., 6 Dec. 1878; S.R.O., q. sess. recs., box 30, cuttings bk. 1877–82, mins. of adjourned q. sess. (24 July 1878) and of an interview (5 Aug. 1878) given to a q. sess. deputation by Mr. Sec. Cross, and copies of corresp. with Home Office (Nov. 1878).

[65] *Eddowes's Jnl.* 7 Jan. 1880. Cf. *18th Rep Comrs. in Lunacy*, H.C. 389, pp. 74–5 (1864), xxiii; *Rep. Medical Supt. 1863*, 5–6.

[66] Under the Poor Law Act, 1879, 42 & 43 Vic. c. 54, s. 8, a provision secured by Leighton himself: *Eddowes's Jnl.* 15 Oct. 1879; 7 Jan. 1880.

[67] Ibid. 7 Apr. 1880.

[68] Notably from Stan. Leighton and R. J. More: S.R.O., q. sess. recs., box 30, cuttings bk. 1877–82.

[69] *Orders of Q. Sess.* iv. 254–5, 258, 262.

[70] *Eddowes's Jnl.* 8 Apr. 1885.

[71] Ibid. (rep. of Salwey's grand-jury charge).

[72] See p. 212.

[73] S.R.O., q. sess. recs., box 30, cuttings bk. 1883–9.

[74] *Orders of Q. Sess.* iv, p. iii.

[75] *Shrews. Chron.* 4 Jan. 1889.

[76] *Eddowes's Jnl.* 18 Oct. 1865; *Orders of Q. Sess.* iv, p. xvi.

[77] Cattle Diseases Prevention Act, 1866, 29 & 30 Vic. c. 2.

a cattle-plague committee; under the energetic Sir Baldwin Leighton the committee greatly improved on the previous lackadaisical efforts of the petty-sessional magistrates to combat the disease[78] which, by 1867, had been eradicated from the county at a cost to the rates of almost £30,000.[79]

From 1869 the court had to appoint a statutory Executive Committee and cattle inspectors. The first inspectors were veterinary surgeons; it was soon found, however, that the police could do the work more cheaply[80] and, despite police and Home Office misgivings,[81] many were employed on the work in the 1870s and 1880s.[82] The Police and Executive Committees were virtually identical in membership.[83] In a period which witnessed several severe outbreaks of animal disease the committee's activities and efficiency were of great importance, and in 1883 six leading agriculturists who were not magistrates were co-opted to it.[84] All were leading guardians or waywardens[85] but for each it was a first experience of county government; they included four future members of the county council, one of them a future chairman.[86]

The Executive Committee's work was progressively circumscribed by statute and government regulation, and from 1878 the Treasury became liable to compensate for the slaughter of cattle-plague victims,[87] though not, for example, that of swine-fever victims.[88]

County Coroners

At the beginning of the period the four county coroners, like their predecessors for 640 years, had been elected to their offices by the freeholders in the county court.[89] In the political excitement following the election of the first reformed House of Commons the parties naturally used vacancies in the office to test or influence public opinion, and in 1833 and 1834 the county witnessed political contests for the office. William Downes, a Whig attorney who had helped to beat the Hon. R. H. Clive at Ludlow in the 1832 general election, was unsuccessful in 1833. Next year Downes engaged in a contest of almost seven weeks in which almost 6,100 voted. Lord Powis, head of Shropshire's die-hard Tories, exerted himself to the utmost: his tenants were brought in at an early stage, later to be reinforced by cottagers and miners and other dubiously qualified voters 'from scarcely inhabitable huts on the hills'. It was in vain. Downes won by 192 votes[90] defeating the Powis interest for a second time in two years.

Such contests were rare. Issues at stake were usually the candidates' places of residence and their professional qualifications.[91] Most Shropshire coroners during the period were solicitors, though some surgeons and other professional men were also elected.[92] Occasionally a candidate protested against the use of aristocratic influence,[93] but by no means all vacancies were contested.[94] In 1861 the county coroners were said

[78] *Eddowes's Jnl.* 3 Jan., 17 Oct. 1866; *T.S.A.S.* lix. 137-8; Leighton, 'Life of Sir B. Leighton' (S.R.O. 783, parcel 194), p. 72.

[79] *Orders of Q. Sess.* iv, p. xvi.

[80] Contagious Diseases (Animals) Act, 1869, 32 & 33 Vic. c. 70, ss. 11-12; *Eddowes's Jnl.* 29 June 1870; 3 Jan. 1872; *Oswestry Adv.* 29 June 1870.

[81] *Rep. Insp. Const.* H.C. 25, pp. 35-6 (1871), xxviii; ibid. H.C. 47, pp. 46-7 (1872), xxx.

[82] Ibid. H.C. 25, pp. 35-6 (1871), xxviii, and subsequent reps.

[83] *Eddowes's Jnl.* 29 June 1870.

[84] *Orders of Q. Sess.* iv, pp. xvi-xvii, 262.

[85] *Shrews. Chron.* 4 Jan. 1884.

[86] *Illustrated Official Handbk. to Co. Council of Salop* (Shrews. 1890), 19, 21-2; *Shrews. Chron.* 28 Oct. 1892 (C. Wadlow's election as co. alderman); below, pp.

166, 185-6.

[87] Under the Contagious Diseases (Animals) Act, 1878, 41 & 42 Vic. c. 74, s. 15 (3).

[88] See p. 151.

[89] See p. 28.

[90] *Salopian Jnl.* 15 May 1833; *Salop. N. & Q.* n.s. iii. 96-9, 104-6, 108-9, 111.

[91] See e.g. *Eddowes's Jnl.* 9 July 1845.

[92] C 202 yields an incomplete list of coroners for the period and the q. sess. rolls in S.R.O. are unreliable; both have been supplemented from sources cited above, p. 149, Table I, and from S.R.O., q. sess. Finance Cttee. rep. bks. Directories and newspaper advertisements and election reps. yield inf. about professions.

[93] *Shrews. Chron.* 30 Nov. 1849. Cf. N.L.W., Aston Hall 529.

[94] See e.g. *Eddowes's Jnl.* 3 and 10 Sept. 1845.

to be a 'very respectable' body of men, 'much more so than formerly'.[95] The Dicken family of Wollerton maintained its hold on one coronership until 1849[96] and in 1845 the Weymans, Ludlow attorneys, established a hold on another which they maintained for almost a century.[97] In 1845 the county was divided into five coroners' districts and an additional coroner was elected;[98] their number was raised to six in 1850.[99] The election of coroners passed to the county council in 1889,[1] though H. T. Weyman, the last Shropshire coroner elected by the freeholders, remained until 1939.[2]

Constitutional and Legal Changes: the Militia, the County Courts, and the Sheriff

Constitutional and legal reforms achieved the supersession of many of the ancient, mostly moribund, institutions for the maintenance of order and the administration of law in the county. Piecemeal legislation, however, was careful to preserve constitutional vestiges which had no practical significance. The ancient conscriptible county militias, for example, the constitutional force of the realm,[3] remained in being, but only nominally. Similarly, new local courts, theoretically within the framework of the ancient county court,[4] were actually quite distinct from it. The hundreds were neither abolished nor retained, simply superseded. The sheriff survived, though without significant duties.

In 1852 the county militias became voluntarily enlisted forces to be raised by the lieutenants and their deputies.[5] Nevertheless, despite the change and later consequent changes, the archaic compulsory system, administered by the lieutenancy and centring on the ballot,[6] maintained a formal,[7] though suspended,[8] existence, even after 1882 when the law of the lieutenancy and militia was consolidated.[9] Indeed the dual system, of conscription in theory and voluntary engagement in practice,[10] was abolished only in 1921.[11] Some reinvigoration of the Shropshire militia, however, seems to have begun after 1845 when Lord Hill became lieutenant: in 1846 he commissioned nine officers, the first new commissions since 1834;[12] one of Hill's friends, Col. Edward Corbett, became major in 1852, took command in 1855, and created an efficient force[13] able to do home garrison duty during the Indian Mutiny.[14]

The history of the Shropshire militia in the late 19th century, however, belongs less to the county's history than to the army's. In 1871 Cardwell's reforms, abridging the lieutenants' powers,[15] began the militias' integration into the Crown's other armed forces. Ten years later, with the army's territorialization, the county militia became the 3rd (Salop Militia) Battalion, the Shropshire Regiment (King's Light Infantry).[16] From 1919 until its formal disbandment in 1953 the battalion existed only in name.[17]

[95] Eddowes's Jnl. 17 Oct. 1860.
[96] C 202/194/17; Shrews. Chron. 16 Nov. 1849 (notice of Jos. Dicken's death).
[97] C 202/235/16; C 202/296.
[98] Under the Coroners Act, 1844, 7 & 8 Vic. c. 92: S.R.O., q. sess. Finance Cttee. rep. bk. 1843–50, pp. 40–8, 56, 86; C 202/235/15.
[99] Orders of Q. Sess. iv. 74–5, 78.
[1] Under the Local Govt. Act, 1888, 51 & 52 Vic. c. 41, s. 5 (1).
[2] Co. Councils Assoc. Jubilee of Co. Councils (1939; Salop. edn.), 101–2; S.C.C. Mins. 1939–40, 329.
[3] C. M. Clode, Military Forces of the Crown (1869), i. 31, 36–7, 44, 61–2, 262–3; ii. 60–1, 79–80.
[4] Sir W. Holdsworth, Hist. Eng. Law, i (1956), 191–2.
[5] Militia Act, 1852, 15 & 16 Vic. c. 50, ss. 11–12.
[6] See p. 132.
[7] Militia (Ballot) Act, 1860, 23 & 24 Vic. c. 120.
[8] See Militia (Ballot Suspension) Act, 1829, 10 Geo. IV,

c. 10; Expiring Laws Continuance Act, 1921, 11 & 12 Geo. V, c. 53, sched., no. 9; above, p. 132.
[9] Militia Act, 1882, 45 & 46 Vic. c. 49.
[10] Cardwell's summary: C. Sebag-Montefiore, Hist. of Volunteer Forces . . . to . . . 1860 (1908), 27 n. 1.
[11] Territorial Army and Militia Act, 1921, 11 & 12 Geo. V, c. 37.
[12] See p. 139 and source there cited.
[13] S.R.O., q. sess. recs., box 302, reg. of coms. in militia; Shrews. Chron. 11 Jan. 1985 (obit.).
[14] i.e. in Dublin 1857–8: G. A. Parfitt, Salop. Militia and Volunteers (Hist. of Corps of King's Salop. Light Inf. iv. [1970]), 169.
[15] See p. 139.
[16] Under the Regulation of the Forces Act, 1881, 44 & 45 Vic. c. 57, s. 4. For the regt.'s changes of name 1881–1920 see Reg. of Regts. and Corps of Brit. Army, ed. A. Swinson (1972), 152, 187.
[17] Parfitt, op. cit. 178–9. From 1921 it was known as the 3rd (Militia) Bn., K.S.L.I.

With vestigial responsibilities for public order in Shropshire[18] the lieutenant retained some administrative links with the armed forces. From 1908, however, those links were not with the units descended from the old militia[19] but with the Territorial Force units: the Shropshire Imperial Yeomanry dating from the 1790s and formed into a single regiment in 1872[20] and the rifle and artillery units[21] descended from the volunteers enrolled by the lieutenant in the anti-French patriotic movement of 1859.[22]

The hundreds were superseded in the 1840s. The County Courts Act, 1846,[23] providing twelve small-debts courts in Shropshire,[24] extinguished the only significant jurisdiction of the ancient county court and of the surviving hundred courts, Bradford, Chirbury, Clun, and Purslow.[25] The county court lingered on for the transaction of a few scraps of formal business, but the hundred courts either ceased altogether or, as Brimstree and Ford had already done,[26] dwindled to mere archaic, formal relics long before the abolition of their civil jurisdiction in 1867.[27] The county's ancient fiscal and administrative divisions, based on the hundreds[28] though generally not conterminous with the jurisdictions of their courts,[29] had already been abandoned: the high constables' duties of summoning jurors to quarter sessions and keeping the court passed to the county police in 1842,[30] their rate-collecting duties to the poor-law guardians in 1844,[31] and their office fell into disuse long before formal abolition in 1870. In Shropshire the cessation of the office revived the process of grand-jury indictment whenever, before 1889, a hundred rate was required for bridge repair.[32] Shropshire hundred names survived in petty-sessional divisions until 1954,[33] land-tax commissioners' divisions until 1963,[34] and coroners' districts until the early 1970s.[35]

The sheriff survived as a relic of the ancient government of the county.[36] By the end of the period, however, almost all his remaining responsibilities had passed to the police[37] and the new prison administration.[38] He was little more than an ornamental figure burdened with the expense of what was, from the 1870s, an increasing amount of ceremonial attendance on the assize justices, 'rather more exacting' in such matters than formerly.[39] The office was unpopular in Shropshire,[40] at least with men like Sir Baldwin Leighton (1835-6)[41] and Sir Offley Wakeman (1887-8),[42] active in county administration and whose work as magistrates was thus interrupted for a year. Energetic sheriffs achieved some reforms[43] but even at the end of the period there was much room for improvement, especially in the financial accountability of the under-sheriff

[18] See p. 224.
[19] i.e. the Special Reserve, so known 1908-21 as a result of the Territorial and Reserve Forces Act, 1907, 7 Edw. VII, c. 9: Parfitt, op. cit. 160.
[20] E. W. Gladstone, *Shropshire Yeomanry, 1795-1945* (Manchester, 1953), 99-100, 167.
[21] O.S. *Map . . . of . . . Imp. Yeomanry, Militia & Volunteer Units in No. 4 Grouped Regtl. Dist.* (1907; copy in S.R.O., q. sess. recs., box 305).
[22] Parfitt, op. cit. 15, 252. [23] 9 & 10 Vic. c. 95.
[24] *Lond. Gaz.* 9 Mar. 1847 (p. 1010).
[25] *Ret. Hund. and Manor Cts.* H.C. 338-III, pp. 5, 8 (1839), xliii; *Ret. Cts. of Requests, Cts. of Conscience,* H.C. 619, pp. 132-7 (1840), xli. Boro. cts. of record are reserved for treatment in later vols. of this *Hist.*
[26] S.R.O. 1190, box 23, papers *re* Brimstree hund. (suit and ct. r. 1831-47); *V.C.H. Salop.* viii. 181.
[27] Co. Cts. Act, 1867, 30 & 31 Vic. c. 142, s. 28.
[28] *T.S.A.S.* 3rd ser. vii. 351-2; *Shropshire Hearth-Tax Roll of 1672,* ed. W. Watkins-Pitchford (1949), pp. vi-vii.
[29] *T.S.A.S.* 2nd ser. iv. 288; *V.C.H. Salop.* viii. 2.
[30] S.R.O., q. sess. Auditing Cttee. and Finance Cttee. rep. bk. 1837-43, pp. 134, 169. By 1842 the high consts. were known as bailiffs.
[31] Under the Co. Rates Act, 1844, 7 & 8 Vic. c. 33: S.R.O., q. sess. order bk. 1843-6, p. 138; q. sess. Finance Cttee.

rep. bk. 1843-50, p. 33. And see *Orders of Q. Sess.* i. pp. xiii-xiv (where the details of allotments are wrongly given: cf. above, p. 102).
[32] *Orders of Q. Sess.* iv, pp. xii, xvii, 190; above, p. 153. Some police supts. were acting as high consts. in the early 1860s: *Rep. Insp. Const.* H.C. 67, pp. 29-30 (1861), lii; ibid. H.C. 26, p. 44 (1864), xlviii.
[33] S.C.C. *Year Bk. 1954-5*; below, p. 227. Some simplification of names had occurred in 1920: S.R.O., q. sess. min. bk. 19, pp. 220-1.
[34] See e.g. S.R.O. 1332, 1348, 1356, 1457. The tax was abolished by the Finance Act, 1963, c. 25, s. 68.
[35] S.C.C. *Year Bk. 1972-3.*
[36] Sheriffs Act, 1887, 50 & 51 Vic. c. 55.
[37] S.R.O., q. sess. Const. Cttee. rep. bk. 1854-65, p. 117; *Eddowes's Jnl.* 30 June 1869; 5 Jan. 1870; *Shrews. Chron.* 8 Jan. 1886.
[38] See p. 157.
[39] *Rep. Sel. Cttee. on High Sheriffs,* H.C. 257, pp. 64, 69 (1888), xii.
[40] Ibid. 15-25, 63-70, 122, 128.
[41] Leighton, 'Life of Sir B. Leighton' (S.R.O. 783, parcel 194), pp. 60-2.
[42] *Rep. Sel. Cttee. on High Sheriffs,* 63, 67-8; *Shrews. Chron.* 6 and 13 Apr. 1888.
[43] Leighton, op. cit. 62.

on whom the occasional correspondence[44] and legal routine[45] of the shrievalty was devolved; that office was virtually monopolized by the formidable E. C. Peele from 1871 to 1911.[46]

The changes to the historic county and its forms of government portended by the Local Government (Boundaries) Act, 1887,[47] and the 1888 Local Government Bill, were dealt with by the magistrates in the practical unsentimental spirit characteristic of their attitude to the ancient office of sheriff. The court's Boundaries Committee (1887–8), set up to confer with the commissioners named in the 1887 Act,[48] recommended that large areas of Cheshire, Flintshire, Herefordshire, and Staffordshire, lying in mainly Shropshire unions, be annexed to the county.[49] In part explanation the court's chairman reported everywhere 'a great affection . . . for the union boundary'. Only one magistrate opposed the proposals, appealing to the court as 'the embodiment of the historical sentiment of the county, as well as of what was conservative in its best sense': Jasper More, the Liberal Unionist M.P., urged no interference with the Welsh border so as to retain 'a monument of this historical district'. His sentiment, briskly dismissed by Lord Powis, a leading member of the committee, was unsupported. The report was adopted.[50] Three months later the Local Government Bill was published and the magistrates' assistance 'in every way' was pledged to the new county authority. The magistrates considered the Bill in a 'very fair and impartial spirit', and their chairman, Salwey, reiterated his, and his predecessor's,[51] hope that many of the court's 'working members' would be found on the new 'county board',[52] as indeed they were.

Next year, when Salwey had become chairman of the county council and its Finance Committee, he invited the chairmen of the council's five other standing committees and representatives of the Asylum Visitors to join him on the bench. Seven men did so.[53] Three were magistrates who had been leading members of quarter sessions' standing committees;[54] two others, J. Bowen-Jones and Thomas Topham, both of whom became magistrates in the next few years,[55] had been co-opted members of the court's Executive Committee;[56] only two[57] had no experience of the court's administrative work. Almost half of the council's members were drawn from the magistracy.[58] Thus the court's traditions of stringent economy were maintained, for good or ill,[59] by a generation whose leadership of the council was guided by the financial principles of quarter sessions.

[44] See e.g. *Eddowes's Jnl.* 4 Jan. 1871 (*re* improvements to shirehall cts.).

[45] *Rep. Sel. Cttee. on High Sheriffs*, 19, 63, 65–6. Cf. below, p. 227.

[46] Occasionally as joint or deputy under-sheriff: Hughes, *Sheriffs*; below, pp. 188, 227–8.

[47] 50 & 51 Vic. c. 61.

[48] *Shrews. Chron.* 21 Oct. 1887.

[49] Small exchanges of territory with Mont. and Worcs. and the cession of 3 remote pars. to Radnors. were also recommended.

[50] *Shrews. Chron.* 6 Jan. 1888; S.R.O. 68/6.

[51] Spearman, *Co. Councillor's Manual* (1889), 2 (introd. chap. by Lowndes).

[52] *Shrews. Chron.* 6 and 13 Apr. 1888.

[53] Ibid. 17 May 1889. Cf. *Illustrated Official Handbk. to Co. Council of Salop* (Shrews. 1890), 23–6.

[54] Sir O. Wakeman, Maj.-Gen. the Hon. W. H. Herbert, and the Revd. L. J. Lee. The last two were spokesmen for the asylum visitors: see e.g. *Shrews. Chron.* 2 July, 22 Oct. 1886; 6 Jan., 6 Apr., 19 Oct. 1888.

[55] *Kelly's Dir. Salop.* (1891; 1895).

[56] See p. 163.

[57] Ric. Groom, Edw. Jones.

[58] See p. 182.

[59] See p. 190.

THE NEW
LOCAL AUTHORITIES

The Poor-Law Unions 1836–1930, p. 169. The School Boards 1872–1903, p. 174. Unification: the Sanitary Authorities, Highway Boards, and District Councils, p. 177.

BY the beginning of the 19th century the only effective organs of local government outside the chartered municipalities were the parishes and townships supervised by the county magistrates. The 1834 Poor Law Amendment Act,[1] however, created a new tier of government, conferring the most expensive branch of local administration on the boards of guardians of the poor-law unions. The unions were not without precedent. In the 18th century parochial unions for poor-law purposes had been effected under local Acts,[2] and more generally the turnpike trusts provided examples of special-purpose statutory authorities[3] reaching back in Shropshire to 1726.[4] In three important respects, however, the unions represented a new departure. First, their supervision, not left to the county magistrates, was conferred on a central organ of the state.[5] Secondly, they formed a nationwide, increasingly uniform system of local authorities. Thirdly, the unions were administered by elected guardians, and a large local-government electorate, though one weighted in favour of property,[6] was thereby created.

The guardians' work coming under the supervision of the Poor Law Board (from 1871 the Local Government Board), the apparent utility of the unions caused successive governments to adopt them for the development of local administration. Consequently in the 1840s, for almost all executive functions, whether old[7] or new,[8] they replaced the ancient hundreds[9] and provided a territorial framework within which new courts and special-purpose authorities could be fitted. In Shropshire the impact of this administrative revolution was softened by the fact that the new authorities were run by the same sort of men as the older-established organs of government. The gentry and clergy ran the unions and the younger sons of the gentry even sought, and occasionally found, official employment within the new system. Uvedale Corbett, for example, was a county-court judge[10] and became also an official under the Poor Law Board. Stanley Leighton seems to have aspired to the same sort of career but failed to obtain Corbett's poor-law auditorship in 1862, the post going to a Ludlow solicitor.[11] Indeed much of the official work in any of the new areas was likely to be engrossed by one or two leading solicitors of its central market

---

[1] 4 & 5 Wm. IV, c. 76.
[2] See p. 169. There were no unions under Gilbert's Act (22 Geo. III, c. 83) in Salop.: V. J. Walsh, 'The Admin. of the Poor Laws in Salop. 1820–1855' (Pennsylvania Univ. Ph.D. thesis, 1970), 63 n. (copy in S.R.O.).
[3] E. Pawson, *Transport and Economy: the Turnpike Roads of Eighteenth-Cent. Brit.* (1977), 76, 87–94.
[4] See p. 115. [5] See p. 154 n. 27.
[6] B. Keith-Lucas, *Eng. Local Govt. Franchise* (1952), 35–7. The poor-law electorate was thrice the size of the post-1832 parl. electorate: S. and B. Webb, *Eng. Poor Law Hist. II: the Last Hundred Yrs.* i. 119–20; Sir Ll.

Woodward, *Age of Reform, 1815–1870* (1962), 88.
[7] e.g. collection of rates: see p. 165, n. 31, and sources there cited.
[8] e.g. registration of vital statistics: see p. 135.
[9] The *Census Reports* gave population figs. for the hunds. until 1881, but did not give their territorial composition after 1841: *V.C.H. Salop.* ii. 204.
[10] See e.g. *Eddowes's Jnl.* 19 Oct. 1859. For the new co. cts. see p. 165.
[11] Loton Hall MSS., Sir B. Leighton's diary, [Feb.], 8 July 1862; *T.S.A.S.* lix. 151; and e.g. *Local Govt. Dir. 1875*, 5.

town. In Wellington, for example, in 1856 R. D. Newill was clerk to the divisional petty sessions and county-court clerk, while George Marcy was clerk to the board of guardians and superintendent registrar. Newill at least embodied some continuity with the older-established legal hierarchy: elected a county coroner in 1849, when Sir Robert Hill's support for him elicited allegations of undue aristocratic influence, he was also steward of the duke of Cleveland's court for Bradford hundred.[12] There was even a tendency, recalling the earliest documented period of county government,[13] for offices within the new system to become hereditary, as in the Atcham union where four members of the Everest family held the clerkship to the guardians throughout the whole of the union's history (1836-1930).[14]

The new local-government system, as it developed, became unduly complex, the statutory relationships between the highway boards, the school boards, and the sanitary authorities on the one hand and the central government on the other by no means corresponding to the pattern established in 1834. Victorian resistance to the growth of central bureaucratic control[15] helped to ensure that the 1862 Highway Act,[16] the 1870 Elementary Education Act,[17] and the Public Health Acts of 1848 and 1872[18] varied the theme set by the legislation of 1834. By reaction there was a striving after unification, gradually achieved during almost sixty years following the 1872 Public Health Act. Completion of the process was hardly possible before the creation of a new county authority in 1888-9. Nevertheless in Shropshire, where in any case the absence of large towns limited the complexities of the new system, the ruling gentry used their influence from an early stage to promote the unification and efficiency of the new local authorities.[19]

The establishment of a new system of local authorities between the parish and the county wrought great changes to the administrative map of England and Wales; in the rural counties, if Shropshire is typical, those changes endured for well over a century. With some modification[20] the boundaries of the Shropshire unions created in 1836-7 were still visible on the map as the boundaries of the rural districts at the beginning of 1966.[21] By then, however, the Shropshire district authorities, like those in England and Wales generally, were recognized as too small for the efficient discharge of their responsibilities,[22] and they were reorganized later that year. The rural districts, reduced from 10 to 9 by the amalgamation of Ellesmere and Wem as North Shropshire, absorbed all the smaller urban authorities. Five of the 6 municipal boroughs and 5 of the 9 urban districts were dissolved; they became merely civil parishes, though the former boroughs retained mayors and the courtesy title of rural borough.[23] The scheme had been prepared by the Salop County Council,[24] one of the few county councils to shoulder its responsibilities under the 1958 Local Government Act[25] and almost the only one to see its reorganization carried through.[26] In the event success was owed to a bargain struck in 1965. Over dinner with the council's leaders R. H. S. Crossman,

[12] P.O. Dir. Salop. (1856), 136-7; Walsh, 'Poor Laws in Salop. 1820-1855', 348; Shrews. Chron. 30 Nov. 1849.

[13] See p. 28.

[14] Walsh, 'Poor Laws in Salop. 1820-1855', 347-8; J. Bowen-Jones, Rep. on Progress of Atcham Union . . . to . . . 1890 (Shrews. 1890), 19; S.R.O. 13/13, pp. 195-6, 202; Kelly's Dir. Salop. (1929), 30. The last remained clk. of Atcham R.D.C. until 1947: S.C.C. Yr. Bk. 1946-7, 131; local information.

[15] See e.g. W. C. Lubenow, The Politics of Govt. Growth . . . 1833-1848 (Newton Abbot, 1971); D.N.B. sub Smith, Joshua Toulmin.

[16] 25 & 26 Vic. c. 61.

[17] 33 & 34 Vic. c. 75.

[18] 11 & 12 Vic. c. 63; 35 & 36 Vic. c. 79.

[19] See pp. 173, 177-80.

[20] Mainly in 1934 when 7 small R.D.s were absorbed by their neighbours: V.C.H. Salop. ii. 213, 216-18. All but 1 (Ch. Stretton) consisted of the amputated parts of unions whose territory crossed the co. boundary, the amputations being those of 1895 (for detail see S.C.C. Mins. 1894-5).

[21] See map on p. 179.

[22] B. Keith-Lucas, Eng. Local Govt. in Nineteenth and Twentieth Cents. (Hist. Assn. 1977), 30, 32, 37.

[23] V.C.H. Salop. ii. 205, 214, 216, 218, 235-7; and see map on p. 179, below.

[24] S.R.O. 1403/1.

[25] 6 & 7 Eliz. II, c. 55, s. 28.

[26] 316 H.L. Deb. 5th ser. 1181.

Minister of Housing and Local Government, persuaded them to accept the expansion of Dawley New Town despite 'very wide incursions into agricultural land', and in return he 'quickly gave in' to the council's proposals for redistricting.[27] The reorganization thus achieved paved the way[28] for the more drastic changes introduced in 1974.[29]

The elective character of the boards of guardians seems to form a striking contrast to the nominated oligarchy of landowning magistrates who ruled the county until 1889. To contemporaries, however, the contrast may have been less apparent. Certainly there was no lack of schemes to combine elective and nominated elements, so incongruous from a later point of view, into a single county authority;[30] moreover the presence, in Shropshire often the dominating presence, of the non-elected magistrates among the guardians gave even those boards a mixed character. The constitutional problem was not urgent during a period in which the stringent economy of local government, in Shropshire at least, gave the ratepayers no ground for complaint either against the guardians, waywardens, and school-board members whom they elected or against the magistrates.[31] Whether elected or nominated they had regard primarily to economy, and the history of Shropshire's poor-law unions, highway boards, school boards, and sanitary authorities, and of the services they provided, cannot be divorced from consideration of the question who ruled the countryside. Under the leadership of its traditional rulers Victorian Shropshire kept its rates low, though often only at the cost of destitution produced by the denial of out-relief,[32] low standards of elementary education,[33] and deplorable levels of domestic sanitation and hygiene largely ignored by an impotent or sycophantic sanitary inspectorate living 'under the landlord'.[34]

The Poor-Law Unions 1836–1930

The Shropshire poor-law unions were formed in 1836–7 by William Day, an assistant poor-law commissioner.[35] In accordance with the commissioners' recommendations Day arranged each union to centre on a convenient market town, and in the south and east of the county ten unions, whose territories lay wholly[36] or mainly[37] in Shropshire, were quickly and easily formed. Formation proceeded less easily in the north and west where the existence of six local-Act incorporations[38] complicated the process.[39] The failure of the Shrewsbury, Oswestry, and Whitchurch incorporations to dissolve themselves resulted in the choice of Wem, rather than the larger town of Whitchurch, as one union centre and in the formation of two unions whose anomalous areas

[27] R. Crossman, *Diaries of a Cabinet Minister*, i(1975), 307–8. See also below, p. 220. The Labour govt. had squashed reorganization under the 1958 Act (316 *H.L. Deb.* 5th ser. 1181) and Crossman was intent on a general review of local govt. (e.g. Keith-Lucas, op. cit. 36–7; Crossman, op. cit. i. 440–1).

[28] 316 *H.L. Deb.* 5th ser. 1181–2.

[29] Under the Local Govt. Act, 1972, c. 70, s. 1(4): *Eng. Non-metropolitan Districts (Definition) Order, 1972* (Stat. Instr. 1972, no. 2039); *Eng. Non-metropolitan Districts (Names) Order, 1973* (Stat. Instr. 1973, no. 551).

[30] *V.C.H. Wilts.* v. 231, 258, 263; J. Redlich and F. W. Hirst, *Hist. of Local Govt. in Eng.* ed. B. Keith-Lucas (1970), 169–74.

[31] The Salop. magistrates' zeal for economy (see pp. 148–52) does not bear out general contemporary radical criticisms of magisterial 'prodigality' (see e.g. Redlich and Hirst, *Local Govt.* 171–2).

[32] See pp. 171–2.

[33] See pp. 176–7.

[34] *Rep. R. Com. on Poor Laws, App. XVII* [Cd. 4690], p. 146 (1909), xliii; cf. ibid. 150, 152–3, 163.

[35] This para. is based on Walsh, 'Poor Laws in Salop. 1820–1855', 60–105, 138–203. For the formation of W. Bromwich union (which included townships which were in Salop. until 1844) see *V.C.H. Staffs.* xvii. 45.

[36] Bridgnorth, Ch. Stretton, Madeley, and Wellington. Wem (see below) was also wholly in Salop.

[37] Cleobury Mortimer (also Worcs.), Clun (also Mont.), Drayton (also Ches. and Staffs.), Ludlow (also Herefs.), Newport (also Staffs.), and Shifnal (also Staffs.). Atcham and Ellesmere unions (see below) also included Welsh territory. A few Salop. parishes or townships lay in Herefs., Mont., Radnors., Staffs., and Worcs. unions.

[38] Shrews. (formed 1784), Oswestry (1791), Ellesmere (1791), Whitchurch (1791), Atcham (1792), and Montgomery and Pool (1792). Oswestry lay partly, Montgomery and Pool mainly, in Wales.

[39] The incorporations seem to have been the only significant obstacles to union formation in Salop. Elsewhere aristocratic interference has been noted: A. Brundage, 'The landed interest and the New Poor Law: a reappraisal of the revolution in govt.', *E.H.R.* lxxxvii. 30–2.

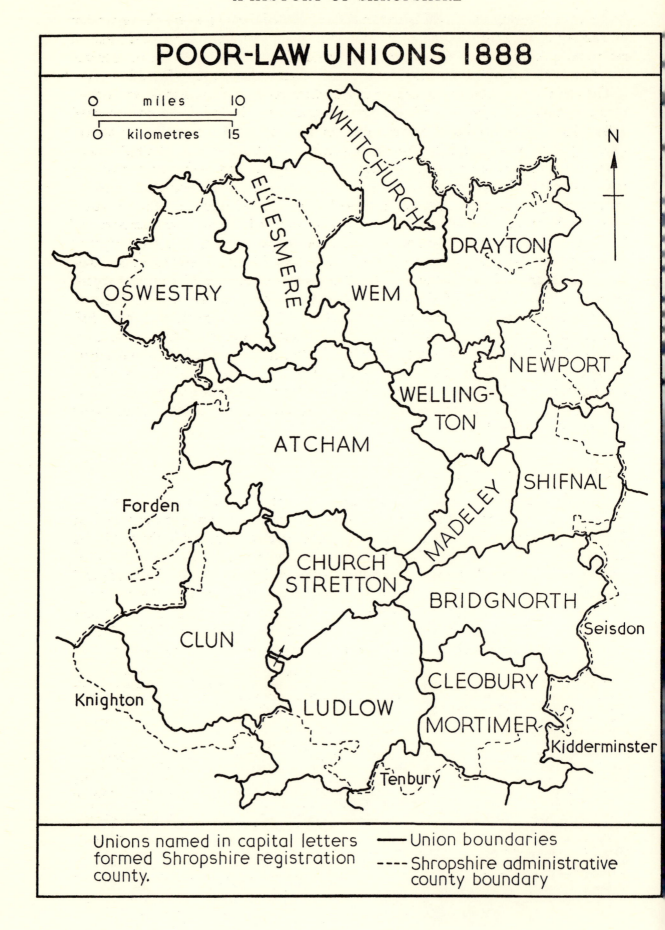

POOR-LAW UNIONS 1888

O miles 10

O kilometres 15

N

WHITCHURCH

ELLESMERE

DRAYTON

OSWESTRY

WEM

NEWPORT

WELLING-TON

ATCHAM

SHIFNAL

Forden

MADELEY

CHURCH STRETTON

BRIDGNORTH

Seisdon

CLUN

CLEOBURY

Knighton

LUDLOW

MORTIMER

Kidderminster

Tenbury

Unions named in capital letters formed Shropshire registration county.

—— Union boundaries

---- Shropshire administrative county boundary

departed from the utilitarian pattern planned by Day and the commissioners. Atcham, the largest Shropshire union, stretched from the Welsh border to the neighbourhood of Wellington and encircled the old Shrewsbury incorporation. Ellesmere, even more eccentric when its formation was completed in 1837, stretched from Worthenbury 6 miles east of Wrexham to Hadnall only 6 miles north of Shrewsbury.

Despite such anomalies the pattern created in 1836–7 endured. It was modified only slightly, as far as Shropshire was concerned, in 1854 when the dissolved Whitchurch parochial incorporation was merged in the new Whitchurch union, to which an extensive tract of Cheshire territory was assigned.[40] More significant was the dissolution of the 'wicked' Shrewsbury incorporation and its amalgamation with the Atcham union,[41] and the histories of Atcham and Shrewsbury illuminate and sharpen the main theme in the history of Shropshire poor relief during the first seventy years after 1836: the theme of contrast, and even of conflict, between town and country.[42]

From its foundation in 1836 the Atcham union was administered in strict accord with the principles which inspired the report of the Poor Law Commission (1832–4) and the resulting Act of 1834. Mere poverty gave the able-bodied no claim on the rates: destitution was their sole entitlement to public relief, the offer of the workhouse at once the test of destitution and the guarantee that relief was less eligible than the lowest independence.[43] The Atcham board's rigorous rules and its close, undeviating application of them were the work and the legacy of Sir Baldwin Leighton, its first chairman (1836–71).[44] Throughout the century and beyond the union's rate of pauperism was by far the lowest in Shropshire, and by the early 20th century Atcham was famed for its 'unique' place in poor-law history.[45]

The Shrewsbury incorporation provides a sharp contrast. Administration of out-relief had been decentralized in 1826;[46] from that time it devolved on the select vestrymen of the six parishes, the incorporation directors controlling only the house of industry. By the 1850s and 1860s neither the level of out-relief[47] nor the bickerings which marked the administration of the house[48] can have impressed the Poor Law Board favourably. The high level of out-relief indeed persisted despite the parishes' agreement to give effect to the Board's prohibitory order in 1850 and was, no doubt with much justification, attributed to the corruption of Shrewsbury politics. In 1869–70 local pressures to merge Shrewsbury and Atcham, encouraged by the Poor Law Board, were naturally resisted by an 'old guard' among the Shrewsbury directors and also by those who feared that the probity of the Atcham administration would be infected by Shrewsbury standards.[49] Prominent among the latter was Leighton, critical of urban guardians' methods of business and seeing the influence of the country gentlemen as the best guarantee of the purity and economy of local government.[50]

Shrewsbury was in fact dissolved by a coup which took place in 1871 a few months after Leighton's death. When it was merged with Atcham, the rural guardians swamped those from Shrewsbury and out-relief was virtually eliminated within a few years. In the 1890s the rural guardians remained keenly aware of the importance of preserving

[40] S.R.O. 131/9, 17 Nov. 1854; *P.O. Dir. Salop.* (1856), 143.

[41] *R. Com. on Poor Laws, App. XVII*, 195.

[42] Walsh, 'Poor Laws in Salop. 1820–1855', 381–2.

[43] W. Chance, *Our Treatment of the Poor* [1899], 9–60; Bowen-Jones, *Progress of Atcham Union*, 6. Cf. S. and B. Webb, *Eng. Poor Law Policy* (1910), 11; *Eng. Hist. Doc. 1833–1874*, ed. G. M. Young and W. D. Handcock (1956), pp. 697–9.

[44] See p. 140 and sources cited ibid. n. 99.

[45] 224 *Parl. Deb.* 3rd ser. 1788–9, 1804; Bowen-Jones, *Progress of Atcham Union*, 19 sqq.; *R. Com. on Poor*

Laws, *App. XVII*, 195, 208; Chance, *Our Treatment of the Poor*, 17–18.

[46] V. J. Walsh, 'Old and New Poor Laws in Salop. 1820–1870', *Midland Hist.* ii. 231.

[47] *R. Com. on Poor Laws, App. XVII*, 195.

[48] i.e. 1861–5: S.R.O. 248/22. The ho.'s admin. had been considerably improved in the 1840s and earlier 1850s: *Midland Hist.* ii. 231–2; Walsh, 'Poor Laws in Salop. 1820–1855', 231–5.

[49] *R. Com. on Poor Laws, App. XVII*, 195; Walsh, 'Poor Laws in Salop. 1820–1855', 323; below, pp. 325, 353.

[50] *T.S.A.S.* lix. 151; above, pp. 141–2.

their majority (33 to 19 in 1890) over the Shrewsbury guardians whenever proposals to increase the borough guardians were mooted. The Atcham policies thus prevailed,[51] though only, according to one Shrewsbury guardian in 1907, at the cost of 'lingering destitution' throughout the union.[52] By then, to judge from the evidence to the Royal Commission on the Poor Laws (1905–9), the memory of Leighton's strong chairmanship was still green, and throughout the county the prestige of his name and of the Atcham policy still prevailed. Among the Shropshire guardians to give evidence the gentry, clergy, and substantial farmers were all strongly opposed to out-relief in principle.[53]

In the early years of the 20th century local supervision of poor-law administration in the county still fell to the traditional rulers of the Shropshire countryside.[54] It had done so from the earliest years despite the fact that the 1834 Act was a Whig measure, the Shropshire squirearchy overwhelmingly Tory.[55] At the boards of guardians, as at quarter sessions,[56] politics were almost invariably[57] set aside[58] and the landowning magisterial class acquired a commitment to the new Poor Law. At quarter sessions magistrate-guardians spoke up for the unions' policies whenever necessary,[59] reminding the court from time to time how great a share of local expenditure was controlled by the unions.[60] In 1838 T. W. Wylde Browne had declined the chair of the Bridgnorth guardians because 'the commissioners in London had too great power over the chairman',[61] but his refusal and the resentment of reduced power which it implied[62] seem to have been unusual in Shropshire. For seventy years the landed classes and the clergy had virtually monopolized the union chairmanships[63] and, since few of them seem to have been mere figureheads,[64] the resulting influence over administrative policy.[65]

That state of affairs did not long outlast the 19th century. In the county's industrial areas indeed out-relief had long been administered more liberally than in the rural areas, even under chairmen like W. Layton Lowndes (Madeley, 1862–79) who revered the Atcham policy.[66] By about 1900 changes were apparent even in Atcham, where no Shrewsbury guardian could be elected without a prior commitment to out-relief,

---

[51] *R. Com. on Poor Laws, App. XVII*, 195 (describing the events of July 1871); Bowen-Jones, *Progress of Atcham Union*, 23, 28–33.

[52] *R. Com. on Poor Laws, App. VII* [Cd. 5035], pp. 89–90 (1910), xlvii.

[53] Ibid. 88–113, 120–33, 137–78; *App. XVII*, 210–29.

[54] In 1905 identifiable landowners and clergy seem to have chaired all the Salop. bds. except Madeley, Oswestry, and Wellington: *Kelly's Dir. Salop.* (1905). Cf. F. M. L. Thompson, *Eng. Landed Society in Nineteenth Cent.* (1963), 288–9.

[55] Opposition to the new poor law was long maintained by the *Shropshire Conservative* (see e.g. issues of 6 Jan. 1844; 19 Sept. 1846), but the paper probably carried little weight with the squires (below, p. 313).

[56] See pp. 141, 155.

[57] W. Wolryche Whitmore's resignation of the Bridgnorth chair in 1838 perhaps resulted from political intrigues on the bd., but Bridgnorth was 'torn by politics' to an unusual degree and the affair was complicated by the fact that the Whig Whitmore's Tory bro.-in-law, A. F. Sparkes, was clk.: corresp. with Whitmore-Jones fam. of Pensax (Worcs.) and Chastleton (Oxon.), Jan.-Apr. 1838 (*penes* Dr. J. F. A. Mason, on loan from the late A. Clutton-Brock of Chastleton). Whitmore evidently remained influential in the union (see the attack on him in *Shropshire Conservative*, 5 June 1841) and in the affairs of the farm (district union) sch. at Quatt (see e.g. *Corresp. of Ld. Overstone*, ed. D. P. O'Brien (1971), ii. 658), founded 1837 (J. C. Symons, *Dist. Labour Schools*

(1856; pamphlet *penes* the late G. C. Wolryche-Whitmore); *Quarterly Review*, cx. 492–4).

[58] Wolryche Whitmore thought it of 'paramount importance' that politics be banished from the bd.: Whitmore-Jones corresp., Whitmore to Sparkes, 7 Feb. 1838.

[59] See p. 161.

[60] *Shrews. Chron.* 9 Apr. 1886 (Salwey's remarks, implying that the Salop. unions' expenditure was thrice that of q. sess.).

[61] Whitmore-Jones corresp., Wolryche Whitmore to J. H. Whitmore-Jones, 3 Apr. 1838.

[62] Cf. P. Dunkley, 'The landed interest and the New Poor Law: a critical note', *E.H.R.* lxxxviii. 837–8.

[63] Based on lists of chmn. (to 1930) of Atcham, Clun, Drayton, Madeley, Newport, Ch. Stretton, and Wellington unions, and of Oswestry incorporation, compiled from guardians' min. bks. in S.R.O.

[64] The Whig John Cotes was perhaps an exception: he was chmn. of the Newport guardians 1836–52 but rarely attended the bd.: S.R.O. 77/50–1.

[65] When the co. and all but 2 unions adopted the way-ticket system of vagrant relief in Apr. 1883 (above, p. 146) Oswestry incorporation deferred consideration of the subject because its chmn., the Revd. F. P. Wilkinson, was out of the country (*Shrews. Chron.* 19 Oct. 1883); it joined only next yr. (ibid. 11 Apr. 1884).

[66] Loton Hall MSS., vol. of Sir Baldwyn Leighton's 'Speeches & Pamphlets on Agriculture, Labour &c.', art. on guardians' conference at Malvern from *Worc. Herald*, dated 13 May 1871.

and out-relief was in fact increasing.[67] Whatever changes were taking place in poor-law administration, however, there was a general and growing feeling by the early years of the 20th century that the unions had outlived their usefulness, as the government conferred new public-assistance responsibilities on other local authorities and agencies. Improvements were made to the guardians' services, especially in respect of pauper children and sick,[68] but in general the guardians' most prominent defenders were those who still revered the obsolete[69] principles of 1834.[70] In Shropshire, as those principles found fewer adherents,[71] poor-law administration was yielded up by the gentry and clergy. In 1909 Col. S. T. H. Burne resigned the chair of the Newport board, unable after a 22-year chairmanship to adapt to 'the new manner and methods which are being introduced'.[72] The changes were being widely felt. In the industrial Madeley and Wellington unions the resignations of Col. J. A. Anstice (1903)[73] and H. H. France-Hayhurst (1904)[74] seem to mark the end of the domination of those boards by the owners of industrial, commercial, and landed wealth,[75] and the Madeley chair was filled by a Labour councillor from 1918 to 1930.[76] In Oswestry the even earlier victory of a leading tenant farmer over an incumbent chairman supported by local landowners and clergy[77] and in Atcham the election of the board's first (and last) Shrewsbury chairman in 1910[78] seem indicative of the same changes.

Despite recommendations of their abolition in 1909[79] and 1918,[80] however, the unions lingered on until 1930, obstacles to local-government unification[81] and increasingly uneconomic anachronisms. During that time the removal of pauper children from the Shropshire workhouses was partly successful. Only the Atcham union provided 'scattered homes' before the retention of children in workhouses became illegal in 1913:[82] two boys' homes were opened in 1908[83] and Besford House in 1911.[84] Wellington union isolated the children's section from the rest of the workhouse in 1913–14 and later transferred the children elsewhere.[85] The other Shropshire unions, less urban and less populous, could board their children with Atcham and Wellington, and some did so;[86] some children, however, remained in the workhouses.[87] Attempts were also made to tackle vagrancy in these years, though without success. The way-ticket system had no better prospects in 1912 than it had thirty years before, and vagrancy remained an intractable problem, though it gave rise to the annual Shropshire Poor Law Conference, founded in 1912,[88] and to its offshoot the Shropshire Joint Vagrancy Committee, formed in 1925.[89]

[67] *R. Com. on Poor Laws, App. VII*, 90, 104–5; *App. XVII*, 197.

[68] *Rep. on Transfer of Functions of Poor Law Authorities in Eng. and Wales* [Cd. 8917], pp. 3–4, H.C. (1917–18), xviii.

[69] The judgement (*R. Com. on Poor Laws, App. XVII*, 368–9) of Thos. Jones, special investigator in Salop. in 1907 and later a distinguished public servant (*D.N.B.* 1951–60).

[70] e.g. Sir Wm. Chance: *Who Was Who, 1929–40*, 237.

[71] See e.g. sources cited above n. 53 (esp. the evid. of J. K. Morris, J. Blud, J. Hood, and R. Pearson).

[72] S.R.O. 77/67, pp. 330, 335.

[73] Chmn. since 1879: S.R.O. 134/8, p. 94; /12, pp. 414–19. Anstice's resignation too was over a policy issue.

[74] Chmn. 1896 and 1901–4: S.R.O. 77/15, p. 396; /17, p. 9; S.R.O. 88/4, pp. 132, 210, 218.

[75] Madeley's five 19th-cent. chmn. comprised two Anstices, a Darby, Geo. Pritchard (the banker: S.R.O. 1190, box 81, 'Pritchard Fam. Memoranda', etc.), and W. Layton Lowndes (above, pp. 141–2, 145). Wellington was chaired by farmers from the north of the union 1838–83, thereafter to 1891 by Ric. Groom (above, p. 166 and n. 57) of Dothill Pk., a timber merchant.

[76] R. A. Rhodes: S.R.O. 134/17, p. 63; /19, p. 180.

[77] John Richards (chmn. 1897–8, 1901–10): S.R.O. 122/10, p. 589; /11, pp. 31, 515; /12 *passim*.

[78] Wm. Adams, a Shrews. chemist: S.R.O. 13/14, p. 25; /18, p. 82; *Shrews. Chron.* 10 Dec. 1943 (obit.).

[79] R. C. K. Ensor, *Eng. 1870–1914* (1936), 517.

[80] P. B. Johnson, *Land Fit for Heroes* (Chicago, 1968), 47–8, 80–5.

[81] Well indicated by Neville Chamberlain (223 *Parl. Deb.* 5th ser. 65 sqq.), whose father had wished to see the guardians' functions transferred to co. councils in 1888.

[82] Ivy Pinchbeck and Margaret Hewitt, *Children in Eng. Society*, ii (1973), 540–1. Boarding out had been sanctioned since 1870 and was later encouraged: ibid. 522–3, 540–1.

[83] *Kelly's Dir. Salop.* (1909), 28.

[84] *Shrews. Chron.* 8 Sept. 1911.

[85] S.R.O. 77/19, pp. 17, 31–2, 70–1, 177–8, 301; /20, pp. 139–40, 146–7, 154, 220; /21, p. 6.

[86] See e.g. ibid. /20, p. 91.   [87] See p. 215.

[88] On the initiative of Oswestry incorporation: S.R.O. 77/68, pp. 239, 325; *Shrews. Chron.* 26 June 1912; above, p. 146.

[89] S.R.O. 77/71, p. 258; *Shrews. Chron.* 24 July, 7 Aug. 1925.

When Chamberlain's reform proposals [90] were published in 1928 the county news-paper pointed out that much the most 'contentious' of the proposals was the transfer of rural highways from the district to the county councils. The abolition of the guardians and their too numerous, under-occupied workhouses was seen as necessary for greater efficiency and economy in 'institutional treatment',[91] and at the end the Shropshire guardians found few arguments in their own behalf. W. H. Smith's condemnation of the 1929 Act as 'one of the most ridiculous pieces of legislation that I remember in my time'[92] embodies a natural historic sentiment, though one surprising in a former leading county councillor.[93] In 1930 many of the former guardians found, as had been predicted, 'new scope for their energies'[94] on the county council's guardians committees.[95] The Poor Law, however, with its essential discrimination against the destitute, was not abolished[96] until 1948, nor, it seems likely, did many of that generation of destitute old, sick, and feeble-minded live to see much improvement to their surroundings as a result of the transformation of the guardians' workhouses into the county council's public-assistance institutions.[97]

The School Boards 1872–1903

The 1870 Elementary Education Act[98] inaugurated developments of the greatest significance for local government when, for the first time, it established rate-financed education in England and Wales, for in the succeeding century education became by far the greatest object of local-government expenditure.[99] Unlike the 1834 Poor Law Amendment Act, however, the 1870 Act, which made elementary education universally available, established no universal system of local authorities; that developed only over the following decade as Lord Sandon's 1876 Elementary Education Act[1] and Mundella's Act of 1880[2] made elementary education compulsory and school attendance committees were set up wherever there was no school board. The dual character of the local elementary education authorities stemmed primarily from sectarian rivalries, but their universal existence[3] eased the transfer of elementary education in 1902–3 almost everywhere in rural England to the county councils. Indeed the threat of absorption by the county councils, real or imagined, had hung over the school boards ever since 1888–9 and in their last years the boards were unpopular, in educational circles at least.[4] As a result of that transfer local education authorities were at last created which had, or acquired, the powers to mount a direct attack on the many chronic problems affecting rural elementary education. In Shropshire, however, the attack was mounted in earnest only during the years between the two world wars.[5]

The availability of government grants from 1833[6] does not alter the fact that elementary education before 1870 is the story of parochial effort.[7] In Shropshire that

[90] *Proposals for Reform in Local Govt.* [Cmd. 3134], H.C. (1928), xix.

[91] *Shrews. Chron.* 13 July 1928.

[92] Ibid. 28 June 1929. He was chmn. of the Whitchurch guardians.

[93] See p. 201. [94] *Shrews. Chron.* 13 July 1928.

[95] Ibid. 4 Apr. 1930 (electn. of Ludlow guardians cttee.). For the cttees. see ibid. 2 Aug. 1929.

[96] 223 *Parl. Deb.* 5th ser. 117–19.

[97] National Assistance Act, 1948, 11 & 12 Geo. VI, c. 29, s.1; below, p. 218.

[98] 33 & 34 Vic. c. 75.

[99] E. E. Rich, *The Education Act, 1870: A study of public opinion* (1970), 99, 103.

[1] 39 & 40 Vic. c. 79. [2] 43 & 44 Vic. c. 23.

[3] See below, n. 17.

[4] J. W. Adamson, *Eng. Education, 1789–1902* (1930), 456–7, 467–8; T. D. M. Jones, 'Development of Educa-

tional Provision in the Rural Co. of Salop. between 1870 and 1914 . . .' (Keele Univ. M.A. thesis, 1969), 95–6; P. R. Sharp, 'The Entry of Co. Councils into Educational Admin., 1889', *Jnl. of Educ. Admin. and Hist.* i. 14, 16–18; cf. below, p. 177 and n. 41. Secondary-education powers were also conferred by the 1902 Act (below, p. 199) which avoided the creation of special local authorities as recommended by the otherwise influential Bryce Commission (1894–5).

[5] Jones, 'Educ. Provision in Salop.', 86–8; below, pp. 201–2. Improvement of rural housing, equally vital to education, was long delayed: below, pp. 208–9.

[6] *Eng. Hist. Doc. 1833–1874*, ed. Young and Handcock, p. 829.

[7] As such its detailed treatment has been reserved for the parish articles of this *Hist.* This section (pp. 174–7) and pp. 198–207, below, constitute the general treatment of (rate-supported) education foreseen in *V.C.H. Salop.* ii. 141.

story is not without its heroes. Gifted boys of the working, or even pauper, classes occasionally rose through education to eminence. Such were Samuel Lee (1783–1852), the Cambridge professor educated at Longnor charity school,[8] and William Farr, F.R.S.,[9] a pauper apprenticed[10] to the founder of Dorrington charity school.[11] Individual successes apart, however, parochial efforts to provide elementary education were unsatisfactory: necessarily intermittent,[12] unco-ordinated, and largely unsupervised. Generally farmers and labourers alike were indifferent, even hostile, to elementary education.[13] In 1870 scarcely half of Shropshire's elementary schools were in receipt of the state grant, and ten years earlier the proportion had been even lower. Educational deprivation was more acute in the rural south of the county than in the more populous north, over two thirds of the Shropshire parishes and townships without a school being south of the Severn.[14]

The 1870 Act, even while it was yet passing through Parliament as a Bill, improved those conditions by stimulating voluntary effort among Shropshire churchmen and landowners. They were moved both by a desire to retain control of religious instruction and by a 'dread of rates' so great that, as the government inspector reported, many 'were ready to spend more in subscriptions than the rate would have come to . . . like the man who cut his throat through fear of dying'.[15] So successful was the voluntary effort that two years after the passing of the Act the only school board formed in the county was that at Wellington (1872).[16] In fact school boards were few in Shropshire: by 1902, the year before their dissolution, there were only 22 and only Shrewsbury, with a population of 26,967, and Wellington (12,339) were of any size; sixteen boards served districts with populations of less than 1,000.[17] Between them the boards had built or acquired fewer than 40 elementary schools.[18]

Twelve of the boards were formed compulsorily[19] but most, whether so formed or not, were elected with little fuss, at worst being accepted as a painful necessity.[20] The gentry and clergy seem to have been able to play a leading part in the affairs of the boards, even of the urban boards, whenever they were inclined to do so. Thus in its last twelve years the Shrewsbury board was chaired by Maj.-Gen. the Hon. W. H. Herbert and G. Butler Lloyd of Shelton Hall, successive vice-chairmen including Canon S. W. Allen, administrator of the Roman Catholic cathedral, and Archdeacon Maude. Other board members in those years included the Revd. Thomas Auden, Edward Corbett, Sir Lovelace Stamer, suffragan bishop of Shrewsbury, and the Revd. A. J. Moriarty, nephew of the Roman Catholic Bishop Allen. The gentry even served as board officials on occasion: in its last years the Shrewsbury board's treasurer was R. A. Slaney Eyton of Walford,[21] and in 1902 W. E. M. Hulton-Harrop, of Lythwood Hall, was actually clerk of the Ratlinghope board, such posts elsewhere

[8] D.N.B.; Shropshire Mag. June 1958, 30; J. and J. A. Venn, Al. Cantab. . . . 1752–1900, iv. 133; Alice M. Lee, A Scholar of a Past Generation . . . (1896).

[9] D.N.B.; J. M. Eyler, 'Wm. Farr on the Cholera: The Sanitarian's Disease Theory and the Statistician's Method', Jnl. of Hist. of Medicine and Allied Sciences, xxviii. 79–100.

[10] S.R.O. 1977/7/1882. Farr had been bap. in Kenley in 1807: S.P.R. Lich. ii(4), pp. iv, 56.

[11] Jos. Pryce: V.C.H. Salop. viii. 57.

[12] For the various ways in which sch. endowments and bldgs. could be lost and misappropriated see J. P. Dodd, 'Rural Educ. in Salop. in the Nineteenth Cent.' (Birm. Univ. M.A. thesis, 1958), chap. 3.

[13] See e.g. ibid. 95–6; Jones, 'Educ. Provision in Salop.', 22–6, 65–6.

[14] Dodd, op. cit. 127–30; Jones, op. cit. 10–11.

[15] Voluntary rates were also raised.

[16] Jones, op. cit. 11–14. The proportion of schs. receiving the govt. grant had also increased by 1872: ibid. 10–11.

[17] List of Sch. Bds. and Sch. Attendance Cttees. in Eng. and Wales, 1st Jan. 1902 [Cd. 1038], p. 75, H.C. (1902), lxxix. In 1901 over two thirds of the co.'s pop. lived under the jurisdiction of sch. attendance cttees., less than a third under the bds.: Jones, op. cit. 28.

[18] Cf. the lists in Jones, op. cit., App. B(2) (list of bd. schs. in 1900); S.C.C. Mins. 1903–4, 124 (list of co.-council schs. 1903, which does not include the former bd. schs. transferred to Shrews. boro.).

[19] Source cited above, n. 17.

[20] Jones, op. cit. 14–15.

[21] Resumé of Work of Sch. Bd. for Boro. of Shrews. 1890–93; 1893–96; 1899–1902 (copies in S.R.O. 3106/9/1–3). Cf. Jones, op. cit. 94–5, calling Allen an 'unenthusiastic administrator' of educational law.

being filled, like the clerkships of most statutory authorities, by solicitors.[22] Sectarian disputes were few, with one or two notable exceptions. In 1871 Pontesbury enthusiasts for a school board, including dissenters and miners in the parish, attempted to establish one by a coup, but local churchmen defeated it. In its early years the Wrockwardine Wood board, formed in 1875, was disrupted by an Anglican minority until, in January 1878, the board elections produced an Anglican victory, a resolution of disputes, and the establishment of a school.[23]

If denominational rivalry was rare, probably owing to the overwhelming influence of the Church of England,[24] parochialism by contrast was widespread and characteristic of the managements of board and voluntary schools alike. The only serious attempt at co-operation between the school boards was initiated in 1882. The Wellington board proposed the establishment of a joint truant industrial school to 7 of the larger Shropshire boards and to 3 Staffordshire boards, but no progress was made and no similar effort was ever repeated.[25] In 1890–1 a Lichfield diocesan scheme to combine church schools in the archdeaconry of Salop was initiated, but by 1896 it had failed in the face of rural inertia and parochialism. The failure was the more notable in so far as the 1890s saw the financial position of the voluntary schools worsen with the abolition of school fees (1891) and the imposition of stricter regulations concerning school buildings.[26]

Generally the real contrasts between elementary schools were those between town and country; the formal distinction between board and voluntary schools counted for less. In Shropshire the achievements of the urban schools seem large only beside the record of the rural ones; in themselves they were modest. No higher-grade school evolved under any Shropshire board, the only one in the county being the Lancasterian school in Shrewsbury.[27] Nevertheless the Shrewsbury and Wellington boards established central cookery kitchens, and in Wellington girls were taught practical laundry work.[28] The Shrewsbury board showed a progressiveness unusual in Shropshire when it appointed a permanent full-time school medical officer in 1901.[29] By the 1890s Wellington school attendance committee seems to have been the only Shropshire local education authority to have adopted standard VI as the leaving standard; two other districts had adopted standard V, but in most of the county children of 12–13 were in standard III and immediately they reached standard IV, the legal minimum, they left school.[30]

In the great urban centres of England the schools were better able to expand their curricula, attract higher government grants, and retain better qualified teachers. The prestige of their school boards and the commitment of significant numbers of board members to secular education and educational expansion were their chief advantages.[31] In Shropshire, however, voluntary schools preponderated, and those who believed in them, and in the associated economical policy,[32] predominated even on the urban boards.[33] In the Shropshire countryside no signs of vigour can be detected: chronic indifference to education characterized both school managements and the labourers for whose children the schools were provided. The most signal example of apathy is provided by a rural board. The indifference to its duties of the Mainstone board,

[22] Source cited above, n. 17.
[23] Jones, op. cit. 15–18.
[24] Cf. ibid. 48.
[25] Ibid. 96–7. There were then 16 Salop. bds.: ibid., App. B(1).
[26] Ibid. 9–10, 88–91; D.N.B. 1922–30, sub Acland, Sir Art. Herb. Dyke.
[27] Jones, op. cit. 73–8.
[28] Ibid. 72–3.
[29] Ibid. 88.

[30] Ibid. 69. By the 1890s standard V or above had been adopted in most cos. Cf. V.C.H. Wilts. v. 355.
[31] Jones, op. cit. 18–19, 33–48, 62–4, 73–4; Adamson, Eng. Educ. 1789–1902, 465 (referring to the 1890s). Cf. D. Rubinstein, 'Socialization and the London Sch. Bd. 1870–1904', Popular education and socialization in the nineteenth cent. ed. P. McCann (1977), 231–64.
[32] Cf. Rubinstein, op. cit. 240–1.
[33] See e.g. above, p. 175 and n. 21.

SIR GEORGE BLOUNT (d. 1581)
Magistrate, M.P., chantry
commissioner

FRANCIS NEWPORT, EARL OF BRADFORD
(d. 1708)
Lieutenant 1660–87 and 1689–1704, Whig

SIR HENRY EDWARDES, BT. (d. 1767)
Leading magistrate, Whig

HENRY ARTHUR HERBERT, EARL OF POWIS
(d. 1772)
Lieutenant 1735–60 and 1764–72,
leader of the Shropshire Whigs

SIR BALDWIN LEIGHTON, BT. (d. 1871)
Chairman of quarter sessions
1855–71, M.P.

ROWLAND HILL, VISCOUNT HILL
(d. 1875)
Lieutenant 1845–75

ALFRED SALWEY (d. 1902)
Chairman of quarter sessions 1883–9
and of the county council 1889–93

EDMUND CRESSWELL PEELE (d. 1911)
Clerk of the peace 1886–1911,
'lord high everything else'

first elected in 1875, compelled the appointment in 1880 of a professional board which quickly provided a school and handed it over to an elected board in 1882.[34] Mainstone was exceptional. The malign influences of apathy were generally more insidious, and may be detected in the poor attendance record of rural schools. To some extent rural absenteeism was due to the fact that the law, progressively tightened up for urban areas, remained much more permissive in the countryside.[35] Even clear infractions of the law, however, were rarely brought to book. Rural school-attendance officers had large areas and, normally, other occupations, while rural labourers, as they became poorer in the last years of the century, became more dependent on their children's casual earnings. Magistrates, sometimes through leniency, were lax in the discharge of their duties and loth to convict.[36] In 1867 one prominent Shropshire magistrate, Edward Corbett, claimed to the Children's Employment Commission that agricultural labourers' children could not have attendance forced upon them.[37] Twenty years later, when compulsory attendance had become the law, the rector of Hopesay told the Cross Commission that strict construction of the law in a scattered farming community would cause open rebellion.[38]

In the Shropshire countryside educational improvement was imperceptibly slow after the great effort to provide extra voluntary-school places in 1870, and educational progress before 1903 was limited either by the parochial views of those to whom the management of elementary schools was confided or by the insanitary condition of rural cottages and schools, blighting the work of pupils and teachers alike.[39] At the turn of the century badly clothed country children from insanitary cottages still walked long distances to school. Tired, and sometimes cold and wet, they sat in poor, even if recently improved, classrooms. Not surprisingly they had a characteristic catarrhal condition common to the county's rural population. The schools had only recently begun to close voluntarily to forestall the epidemics of scarlet fever, diphtheria, and measles which they had earlier been accused of fomenting.[40] The country child's problems were not primarily educational but social: those of health, housing, and transport. In 1903 elementary schools, except those in Shrewsbury,[41] passed to the county council,[42] an authority which possessed, or eventually acquired, the powers to act in those fields.[43]

Unification: the Sanitary Authorities, Highway Boards, and District Councils

No single piece of legislation between 1834 and 1888 did more to unify English local government than the Public Health Act of 1872.[44] The origins of the movement for public health and sanitary reform[45] were urban, as were, accordingly, the first sanitary districts, created under the 1848 Public Health Act[46] or the 1858 Local Government Act.[47] By 1888–9 the Shropshire urban sanitary districts numbered ten: the municipal boroughs of Bishop's Castle, Bridgnorth, Ludlow, Oswestry, Shrewsbury, and Much Wenlock,[48] and the districts of Dawley, Ellesmere, Newport, Wellington, and Whitchurch and Dodington.[49] To the urban districts the 1872 Act

[34] Jones, op. cit. 18. [35] Ibid. 22–8.
[36] Ibid. 29–31. [37] Dodd, op. cit. 136–7.
[38] Jones, op. cit. 28–30.
[39] Ibid. 66–8. [40] Ibid. 84–8.
[41] See S.R.O. 3106/4–5. In 1900 there were 5 schs. under the jurisdiction of the Shrews. bd., 2 of them former voluntary schs.: Jones, op. cit., App. B(2).
[42] S.C.C. Mins. 1903–4, 118–24.
[43] See pp. 208–10.
[44] 35 & 36 Vic. c. 79. See S. and B. Webb, Story of the King's Highway (1913), 212.

[45] In which one Salop. J.P. and M.P., R. A. Slaney, was very prominent: D.N.B.; Eng. Hist. Doc. 1833–1874, ed. Young and Handcock, p. 753. See also Loton Hall MSS., Sir B. Leighton's diary, 19 May 1862.
[46] 11 & 12 Vic. c. 63.
[47] 21 & 22 Vic. c. 98.
[48] Cr. 1889, it absorbed the earlier U.S.D.s of Broseley, Madeley, and Much Wenlock and part of Madeley R.S.D.
[49] V.C.H. Salop. ii. 204, 229; Rep. Boundary Com. Eng. and Wales, H.C. 360, map facing p. 307 (1888), li.

had added rural districts so that every part of the country was assigned to a sanitary district. The rural sanitary districts were to coincide with the poor-law unions after any urban sanitary districts had been left out, and the rural sanitary authorities were to be the boards of guardians.[50] The poor-law authorities thus began to develop into general-purpose local authorities, and six years later that progress was advanced by another Act,[51] which enjoined the county courts of quarter sessions to arrange for the coincidence of the highway districts with newer rural sanitary districts as far as was practicable.[52] This policy the Shropshire magistrates had already followed for many years, and in 1878 it was accordingly reported to the court that 'no very extensive change' was necessary to comply with the new legislation.[53]

The long-established Shropshire practice of administering highways and sanitary affairs within coincident territorial limits meant that the county could adjust quickly and easily to the provisions of the 1894 Local Government Act (coming into force in 1895)[54] whereby both rural sanitary and highway districts were abolished, and their responsibilities, along with some of the guardians' general administrative responsibilities,[55] conferred on the new urban and rural district authorities. The work of the Shropshire district authorities cannot be fully examined here,[56] though as an example of the developing relationship between the county and the pre-1895 authorities the story of the Shropshire highway boards may be told.

The 1862 Highway Act[57] passed at a time when centralizing, bureaucratic measures were widely disliked. Opposition to the sanitary legislation of the 1840s[58] and the activities of the Anti-Centralisation Union in the 1850s[59] had produced an atmosphere unfavourable to compulsory legislation.[60] Unlike the 1834 Poor Law Amendment Act, therefore, the 1862 Act was an enabling measure only: no government commissioners were appointed to cover the country with new highway authorities; instead county courts of quarter sessions were merely empowered to unite parishes and townships into highway districts.

There was, not surprisingly, much opposition in Shropshire both to the adoption of the Act in the first instance and later to the detail of district formation. In 1880–1 moreover one highway district was dissolved by quarter sessions on the insistence of its ratepayers. During the initial debates in court (1862–3) magistrates like T. C. Whitmore, Uvedale Corbett, and T. C. Eyton opposed the measure as representatives both of their own districts' known opposition to the Act and also of the vast majority of those whose views had been canvassed.[61] In spite of those views, however, the Act was adopted, though over the next few years the frequency of orders reassigning places to different districts,[62] and the debates on those orders,[63] well illustrate the parochial pressures to which the magistrates were subject. More clearly than any other branch of local government, highway administration shows how Shropshire quarter sessions, though composed of a hereditary landowning class, was responsive to local feeling, and yet willing to give leadership to the localities.

In 1880 Egerton Harding moved the dissolution of the Market Drayton highway

[50] Since 1846 the rural authority under the Nuisances Removal Act, 1846, 9 & 10 Vic. c. 96, etc.: *T.S.A.S.* lix. 169.
[51] Highways and Locomotives (Amendment) Act, 1878, 41 & 42 Vic. c. 77, s. 3.
[52] The Act (s. 4) also provided for the merging of rural sanitary and highway authorities under certain conditions.
[53] *Eddowes's Jnl.* 1 Jan. 1879.
[54] 56 & 57 Vic. c. 73.
[55] e.g. collection of rates.
[56] Where their story impinges on that of the county authority, however, notice has been taken of the district

authorities: see e.g. below, pp. 194, 207. For an official hist. of one authority see *Dawley U.D.C., A Story 1966–1974* (copy in S.R.O. 3120/1).
[57] 25 & 26 Vic. c. 61.
[58] Lubenow, *Politics of Govt. Growth*, 84 sqq.
[59] Ibid. 90.
[60] See q. sess. debate reported in *Eddowes's Jnl.* 15 Oct. 1862 (ref. to withdrawal of a compulsory Highway Bill of Ld. Derby's 1858–9).
[61] Ibid. 15 Oct. 1862; 7 Jan., 18 Mar. 1863.
[62] *Orders of Q. Sess.* iv, pp. xviii, 151.
[63] Source cited above, p. 143, n. 60.

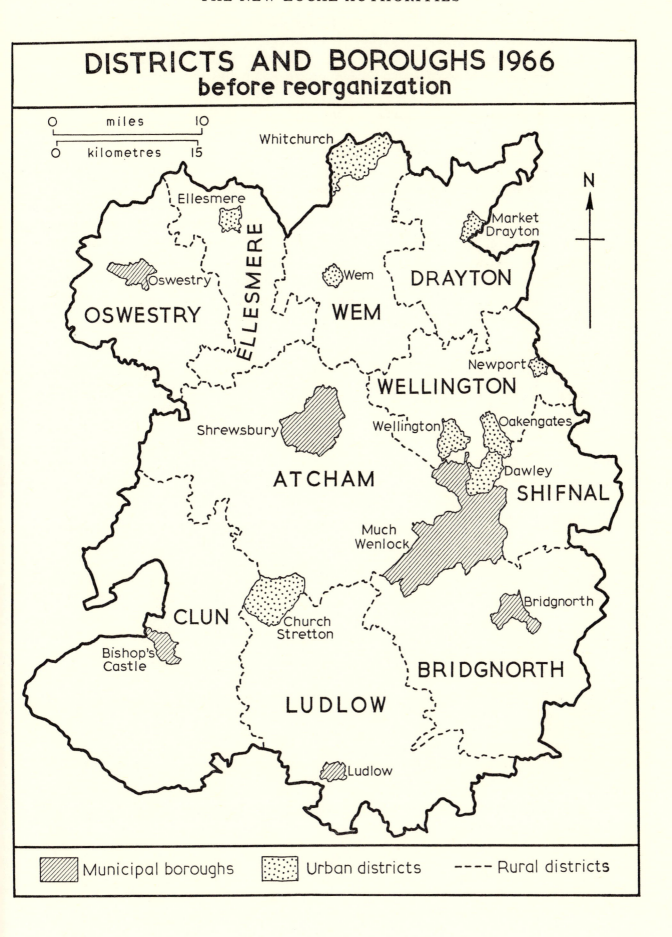

DISTRICTS AND BOROUGHS 1966
before reorganization

miles

kilometres

Whitchurch

Ellesmere

ELLESMERE

Market Drayton

Wem

DRAYTON

Oswestry

OSWESTRY

WEM

Newport

WELLINGTON

Shrewsbury

Wellington

Oakengates

Dawley

ATCHAM

SHIFNAL

Much Wenlock

Bridgnorth

CLUN

Church Stretton

Bishop's Castle

BRIDGNORTH

LUDLOW

Ludlow

N

Municipal boroughs   Urban districts   ---- Rural districts

board under whose administration costs had increased; emphasizing to quarter sessions that it was 'solely because they had their pockets touched' that the ratepayers had 'urgently requested' him to do so, he caused great laughter and applause in court when he claimed that 'if he could not return home and give them some hopes of redress, he did not know what his reception might be'.[64] The Drayton board was dissolved next year[65] and thereafter until 1895 the highway authorities were the parishes and townships of north-east Shropshire[66] acting under the 1835 Highway Act.[67] Elsewhere in the county, however, the new authorities survived. The immediate adoption of the 1862 Act in 1862–3 had been largely due to the influence of Sir Baldwin Leighton, chairman of quarter sessions.[68] Leighton's success in reducing the poor-rates of the Atcham union by a thorough application of the principles of the 1834 legislation[69] had convinced him that similar benefits were to be expected from the formation of unions for highway administration.[70] He had also seen the creation of highway districts by quarter sessions as an enhancement of the influence already exercised by the landed gentry over the existing highway authorities.[71] One effect of that influence in the hands of his successors in quarter sessions was to preserve the new authorities largely intact until their disappearance in the unification of 1895.

[64] S.R.O., q. sess. rec., box 30, cuttings bk. 1877–82, 28 June, 18 Oct. 1880.
[65] Orders of Q. Sess. iv. 250, 252.
[66] S.R.O. 62/1. [67] 5 & 6 Wm. IV, c. 50.
[68] Sir B. Leighton, 'Life of Sir B. Leighton' (S.R.O. 783, parcel 194), p. 72.
[69] See p. 171.
[70] Eddowes's Jnl. 15 Oct. 1862; 7 Jan. 1863.
[71] 156 Parl. Deb. 3rd ser. 249–50 (his maiden speech: Loton Hall MSS., Sir B. Leighton's diary, 28 Jan. 1860).

THE COUNTY COUNCIL
1889-1974

Finance, p. 190. Roads and Bridges, p. 193. Public Protection and Licensing, p. 196. Agriculture, p. 196. Education, p. 198. Health, p. 207. Social Services for the Handicapped, the Poor, and the Homeless, p. 213. Planning, p. 219. Civil Defence and Fire Brigade, p. 221. The Shirehall, p. 222. Records, p. 222.

DURING the forty years from 1889 to 1930 county government was gradually unified under a single elected body, the county council created by the Local Government Act of 1888.[1] In 1888 the elective principle in local government was already firmly established. For half a century important sections of local administration had been entrusted by Parliament to special-purpose elected boards, each representative of, and responsible to, the ratepayers of its own small district. The creation of *ad hoc* bodies, however, eventually resulted in a tangle of overlapping boards and rating authorities. Before the passing of the 1888 Act there were widespread hopes, in Shropshire as elsewhere, that 'county boards' would be created, with responsibilities sufficiently comprehensive to restore the historic county as the principal unit of local government.[2] That did not happen at once, for many existing boards were left intact in 1889. Nevertheless the 1888 Act, in creating the county council, and the Local Government Act of 1894,[3] which created new district and parish councils, together established a simple hierarchy of authorities, to which Parliament was able by stages to entrust not only the work of the remaining *ad hoc* bodies but also such new work as it required to be done. The principal stages in that process were marked by the Education Act of 1902 and the Local Government Act of 1929. No sooner was the pattern complete, in the 1930s, than a fresh tendency towards fragmentation began, this time in favour of *ad hoc* regional agencies of government.[4]

So durable, however, was the constitutional framework established by the Acts of 1888 and 1894 that it survived the important changes wrought in the nature of local government in the following eighty years, and the full implications of those changes were only gradually perceived by members and officers. Of more immediate concern to contemporaries were the changeless round of elections and budgets, and the current influence, real or supposed, of individuals and parties. Those were matters that varied greatly from one county to another. Some councils, particularly in those counties that experienced massive urban growth, underwent painful social and political transformation between 1889 and 1974. Shropshire, however, was among the counties that experienced least urban growth.[5] There were some changes, both political and

[1] 51 & 52 Vic. c. 41. This article was written in 1973 and revised in 1974. For substantial comment and information thanks are due to Ld. Bridgeman (H.M. Lieut. 1951–70), the late Sir O. Wakeman (chmn. of co. council 1943–63), Dr. Linnie A. Hamar (chmn. of Health Cttee. 1966–74), and Messrs. N. Bennett (co. planning offr. 1945–69), L. Copplestone (co. treasurer 1950–74), the late F. G. Fawcett (co. welfare offr. 1948–68), G. C. Godber (clk. of co. council 1944–66), W. N. P. Jones (clk. of co. council 1966–74), and H. Martin Wilson (sec. for educ. 1936–65).

[2] S.R.O. 148/15, Venables C.C. newscuttings 1888–92, pp. 30–2; J. P. D. Dunbabin, 'Expectations of the new Co. Councils and their realization', *Hist. Jnl.* viii. 363 n.

[3] 56 & 57 Vic. c. 73.

[4] K. B. S. Smellie, *Hist. of Local Govt.* (1957), 117–18.

[5] J. M. Lee, *Social Leaders and Public Persons: a Study of Co. Govt. in Ches. since 1888* (1963), 215–45. Taking into account the combined circumstances of population density, housing growth rate, proportion of contested co.-council seats, proportion of rate deficiency grant, and ratios of co. roads and school children to population, the following administrative cos. were roughly comparable to Salop. in 1960: Ang., Carms., Denb., Devon, Ely, Lincs. (Kesteven), Norf., Northumb., E. Suff., W. Suff., Yorks. E.R.: ibid. 235–45. No co., however, has ever been exactly comparable with another.

social, in the composition of its county council, but they were barely perceptible against a background of local stability in which neither political nor social distinctions were of first importance.

In 1889 only sixteen of the 51 divisions represented on the new council were contested, one of the lowest proportions in the country,[6] and only two were fought on party lines.[7] Most candidates appealed to their record in public work and promised to protect the ratepayers; some had views on the future of local-government legislation; few made specific promises of action on any matter within the council's purview.[8] Of the 51 councillors returned in 1889 the private political allegiances of some 35 are readily known: 25 were Conservatives, 10 Liberals.[9] County magistrates were returned in 17 of the 35 uncontested divisions; in the 10 divisions where county magistrates faced contests, 5 were successful.[10]

To advocates of sweeping reform the new council may have seemed disappointingly familiar. The former chairman of quarter sessions, Alfred Salwey, was chairman of the council; Lord Bradford and Lord Powis, lord lieutenants of Shropshire and Montgomeryshire respectively, were elected aldermen and sat in their old seats on the bench;[11] 22 of the 51 councillors and 10 of the 17 aldermen were county magistrates, and others had family connexions with the magistracy.[12] According to Richard Stone, a radical Liberal councillor,[13] the magistrates were seeking to retain control of county government.[14] The magistrates certainly regarded themselves as a separate group; Lord Bradford seconded Salwey's election to the chair 'on behalf of the magistrates', and rival candidates for the vice-chairmanship were backed by the magistrates and the non-magistrates.[15] Salwey, however, hoped that the distinction would soon die out,[16] and it was not heard of after 1889. The number of members who were also county magistrates gradually rose, reaching 43 in 1913, but fell steadily after the First World War; by 1970 only fifteen members were on the 'active list' of justices.[17]

There was a notable continuity in the tenure of most seats. The largest number of divisions contested at one election was 27 in 1946 — fewer than half[18] and again one of the lowest proportions in England.[19] In some parts of the county seats were held for long periods by members of one family: Bishop's Castle was held by three generations of the Sykes family from 1904 to 1958; three Cambidges sat for Ruyton-XI-Towns between 1922 and 1974; and at least fifteen other divisions were similarly represented.[20]

Throughout the council's history an overwhelming majority of councillors sat as Independents, and successive chairmen insisted that party politics should play no part in the debates;[21] indeed, few local issues were felt to lend themselves to debate on political lines. The proceedings were still free of party strife in 1974.[22] The arrange-

[6] Lee, *Social Leaders*, 228.

[7] *Shrews. Chron.* 18 Jan. 1889. Party feeling in the election was negligible in some 14 co., including Herefs., Staffs., and Worcs.: *Hist. Jnl.* viii. 361.

[8] S.R.O. 148/15, Venables C.C. newscuttings 1888–92, pp. 30–2.

[9] Ibid. pp. 30–3.   [10] *Shrews. Chron.* 18 Jan. 1889.

[11] Ibid. 8 Feb. 1889. In Worcs. the peers sat by the chmn.: *Hist. Jnl.* viii. 361.

[12] *Kelly's Dir. Salop.* (1891), 251–2. Other sources suggest that 19 magistrates became councillors: *Hist. Jnl.* viii. 378.

[13] S.R.O. 148/15, Venables C.C. newscuttings 1888–92, p. 32.

[14] *Shrews. Chron.* 25 Jan. 1889.

[15] Ibid. 8 Feb. 1889. The magistrates wanted a non-magistrate and *vice versa*.

[16] Ibid.

[17] *Kelly's Dir. Salop.* (1900 and later edns.); S.C.C. *Year Bk.* 1955–71 (copies in S.R.O. 115).

[18] *Shrews. Chron.* 8 Mar. 1946. The no. of divisions was increased to 57 in 1934: S.C.C. *Year Bk. 1934–5.*

[19] Lee, *Social Leaders*, 229–30.

[20] Prees (Batkin fam.), Montford (Everall), Broseley (Weld-Forester), Lydbury (Hamar), Hadley (Hayward), Hodnet (Heber-Percy), Ellesmere (Jebb, Mainwaring), Oswestry, Western (Parry-Jones), Wombridge (Patchett), Clee Hill (Rouse-Boughton, Winder), Whitchurch (Smith), Shrewsbury, Abbey and Stone Within (Southam), Bridgnorth (Southwell), Chirbury (Wakeman), and Albrighton (Yates): S.C.C. *Year Bk.* 1889–1973.

[21] *Shrews. Chron.* 8 Feb. 1889; 22 Mar. 1901; 7 Nov. 1930.

[22] Local information (1974). See also e.g. *Shrews. Chron.* 18 Apr. 1958.

ment suited all parties. Most of the Independent majority were, in other spheres, Conservatives; most of them, in safe seats, had nothing to gain by adopting a party label at election time.[23] The official Liberal and Labour members of the council, if they ever attempted to press their party views, were inevitably cast in an unsympathetic role; Independents maintained that national politics were irrelevant to local affairs.[24] Independents, however, felt free to put Conservative views. The position is well illustrated by an incident that occurred at a council meeting in 1924. The chairman of the council, Lt.-Col. H. H. Heywood-Lonsdale, 'without going into politics at all', referred to the recent election of a Labour government: he said that it was 'credited' with a great desire for reform which was 'much appreciated by . . . many people, though it was, perhaps, distasteful to other people'. William Latham, a Labour councillor, interjected 'To men of wealth, yes'. His interruption brought cries of 'Order' from all parts of the chamber, but his reply, that it was the chairman who should be called to order, went unheeded.[25] Such clashes were rare. The avoidance of partisan debate was as much an advantage to Liberal and Labour as to Conservative, for minority views could thus gain a hearing on particular issues without seeming to offer a general threat to the majority.

Until after the Second World War most of the triennial county-council elections passed off with little political activity, and wrought no important changes in the composition of the council.[26] There was, however, unusual activity in those of 1904, 1907, and 1922.

The 1904 election was held at the height of the national controversy over the religious implications of the Education Act, 1902, strongly resented by the nonconformists, many of whom were Liberals.[27] Under the active leadership of Alfred Billson[28] the Shropshire Liberals were said by their opponents to have intended to contest all 51 divisions on the education issue.[29] In the event there were only fifteen contests, and official Liberal candidates stood in eleven; in three they were opposed by official Liberal Unionists, in six by official Conservatives. They beat two of the Unionists and two of the Conservatives and also retained the two contested seats they had previously held.[30] The effect on the composition of the council of their net gain of four seats was negligible.

The Liberals, still organized by Billson, made another concerted effort in 1907. Official Liberals stood in all eight contests. They won two of the three divisions in which they had been beaten in 1904 and retained the one contested seat that they already held, but failed in the four divisions that they were contesting for the first time.[31] Once more the Liberal gain was negligible, but the election did introduce the first working man to the council: William Latham, a miner and trade-union official who won Lilleshall at the second attempt.[32] He stood as a Liberal, but in 1925 regarded himself as having been the first Labour councillor. He recalled the difficulty that a working man had in attending meetings; he often had to come straight from the pit with time to wash only his hands and face.[33]

During the First World War triennial elections were suspended, and vacant seats were filled by a ballot of council members. This arrangement favoured the Conservatives; for example Lt.-Col. H. P. Sykes, an unsuccessful Conservative candidate in

[23] *Hist. Jnl.* viii. 363.

[24] A view persisting in many cos. (e.g. Northumb., E. Suff., W. Suff.) in the 1960s: Lee, op. cit. 222-3.

[25] *Shrews. Chron.* 21 Mar. 1924. Heywood-Lonsdale's father had died a millionaire: W. D. Rubinstein, 'British Millionaires, 1809-1949', *Bull. Inst. Hist. Res.* xlvii. 210.

[26] *Shrews. Chron.* 11 Mar. 1892; 8 Mar. 1895; 4 Mar. 1898; 15 Mar. 1901; 4 and 11 Mar. 1910; 14 Mar. 1913; 7 Mar. 1919; 13 Mar. 1925; 9 Mar. 1928; 6 Mar. 1931; 9 Mar. 1934; 5 Mar. 1937.

[27] See p. 199.

[28] See p. 345.

[29] *Shrews. Chron.* 11 Mar. 1904.

[30] Ibid. 4 and 11 Mar. 1904.

[31] Ibid. 1, 8, and 15 Mar. 1907.

[32] Ibid. 15 Nov. 1907.

[33] Ibid. 31 July 1925.

1907,[34] gained a seat in 1918 by council ballot[35] only to lose it at the 1919 triennial election.[36] In 1922 the county branch of the National Farmers' Union made a bid for council seats. Its candidates contested five divisions, pledging themselves to fight for a reduction of rates through cuts in expenditure. They won four of the five, unseating four councillors including Lt.-Col. R. C. Donaldson-Hudson, vice-chairman of the council. The 1922 election introduced the first woman councillor, Mrs. Margaret J. Rotton.[37]

The main feature of elections after the Second World War was the strong but unsuccessful effort of the Labour party significantly to increase its representation on the council. It contested many divisions but its net gains and losses were small and tended to cancel each other out.[38] Thus in 1949, despite a massive Labour effort at the election, there were 6 Labour, 5 Conservative, and 46 Independent councillors.[39] The small Labour group had a recognized leader[40] but made little contribution to debate. Its silence was attributed by a local newspaper to the council's zeal in carrying out its statutory duties regardless of the political character of the government that had imposed them, so that Labour members had 'not had very much to complain about'.[41] One effect of Labour efforts in the post-war elections was to provoke an increase, as in other counties,[42] in the number of official Conservative candidates. Nevertheless most Conservatives, to the annoyance of the local Labour and Liberal parties, continued to stand as Independents; some were alleged to be covertly backed by their divisional Conservative associations.[43] Official Liberals made a strong effort at the 1964 election, but succeeded only in retaining their one seat, gained at a previous by-election.[44] After the 1970 election there were 9 Conservative, 6 Labour, 2 Independent Conservative, 1 Liberal, and 41 Independent councillors.[45] By 1974 it was expected that local-government reorganization would lead to an increased proportion of urban members and thus to greater Labour–Conservative rivalry.[46]

Between 1889 and 1974 the social composition of the council changed more than the political. In 1889 some 20 of the 51 councillors and 8 of the 17 aldermen were principally landowners; another 14 councillors and 2 aldermen were business or professional men; 9 councillors and 5 aldermen were farmers; 3 councillors and 2 aldermen were clergy.[47] Landowners and farmers on the council were conscious of representing distinct interests.[48] By 1913 there were slightly fewer landowners and no clergy; there were a few more business and professional men and farmers. On the whole, however, there was little change.[49] By 1955 businessmen formed the largest single class; only slightly fewer were the farmers; professional men, some of them retired, formed another large class; wage-earners and housewives came behind; only five councillors, other than those retired, claimed no regular occupation.[50]

The office of alderman, bringing with it prestige and security of tenure, was sought by 57 candidates in 1889, 14 of them councillors. In Shropshire, as in a few other most strongly conservative counties,[51] the council elected non-councillors to all 17 aldermanic seats,[52] three of them men who had failed at the recent polls.[53] At the end of

[34] *Shrews. Chron.* 15 Mar. 1907.
[35] Ibid. 15 Mar. 1918. [36] Ibid. 7 Mar. 1919.
[37] Ibid. 10 Mar. 1922.
[38] Ibid. 8 Mar. 1946; 15 Apr. 1949; 11 Apr. 1952; 8 Apr. 1955; 18 Apr. 1958; 21 Apr. 1961; 17 Apr. 1964; 21 Apr. 1967; *Tuesday Chron.* (special issue of *Shrews. Chron.*), 14 Apr. 1970.
[39] Ibid. 15 Apr. 1949.
[40] Ibid. 8 Apr. 1955.
[41] Ibid. 11 Mar. 1949.
[42] A local-govt. dept. was opened at Conservative central office in 1946: Smellie, *Hist. Local Govt.* 99.

[43] *Shrews. Chron.* 11 Mar., 15 Apr. 1949; 18 Apr. 1958; 10 Apr. 1964.
[44] Ibid. 10 and 17 Apr. 1964.
[45] Ibid. 14 Apr. 1970. The no. of divisions was increased to 59 in 1955: S.C.C. *Year Bk. 1955–6.*
[46] Local information (1974).
[47] S.R.O. 113/1, pp. 1–3.
[48] Local information (1974).
[49] *Shrews. Chron.* 7 Mar. 1913.
[50] *S.C.C. Mins.* 1955–6, 3–5.
[51] Lee, *Social Leaders*, 228.
[52] *Shrews. Chron.* 25 Jan. 1889.   [53] Ibid. 18 Jan. 1889.

his term an alderman was invariably re-elected if he so wished, but in the 1890s a vacancy was otherwise filled by the nominee of a small committee, informal and private, which expected the full council to follow its lead at the formal election.[54] The practice was still observed in the 1900s and 1920s,[55] and most councillors presumably acquiesced in it. It was, however, occasionally attacked by members who preferred to make up their own minds.[56] Such was the influence of the private committee that, at an aldermanic election in May 1906, some members of the council were outraged to find that official voting papers were handed out with the name of the private committee's nominee, H. H. Heywood-Lonsdale, already filled in.[57] Heywood-Lonsdale had been an unsuccessful candidate in the 1904 triennial election;[58] eleven of the existing aldermen had never served as councillors,[59] but only one, W. H. Whitaker, had been an unsuccessful triennial-election candidate.[60] The bad feeling that attended Heywood-Lonsdale's election as alderman ended the practice of choosing aldermen from outside the council.[61] Between 1906 and 1974, with four deliberate exceptions, aldermen were always elected from among the councillors.[62] For some time it was customary to elect a landowner and a farmer alternately.[63] In the 1930s the choice was an open one[64] and was still so in theory in 1964,[65] but by 1973 it had long been the custom to elect by seniority.[66] Even in its early days the office was not merely honorific; in the 1890s aldermen attended, on average, rather more meetings than councillors.[67] Nevertheless, few aldermen in the history of the council attained important chairmanships unless they had already done so as councillors.[68]

The real leaders of the council were not the magistrates or the aldermen but the chairmen of its committees. They owed their chairmanships to the respect of their colleagues and retained them only by ability and hard work; brilliance in debate, political views, and social position counted far less. Only a small proportion of committee members felt able to sacrifice their time to mastering the administrative and legislative intricacies of their duties; the rest were grateful to elect men who could. Mastery of detail was, for example, publicly acknowledged in Sir J. B. Bowen-Jones,[69] Alfred Salwey,[70] W. H. Smith,[71] R. G. Venables,[72] and Sir Offley Wakeman.[73] Loyalty to a chairman could lead to his being prevailed on to remain in office longer than his health would allow. Salwey's health broke down permanently in 1894 as a result of the 'overwhelming share' of council work that he undertook.[74] Bowen-Jones, conscious of failing strength, had by 1915 retired from all public office except the chairmanship of the council,[75] but was kept in office until 1920. In the absence on military service of those members considered best fitted to succeed him[76] his knowledge was deemed indispensable.[77]

[54] Ibid. 29 May 1891.
[55] Ibid. 5 May 1906; 20 Mar. 1925.
[56] Ibid. 29 May 1891; 11 May 1906.
[57] Ibid. 11 May 1906. [58] Ibid. 11 Mar. 1904.
[59] S.C.C. *Year Bk.* 1889-1907.
[60] *Shrews. Chron.* 18 Jan. 1889. [61] Ibid. 7 Nov. 1930.
[62] S.C.C. *Year Bk.* 1906-73. The exceptions were Brig.-Gen. A. H. O. LLoyd (in 1931), Ld. Harlech (1938), Lady Boyne (1941), and Ld. Bridgeman (1951).
[63] Local information (1974). [64] S.R.O. 34/4.
[65] *S.C.C. Mins.* 1964-5, 242.
[66] Ex inf. clk. of co. council (1973).
[67] S.C.C. *Abstr. of No. of Meetings of Co. Council,* 1892-3, 1894-5 (copies in S.R.O.).
[68] In the rest of this section inf. on the careers of members, chmn. and offrs. is, unless otherwise stated, taken from: S.R.O. 113/1; *S.C.C. Mins.* 1891-1974; S.C.C. *Year Bk.* 1889-1973; S.R.O., S.C.C. cttee. mins. 1889-1974.
[69] *Shrews. Chron.* 17 Mar. 1916; 31 July 1925. He was

chmn. of Finance and Gen. Purposes Cttee. 1894-1920, council 1895-1920.
[70] S.R.O. 148/15, Venables C.C. newscuttings 1888-92, p. 31; *Shrews. Chron.* 7 Nov. 1902 (suppl.). He was chmn. of council 1889-93, Finance and Gen. Purposes Cttee. 1889-94.
[71] S.R.O. 148/15, Venables educ. newscuttings 1906-7, p. 3; *Shrews. Chron.* 29 July 1921. He was chmn. of Educ. Cttee. 1906-21.
[72] S.R.O. 148/15, Venables educ. newscuttings 1904-6, p. 3. He was chmn. of Roads and Bridges Cttee. 1897-1903, Educ. Cttee. 1903-6, vice-chmn. of council 1897-1920.
[73] *Oswestry Adv.* 11 Oct. 1944. He was chmn. of Educ. Cttee. 1937-40, 1944-67, Finance and Gen. Purposes Cttee. 1940-5, council 1943-63.
[74] *Shrews. Chron.* 22 Aug., 7 Nov. 1902 (suppl.)
[75] Ibid. 19 Mar. 1915.
[76] e.g. Lt.-Col. R. C. Donaldson-Hudson and Lt.-Col. H. H. Heywood-Lonsdale: ex inf. Lord Bridgeman (1974).
[77] *Shrews. Chron.* 17 Mar. 1916; 15 Mar. 1918.

A businesslike and conciliatory approach was more highly esteemed than vehemence, wit, or simple idealism. The council career of John (later Sir John) Bayley, which lasted from 1889 to 1931, illustrates the point. Founder of Wellington College,[78] he was one of the most gifted men ever to enter the council. A fluent debater, he had exceptional energy and organizational ability and a forceful personality. Such gifts did not, however, conform easily to the slow and orderly procedures of the council in which all expressions of opinion, of whatever degree of sophistication, had to receive fair consideration. The council had no place of trust for 'a visionary who breathed out fire and brimstone on any who would thwart the realization of his dreams, a young lion of a man who could not be caged by . . . the limits of finance committees'.[79] Despite the general recognition of his ability, Bayley never attained a chairmanship, even in his special field of education. Wits like the Revd. C. H. Bowman,[80] and fierce debaters like Lt.-Col. James Patchett,[81] likewise were not called to office.

Those who became chairmen were often reserved, even taciturn, men. W. M. W. Fell,[82] though exercising much influence, spoke very little in public.[83] E. B. Fielden[84] rarely spoke on the council except on financial questions.[85] H. H. Heywood-Lonsdale[86] was notably reserved and in later years showed an 'unwillingness to commit himself before having worked out his decision'.[87] R. G. Venables spoke little in the council chamber[88] and always 'set a good example by the brevity of his remarks'.[89] Bowen-Jones, Fielden, Salwey, and W. H. Lander[90] were among those admired for their impartiality and ability to conciliate.[91] Such were the general tendencies, but exceptions did occur. One was the Revd. R. A. Giles, an Australian.[92] His frequent and colourful contributions to council debates sometimes reached extremes of vehemence and were much reported in the local press.[93] He was considered a useful spokesman by those members who wanted economies[94] and was nominated for the chairmanship of the Education Committee in 1944.[95] He later succeeded in becoming chairman of the Public Assistance (1946–8), Welfare (1948–52), and Health (1952–62) committees.

Most chairmen were landowners, industrialists, businessmen, or substantial farmers, rather than professional men or wage-earners. Those classes usually had more time and were often better prepared by education or experience to handle public affairs. On the other hand social position, without special ability or effort, did not carry with it strong influence on the council. Six descendants of the 2nd earl of Powis (d. 1848)[96] sat on the council between 1889 and 1974, but none was elected to a chairmanship. There were some instances in which rank may have proved a useful adjunct to natural ability; the progressive policy propounded by Sir Offley Wakeman after the Second World War for example might have gained less support on the council but for his social standing.[97] The first woman to attain an important chairmanship did so only in 1966.[98]

[78] *V.C.H. Salop.* ii. 163.

[79] S.R.O. 148/15, Venables C.C. newscuttings 1888–92, p. 30; S.R.O. 649/1.

[80] *Shrews. Chron.* 1889–98. He was a councillor 1889–98.

[81] Ibid. 1889–1925. He was a councillor 1889–1910, and alderman 1910–25.

[82] Chmn. of Roads and Bridges Cttee. 1948–53, Finance Cttee. 1953–74, council 1963–6.

[83] Local information (1974).

[84] Chmn. of Finance and Gen. Purposes Cttee. 1920–40.

[85] *Shrews. Chron.* 3 Apr. 1942.

[86] Chmn. of Standing Joint Cttee. 1910–20, council 1920–30.

[87] *Shrews. Chron.* 21 Nov. 1930.

[88] Oswestry Adv. *Unconventional Portraits* (1910), 19.

[89] *Shrews. Chron.* 14 Mar. 1919.

[90] Chmn. of Executive Cttee. 1901–21, vice-chmn. of council 1922–7.

[91] *Shrews. Chron.* 7 Nov. 1902 (suppl.); 31 July 1925; 13 May 1927; 3 Apr. 1942; S.R.O. 148/15, Venables C.C. newscuttings 1888–92, p. 31; ibid., Venables educ. newscuttings 1906–7, p. 38.

[92] Councillor 1934–50, alderman 1950–65.

[93] *Shrews. Chron.* 1945–50.

[94] Local information (1974).

[95] *Oswestry Adv.* 11 Oct. 1944.

[96] The 3rd Ld. Powis, the Hon. R. C. Herbert, Maj.-Gen. the Hon. W. H. Herbert (sons), the 4th Ld. Powis (grandson), Col. E. R. H. Herbert (later the 5th Ld. Powis; gt.-grandson), and V. M. E. Holt (gt.-gt.-grandson): Burke, *Peerage* (1967), 2038. The last-named, however, became a chmn. after the close of the period here treated.

[97] Local information (1973).

[98] *S.C.C. Mins.* 1966–7, 42.

Political beliefs, other than those of the extreme left, seem to have been no bar to office. Even in so sensitive an area as elementary education in the 1900s it was possible for a Liberal,[99] W. H. Smith, to be elected chairman of the Education Committee.[1] Other Liberals who attained chairmanships were Richard Groom (1889–93),[2] A. P. Heywood-Lonsdale (1895–7),[3] W. H. Lander (1901–27),[4] J. V. Wheeler (1921–36)[5] T. Ward Green (1931–43),[6] and T. C. Ward (1930–56),[7] though Heywood-Lonsdale and Wheeler were old-fashioned land-owning Whigs rather than conventional Liberals.[8] By the 1960s a Labour councillor might also be a chairman, as were Peter Morris[9] and Clifford Smith.[10]

Chairmen were in theory elected annually by their committees, but until 1907 they were in fact automatically reinstated every year at the spring meeting of the council, before their committees had met. In the 1890s the Revd. C. H. Bowman feared that a clique had gained control of the council, but his proposals to limit chairmanships to a fixed number of years, to elect chairmen only at annual meetings of their committees, and to hold that election by ballot were not adopted.[11] Re-election in full council seems to have ceased in 1907,[12] but in 1945 proposals to elect by ballot were again defeated.[13] If the chairmanship of the council went to a landowner it was customary for a farmer to be elected vice-chairman and *vice versa*.[14] Early in 1945 there was renewed concern about the concentration of power.[15] Sir Offley Wakeman was elected chairman of the Education Committee in October 1944 on the death of Major C. U. Corbett. Wakeman was already chairman of the Finance and General Purposes Committee and of the council. He had agreed to resign the Finance chairmanship if elected to that of Education[16] and did so.[17] In March 1945 the council resolved that it was 'undesirable' for anyone to be chairman of more than one standing committee. A motion that it was undesirable for the chairman of the council to be chairman of any standing committee without the council's consent was defeated[18] but some members remained uneasy for many years at the apparent advantage enjoyed by the Education Committee in having the chairman of the council as its chairman.[19] Wakeman retired from the council chairmanship in 1963. In 1965 it became the custom for the chairmanship to be limited to three years; it was also agreed that at future vacancies an informal committee of the aldermen and chairmen should propose a new chairman to an informal meeting of the council; if then approved he would proceed to be formally elected.[20]

Assignment of members to the various committees was worked out by the Finance and General Purposes Committee (from 1946 the General Purposes Committee)[21] and was usually adopted by the council without discussion.[22] In principle it was intended to give every part of the county fair representation on each committee,[23] a procedure that was flexibly applied. A member's own preference might be taken into account[24] and,

[99] W. Mate & Sons Ltd. *Shropshire: Historical, Descriptive, Biographical* (1906), pt. 2, p. 127.

[1] See p. 199.

[2] S.R.O. 148/15, Venables C.C. newscuttings 1888–92, p. 32. Chmn. of Sanitary and Rivers Pollution Cttee. 1889–93.

[3] Ibid. Chmn. of Roads and Bridges Cttee. 1895–7, vice-chmn. of council 1895–7.

[4] Mate, op. cit. pt. 2, p. 181; and see above, n. 90.

[5] J. Dale, *County Biographies, 1904* (*Shropshire*), 98. Chmn. of Agric. Ctee. 1921–30, Public Assistance Cttee. 1930–6.

[6] Ibid. 84. Chmn. of council 1931–43.

[7] Local information (1974). Chmn. of Agric. Cttee. 1930–45, Finance and Gen. Purposes Cttee. 1945–6, Finance Cttee. 1946–53, vice-chmn. of council 1946–56.

[8] Local information (1974).

[9] *Shrews. Chron.* 8 Mar. 1946. Chmn. of Welfare Cttee. 1960–4.

[10] Ibid. 8 Apr. 1955. Chmn. of Children Cttee. 1963–70.

[11] Ibid. 13 Nov. 1896; 21 Mar. 1902.

[12] Ibid. 28 Mar. 1907 (the first time no rep. of such election appears).

[13] *S.C.C. Mins.* 1945–6, 350.

[14] Local information (1974).

[15] *Shrews. Chron.* 9 Mar. 1945.

[16] Local information (1974).

[17] S.R.O., Finance and Gen. Purposes Cttee. min. bk. 14, p. 355.

[18] *S.C.C. Mins.* 1945–6, 2.

[19] Local information (1974).

[20] *S.C.C. Mins.* 1965–6, 2, 58–9, 117.

[21] Ibid. 1945–6, 351.

[22] *Shrews. Chron.* 1889–1974.

[23] Ibid. 5 Apr. 1889; 22 Mar. 1907.

[24] *S.C.C. Mins.* 1945–6, 351.

to judge from an allegation made in 1916 by William Latham (Labour), some intrigue attended the distribution of places.[25] In 1926 it became official practice for the Finance and General Purposes Committee to adopt a list of appointments to committees drawn up by the Committee of Chairmen;[26] a chairman was thus allowed some official word in the composition of his own committee. That procedure ceased after 1938.[27]

On 1 April 1889 the council inherited three chief officers, all part-timers: a clerk, a treasurer, and a surveyor.[28] The clerk, E. C. Peele, and the treasurer, G. M. Salt, were first cousins[29] and partners in the Salop Old Bank (Eyton, Burton, Lloyd & Co.)[30] where the county funds were kept. Counsel's opinion, taken by the council in 1889, was that Salt's connexion with Peele did not legally disqualify him from the treasurership.[31] Some members were uneasy because the county financial clerk, William Baxter, who actually kept the accounts and advised on financial policy, was under Peele's control.[32] Peele held numerous offices concurrently with the clerkship. At various times between 1889 and 1911 he was under-sheriff, town clerk of Shrewsbury (until 1890), mayor of Shrewsbury (in 1891 and 1897), deputy chairman of the governors of Shrewsbury School, and colonel of the 1st Shropshire and Staffordshire Volunteer Artillery. His business interests included a local directorship of the Alliance Assurance Co. He was a known Conservative and tariff reformer.[33] In 1892 Sir T. F. Boughey, a councillor, likened him to the 'lord high everything else' of *The Mikado*.[34] In 1893 Sir C. H. Rouse-Boughton, a 'quiet onlooker on the back benches', privately warned Salwey, the chairman of the council, that if he 'did not keep his hands down, he would find his clerk before long getting away with him'; at about that time others too were apprehensive about the effects of Peele's forceful personality.[35] The council, however, had no power to remove its clerk; because he had been appointed clerk of the peace before 1 April 1889 Peele could be removed only by quarter sessions.[36] Despite a unanimous recommendation by the council in 1903,[37] the law was not changed until the Local Government (Clerks) Act, 1931, made the clerkships of the peace and of the council separable.[38]

The influence of the Salop Old Bank and its partners was weakened in 1906 when, shortly after his announcement of resignation, it was discovered that Salt, on the basis of a 'verbal' agreement with unnamed 'officers' of the council, had been charging no commission and allowing no interest on the education account opened in 1903 — an arrangement that favoured the bank.[39] A move to offer the treasurership to G. Butler Lloyd, another partner in the Salop Old Bank,[40] was stopped by protests from the council floor. The office was publicly advertised and went to Arthur Gill, then manager of the Shrewsbury branch of the Birmingham District & Counties Banking Co. Ltd.[41] For the first time since 1764 the county treasurership had passed to someone not related to his predecessor.[42] When Peele died in 1911 he was succeeded by the deputy clerk of the council, Frederick Crowte, who had come to Shropshire as recently as 1903, having previously served with Cardiff town council.[43] All subsequent clerks

[25] *Shrews. Chron.* 11 Feb. 1916.
[26] S.R.O., Special Cttees. (Cttee. of Chmn.) min. bk. 1912–35, p. 201 (the first ref.).
[27] S.R.O., Cttee. of Chmn. min. bk. 2, p. 49 (the last ref.).
[28] Under the Local Govt. Act, 1888, 51 & 52 Vic. c. 41. The clk. was a partner in Peele & Peele, solicitors, the treasurer a partner in Salt & Sons, solicitors: *Kelly's Dir. Salop.* (1891), 584. For the surveyor see below, p. 193.
[29] S.P.L., MS. 2794, pp. 489, 620–1; *S.P.R. Heref.* ix. 270, 272.
[30] S.R.O. 2620, box 25, articles of partnership 1884 (copy) and 1900 (draft), declaration of trust 1906 (draft).
[31] *Shrews. Chron.* 16 Aug. 1889.   [32] Ibid.
[33] Ibid. 25 Aug. 1911; Mate, *Shropshire*, pt. 2, p. 148.

[34] *Shrews. Chron.* 29 Jan. 1892.
[35] S.R.O. 1033/34–43.
[36] A. Macmorran and T. R. Colquhoun Dill, *Local Govt. Act, 1888* (3rd edn. 1898), 158.
[37] *Oswestry Adv.* 11 Nov. 1903.
[38] 21 & 22 Geo. V, c. 45.
[39] *Shrews. Chron.* 11 May 1906.
[40] S.R.O. 2620, box 25, decl. of trust 1906.
[41] S.R.O. 148/15, S.C.C. newscuttings 1905–20 (meetings 10 Mar., 5 May 1906).
[42] See p. 361.
[43] S.R.O. 148/15, Venables C.C. newscuttings 1902–4, p. 35; E. Stephens, *Clerks of the Counties 1360–1960* (1961), 153.

were men whose careers had been spent entirely in local-government service. Thus after some 140 years[44] the grip on county administration of the Peeles and their family and business connexions, the Loxdales and Salts, was at an end.

The council's chief officers were always notable for their length of service. Few left in order to work for another authority. In the lower grades, however, the council lost capable men. In 1921 the vice-chairman of the council, R. C. Donaldson-Hudson, remarked that, because of the low salaries offered, Shropshire had been a 'stepping-stone' council for the previous twenty years.[45] The Finance and General Purposes Committee admitted in 1922 that the council's salaries were among the lowest in the country.[46] Between 1889 and 1924 there was no superannuation scheme,[47] and officers were inevitably tempted to postpone their retirement, even to a point where their efficiency might be impaired. For example, A. T. Davis, county surveyor from 1889 to 1923, was evidently unable to cope with his duties during his last few years of service.[48] Yet he could not afford to resign until the council offered him the sinecure post of consulting surveyor with a small salary.[49] A few months later the council adopted the Local Government and other Officers' Superannuation Act, 1922.[50] Before the Second World War two or three outstanding chief officers were appointed, but the council kept salaries low and some of the principal posts failed to attract able men.[51]

Over the period 1889–1974, by a subtle process, control of policy tended more and more to elude the ordinary council member. Parliament imposed on county councils increasingly technical duties that called for judgements that could come only from specialized knowledge, and the salaried officer, as interpreter of the legislation to elected members, became correspondingly more influential. It was perhaps partly for that reason that after the First World War selection of candidates for senior posts was always delegated to an appropriate committee.[52] The committees met in private whereas previously the candidates had been interviewed and voted for in full council with press and public present;[53] the change must have helped to improve senior officers' standing. Similarly, increasing deference is implied in the council's resolution of 1931 that senior officers' salaries must be discussed by the council only in committee.[54] During the council's history the volume of work increased so greatly that it would, in any case, have overwhelmed any but the professional administrator. Growth of work may be measured by the growth of staff. The council's central staff[55] numbered 33 in 1907[56] and by 1924 had grown to 77;[57] by January 1974 there were some 820 people on the central staff and some 5,400 full-time employees outside it.[58] In the 1930s some members were already fully aware of the council's dependence on its officers. Capt. Richard Jebb complained in 1934 that it was 'really difficult' for a member to have any influence except in matters of detail: 'the big questions were slipped through without being properly investigated'.[59] Commenting on the situation in 1939, Lord Powis, a county alderman and the lord lieutenant, wrote that it would be 'an evil day for England' should the unpaid council members find their duties beyond them.[60]

After the Second World War the council found itself with a chairman, Sir Offley

[44] See pp. 146–7.
[45] *Shrews. Chron.* 11 Feb. 1921.
[46] Ibid. 10 Feb. 1922.
[47] Ibid. 21 June 1889.
[48] See p. 194.
[49] *S.C.C. Mins.* 1923–4, 136.
[50] 12 & 13 Geo. V, c. 59; *Shrews. Chron.* 5 Oct. 1923.
[51] Local information (1974); *Shrews. Chron.* 3 Aug. 1945.
[52] e.g. *S.C.C. Mins.* 1 Feb. 1902, 46.
[53] e.g. ibid. 1923–4, 210. The right to order an election in full council remained implicit in the standing orders

in 1972: S.C.C. *Year Bk. 1972–3*, 53.
[54] *S.C.C. Mins.* 1931–2, 114.
[55] Defined as full-time central administrative, professional, technical, and clerical staff.
[56] *S.C.C. Mins.* 1907–8, 76–7.
[57] S.R.O. 559/I/5/5, income tax return 1924–5.
[58] S.C.C. *Digest and Development Budget 1974–5* (copy in possession of S.C.C. personnel offr.), 13.
[59] *Shrews. Chron.* 22 June 1934.
[60] Co. Councils Assoc. *Jubilee of the Co. Councils* (1939; Salop. edn.), 65.

Wakeman (1943–63), who was a progressive by temperament. Through his growing influence chief officers' salaries were improved and members came to understand that only through the employment of able men could their own exertions be attended with success. Wakeman encouraged the initiative of the chief officers, who had in G. C. Godber, clerk of the council 1944–66, a leader who would stimulate and support them. As the expansionist outlook of government came to be that of the council's leaders so were the officers made free to put their ideas into practice.[61]

Finance

In the early years of the council Alfred Salwey, first chairman of the Finance and General Purposes Committee, assumed that local-government expenditure would remain constant and that there was a 'normal' county rate of between 3d. and 3½d. in the pound.[62] In 1889–90 only 28 per cent of the council's income of £75,000 was obtained from the ratepayers; the rest was derived almost wholly from government grants.[63] The county debt, incurred by quarter sessions on the asylum and the shirehall, was being repaid by regular annual sums, and Salwey hoped that the council's own borrowing powers would never be used.[64] The motto he favoured was 'efficiency with economy'.[65] As the departments moved into full activity, however, so expenditure rose. In 1893–4 the rate was increased from 3½d. to 5¼d. It proved possible, by various expedients, to hold the rate below 6d. for the next ten years; expenditure was held down at between £100,000 and £110,000 a year, the technical-instruction programme was curtailed in 1894,[66] government grants were increased in 1897,[67] and repayment of the county debt was suspended in 1901–2 and 1902–3.[68] By 1902–3 the rates were contributing only 24 per cent of the council's income; that result, satisfactory enough to the ratepayers as such, was not attained without neglect of public health, smallholdings, and the asylum.[69]

The Education Act, 1902, the pre-war legislation of the 1905–15 Liberal government, and the rapid growth of motor traffic put an end to the idea that expenditure and rates could remain constant from year to year. In 1903–4 annual expenditure leapt to £192,000; reaching a peak of £342,000 in 1911–12, it stood at £319,000 by 1913–14. The ratepayers' contribution rose to 41 per cent by 1913–14, and the poundage to 1s. 9¼d., as government grants became increasingly inadequate. The council first borrowed in 1906–7; thereafter borrowing became a regular part of its annual budget. In 1911–12, with secondary-school building at its height, loans formed 31 per cent of income. In 1910 J. B. Bowen-Jones, chairman of the Finance and General Purposes Committee, blamed rate increases on the 'almost despotic power' of government departments;[70] in 1913 he claimed that ratepayers were being taxed nearly to the limit.[71] By 1915 he had to contend with a minority on the council who wanted expenditure cut at whatever sacrifice of public services.[72]

Expenditure had risen to £906,000 by 1920–1; the government contributed only 37 per cent of income — the lowest proportion since 1889 — while the rate rose from

[61] Local information (1974).
[62] Shrews. Chron. 29 Apr. 1892.
[63] The financial statistics on which this section is based are, unless otherwise stated: for 1889–1914 and 1919–34, the Annual Local Taxation Returns (those for 1889–1913 are parliamentary papers; those for 1914 and 1919–34 are H.M.S.O. publications); for 1934–7, the annual Local Govt. Financial Statistics (H.M.S.O.); for 1914–19 and 1937–50, the annual S.C.C. Abstr. of Accts. (copies in S.R.O.); for 1950–74, the annual S.C.C. Accts. (copies in S.R.O.). Sums of money in the text are given to the nearest thousand pounds when they exceed £10,000. The terms 'income' and 'expenditure' are used to denote income from all sources and expenditure of all kinds.
[64] Shrews. Chron. 28 Apr. 1893.
[65] Ibid. 8 Feb. 1889. [66] See p. 198.
[67] Under the Agricultural Rates Act, 1896, 59 & 60 Vic. c. 16.
[68] Shrews. Chron. 9 May 1902. [69] See pp. 197, 207–8, 212.
[70] Shrews. Chron. 18 Mar., 11 Nov. 1910.
[71] Ibid. 9 May 1913.
[72] Ibid. 30 July 1915; 12 May 1916.

3s. 5⅛d. in 1919–20 to 6s. 2⅜d. in 1920–1, representing 45 per cent of income. Calls for expenditure cuts were headed by two back-benchers, Lord Forester and W. F. Beddoes. In February 1921 the council unanimously adopted Forester's resolution deploring increasing government control of county administration and its consequent financial burden;[73] at the same meeting the council agreed that each committee should present a quarterly account of its expenditure.[74] It proved possible to reduce the rate in 1921–2, mainly because the previous year's rate had been based on an over-estimate.[75] At the 1922 council election some members were returned on a pledge to secure economies,[76] but the chairman of the council, Heywood-Lonsdale, and the chairman of the Finance and General Purposes Committee, E. B. Fielden, resisted appeals for extreme cuts.[77] As Fielden pointed out, the council had practised strict economy since 1889, and had little margin for further reduction.[78] Expenditure was, however, reduced over the years 1922–4 and held fairly steady for the remainder of the 1920s, except in 1925–7 when road reconstruction was at its height; government grants fluctuated between 51 and 60 per cent and rates remained correspondingly steady.

The Local Government Act, 1929, caused a sudden rise in expenditure in 1930–1 to £1,470,000; the rate poundage rose from 5s. 7d. in 1929–30 to 11s. 4½d. in 1930–1, but the burden on some ratepayers was alleviated by the de-rating of agricultural and other property;[79] the proportions of income from rates and grants remained as they had been in the 1920s. In 1931 the council improved its scrutiny of expenditure. Until then each committee's annual estimate had been examined by the Committee of Chairmen before submission to the Finance and General Purposes Committee. Thereafter that scrutiny was transferred to an Estimates Sub-Committee, a body more disinterested in that it did not consist mainly of chairmen. Instructed to insist on economies wherever possible,[80] the sub-committee during the 1930s often sent a committee's estimate back with a request for reduction;[81] expenditure was held steady, as were grants and rates. The work of the sub-committee was all the more acceptable in the 1930s, for the National Farmers' Union members, who had entered the council in 1922 pledged to cut expenditure, were felt by some observers to have lost their keenness as a pressure group as soon as their farms were de-rated in 1930.[82]

The economies practised by the council in the 1930s left Shropshire among those counties that found themselves in 1945 with exceptionally heavy arrears of capital development.[83] New legislation was adding new burdens; the Education Act, 1944, and the social legislation of the 1945–51 Labour government called for unprecedented capital expenditure. In 1944 G. C. Godber was appointed clerk of the council. Unlike his recent predecessors Godber had great administrative gifts and a strong belief that the council should be making up lost ground. His tenure of office from 1944 to 1966 was the vital local influence in the council's post-war expansion.[84] Expenditure rose from £1,481,000 in 1936–7 to £5,251,000 in 1951–2; in 1951–2 rates, though higher than before the war, provided only 20 per cent of income; 60 per cent came from government grants.

Such developments help to explain why, in the late 1940s, some council members complained bitterly of government domination.[85] Other critics on and off the council, accused the council, and especially its Education Committee, of extravagance in exceed-

[73] *Shrews. Chron.* 11 Feb. 1921.
[74] Ibid. 18 Mar. 1921.   [75] Ibid. 13 May 1921.
[76] Ibid. 17 Mar. 1922; 16 Mar. 1928.
[77] Ibid. 17 Mar. 1922; 16 Mar., 11 May 1923; 21 Mar., 9 May 1924; 20 Mar. 1925.
[78] Ibid. 12 May 1922.
[79] 19 Geo. V, c. 17.
[80] S.C.C. *Mins.* 1931–2, 370.

[81] S.R.O., Finance and Gen. Purposes Cttee. min. bk. 12, p. 105; 13, pp. 84–5, 200, 308, 431, 537.
[82] *Shrews. Chron.* 22 June 1934.
[83] S.C.C. *Salop Co. Council: the Post-War Years and the Future* (1965; copy in S.R.O.); S.C.C. *Mins.* 1966–7, 281.
[84] Local information (1974).
[85] *Shrews. Chron.* 9 Mar. 1945; 4 Mar. 1949; *Oswestry Adv.* 26 Nov. 1947.

ing the government's minimum demands.[86] Yet others were simply baffled by the transition from the static policy of the 1920s and 1930s to the expansionist one of the post-war period; in 1949 Lt.-Col. W. G. Dugdale, chairman of the Fire Brigade Committee, asked during a budget debate 'Are we going to go on year after year with increases? . . . Can nothing be done?'[87] The critics, however, exercised little influence in the council, perhaps largely because the general public silently accepted the council's ever-increasing expenditure; ratepayers' associations failed to arouse widespread opposition to it.[88]

Power in the council during the post-war period was exercised by members who were keenly aware of the effects of what the Revd. J. E. G. Cartlidge called in 1945 the 'cursed economy for which this council is becoming famous'.[89] Sir Offley Wakeman, as chairman of the council, was among those who in 1945, from long and varied experience of local government,[90] understood the greatly enlarged role that the council would be expected to play in the lives of Shropshire people. In 1948 he urged members not to give way to 'panic, and fear of not being able to carry out their duties',[91] and in 1949 the council, though largely composed of Conservatives, seemed to one local newspaper to be 'almost Socialistic' in outlook.[92] By the mid 1950s even those members who had most strongly opposed the large expenditure incurred under Wakeman's chairmanship had come to accept his outlook.[93]

Expenditure increased yearly; in 1968–9 it reached almost £20 million. In the 1950s and 1960s government grants tended to increase at the same pace as expenditure, income from rates more rapidly; poundages were not allowed to rise much, but upward revaluation of property added to the yield. The average annual amounts of grants and rates were not, however, enough to finance short periods of unusually heavy capital expenditure such as occurred in 1957–9, 1961–5 and 1966–9. Borrowing therefore came to play a more important part than ever before in the history of the council. In the mid 1950s interest rates rose sharply and the normal method of borrowing for terms of years became difficult; in the late 1950s and the 1960s increasing reliance was placed on 'temporary' loans of less than twelve months' duration.[94] In the late 1960s those too became costly,[95] a circumstance contributing in 1969–70 to a reduction in capital development.[96]

Though government grants remained at a fairly constant level relative to expenditure, the council's increasing need in the 1950s and 1960s for government loan-sanction meant a general extension of central control over council policy and intensification of pressures from the national economy. At the same time the council's initiative was reduced by new *ad hoc* bodies such as the Dawley Development Corporation, the Midland Road Construction Unit, and the West Midland Children's Regional Planning Committee.[97] A note of crisis was sounded by the county treasurer in 1969; viewing the prospect of local-government reorganization in the early 1970s, he called for additional income under the council's own control and warned that, without it, local government would in future be 'little more than a façade', with initiative and achievement lost to the government and its regional agencies.[98] Similar fears were widely shared by council members in 1974.[99]

[86] *Shrews. Chron.* 7 Mar. 1947; *Sunday Express*, 13 Oct. 1947; *Oswestry Adv.* 23 Mar. 1949.
[87] *Wellington Jnl.* 5 Mar. 1949.
[88] Ibid. 16 Apr. 1949; *Shrews. Chron.* 7 Mar. 1947.
[89] *Manchester Guardian*, 20 July 1945.
[90] *Who's Who, 1952.*
[91] *Oswestry Adv.* 2 June 1948.
[92] *Shrews. Chron.* 11 Mar. 1949.
[93] *Oswestry Adv.* 10 Mar. 1954.

[94] S.C.C. *Shropshire Financial Facts*, vi–ix (1956–9); S.C.C. *Shropshire Local Govt. Finance*, x–xx (1960–70).
[95] *Shropshire Local Govt. Finance*, xvi. 5; xix. 5.
[96] Ibid. xx. 5.
[97] See pp. 195, 216, 220.
[98] *Shropshire Local Govt. Finance*, xix. 4.
[99] Remarks passed at the last meeting of the co. council in Mar. 1974.

CAPTAIN SIR OFFLEY WAKEMAN, BT., C.B.E.
(d. 1975)
Chairman of the county council 1943–63

WILLIAM HENRY BUTLER (d. 1965)
County surveyor 1924–48

THE SHIREHALL, SHREWSBURY, BUILT 1963–6
Column House, headquarters of the county library from 1967, with huts behind, is top right; the central
ambulance station, opened 1954, is bottom left

ROBERT JASPER MORE, M.P. (d. 1903)
'The Farmer's Friend'

JOHN FRAIL (d. 1879)
Tory organizer

Roads and Bridges

Under the Local Government Act, 1888, the county council inherited all the administrative responsibilities of quarter sessions for roads and bridges, and acquired the new responsibility of maintaining all main roads.[1] The Shropshire urban authorities chose under the Act to maintain their own main roads and the county council at first delegated its main roads to the rural highway authorities.[2] In May 1889 the council required its surveyor to assume the responsibility, previously exercised by the police, of inspecting the main roads maintained by the minor highway authorities, and to devote his whole time to Shropshire.[3] Accordingly W. N. Swettenham (county surveyor 1887-9), who was also surveyor of Montgomeryshire, was replaced by A. T. Davis (1889-1923).[4] The council took over direct maintenance of some rural main roads in 1890 and, with a little hesitation, took over the remainder in 1892-3, earlier than in some comparable counties;[5] six divisions were created, each with a surveyor equipped with a horse and trap.[6] When the council took over the main roads most through traffic went by railway; some main roads were so little used that money could have been saved by reducing them in width.[7] The surfaces were in poor condition at that time.[8] The normal surfacing method was to lay dry stones and allow traffic to grind them in. To aid that process the council bought its first steam roller in 1890[9] and by 1896 nearly all the 697 miles of county roads had been resurfaced and rolled.[10] Day-to-day maintenance was carried out by local 'lengthsmen', each responsible for a piece of road.[11] Supervision of the men proved difficult in the 1890s.[12]

The effects of motor traffic were first felt in the 1900s. In 1903, when there were only some 125 cars on Shropshire roads,[13] complaints of dust and speed were received,[14] and in the same year the effect of cars on traditional road construction was first noticed by local people.[15] The surveyor first acknowledged the abnormal wear in 1906,[16] and in 1907 the committee was pressed by eleven district councils to alleviate the dust nuisance.[17] The committee at first refused to use water-proofing and dust-preventing surface binders, arguing that they would double the roads expenditure.[18] Government grants, however, became available in 1909[19] and in 1911 the committee began to tar roads in and near towns and villages and, where necessary, to resurface them with tarred stones ('tar macadam').[20] Because of the cost the work proceeded slowly[21] and failed to keep pace with the wear from motor traffic.[22] By 1914 the roads were evidently deteriorating but were claimed to be still among the best in England.[23]

During the First World War, with materials and labour in very short supply[24] and with the roads subjected to unprecedented wear by military and goods traffic,[25] there

[1] 51 & 52 Vic. c. 41.
[2] S.C.C. *Resumé of Work of First Co. Council of Salop* [1893], 1.
[3] *S.C.C. Mins.* Officers, etc., Cttee. rep. 23 Mar. 1889, 9; *Shrews. Chron.* 5 Apr., 17 May 1889.
[4] *S.C.C. Mins.* 15 June 1889, 33.
[5] *V.C.H. Wilts.* v. 277; *Hist. of N. Riding of Yorks. C.C. 1889-1974*, ed. M. Y. Ashcroft (Northallerton, 1974), 35. By 1892 some 25 cos. had assumed direct maintenance of main roads: *Hist. Jnl.* viii. 375.
[6] *Resumé of Work of First Co. Council*, 5-7.
[7] S.C.C. *Co. Surveyor's Rep.* 28 June 1892 (copy in S.R.O., *S.C.C. Mins.* (R. G. Venables's copy), 1892-5, p. 736), 6; *T.S.A.S.* lviii. 184; *Shrews. Chron.* 28 July 1916.
[8] *Shrews. Chron.* 7 Feb. 1896.
[9] *Resumé of Work of First Co. Council*, 6; S.R.O. 148/15, Venables C.C. newscuttings 1888-92, p. 65.
[10] *Shrews. Chron.* 7 Feb. 1896.
[11] Ibid. 9 Feb. 1917; 2 June 1939 (suppl.).

[12] *S.C.C. Mins.* Main Roads Cttee. rep. 13 Oct. 1894, 2.
[13] *S.C.C. Mins.* 1904-5, 93.
[14] S.R.O. 148/15, Venables C.C. newscuttings 1902-4, pp. 28, 43.
[15] *S.C.C. Mins.* 1903-4, 173.
[16] S.C.C. *Co. Surveyor's Rep.* July 1906 (in *S.C.C. Mins.* 1906-7), 4.
[17] *S.C.C. Mins.* 1907-8, 91.
[18] *Shrews. Chron.* 10 May 1907.
[19] Under the Development and Road Improvement Funds Act, 1909, 9 Edw. VII, c. 47.
[20] S.C.C. *Co. Surveyor's Rep.* Jan. 1912 (in *S.C.C. Mins.* 1911-12), 6.
[21] *Shrews. Chron.* 10 May 1912.
[22] S.C.C. *Co. Surveyor's Rep.* Jan. 1913 (in *S.C.C. Mins.* 1912-13), 9.
[23] *Shrews. Chron.* 7 Nov. 1913.
[24] Ibid. 28 July, 10 Nov. 1916; 9 Feb. 1917.
[25] *S.C.C. Mins.* 1915-16, 155; 1917-18, 29.

was a rapid general deterioration. Nevertheless during those years the council decided to curtail its roads expenditure in order to relieve the rates.[26] After the war resurfacing with tar macadam was resumed on a large scale,[27] the committee acknowledging reluctantly that no cheaper surface could withstand modern traffic.[28] In 1922, however, the council, despite the committee's warnings, imposed new economies,[29] so that by 1923 further serious deterioration seemed inevitable.[30] Davis, who had suffered periodic ill health,[31] had been surveyor since 1889; in 1922 and 1923 he was attacked in council for using inefficient methods[32] and in 1923 he asked to be relieved of the 'ever increasing responsibilities of office'.[33]

His successor W. H. Butler (1924–48) inherited a very difficult situation.[34] Cheap, short-term methods, and work left half finished, were leading to premature deterioration.[35] Butler, insistent and allegedly ruthless,[36] persuaded the committee to adopt a long-term policy of wholesale resurfacing and renewal, and an increased expenditure. Ordinary revenue would not suffice, so the committee asked the council to approve a loan, arguing that the repayments would be offset by the eventual saving in annual maintenance costs.[37] The council debate, one of the longest on record, ranged over the whole future of roads in Shropshire; the loan policy was approved by 37 votes to 23[38] and opened the way to a huge programme of reconstruction. In 1925–6 112 miles of main roads were rebuilt and resurfaced, an achievement said at the time to be a record for road-making in England.[39] Soon after Butler's appointment administration improved noticeably;[40] in 1925 he spent at least four days a week out on the roads, travelling an average of five hundred miles a week in his car.[41] The surveyor was able to concentrate almost wholly on roads and bridges after 1929 when his original responsibility for county buildings was transferred to the newly created post of county architect.[42] By 1927 the arrears of work had been mostly dealt with,[43] and by 1928 the county roads were in excellent condition. Annual maintenance costs fell so markedly that it became possible for the first time to undertake large-scale widening, re-alignment, and other improvements, and also to reduce the amounts required from rates.[44] All this had been achieved despite a 62 per cent increase in traffic on Class I roads in Shropshire between 1925 and 1928.[45] Work on main roads became a succession of major improvement schemes;[46] the most ambitious were the new Atcham bridge opened in 1929 and the first part of the Shrewsbury by-pass opened in 1933.[47] Work on the by-pass was begun solely as a result of Butler's insistence.[48]

In 1930 the council took over urban classified roads and all roads formerly maintained by rural districts[49] — an increase of mileage from 767 to 3,308. Certain boroughs and urban districts continued to maintain their classified roads, but as agents of the council. The poor condition of rural unclassified roads in 1930 recalled that of the main roads

[26] *Shrews. Chron.* 10 Nov. 1916.
[27] Ibid. 1 Aug. 1919. [28] Ibid. 12 Nov. 1920.
[29] Ibid. 10 Nov. 1922; 21 Mar. 1924.
[30] S.C.C. *Co. Surveyor's Rep.* Jan. 1923 (in *S.C.C. Mins.* 1922–3), 8.
[31] *Shrews. Chron.* 28 Oct. 1892; 10 May 1912; *S.C.C. Mins.* 1933–4, 373.
[32] *Oswestry Adv.* 10 May 1922; *Shrews. Chron.* 3 Aug. 1923.
[33] *S.C.C. Mins.* 1923–4, 135.
[34] *Shrews. Chron.* 21 Mar. 1924.
[35] S.R.O., Roads and Bridges Cttee. min. bk. 9, p. 8 (Finance Sub-Cttee. rep. 5 Apr. 1924, pp. 2–3).
[36] Local information (1974).
[37] Roads and Bridges Cttee. min. bk. 9, p. 8 (Finance Sub-Cttee. rep. 5 Apr. 1924, p. 3); *Shrews. Chron.* 20 Mar. 1925; *Oswestry Adv.* 6 May 1925.
[38] *Oswestry Adv.* 6 May 1925.

[39] S.C.C. *Co. Surveyor's Rep.* 15 Apr. 1926 (in *S.C.C. Mins.* 1926–7), 1–2.
[40] *Shrews. Chron.* 8 May 1925.
[41] Ibid. 13 Nov. 1925.
[42] S.R.O., Finance and Gen. Purposes Cttee. min. bk. 11, pp. 135–6.
[43] S.R.O., Roads and Bridges Cttee. min. bk. 10, p. 60 (*Ann. Estimate*, 1927–8, 1).
[44] Ibid. p. 158 (*Ann. Estimate*, 1928–9, 1–2).
[45] *S.C.C. Mins.* 1928–9, 292. Roads were classified by the Ministry of Transport under the Ministry of Transport Act, 1919, 9 & 10 Geo. V, c. 50.
[46] Listed in *Shrews. Chron.* 2 June 1939 (suppl.).
[47] S.C.C. *Co. Surveyor's Rep.* 14 Oct. 1929 (in *S.C.C. Mins.* 1929–30), 6; *S.C.C. Mins.* 1933–4, 10.
[48] Local information (1974).
[49] Under the Local Govt. Act, 1929, 19 & 20 Geo. V, c. 17: *S.C.C. Mins.* 1929–30, 5.

in 1924.[50] Not until 1934, however, was a corresponding renewal programme financially possible.[51] By 1939 their reconstruction was complete,[52] and the county's roads were sound enough to stand up well in wartime to enforced neglect and the wear and tear of heavy vehicles.[53]

After 1945 the council had difficulty in maintaining the standards it had set before the war. Much work was needed to restore the roads, additionally damaged by the exceptionally severe winter of 1946–7.[54] Throughout the 1940s and 1950s work was delayed by government restrictions[55] and the high cost of materials. In 1948 the council's force of roadmen, already half its pre-war size, was further reduced by government order.[56] Despite mounting complaints from the public the committee in 1948 felt powerless to prevent the rapid deterioration of road surfaces,[57] and the lengthsmen system had by then largely broken down; in 1949 only 56 per cent of the 607 lengths were permanently manned.[58] By 1951 the committee feared that government restrictions would lead to the 'complete collapse' of some county roads.[59] Those restrictions coincided with a great increase in the volume of traffic, and accident figures rose alarmingly; in 1951 the Shropshire accident rate equalled the national average, but by 1958 it was 30 per cent above it, with deaths and serious injuries 60 per cent above.[60]

Improvements came slowly. The committee, aiming to save man-power, decided in 1955 gradually to replace the lengthsmen by mechanized mobile gangs;[61] over the years the new system was found also to induce better standards of work.[62] Major improvements, however, came only when the Ministry of Transport allowed the resumption of large-scale capital expenditure in the 1960s. The ministry announced a ten-year programme of grants for classified roads in 1964, and for the first time since the 1930s the committee was able to adopt a comprehensive programme to bring its classified roads up to an acceptable standard.[63] The worst fears expressed by the committee in 1951 about the effects of government financial restrictions were thus dispelled by the early 1960s.[64] The situation was further eased in 1967 when the government lifted all restrictions on the council's capital expenditure on roads other than Class I (renamed 'principal') roads.[65] The same year, however, saw a diminution of the committee's powers; Shropshire was included in the area of the Midland Road Construction Unit, one of six units set up by the government to carry out all road schemes costing over £1 million.[66] The committee did not welcome the innovation[67] and its Roads and Bridges Department, because it had insufficient experience of large-scale works, was not invited to participate in running the unit.[68] In 1970 and 1973 the council again applied to take part, but without sucess.[69]

In 1937 the Ministry of Transport took over 118 miles of Shropshire trunk roads,[70] a development that the committee felt to be a threat to its independence.[71] The ministry, despite repeated representations by the council, made no plans for major improvements to trunk roads before 1967; the county, it argued, was too far from the

[50] S.R.O., Roads and Bridges Cttee. min. bk. 12, p. 2 (*Ann. Estimate, 1931–2*, 1); *S.C.C. Mins.* 1930–1, 103.

[51] *S.C.C. Mins.* 1932–3, 113; 1933–4, 382–3, 585; *S.C.C. Ann. Rep. of Co. Surveyor, 1934–5*, 2 (copy in S.R.O. 1676/3).

[52] *Shrews. Chron.* 2 June 1939 (suppl.).

[53] S.R.O., Roads and Bridges Cttee. min. bk. 14, pp. 113, 127 (Co. Surveyor's reps. Jan.–Mar., July–Sept. 1944).

[54] Ibid. p. 234 (Co. Surveyor's rep. Apr.–June 1947); *S.C.C. Mins.* 1946–7, 518–19; 1947–8, 137.

[55] *S.C.C. Mins.* 1950–1, 379; 1956–7, 30; 1957–8, 13; 1958–9, 303.

[56] Ibid. 1947–8, 262–3.

[57] Ibid. 262; S.R.O., Roads and Bridges Cttee. min.

bk. 14, p. 315 (Co. Surveyor's rep. Oct.–Dec. 1948).

[58] *S.C.C. Mins.* 1949–50, 178.

[59] Ibid. 1950–1, 379.

[60] Ibid. 1957–8, 290.

[61] Ibid. 1954–5, 332.

[62] 1963–4, 37.

[63] 1964–5, 162.

[64] Co. Surveyor's rep. June–Sept. 1964 (in S.R.O. 1731/2).

[65] *S.C.C. Mins.* 1966–7, 147, 390.

[66] Ibid. 353.

[67] Ibid. 1967–8, 59.

[68] Ibid. 211.

[69] Ibid. 1970–1, 269; 1973–4, 243, 301.

[70] Under the Trunk Roads Act, 1936, 1 Edw. VIII & 1 Geo. VI, c. 5: *Shrews. Chron.* 2 June 1939 (suppl.).

[71] *S.C.C. Mins.* 1936–7, 153.

country's main lines of communication to warrant immediate attention.[72] In 1967, however, trunk-road improvement schemes were promised for the early 1970s.[73]

Public Protection and Licensing

In 1890, following the Weights and Measures Act, 1889,[74] the County Rate and Weights and Measures Committee appointed two inspectors for North and South divisions of the county respectively; at first the committee allowed too little time for the initial testing of existing weights and measures, and great confusion ensued.[75] The inspectors sometimes failed to turn up at the times and places advertised.[76] By 1892 the inspectors finished their stamping but much necessary work remained untouched,[77] as was evident in the last quarter of 1904 when 938 of the 1,473 items tested proved faulty.[78] Efficiency, however, improved with better communications, and in 1935 the separately staffed divisions were amalgamated under a chief inspector.[79]

The committee's duties were gradually enlarged by Acts regulating conditions in shops, misdescription of fabrics, markets and fairs, merchandise marks, pharmacy and poisons, Sunday trading, and the employment of young people.[80] In 1946 it absorbed the Betting and Lotteries Committee[81] to form the Public Protection Committee.[82] Its scope was widened in 1951, when it took over theatre and cinema licensing from the magistrates,[83] and in 1959 when the council made it responsible for road-safety instruction.[84] By 1973, as a result of recent legislation,[85] the Weights and Measures Department was investigating more trading offences than ever, and often found itself the resort of those hoping for relief from 'the troubles involved in ill-conceived purchases'.[86]

Agriculture

The Executive Committee, responsible for control of animal diseases, met more often than any other in the early 1890s.[87] Its principal enemies were swine fever, sheep scab, and anthrax.[88] The restriction of trade imposed when swine fever was reported made the committee unpopular,[89] but in 1891 it adopted a slaughter policy, avoiding the closure of markets and declaration of infected areas.[90] The Contagious Diseases (Animals) Act, 1893,[91] deprived the council of much of its initiative in swine-fever control and the committee resolved to meet only monthly.[92] In the 1890s trade in sheep between counties on the Welsh border was hampered by sheep scab; counties whose internal control was good had often to ban imports from less efficient neighbours. In 1899, on the initiative of J. Bowen Jones, chairman of the council and a leading agriculturist, a 'combined area' of Welsh and English counties, including Shropshire, was formed to adopt uniform sheep-scab regulations[93] (superseded by

[72] S.C.C. Mins. 1966–7, 139; S.C.C. Salop Co. Council: the Post-War Years and the Future (1965).
[73] S.C.C. Mins. 1966–7, 457.
[74] 52 & 53 Vic. c. 21.
[75] S.C.C. Resumé of Work of First Co. Council of Salop [1893], 10–12.
[76] See e.g. Shrews. Chron. 13 Nov. 1891.
[77] Resumé of Work of First Co. Council, 10–12.
[78] Shrews. Chron. 10 Feb. 1905.
[79] Co. Councils Assoc. Jubilee of the Co. Councils (1939; Salop. edn.), 97.
[80] S.C.C. Year Bk. 1900–40.
[81] S.C.C. Mins. 1945–6, 265. The Betting and Lotteries Cttee. was set up in 1935 under the Betting and Lotteries Act, 1934, 24 & 25 Geo. V, c. 58: ibid. 1934–5, 574.
[82] Ibid. 1945–6, 335.

[83] 1950–1, 110.
[84] 1958–9, 244.
[85] Weights and Measures Act, 1963, c. 31; Trade Descriptions Act, 1968, c. 29.
[86] S.C.C. Salop Co. Council Review (1973), 17.
[87] S.C.C. Abstr. of No. of Meetings of Co. Council, 1892–5.
[88] Shrews. Chron. 18 Mar. 1910.
[89] S.C.C. Mins. Executive Cttee. rep. 9 Mar. 1892, 6; 14 Jan. 1893, 13.
[90] Ibid. Executive Cttee. rep. 14 Jan. 1893, 12.
[91] 56 & 57 Vic. c. 43.
[92] S.C.C. Mins. Executive Cttee. rep. 6 Jan. 1894, 12.
[93] Ibid. Executive Cttee. rep. 1 July 1899, 3; S.C.C. Mins. Rep. of Conference held at Shrews. 11 Nov. 1898, 3.

government measures in 1903);[94] but the disease remained as common in Shropshire in 1929 as in the 1890s.[95] In dealing with anthrax the Shropshire committee was, in 1901, one of the first to require the burning of carcasses.[96] With little independent initiative after 1904 the committee remained in being until 1959.[97] It conducted a bounty scheme against rats in 1919–20[98] and between 1932 and 1935 exterminated a plague of musk rats.[99] From 1937 to 1950, when its responsibility for rats ended,[1] it employed paid rat catchers.[2] In 1968 the council appointed an animal diseases inspectorate to perform the day-to-day duties[3] that it had until then delegated to the police.[4]

In the 1890s the council made little effort to publicize its power to provide smallholdings.[5] No applications for smallholdings were invited between 1893 and 1907;[6] seventeen were made but none was granted.[7] The Allotments and Small Holdings Committee claimed that there was little demand for smallholdings,[8] but in 1907 a survey revealed that there were some 290 potential applicants.[9] Sir Offley Wakeman (d. 1929), the committee's chairman, then argued that it was difficult to conceive of a scheme that would be both 'healthy from the moral point of view' and prosperous.[10] He warned the council against 'impulsive action' in its operation of the compulsory Act of 1907.[11] The council's scheme, however, developed quickly and was a financial success. By 1913 the council had acquired some 2,000 acres and granted 94 applications; larger holdings were being increasingly requested.[12] After the First World War a further 3,500 acres were purchased for ex-service men;[13] another 3,500 were acquired in the late 1920s and 1930s, with a government financial guarantee.[14] The guarantee proved unnecesary; the council made a profit every year from 1926 to 1939. By 1939 it had 380 smallholdings; arrears of rent were negligible and the number of good applicants was embarrassingly large.[15] The estate was held to be one of the best run in the country.[16] After the Second World War little new land could be acquired; the committee concentrated instead on improving the existing holdings. By 1972, in response to changes in farming economics, the sizes of holdings had been increased by amalgamation so that their number had fallen to 260. In that year the committee decided to aim, through further amalgamations, at a total of 161 large holdings by the end of the century.[17]

A Drainage Committee was set up in 1920 to supervise the existing drainage authorities in the county and to carry out small schemes of its own.[18] In 1930 the supervisory duties were taken over by the new River Severn Catchment Board[19] but the council kept the power to initiate schemes in areas not covered by internal drainage boards; it had also to enforce maintenance of watercourses, and by 1939 had dealt

[94] Under the Diseases of Animals Act, 1903, 3 Edw. VII, c. 43: *Shrews. Chron.* 27 Feb. 1925.

[95] *S.C.C. Mins.* 1929–30, 114.

[96] *Shrews. Chron.* 8 Nov. 1901; 27 Feb. 1925.

[97] *S.C.C. Mins.* 1958–9, 327–8.

[98] Ibid. 1919–20, 62; 1920–1, 71.

[99] *Shrews. Chron.* 2 June 1939 (suppl.); *Jubilee of Co. Councils,* 82–3.

[1] Under the Prevention of Damage by Pests Act, 1949, 12 & 13 Geo. VI, c. 55.

[2] *S.C.C. Mins.* 1937–8, 232–3; 1949–50, 195.

[3] Under the Diseases of Animals Act, 1950, 14 Geo. VI, c. 36.

[4] *S.C.C. Mins.* 1968–9, 132.

[5] Under the Allotments Act, 1890, 53 & 54 Vic. c. 65, and Small Holdings Act, 1892, 55 & 56 Vic. c. 31.

[6] *S.C.C. Mins.* Allotments and Small Holdings Cttee. rep. 25 Mar. 1893, 26 (the last ref. in the mins.).

[7] *Shrews. Chron.* 10 May 1907.

[8] S.C.C. *Résumé of Work of First Co. Council of Salop* [1893], 47; S.R.O., Allotments and Small Holdings

Cttee. min. bk. 1890–4, p. 4; *S.C.C. Mins.* Allotments and Small Holdings Cttee. rep. 14 Oct. 1893, 22.

[9] S.R.O., Local Govt. etc. Cttee. min. bk. 1904–26, p. 73.

[10] *Shrews. Chron.* 10 May 1907.

[11] Ibid. 8 Nov. 1907; Small Holdings and Allotments Act, 1907, 7 Edw. VII, c. 54.

[12] *Shrews. Chron.* 13 Feb. 1914.

[13] Under the Land Settlement (Facilities) Act, 1919, 9 & 10 Geo. V, c. 59: *Shrews. Chron.* 7 Feb. 1919; 2 June 1939 (suppl.).

[14] Under the Small Holdings and Allotments Act, 1926, 16 & 17 Geo. V, c. 52: ibid. 2 June 1939 (suppl.).

[15] Ibid.

[16] Local information (1974).

[17] Under the Agriculture Act, 1970, c. 40: *S.C.C. Mins.* 1971–2, 518, 520–1.

[18] Under the Land Drainage Act, 1918, 8 & 9 Geo. V, c. 17: ibid. 1919–20, 115; 1920–1, 22.

[19] Under the Land Drainage Act, 1930, 20 & 21 Geo. V, c. 44.

with some 400 cases.[20] Between 1963 and 1973 the Land Drainage Department reclaimed some 60,000 acres in Shropshire.[21]

Education

Between 1889 and 1903 the council was directly concerned only with further education; that is, part-time instruction for those who had left school. In 1891 the council approved a scheme prepared by the Intermediate, Technical, and Agricultural Education Committee.[22] It provided for domestic-science classes and lectures in science with special reference to industry and agriculture. In addition it provided for grants to the schools of art and science at Oswestry, Shrewsbury, and Wellington, and to local committees set up in each poor-law union. Those bodies were to provide classes in subjects that were in local demand, such as handicrafts, modern languages, forestry, book-keeping, and nursing. Some scholarships, tenable at grammar schools and universities, were to be set up.[23] An organizing secretary, F. R. Armytage, was appointed in the same year.[24] The scheme aimed to provide technical instruction in every part of the county and to any person, however poor, who might care to attend.

The scheme was too idealistic to succeed. In country areas the standard of elementary education was so low that academic subjects could not successfully be taught.[25] Domestic science, at first popular, lost its appeal[26] and football claimed many male students.[27] There were too few applicants for the scholarships,[28] and hardly any of the university scholarships went to former elementary-school pupils.[29] The main beneficiaries of the scheme were the middle classes, not the poor. The disappointments intensified the disquiet with which the scheme had, in some quarters, been received.[30] Landowners throughout the country feared that technical education would harm an already declining agriculture.[31] A few council members disapproved of further education for the working classes; others doubted whether the scheme could be effective; many more, however, felt that the money, which came wholly from government sources, would be better used to relieve the rates.[32] In 1894, in response to mounting pressure,[33] the committee agreed that the scheme should be curtailed and that more than a third of the annual government grant should be diverted to relieve the general rate.[34]

Thereafter the council became more selective in its use of technical-education funds. Evening classes, open to all, were reduced in number.[35] Expenditure on competitive scholarships was increased from £28 in 1893–4 to £510 in 1894–5 and continued to increase until 1907–8, when free places at the new county secondary schools began to reduce demand.[36] In 1895 the council began to support the proposed Harper Adams Agricultural College at Edgmond, and in 1896 the proposed Shropshire Technical School for Girls at Radbrook.[37] By 1913, however, Shropshire had made

[20] *Jubilee of Co. Councils*, 82; *Shrews. Chron.* 2 June 1939 (suppl.).
[21] S.C.C. *Salop. Co. Council Review* (1973), 19.
[22] *S.C.C. Mins.* 23 May 1891, 2–5.
[23] *S.C.C. Mins.* Intermediate Educ. Cttee. rep. 9 May 1891, 22–6.
[24] *S.C.C. Mins.* 23 May 1891, 4.
[25] Ibid. Intermediate Educ. Cttee. rep. 11 Jan. 1892, 10; 12 July 1892, 41–7.
[26] Ibid. 9 May 1891, 27; 11 Jan. 1892, 10; 8 July 1893, 45.
[27] Ibid. 30 June 1894, 41.
[28] Ibid. 11 Jan. 1892, 9; 12 July 1892, 35; 14 Oct. 1893, 14.
[29] S.C.C. *Rep. on After-Careers of Co. Council University Scholarship Holders, 1894–1913*, 2 (copy in S.R.O.).
[30] *S.C.C. Mins.* Intermediate Educ. Cttee. rep. 31 Oct. 1891, 29; 11 Jan. 1892, 10; S.R.O. 784/50, meeting 23 May 1891.
[31] P. Keane, 'An Eng. County and Education: Som. 1889-1902', *E.H.R.* lxxxviii. 288–9.
[32] S.R.O. 784/50, meeting 22 Oct. 1892; *S.C.C. Mins.* Intermediate Educ. Cttee. rep. 8 July 1893, 28; *Shrews. Chron.* 9 Nov. 1900; 6 Nov. 1925.
[33] S.R.O. 784/50, meetings 22 Apr., 22 July 1893.
[34] Ibid. meeting 27 Apr. 1894.
[35] *S.C.C. Mins.* Intermediate Educ. Cttee. rep. 14 July 1900, 6; S.C.C. *Higher Educ. Dept. Rep. 1905–6*, 27 (copy in S.R.O.).
[36] *Rep. on After-Careers*, 1.
[37] *S.C.C. Mins.* 1897–8, 506; ibid. 4 May 1901, 1.

less progress in technical education than had other rural counties.[38] Evening classes in country areas continued until 1914 to meet with apathy among the inhabitants and some hostility from employers; the lower-paid were in any case discouraged from attending by long working hours and lack of transport.[39]

The Education Act, 1902,[40] aroused strong feelings among Shropshire nonconformists;[41] they objected to the fact that, under the Act, Anglican elementary schools would be supported by the ratepayers and allowed to continue to provide denominational religious instruction. Of the 279 elementary schools that came under the council's control in 1903 all but 30 were 'voluntary' and most of them Anglican.[42] Nonconformists were well represented on the council, but sectarian attitudes were carefully avoided by both sides.[43] In 1902, in discussing the Education Bill, the council was in favour of half the managers of each elementary school being appointed by the council, rather than the one third required by the Bill and the eventual Act;[44] feeling on the council thus did not reflect Anglican opinion in Shropshire.[45] Under the chairmanship of R. G. Venables (1903–6), genial, popular, and scrupulously fair,[46] the Education Committee was able to put the Act into effect with very little ill-feeling. A few Shropshire nonconformists tried to organize non-payment of the elementary education rate but they failed to attract support or even interest.[47] T. Ward Green, a nonconformist newcomer to the council in 1904, was surprised to find himself warmly received by its members,[48] and by 1905 it was possible to refer to a 'general spirit of content' that distinguished Shropshire in the matter of education from the Welsh counties.[49] In 1906 the Anglican majority on the council made a conscious gesture of goodwill in supporting the election of a staunch nonconformist, W. H. Smith, as Venables's successor.[50]

In 1903 Armytage, the organizing secretary, was offered the post of secretary for education. Finding the salary unacceptable, he asked to be dismissed with the statutory compensation, but the council refused. He remained responsible for higher education and a separate secretary for elementary education, H. E. Wale, was appointed.[51] Armytage resigned soon afterwards[52] but the dual administration could not be abandoned without dismissing Wale, and it therefore continued until Wale's retirement in 1924.[53] Until the 1920s little change in the pattern of elementary education in Shropshire resulted from the council's assumption of responsibility in 1903; in the field of secondary education, however, an entirely new system of county schools was created under the direction of W. H. Pendlebury, secretary for higher education 1903–24 and secretary for education 1924–36.

In 1900 secondary education for boys in Shropshire was provided by 10 endowed, 1 proprietary, and 18 private schools. For girls there were 1 proprietary and 78 private schools.[54] In England in 1904 some 48 per cent of boys estimated to be capable of benefiting from secondary education were receiving it. In none of Shropshire's fifteen registration districts did provision reach that level, and only in the Wem and

[38] T. D. M. Jones, 'Development of Educational Provision in the Rural Co. of Salop. between 1870 and 1914' (Keele Univ. M.A. (Ed.) thesis, 1969), 365–6. This article was completed before Mr. Jones's thesis was seen. Mr. Jones's conclusions are similar to those expressed here.
[39] *Higher Educ. Dept. Rep. 1912–14*, 19.
[40] 2 Edw. VII, c. 42.
[41] *Oswestry Adv.* 13 Nov. 1946.
[42] *S.C.C. Mins.* 1903–4, 118–23.
[43] S.R.O. 148/15, Venables C.C. newscuttings 1902–4, p. 10; ibid. Venables educ. newscuttings 1906–7, p. 3.
[44] *S.C.C. Mins.* 3 May 1902, 25.
[45] *The Times*, 4 June 1902.

[46] *Shrews. Chron.* 11 Mar. 1905.
[47] Jones, 'Devt. of Educ. Provision', 234–6.
[48] *Oswestry Adv.* 13 Nov. 1946.
[49] *Shrews. Chron.* 17 Mar. 1905.
[50] S.R.O. 148/15, Venables educ. newscuttings 1906–7, p. 7.
[51] *S.C.C. Mins.* rep. of sub-cttee. appointed by Special Educ. Cttee. 21 Mar. 1903, 1–2; S.R.O. 148/15, Venables educ. newscuttings 1903–4, p. 23; ibid. Venables C.C. newscuttings 1902–4, p. 32.
[52] *S.C.C. Mins. (Educ.)*, 1903–4, 40.
[53] *Shrews. Chron.* 6 Feb. 1925.
[54] *S.C.C. Mins.* Intermediate Educ. Cttee. rep. 21 Apr. 1900, 4.

Newport districts did the proportion even approach it. Provision for girls, though better numerically, was worse than that for boys, for the academic standard of the many girls' private schools was low.[55] Even in boys' schools the standard was not high; only a third of the pupils there learned any science.[56] In 1905 Pendlebury presented a scheme to the Education Committee with the aim that each ratepayer 'should have within reach as good facilities for the secondary education of his children as he has for elementary education'. He proposed the building of six new boys' schools and eight 'dual' schools (with boys and girls in separate classrooms), and it was hoped that existing grammar and private schools would agree to be absorbed into the scheme with financial support from the council. Pendlebury recommended a system of differential rating, by which maintenance of a school would be supported by a rate leviable only in the union that it served.[57] The scheme did not of course aim at secondary education for all; in 1915 Pendlebury stated that the secondary school was framed to suit 'the needs of the middle-class parent' looking forward to a profession for his son, and to help young people who would not otherwise have a chance of further study.[58]

Opposition to the 1905 scheme in the county at large centred on its financial arrangements and on its possible social effects. Many felt that differential rating would unfairly burden the remoter parishes of unions where schools were built. Others felt that boys in rural areas would be better off learning practical farming, and held higher education to blame for the loss of good labourers.[59] Rural depopulation and agricultural depression had long been serious problems. School leavers often made for Canada, the south of England, or the south Lancashire mills. A petition signed by eight farmers from Hopton Cangeford and Cold Weston stated that they had no money to spare for secondary education, no land to spare, and no time to spare as 'farm work is never done'.[60] The council's debate on the scheme kept mainly to the financial question. A proposal to refer the scheme back was defeated only by the chairman's casting vote.[61] The first new schools were to be at Bridgnorth and Shifnal.[62]

Local opposition forced the council to abandon the Shifnal scheme.[63] In 1909, however, the objections of many ratepayers were met by the introduction of a 'zonal' rating system, under which parishes were rated according to their distance from the secondary school provided in their poor-law union.[64] Progress after 1909 was rapid; by 1914 thirteen new secondary schools had been opened.[65] Most of the grammar schools had joined the county system, and about half the girls at independent secondary schools had come within the scheme.[66] In 1915 Pendlebury claimed that Shropshire had 'the most complete system of secondary schools under public management of any rural county in England'.[67] The adoption of the scheme had not immediately dispelled the mood of caution and scepticism, and the new schools were referred to as 'Smith's follies' after the chairman of the committee.[68] The committee had consequently been anxious not to overestimate the number of secondary places needed,[69] but by 1915 so many pupils were being attracted by the schools that there was perceptible

[55] S.C.C. Mins. 1903–4, 256, 258.
[56] S.C.C. Seventeen Years of Secondary Educ. in Salop. (1920), 4 (copy in S.R.O.).
[57] S.C.C. Secondary Educ. Scheme (1905), 1–14 (copy in S.R.O.).
[58] Higher Educ. Dept. Rep. 1912–14, 7.
[59] Secondary Educ. Scheme, 60, 66, 72, 76, 78.
[60] Ibid. 71.
[61] Shrews. Chron. 28 July 1905.
[62] S.C.C. Mins. 1905–6, 109–10.

[63] Higher Educ. Dept. Rep. 1905–6, 1; 1906–7, 27.
[64] Ibid. 1908–9, 1.
[65] Shrews. Chron. 2 June 1939 (suppl.).
[66] S.C.C. Public Secondary Schs. in Salop. 1903–10 (1911), 1 (copy in S.R.O.); Seventeen Years of Secondary Educ. 3.
[67] Higher Educ. Dept. Rep. 1912–14, 3.
[68] Shrews. Chron. 5 Jan. 1940.
[69] Seventeen Years of Secondary Educ. 8.

pressure on the available space.[70] By 1919 ten council secondary schools were in urgent need of enlargement.[71]

The extension of secondary education in Shropshire was accompanied by an improvement in its quality. Headmasters were allowed exceptional independence and could, for example, appoint their own staff.[72] In 1903 graduates formed only 35 per cent of staff in boys' schools and 5 per cent in girls' schools; by 1920 those proportions were 80 per cent and 51 per cent. By 1920 all boys and 90 per cent of girls learned science. All girls then learned mathematics, though only 24 per cent had done so in 1903.[73] By 1928 nearly 10 per cent of secondary-school leavers each year went to universities, compared with a national average of under 5 per cent.[74] Nevertheless the number of pupils remaining at secondary schools after the age of sixteen showed no increase over 1903. In 1911 Pendlebury condemned as 'pure waste' the attitude of many parents that a year or two's 'veneer' of secondary education was enough.[75]

The success of the secondary-education scheme was considered a personal triumph for Smith, chairman of the committee from 1906 to 1921.[76] Smith's powers of persuasion helped to overcome early opposition, and his 'silvery speech' was effective in obtaining the necessary finance.[77] On the other hand Smith's very success, and Pendlebury's insistence that the secondary scheme should have foremost place in the council's education programme,[78] led to relative neglect of the elementary schools[79] and of technical education.[80]

Under the 1902 Act maintenance of voluntary-school buildings remained the responsibility of the voluntary organizations. By 1906, however, subscriptions to those organizations were seriously falling off, as the public seemed to suppose that the local authority was maintaining the buildings.[81] In 1903 some county councils encouraged the continuance of local initiative by forming area committees with local representatives. In Shropshire, however, the council favoured strong central control, which led to a decline of local interest in the schools.[82] The council was disinclined to spend money on elementary education, having one of the lowest rates for that purpose in England.[83] Neglect ensued and was aggravated by the austerity of the First World War and its aftermath.[84] Before the Education Act, 1918, the council could build a new elementary school only by raising a special local rate; its attempts to do so always met 'enormous local pressure' to patch up the existing school, however unsuitable.[85] Local opposition also frustrated its attempts to close down certain schools altogether.[86] The 1918 Act[87] did away with the need for a local rate, but until 1925 the building of new council schools was opposed both by council members and by the voluntary-schools associations.[88] By that time the condition of some school buildings was very bad.

In 1925 the Board of Education issued a 'black list' of Shropshire elementary schools: 19 (18 of them voluntary) were beyond improvement and 30 (27 of them voluntary) needed extensive repair.[89] The Education Committee worked out a 'concordat' with the voluntary-schools associations based on a scheme adopted in the

[70] *Higher Educ. Dept. Rep. 1912–14*, 3.
[71] *Shrews. Chron.* 1 Aug. 1919.
[72] Ex inf. Sir Offley Wakeman (1974).
[73] *Seventeen Years of Secondary Educ.* 4.
[74] *Shrews. Chron.* 16 Mar. 1928.
[75] *Public Secondary Schs. 1903–10*, 3; *Seventeen Years of Secondary Educ.* 10.
[76] *Shrews. Chron.* 5 Jan. 1940.
[77] Ibid. 27 May 1910.
[78] *Seventeen Years of Secondary Educ.* 3.
[79] *Shrews. Chron.* 12 Nov. 1937; *Wellington Jnl.* 4 Oct. 1947; local information (1974).

[80] Jones, 'Devt. of Educ. Provision', 366.
[81] S.R.O. 148/15, Venables educ. newscuttings 1906–7, p. 13.
[82] Jones, op. cit. 250–1, 261.
[83] Ibid. 301–2.
[84] *Shrews. Chron.* 6 Feb. 1925.
[85] Ibid. 1 Aug. 1924.
[86] Ibid. 7 May 1926.
[87] 8 & 9 Geo. V, c. 39.
[88] *Shrews. Chron.* 1 Aug. 1924.
[89] *S.C.C. Mins. (Educ.)*, 1925–6, 80–1.

West Riding of Yorkshire; the council would take responsibility for a school building while allowing denominational religious instruction to be continued in it. In other words, Anglican schools that would otherwise have to close would, thanks to public funds, be enabled to continue giving denominational religious instruction. The proposal threatened to split the council on sectarian lines. The alternative, for the council to spend large sums building entirely new schools of its own, was equally unwelcome to some members. The concordat proposal was carried by a small majority[90] but never needed to be put into effect, for by 1927 the voluntary associations had sufficient funds to carry out the work unaided.[91] By 1939 most of the 'black list' schools had been closed or in some way improved.[92] In 1925, owing to the efforts of A. R. Clegg, chairman of the Education Committee 1922–37,[93] there began a ten-year campaign to renew the elementary schools' equipment and books,[94] which had been in a state of neglect since before the First World War.[95]

In 1929 the organization of public elementary education in Shropshire had changed little since 1903:[96] 1·2 per cent of the child population was in secondary schools;[97] all other children not educated privately stayed at a single elementary school until they were fourteen. In 1926 the Hadow Report recommended that elementary-school children between eleven and fourteen should be taught in separate senior schools or departments, large enough in either case to provide a practical education suited to their special needs. In 1929, therefore, Pendlebury recommended the creation of senior schools in towns and of senior departments (known as 'senior tops') at selected rural schools. Many of the 42 new schools and departments needed might have to be provided by the voluntary-schools associations. The associations were expected not only to resist the financial burden but also to oppose the scheme on the ground that some children would be transferred at eleven from a church school to a council one; nonconformists, for their part, might object to the transfer of their children at that age from a council to a church school.[98] Some people in rural areas feared the social effects of sending children to schools outside their home parishes.[99] Those difficulties hampered progress[1] and were not mitigated until the Education Act, 1936,[2] enabled the council to make grants to the associations towards senior-school provision; the Act also directed that pupils transferred to a senior school at eleven must be allowed to continue to receive the form of religious instruction that they had had at their elementary school.[3] Co-operation between the associations and the council ensued[4] and twelve senior schools were in use when war intervened in 1939.[5]

The extension of secondary education, together with a more selective policy, made the council's technical-instruction programme moderately successful in the 1920s and 1930s. By 1925 evening classes had been discontinued in the smaller towns in face of competition from the cinema and other popular entertainments. Instruction was concentrated at the Shrewsbury Technical School and School of Art, the Oswestry Technical Institute and School of Art, and at sixteen centres in the industrial east of the county. The Walker Technical College at Oakengates was opened in 1927[6] and a new purpose-built technical college at Shrewsbury in 1938.[7] The centres were in-

[90] *Oswestry Adv.* 10 Feb. 1926; *Shrews. Chron.* 12 Feb. 1926.
[91] *Shrews. Chron.* 29 July 1927.
[92] Ibid. 2 June 1939 (suppl.).
[93] Ibid. 12 Nov. 1937. In 1939 Clegg was knighted for political and public services in Salop.: *Lond. Gaz.* 2 Jan. 1939, p. 2.
[94] *Shrews. Chron.* 7 May 1926.
[95] Ibid. 6 and 13 Feb. 1925; 7 May 1926.
[96] Ibid. 2 June 1939 (suppl.).
[97] Ibid. 16 Mar. 1928.
[98] S.R.O. 2699/10, pp. 117–43.
[99] Local information (1974).
[1] *S.C.C. Mins. (Educ.)*, 1930–1, 39; *S.C.C. Mins.* 1931–2, 367.
[2] 26 Geo. V & 1 Edw. VIII, c. 41.
[3] *S.C.C. Mins.* 1936–7, 86–7.
[4] *Oswestry Adv.* 9 Mar. 1938.
[5] S.C.C. *Educ. in Salop. 1945 to 1965* (1965), 12 (copy in S.R.O. 1631/1).
[6] *S.C.C. Mins. (Educ.)*, 1927–8, 60, 66.
[7] Ibid. 1938–9, 74.

creasingly popular and attracted better students than before the First World War. Some day classes were provided. The courses were almost exclusively vocational, but there were some signs in Shrewsbury that people were becoming interested in cultural and recreational subjects. Those subjects, however, remained the province of other bodies, such as the Workers' Educational Association, the Women's Institutes, and the universities.[8]

Before the Second World War, despite the success of the secondary-education scheme, Shropshire was in many ways behind the times in educational matters.[9] A wider view of education policy was introduced by Sir Offley Wakeman, chairman of the Education Committee from 1944.[10] He had already had great experience in educational administration, first with the London County Council, then, from 1926, with the Shropshire Education Committee,[11] of which he had been chairman 1937-40.[12] A member of the Education Advisory Committee of the County Councils Association, he had taken part in the negotiations preparatory to the Education Act of 1944.[13] He remained chairman of the Shropshire committee until 1967[14] and in partnership with H. Martin Wilson, secretary for education 1936-65,[15] reorganized the county's education services on the lines of the Act. Wilson, too, was exceptionally well qualified for his task. He was noted for vision and drive and the ability to communicate them to others.[16] It was sometimes alleged, however, that he would push his policies through without due regard to the committee's views.[17] He had personal influence in Whitehall and studied developments in other parts of the country and abroad.[18] By the time he retired Shropshire had moved from a backward to a leading position in education[19] and Wilson's own reputation was by then international.[20]

In 1947 Wilson presented a county development plan for education, calling for capital expenditure of over £7½ million spread over eighteen years. According to the plan many of the 292 primary schools were too small to be economically or educationally viable and the closure of 153 was recommended. Of those retained, 96 were to be rebuilt. Forty new primary schools were to be set up. There were to be secondary 'modern' schools throughout the county, 23 of them in new buildings, providing secondary education for every child irrespective of academic ability.[21] Many ratepayers were dismayed at the proposed expenditure,[22] and most of the opposition to the plan, when it came before the council, was directed against the costs.[23] A few members objected on religious grounds. Under the Act voluntary schools that could not be rebuilt or substantially improved without council assistance, and had therefore to acquire 'controlled' status, would no longer be allowed to give denominational religious instruction except to those pupils whose parents requested it. Such schools formed the majority of those retained in Wilson's plan.[24] The diocesan authorities made no serious difficulties during preparation of the plan[25] but a few council members, among them the Revd. R. A. Giles, objected that the spiritual aspects of education were being sacrificed in favour of 'bricks and mortar'. On the other hand Peter Morris (Labour) held that parents were tired of religious denominations trying to 'seek power through

[8] S.C.C. *Technical and Evening Classes, 1924-25,* 2-17 (copy in S.R.O.); *Shrews. Chron.* 2 June 1939 (suppl.).
[9] *Shrews. Chron.* 23 Oct. 1964; *S.C.C. Mins.* 1965-6, 8.
[10] *S.C.C. Mins.* (*Educ.*), 1944-5, 63-4.
[11] *Shrews. Chron.* 19 Mar. 1926.
[12] *S.C.C. Mins.* (*Educ.*), 1937-8, 107; 1940-1, 52.
[13] 7 & 8 Geo. VI, c. 31; *Oswestry Adv.* 11 Oct. 1944.
[14] *S.C.C. Mins.* (*Educ.*), 1967-8, 112.
[15] *S.C.C. Mins.* 1936-7, 221; *S.C.C. Mins.* (*Educ.*), 1964-5, 337.
[16] *Shrews. Chron.* 23 Oct. 1964.
[17] Ibid. 4 July 1947; 3 Feb. 1950; *Oswestry Adv.*

23 Mar. 1949.
[18] Local information (1974).
[19] *Shrews. Chron.* 23 Oct. 1964; *S.C.C. Mins.* 1965-6, 8.
[20] *Shrews. Chron.* 10 Jan., 23 Oct. 1964; *S.C.C. Mins.* (*Educ.*), 1965-6, 62.
[21] S.C.C. *Development Plan of Primary and Secondary Educ.* (1947; copy in S.R.O.).
[22] *Oswestry Adv.* 18 June 1947.
[23] *Shrews. Chron.* 23 May 1947.
[24] Unless otherwise stated, the rest of this section is based on S.C.C. *Educ. in Salop. 1945-65.*
[25] *Wellington Jnl.* 24 May 1947.

the schools'.[26] The financial question, however, was uppermost and a motion was put that it was 'financially impracticable' to carry the plan into effect. The motion was defeated by only 34 votes to 32. Replying to the debate Wakeman hoped that council members 'would do nothing which might indicate to the public or the government that they were not really keen on educational progress'.[27] At the end of the debate the plan was adopted.[28]

The plan proposed to emphasize in the early years the building of new secondary schools, but in the event primary schools had to take precedence as successive post-war 'bulges' and the development of new housing areas brought an unforeseen increase in the number of younger children. From 1949 to 1953 the council's capital expenditure on primary schools exceeded that on any of its other educational services. There was an impression of new schools appearing everywhere, but much in fact remained to be done. In 1953 only 40 per cent of Shropshire primary schools had water-borne sanitation, and 27 per cent were lit only by oil lamps. In 1950 over-crowding was said by one councillor to be 'beyond words',[29] but it grew worse. In 1946 there had been 88 primary-school classes with more than 40 pupils; by 1954 there were 214. As church schools one by one became 'controlled', some improvements were possible. For primary schools, however, traditional building methods were proving too slow and expensive to fulfil the objects of the 1947 plan, let alone to provide extra space for the unforeseen numbers. Experiments with buildings of light construction began in 1948 and in 1965 they remained the only feasible form of relief to many small schools. Provision of permanent buildings was accelerated in 1962 when, on the initiative of the county architect, R. V. Crowe, the Second Consortium of Local Authorities ('SCOLA') was formed. Several education authorities co-operated to develop a system of building based on a small range of mass-produced structural components; it had the advantages of bulk purchase and rapid erection and by 1965 was the only method used in Shropshire to put up permanent school buildings.[30] By 1965 some 42 per cent of primary-school children in the county were being taught in post-war buildings, but only 58 permanent new schools had been built, against the 136 indicated for that date in the 1947 plan.

Teaching methods in primary schools changed considerably in the twenty years following the Second World War. Wilson encouraged experiment and innovation in the classroom:[31] flexible timetables, group activity, self-expression, and opportunities for individual discovery modified for many children the disciplined learning which had been normal in the 1940s. By 1965 some schools were experimenting with classes of mixed age and ability, in which children were said to acquire a sense of interdependence.

Secondary-school building did not assume priority until 1953–4; thereafter progress was rapid and by the late 1950s most parts of the county had secondary modern schools. In the immediate post-war years a limited programme was conducted, using makeshift accommodation and offering a minimum of two years' secondary education to most primary-school leavers. To allow rapid coverage of the county the new buildings were designed to minimal specifications, and although 24 had been erected by 1965 there was a serious deficiency of special rooms for practical subjects, made worse by an increasing number of pupils staying for four or five years. Nevertheless the aim of secondary education for all had been virtually achieved; in 1965 only one all-age primary school remained from the 207 existing in 1945.

[26] Ibid.; *Shrews. Chron.* 23 May 1947.
[27] *Oswestry Adv.* 21 May 1947.
[28] *S.C.C. Mins.* 1947–8, 7

[29] *Express & Star*, 14 Oct. 1950.
[30] *S.C.C. Mins.* 1966–7, 336.
[31] *S.C.C. Mins. (Educ.)*, 1965–6, 62.

At first the secondary modern schools were little concerned with external examinations. Headmasters, encouraged by the committee, could develop curricula according to their own estimate of pupils' needs. The demand of employers and parents for formal qualifications, however, forced the schools to concede that some external examination should be provided.[32] Groups of secondary modern schools in Shropshire devised their own school-leaving certificates, and a few pupils were entered for the General Certificate of Education. The first examination to be devised by the government expressly for secondary modern schools, the Certificate of Secondary Education, was taken for the first time in 1965. The extension of examinations to the whole of the secondary-modern field was greeted by the committee 'without enthusiasm'.

Comprehensive schools (secondary schools taking pupils undifferentiated by ability) were included in the 1947 plan for areas where the population was too small to sustain two efficient selective schools, and in other places where local circumstances seemed favourable.[33] In 1951 hardly any council member supported P. H. Griffiths, representing Drayton, when he attacked the principle of comprehensive schools and called for their deletion from the 1947 plan.[34] Local opinion in Market Drayton, where the grammar school was to become part of a comprehensive school, was so strongly divided, however, that even in 1965 when the new school, the Grove, was opened,[35] some local people remained hostile. On the other hand in 1963 the council approved a system of comprehensive schools for Dawley new town and met little local opposition.[36] In 1965 the Labour government required local authorities to reorganize their secondary-education schemes on completely comprehensive lines. Neither the Education Committee nor the council wished to oppose the government in principle,[37] and by 1968 the council had introduced or approved schemes for comprehensive education in thirteen areas.[38] Comprehensive schools worked well in Shropshire because they never attained an unmanageable size.[39] Even when compulsion was withdrawn by the Conservative government in 1970, the council decided to press on with such comprehensive schemes as were already planned.[40] The committee and the council could not, however, agree on a scheme for Shrewsbury. Although most Shrewsbury parents and teachers favoured comprehensive education,[41] the council rejected in 1968 and 1971 the committee's recommendations for a comprehensive system in the town.[42]

The technical-education scheme was expanded after 1945. Between 1945 and 1950 the scope of evening classes was enlarged to include a wider range of cultural subjects. Area tutors were appointed to organize cultural and recreational classes in co-operation with the Workers' Educational Association and Birmingham University, and in 1948 the council was associated with the establishment of the Shropshire Adult College at Attingham Park,[43] one of the first such ventures in England.[44] The Shropshire Farm Institute at Walford was opened by the council in 1949 and proved an outstanding success; it offered a one-year residential course and quickly developed as a centre for other courses and activities.[45] There was a great need for more 'day-release' courses in vocational subjects for people in employment between the ages of sixteen and eighteen.[46] In 1950 the council approved a further-education scheme prepared by Wilson, which

[32] *Oswestry Adv.* 30 June 1948.
[33] *Devt. Plan of Primary and Secondary Educ.* 5.
[34] *Shrews. Chron.* 19 Oct. 1951.
[35] *V.C.H. Salop.* ii. 145.
[36] *S.C.C. Mins. (Educ.),* 1962-3, 177; 1969-70, 241; 1970-1, 242.
[37] Ibid. 1965-6, 252.
[38] Ibid. 1968-9, 278.
[39] Local information (1974).

[40] *S.C.C. Mins. (Educ.),* 1970-1, 226, 242; *S.C.C. Mins.* 1970-1, 334.
[41] *S.C.C. Mins. (Educ.),* 1971-2, 85, 87.
[42] Ibid. 1968-9, 279; 1972-3, 87.
[43] Ibid. 1950-1, 70-9.
[44] Local information (1974).
[45] *S.C.C. Mins. (Educ.),* 1950-1, 76, 83; 1961-2, 273; local information (1974).
[46] *S.C.C. Mins. (Educ.),* 1950-1, 79.

required among other things the expansion of the three existing technical colleges and the establishment of five others. They would concentrate on providing day-release courses.[47] By 1965 progress had been slower than expected. It was hoped to start by 1953 on new college buildings at Bridgnorth, Oakengates, Oswestry, and Shrewsbury,[48] but only the first instalments of work at those places had been finished by 1965.[49] The number of students more than trebled between 1945 and 1965, but even then only 28 per cent of employed young people of 16–18 attended day-release courses. Agricultural day-release courses, however, were offered at ten centres by 1962 and were attended by most young people entering agriculture.[50] There had, on the other hand, been no development of 'block-release' (short residential) courses,[51] preferred by farmers and recommended by Wilson in 1950.[52]

From the outset the council could send handicapped children to special schools outside the county. Parents, however, often withheld their consent and kept the children at home, in some cases sending them to ordinary elementary schools. According to Lt.-Col. James Patchett, addressing the Education Committee in 1905, many such children — blind, deaf and dumb, and epileptic — were 'living the lives of animals'.[53] In 1906 the elementary schools were known to contain 171 mentally deficient, 52 epileptic, 17 blind, and 9 deaf children.[54] More were discovered when school medical inspection began in 1908.[55] By 1913 some progress had been made in the placing of mentally deficient children under permanent care outside the county.[56] Until after the Second World War, however, the council did not consider that there were enough children of any one disability to justify the provision of a special school for them.[57] In 1947 it opened a school for educationally subnormal boys at Petton Hall. In 1949 it opened one for maladjusted and delicate children at Trench Hall, and in 1950 a school for subnormal girls at Haughton Hall. Children with other disabilities were helped, as before, by arrangement with other local education authorities, through the Regional Conference on Handicapped Children in the West Midlands (later the West Midlands Advisory Council for Special Educational Treatment), set up in 1946 with Wilson as its first secretary. In 1958 the Education Committee, urged by Wilson to combat the undue segregation of handicapped children,[58] opened a day school and advice centre in Shrewsbury for such children under seven and their parents; in the same year the committee began to provide special classes attached to ordinary primary schools.

The Education Committee, with some reluctance, set up a county library in 1925,[59] taking advantage of a capital grant from the Carnegie United Kingdom Trust. The committee's scheme provided for 300 centres throughout the county,[60] housed in makeshift accommodation, manned by volunteers, and open for a few hours each week. Boxes of books were sent from headquarters by train or bus. By 1930 most people were within reach of a centre, and deliveries were being made in a hired van. By 1939, however, the voluntary system was inadequate to the demand. The committee at first resisted the employment of paid librarians but in 1949 opened its first professionally staffed branch library;[61] it was open full-time. As branch libraries were opened in towns,

[47] S.C.C. Mins. (Educ.), 1950–1, 81–2.
[48] Ibid. 98–9.
[49] S.C.C. Salop Co. Council: the Post-War Years and the Future (1965).
[50] Local information (1974).
[51] S.C.C. Mins. (Educ.), 1961–2, 269, 271, 273.
[52] Ibid. 1950–1, 82.
[53] S.R.O. 148/15, Venables educ. newscuttings 1904–6, p. 37.
[54] S.C.C. Mins. (Educ.), 1906–7, 65.
[55] Ibid. 1908–9, 117; S.C.C. Ann. Rep. of Sch. M.O. 1908, 13 (copy in S.R.O.).

[56] Jones, 'Devt. of Educ. Provision', 275–6.
[57] Devt. Plan of Primary and Secondary Educ. 8.
[58] Local information (1974).
[59] Under the Public Libraries Act, 1919, 9 & 10 Geo. V, c. 93. Except where otherwise stated, the rest of this section is based on R. C. Elliott, 'Development of Public Libraries in Salop.' (Loughborough Univ. M.A. thesis, 1970; copy in Salop. Co. Libr.).
[60] S.C.C. Mins. (Educ.), 1924–5, 124.
[61] By 1938 Devon had 12 branch libraries and E. Suff. 3: Jubilee of Co. Councils (Devon edn.), 72; ibid. (E. Suff.), 72.

mobile libraries, introduced in 1948, began to replace the village centres, and the book-box system ceased altogether in 1959.[62] In 1961 eight area headquarters were set up, and by 1973 each was linked by Telex to central headquarters. By 1973 the central catalogue was recorded on a computer.[63]

As the county library grew, special services were introduced to meet changes in public demand. In 1927 most readers were women or children and the greatest demand was for fiction.[64] By 1938, with the growth of adult education, requests for non-fiction were increasing.[65] In the late 1940s new best-sellers were much in demand but by 1963 such requests were insignificant beside an increased demand for purely educational reading.[66] A collection of gramophone records for loan was started in 1946. A children's librarian was appointed in 1953, followed in the 1960s by other specialist appointments, including a reference librarian and an arts librarian. After 1967, when the Department of Education and Science reported unfavourably on the library's reference and information services, particular emphasis was placed by the library on its function as an information centre.[67]

Health

Until the 1900s the council's main role in health matters was one of supervising the work of the sanitary districts and their successors, the urban and rural districts, each of which had a medical officer of health and an inspector of nuisances, both of them part-timers. In 1890 the council appointed a part-time county medical officer, Dr. W. N. Thursfield, who was early to recognize the value of Pasteur's treatments and was a district medical officer in several counties.[68] His duties did not go beyond collating the reports of the district medical officers and advising on their implications. His reports provided copious information on water supplies, housing, mortality, and infectious diseases, but the council had little power to act on them. The council normally gave a minor authority twelve months before enquiring whether it had taken action as recommended in the county medical officer's report;[69] if it failed to act, the county council could, and sometimes did, threaten to overrule it and to take action independently.[70] The district council, however, could easily claim poverty and ask for more time,[71] and the county council never used its ultimate power. In the 1890s the successive committees responsible for health[72] were inactive. In 1893 the Sanitary and Rivers Pollution Committee reported that its duties had been 'of a passive and not very arduous nature' and found cause for congratulation in the 'very efficient manner' in which the local sanitary authorities had carried out their duties. It expressed the hope that the work of succeeding committees might be 'of the same light, though far from unimportant, character'.[73] By 1896 the council had done nothing to prevent river pollution,[74] to obtain information on houses unfit for habitation,[75] to provide isolation hospitals,[76] or to investigate any particular disease; above all, the Sanitary

[62] *Educ. in Salop. 1945–65*, 110.

[63] S.C.C. *Salop Co. Council Review* (1973), 9 (copy in S.R.O.).

[64] S.C.C. *Salop. Co. Library: First Ann. Rep.* (1927), 7 (copy in S.R.O.).

[65] *Shrews. Chron.* 2 June 1939 (suppl.).

[66] *Educ. in Salop. 1945–65*, 109.

[67] In 1974 the motto 'Information is our business' was in use on the library's vehicles and stationery.

[68] S.R.O. 113/1, p. 102; W. Mate & Sons Ltd. *Shropshire: Historical, Descriptive, Biographical* (1906), pt. 2, p. 207.

[69] *Shrews. Chron.* 15 Feb. 1901.

[70] Under the Local Govt. Act, 1894, 56 & 57 Vic. c. 73, and Housing of the Working Classes Act, 1900, 63 & 64 Vic. c. 59: *S.C.C. Mins.* 1904–5, 139, 182; 1912–13, 114.

[71] *S.C.C. Mins.* 1930–1, 208; 1936–7, 34.

[72] The Co. Buildings, Music Licences, and Rivers Pollution Cttee. 1889; the Sanitary and Rivers Pollution Cttee. 1889–93; the Sanitary and Roads and Bridges Cttee. 1893–5; the Sanitary Cttee. 1895–1910: S.R.O. 113/1, pp. 18, 57; *S.C.C. Mins.* 11 Mar. 1893, 4; ibid. 1895–6, 4; S.R.O., Sanitary Cttee. min. bk. 3, p. 244.

[73] S.C.C. *Resumé of Work of First Co. Council of Salop* [1893], 15.

[74] Under the Rivers Pollution Prevention Act, 1876, 39 & 40 Vic. c. 75.

[75] Under the Housing of the Working Classes Act, 1890, 53 & 54 Vic. c. 70.

[76] Under the Isolation Hospitals Act, 1893, 56 & 57 Vic. c. 68.

Committee would not acknowledge the need for a full-time county medical officer to exercise effective supervision of the districts.[77]

One member of the committee, Dr. J. McC. McCarthy, was not satisfied. He alleged in 1896 that the committee had been determined to 'shelve' sanitary work; the 'insanitary condition of Shropshire' had been repeatedly pointed out but there had been hardly any improvement.[78] District health administration was indeed unsatisfactory: many of the inspectors of nuisances were, as one council member put it, 'men who had failed in various walks of life'; tenants were afraid to lodge complaints against their landlords;[79] and district medical officers whose private practices lay in their own districts were reluctant to cause offence by reporting insanitary conditions.[80] The committee at first held out against appointing a full-time county medical officer[81] but McCarthy found much support on the council[82] and succeeded in converting its vice-chairman, A. P. Heywood-Lonsdale.[83] The council was persuaded in 1897 to appoint Thursfield as full-time county medical officer.[84] Neither Thursfield, who died in 1899,[85] nor his successor was able to do much. In 1902, however, Dr. James Wheatley was appointed,[86] and in the same year McCarthy became chairman of the Sanitary Committee.[87] The partnership lasted more than twenty years: McCarthy was chairman until 1924 and Wheatley medical officer until 1928;[88] they saw a considerable expansion in the county's health services, in the course of which Wheatley, 'a man of long views', became internationally known as an authority on public health.[89]

It was not until 1930 that the council had real power to improve water supplies, sewerage, or housing, which were still responsibilities of the district councils. The Local Government Act, 1929, enabled the council to help district councils to pay for sewerage and water-supply schemes. Despite the Public Health and Housing Committee's recommendation that it should do so, however, the council refused to act without a government grant; the district councils, for their part, claimed that their water supplies and sewerage were adequate.[90] Following severe droughts the government made grants available in 1934,[91] and within three years the district councils in Shropshire made more progress in improving water supplies than in the preceding quarter of a century.[92] The grants ceased in 1937 and the council soon concluded that progress could be made only if the districts combined to carry out larger water-supply schemes.[93] As a result of a survey commissioned by the council[94] the East Shropshire Water Board was formed by six minor authorities in 1949;[95] it was enlarged in 1963,[96] and in 1964 the rest of the county combined to form the West Shropshire Water Board.[97] The district councils, and later the boards, received county-council grants under the Rural Water Supplies and Sewerage Act, 1944.[98] Under the Housing Act, 1930, the council was required to subsidize new houses built by rural district councils.[99] In 1931 many Shropshire houses were admitted by the district

[77] S.C.C. Mins. 1895–6, 169–87.
[78] S.R.O. 784/50, meeting 1 Feb. 1896.
[79] Ibid. meeting 2 May 1896.
[80] S.C.C. Mins. 1896–7, 372.
[81] Ibid. 235.
[82] S.R.O. 784/50, meetings 1 Feb., 2 May 1896.
[83] Shrews. Chron. 19 Mar. 1897.
[84] S.C.C. Mins. 1897–8, 440, 489. Some comparable cos. appointed no co. medical offr. at all until the compulsory Housing, Town Planning, &c. Act, 1909, 9 Edw. VII, c. 44: Jubilee of Co. Councils (Carms. edn.), 74; ibid. (Devon), 72; ibid. (E. Suff.), 68.
[85] S.R.O., Sanitary Cttee. min. bk. 1, p. 149; Mate, Shropshire, pt. 2, p. 207.
[86] S.C.C. Mins. 1 Feb. 1902, 46.
[87] S.R.O., Sanitary Cttee. min. bk. 2, p. 79.

[88] S.R.O., Public Health and Housing Cttee. min. bk. 5, p. 31; Shrews. Chron. 16 Mar. 1928.
[89] S.C.C. Mins. 1926–7, 155; Shrews. Chron. 16 Mar. 1928.
[90] S.C.C. Mins. 1930–1, 208; 1934–5, 343; 1936–7, 34.
[91] Under the Rural Water Supplies Act, 1934, 24 & 25 Geo. V, c. 7.
[92] S.C.C. Mins. 1937–8, 381.
[93] Ibid. 549; Jubilee of Co. Councils (Salop. edn.), 92.
[94] S.C.C. Mins. 1944–5, 239; 1945–6, 84; 1946–7, 130.
[95] Ibid. 1948–9, 355.
[96] Ibid. 1962–3, 386.
[97] Ibid. 1963–4, 268.
[98] 7 & 8 Geo. IV, c. 26: S.R.O. 2452/6, Health (Water) Sub-Cttee. mins. 2 Nov. 1967, App.
[99] 20 & 21 Geo. V, c. 39.

councils to be unfit for habitation or overcrowded,[1] but by 1939 only 200 houses had been built under the Act, by only eight district councils.[2]

Standards of domestic hygiene, quite apart from housing standards, appear to have been low in the 1900s, especially among the poor, some of whom regarded dirt and stuffiness as 'homely'.[3] Conditions for child-birth were often primitive, especially in rural areas. A local doctor recalled that near Wellington midwives were few. The doctor's only assistant was generally an untrained neighbour, and washing facilities were of the barest kind.[4] Between 1889 and 1900 annual infant mortality in Shropshire ran at 12 per cent of live births.[5] In 1902 the council decided to spend £100 on lectures and home visits in an effort to reduce infant deaths.[6] Midwives came under its supervision in 1903,[7] and in 1905 they were given a simple leaflet of feeding instructions to distribute to mothers.[8] In 1907 the council began making grants to the Shropshire Nursing Federation towards the training of midwives.[9] Midwives remained scarce, and were more so when, in 1910, those without certificates were forbidden by the government to practise.[10] Nevertheless by 1914 infant mortality in Shropshire had been reduced to 8·8 per cent.[11] Systematic home visiting became feasible in 1914 when the council adopted the Notification of Births Act, 1907.[12] Six health visitors had been appointed by 1919, but most visiting was carried out by district nurses of the Shropshire Nursing Federation.[13] The low salaries offered by the council made the recruitment of council health visitors difficult in the 1920s,[14] but their work was lightened by the establishment of county-council child-welfare centres. The first was opened at Newport in 1919[15] and by 1925 there were fourteen; there was some initial scepticism on the council, but the centres proved very popular.[16] Between 1914 and 1939 infant mortality in Shropshire was halved.[17]

In 1948 the council took over the district nursing and midwifery services of the Shropshire Nursing Association.[18] There was an acute shortage of nurse-midwives and health visitors in the 1950s and 1960s.[19] At the same time under the free National Health Service most mothers preferred to be delivered in hospital rather than at home. The council was accordingly anxious to amalgamate some of the small nursing areas into which the county was divided, but local opposition made it difficult and sometimes impossible.[20] In 1971 a complete reorganization on lines recommended by the government took place; the old nursing areas, each served by one nurse-midwife, were replaced by sixteen teams of nurses, midwives, and health visitors, working in consultation with groups of general practitioners.[21] After the Second World War some of the council's welfare centres, most of which had been set up in adapted premises, needed replacement;[22] indeed the need for more purpose-built accommodation had been recognized as early as 1934.[23] The first of the new welfare centres was opened at Newport in 1953.[24] In 1967, however, the government urged the council to give up the building of welfare centres in favour of health centres, buildings to be shared

[1] S.C.C. Mins. 1931–2, 135.
[2] Jubilee of Co. Councils, 92.
[3] S.C.C. Mins. (Educ.), 1906–7, 40.
[4] H. W. Pooler, My Life in General Practice (1950), 23.
[5] S.C.C. Rep. by Co. M.O.H. 1890–1900 (copies in S.R.O.).
[6] Shrews. Chron. 7 Feb. 1902.
[7] Under the Midwives Act, 1902, 2 Edw. VII, c. 17.
[8] S.C.C. Mins. 1905–6, 116.
[9] S.C.C. Mins. (Educ.), 1907–8, 96.
[10] Shrews. Chron. 18 Mar. 1910.
[11] Rep. by Co. M.O.H. 1900–14.
[12] 7 Edw. VII, c. 40: S.C.C. Mins. 1914–15, 78.
[13] Ibid. 1918–19, 192.
[14] Ibid. 1925–6, 236.

[15] Ibid. 1919–20, 283. A child-welfare centre at Ironbridge had been opened by voluntary effort in 1918: G. G. P. Heywood, The Mary Heywood Child Welfare Centre [c. 1950] (copy in libr. of Ironbridge Gorge Museum Trust), 5.
[16] Shrews. Chron. 30 Jan., 6 Feb., 31 July 1925.
[17] Rep. by Co. M.O.H. 1914–17; S.C.C. Ann. Rep. of Co. M.O.H. 1918–39 (copies in S.R.O.).
[18] Shrews. Chron. 14 Nov. 1947.
[19] S.C.C. Mins. 1950–1, 73–4; 1956–7, 357; 1963–4, 263; 1966–7, 314; Express & Star, 6 Mar. 1952.
[20] S.C.C. Mins. 1952–3, 241.
[21] Ibid. 1970–1, 371; 1971–2, 88.
[22] Ibid. 1949–50, 53.
[23] Ibid. 1934–5, 344.
[24] Ibid. 1953–4, 11.

between the council, general practitioners, and the regional hospital board.[25] Eight such centres were planned and the first was opened by the council in 1971 at Wellington.[26]

After the Second World War the council extended its welfare services to include a Shrewsbury birth-control clinic, taken over in 1950 from the Family Planning Association.[27] Further clinics were promised under the National Health Service (Family Planning) Act, 1967.[28] In 1946 the Women's Voluntary Service, with council support, began a home-help service designed to assist expectant mothers, old people, and the chronically sick.[29] It was very popular and expanded rapidly but in 1952 the council took the service over after a disagreement about its financial administration.[30] Some 400 home helps were employed in 1973.[31] In 1960 the council began to support a chiropody service run by voluntary organizations[32] and in 1967 it started a geriatric clinic.[33]

Regular inspection of school children by council medical officers began in 1908.[34] The defects found among children were more numerous than expected;[35] besides 28 per cent who were in need of medical attention, 10 per cent were undernourished, 56 per cent had three or more decayed teeth, and 12 per cent had head lice.[36] By 1914 tooth decay and head lice were worse, and nourishment had not improved.[37] By 1920, however, children's health was much better, and the general improvement continued through the 1920s and 1930s, though undernourishment increased in the period 1935–7 and head lice in 1937.[38] In the three decades following the Second World War children's health continued to improve generally, though tooth decay increased again in the 1950s.[39] By the 1960s, with infectious disease much diminished, the department devoted increasing attention to the prevention and early detection of congenital disorders and malformations.[40] In the late 1960s the council developed a scheme for the systematic inspection, independently of parental initiative, of every newly born child in the county and for his inspection at all critical stages of his childhood.[41] The scheme came into full operation in 1971, and by 1973 every child's progress from birth was recorded in a computer which automatically invited his attendance at a council clinic at the necessary intervals.[42]

Before the First World War Wheatley, a dental specialist,[43] pointed out to the Education Committee the dangers of tooth decay to children's health, but most parents remained unaware of them.[44] In 1914 71 per cent of school children had more than three decayed teeth.[45] In 1919 Wheatley drew up a comprehensive scheme for free school dental treatment and dental education, requiring 7 full-time dentists and 21 clinics. As Wheatley recognized, the national shortage of dentists would allow only a limited service to be introduced.[46] Only three dentists were employed in the 1920s and 1930s.[47] Tooth decay increased during the 1930s,[48] and a quarter of the lost teeth decayed because the school dentist could not see the child often enough to detect the early stages or to complete the necessary treatments.[49] Shortage of dentists continued

[25] S.C.C. Mins. 1967–8, 177.
[26] Ibid. 1971–2, 85.
[27] Ibid. 1949–50, 262.
[28] 1967, c. 39: ibid. 1968–9, 20.
[29] Ibid. 1946–7, 208.
[30] Ibid. 1951–2, 45, 328; local information (1974).
[31] S.C.C. Salop Co. Council Review (1973), 13.
[32] S.C.C. Mins. 1959–60, 354.
[33] Ibid. 1966–7, 436.
[34] Under the Education (Administrative Provisions) Act, 1907, 7 Edw. VII, c. 43: S.C.C. Mins. (Educ.), 1907–8, 173.
[35] Ibid. 1908–9, 117.
[36] Ann. Rep. of Sch. M.O. 1908, 13, 16, 20, 22.
[37] Ibid. 1914, 25, 39–40.
[38] Ibid. 1920, 14, 16; 1938, 9, 12, 14.
[39] S.C.C. Rep. of Sch. M.O. 1946–54 (copies in S.R.O.); S.C.C. Rep. of Principal Sch. M.O. 1955–71 (copies in S.R.O.).
[40] Local information (1974).
[41] S.C.C. Mins. 1970–1, 372.
[42] Salop Co. Council Review, 15.
[43] Shrews. Chron. 16 Mar. 1928.
[44] S.C.C. Mins. (Educ.), 1919–20, 15–16.
[45] Ann. Rep. of Sch. M.O. 1914, 25.
[46] S.C.C. Mins. (Educ.), 1919–20, 15–20.
[47] Ann. Rep. of Sch. M.O. 1930, 2; S.C.C. Mins. (Educ.), 1939–40, 30.
[48] Ann. Rep. of Sch. M.O. 1938, 12.
[49] S.C.C. Mins. (Educ.), 1938–9, 100.

to hinder the service until the late 1960s when an adequate staff was at last built up.[50]

Apart from such general services the council took special measures to deal with particular diseases. In the 1900s lung tuberculosis caused more deaths in Shropshire than all the common infectious diseases put together: some 120 a year.[51] Wheatley pointed out in 1907 that many cases could be cured in the early stages if there were a sanatorium in the county.[52] In 1910 the King Edward VII Memorial Sanatorium was opened at Shirlett by the Association for the Prevention of Consumption,[53] but the council refused to take any action of its own[54] until assured in 1913 of a government grant under the National Insurance Act, 1911. In 1913 it approved a scheme prepared by Wheatley for the appointment of a tuberculosis officer, the opening of nine dispensaries, financial aid to enlarge the sanatorium, and the provision of 50 beds for advanced cases unable to benefit from sanatorium treatment.[55] By 1918 the Shropshire death rate from consumption was higher than at any time since 1906,[56] but only two dispensaries had been opened by 1919.[57] Almost no accommodation for advanced cases was available until 1921 when the council provided eleven beds at a former smallpox isolation hospital at Prees Heath.[58] Efforts to provide more beds failed in the 1920s and 1930s.[59] In 1947 T. O. Steventon, chairman of the Public Health and Housing Committee, remarked that 'we have been treating these poor folk almost like animals',[60] but by then the urgent need had passed. There were six dispensaries by 1939 and the death rate had been halved since 1919.[61] Inoculation against tuberculosis first became available through the council in 1950[62] and it was extended to school children in 1954.[63] By 1958 the death rate had fallen to ·0003 per cent of the population; it rose again in the early 1960s, reaching its 1949 level in 1963, but fell again in the later 1960s.[64]

In 1918 a high incidence of venereal disease was expected to follow demobilization.[65] The council set up a venereal-disease clinic in Shrewsbury in 1918[66] but was prevented by local opposition from opening another at Oswestry in 1920.[67] The Shrewsbury clinic was the only one in the county until 1941, when a second was opened at Oswestry to meet the needs of another war.[68] After reaching a peak in 1921 the number of cases remained fairly steady in the 1920s and 1930s. A large increase occurred during and immediately after the Second World War; numbers then fell off gradually until 1960 when a new increase began which had not been brought under control by 1971.[69] In 1941 diphtheria was running at a rate of 237 cases a year in Shropshire; there had been no improvement since records began in 1900.[70] Immunization was in the hands of district councils;[71] it had been a subject of popular controversy on medical and ethical grounds[72] and only 22 per cent of children under five and 58 per cent between five and fourteen were protected.[73] In 1942 the county council decided to take over the immunization of children[74] and by 1945 some 85 per cent were protected.[75] The

[50] Rep. of Principal Sch. M.O. 1961, 30; ibid. 1966-71.
[51] S.C.C. Rep. on Phthisis in the Co. (1907), 3, 13 (copy in S.R.O., Sanitary Cttee. min. bk. 3, p. 68).
[52] Rep. on Phthisis, 15.
[53] Kelly's Dir. Salop. (1913), 29.
[54] Shrews. Chron. 8 Nov. 1912.
[55] Ibid. 21 Mar. 1913.
[56] Rep. by Co. M.O.H. 1906-17; Ann. Rep. of Co. M.O.H. 1918, 7.
[57] S.C.C. Mins. 1918-19. 182.
[58] Shrews. Chron. 13 Feb. 1920; S.C.C. Mins. 1921-2, 227; 1925-6, 70. For a short time previously 2 or 3 beds had been available at a former smallpox hosp. at Steer-away: S.R.O., Public Health and Housing Cttee. min. bk. 4, p. 247.
[59] S.C.C. Mins. 1925-6, 70; 1926-7, 33, 96; 1927-8, 241; 1932-3, 216; 1935-6, 310; 1937-8, 383; 1938-9, 186.

[60] Shrews. Chron. 14 Nov. 1947.
[61] Ann. Rep. of Co. M.O.H. 1918-39.
[62] S.C.C. Mins. 1949-50, 263.
[63] Ibid. 1954-5, 57.
[64] Ann. Rep. of Co. M.O.H. 1940-71.
[65] Rep. by Co. M.O.H. 1917, 17.
[66] S.C.C. Mins. 1918-19, 184.
[67] Ibid. 1920-1, 51.
[68] Ibid. 1942-3, 12.
[69] Ann. Rep. of Co. M.O.H. 1919-71.
[70] Rep. by Co. M.O.H. 1900-17; Ann. Rep. of Co. M.O.H. 1918-41.
[71] S.C.C. Mins. 1940-1, 301.
[72] Local information (1974).
[73] S.C.C. Mins. 1941-2, 267.
[74] Ibid. 1942-3, 137.
[75] Ibid. 1944-5, 241.

number of Shropshire cases of diphtheria fell to seven in 1945 and the disease was eradicated from the county by 1953.[76] Poliomyelitis became an increasing threat after the Second World War. Since records began in 1912 there had rarely been more than ten Shropshire cases a year, but from 1944 until the late 1950s they became more numerous, reaching a peak of 62 in 1950.[77] In 1956 vaccination became available to children through the council,[78] and the disease may be considered to have been eradicated from Shropshire by 1962.[79] Tests for cervical cancer were first provided by the council in 1967.[80] In 1968 the council began payments to victims of kidney disease, to enable their homes to be adapted for the installation of life-sustaining machines.[81]

The council had from the first a considerable responsibility for hospitals. As part-owner of the Salop and Montgomery Counties and Wenlock Borough Lunatic Asylum at Shelton the council had partial control of capital expenditure there, but administration was otherwise in the hands of a Committee of Visitors, comprising members of the participating councils.[82] The buildings had been enlarged between 1882 and 1885[83] but by 1900 further extensions were necessary.[84] The visitors nevertheless continued to avoid new building by the costly expedient of boarding patients in workhouses or in asylums in other counties.[85] In 1911 the partnership with Montgomeryshire was dissolved at the request of the Salop County Council, releasing more places for Shropshire patients.[86] By 1922, however, overcrowding was again a problem and was affecting the patients' health;[87] there was a grave incidence of dysentery.[88] Copthorne House was acquired by the visitors and opened in 1929 as a hostel for higher-grade male patients,[89] and similar provision was made for women in 1932 at Oxon Hall.[90] By 1939 overcrowding was again serious,[91] but no improvement was effected before 1948, when the hospital passed to the Birmingham Regional Hospital Board as part of the National Health Service.[92]

In the early 1900s few minor local authorities in Shropshire had adequate isolation hospitals for smallpox; some had a cottage or a wooden hut, others relied on a firm of contractors who undertook to erect a large tent within 48 hours of an outbreak.[93] From 1902 to 1905 an epidemic occurred in the county, and the council tried in vain to persuade district authorities to combine to provide proper hospitals; by good fortune, however, the outbreaks were confined to those districts with adequate isolation hospitals.[94] Subsequent efforts by the council to form joint hospital districts and to provide a county isolation hospital achieved little[95] but smallpox never again became an urgent threat.[96]

In 1930 the Public Assistance Committee inherited the poor-law general hospital at Cross Houses (formerly Atcham union workhouse). It passed to the Public Health and Housing Committee in 1934,[97] and it was hoped that it would become the council's centre for all institutional medical treatment, including maternity, tuberculosis, and

[76] Ann. Rep. of Co. M.O.H. 1942–53. A single case occurred in 1961: ibid. 1961, 13.
[77] Rep. by Co. M.O.H. 1912–17; Ann. Rep. of Co. M.O.H. 1918–57.
[78] S.C.C. Mins. 1955–6, 353.
[79] Ann. Rep. of Co. M.O.H. 1958–71.
[80] S.C.C. Mins. 1966–7, 437.   [81] Ibid. 1968–9, 21.
[82] Ann. Rep. of Lunatic Asylum, 1889, 4 (copy in S.R.O.).
[83] See p. 162.
[84] Shrews. Chron. 3 Aug. 1900.
[85] Ibid. 3 Aug. 1906.
[86] S.C.C. Mins. 1909–10, 123; Ann. Rep. of Lunatic Asylum, 1910, 3, 10. From 1911 to 1921 the asylum was called the Salop County and Wenlock Borough Lunatic Asylum, from 1921 to 1948 the Salop Mental Hospital:
S.R.O., Visiting Cttee. min. bk. 12, p. 169; Ann. Rep. of Salop Mental Hosp. 1921, 6 (copy in S.R.O.).
[87] Ann. Rep. of Salop Mental Hosp. 1921, 8.
[88] Ibid. 1922, 9.   [89] Ibid. 1929, 9.
[90] Ibid. 1932, 8.
[91] Ibid. 1939, 8.
[92] S.C.C. Mins. 1948–9, 88–9.
[93] S.C.C. Mins. Sanitary Cttee. rep. 3 May 1902, 1, 4.
[94] Ibid. 1; ibid. 26 July 1902, 7; Rep. by Co. M.O.H. 1903, 9, 11; 1906, 16.
[95] S.C.C. Mins. 1913–14, 160, 226; 1918–19, 98–9; 1932–3, 216; 1935–6, 311; 1937–8, 383, 550; 1938–9, 45, 354.
[96] Ibid. 1933–4, 254; 1945–6, 87; 1946–7, 367.
[97] Ibid. 1933–4, 252.

isolation cases.[98] Despite the inadequacy of the building and patients' reluctance to enter a former workhouse,[99] a high standard of nursing was maintained in the 1930s,[1] and a complete reconstruction was contemplated when war intervened.[2] Nothing more could be done before the hospital was absorbed by the National Health Service in 1948.[3] In 1946 the council took over the former Copthorne Military Hospital, Shrewsbury, at the request of the Minister of Health, but was unable to convert it for civilian use before 1948.[4]

Until 1948, when the council became responsible for ambulances throughout the county,[5] there were seventeen ambulance authorities in Shropshire, of which the council was one;[6] it had four vehicles in 1945.[7] In 1948 the new council fleet was stationed at the Cross Houses hospital but, after a fire in Shrewsbury in that year, as a result of which four people died, one vehicle was immediately stationed at Copthorne in response to strong public pressure.[8] A second central depot was set up at Meole Brace in 1949, and by 1950 there were 11 stations and 41 vehicles.[9] Radio control was introduced in 1954,[10] and in the same year a purpose-built central ambulance station was opened in Shrewsbury, replacing the Cross Houses and Meole Brace depots.[11] By 1973 there were 65 vehicles, travelling some $1\frac{1}{2}$ million miles a year.[12]

How far the council was directly responsible for the great improvement in public health between 1889 and 1974 is difficult to assess. Its role was shared with minor authorities, voluntary bodies, general practitioners, and, from 1948, the National Health Service. The gradual alleviation of poverty also played a part. By the 1970s, however, there were few Shropshire people who had not at some time used one of the council's health services.

Social Services for the Handicapped, the Poor, and the Homeless

Until 1930 the only council committee concerned exclusively with social services was the Mental Deficiency Committee set up in 1914[13] under the Mental Deficiency Act, 1913, which required the council to ensure the proper care of mental defectives.[14] In the 1920s and 1930s the council tried to provide a special residential institution for mentally defective adults, but without success:[15] in 1930 most remained at home; some occupied 'certified' beds in public-assistance institutions (the former workhouses); others lived in special institutions outside the county, and a few in the Salop Mental Hospital.[16] Major improvements in accommodation and training came only after the Second World War. In 1947 many mentally defective men in public-assistance institutions were intended to be transferred to the disused casual wards at Shawbury,[17] and there were similar plans for mentally defective women. Those were abandoned when Shropshire was promised places in a new home planned at Bromsgrove (Worcs.) by the West Midlands Joint Board for the Mentally Defective. The home was opened in 1949[18] but Shropshire patients were admitted only gradually.[19] In 1965 some 40 to 50 subnormal adults were sent from hospitals and old people's homes to Morda

[98] Ibid. 1937–8, 383.
[99] Local information (1974).
[1] S.C.C. Mins. 1934–5, 171; 1938–9, 46.
[2] Ibid. 1938–9, 519; 1945–6, 86.
[3] Under the National Health Service Act, 1946, 9 & 10 Geo. VI, c. 81.
[4] Oswestry Adv. 4 Sept. 1946; Shrews. Chron. 1 Aug. 1947.
[5] Under the National Health Service Act, 1946.
[6] Shrews. Chron. 9 Apr. 1954.
[7] S.C.C. Mins. 1945–6, 188.
[8] Ibid. 1948–9, 57; Express & Star, 10 May 1948; Oswestry Adv. 28 July 1948.

[9] S.C.C. Mins. 1949–50, 264.
[10] Shrews. Chron. 30 Apr. 1954.
[11] S.C.C. Mins. 1954–5, 132.
[12] S.C.C. Salop Co. Council Review (1973), 19.
[13] S.C.C. Mins. 1914–15, 152.
[14] 3 & 4 Geo. V, c. 28.
[15] S.C.C. Mins. 1920–1, 327; 1934–5, 82; 1935–6, 102; 1946–7, 194; S.R.O. 1211/2. The council's provision for the education of mentally deficient children is treated above, p. 206, and below, p. 214.
[16] S.C.C. Mins. 1930–1, 79.
[17] Ibid. 1946–7, 357.
[18] Ibid. 494; 1949–50, 462.
[19] Ibid. 1949–50, 53, 462.

House (the former Oswestry public-assistance institution).[20] From 1948 the council had to provide training for mentally defective people capable of benefiting from it.[21] An occupational therapist was appointed in 1953;[22] a residential training centre for children, one of the first in the country, was opened at Shrewsbury in 1959;[23] a residential training centre for adults was opened in 1968 and another in 1969.[24]

Other social services provided by the council before 1930, for the physically handicapped and the blind, were administered by the Health Committee. The council began to help physically handicapped people by subsidizing the treatment of tuberculous adults from 1917 and crippled children from 1918 at the Shropshire Convalescent and Surgical Home, founded at Baschurch in 1900 by Agnes (later Dame Agnes) Hunt.[25] According to Dame Agnes the council was 'the first public body in the world to realize and tackle the responsibility of the crippled child'.[26] In the 1920s and 1930s the council allowed the home to hold prevention and after-care clinics at the new council welfare centres. The clinics worked so well that the number of patients needing council-subsidized treatment at the home fell steadily, and the clinics themselves were less needed by the late 1930s.[27] The council increased its support to the home in 1938 by aiding all needy adults requiring treatment there.[28]

In 1922 the county medical officer of health presented a scheme for the care of blind people.[29] Under it, the council was responsible for registering the blind, discovering new cases, visiting those under five years old, and arranging for vocational training at institutions. It would delegate the supervision of blind 'home workers' and teaching of 'pastime occupations' to the Birmingham Royal Institution for the Blind. Supervision of blind people's welfare would be delegated to the Shropshire Society for Home Teaching of the Blind. Financial support of the unemployable blind was to remain with the boards of guardians. The annual cost of the scheme to the council was estimated at £325.[30] E. B. Blake, a Labour councillor, described it as the worst scheme presented in any county; Cheshire had proposed spending £2,000 a year on its scheme and the Shropshire Society, he claimed, had been 'practically dead' for six years.[31] The scheme was adopted, but a Care Committee, on which the council and voluntary bodies were represented, was substituted for the Shropshire Society.[32] Financial assistance to blind people improved gradually during the next twenty years. In 1923 the council began to make grants to the newly formed Shropshire Association for the Blind for financial help to those not eligible for poor relief,[33] and in 1929 the council began to supplement, where necessary, the incomes of home workers.[34] In 1943, however, the rates of assistance paid in Shropshire were found to be among the lowest in the country and were accordingly raised.[35]

The National Assistance Act, 1948, empowered the council to secure the welfare of all blind, deaf and dumb, and handicapped people,[36] though financial assistance to the blind became a government responsibility.[37] The council did so by working through or subscribing to voluntary bodies.[38] It had supported the Shropshire Voluntary

[20] *S.C.C. Mins.* 1964–5, 281.
[21] Under the National Health Service Act, 1946: ibid. 1952–3, 242.
[22] Ibid. 243.
[23] *Ann. Rep. of Co. M.O.H. 1959,* 69; *S.C.C. Mins. 1960–1,* 63.
[24] *S.C.C. Mins.* 1968–9, 18; *Ann. Rep. of Co. M.O.H. 1969,* 58.
[25] *S.C.C. Mins.* 1917–18, 109; 1918–19, 174; *Kelly's Dir. Salop.* (1913). The council's provision for the education of handicapped children is treated above, p. 206.
[26] H. W. Pooler, *My Life in Three Counties* (1950), 43.
[27] *S.C.C. Mins.* 1929–30, 303; 1935–6, 453.
[28] Ibid. 1938–9, 362.
[29] Under the Blind Persons Act, 1920, 10 & 11 Geo. V, c. 49.
[30] *S.C.C. Mins.* 1922–3, 45–6.
[31] *Shrews. Chron.* 17 Mar. 1922.
[32] *S.C.C. Mins.* 1922–3, 159.
[33] Ibid. 1923–4, 53.
[34] Ibid. 1929–30, 224.
[35] Ibid. 1942–3, 207.
[36] 11 & 12 Geo. VI, c. 29.
[37] *S.C.C. Mins.* 1947–8, 335.
[38] Ibid. 1948–9, 372; 1952–3, 76.

Orthopaedic Association, a body concerned with the welfare, as distinct from the treatment, of cripples, since its foundation in 1929;[39] the association's work was carried on from 1955 with council support, by the Shropshire Voluntary Helping Hand Association for the Home-Bound Disabled.[40] The council began in 1959 to provide social centres and holidays for handicapped people.[41] In 1962 it took over direct responsibility for training and finding employment for the disabled, the mentally handicapped, and the blind.[42] In 1971 it began to contribute to the cost of television and telephones for people confined to their homes.[43]

In 1930 the council inherited the functions of the guardians.[44] Among them was the administration of institutions for the sick and destitute. The Public Assistance Committee inherited fourteen workhouses (renamed public-assistance institutions) and a general hospital in 1930,[45] buildings whose condition ranged from fair to bad.[46] Opinion on the council had for some years been evenly divided as to the need to reform the methods of the guardians.[47] The government, however, required changes, especially the segregation of the sick, the poor, and mental defectives from each other. In 1931 there were some 1,025 residents; about 525 were classed as infirm (most of them old or chronically sick) and about 500 were able-bodied (half of them mentally deficient); there were also some 125 children in the institutions, half of them healthy and normal.[48] The committee's plans to segregate the different classes of residents into separate public-assistance institutions[49] came to little before 1939; lack of money prevented the alterations and new building which were necessary to prepare the way for a redistribution of residents.[50] Four of the institutions were closed by 1939;[51] most of those that remained contained a mixture of residents as in 1930, though by 1939 there were few children in the general wards.[52]

In 1932 there were about 125 children in public-assistance institutions; some 160 lived in two council homes inherited from the guardians; and another 80 were in council foster homes.[53] In 1934 the committee began to send some of those in institutions to children's homes in other counties or to voluntary children's homes in Shropshire; children under three were housed in the former hospital block at the Church Stretton institution;[54] in 1935 the former hospital block at Newport was opened as a home for those under five; and in 1936 the committee established a receiving home in Shrewsbury.[55] A system was thus completed in which a child would progress from Shrewsbury, to Church Stretton, to Newport, and at the age of five to a council, voluntary, or foster home.[56]

The Second World War, bringing homeless children from bombed areas to Shropshire, forced the council to keep increasing numbers in public-assistance institutions and foster homes.[57] The methods of supervising the latter, however, were inadequate. A part-time boarding-out visitor was appointed in 1938[58] and in 1945 the council was responsible for 118 boarded-out children.[59] In that year Dennis O'Neill, a 12-year-old boy, died from ill treatment and neglect in a council foster home. An inquiry revealed

[39] Ibid. 1928–9, 304.
[40] Ibid. 1955–6, 162.
[41] Ibid. 1958–9, 207.
[42] Ibid. 1961–2, 83, 174–5.
[43] Ibid. 1970–1, 506–7.
[44] Under the Local Government Act, 1929, 19 Geo. V, c. 17.
[45] S.C.C. Mins. 1929–30, 355; Kelly's Dir. Salop. (1929), 35.
[46] S.R.O. 1211/2.
[47] Shrews. Chron. 12 Feb. 1926.
[48] S.R.O. 1211/2.
[49] Ibid.
[50] S.C.C. Mins. 1932–9; S.C.C. Salop Co. Council: the Post-War Years and the Future (1965).
[51] S.C.C. Mins. 1930–1, 68, 263; 1934–5, 82; 1938–9, 569; 1939–40, 284. The general hosp. at Cross Houses was transferred from the Public Assistance Cttee. to the Public Health and Housing Cttee. in 1934: see above, p. 212.
[52] S.C.C. Mins. 1939–40, table facing p. 409.
[53] Ibid. 1929–30, 355; S.R.O. 1211/2.
[54] S.C.C. Mins. 1933–4, 493; 1934–5, 410.
[55] Ibid. 1935–6, 234, 378.
[56] Ibid. 1936–7, 403–4.
[57] Ibid. 1940–1, 339; 1944–5, 42.
[58] Ibid. 1937–8, 699.
[59] Ibid. 1945–6, 128.

administrative deficiencies in the Public Assistance and Education departments[60] and led the council to set up a special staff to deal with boarding out.[61] The decision partly anticipated the requirements of the Children Act, 1948,[62] and the O'Neill case figured prominently in the report of the Curtis Committee on whose recommendations the Act was based.[63]

In 1945 the council's existing children's homes were overcrowded and, it was said, rather severe in their regime. Some 140 new places were needed[64] but financial restrictions retarded their provision.[65] In 1946 there were still 42 children in public-assistance institutions,[66] but by 1951 the council had nine homes and three nurseries, housing 300 children.[67] At the Vineyard, Wellington, opened in 1947, a more homely atmosphere was induced by grouping the children in 'families',[68] and in 1954 the first of twelve proposed 'cottage homes' was opened in the Vineyard's grounds.[69] By 1955 the end of overcrowding could be foreseen: the demand for places for younger children was falling off and a long-deferred reconstruction of homes was taking place.[70] Four homes and two nurseries were closed between 1951 and 1965 and only five of the proposed cottage homes were built.[71] Pressure on foster homes fell after 1962 as the number of older children in care ceased to rise.[72]

Between 1955 and 1965 the children's homes ceased to be needed principally as permanent homes for children without families and became more often the temporary shelter of those whose behaviour was abnormal or whose families were in difficulties.[73] Under the Children and Young Persons Act, 1969,[74] the council lost its control of policy in that field to the West Midland Children's Regional Planning Committee, required by the government to merge the Home Office's 'approved schools' and 'remand homes' with local-authority children's homes into a single category of 'community homes'.[75] The regional committee's plan, presented in 1972, retained the existing Shropshire council homes as well as approving five new ones previously planned by the council.[76]

Vagrants were a considerable burden on the council before the Second World War; they consisted not only of social misfits but also of men travelling in search of work. In 1930 vagrants might seek shelter in any of the council's public-assistance institutions; in 1930–1 some 87,000 'maintenance days' were spent in the Shropshire casual wards, and the figure rose sharply to 110,000 in 1932–3.[77] Government policy was to concentrate vagrants at fewer centres and the council accordingly closed many of the casual wards at its public-assistance institutions during the 1930s.[78] It opened new wards in 1935 where vagrants could be concentrated; badly sited at Shawbury, they were little used.[79] From 1937 the older men were encouraged to settle in the general wards of the institutions.[80] Of the seven casual wards that remained in 1939 the last had been closed by 1946.[81] Most vagrants deserted Shropshire for towns east of the county;[82]

[60] *Rep. on boarding out of Dennis and Terence O'Neill* [Cmd. 6636], H.C. (1944–5), iv.
[61] *S.C.C. Mins.* 1945–6, 135.
[62] 11 & 12 Geo. VI, c. 43.
[63] *Rep. of Care of Children Cttee.* [Cmd. 6922], pp. 116, 120–1, 139, 146, 153, H.C. (1945–6), x; *Summary of Main Provisions of Children Bill* [Cmd. 7306], p. 2, H.C. (1947–8), xxii.
[64] *S.C.C. Mins.* 1946–7, 42; *Oswestry Adv.* 31 July 1946; *Shrews. Chron.* 23 Aug. 1946.
[65] *S.C.C. Mins.* 1952–3, 265.
[66] Ibid. 1946–7, 361.
[67] *Salop Co. Council: the Post-War Years and the Future.*
[68] *S.C.C. Mins.* 1945–6, 326; 1947–8, 11.
[69] Ibid. 1946–7, 42; 1954–5, 22.
[70] Ibid. 1954–5, 175.

[71] *Salop Co. Council: the Post-War Years and the Future.*
[72] *S.C.C. Mins.* 1957–8, 299; 1961–2, 414; 1965–6, 396.
[73] Ibid. 1969–70, 138; *Salop Co. Council: the Post-War Years and the Future.*
[74] 1969, c. 54.
[75] *S.C.C. Mins.* 1969–70, 255, 370; 1970–1, 196.
[76] Ibid. 1971–2, 552.
[77] Ibid. 1931–2, App. facing p. 84; 1932–3, Apps. facing pp. 173, 284, 391; 1933–4, App. facing p. 88.
[78] S.R.O. 1211/2; *S.C.C. Mins.* 1934–9.
[79] *S.C.C. Mins.* 1935–6, 377; local information (1974). Similar provision was made at that time in Carms. and E. Suff.: *Jubilee of Co. Councils* (Carms. edn.), 77; ibid. (E. Suff.), 78.
[80] *S.C.C. Mins.* 1938–9, 116.
[81] Ibid. 1946–7, 191.
[82] Ibid. 1947–8, 9.

the few remaining were given casual accommodation in the general wards.[83] Government reception centres, administered by the council and charged with the rehabilitation of vagrants, were set up at three institutions in 1948,[84] but all had been closed by 1956.[85] In the late 1960s the council was trying to find a permanent camp site for gipsies.[86] The provision of a site became obligatory under the Caravan Sites Act, 1968,[87] but none had been provided by 1974.[88]

In 1930 the council inherited the guardians' obligation to pay outdoor poor relief. The proportion of the county's population receiving relief rose from 1·1 per cent in September 1930 to 1·9 in December 1932, and fell only in 1937 when unemployed persons not eligible for national-insurance benefits became chargeable to the Unemployment Assistance Board.[89] In 1948 all the council's out-relief responsibilities passed to the National Assistance Board.[90]

In 1940, when a German invasion seemed imminent, the council set up housing and feeding centres on the border with Staffordshire to cope with an expected rush of disorganized refugees from devastated towns to the east;[91] some 120 centres had been set up by 1941.[92] Such an influx never occurred, but the council had nevertheless the problem of looking after numerous organized evacuees, for many of whom billets could not be found. At first they were housed in public-assistance institutions[93] or at the housing centres, but late in 1941, as those arrangements were strained by increasing numbers,[94] the council began to set up 'intermediate hostels' and 'emergency meals centres'.[95] In 1945 most of those services were closed down.[96]

Apart from children and the mentally deficient, whose special needs were gradually met after the Second World War, the ten public-assistance institutions administered by the Public Assistance Committee in 1945 housed many old and chronically sick people. Staff was difficult to obtain, partly because of the bad accommodation,[97] and staff shortages forced the Madeley and Oswestry sick wards to refuse admissions in 1946.[98] The chronically sick, of whom there were some 600 in 1946,[99] were especially burdensome; the Public Assistance Committee had to admit that, despite government pressure, there was virtually no segregation of the types of sick patient, while the provision of curative treatment and rehabilitation was 'negligible'.[1] The public-assistance officer, J. H. Hargreaves, gave warning in 1946 of a partial breakdown in the service.[2] The National Health Service Act, 1946, transferred the care of the sick from the council to the Birmingham Regional Hospital Board.[3] The National Assistance Act, 1948, required institutions used principally for the sick to be vested solely in the Minister of Health. Nine of the ten institutions contained a mixture of sick and able-bodied residents; the five in which the sick were in the majority were transferred to the Minister. All nine were to be under the joint administration of the board and the council.[4] The arrangement did not work well, and in 1950 the board and the council agreed to take their own patients into separate institutions,[5] a process virtually completed by the mid 1950s.[6]

[83] Ibid. 1946-7, 191.
[84] Under the National Assistance Act, 1948, 11 & 12 Geo. VI, c. 29: ibid. 1948-9, 210.
[85] Ibid. 1956-7, 110.
[86] Ibid. 1966-7, 12; 1967-8, 223, 447; 1970-1, 209.
[87] 1968, c. 52.
[88] S.C.C. Mins. 1970-4.
[89] Ibid. 1930-9, Apps. to Public Assistance Cttee. reps.
[90] Under the National Assistance Act, 1948.
[91] S.C.C. Mins. 1940-1, App. following p. 73.
[92] Ibid. 339.
[93] Ibid. 338.
[94] Ibid. 1941-2, 149.
[95] Ibid. 225-6, 294; 1942-3, 170, 233.

[96] Ibid. 1944-5, 204.
[97] Ibid. 1946-7, 38, 356.
[98] Ibid. 1945-6, 136; 1946-7, 198.
[99] Ibid. 1946-7, 361.
[1] Ibid. 39.
[2] Ibid. 356.
[3] 9 & 10 Geo. VI, c. 81.
[4] S.C.C. Mins. 1947-8, 316.
[5] Ibid. 1949-50, 286-7; 1950-1, 23. Stone Ho. (the former Clun institution) remained in joint use for economic reasons: 1957-8, 105.
[6] Local information (1974). The last board patients were not removed from Morda Ho. until 1967: S.C.C. Mins. 1968-9, 268.

A small beginning to the removal of able-bodied old people from the public-assistance institutions was made in 1946, when a few of them were placed in three former evacuees' hostels[7] where a homely atmosphere was fostered.[8] Most, however, remained in the institutions in the late 1940s[9] and for them conditions were bleak. The obsolete buildings had been neglected during the war;[10] many improvements authorized by the council had not been carried out by the county architect.[11] A councillor visiting East Hamlet Hospital (the former Ludlow institution) in 1949 found that the old men and women were housed in separate buildings each having 'one long common room with cold stone floors, and one fireplace, around which all huddle on cold days'. The low-ceilinged rooms had drab walls whose age-rotted plaster could not take paint. There was no privacy even in the long dormitories.[12] A visitor to the Beeches Hospital (the former Madeley institution) in the same year described the day rooms as 'horrible places'. None of the downstairs rooms had a ceiling but only bare beams and on top of them the floorboards of the upper storey. There were cracks between the boards and 'ugly streaks on the walls where liquids spilt above had trickled down'. None of the old people had room for personal possessions save that a few had managed to beg 'a cardboard box to put under the bed and keep a few treasures'.[13]

In the early 1950s the institutions were at last redecorated and provided with comfortable furniture;[14] in 1955 open days at Innage House (the former Bridgnorth institution) helped to dispel public concern about conditions.[15] At the same time the council, as required by the National Assistance Act, 1948, was trying to place as many old people as possible in special homes away from the institutions,[16] and in 1953 it completed at Shrewsbury the first purpose-built old people's home in the country.[17] Shropshire was later one of the first counties to build homes subdivided into 'family units';[18] its first was opened in 1965.[19] Shropshire was also a pioneer in helping minor authorities to provide grouped bungalows, in which old people could live independently but with access to a warden living near by;[20] with county-council assistance Shrewsbury borough council opened Shropshire's first such group in 1958.[21] Other authorities in the county soon followed suit,[22] and by 1974 grouped dwellings provided some 1,050 places.[23] By 1962 some 250 able-bodied old people were living in special homes, but some 450 remained in the former public-assistance institutions.[24] Stone House (the former Clun institution at Bishop's Castle) was rebuilt between 1962 and 1964.[25] Because of the increasing demand for places, however, the council was forced to resist government pressure for the remaining four institutions to be closed.[26] Some relief came through the home-help and 'meals-on-wheels' schemes, started in 1946 and 1951 respectively by the Women's Voluntary Service with council support;[27] they enabled old people to remain longer in their own homes.

Under the Local Authority Social Services Act, 1970,[28] the council's welfare services were co-ordinated by a single powerful committee with a director of social services. The change was regarded as the council's most far-reaching administrative develop-

[7] S.C.C. Mins. 1945–6, 242; 1946–7, 40.
[8] Oswestry Adv. 22 May 1946.
[9] S.C.C. Mins. 1948–9, 502.
[10] Shrews. Chron. 28 Mar. 1952.
[11] Local information (1974).
[12] Express & Star, 4 Feb. 1949.
[13] Ibid. 7 Feb. 1949.
[14] Shrews. Chron. 28 Mar. 1952.
[15] S.C.C. Mins. 1955–6, 161.
[16] 11 & 12 Geo. V, c. 29: ibid. 1948–9, 502–3.
[17] Ibid. 1953–4, 26; Salop Co. Council: the Post-War Years and the Future.

[18] Local information (1974).
[19] S.C.C. Mins. 1965–6, 31.
[20] Ed. J. Burrow & Co. Ltd. Salop. Co. Handbook [1967], 13.
[21] S.C.C. Mins. 1957–8, 350.
[22] Ibid. 1964–5, 47.
[23] S.C.C. Digest and Development Budget 1974–5, 15.
[24] S.C.C. Mins. 1962–3, 58.
[25] Official opening of Stone House (1965; copy in possession of Mr. F. G. Fawcett); local information (1974).
[26] S.C.C. Mins. 1967–8, 221–2.
[27] Ibid. 1946–7, 208; 1951–2, 64.
[28] 1970, c. 42.

ment since the late 1940s.[29] In 1973 it was estimated that there were 12,000 elderly and handicapped people in Shropshire needing help, of whom fewer than half were known to the council's Social Services Department, and a campaign was planned to find out and register every such person.[30] The council's social concerns had broadened greatly since 1930. Relief of poverty had ceased to be a direct responsibility of local government but the council had taken on more of the pastoral care formerly given by voluntary bodies alone.

Planning

The council's earliest planning powers were exercised through the county surveyor and the Roads and Bridges Committee. From the later 1920s the council had some powers to control roadside development,[31] which were enlarged in 1935 when the council's consent to any development near classified roads became necessary; in 1937 the council elected to extend its control to certain unclassified roads.[32] By 1939 the issuing of consents and resisting of appeals were an important part of the committee's work.[33]

Following the Town and Country Planning Act, 1932,[34] the surveyor, W. H. Butler, recommended the Shropshire minor local authorities to combine in four regional joint planning committees, offering to undertake the technical part of their work in his department.[35] Some declined to participate, and the remainder would do so only on a policy-making level, keeping their separate powers of enforcement.[36] The council's Town and Country Planning Committee was set up in 1932 as a co-ordinating body.[37] Little, however, was achieved before the outbreak of war. The surveyor's staff had no special training in planning and relied on a firm of consultants, Allen & Potter, of London.[38] Only a quarter of the county was subject to control other than that of ribbon development,[39] and no planning schemes had been completed by September 1939.[40] The committee was dissolved in 1939.[41]

In 1945, in anticipation of more far-reaching legislation, a planning officer, Norman Bennett, was appointed,[42] and in 1947 he was made head of his own department.[43] Under the Town and Country Planning Act, 1947, the council became a planning authority.[44] In 1948 the council, on Bennett's advice, decided not to delegate its development control powers to district councils,[45] except for a limited delegation to Shrewsbury borough.[46] The Planning Department had first to prepare a county development plan, less detailed and rigid in conception than the schemes required by the 1932 Act, and subject to periodic review. Its draft plan, completed in 1952, served thereafter as the basis for county planning decisions.[47] The committee's policy was to promote the better siting of rural housing by discouraging scattered development, to allow some light industry in depressed areas, to control the unsightly effects of mining, to improve existing roads, and to encourage, and in some cases enforce, the preservation of historic buildings and the countryside.[48] Applications for planning permission rose

[29] Ex inf. the chief executive, S.C.C. (1974).
[30] Under the Chronically Sick and Disabled Persons Act, 1970, c. 44: *S.C.C. Mins.* 1972-3, 199, 340-1.
[31] Under the Roads Improvement Act, 1925, 15 & 16 Geo. V, c. 68, and Public Health Act, 1925, 15 & 16 Geo. V, c. 71.
[32] Restriction of Ribbon Development Act, 1935, 25 & 26 Geo. V, c. 47; *S.C.C. Mins.* 1936-7, 455-64; 1937-8, 372.
[33] *Shrews. Chron.* 2 June 1939 (suppl.).
[34] 22 & 23 Geo. V, c. 48.
[35] *S.C.C. Mins.* 1933-4, 425-6.
[36] Ibid. 1934-5, 291, 594.
[37] Ibid. 1932-3, 241.
[38] Ibid. 1933-4, 539; 1939-40, 20.
[39] Ibid. 1944-5, 12.
[40] Ibid. 1943-4, 137; 1944-5, 171.
[41] Ibid. 1939-40, 20.
[42] Ibid. 1944-5, 236.
[43] Ibid. 1947-8, 84.
[44] 10 & 11 Geo. VI, c. 51.
[45] *S.C.C. Mins.* 1947-8, 193.
[46] Ibid. 195.
[47] Ibid. 1952-3, 65-6.
[48] S.C.C. 'Development Plan Survey Rep.' (TS. 1952; copy in S.R.O. 1090/1).

from 920 in 1951 to some 6,500 in 1972. In 1972 there were 126 appeals against refusals, each necessitating a public inquiry at which officers could be cross-examined.[49]

A major intrusion was made into the 1952 plan when, in the mid 1950s, proposals were made to expand Dawley by taking excess population from Birmingham by arrangement with the city council. The idea was suggested in 1955[50] by A. W. Bowdler, a local journalist. It was immediately taken up by Charles Savage, engineer and surveyor of Dawley U.D.C.,[51] and the county Planning Committee received the idea favourably as a means of securing the reclamation of derelict land on a scale beyond its own resources.[52] In 1962, however, when the Minister of Housing and Local Government announced detailed proposals for a 'new town' the committee was concerned at learning the extent of agricultural land that would also be lost.[53] The Dawley Development Corporation was set up in 1963.[54] In 1965 the minister proposed to double the area of the new town,[55] trebling its projected population to some 220,000;[56] his decision, renaming the town Telford, was formally announced in 1968.[57] The county council, which would have to invest in schools, health centres, and other services, was afraid that it would suffer heavy financial loss if population failed to be attracted as rapidly as the ministry predicted.[58] It was generally admitted that in the 1960s industry had not been attracted to the new town at a satisfactory pace,[59] and there was no improvement in the early 1970s.[60] By 1972 Telford's rate of growth was seen to depend increasingly on the vagaries of strategic planning at government level.[61]

The abundance of natural scenery and historic buildings in Shropshire made conservation a matter of special concern to the committee. In 1939 the council helped to acquire part of Ercall Wood near Wellington — the first area of open space or woodland secured by the council for public enjoyment;[62] other areas were acquired from 1952, notably the Mere at Ellesmere.[63] Bennett did much to secure the designation in 1959 of the south Shropshire hills, together with Wenlock Edge and the Wrekin, as an 'area of outstanding natural beauty'.[64] In the same year the Planning Department completed a survey of public rights of way.[65] Some 3,700 historic buildings were listed in Shropshire by the Ministry of Housing and Local Government,[66] but the committee found it financially difficult to help to preserve them, except in a few cases.[67] The county planning officer advised the committee in 1971 to declare only a small number of 'conservation areas' under the Civic Amenities Act, 1967,[68] and by 1973 nine had been designated;[69] applications for preservation grants from them were to receive preference.[70]

During the 1960s and early 1970s the Planning Department, already short of qualified staff, laboured under an increasing burden of legislation;[71] by 1973 it had difficulty

[49] S.C.C. *Salop Co. Council: the Post-War Years and the Future* (1965); *S.C.C. Mins.* 1972–3, 436.
[50] *Birmingham Gaz.* 16 Feb. 1955. Similar ideas had been circulating locally for years: local information (1976).
[51] S.C.C. Co. Secretary's Dept., file T.P. 65.
[52] *S.C.C. Mins.* 1956–7, 215; 1960–1, 126; 1966–7, 273.
[53] Ibid. 1962–3, 36, 148.
[54] Ibid. 1964–5, 272.
[55] R. Crossman, *Diaries of a Cabinet Minister*, i (1975), 307–8.
[56] S.R.O. 2755/1, Roads and Bridges Cttee. mins. 31 Dec. 1971, App. G, pp. 1–2.
[57] *Dawley New Town (Designation) Amendment (Telford) Order, 1968* (Stat. Instr. 1968, no. 1912).
[58] *S.C.C. Mins.* 1968–9, 110, 223; 778 *H.C. Deb.* 5th ser. 912–32.
[59] *S.C.C. Mins.* 1969–70, 88; 1971–2, 229–30, 378; F. Schaffer, *The New Town Story* (1970), 113.
[60] *The Times*, 17 Mar. 1976.

[61] *S.C.C. Mins.* 1972–3, 205.
[62] Under the Open Spaces Act, 1906, 6 Edw. VII, c. 25: ibid. 1954–5, 135.
[63] Ibid. 1953–4, 226; 1961–2, 277; 1969–70, 89; 1971–2, 236; 1972–3, 207.
[64] By the Ministry of Housing and Local Govt. under the National Parks and Access to the Countryside Act, 1949, 12, 13 & 14 Geo. VI, c. 97: ibid. 1958–9, 344; local information (1974).
[65] Under 12, 13 & 14 Geo. VI, c. 97: *S.C.C. Mins.* 1959–60, 163.
[66] Ibid. 1969–70, 271.
[67] S.R.O. 2646/1, Planning Cttee. mins. 17 Dec. 1969, App. G, p. 2.
[68] 1967, c. 69; S.R.O. 2952/1, Planning Cttee. mins. 1 Dec. 1971, Rep. on Urban Conservation, p. 7.
[69] *S.C.C. Mins.* 1972–3, 444.
[70] Ibid. 1967–8, 428.
[71] Ibid. 1964–5, 35; S.R.O. 2646/1, Planning Cttee. mins. 29 June 1970, Staff Review, p. 1.

even with the day-to-day handling of planning applications.[72] At the same time a new climate of opinion expected planning to embrace the environment, society, and the economy in all its aspects.[73] Michael Law, appointed planning officer in 1969, pressed for more staff, and in 1971 introduced a 'design and conservation' section to advise on aesthetic, environmental, and economic matters.[74] In 1972 a successful experiment in public participation was conducted at Ludlow where, through an exhibition and public meeting, the townspeople were encouraged to comment on the department's plans for the town.[75] In 1970 the committee was called on to prepare a county 'structure plan', more general in scope than the 1952 plan and designed to supersede it.[76]

Civil Defence and Fire Brigade

In 1936 the council organized an air-raid precautions (A.R.P.) scheme co-ordinating all the local authorities and many voluntary bodies.[77] Shropshire had little industry but several airfields and vital railways.[78] In September 1939 the county A.R.P. organization was dangerously ill equipped, but the deficiencies were made up within a year.[79] Some 800 high-explosive bombs and thousands of incendiary bombs were dropped on Shropshire during the war, but only eight people were killed.[80] Beginning in 1942, the council set up some 80 local invasion committees to aid the armed forces and regulate civil life in the event of an invasion; the committees lapsed as the danger of invasion receded and were wound up in 1944.[81] The county A.R.P. organization, employing some 7,000 volunteers, was disbanded in 1945.[82]

In 1949, after the outbreak of the 'cold war', the council had to raise a volunteer civil defence corps[83] trained to deal with the effects of atomic bombs.[84] A full-time officer[85] and volunteer instructors[86] were appointed. The corps was the first in the country to demonstrate the peace-time value of civil defence when it assisted at an explosion at Madeley Wood in 1950.[87] Recruitment, at first slow,[88] was soon better than in most parts of Britain.[89] By 1960 the force numbered some 3,000 but recruitment barely kept pace with resignations.[90] In 1968 the corps was disbanded[91] and the council remained responsible only for contingency plans.[92]

The National Fire Service's county brigade, formed in 1941 from the local-authority brigades, was brought under the council's control in 1948.[93] The council's brigade inherited 'expensive ideas . . . and some well worn equipment',[94] and many of its buildings were dilapidated. In 1950 it consisted mainly of part-time men and was 15 per cent below strength.[95] In that year four part-timers were seriously injured at the Madeley Wood explosion, and the government prevented the council from reaching

[72] S.C.C. Mins. 1972–3, 570.
[73] S.R.O. 2646/1, Planning Cttee. mins. 17 Dec. 1969, App. G, p. 1; S.C.C. Mins. 1969–70, 153.
[74] S.R.O. 2952/1, Planning Cttee. mins. 1 Dec. 1971, Rep. on Urban Conservation, p. 1.
[75] Sunday Times, 3 Dec. 1972; S.C.C. Salop Co. Council Review (1973), 7, 9.
[76] Under the Town and Country Planning Act, 1968, c. 72: S.C.C. Mins. 1970–1, 280.
[77] S.C.C. Mins. 1936–7, A.R.P. Scheme. It was revised in 1938: ibid. 1938–9, A.R.P. Scheme. Schemes became compulsory under the Air-Raid Precautions Act, 1937, 1 & 2 Geo. VI, c. 6.
[78] Co. Councils Assoc. Jubilee of the Co. Councils (1939; Salop. edn.), 98.
[79] S.R.O. 405/2.
[80] Oswestry Adv. 7 Nov. 1945.
[81] S.R.O. 106/1.
[82] S.R.O. 405/9.
[83] Under the Civil Defence Act, 1948, 12 & 13 Geo. VI,

c. 5: S.C.C. Salop Co. Council: the Post-War Years and the Future (1965).
[84] Shrews. Chron. 25 Sept. 1953.
[85] Express & Star, 1 Nov. 1949.
[86] Shrews. Chron. 17 Mar. 1950.
[87] Ibid. 26 May 1950.
[88] Express & Star, 25 July 1950.
[89] Ibid. 24 Aug., 25 Oct. 1950; 21 July 1953; Shrews. Chron. 25 Sept. 1953.
[90] S.C.C. Mins. 1959–60, 322.
[91] On govt. orders: ibid. 1964–8.
[92] Ibid. 1968–9, 122–3.
[93] Under the Fire Services Act, 1947, 10 & 11 Geo. VI, c. 41.
[94] Salop Co. Council: the Post-War Years and the Future.
[95] H. D. G. Foxall, 'Short Hist. of Fire-Fighting in Salop.' (1973), 4 (TS. in possession of co. archivist); Shrews. Chron. 28 Apr. 1950; Express & Star, 9 Oct. 1951.

a mutually satisfactory agreement with the men on compensation;[96] 30 part-time men resigned as a result.[97] By 1953 resignations were increasing through dissatisfaction with the brigade's uncongenial premises.[98] It soon became possible, however, to begin replacing old fire stations; between 1953 and 1973 16 of the 25 stations were rebuilt. In 1973 three of them were manned by full-time firemen.[99] Some 2,500 calls were answered in 1973 and some 5,200 premises were inspected with a view to fire prevention.[1] The rescue of people from crashed motor vehicles was then an important part of the brigade's work.[2]

The Shirehall

Until the late 1900s Shrewsbury borough council's use of rooms in the shirehall caused continual friction between the borough on the one hand and the county council and magistrates on the other.[3] Both councils had a growing need for more space. The county council, whose needs had been increased by the Education Act, 1902, alleged in 1909 that the borough had acquired a disproportionate share of the accommodation by 'subtle procedure' and was likely to 'over-run' the building.[4] On 13 May 1912 the clerk of the county council refused to unlock the Grand Jury Room for a borough committee meeting and the borough's men broke open the door;[5] a few days later the Standing Joint Committee asked the borough to join in a 'final and legal settlement' of the shirehall question.[6] Settlement was reached in 1915 with the Salop County Council (Shirehall and Guildhall) Act, and the county bought out the borough for £12,500.[7]

Extensions to the shirehall were completed in 1908[8] and others were added in 1938 and 1940 in response to needs created by the Local Government Act, 1929.[9] For a time nearly all the departments were housed in the extended shirehall; with the growth of business arising from legislation in the 1940s, however, more and more were forced to find offices elsewhere.[10] In 1945 it was proposed to build a new shirehall at the Column, Shrewsbury, to house all the departments. The site was acquired, but periods of financial stringency and the priority given to new schools were among the circumstances that delayed the decision to build. From first to last there was considerable opposition to the scheme and it was finally approved in 1963 by a margin of only one vote.[11] The new shirehall was completed in 1966 and officially opened by Elizabeth II in 1967.[12]

Records

Quarter sessions set up a Records Committee in 1899 to report on the records held by the clerk of the peace,[13] which were then housed in the shirehall basement.[14] Later in 1899 the committee was made a sub-committee of the Standing Joint Committee so that expenditure could be incurred.[15] By 1901 the committee had arranged and listed the records,[16] and between 1901 and 1916 it published abstracts of the sessions order

96 *Shrews. Chron.* 26 May 1950.
97 *Express & Star*, 26 July 1950. The council eventually helped the injured men with 'unofficial' funds: ex inf. Mr. G. C. Godber (1974).
98 *Shrews. Chron.* 4 Sept. 1953.   99 Foxall, op. cit. 4.
1 S.C.C. *Digest and Development Budget 1974–5*, 17.
2 Foxall, op. cit. 3.
3 A. Heber-Percy, *Shirehall and Guildhall: Statement of Facts* (Shrews. 1897), 14–17 (copy in S.R.O. 284/1).
4 S.R.O. 348/771; *S.C.C. Mins.* 1939–40, 558.
5 S.R.O. 348/693–9.   6 S.R.O. 1819/9, p. 185.
7 5 & 6 Geo. V, c. 18 (Local).

8 Mary C. Hill, *Hist. of Shropshire's Many Shirehalls* (Shrews. 1963), 9 (copy in S.R.O. 1303/1); *S.C.C. Mins.* 1907–8, 247.
9 *S.C.C. Mins.* 1939–40, 558–60.
10 S.C.C. *New Shirehall, Shrews.: Rep. of the Clerk* [1963], 2–3 and App. I (copy in S.R.O. 1303/1).
11 Ibid. 3–5; *S.C.C. Mins.* 1963–4, 24a–g.
12 *S.C.C. Mins.* 1966–7, 66; *Shrews. Chron.* 24 Mar. 1967.
13 S.R.O., q. sess. min. bk. 18, p. 23.
14 S.R.O. 347/1, meeting 17 Oct. 1899.
15 S.R.O. 1818/7, pp. 230–1.
16 Ibid. 8, p. 51; S.R.O., q. sess. min. bk. 18, p. 26.

books 1638-1889 and of the sessions rolls 1696-1820, and lists of the inclosure awards and deposited plans.[17] Shropshire was one of the first counties to publish its quarter-sessions records systematically.[18] The committee met only five times after 1902, ceasing to meet in 1916.[19] The muniment rooms were, in 1901, dark, cramped, susceptible to fire, and already full.[20] A new Records Committee was set up in 1934[21] and in 1935 an honorary archivist was appointed.[22] Lack of space prevented the committee from inviting deposits of records.[23] It met only three times between 1935 and 1938, and not thereafter until 1945.[24] In 1945 the clerk of the council called in Joyce Godber, acting clerk of records in Bedfordshire, to report on the records; she found them dirty and ill-housed, and noted the lack of space for searchers.[25] A full-time archivist was appointed in 1946. For the first time encouragement was given to outside depositors.[26] A *Guide to the Shropshire Records* was published in 1952. In 1966 the office and its contents were moved to purpose-built accommodation in the new shire-hall.

As early as 1895 the Local Government, Allotments, and Small Holdings Committee began a survey of Shropshire parish records;[27] its inventory was one of the first of its kind when it was published in 1903.[28] After 1946 the county archivist resumed the inspection of parish records and advised on their preservation.[29] A Records Committee sub-committee was formed when, in 1960, the council in association with the University of London revived the *Victoria History of Shropshire*.[30]

[17] *Orders of Q. Sess.* (Salop. Co. Rec. nos. 2-5, 7, 9, 11-17 [Shrews. 1901-16]); *Q. Sess. Rolls* (Salop. Co. Rec. nos. 6, 10 [Shrews. 1901-5]); *Commissioners' Awards for Inclosing Lands, 1773-1891* (Salop. Co. Rec. no. 1 [Shrews. 1901]); *Plans and Documents deposited with the Clk. of the Peace for Salop* (Salop. Co. Rec. no. 8; Shrews. 1902).

[18] Yorks. N.R. began in 1884, Worcs. in 1900; neither series was as comprehensive as that of Salop. and neither was carried so far: F. G. Emmison and I. Gray, *County Records* (1967), 27-31.

[19] S.R.O. 1818/8, p. 183; 9, pp. 51, 190; 10, pp. 21, 63. The sub-cttee. was formally dissolved in 1934: ibid. 13, p. 174.

[20] Ibid. 8, p. 51.

[21] Under the Local Govt. Act, 1933, 23 & 24 Geo. V, c. 51: *S.C.C. Mins.* 1934-5, 309.

[22] Ibid. 1935-6, 63.

[23] Ibid. 1945-6, 147; S.R.O. 1076/1, p. 5.

[24] *S.C.C. Mins.* 1935-6, 1; 1936-7, 3; 1938-9, 8; 1945-6, 16.

[25] Ibid. 1945-6, 146-55.

[26] Ibid. 309.

[27] Under the Local Govt. Act, 1894, 56 & 57 Vic. c. 73: S.R.O., Local Govt. etc. Cttee. min. bk. 1894-1903, pp. 66-7, 105.

[28] *Shropshire Parish Documents* (Shrews. [1903]): Local Govt. etc. Cttee. min. bk. 1894-1903, p. 268; *Shrews. Chron.* 18 Mar. 1910. E. C. Peele and R. S. Clease appear on p. iv as joint compilers, but the whole work was carried out by Clease: S.R.O., Local Govt. etc. Cttee. min. bk. 1894-1903, p. 244.

[29] *S.C.C. Mins.* 1946-7, 225-31.

[30] *V.C.H. Gen. Intro.* 18-19; *V.C.H. Salop.* viii, p. xv; *T.S.A.S.* lix. 181-2.

LAW AND ORDER AFTER 1889

The Lieutenant and the Magistrates

In 1896 Lord Bradford resigned the lieutenancy on grounds of age and infirmity.[1] Lord Powis, aged 34,[2] was his natural successor.[3] Three earls of Powis had held the Shropshire lieutenancy since 1735, and Lord Salisbury, the prime minister, was anxious to have young lieutenants appointed to secure some Conservative influence in the counties against future changes of government.[4] Powis resigned in 1951[5] after a term unequalled in length by any lieutenant of an English county then in office,[6] having remained active throughout.[7] By 1945, however, his age and reluctance to retire were causing some concern.[8] Powis was taken ill in Italy c. 1947. He had always refused to appoint a vice-lieutenant, and could not then do so because the necessary document had to be executed in the United Kingdom. Thus the lieutenancy, for the first time since 1804,[9] was put in commission until Powis's return, when a vice-lieutenant was appointed.[10] Powis's successors were bound by their commissions to retire at the age of 75,[11] as were all other lieutenants by that time.

As local representative of the Sovereign the lieutenant was often elected county president of organizations of which the Sovereign was head, such as the British (later Royal British) Legion.[12] Vestiges of the lieutenant's ancient responsibilities for military affairs and for the general security of the county survived into the 20th century. In 1907, as a result of Haldane's reorganization of army reserve forces,[13] the lieutenant became *ex officio* president of the Territorial Force Association (from 1921[14] the Territorial Army Association and from 1947[15] the Territorial and Auxiliary Forces Association) for the County of Salop,[16] which from 1908 administered, but did not command, the county's force. In 1968[17] the Shropshire association was absorbed into the new Territorial Auxiliary and Volunteer Reserve Association for the West Midlands, the lieutenant being eligible for appointment as president by the Secretary of State for Defence.[18] In 1919 the lieutenant was involved in the proposed recruitment of 'citizen guards' and in 1921 with the proposed Shropshire Defence Force, bodies designed by the government to prevent civil disorder during industrial disputes.[19] In 1940 he was charged with duties connected with the Local Defence Volunteers, later renamed the Home Guard.[20]

[1] S.R.O., q. sess. min. bk. 17, Mids. 1896. This article was written in 1976.

[2] Burke, *Peerage* (1967), 2038.

[3] S.R.O. 1665/23.

[4] J. M. Lee, *Social Leaders and Public Persons: a Study of Co. Govt. in Ches. since 1888* (1963), 226–7.

[5] *S.C.C. Mins.* 1951–2, 194.

[6] S.R.O., S.C.C. special occasion files, G. C. Godber (clk. to the lieutenancy) to Maj. B. E. P. Leighton, 31 Oct. 1945.

[7] S.R.O. 45/1, 'notes as to Ld. Powis', 1946; S.R.O. 1839/1.

[8] S.R.O. 45/1, Godber to J. B. Graham, 29 Oct. 1945.

[9] See p. 131.

[10] Local information (1976).

[11] See p. 360 and sources there cited.

[12] Local information (1976).

[13] Territorial and Reserve Forces Act, 1907, 7 Edw. VII, c. 9.

[14] Under the Territorial Army and Militia Act, 1921, 11 & 12 Geo. V, c. 37.

[15] *Lond. Gaz.* 28 May 1968, suppl., p. 6131.

[16] S.R.O. 119/8.

[17] Under the Reserve Forces Act, 1966, 14 & 15 Eliz. II, c. 30.

[18] *Lond. Gaz.* 28 May 1968, suppl., pp. 6131–2.

[19] S.R.O., S.C.C. clk.'s in-letters, box 10, Powis to borough and district councils, 4 Oct. 1919; Powis to employers, 16 Apr. 1921.

[20] [J. Moulsdale,] *Hist. of Corps of King's Shropshire Light Infantry*, iii [Shrewsbury, c. 1970], 355 (copy in S.R.O.).

The lieutenant's most important surviving duty was that of making, as *custos rotulorum*, the nominations to the lord chancellor of people to be appointed as county magistrates. At the beginning of the period the lieutenant had no formal obligation to take advice about his recommendations. A long succession of Conservative governments coinciding with Lord Halsbury's chancellorships produced, even in counties less Conservative than Shropshire, predominantly Conservative benches. The Shropshire bench was said by C. S. Henry, Liberal M.P. for Wellington, to consist in 1905 of some 240 Tories and no more than 10 Liberals.[21] Henry alleged that Lord Powis, in recommending appointments, took advice only from strong Unionists and refused nominations of men who had shown 'pronounced political activity'.[22] Sir Offley Wakeman, chairman of quarter sessions 1889–1914, emphasized the difficulty of finding suitable Liberal gentlemen; small tradesmen were not wanted because it was supposed that they could not deal impartially with people who might be their customers, while suitable artisans were unknown and in any case unable to attend sessions. Less controversially, Wakeman regretted an increasing tendency to regard appointment to the bench merely as a reward for past services.[23]

The Liberal victory of 1906 led to changes that went some way to removing magisterial appointments from the political arena. Halsbury's successor, Lord Loreburn, was firmly opposed, as was Lord Powis, to political jobbing of the bench. He was nevertheless subjected to immense pressure from his own party to make more Liberal magistrates. Henry, with George Whiteley of Hawkstone, the Liberal chief whip, was insistent that the political balance of the Shropshire bench be altered; so much so that Loreburn accused them of trying to force upon him a 'prostitution' of his office.[24]

Instead lieutenants' advisory committees, with power to by-pass the lieutenant if necessary, were appointed in 1911 in most of those counties in which none already existed, among them Shropshire. The committee consisted of five or six prominent local people appointed by the lieutenant for life.[25] From 1924 half the committee had to retire every three years, and new appointments had to be approved by the lord chancellor.[26] In practice retiring members were reappointed if they so wished.[27] Throughout his lieutenancy Powis took much, some thought excessive,[28] personal trouble over the details of appointments to the magistracy[29] and was anxious to secure fair representation of political and religious views on the advisory committee.[30] Liberals were appointed to it from the first[31] and there was a representative of Labour from at least 1924.[32] In 1941 the committee consisted of two Conservatives, one Liberal, one Labour member, and one Independent;[33] in a predominantly Conservative county it was a fair balance.

The property qualification for county magistrates was abolished in 1906[34] and at least one working-class justice had been appointed in Shropshire by 1918.[35] Powis and his committee made conscientious efforts to secure a proportion of working-class appointments[36] but by 1940 there were only ten such magistrates.[37] Since the member-

[21] The total no. of Salop. J.P.s was really c. 226: *Kelly's Dir. Salop.* (1905), 10–12.

[22] *Rep. R. Com. on Selection of J.P.s, 1910: Mins. of Evidence* [Cd. 5358], pp. 184–5, 189–90, H.C. (1910), xxxvii.

[23] Ibid. pp. 193–4.

[24] R. F. V. Heuston, *Lives of the Ld. Chancellors 1885–1940* (1964), 153–7.

[25] Esther Moir, *Justice of Peace* (1969), 185.

[26] S.R.O. 1839/1, pp. 31, 42.

[27] Ibid. *passim.*

[28] S.R.O. 1193/2, H. C. Kenyon to Sir O. Wakeman, 2 Jan. 1950.

[29] S.R.O. 1193/1.

[30] Ibid., Powis to W. L. Edge (clk. to the lieutenancy),

19 June 1940.

[31] S.R.O. 1839/1, p. 1. For Smith and Wheeler see above, p. 187; for Patchett see *Shrews. Chron.* 4 and 11 Mar. 1904.

[32] S.R.O. 1839/1, pp. 31, 57.

[33] S.R.O. 1193/1, questionnaire [4 Apr. 1941].

[34] Under the Justices of the Peace Act, 1906, 6 Edw. VII, c. 16. Under the Local Govt. Act, 1894, 56 & 57 Vic. c. 73, chairmen of district councils could be *ex officio* J.P.s without the property qualification.

[35] S.R.O. 1193/1, Edge to Powis, 21 June 1940.

[36] S.R.O. 1839/3, Dec. 1943; S.R.O. 1193/2 Godber to Dr. W. B. Clegg, 6 July 1950.

[37] S.R.O. 1193/1, Edge to Powis, 21 June 1940.

ship and proceedings of the advisory committee were confidential there were suspicions that working-class people were being unfairly excluded from the magistracy, and that view was probably reinforced whenever a working-class candidate was proposed to the committee and rejected.[38] The practice, followed in some parts of the country, of receiving nominations from political agents and organizations and from trades unions[39] was not encouraged in Shropshire under Powis; it was thought undesirable to seek political or sectional nominations for an independent office.[40] It is nevertheless true that, despite the committee's efforts, the proportion of Labour magistrates appointed in Shropshire between 1930 and 1946 was considerably lower than that of the county's Labour voters in 1945, a point that the newly elected Labour government did not fail to press.[41] That there was a lingering local prejudice in favour of the middle and upper classes may be suggested by a note made by Powis during the Second World War that a lady was being considered, 'being wife of M.F.H.';[42] it is equally significant, however, that she was not appointed.[43]

Labour governments and local Labour and trades-union organizations pressed the advisory committee to appoint more working people;[44] local people were sometimes unaware even that Labour was represented on the committee.[45] The committee, however, faced a practical difficulty that was hard to reconcile with democratic ideals; for historical reasons that could not suddenly be discounted, few working people had the right experience and sense of authority to make acceptable magistrates. Moreover, when such a person was found and offered a place, he often declined it.[46] In 1930 the Labour member of the committee could find no Labour party supporter in the Oswestry area suitable for appointment to the bench.[47] In 1954 his successor on the committee was asked by the lieutenant to find a suitable working man from the same area, only to have to report eighteen months later that none could be found.[48] The committee would not proceed to a nomination without good knowledge of a candidate's record and reputation. Since fewer of the working-class candidates were well known to the committee members and their close friends, there was thus a further practical obstacle to finding suitable working-class magistrates; for there was a limit to the outside enquiries that could be made about a person if the confidentiality of the appointment procedure was not to be breached.[49] Women became eligible for appointment in 1919[50] and the first women magistrates in Shropshire were appointed in 1922.[51]

The successive chairmen of quarter sessions were all men with legal qualifications, well before 1939 when legal experience became compulsory.[52] Sir Offley Wakeman (1889–1914) and R. Ll. Kenyon (1914–27) were barristers;[53] both were also men of scholarly interests.[54] Kenyon, who had a reputation for severity on the bench,[55] was the third generation of his family to occupy the chair and was the last chairman of quarter sessions to participate in county administration, having been a county alderman since 1889.[56] Sir W. F. K. Taylor (later Lord Maenan), chairman 1927–47, was

[38] S.R.O. 1839/2, p. 2.
[39] A. J. P. Taylor, *Eng. Hist. 1914–1945* (1966), 175.
[40] S.R.O., lieutenancy letter bk. 1914–34, pp. 230, 401, 415, 498; S.R.O. 1193/1, 10 Feb. 1942; S.R.O. 1839/1, p. 49; ibid. 3, 6 Apr. 1943.
[41] S.R.O. 1193/1, sec. of commissions to Powis, 15 July 1946.
[42] S.R.O. 1839/3, p. [19].
[43] S.R.O. 1839/1.
[44] Ibid. pp. 49, 54, 106.
[45] Ibid. p. 57; S.R.O. 1839/2, p. 2.
[46] S.R.O. 1193/1, Godber to L. E. Bury, 20 Dec. 1948.
[47] S.R.O., lieutenancy letter bk. 1914–34, p. 422.
[48] S.R.O. 1839/1, pp. 155, 158.
[49] S.R.O 1193/2, Godber to Maj. W. H. B. Whitaker,

25 Apr. 1950; Godber to Powis, 28 July 1950; [Powis] to R. A. Bowen, 20 Sept. 1950.
[50] Under the Sex Disqualification (Removal) Act, 1919, 9 & 10 Geo. V. c. 71.
[51] S.R.O. 1839/1, pp. 29–30.
[52] Under the Administration of Justice (Misc. Provisions) Act, 1938, 1 & 2 Geo. VI, c. 63.
[53] *Who Was Who, 1929–40*, 747, 1398.
[54] They edited *Orders of Q. Sess.* and were contributors to *T.S.A.S.* Kenyon wrote important numismatic works: B.M. *Gen. Cat. of Printed Books . . . to 1955* (photolithographic edn. 1959–66), cxxii, col. 322.
[55] Oswestry Adv., *Unconventional Portraits* (1910), 9.
[56] *Who Was Who, 1929–40*, 747.

presiding judge of the Liverpool Court of Passage 1903–48.[57] He retired from the chairmanship at the age of 93, remaining alert and efficient throughout.[58] Sir W. N. Stable (1948–67) was a high court justice 1938–68 and chairman of Merionethshire quarter sessions 1944–71.[59] R. M. A. Chetwynd-Talbot (1967–71) was recorder of Banbury (Oxon.) 1955–71 and became a circuit judge in 1972[60] when quarter sessions were abolished.[61]

With the abolition of quarter sessions the corporate character of the bench was lost. The annual quarter-sessions dinner was discontinued.[62] A magistrate's duties were thereafter confined to his petty-sessional division. There was virtually no change in those divisions before the 1950s.[63] The borough quarter sessions of Bridgnorth, Ludlow, Oswestry, and Much Wenlock were abolished under the Justices of the Peace Act, 1949,[64] and their areas became petty-sessional divisions, making a county total of twenty-two; Shrewsbury was then the only borough to retain its own quarter sessions.[65] In 1944 ten of the Shropshire divisions were among only eighteen in England and Wales that held sessions less often than once a month. The Shropshire divisions were too small to be efficient[66] and over the period 1954–9 were reduced by amalgamation to eight.[67] In 1974 Shrewsbury's separate peace commission was abolished[68] and its area absorbed by the surrounding division.[69]

The Sheriff

The sheriff's work continued to be governed by the Sheriffs Act, 1887.[70] The office of high sheriff remained a costly one to the holder. In 1911–12, for instance, he had to find £199 for the essential expenses of the under-sheriff, beyond what was reimbursed by the Treasury;[71] in 1934–5 the figure was £245.[72] Beyond that were the high sheriff's personal expenses connected with hospitality and ceremonial, which he was compelled by custom to incur.[73]

Few high sheriffs had any detailed understanding of their statutory duties and, except for their personal attendance upon the judges who came into the county, virtually all the work was carried out by the under-sheriff.[74] Until 1974 the under-sheriff of Shropshire was always a partner in Peele & Peele (from 1934 Peele & Aris), solicitors, of Shrewsbury.[75] The office then passed to Joseph Newell,[76] a partner in Sprott, Stokes, & Turnbull, solicitors, of Shrewsbury.[77] E. C. Peele, under-sheriff until 1911, whose forceful conduct was a source of disquiet in some county-council circles,[78] formed an exaggerated estimate of his own standing. At the 1893 Summer assizes the sheriff could not attend and Peele, 'carried away' with his importance as 'acting' sheriff,[79] took it as a deliberate slight when he was not invited to the grand-jury

[57] Ibid. *1951–60*, 723.
[58] S.R.O. 45/1, Godber to J. B. Graham, 3 Nov. 1945.
[59] *Who's Who, 1975*, 2976. He was known as 'the kindly judge': *Shropshire Star*, 24 Nov. 1977 (obit.).
[60] *Who's Who, 1975*, 3085.
[61] Under the Courts Act, 1971, c. 23.
[62] Local information (1976).
[63] S.R.O. 900/1, p. 10a.
[64] Justices of the Peace Act, 1949, 12, 13 & 14 Geo. VI, c. 101.
[65] S.C.C. *Year Bk. 1952–3*, 134–5, 137–60.
[66] S.R.O. 900/1, p. 10a.
[67] 12, 13 & 14 Geo. VI, c. 101; S.R.O. 900/1, p. 39; 3474/3, pp. 25–32; S.C.C. *Year Bk. 1960–1*, 138–52.
[68] Under the Local Govt. Act. 1972, c. 70.
[69] S.C.C. *Year Bk. 1974–5*, 120.
[70] 50 & 51 Vic. c. 55.

[71] S.R.O. 1166/15.
[72] S.R.O. 2572, under-sheriff's acct.
[73] *Rep. Sel. Cttee. on High Sheriffs, 1888*, H.C. 257, pp. 64, 69 (1888), xii.
[74] Ibid. p. iv.
[75] Local information (1976); *Kelly's Dir. Salop.* (1891 and later edns.). Sir Oliver Leese (1958–9) appointed a Liverpool solicitor as his under-sheriff, but the actual work remained with the usual firm: ex inf. Mr. M. C. de C. Peele, under-sheriff 1949–58, 1959–74.
[76] S.R.O. 3150/3.
[77] Stevens & Sons Ltd., *Law List, 1975*, 993.
[78] See p. 188.
[79] It is doubtful whether Peele was entitled to the privileges of acting sheriff; it was customary then (S.R.O. 1033/42) as in 1974 (ex inf. Mr. M. C. de C. Peele) for the high sheriff to be represented, in the event of unavoidable absence, by his predecessor.

luncheon; for some years it had been customary in Shropshire to invite the high sheriff,[80] who paid for the jurors' meal.[81]

The sheriff's duties were gradually diminished. In 1933 the grand jury was abolished.[82] In 1965 the duty of supervising hangings came to an end with the abolition of capital punishment.[83] That of recovering fines ceased after 1967.[84] In 1971 the task of impanelling jurors was transferred to the Lord Chancellor's Department.[85] By 1976 the main surviving duty, carried out by the under-sheriff, was the execution of writs of *fieri facias* and writs of possession.[86]

The Police

In 1889 the Shropshire Constabulary came under the control of a Standing Joint Committee consisting of equal numbers of magistrates and county-council members.[87] The committee's proceedings were not subject to debate by the council, though it was the practice in Shropshire for the committee to present formal reports for the council's information.[88] The Bridgnorth and Ludlow police were absorbed by the county force,[89] leaving Shrewsbury with the only separate constabulary.

Until the late 1900s Shropshire had a reasonably efficient force, though it was less well paid than those of neighbouring counties and less attractive to recruits.[90] Capt. G. C. P. Williams-Freeman, chief constable 1890–1905, ran the police on military lines. He introduced merit badges, with extra pay, for special devotion to duty and founded an annual drill competition.[91] He began constabulary sports, a development seen in many forces in the 1890s,[92] and insisted on ambulance training for every member of the force including himself.[93] Bicycles were first provided in 1897,[94] and in 1900 the chief constable led his men in a ceremonial cycle ride from Shrewsbury to Wellington.[95] A new county police headquarters was opened in Shrewsbury in 1903.[96] Maj. (later Maj.-Gen. Sir) L. W. Atcherley, chief constable 1906–8, was another man of noted ability.[97] There seems to have been a marked rise in the number of indictable offences committed in Shropshire during the 1900s[98] but a high detection rate for such crimes was apparently maintained until Atcherley's resignation. Thereafter the detection rate seems to have fallen.[99]

During the First World War, with so many men under military discipline, the number of crimes fell; but so too, it seems, did the Shropshire detection rate.[1] Leadership of the quality given by Williams-Freeman and Atcherley was lacking. Capt. G. L. Derriman, chief constable from 1908, was given leave of absence in 1914[2] and died on active service in 1915.[3] The Standing Joint Committee appointed its vice-chairman, Augustus Wood Acton, then in his seventies,[4] as honorary chief constable for the duration of the war.[5] Early in 1918, however, the Home Office forced the committee to appoint a permanent chief constable; the appointment went to Maj.

[80] S.R.O. 1033/34, 38–43.
[81] *Rep. Sel. Cttee. on High Sheriffs, 1888,* p. 65.
[82] Under the Administration of Justice (Misc. Provisions) Act, 1933, 23 & 24 Geo. V, c. 36.
[83] Under the Murder (Abolition of Death Penalty) Act, 1965, c. 71.
[84] Under the Criminal Justice Act, 1967, c. 80.
[85] Under the Courts Act, 1971, c. 23.
[86] Ex inf. Mr. M. C. de C. Peele.
[87] Under the Local Govt. Act, 1888, 51 & 52 Vic. c. 41.
[88] S.R.O. 1818/6, p. 11.
[89] S.C.C. *Resumé of Work of First Co. Council of Salop* [1893], 23.
[90] *Shrews. Chron.* 16 Mar. 1901; S.R.O. 1818/9, p. 167.
[91] S.C.C. *Mins.* S.J. Cttee. rep. 10 Oct. 1891, 17; J. Durrell and V. H. Roberts, *Salop. Constabulary: the First Hundred Years 1839–1939* (Salop. Constabulary, 1963;

copy in S.R.O. 1818/112), 13–14.
[92] T. A. Critchley, *Hist. of Police in Eng. and Wales 900–1966* (1967), 166.
[93] S.C.C. *Mins.* S.J. Cttee. rep. 10 Oct. 1891, 16; S.C.C. *Mins.* 1905–6, 203–4.
[94] S.R.O. 1818/7, p. 130.
[95] *Ann. Rep. of Ch. Const.* (copies in S.R.O.) 1952, 9.
[96] Durrell and Roberts, op. cit. 18.
[97] *Who Was Who, 1951–60,* 43.
[98] S.C.C. *Mins.* 1910–11, 64.
[99] S.C.C. *Mins.* S.J. Cttee. rep. 7 Apr. 1900, 5; S.C.C. *Mins.* 1910–11, 64; 1914–15, 97.
[1] S.C.C. *Mins.* 1920–1, 73.
[2] S.R.O. 1818/10, p. 19.   [3] Ibid. p. 42.
[4] W. Mate & Sons Ltd. *Shropshire: Historical, Descriptive, Biographical* (1906), pt. 2, p. 63.
[5] S.R.O. 1818/10, p. 45.

(later Sir) Jack Becke[6] who served until 1935. Pay in Shropshire remained lower than in the neighbouring English counties, and that fact aggravated in Shropshire[7] the considerable discontent that was felt about pay by men of all forces during the war.[8] A higher pay scale, which improved Shropshire's relative position, was introduced in 1918[9] but the general dissatisfaction over pay remained. In 1919 police strikes occurred in Birmingham, Liverpool, and other places[10] and serious unrest threatened to spread to the Shropshire police.[11] Later in the year, however, the committee adopted, albeit under protest, an increased national pay scale.[12]

Between 1918 and the mid 1930s there was little increase either in the population of Shropshire[13] or, apparently, in the number of indictable offences committed there.[14] Nevertheless the detection rate for such offences seems to have continued to fall until the mid 1930s.[15] The force failed to adapt to changing conditions occasioned by the very great increase of motor transport.[16] Criminals were able more quickly to reach, and to escape from, the scenes of crimes, and they were harder to trace because they came from farther afield. Moreover, men occupied in traffic control could not aid the solving of crimes.[17] A car for the chief constable's use had first been provided in 1907,[18] but the force needed more cars, more comprehensive criminal records, and more men.[19] In fact the establishment was fixed at 185 in 1919[20] and not increased again until 1935.[21] In the early 1920s the Home Office would allow no increase, for reasons of economy.[22] Thereafter no formal application by the committee seems to have been made.[23] Since 1913 officers had been granted an allowance for using their own cars for police work.[24] By 1931, however, only 21 men owned cars; 43 others owned motor cycles.[25] There were no traffic patrols. Government grants became available in 1930[26] to provide patrol cars for enforcing traffic regulations, and in 1930 the committee bought one car.[27] Becke was reluctant to use patrol cars without an increased establishment because they kept men away from general duties.[28] Two more cars were bought in 1935.[29]

Some improvement in efficiency was attempted in the years immediately before the Second World War. In 1935 the establishment was increased to 189.[30] Maj. (later Lt.-Col.) H. A. Golden succeeded Becke as chief constable in 1935. He introduced a modern system of filing criminal records[31] and made reforms in general administration.[32] Three more patrol cars were bought, bringing the total to six by 1936,[33] and by 1939 most of the men were using their own cars for police work.[34] The 1935 establishment increase did not mean an immediate increase in actual strength; in 1936 the strength stood at 182,[35] three below the 1919 establishment. Recruiting was slow, an unattractive feature of the Shropshire force being its poor housing. It had been the committee's policy to save money by renting and buying existing houses rather than building new ones.[36] By 1936, as Golden reported, the county was burdened with many old police houses that were not only inadequate but also expensive to maintain.[37]

[6] Ibid. pp. 95–6, 102–4, 106–7, 117.
[7] Ibid. pp. 58, 115; *Shrews. Chron.* 7 May 1915.
[8] Critchley, *Hist. of Police,* 184–5.
[9] *S.C.C. Mins.* 1918–19, 145.
[10] Critchley, op. cit. 188–9.
[11] S.R.O. 1818/52, pp. 45–6, 59.
[12] *S.C.C. Mins.* 1919–20, 233.
[13] *V.C.H. Salop.* ii. 219, 227 (i.e. Salop. less Shrews.).
[14] Crime was increasing in Eng. as a whole: Critchley, op. cit. 253.
[15] *S.C.C. Mins.* 1929–30, 36; 1937–8, 67.
[16] Ibid. 1928–9, 292; 1935–6, 298.
[17] *Shrews. Chron.* 2 June 1939 (Suppl.).
[18] S.R.O. 1818/9, p. 7; *S.C.C. Mins.* 1907–8, 51.
[19] S.R.O., S.C.C. bundle system, box 75, 'Ch. Constable's Rep. on Augmentation of Force, March 1939', p. 2.

[20] S.R.O. 1818/10, p. 145.
[21] S.R.O. 1818/13, p. 226.
[22] S.R.O. 1818/11, pp. 81–2.
[23] S.R.O. 1818/11–13.
[24] S.R.O. 1818/9, p. 227.
[25] S.R.O. 1818/12, p. 19.
[26] Under the Road Traffic Act, 1930, 20 & 21 Geo. V, c. 43.
[27] Durrell and Roberts, *Salop. Constabulary,* 32.
[28] S.R.O. 1818/12, p. 19; 13, p. 216.
[29] S.R.O. 1818/13, p. 226.   [30] Ibid.
[31] *S.C.C. Mins.* 1938–9, 84.
[32] S.R.O. 1818/13, p. 30.
[33] *S.C.C. Mins.* 1936–7, 362.
[34] *Shrews. Chron.* 2 June 1939 (Suppl.).
[35] S.R.O. 1818/13, p. 54.
[36] Ibid. p. 128.   [37] Ibid. pp. 54–5.

In 1938 he recommended that 48 of them should be replaced within five years.[38] The committee agreed[39] but could do little before war intervened.

The Second World War brought a temporary halt to consideration of the force's long-term improvement, but by 1944 post-war needs were under discussion. By then 95 police houses were reckoned to need replacement.[40] A new county police headquarters was also needed.[41] In 1945, the year before he resigned, Golden recommended a post-war establishment of 273, including 8 policewomen, 25 civilian clerks, and 12 patrol cars with 24 crew members.[42] In 1946 his successor, Douglas (later Sir Douglas) Osmond, who served until 1962, recommended an establishment of 362.[43] The committee agreed that such an increase was long overdue, for Shropshire was by then one of the most lightly policed counties in England.[44] The following period, until the 1960s, was marked by successive increases in establishment and by technical innovations, willingly supported by the committee under the chairmanship (1947–65) of Lt.-Col. Arthur Heywood-Lonsdale.[45] They were needed to meet an unprecedented rise in the county's population,[46] in the number of crimes,[47] and in motor traffic.[48] Against bitter opposition in the borough,[49] the Shrewsbury force was absorbed by the county in 1947,[50] and later in the year the Home Office authorized an establishment of 378.[51] In 1948, to accommodate that increase and to remedy the inheritance of poor police houses, the committee resolved to build 148 new houses by 1953.[52] That total could not be reached before 1956,[53] by which time the establishment had grown to 389.[54] Nevertheless the housing problem was substantially dealt with; by 1964 over 80 per cent of police houses were of post-war construction.[55] Recruiting, however, remained slow;[56] in 1950, for example, the strength was 53 below establishment.[57] Pay and conditions did not compare well with those offered even to unskilled workers[58] and it was not until 1963, after improved pay and conditions had been granted, that the force came up to its establishment, which had stood at 407 since 1957.[59] By the end of 1964, after further increases of establishment, the force was again under strength.[60]

New methods were readily adopted, and enabled more efficient use to be made of the force's existing strength. In 1949 Shropshire was one of the first counties to introduce the radio control of patrol cars[61] and a dramatic increase in arrests by car crews resulted.[62] In the same year a probationary training scheme was introduced in Shropshire, to which all recruits were subject for their first two years' service;[63] the system was later widely adopted by other forces.[64] In 1953 a successful crime-prevention policy was adopted, of a kind later used by forces throughout the country.[65] Experiments in 1951 and 1952, however, convinced Osmond that 'team' policing, a system recently advocated by some forces, in which a team of officers would be responsible jointly for policing a single urban area (and so save some man-power), would not be a good substitute for the traditional 'beat' system used in Shropshire towns.[66] In 1945 the

[38] S.R.O. 1818/13, p. 184.
[39] Ibid. p. 189.
[40] Ibid. p. 423; S.C.C. Mins. 1944–5, 253.
[41] S.R.O. 1818/13, pp. 406–7.
[42] S.C.C. Mins. 1945–6, 197.
[43] Ibid. 1946–7, 250.
[44] Ibid. 251.
[45] Ex inf. Sir Douglas Osmond (1976).
[46] V.C.H. Salop. ii. 219, 227.
[47] Ann. Rep. of Ch. Const. 1949–61; Rep. of Ch. Const. 1962–6 (copies in S.R.O.).
[48] Ann. Rep. of Ch. Const. 1957, 1.
[49] Local information (1976).
[50] Under the Police Act, 1946, 9 & 10 Geo. VI, c. 46: S.C.C. Mins. 1946–7, 66.
[51] S.R.O., S.J. Cttee. min. bk. 1946–52, p. 118.
[52] S.C.C. Mins. 1947–8, 400.
[53] S.R.O., S.J. Cttee. min. bk. 1952–7, p. 557.
[54] Ann. Rep. of Ch. Const. 1956, 36.
[55] Rep. of Ch. Const. 1964, 43.
[56] Ann. Rep. of Ch. Const. 1956, 4.
[57] Ibid. 1950, 3.
[58] Ibid. 5.
[59] S.C.C. Mins. 1962–3, 375.
[60] Rep. of Ch. Const. 1964, 1.
[61] Ann. Rep. of Ch. Const. 1956, 15; S.C.C. Mins. 1966–7, 40.
[62] Ann. Rep. of Ch. Const. 1952, 14.
[63] Ibid. 1950, 6–7.
[64] Ex inf. Sir Douglas Osmond (1976).
[65] Ann. Rep. of Ch. Const. 1953, 26; S.C.C. Mins. 1959–60, 324.
[66] Ann. Rep. of Ch. Const. 1952, 11–14.

force had 10 cars and 3 motor cycles, for all duties including traffic patrols.[67] By 1964 there were 84 vehicles, including 13 patrol cars and 54 motor cycles.[68] By the early 1960s there was a tendency in Shropshire to make more use of motor cycles for traffic patrols.[69] In 1967 personal radio sets were first issued to policemen on foot.[70]

By contrast with the 1920s and 1930s, expansion and innovation after the Second World War allowed the Shropshire police to keep up with the changing character of crime. From the late 1940s to the 1960s a better detection rate for indictable offences than any attained there in the 1920s and 1930s was consistently achieved in Shropshire.[71]

After a lapse of many years special constables were recruited in Shropshire in 1911 at the instigation of the government.[72] They were civilians who agreed to be called up in an emergency. Until the general strike of 1926, whose failure began a long period of industrial calm,[73] the government was concerned by the possibility that industrial unrest might lead to dangerous disorders.[74] The newly-recruited Shropshire specials were first called out in 1912 during the coal strike,[75] but Shropshire strikers proved so orderly that the specials were not needed in the railway strike of 1919[76] nor in the general strike.[77] They remained a valuable reserve during the two world wars and for routine duties in peace time.[78] Two policewomen were appointed in Shropshire in 1918 in response to local concern about moral dangers to girls, women, and young service-men near camps in the Market Drayton and Whitchurch areas.[79] They were dismissed as an economy measure in 1921.[80] In 1939 there were four policewomen, to meet similar needs near Cosford and Oswestry.[81] There were eleven policewomen by 1964.[82]

In 1965 Standing Joint Committees were replaced by Police Committees, on which county-council representation was increased to two-thirds and whose proceedings were for the first time subject formally to some county-council scrutiny.[83] Little change resulted in Shropshire, where the Standing Joint Committee had always worked closely with the council.[84] In 1966, by which time there were definite proposals for a new county police headquarters to replace the 1903 building,[85] the government, contrary to recent assurances, announced that the Shropshire force would be amalgamated with those of Herefordshire, Worcestershire, and Worcester City to form a new regional force.[86] Mutual aid agreements with other authorities had been entered into by Shropshire as early as 1909,[87] at a time when such arrangements were still uncommon,[88] and a regional approach to serious crime had been welcomed by the committee in 1964 when a 'regional crime squad' was proposed, providing a pool of detectives upon whom each chief constable could call.[89] The Police Committee, however, at first had some misgivings about the dissolution of the Shropshire force, suspecting political motives behind the government's decision and arguing that friendly relations with the public might be endangered by the loss of local control.[90] The committee nevertheless accepted that change was inevitable, even desirable;[91] the amalgamation took effect in 1967 with the creation of the West Mercia Constabulary.[92]

[67] Ibid. 1956, 14.
[68] *Rep. of Ch. Const.* 1964, 29.
[69] *Ann. Rep. of Ch. Const.* 1961, 10–11.
[70] *S.C.C. Mins.* 1967–8, 169.
[71] *Ann. Rep. of Ch. Const.* 1949–61; *Rep. of Ch. Const.* 1962–6.
[72] S.R.O. 1818/9, p. 162.
[73] Taylor, *Eng. Hist., 1914–1945*, 248–50.
[74] S.R.O. 1818/10, p. 179; Critchley, *Hist. of Police*, 179, 198.
[75] S.R.O. 1818/9, p. 175.
[76] S.R.O. 1818/52, p. 74.
[77] No such mention in S.R.O. 1818/11.
[78] *Rep. of Ch. Const.* 1964, 9.
[79] S.R.O. 1818/10, pp. 93–5, 110.
[80] *S.C.C. Mins.* 1921–2, 251. A similar course was followed by many police authorities at about that time: Critchley, op. cit. 217.
[81] *S.C.C. Mins.* 1939–40, 370.
[82] *Rep. of Ch. Const.* 1964, 7.
[83] Under the Police Act, 1964, 12 & 13 Eliz. II, c. 48.
[84] *S.C.C. Mins.* 1954–5, 277; 1964–5, 138.
[85] Ibid. 1965–6, 210–11.   [86] Ibid. 1966–7, 39–41.
[87] Under the Police Act, 1890, 53 & 54 Vic. c. 45: ibid. 1909–10, 201.
[88] Critchley, op. cit. 179.
[89] *S.C.C. Mins.* 1964–5, 137.   [90] Ibid. 1966–7, 40–1.
[91] Ex inf. the chief executive, S.C.C. (1976).
[92] Under the Police Act, 1964: *W. Mercia Police (Amalgamation) Order, 1966* (Stat. Instr. 1966, no. 1617). Similar amalgamations were to be made throughout the country: Critchley, op. cit. 312.

PARLIAMENTARY REPRESENTATION

FROM Edward I's reign to Edward IV's Shropshire sent six members of the Commons to Parliament: two knights of the shire and two burgesses each for Shrewsbury and Bridgnorth. Two more boroughs, Ludlow and Much Wenlock, were enfranchised after the Yorkist triumph of 1461 and a fifth, Bishop's Castle, in Elizabeth I's reign. In the 1650s, under the Cromwellian protectorate, the county representation was temporarily reduced to eight members. With that exception, however, for nearly three centuries (1584–1868) the county was represented in the Commons by twelve M.P.s. The Reform Act of 1832 disfranchised Bishop's Castle but created two two-member county divisions.[1] The Reform Act of 1867 reduced the number of Shropshire M.P.s to ten, a figure which was halved by the redistribution of seats effected in 1885. Since 1918 the county has had only four constituencies.

Before 1832 the five parliamentary boroughs were all 'freemen boroughs', and disputes about the franchise or the extent of the parliamentary borough were common in each. In the period for which the evidence is most ample all the boroughs except the county town were cleverly controlled, often at great expense, by four families: the Herberts, the Clives, the Whitmores, and the Foresters. One of the boroughs, Bishop's Castle, developed a tradition of extreme venality during the years before the imposition of Clive control. Shrewsbury was an 'open' borough, though eventually it may have owed the preservation of its freedom from joint control by the Clives and the corporation to the wealth of William Pulteney. The county itself was seldom amenable to pressure from the peerage, nor any borough to pressure from the government or its local agencies. Some families have been active over long periods and one of them still provided an M.P. in October 1974;[2] particular houses and estates[3] wielded political influence over even longer periods and in widely varying conditions.[4]

TO 1629

THE economic standing of the Shropshire parliamentary boroughs in the period before 1629 varied widely, and there are parallels between each borough's prosperity and the character of its representatives in the Commons; the more prosperous a

---

[1] Between 1895 and 1930 H. T. Weyman (1850–1941) published articles on Salop. parl. hist. in *T.S.A.S.* 2nd ser. vii. 1–54; x. 33–68; 3rd ser. ii. 297–358; 4th ser. iii, pp. *iii–iv*; v. 1–76; x. 1–32, 161–92; xi. 1–48, 153–84; xii, pp. 1–47, 113–272, *xvi*; xlvii, pp. *i–ii*. They are not uniform in plan, and pitfalls include mistaken identifications and inadequate party classifications. Nevertheless Weyman's work is of great value. His knowledge of the county, esp. Ludlow, was extensive, and his recollections of the political personalities of his own time remain particularly helpful.

[2] Jasper More: see p. 358.

[3] Notably Apley Pk.

[4] Thanks are due to the editors of, and contributors to, the History of Parliament for 1386–1422, 1509–58, 1558–1603, 1660–90, 1690–1715, and 1790–1820 for permission to consult unpublished material. Among those to whom gratitude is due for hospitality and permission to use papers in their possession are the late Lady Rayleigh, the late Sir Robert Pigot, Bt., the late Sir Francis Whitmore, Bt., and the late Capt. G. C. Wolryche-Whitmore. The late Mr. S. Morley Tonkin kindly lent a microfilm of the *Shrews. Chron.*

borough, the more successful its resistance to the inevitable pressure of outsiders ambitious to control its elections.

Of Shropshire's medieval boroughs only Shrewsbury and Bridgnorth were represented at all before the later 15th century. They were the two richest towns of Shropshire in the early 14th century, and Shrewsbury was then among the dozen richest in England.[5] In the early 17th century Shrewsbury remained a town of wealthy merchants[6] and only in the late 16th showed signs of responding to electoral pressure from the county gentry and the peers. Paradoxically, however, in elections of knights of the shire Shrewsbury's independence could be used by outsiders seeking a county seat; from at least the 15th century the county electors who lived in Shrewsbury could readily be mobilized to secure the return of someone not nominated by the small circle of gentry families which otherwise monopolized the county seats. Bridgnorth's declining fortunes[7] meant that by the mid 15th century its representation was beginning to fall into the hands of outsiders. By the mid 16th century Bridgnorth had virtually ceased to be represented by its own townsmen; by then the gentry and the Council in the Marches of Wales controlled its elections.

Of the two boroughs that owed their representation to Edward IV Ludlow was small but prosperous in the late 15th century[8] and throughout the 16th kept an element of representation by townsmen. By Elizabeth I's reign, however, the presence of the Council in the Marches at the castle meant that at least one of the two seats usually went to someone connected with the council. Much Wenlock owed its parliamentary status to the personal influence of the Yorkist Lord Wenlock,[9] for the town had little economic importance. It was never strong enough to resist the electoral control of his cousins and heirs,[10] the Lawleys, and other gentry families of the neighbourhood. Bishop's Castle, a medieval planned town that had never developed economically,[11] was prey, from its first return of members in 1584, to a variety of outside interests and was often represented by virtual strangers to the county.

The constitutional theory that knights of the shire were elected by the county court after due consideration of their fitness for the duties had some reality in Shropshire in the 14th and 15th centuries, when the men most often elected seem also to have been the most able. When there was baronial or royal interference it probably helped rather than hindered the county court in choosing wisely, for the men of most skill and worth were often the magnates' or the king's own officers and advisers. With the decline of baronial households, however, the influence of the rich or powerful relative supplanted that of the well-served patron in county elections, so that by the later 16th century the wealthiest county families, the Corbets and the Newports, and those with relatives at Court, like the Leightons and the Bromleys, monopolized the county constituency.

Shropshire

The earliest Parliament for which the names of the Shropshire knights of the shire are known is that of 1290.[12] The pattern of county elections 1290–1628 falls into two

[5] *New Historical Geog. of Eng.* ed. H. C. Darby (1973), 183–4.
[6] Ibid. 243, 459; T. Rowley, *Shropshire Landscape* (1972), 200–1.
[7] Rowley, op. cit. 191. [8] Ibid. 185–6.
[9] J. S. Roskell, *The Commons and their Speakers in Eng. Parliaments 1376–1523* (1965), 259.
[10] J. S. Roskell, 'John, Ld. Wenlock of Someries', *Beds. Historical Rec. Soc.* xxxviii. 40, 48.

[11] Rowley, *Shropshire Landscape*, 175.
[12] This section (pp. 233–9) was written in 1977. The writer's thanks are due to Dr. Mason for some material, including information from the editors of the Hist. of Parliament. Unless otherwise stated, names of men elected are taken from *Return of the Name of every Member of the Lower House*, i, H.C. 69 (1878), lxii. Biographical information, unless otherwise stated, is taken from *T.S.A.S.* 4th ser. x. 15–32, 161–92; xi. 1–48, 153–68.

periods. Until Edward IV's reign there was, on average, a general election every seven or eight months. Thereafter the average interval between elections was nearly two years. Elections were only a third as frequent after 1485, but the proportion of re-elections was reduced in Shropshire by less than a half; such opportunities for election as existed after 1485 were thus less widely enjoyed. Indeed, during the later 16th and early 17th centuries the proportion of Shropshire elections at which a new county member was returned dropped steadily. The Reformation Parliament permanently enhanced the Commons' prestige, and election as a knight of the shire is found in Elizabethan and early-Stuart Shropshire to have become usually the preserve of a few county families. Nevertheless the urban county electors of Shrewsbury were occasionally mobilized, from the late 15th century if not earlier, to secure the return of an alternative candidate.[13]

In Shropshire before 1399 hardly more than a third of the knights of the shire served as sheriffs, for annual appointment of sheriffs was unusual there before 1376.[14] Three quarters of the Shropshire knights elected in the periods 1399–1485 and 1485–1558 served as sheriffs. In the first period, however, the shrievalty tended to come earlier in a man's career than election as a knight. Henry V's reign was unusual in Shropshire, for then there was a marked tendency for election to come earlier in life than the shrievalty; the few years after 1415, when power in Shropshire shifted from the FitzAlans to the Talbots, saw a high proportion of new and inexperienced men returned for the county.[15] In the period 1485–1558 election as a knight was tending to come earlier in life than the shrievalty, but the tendency was reversed after Elizabeth I's accession. Thereafter a smaller proportion of the elected knights were sheriffs at all, and those that were tended to be sheriffs first. The sheriff's standing in the county was as great as before,[16] but that of the elected knight had become appreciably greater.

A little Shropshire evidence illustrates electoral procedure. In 1324 and 1485 we learn that the election writ was delivered to the sheriff's home,[17] which implies that the parliamentary writ was reckoned especially important, or at least especially urgent. Contests were probably as exceptional in Shropshire as elsewhere. Several methods of estimating the majority at a contest were in use in 16th-century England,[18] but by 1588 it was said that at least some Shropshire county elections had within living memory been decided by a poll.[19]

In the 14th century sheriffs quite often returned themselves at county elections, especially in Shropshire, Staffordshire, and Lincolnshire. There were hardly any Shropshire instances before Edward III's first Parliament; thereafter there were at least seventeen until 1372, in which year an Ordinance forbade the practice.[20] Sir John Burgh's self-return in 1453 seems to have been the only one in Shropshire after 1372, and would probably not have been allowed in more settled times. In 1390 Thomas of Whitton, said to be of the 'affinity and alliance' of his fellow member, Sir Richard of Ludlow, was found to have been appointed sheriff of Shropshire, allegedly through Ludlow's influence, between his election for the county and the assembling of that Parliament;[21] he was then removed from the shrievalty as dis-

[13] In some shires the electors in the co. town regularly determined the outcome of co. elections: D. Hirst, *The Representative of the People?: Voters and Voting in Eng. under the early Stuarts* (1975), 40.

[14] Above, pp. 17–20, 74. Unless otherwise stated, details of shrievalties are taken from *List of Sheriffs* (P.R.O. Lists & Indexes, ix; corrected reprint 1963), 117–19.

[15] See p. 236.

[16] See p. 75.

[17] *Parl. Writs* (Rec. Com.), ii(2), 323; *Intrationum Excellentissimus Liber* (London, 1511; printed by Nic. Pynson),

f. 127v.

[18] J. G. Edwards, 'The Emergence of Majority Rule in Eng. Parl. Elections', *Trans. R.H.S.* 5th ser. xiv. 189–90.

[19] J. E. Neale, 'Three Elizabethan elections', *E.H.R.* xlvi. 233.

[20] Kathleen L. Wood-Legh, 'Sheriffs, Lawyers, and Belted Knights in the Parls. of Edw. III', *E.H.R.* xlvi. 373–4.

[21] S.C. 8/220 no. 10994. Thanks are due to Dr. J. R. Maddicott for this ref.

qualified by statute.[22] During the earl of Arundel's life shrievalty (1345–76) his under-sheriffs were virtually sheriffs,[23] and at more than a third of the general elections they returned themselves for the county. In nominating under-sheriffs the earl was nominating potential knights of the shire, whether or not he realized it.

In the Middle Ages many Shropshire knights of the shire may be identified as officers or retainers of particular magnates, but it cannot be proved that they owed their election to their patrons' influence. In the 14th century about half of the individual county elections in Shropshire were of men who had never sat for the county before. A few men, however, were returned so often that they, at least, may be credited personally with the electors' confidence and perhaps, from their accumulated experience, with personal standing in the Commons. In the earlier 14th century the knights most consistently elected for Shropshire were Richard of Harley (8 times 1300–16), Sir Roger Corbet of Caus (15 times 1309–41), Sir William of Ercall (10 times 1324–40), and Sir Walter of Hopton (6 times 1337–63). Harley and Hopton were long-serving keepers or justices of the peace,[24] and Corbet and Ercall also served in those offices. Harley and Ercall were sheriffs. They and Hopton[25] were commissioners of array. In other words they were repeatedly recognized as suitable for high local office, not only by the Shropshire electors but by the government. In the later 14th century the men most often elected were William Banaster of Hadnall (7 times 1351–66), Sir John of Ludlow (6 times 1358–77), Sir Brian de Cornewall (6 times 1369–83), Sir Robert de Kendale (7 times 1371–82), and Edward of Acton (6 times 1378–88). They were of similar calibre to those elected in the earlier 14th century. None of them, however, equalled Corbet, Harley, or Ercall in the number of his elections, and no one of such long service as their own was elected in Shropshire between 1388 and 1399.

In England as a whole Richard II's reign saw an increase both in the proportion of county elections that returned men with previous parliamentary experience and in the average number of times that any one knight of the shire was elected.[26] In Shropshire on the other hand there was a marked decrease, especially after 1388. It was perhaps attributable to outside interference. Political instability, linked with the fortunes of Richard, earl of Arundel, has been noted in the Shropshire peace commission of that period.[27] The Shropshire knights in the Parliament that condemned Arundel in 1397 were Sir Fulk of Pembridge, a friend of the Beauforts, supporters of the king,[28] and Richard Chelmick, steward of the county of Cornwall and a king's esquire,[29] who first appeared on the Shropshire peace commission during the course of that Parliament.[30] Neither had been elected for Shropshire before. At the dissolution of that Parliament Chelmick was one of the king's committee set up to conclude the session's business. He died in 1398.[31] Pembridge lived until 1409 but never again sat for Shropshire.

In the 15th century Shropshire county elections were dominated by lawyers and professional administrators, men who were elected repeatedly in recognition of their ability. There are, however, indications of some outside interference.

A much higher proportion of experienced men was returned for Shropshire during Henry IV's reign than in any of his predecessors' time. The most frequently elected were John Burley (6 times 1399–1411) and David Holbache (5 times 1406–14). They were important officers of Thomas, earl of Arundel. Burley, however, had earlier been

[22] S.C. 1/40 no. 178.
[23] See p. 76.
[24] Cal. Pat. 1292–1301, 517; 1307–13, 31, 54; 1313–17, 108, 123; 1350–4, 91, 284, 449; 1354–8, 388; 1361–4, 64, 292, 529.
[25] Ibid. 1338–40, 355; 1364–7, 364.
[26] N. B. Lewis, 'Re-election to Parl. in Reign of Ric. II',

E.H.R. xlviii. 371–2, 377.
[27] See p. 56.
[28] J. S. Roskell, The Commons and their Speakers in Eng. Parls. 1376–1523 (1965), 189.
[29] Tout, Chapters, iv. 37.
[30] Cal. Pat. 1396–9, 235.
[31] Tout, Chapters, iv. 35–7.

steward of Blakemere for Richard, Lord Talbot,[32] and a member of the earl of Stafford's council.[33] He was the leading Shropshire justice of the peace.[34] Holbache had been appointed justice of South Wales in 1389. He occurs 1411–20 as steward of the lordship of Powys for Lord Charlton, and in 1415 was appointed steward of Bishop's Castle for the bishop of Hereford. He occurs as *custos rotulorum* of Shropshire in 1413. In 1406 he was one of the parliamentary committee set up at the Commons' insistence to audit the war treasurers' accounts.[35]

Arundel's death without issue in 1415 enabled the Talbots to become the dominant aristocratic force in Shropshire politics,[36] and the effect was soon felt in county elections. In the first half of Henry V's reign an unusually high proportion of the knights returned for Shropshire had not sat for the county before. Holbache, though active until 1421, was not returned for Shropshire after 1414. After 1415 the Shropshire knights most often returned were three officers of John Talbot, Lord Furnivalle (cr. earl of Shrewsbury 1442): Sir Richard Lacon[37] (6 times 1413–33), Hugh Burgh[38] (5 times 1415–25), and William Burley of Broncroft, John Burley's son[39] (17 times 1417–55). Between 1413 and 1453, when Shrewsbury died, about half of the individuals returned for Shropshire were his followers. More often than not both knights were his men.[40] Nevertheless his influence could not be maintained without effort. For example Burley and another Talbot officer seem to have given fish to the county electors in Shrewsbury in 1435[41] when Burley was returned with Thomas Corbet of Moreton. Neither Talbot nor any other peer built up a significant group in the Commons.[42] Nor was Burley a Talbot cipher. All the local magnates employed him and by the 1430s he was the leading Shropshire justice of the peace.[43] His Commons career surpassed that of any contemporary in length and continuity. He was twice speaker (1437 and 1445–6) and in 1455 thrice headed Commons deputations asking the Lords for York's appointment as protector. Burley's career strengthens the view that aristocratic influence in county elections did not necessarily imply the return of passive placemen.[44]

In Edward IV's reign it is no surprise to find, more often than any others, the names of Thomas Horde (1459, 1467, 1472) and his nephew John Leighton (1467, 1472, 1478).[45] Horde, a lawyer, succeeded William Burley in the 1450s as the leading Shropshire justice of the peace and kept that position with little interruption until the 1490s.[46] A Lancastrian, he nevertheless held high local office under every king from Henry VI to Henry VII.[47] Like Burley's, Horde's abilities seem to have commended him to all parties. Leighton too held local office under Edward IV, Richard III, and Henry VII,[48] and he was employed by several local magnates. The Shropshire elections of Edward IV's reign were not always quiet. On election day 1463 guards were posted at the gates of Shrewsbury because of a dispute ('discordia et lis') between Lord Grey of Powis and Maurice Ludlow.[49] The quarrel probably had a domestic element. The sheriff, Roger Kynaston,[50] was Grey's brother-in-law and uncle to Grey's daughter,

[32] Barbara Ross, 'Accts. of the Talbot Household at Blakemere . . . 1394–1425' (Canberra Univ. M.A. thesis, 1970; copy in S.R.O.), i. 121.

[33] *Salop. Peace Roll, 1400–14*, 22.   [34] See pp. 62–3.

[35] *Salop. Peace Roll, 1400–14*, 23–4; R. A. Griffiths, *Principality of Wales in Later Middle Ages*, i (1972), 121.

[36] See p. 57.

[37] A. J. Pollard, 'Fam. of Talbot, Lds. Talbot and Earls of Shrews. in the XVth Cent.' (Bristol Univ. Ph.D. thesis, 1968), 231.

[38] J. S. Roskell, *The Commons in the Parl. of 1422* (1953), 158–9.

[39] *T.S.A.S.* lvi. 263–72; Pollard, op. cit. 229–30.

[40] Pollard, op. cit. 240.

[41] Ibid. 242–3; S.R.O. 212, box 82, acct. roll 1434–5.

[42] Pollard, op. cit. 241–2.   [43] See p. 63.

[44] K. B. McFarlane, 'Parl. and "Bastard Feudalism"', *Essays in Medieval Hist.* ed. R. W. Southern (1968), 253–63.

[45] The 1467 names are in Wedgwood, *Hist. Parl. 1439–1509: Reg.* 356. Sir John Burgh, not Thos. Horde, was elected 1455: ex inf. Hist. of Parl.

[46] See pp. 63–4.

[47] Wedgwood, *Hist. Parl. 1439–1509: Biogs.* 469; Pollard, op. cit. 241 n.

[48] Wedgwood. *Hist. Parl. 1439–1509: Biogs.* 535.

[49] S.R.O. 3365/391, rot. 1d.

[50] *List of Sheriffs*, 118.

who later married John Ludlow,[51] probably Maurice's nephew.[52] The result of the election is not known.

In 1485, at the first election after Henry VII's accession, John Leighton's young son Thomas (later Sir Thomas) was returned unopposed. The other seat was contested between John Ludlow's father, Sir Richard, a Yorkist,[53] and the Lancastrian Sir Richard Corbet of Moreton. Ludlow was returned and Corbet sued the sheriff, Sir Gilbert Talbot, claiming that Ludlow had not had a majority of the votes;[54] the majority had evidently been determined by estimation. Talbot had probably returned Ludlow reluctantly, for both Talbot and Corbet had played an important part in Henry VII's victory at Bosworth, and at the next election (1491) they were returned together.[55] It seems, however, that the 1485 Shropshire election had seen town prevail over country; the witnesses to Ludlow's return were headed by Thomas Mytton,[56] the Yorkist bailiff of Shrewsbury, who for many years had been among its most influential burgesses.[57]

To the Reformation Parliament (1529–36) were elected as Shropshire county members John Blount and Sir Thomas Cornewall.[58] Royal interference may be suspected, for Blount's daughter had been the king's mistress and was the duke of Richmond's mother, and Cornewall was employed locally in administering some of that Parliament's ecclesiastical legislation.[59] Blount died soon after election. At the next general election (1536) his widow, with support from the Shropshire gentry, campaigned for their son George (later Sir George), himself occupied at Court. A vociferous body of Shrewsbury townsmen, however, encouraged by the sheriff, secured instead the return of one of the Trenthams of Shrewsbury.[60] Sir George was nevertheless returned for Shropshire in 1547.[61] He and his fellow member in the 1547–52 Parliament, Richard (later Sir Richard) Newport, were employed locally in administering its ecclesiastical legislation.[62]

Some of the Shropshire county members in Mary I's Parliaments were reputed papists or their sympathizers, including William Charlton of Wombridge,[63] Richard Mytton,[64] his brother-in-law[65] William Gatacre,[66] Sir Henry Stafford, and Thomas Fermour. None of them was returned for Shropshire under Elizabeth I. Under Mary Sir George Blount, compromised by a connexion with Northumberland,[67] had to be content with a borough seat. A Shropshire county member, however, could be elected in spite of a connexion with Northumberland if his family's local standing was good. Edward (later Sir Edward) Leighton was the duke's kinsman,[68] but his great-grandfather, grandfather, and probably[69] father had been Shropshire knights of the shire. He sat in 1553 and again 1563–7. Richard (later Sir Richard) Corbet may have supported Northumberland's attempted coup in 1553,[70] but his ancestors had been Shropshire members for generations. He and his nephew,[71] Sir Andrew, between them sat for Shropshire in every Parliament from 1555 to 1567.

[51] Complete Peerage, vi. 139–40, 699. She may have been Grey's stepdau.

[52] Visit. Salop. 1623, ii. 341. Maurice's intervention in the 1463 election suggests that he was hardly young enough to be John's bro., as some pedigrees state (e.g. S.P.L., MS. 2790, pp. 209–10): see Wedgwood, Hist. Parl. 1439–1509: Biogs. 560–1.

[53] Wedgwood, Hist. Parl. 1439–1509: Biogs. 560.

[54] Intrationum Excellentissimus Liber, ff. 126v.–128.

[55] Wedgwood, Hist. Parl. 1439–1509: Reg. 557.

[56] Intrationum Excellentissimus Liber, f. 127v.

[57] Wedgwood, Hist. Parl. 1439–1509: Biogs. 620–1.

[58] Sir Thos. Leighton had sat again since 1485, perhaps in 1497 and 1512: ibid. 535. His son John had almost certainly been returned in 1523: T.S.A.S. 4th ser. xi. 31.

[59] See p. 89.

[60] L. & P. Hen. VIII, x, p. 439.

[61] According to T.S.A.S. 4th ser. xi. 35–6, he was also returned in 1545, with Ric. Mytton.

[62] See p. 89.

[63] Camd. Misc. ix (Camd. N.S. liii), 45.

[64] Ibid. 15; S.P.L., Deeds 16137.

[65] Visit. Salop. 1623, ii. 362.

[66] Camd. Misc. ix. 15.

[67] T.S.A.S. 3rd. ser. viii. 125.

[68] He was Northumberland's 2nd cos. once removed: Visit. Salop. 1623, ii. 324; Complete Peerage, iv. 480–1.

[69] T.S.A.S. 4th ser. xi. 31.

[70] His involvement is not certain: ibid. 44.

[71] Visit. Salop. 1623, i. 136–8.

In the period 1399–1459 25 surnames were represented by 32 known individuals returned for Shropshire. In the period 1559–1629 32 known individuals sat but only 18 surnames occur. In fact the parliamentary representation of Shropshire in that period was dominated by the Corbets of Moreton and their cousins, especially, in the early 17th century, the wealthy Newports. Outside interference, probably exercised through the urban electors of Shrewsbury, only occasionally resulted in the return of men not of the Corbet circle. It was, however, those comparative outsiders who made most mark in the Commons.

In Elizabeth I's early years the head of the Corbets was Sir Richard (d. 1566). Two of his nephews, Sir Andrew Corbet and Sir Arthur Mainwaring, were returned for the county to her first Parliament (1559); in her second (1563–7) Sir Richard himself shared the representation with Edward Leighton, a former county member and a relative[72] and friend[73] of the earl of Leicester. At the next election (1572) any hopes that Leighton may have had of keeping the seat were disappointed when it went to George Bromley of Hallon, attorney general of the Duchy of Lancaster and brother of the solicitor general. The other seat went to the young George Mainwaring, son of the 1559 member and cousin of Sir Andrew Corbet,[74] the new head of the family. Bromley, to a contemporary 'one of the ripest wits' in the Commons,[75] was nominated in that Parliament as speaker.[76] His son Francis, nephew of the lord chancellor, was given the seat at the next election (1584), the other seat going to Walter (later Sir Walter) Leveson of Lilleshall, brother-in-law of Richard Corbet, by then head of the family. Leveson was returned again at the next two elections, accompanied at the first (1586) by Richard Corbet, and at the second (1588) by his own young son Richard (later Sir Richard), Corbet's nephew, son-in-law of Lord Howard of Effingham, and possibly a kinsman of the earl of Essex.[77] In 1593 the Newports, cousins of the Corbets[78] and probably the richest family in Shropshire,[79] reasserted their claim to a county seat, which had lapsed in 1570 when the headship of the family had passed to a boy, Francis. Francis (later Sir Francis) Newport was returned in 1593 with Corbet's kinsman[80] Robert (later Sir Robert) Needham (d. 1631).

In 1597, however, the Corbet and Newport interest was disregarded and two protégés of the earl of Essex were returned: Sir Henry Bromley, nephew of the chancellor of the Exchequer,[81] and Essex's kinsman[82] Thomas Leighton, son of the late Sir Edward. Bromley's career was unfortunate. He had been imprisoned in 1593 when, as a member for Worcestershire, he took part in Peter Wentworth's conspiracy to raise the succession issue in the Commons,[83] and in 1601 he was imprisoned and disgraced for complicity in Essex's revolt. Leighton died prematurely in 1600. At the 1601 election the Corbets and Newports were again disregarded. The lord keeper's young son, John Egerton, was returned with Roger (later Sir Roger) Owen, son of the late Thomas Owen, a justice of Common Pleas and recorder of Shrewsbury.[84] The Owens were of Shrewsbury burgess stock[85] and both had represented the borough in Parliament. Roger's return for the county was probably achieved through his personal

[72] They were 3rd cos.: *Visit. Salop. 1623*, ii. 324; *Complete Peerage*, iv. 480–1; vii. 549.
[73] Blakeway, *Sheriffs*, 91.
[74] They were 1st cos. once removed: *Visit. Salop. 1623*, i. 136–8; ii. 348–9.
[75] J. E. Neale, *Eliz. I and her Parls. 1559–81* (1953), 285.
[76] J. E. Neale, *Elizabethan Ho. of Commons* (1949), 358.
[77] *D.N.B. sub* Leveson, Ric.; *Complete Peerage*, vii. 550–1.
[78] Sir Ric. Newport, M.P. (d. 1570), head of the fam., was neph. of Sir Ric. Corbet, M.P. (d. 1566).
[79] Eyton, ix. 97; Mary F. Keeler, *Long Parl. 1640–1641:*

a Biog. Study of its Members (1954), 284–5.
[80] They were 1st cos. once removed: *Visit. Salop. 1623*, i. 136; ii. 372.
[81] Neale, *Elizabethan Ho. of Commons*, 314–15. He was also son of the late ld. chancellor and neph. of Geo. Bromley, M.P.
[82] Both were nephs. of Sir Thos. Leighton, capt. of Guernsey: *Visit. Salop. 1623*, ii. 324–5; *D.N.B. sub* Knollys, Fra.
[83] Neale, *Eliz. I and her Parls. 1584–1601* (1957), 260.
[84] Owen and Blakeway, *Hist. Shrews.* i. 538.
[85] Ibid. 191.

influence with the county electors in Shrewsbury, for he publicly scorned aristocratic patronage.[86] He represented Shropshire in every Parliament thereafter until his death in 1617. As sheriff he could not stand in 1604, when Sir Richard Leveson and Sir Robert Needham were again returned, but was returned at a by-election on Leveson's death in 1605. Owen, a considerable scholar, was one of the leading anti-Court speakers in the Parliaments of 1604–11 and 1614,[87] becoming sometimes so excited that 'his brains flew up and down in his head as a bird flies in the air'.[88] Needham supported the Court.[89] In the 1614 Parliament Owen's colleague was Sir Francis Newport's young son Richard (later Sir Richard).

In 1620, with Owen dead, the return of two Court supporters outside the Corbet and Newport circle was arranged, possibly by Needham whose relatives the newcomers were. Needham's loyalty to the Crown was rewarded at Charles I's accession when he was created Viscount Kilmorey. Sir Robert Vernon, cofferer of the Household[90] and Needham's brother-in-law, was elected in 1620 with Sir Francis Kynaston of Oteley. Plans for Vernon's return were in hand before the election writ reached Shropshire. The importance of the Shrewsbury vote was recognized, for Vernon reminded his supporter Richard Mytton 'to prepare your tenants in Salop and thereabouts by 8 of the clock in the morning' on election day.[91] Kynaston's first cousin had married Needham's brother.[92] Kynaston was a poet and orator, and was made an esquire of the body on Charles I's accession.[93] His view of Parliament was lyrical, likening its members to 'the high court of Heaven, sitting as angels to judge the world at the Last Day';[94] he nevertheless remained an ornament of the Court.[95] The elections between 1622 and 1628 saw the triumphant reassertion of the Corbet and Newport interest. The heads of the families, Sir Andrew Corbet and Sir Richard Newport, sat together for Shropshire in three of the four Parliaments. Only in the 1626 election was there perhaps some compromise: Newport's brother-in-law, Sir Richard Leveson of Lilleshall,[96] was returned with Lord Kilmorey's neighbour[97] and former son-in-law Sir Rowland Cotton. Both members had earlier represented Newcastle-under-Lyme (Staffs.),[98] where the Needham interest was strong.[99]

Shrewsbury

Shrewsbury, a town of some 3,000 people in the later 14th century,[1] was one of a small number of boroughs known to have achieved regular early representation. It was one of 27 boroughs summoned to an assembly in March 1268, and one of 21 summoned to the Shrewsbury Parliament of 1283; only 13 boroughs were summoned to both. Shrewsbury returned two burgesses in 1295 and regularly thereafter.[2]

The electorate seems to have been fairly large from quite early times.[3] An isolated indenture surviving from 1407 purports to have been made in the presence of burgesses assembled in the common hall, though only ten are named. According to a composition on the government of the borough made in 1433 its M.P.s were to be chosen by the

[86] T. L. Moir, *Addled Parl. of 1614* (1958), 98.
[87] W. M. Mitchell, *Rise of Revolutionary Party in Eng. Ho. of Commons* (1957), 44, 74.
[88] Moir, op. cit. 85.
[89] Ibid. 194.
[90] *Commons Debates 1621*, ed. W. Notestein and others (1935), ii. 134 n.
[91] S.P.L., Deeds 16140.
[92] *Visit. Salop. 1623*, ii. 299, 372. Their kinsmen, Sir Nic. and Sir Hen. Bagnall, were father and son: *D.N.B. Suppl.*
[93] *D.N.B.*
[94] *Commons Deb. 1621*, vi. 120.

[95] *D.N.B.*
[96] A 3rd cos. and adopted son of Sir Ric. Leveson, M.P. Shropshire 1589, 1604–5: S. Shaw, *Hist. . . . of Staffs.* ii (1801), 169; *S.H.C.* 1920 and 1922, 8.
[97] Cotton's seat at Bellaport (in Mucklestone) was in a near-by par. to Kilmorey's at Adderley.
[98] *S.H.C.* 1920 and 1922, 8, 31.
[99] Ibid. 16.
[1] J. C. Russell, *Brit. Medieval Population* (1948), 142.
[2] May McKisack, *Parl. Rep. of Eng. Boros. during the Middle Ages* (1932), 3, 6, 19.
[3] This para. is based on inf. from Hist. of Parl.

community of the borough in the manner laid down for the borough's auditors, that is by the whole body of burgesses. That may have been the earlier, or even the original, method. The 1453 indenture speaks of an election by the bailiffs with the consent of the commonalty, and the 1478 indenture was witnessed by 105 burgesses.[4] At the latter election all the burgesses had been summoned to the booth hall, the result being determined by the 'greater number' of those who appeared.[5] At the first known poll, in 1584, at least 475 voted, and Shrewsbury's was probably by then the largest borough electorate in England.[6]

In most Parliaments Shrewsbury was represented by M.P.s who had served at least once before. Of 115 known M.P.s returned between 1295 and 1523,[7] 55 served in only one Parliament, 26 in two, and 16 in three; on exactly half the possible occasions, however, the M.P.s had served at least 4 times, but Roger Pride's 18 returns (1312–40) and Thomas le Skinner's 13 (1370–96) were exceptional. On few occasions were both M.P.s serving for the first time and sometimes both M.P.s were men of considerable parliamentary experience. In 1515 re-election of the two previous M.P.s was required of the borough by the king.[8] Most Shrewsbury M.P.s were men who had reached, or would shortly reach, the top of the municipal hierarchy. Of 115 known M.P.s before 1523, 42 had been bailiffs;[9] a further 24 became bailiffs afterwards, some very soon after. Forty-three were never bailiffs.[10]

Those 115 known M.P.s bore 76 surnames. Fifty-four surnames supplied only one M.P. each, 15 supplied two, 3 supplied three; the Colles produced four. The dominant families in the borough's representation, however, were the Prides (five 1298–1411), the Myttons (seven 1354–1554), and the Thornes family (eight or nine 1357–1539). Many of the families were linked by marriage. There was, moreover, much continuity of property: the Skinner property came to Reynold de Mytton by his first marriage and the Vaughan property by his second, so that Vaughan's Place became the property of the Myttons of Halston. In the next generation marriage brought the Myttons of Halston the Pride estate, which had descended through the Tour and Burley (of Malehurst) families, and in the generation after that part of the Burgh estate in Habberley.[11] In early years there were at least three occasions when father and son were returned together: Geoffrey and William Randulf (1318) and the elder and the younger William Skinner (1335, 1336). John and Richard of Weston (1340) may have stood in the same relation. In 1410 two members of the Thornes family were elected. In general Shrewsbury's medieval M.P.s were substantial men closely connected with the town. One M.P., William Bastard in 1447, sent messages to the borough from Parliament,[12] and in 1472 another, John Horde, was paid for his labours in resisting a Bill on murage.[13] The regular wage paid by the borough to its M.P.s was not the customary 2s. a day but only 1s.[14]

Of the ten M.P.s 1529–59 seven were former or future bailiffs and two were sons of bailiffs. The exception, Reynold Corbet (1547, Oct. 1553, 1555), came of the county gentry but by 1559 was recorder. In 1557 the borough forbade canvassing,[15] which had presumably occurred. Nine years later, in Elizabeth I's second Parliament, Richard

[4] McKisack, *Parl. Rep. Eng. Boros.* 58.
[5] *T.S.A.S.* lvii. 164.
[6] J. H. Plumb, 'Growth of Electorate in Eng. from 1600 to 1715', *Past and Present*, xlv. 100 n. It had been large a century earlier, though perhaps then exceeded by Gloucester's: Wedgwood, *Hist. Parl. 1439–1509: Reg.* 646, 673.
[7] Except where otherwise stated this para. and the next are based on *T.S.A.S.* 4th ser. xii. 113–26, 130–81, 269–72.
[8] *T.S.A.S.* xi. 154.
[9] Listed (to 1545) ibid. 3rd ser. i. 7–32, 153–84, 289–320; ii. 269–86; iii. 363–88; iv. 259–74. Cf. *T.S.A.S.* lix. 43–7.
[10] In 6 of those instances there is uncertainty.
[11] *V.C.H. Salop.* viii. 240.
[12] McKisack, *Parl. Rep. Eng. Boros.* 144.
[13] Ibid. 138.
[14] Ibid. 97.
[15] T. C. Mendenhall, *Shrews. Drapers and the Welsh Wool Trade in the XVI and XVII Cents.* (1953), 124 n. 2.

Purcell, a draper, won over his colleague Robert Ireland, a mercer, to secure the passage of a Bill giving the Drapers' Company a virtual monopoly of the Welsh wool trade. The Drapers' triumph was short-lived, for Purcell was replaced in 1571 by a former M.P., George Lee; but next year, amid much controversy, Ireland was replaced by Purcell. In 1572, however, Purcell was unable to prevent Lee from achieving partial repeal of the Act that Purcell himself had secured. The high cost of this operation was financed by admitting 50 new burgesses at £5 each.[16]

These admissions and the borough's financial difficulties opened the way to the county gentry at the next election (1584).[17] It was contested by three gentlemen lawyers of the neighbourhood, all sons of former bailiffs. The burgesses went 'through the door by poll', and Thomas Owen of Condover, who had rendered professional services to the borough, received 366 votes, Richard Barker of Haughmond 299, and Thomas Harris of Shrewsbury 176. In the next Parliament both Owen and Barker were displaced. Reginald Scriven of Frodesley sat for the first of five times, with Thomas Harris the defeated candidate of two years before. Before the 1588 election the borough secured an opinion from its recorder that it could elect non-residents, and Scriven's next colleague was Andrew Newport, younger brother of Francis Newport of High Ercall. John Thynne of Caus offered himself in 1593 but was rejected; the new M.P., Robert Wright, was steward of the earl of Essex, then seeking to build up parliamentary influence. Wright, however, was a native of Shrewsbury, and not a stranger. Four years later Essex boldly asked for the nomination of both M.P.s but was rebuffed; instead the borough accepted a request from Thomas Owen (d. 1598), the former M.P. and by then recorder of the borough, to elect his son Roger. Roger moved on to the county in 1601, when his successor was John Barker, Francis Newport's son-in-law. By the end of Elizabeth I's reign outside influences had been brought to bear on the borough but no stranger had been elected; neighbouring gentry families were establishing hereditary links with the representation just as resident burgess families had once done.

There was a contest in 1601 but little is known of it. In 1603 the corporation ordered that only resident burgesses should thenceforth be returned,[18] but in 1604 another outside influence sought to determine the representation, this time in favour of a stranger. Lord Zouche, lord president of the Council in the Marches of Wales, conceded that the first seat should be Richard Barker's; besides being the borough recorder he was a council member. For the second seat, however, Zouche urged the borough to return his connexion by marriage, Francis Tate of Delapré Abbey (Northants.). Barker, however, had aroused the enmity of the sheriff, Roger Owen, the former M.P. Owen and his friends tried to disrupt the election but could not prevent Barker from being chosen. Nevertheless Owen had an indenture made out several days later returning Thomas Harris, the 1586 M.P.,[19] and Tate. The Commons ordered a fresh election. Owen moved his 'household' to Shrewsbury and again sought to disrupt the election. Owen's behaviour appears sometimes irrational, but his eventual decision to return Barker and Tate, and the respect in which his late father was held by the House of Commons, saved him from any penalty.[20]

[16] Ibid. 123 sqq.; *T.S.A.S.* 4th ser. xii. 126, 187–91; Shrews. Drapers &c. Act, 1566, 8 Eliz. I, c. 7; Shrews. Drapers &c. (Partial Repeal) Act, 1572, 14 Eliz. I, c. 12.

[17] For this para. see *T.S.A.S.* 4th ser. xii. 191–9; Hist. MSS. Com. 4, *5th Rep., Cholmondeley (Condover MSS.)*, p. 342; Owen and Blakeway, *Hist. Shrews.* i. 538.

[18] The record, dated 1 Jas. I (*T.S.A.S.* xi. 165), seems to place the order earlier in that regnal yr. than an order making Ld. Zouche a burgess (dated 29 Sept. 1603: ibid. 2nd ser. x. 306).

[19] Called 'Serjeant Harris the younger' in 1604: *C.J.* i. 170–1. Sjt. Thos. Harries of Cruckton, bap. 1550 (*S.P.R. Heref.* xii (1), 11), was the elder, for Sjt. Thos. Harris of Shrews. was not admitted to Shrews. Sch. until 1571 (*T.S.A.S.* 4th ser. xii. 195). In 1586 Thos. Harris of Lincoln's Inn (i.e. of Shrews.: ibid. 2nd ser. ix. 92), was M.P. for Shrews., while Thos. Harries of the Middle Temple (i.e. of Cruckton: ibid.) was M.P. for Portsmouth: *Return of every M.P.* i. 419, 425.

[20] For this para. see *T.S.A.S.* lix. 272–7.

Until 1640 the borough quietly returned a succession of borough officials and local gentlemen, and thus the tendency to elect men fairly closely connected with the borough was continued.[21]

Bridgnorth

Bridgnorth was a freeman borough with, eventually, a very large electorate. Medieval and Tudor elections may have been made by comparatively few voices; the surviving indentures purport to be made by the bailiffs and the Twenty-Four (the aldermen), but the commonalty's 'consent' is sometimes alleged.[22] However that may be, the burgesses at large voted in a 1610 by-election,[23] and at the election of March 1640 over three hundred were polled.[24]

Between 1295 and 1523 the borough had 106 known M.P.s[25] and 60 were returned only once. Three M.P.s were returned to nine Parliaments: Robert le Palmer (1311–32), Richard Horde (1414–32), and Richard Blyke (1429–59). The two M.P.s most often returned were William Palmer (14 times 1379–99), and Henry Geffrey (15 times 1321–36). In the period 1295–1523 Bridgnorth may have sent up slightly fewer M.P.s with previous parliamentary experience than did Shrewsbury. Nearly a third, and probably more, had been bailiffs of the borough.[26]

Between 1295 and 1523 78 surnames occur among the M.P.s, 52 of the names only once and another 12 only twice. Most of the M.P.s came from the town or its immediate surroundings.[27] In those respects the first two M.P.s were typical: Andrew Bolding seems to have been a resident and had been bailiff;[28] Fremund of Eardington had bought an estate near the town at the Hay, in Eardington.[29] The Palmer family supplied more M.P.s than any other: seven between 1311 and 1399. Their property was much the most important in Bridgnorth and included an *aula* in High Street.[30] Their property passed to the Horde family (which supplied four later medieval M.P.s) by the marriage of John Palmer's daughter to Thomas Horde, who first sat in 1391. The Hordes, however, while retaining their Bridgnorth property, became important county gentry, with property at Hoards Park in Astley Abbots and interests elsewhere. Two later Hordes were M.P.s under Mary I, and another sat in 1601. The Horde property was later held by the Whitmores and then by the Fosters, and from 1311 to 1885 constituted the most important single influence in the representation of the borough.[31] Another property in the town, much smaller than the Palmers', was held by the Bruyn family and supplied three M.P.s between 1302 and 1402 before passing to the Ottleys together with the farm at the Hay already mentioned.[32]

In the 14th century the only prominent county family to represent the borough was that of Pitchford, which had property in the suburb of Little Brug and returned three M.P.s in the 1340s. From an early date, however, outsiders were returned. Among the first was John de Kington in 1319, and the return of William Bolas four times in the 1370s suggests royal influence, for he was keeper of the king's forests in Shropshire. Royal influence cannot, however, be regarded as responsible for the return of more than a very few Bridgnorth members. In the earlier 15th century the Stafford family

[21] *T.S.A.S.* 4th ser. xii. 199–207.
[22] Ex inf. Hist. of Parl.
[23] *C.J.* i. 407.
[24] Bridgnorth boro. rec., 'elections' box.
[25] *T.S.A.S.* 4th ser. v. 9–16.
[26] List of bailiffs printed in Eyton, i. 313–19 (to 1335); *Salopian Shreds and Patches*, viii. 150, 154, 157, 166, 170, 174 (from 1559). A list of bailiffs 1386–1422, compiled by Dr. Linda S. Woodger, is *penes* Hist. of Parl. The present

writer, using Bridgnorth boro. rec., has compiled a list from 1442.
[27] Except where otherwise stated, the rest of this section is based on *T.S.A.S.* 4th ser. v. 1–16, 22–58, 75–6.
[28] Eyton, i. 317.
[29] Ibid. 124.
[30] Ibid. 364–74.
[31] See pp. 244, 275, 336.
[32] Ex inf. Hist. of Parl.

interest may fairly be regarded as responsible for the return of three M.P.s who at other times sat for their borough of Newcastle-under-Lyme: John Cooke (1407), Hugh de Stanford (1411, 1413), and Thomas Mayne (1447, 1449).[33]

In the mid 15th century there are signs of increasing domination of the borough's representation by the local gentry. Such are the returns of Richard Horde (9 times 1414–32), of his son Thomas (1442, 1449), of William Lawley (1429) and John Lawley (1447, 1455), of Richard Blyke of Astley, in Alveley (9 times 1429–59), of Andrew Wolryche of Dudmaston (1435), and of Roger Haughton (1459), who married a Wolryche. Returns of townsmen became much rarer than before.

Humphrey Blount of Kinlet (1460) was the first member of one of the more powerful Shropshire families to sit for the borough for over a century. Such names of Bridgnorth M.P.s as are known during the next sixty years suggest a mixture of gentlemen, royal officials, and townsmen. Under Henry VIII the mixture of members continued, but in the later 16th century townsmen all but ceased to represent the borough. Thomas Lacon of Willey and Edward Grey of Enville (Staffs.), who appear to have been the M.P.s in 1510, came from powerful local families; each, however, had also married a Horde, and the Hordes seem often to have been content to leave the representation to others. In 1529 both M.P.s, Humphrey Goldiston and George Hayward, were residents and both were former and future bailiffs. In 1542 neither member was a resident: Edward Hall the historian had sat for Much Wenlock in the Reformation Parliament but is not known to have had local connexions; William Grey of Enville, however, was son of the probable M.P. of 1510 and nephew of Richard Horde, then recorder. Hall sat again in 1545, when his colleague was Henry Blount, younger brother of the powerful Sir George.[34] Sir George himself sat for Bridgnorth in Mary I's first Parliament and in Elizabeth's first; his nephew Francis Lacon was returned in 1610, but was the last of that family to sit. In the middle of the 16th century two local landed families with some property in the town each supplied one M.P. Roger Smythe of Morville (1547) had engrossed some former religious property in the borough,[35] but neither he nor William Acton of Aldenham (1554, 1555) held property there comparable in extent to the Hordes', and their families did not again produce M.P.s until 1623 and 1640 respectively.

After 1547 the representation of Bridgnorth was shared between local gentry and the Council in the Marches of Wales. The council, which occasionally met in the town, was probably responsible for the return of men with council connexions, whether outsiders or Shropshire gentlemen.[36] The outsiders included Ambrose Gilbert, son-in-law of Sir Robert Townshend chief justice of Chester, returned in March 1553 when Northumberland was anxious to have members favourable to himself;[37] Edward Cordell (1563), brother of the master of the rolls; Townshend's son Henry (1571, 1572); and Thomas Sackford (1572), porter of Ludlow castle and a relative of Lord President Sidney. Shropshire gentlemen connected with the council included the Shrewsbury lawyer Richard Prince (1559), son-in-law of a council member; Thomas Ottley of Pitchford (1571), who held the former Bruyn property in the town but was also a kinsman of the influential council member Sir Andrew Corbet; Corbet's brother Jerome (1584), another council member; and Edward Bromley, son of Sir George Bromley, chief justice of Chester and recorder of Bridgnorth, returned in 1586 and at the five succeeding elections. The Bromleys held an estate at Hallon near Bridgnorth,[38] but Edward's official connexions, which also included an uncle who was lord chancellor,

[33] Ibid.
[34] See p. 89.
[35] Hist. MSS. Com. 13, *10th Rep. IV, Bridgnorth*, p. 426.
[36] Penry Williams, *The Council in the Marches of Wales under Eliz. I* (Cardiff, 1958), 347, 359.
[37] Ex inf. Hist. of Parl.
[38] *Visit. Salop. 1623*, i. 78.

probably explain his initial election for the borough. In 1586, 1589, 1593, and 1597, however, Bromley's colleague was John Lutwyche, who was merely a younger son of a Lutwyche of Lutwyche and had twice been bailiff; in 1601 Bromley's colleague was Thomas Horde, son of the M.P. of 1554 and the last Horde to sit for the borough, of which he was recorder and was later to be bailiff. Horde had a connexion with the council through his marriage to Mary Foxe, grand-daughter of its secretary; nevertheless it is likely that the sharing of the seats represented a compromise that gave more weight than usual to the interests of the town. If so, the influence of the council was reasserted in 1604 when Bromley's last colleague, Lewis Lewkenor, was the relative of yet another chief justice of Chester.

Competition between outside interests eventually led to an enlargement of the electorate. In 1610 Sir Francis Lacon, who united the Lacon and Blount interests, was opposed by Sir George Howard; there was a disputed return, and the bailiffs were summoned to give evidence before the Committee of Privileges. It appears that Lacon had been elected by foreign as well as resident burgesses,[39] but his return was upheld, and that decision gave the vote at Bridgnorth thenceforth to both residents and non-residents. The number of non-residents was at first small, but their admission was to impart a special character to Bridgnorth elections from the late 17th century until 1832.

In 1614 both M.P.s, John Peirse and Richard Synge, were probably townsmen, the last residents to sit for Bridgnorth. At the next election (1620) both seats were taken by *nouveaux riches*, Sir John Hayward and Sir William Whitmore. Hayward was a descendant of the 1529 M.P., and his father had prospered in London; Whitmore descended from a long line of Claverley copyholders,[40] and his father had done well enough in the capital to buy an estate at Apley Park near Bridgnorth. The son bought up the Hordes' property between 1614 and 1621[41] and sat for the borough at the first opportunity. Hayward dissipated his estate and died childless, but Whitmore and his descendants overcame losses in the Civil Wars, to dominate Bridgnorth and its vicinity until 1867.

Whitmore sat again in 1624 and 1625; his next colleague was George Smythe, descendant of the 1547 M.P. In 1625 there was a contest for one seat between George Vernon of Haslington (in Barthomley, Ches.) and an outsider Sir George Paule, a client of the duke of Buckingham. There may have been a double return resulting in some compromise, for in 1626 Vernon was returned with another client of the duke, Sir Richard Shelton, the solicitor general, while in 1628 Shelton was returned with Paule. Again the borough's representation appeared to be on the verge of capture by outside interests.

Ludlow

Ludlow received its charter from Edward IV in 1461 in return for the services that its burgesses had rendered towards his gaining of the Crown, and for the damage that they had thereby suffered. The charter gave the borough two members, to be elected by the burgesses from among themselves or others.[42] The borough's first known M.P.s were those returned in 1467: John Dodmore and Richard Sherman, both Ludlow men.[43]

Most of the earliest known M.P.s had strong connexions with the town, and in the

[39] *C.J.* i. 397–8, 407–10.
[40] Eyton, iii. 171 n. 60; S.P.L., MS. 2792, pp. 451–68.
[41] Deeds in Apley Estate Office, Bridgnorth.
[42] *Cal. Chart. R.* 1427–1516, 155–61; *Brit. Boro. Charters,*

1307–1660, ed. M. Weinbaum (1943), 96.
[43] *T.S.A.S.* 2nd ser. vii. 3, 8; Wedgwood, *Hist. Parl. 1439–1509: Biogs.* 277, 763; ibid. *Reg.* 330, 356. The 1463 M.P.s are unknown.

early decades at least one, sometimes both, came from it.[44] Occasionally an M.P. had outside interests: thus Piers Beaupie (1472–5) was not only recorder of Ludlow and founder of a chantry in St. Lawrence's church but also clerk of the Green Cloth to Edward IV.[45] William Foxe (?1523, 1529–36, 1536) founded a leading Ludlow family; his son Charles (1539–40, 1542–4, 1547–52, March 1553) acquired much former ecclesiastical property, notably the Bromfield priory estates[46] including Oakly Park whence electoral control of Ludlow was to be exercised at intervals for over three centuries. Charles Foxe was the first M.P. to have strong links with the Council in the Marches of Wales.[47] His parliamentary colleague 1539–40 was his brother-in-law Thomas Wheeler, recently bailiff[48] of Ludlow; in 1542–4 it was his brother Edmund Foxe of Ludford. Wheeler sat 1545–7 with John Bradshaw, who had married a kinswoman of the lord president, Bishop Lee; Bradshaw, too, acquired former ecclesiastical property. Outside influence possibly returned Robert Blount, Sir George's brother, in 1547, but he was apparently gentleman usher to the council and his wife was one of the Crofts, a Herefordshire family with much influence in the council.[49] In 1547 and March 1553, however, Charles Foxe took one seat, his colleague on the latter occasion being his brother-in-law Wheeler.

Ten men sat for Ludlow in Mary I's five Parliaments. In her first the M.P.s, John Passie and Thomas Wheeler, were members of the corporation. Only two such men, however, sat in the other four: Thomas Blashfield and Robert Mason. Others had links with the council: Sir John Price from Herefordshire; William Heath, who was doubtless related to the council's president, Archbishop Heath; and Richard Prince of Shrewsbury. The other two M.P.s under Mary, James Warncombe and Thomas Croft, were Herefordshire gentry. The total absence of re-election and the election of fewer townsmen may perhaps be attributed to reluctance to become involved in Mary's legislation.[50]

Only seven men sat for Ludlow in Elizabeth I's reign, three fewer than in the five years of Mary. Six of them were members of the Twelve and the Twenty-Five and between them were bailiffs 18 times between 1544 and 1611. In most Elizabethan Parliaments one Ludlow M.P. (and, except in that of 1562–7, the senior) was in some way connected with the Council in the Marches:[51] thus Robert Berry, returned on every occasion but one between 1584 and 1614, was the porter of Ludlow castle. Charles Foxe's standing was enhanced in the 1570s by his second marriage, to a Leighton, and by his son's to a daughter of Sir Richard Newport. Foxe's presence and the longevity of the six local M.P.s may have determined the representation, though the fact that Foxe was returned for Much Wenlock in 1562 suggests that he could not at that period get himself returned at Ludlow.

The sequence of town elders was broken in 1597. The popular faction then strong in the borough was joined by one of the bailiffs, John Crowther; apparently without consulting the Twelve and Twenty-Five Crowther returned Thomas Candland and Hugh Sanford, an outsider. Berry, who had sat in the previous four Parliaments, was excluded. Sanford was secretary to Lord President Pembroke and later sat in his interest for Wilton; Crowther was thus probably trying to gain the lord president's support. The Commons, however, voided the election, and in December Berry and Candland were returned by the Twelve and the Twenty-Five, then presided over by

[44] Except where otherwise stated the rest of this section is based on *T.S.A.S.* 2nd ser. vii. 1–26, 54.
[45] *Household of Edw. IV*, ed. A. R. Myers (1959), 295.
[46] *V.C.H. Salop.* ii. 29. For the fam. see *T.S.A.S.* 2nd ser. xii. 113–90.
[47] *T.S.A.S.* 2nd ser. xii. 124, 138–40; Williams, *Council*

in Marches, 159 sqq., 333.
[48] Bailiffs listed 1462–1783, 1786–1834 in T. Wright, *Hist. of Ludlow* (Ludlow, 1852), 486–503.
[49] Williams, op. cit. 236–7.
[50] E. Coke, *Fourth Inst.* (1681), 19.
[51] *T.S.A.S.* lvi. 289.

new bailiffs. The council's serjeant-at-arms, one of the popular faction, tried to prevent Berry from taking his seat by serving a writ on him, but in vain, and was disciplined at the bar of the Commons.[52] Berry was 'greatly frowned at' by all the other Shropshire members in 1598 when he tried to make the county subject to a Bill declaring that land converted to pasture since 1558, after twelve years in tillage, should be restored for ever to tillage.[53]

The previous pattern was resumed; Berry and Candland were returned in 1601, and in 1604 Berry was returned with Richard Benson, twice a bailiff. Benson's death in 1609 began a new and more contentious era. The borough was solicited by Lord President Eure[54] on behalf of his brother Sir Francis Eure, and also by the king's chief minister, the earl of Salisbury, on behalf of another stranger, John Leveson. To Salisbury the borough asserted (in open contradiction of the 1461 charter) that it could elect 'none but a resident'[55] and must refuse his request as it had refused Eure's. The M.P. elected was Richard Fisher, a bailiff.[56] It was, however, the last time that Ludlow returned both M.P.s from its own corporation.

In 1614 disputes began again in earnest, opening a period in which borough worthies no longer represented Ludlow in Parliament.[57] Richard Tomlyns, a Ludlow native living in London, offered himself but was rejected on the ground that he was not a sworn burgess. The corporation co-opted Sir Henry Townshend to the Twenty-Five and elected Bailiff Berry and Townshend to represent the borough in Parliament. At the same time it resolved that both M.P.s should be chosen from the Twelve and Twenty-Five.[58] Townshend, an influential member of the Council in the Marches,[59] recorder of Ludlow, and an occasional resident in the borough, had been a burgess since 1584. Berry's election, however, was invalidated on the ground that he had returned himself, and he was replaced by the queen's sewer Robert Lloyd, who was simultaneously made a burgess and agreed to serve without pay. Lloyd was neither a resident nor one of the Twelve or Twenty-Five, and in electing this new type of candidate the Twelve and Twenty-Five ignored its previous order, though 'for this time and Parliament only'.[60]

In 1621 the absentee Tomlyns, by then a burgess, renewed his suit; his letter demonstrates the sorry state of Ludlow's finances, for he not only promised that he would take no wages but also revealed that he had long intended 'to do some good for the town'. Tomlyns knew that the corporation would be 'importuned by letters from greater persons' but hoped that it would be 'constant to hold your ancient and laudable custom, namely to choose none but your native and sworn burgesses'. His plea was successful only in his own case for his colleague was Lord Compton, heir of the earl of Northampton, by then lord president.

Tomlyns was returned to the next four Parliaments. His letters of solicitation before three of those elections were not the only ones received; the bailiffs stated in 1650 that the borough had, to its own prejudice, elected Tomlyns in preference to 'persons of honour'. Tomlyns's colleague in all those Parliaments was Ralph Goodwin, a Ludlow burgess and, from 1628, deputy secretary and clerk of the Council in the Marches.

Much Wenlock

In 1468, after an approach from Lord Wenlock, Edward IV granted the right of

[52] T.S.A.S. lvi. 282–8.
[53] J. E. Neale, Eliz. I and her Parls. 1584–1601 (1957), 339, 344.
[54] S.R.O. 356/2/1, f. 81v.
[55] Cal. S.P. Dom. 1603–10, 566.
[56] S.R.O. 356/2/1, ff. 80v., 81v.–82.
[57] T.S.A.S. lvi. 290.
[58] S.R.O. 356/2/1, ff. 103v.–104.
[59] Williams, Council in Marches, 140–1, 143, 268–9, 291–4, 300, 358–9; T.S.A.S. liv. 184–5.
[60] T.S.A.S. lvi. 289.

parliamentary representation to Much Wenlock. The borough was empowered to return one member, to be chosen, as at Ludlow, by the burgesses from their own number or from outside. The charter defined the borough as the parish of Holy Trinity. That, however, was of great extent and was understood to consist of the whole liberty of the priory.[61] The charter was soon ignored in one important respect, for by 1491 Much Wenlock was returning two M.P.s.[62] The first known M.P. (1472–5) was William Clerk, a Yorkist and constable of Bridgnorth castle; he was elected for Bridgnorth in 1477, when Much Wenlock's M.P. was the obscure Thomas Cambray (Chambre). In 1529 the borough returned Edward Hall the historian[63] with John Forester of Watling Street. Forester was the first known member of his family to sit for the borough. The family later controlled the borough for two centuries but in 1529 was merely one of a number, from a wide surrounding area, that occupied borough seats; it provided only one more M.P. before 1679.

The borough's representation 1544–1629 was mostly dominated by the Lacons and the Lawleys. The influence of the Lacons' Willey estate, later acquired by the Welds and transmitted by them to the Foresters, emerged in 1540 when one member was William Blount, whose sister Agnes married Richard Lacon of Willey. Four years later Richard Lawley of Spoonhill, a son of the first bailiff under the 1468 charter, was returned; his brother Thomas acquired the site of Wenlock priory in 1545. Richard and Thomas Lawley were returned in 1547; the latter (bailiff 1546–7, 1550–1) was elected again in February 1553. After Mary I's accession, however, neither brother sat again. A Lee and an Eyton sat in Mary's first Parliament, but in her remaining four and the first three of Elizabeth I the influence of the Lacons was apparently constant; after 1559 their connexion Thomas Blount held the wardship of the young Thomas Lawley,[64] son of the purchaser of Wenlock priory. In the Parliaments of 1554–5, 1555, 1558, and 1562–7 one M.P. was Sir George Blount, another brother of Agnes Lacon and powerful in his own right. In 1559 and 1571 one M.P. at each election was a Lacon nephew of his. Sir George sat with his brother-in-law Thomas Ridley in 1555 and with George Bromley, his own and the Lacons' relative and a rising lawyer, in 1558. Blount was M.P. 1572–83 with the second Thomas Lawley, then of age.

In the late 16th century the Lawleys of Wenlock Priory appear to have relinquished their interest to other gentry families and to Crown officials. Between 1604 and 1629, however, the Lawleys normally controlled one seat, the other, and on one occasion both, being usually held, in this most rural of boroughs, by a leading gentleman of the district. Before 1572 those M.P.s not closely connected with the Lawleys or the Lacons had belonged to county gentry families. After 1572 there was a change. Thomas Lawley sat in three Parliaments (1572–83, 1584–5, 1586–7) and his brother Robert in the next (1588–9), but their colleague from 1584 was the first real stranger to sit. He was William Baynham of Westbury on Severn (Glos.), who probably owed his return for Much Wenlock at five successive elections (1584–97) to his position as the Crown's receiver general in Shropshire.[65] Baynham's 1593 colleague, Sir John Poole, is obscure; his fellow M.P. in 1597 was William Lacon. Baynham died in 1597 and was replaced by Thomas Fanshawe of Ware (Herts.), the queen's remembrancer and probably an acquaintance of the influential Townshend family.[66] Of the 1601 M.P.s John Brett was perhaps connected with the Council in the Marches, and William Leighton was the son of the owner of Plaish. Yet in six of the next seven Parliaments the Lawleys supplied

[61] *Cal. Chart. R.* 1427–1516, 229–32; Eyton, iii. 232–3, 238, 264 sqq.

[62] For the rest of this section see *T.S.A.S.* 3rd ser. ii. 297–327, 357–8.

[63] *D.N.B.*

[64] Ex inf. the History of Parliament.

[65] Ex inf. Hist. Parl.

[66] He was a trustee of Sir Rowland Hayward, deceased father-in-law of Hen. Townshend of Cound. For Townshend see above, pp. 243, 246; below, p. 248.

at least one M.P. Robert and George Lawley were elected in 1604. Edward Lawley, son of the aged former M.P. Thomas, was elected in 1614 and 1621; his colleague in 1614 was a Lacon, and in 1621 Thomas Wolryche, who owned land near Much Wenlock. In 1624 no Lawley stood and the M.P.s were Wolryche and Henry Mytton of Shipton, but in the next three Parliaments Thomas Lawley of Spoonhill held one seat, dividing the representation with Wolryche (1625), Francis Smalman of Wilderhope (1626), and George Bridgeman (1628–9), whose father was recorder of Much Wenlock and vice-president of the Council in the Marches of Wales.

Bishop's Castle

Bishop's Castle received a royal charter in 1573; it conferred no right to elect M.P.s,[67] but writs to elect two members were received in 1584 and thereafter.[68] The franchise was in the resident burgesses.[69] The first two M.P.s, Thomas Jukes and John Cole, had married nieces of Edmund Plowden, named first among the charter chief burgesses; they were thus well connected among the Shropshire gentry. Jukes was second cousin to Edward Leighton, the earl of Leicester's kinsman and friend,[70] and was a client of the earl of Pembroke, Leicester's nephew. Plowden was an eminent lawyer but, as a Roman Catholic recusant,[71] probably had little public influence[72] and the interest behind the borough's sudden enfranchisement was probably Pembroke's. It must in any case have been an influence of some weight, for the queen's opinion, and opinion at Court generally, had for some years been hardening against municipal incorporations and against increases in the size of the Commons.[73]

Whoever secured the enfranchisement obtained little lasting influence thereby, for until James I's reign no clear pattern of representation emerges. Gentlemen of the immediate neighbourhood represented the borough as early as 1586–7 and 1588–9 when one M.P. was Charles Walcot of Walcot, the first of several generations of his family to sit for the borough. Walcot's first colleague, Thomas Dayrell, a Buckinghamshire squire, was Edward Leighton's brother-in-law;[74] his second, Alexander King, was an auditor of the Exchequer. King's 1593 colleague, Dr. Francis Beavans, was chancellor of Hereford diocese. The 1597 election added further to the variety of M.P.s returned: Hayward Townshend, the parliamentary diarist, was son of the influential Henry Townshend of Cound; his fellow M.P., the turbulent Edmund Baynham, was son of William Baynham, M.P. for Much Wenlock. Both were under age. Edmund Baynham was a rebel with Essex in 1601, and a conspirator in 1605. Samuel Lewkenor and William Twinehoe, elected in 1604, may have had a common background in Sussex; Lewkenor, who had a Shropshire wife,[75] was probably related to the chief justice of Chester.[76]

In James I's reign the exercise of influence can sometimes be detected. In 1610, after Twinehoe's death, the earl of Northampton, who owned the manor of Bishop's Castle, had already aided the town by preventing the erection of a rival market at Church Stretton;[77] in return he requested the election of Sir William Cavendish (still

[67] Cal. Pat. 1572–5, pp. 14–15.
[68] Except where otherwise stated this section is based on T.S.A.S. 2nd ser. x. 33–46, 68.
[69] Ex inf. Hist. of Parl.
[70] Visit. Salop. 1623, ii. 324; Complete Peerage, iv. 480–1; vii. 549; Blakeway, Sheriffs, 91. Leicester had property in Bp.'s Cas.: Cal. Pat. 1572–5, pp. 181, 272.
[71] G. de C. Parmiter, Elizabethan Popish Recusancy in the Inns of Ct. (Bull. Inst. Hist. Res. Special Suppl. xi), 6–7, 10, 21, 28–9, 46–7, 49–50.
[72] D.N.B.

[73] Evangeline de Villiers, 'Parl. Boros. Restored by the Ho. of Commons 1624–41', E.H.R. lxvii. 176, 200; Shelagh Bond and N. Evans, 'The process of granting charters to Eng. boros. 1547–1649', ibid. xci. 110–11. Eliz. I's last enfranchisement was in 1586 (Andover which had returned M.P.s temp. Edw. I and II): de Villiers, op. cit. 176; V.C.H. Hants, iv. 351.
[74] Visit. Salop. 1623, ii. 324. [75] T.S.A.S. 4th ser. vi. 217.
[76] G. Ormerod, Hist. of Co. . . . of Chester (1882), i. 65; cf. above, p. 244.
[77] T.S.A.S. x. 125, 132–3.

under age), 'for though the election be yours by right, the inheritance of the borough is mine'.[78] The borough had incurred debts to its former M.P., Lewkenor,[79] and from 1614 onwards carefully recorded the sworn oaths of M.P.s not to take wages.[80] The town's poverty, however, was insurmountable; foreign burgesses were needed for the fees and services that they paid and rendered, though in 1620 and 1626, when foreign burgesses actually turned up, the borough stipulated that they should not vote.[81] Francis Nichols's return in 1620 may have been due to Cavendish's influence, for in 1617 Cavendish had asked for one seat for himself or a nominee at the next election in return for help in securing a new charter.

From 1624 onwards, however, the owners of local estates asserted their control. In that year the M.P.s were Sir Robert Howard, who had succeeded to the manor of Bishop's Castle, and Richard Oakeley of Oakeley. Howard's colleague in 1625 and 1626 was William Blunden of Blunden Hall in Bishop's Castle, a distant connexion of the Plowdens[82] and the first M.P. ever to be bailiff (in 1628). In 1628–9 Howard's fellow M.P. was Sir Edward Foxe, a member of the Council in the Marches.

1640-60

ONLY four former Shropshire M.P.s were returned to the Short Parliament in 1640. At least three constituencies were contested: the county, Ludlow, and Bridgnorth. Information on the county election is meagre: by 6 March there were four candidates,[83] among whom were Vincent Corbet of Moreton Corbet, later a royalist, and William Pierrepont, a peer's son and newcomer to the county who had acquired Tong Castle by marriage, had been sheriff in 1637–8, and was later a Parliamentarian. Corbet and Pierrepont stood jointly but had 'broken' by 14 March,[84] when Lady Brilliana Harley wrote that the contest was between her cousin Andrew Corbet, another future Parliamentarian Sir John Corbet, and Pierrepont;[85] Vincent Corbet apparently had little chance. Pierrepont, a committee member in that Parliament,[86] must have been returned with one of the Corbets, probably Sir John[87] whose intervention suggests that an attempt to compromise failed in the face of more extreme passions. No Newport is mentioned among the contenders for the county. Sir Richard Newport, knight of the shire in the 1620s, was not yet a strong partisan, and his son Francis, though still a minor,[88] was returned for Shrewsbury with Thomas Owen, M.P. for the borough 1628–9.[89] Nevertheless a report three days before the declaration that Francis Newport and Sir Richard Lee, of Langley, had been returned[90] may suggest that Shrewsbury too was contested, though presumably not to a poll. At Bridgnorth there was a poll, though the contest does not seem to have been long premeditated.[91] All three candidates were later royalists and all were heirs to their fathers' properties: Thomas Whitmore's father had sat in the 1620s and Edward Acton's father held an interest in and near the town second only to the Whitmores'; the family of the third candidate, however, the solicitor general's son-in-law Thomas Littleton of Stoke St. Milborough, had little or no

[78] Bp.'s Cas. boro. rec., 1st min. bk. (at end), f. 4v.
[79] T.S.A.S. x. 126.
[80] Bp.'s Cas. boro. rec., 1st min. bk. ff. 73, 102v., 147v.
[81] Ibid. ff. 102, 147.
[82] Visit. Salop. 1623, i. 49–50; T.S.A.S. lii. 182–3.
[83] Hist. MSS. Com. 29, 14th Rep. II, Portland, iii, pp. 40, 60.
[84] Ibid. 61.
[85] Letters of the Lady Brilliana Harley (Camd. Soc. [1st ser.], lviii), 86. All discussed by D. Brunton and D. H. Pennington, Members of Long Parl. (1954), 11–14; Mary

F. Keeler, The Long Parl. 1640–1641: a Biog. Study of its Members (1954).
[86] C.J. ii. 4; T.S.A.S. 4th ser. xi. 169–70.
[87] T.S.A.S. 4th ser. xi. 172–3.
[88] Ibid. 2nd ser. xii. 7–8.
[89] Ibid. 4th ser. xii. 207–9.
[90] Letters of Lady Brilliana Harley, 86.
[91] Thirteen new burgesses were admitted 22 Oct. 1639, thereafter only 4 in Jan.–Feb. and 4 in Mar. 1640: Bridgnorth boro. rec., 9/3, pp. 623–5.

interest in Bridgnorth. The figures (Whitmore 265, Acton 241, Littleton 74)[92] suggest that the Whitmore and Acton interests had coalesced, as they were to do at intervals for the next sixty years. Stoke St. Milborough was in the borough of Much Wenlock, for which Littleton found a seat, his father being recorder; his colleague was Richard Cressett.[93]

At Ludlow the Council in the Marches could still secure one seat, but only with some difficulty. Timothy Tourneur, solicitor to the council, withdrew in January, after an unfavourable reception, and recommended his friends to vote for Charles Baldwyn of Elsich,[94] a local squire. Lord President Bridgwater recommended his son-in-law Sir Robert Napier of Luton (Beds.), later a lukewarm Parliamentarian, but the town refused him.[95] Ralph Goodwin, M.P. 1628–9, had been a member of the Twenty-Five at Ludlow since 1635 and stood again, presumably singly; the burgesses were not well affected towards him, but he feasted them and was elected. Baldwyn succeeded by the same means, labouring 'importunately' with his friends and using his purse with the burgesses;[96] four later generations of his family were to represent Ludlow. Bishop's Castle returned Sir Robert Howard, M.P. 1628–9, and Richard More of Linley who had been a burgess for thirty years.[97]

The number of contests for the Short Parliament may reflect the novelty of that election rather than strong political feeling. The October returns to the Long Parliament[98] apparently produced no contest, though there is again some evidence of eagerness to gain a seat. H. F. Thynne vainly tried to secure what he professed to regard as the vital interest of the town clerk of Bridgnorth with a view to standing for the borough,[99] in which he himself certainly had no interest. Pierrepont, unable to keep his county seat, stood for Much Wenlock, where he replaced Cressett. There were naturally fewer new M.P.s in October than in March: Sir Richard Lee of Langley for the county and, in place of Owen, William Spurstow for Shrewsbury. Bridgnorth, Ludlow, and Bishop's Castle returned the same men in March and October. Bridgnorth and Ludlow sent up four future royalists, the other four constituencies one future royalist and one future Parliamentarian each. It may have been a fair reflection of opinion in the county, which was not so exclusively royalist as might be suggested by the military predominance which the king's local supporters so early and determinedly set out to acquire.[1] There is little doubt that Ludlow was as royalist[2] and Shrewsbury as divided[3] as the representation of each suggests. The samples are unrepresentative in the sense that five of the eight Shropshire royalist M.P.s were older than any of their opponents. Both sides contained representatives of well established gentry families. The only M.P. outside the gentry circle was Spurstow, who had become a rich London merchant.

The eight royalists were all disabled, Lee and Howard in September 1642, the rest early in 1644. Meanwhile Richard More had died in 1643. They were all replaced in 1645–6 by 'recruiters', almost all of them men of some standing and estate in the county. Parliamentarian troops took Shrewsbury in February 1645, and the way was open to the first of the necessary by-elections. The recruiter elections illustrate well the grip on the county held by Parliamentarian officers, though the capture of Shrewsbury had widened the split among them.[4] In November Thomas Hunt, governor of Wem and much admired by Richard Baxter, was returned for his native Shrewsbury in

[92] Bridgnorth boro. rec., 24/1.
[93] *T.S.A.S.* 3rd ser. ii. 327–9.   [94] Ibid. 2nd ser. vii. 26.
[95] *Letters of Lady Brilliana Harley*, 86.
[96] *T.S.A.S.* 2nd ser. vii. 25–6.
[97] Ibid. x. 133; 2nd ser. x. 46.
[98] For the rest of this section see ibid. 2nd ser. vii. 27–31;

x. 46–50; 3rd ser. ii. 329–32; 4th ser. v. 16, 56–61; xi. 171–84; xii. 127, 209–15.
[99] Bridgnorth boro. rec., 26/1.   [1] *T.S.A.S.* li. 24–5.
[2] *Letters of Lady Brilliana Harley*, 167, 172, 174.
[3] W. J. Farrow, *Gt. Civil War in Salop.* (Shrews. 1926), 20–1.   [4] See p. 112.

Newport's place. Two months later, following Spurstow's death, the other Shrewsbury seat was filled by William Masham, apparently unconnected with the borough but the son of a kinsman and strong supporter of Cromwell. In February 1646 John Corbet, of Halston (in Pontesbury), and Esay Thomas were returned for Bishop's Castle; Thomas was the town clerk and an opponent of the king. In May Humphrey Briggs, of Haughton (in Shifnal), was returned for Much Wenlock. Bridgnorth and Ludlow, the last Shropshire towns held for the king, fell in March and May 1646, and further by-elections could be held. In May the Parliamentarian commander in Cheshire, Sir William Brereton, short of seats in his own county, attempted an intervention similar to one he had tried in Staffordshire:[5] hopefully he recommended one of his subordinates, William Steel, to the Shropshire parliamentary committee for election at Bridgnorth or Ludlow.[6] In Shropshire, as in Staffordshire, he was unsuccessful. The local committee did not go outside the county for any of its nominees: Robert Clive of Styche and Robert Charlton of Apley were elected for Bridgnorth on 22 June, Thomas Mackworth of Betton Strange, a minor, and Thomas More of Linley for Ludlow on 8 August. All the recruiters but two were Shropshire country gentlemen, though for the most part of minor standing; none, however, had any close connexion with, or indeed lived near, the borough for which he was returned. It is probably a reflection of the strength of anti-royalist feeling in Shrewsbury that there alone was a townsman of standing returned as a recruiter: Thomas Hunt's father had been a bailiff of the borough. The military qualifications of other new borough members are clear: Clive and Charlton had been particularly active under the committee, and Mackworth was the son of Humphrey Mackworth the new governor of Shrewsbury, who requested his election in a flowery letter to the bailiffs of Ludlow.[7]

The most important by-election was held on 27 August 1646. According to those who objected to his actions, the sheriff, Gen. Thomas Mytton, had appointed Oswestry, of which he was governor, as the polling place for the new knight of the shire. Nearly a thousand of 'the best knights, esquires, gentlemen, and freeholders' gathered there to support Andrew Lloyd of Aston at the county court appointed for nine o'clock. They found that before five o'clock that morning Mytton had ridden to Alberbury thirteen miles away, ostensibly leaving his under-sheriff to conduct the election. The under-sheriff, however, adjourned the court to Alberbury, where Mytton had already completed the election. Freeholders there present voiced their demand for Lloyd, but Mytton refused a poll and returned his kinsman Humphrey Edwardes of Shrewsbury, though his supporters were allegedly few 'and the greater part of them of mean quality and many of them verily thought not freeholders'. Lloyd petitioned and secured over 300 signatures, among which the names of Humphrey Briggs, John Corbet, Thomas More, and Robert Charlton[8] doubtless indicate the recently elected recruiters and reveal the split in the county committee. Lloyd had been among those who, in March 1645, had denied Mytton the governorship of Shrewsbury. By fixing the election for 'the remotest part of the county', then removing it elsewhere and lying about his actions to Lloyd's supporters whom he met on the road, Mytton had taken revenge. At one moment the Commons' decision in the petition was on 'the point of the poll', but Edwardes defended his actions skilfully[9] and was not unseated.

Pride's Purge in December 1648[10] left Shropshire with four M.P.s in the Rump of

[5] D. Underdown, 'Party management in the recruiter elections, 1645-1648', *E.H.R.* lxxxiii. 252.

[6] Birm. Ref. Libr. 595611, pp. 211-12.

[7] *T.S.A.S.* 2nd ser. vii. 28.

[8] *T.S.A.S.* iii. 141-6 (copy, perhaps draft, in Oswestry boro. rec.); N.L.W., Aston Hall 2334, 2462-7, 3028.

[9] *C.J.* iv. 671; B.L. Add. MS. 10114, f. 19.

[10] Described by Adam Ottley in a letter to his mother: *T.S.A.S.* 3rd ser. xi. 249. Members classified by D. Underdown, *Pride's Purge: Politics in the Puritan Revolution* (1971), App. A.

1649–53: one knight of the shire (Edwardes), one member each for Shrewsbury (Masham), Ludlow (Thomas Mackworth), and Bishop's Castle (John Corbet). By expulsion or voluntary withdrawal Bridgnorth and Much Wenlock thus lost both M.P.s, the other constituencies one; of those, Pierrepont, member of a middle grouping which wanted a return to legality,[11] was not excluded by the army but was a firm and declared opponent of the purge: immediately after it he led his followers away from the House and denounced those who stayed.[12] Mackworth, doubtless kept busy in Shropshire, and Masham seldom attended Rump meetings, but Corbet and Edwardes were active Rumpers.[13] Both were among the 135 commissioners appointed for the king's trial, but Corbet, otherwise an active lawyer,[14] did not take part in it. Edwardes, the one revolutionary among the Shropshire M.P.s, had attended Parliament infrequently in 1648; after the purge, however, he immediately became a very prominent Rumper and, in January 1649, a regicide.[15]

No member excluded in 1648 ever re-entered the Commons. Meanwhile the processes of sequestration, composition, and fine and the occasional arrest of royalists had been organized since 1643.[16] Allegiances were shifting: Silius Titus was among the ex-Parliamentarians who supported Charles II in 1651.[17] The old royalists from time to time gave the government cause for alarm,[18] and in April 1650 Humphrey Mackworth, governor of Shrewsbury, reportedly thought Shrewsbury 'a divided place'.[19] Amidst all this Mackworth[20] and his connexions[21] were the main prop of the Commonwealth and Protectorate regimes in the county,[22] and the Mackworths were highly influential in the elections of 1653, 1654, and 1656. In the Nominated (Barebones) Parliament of 1653 the Shropshire M.P.s were Thomas Baker of Sweeney and William Botterell, bailiff of Ludlow 1648–9 and 1651–2 and governor there since 1649. Their nomination was possibly an attempt, when the county was given only two M.P.s, to represent the north and south of the shire. Baker was a great patron of Independent preachers such as Vavasour Powell, and he served on Powell's Committee for Propagating the Gospel in Wales. Powell's favour determined elections to that Parliament, but Baker was a neighbour of Gen. Mytton and Col. Lloyd, and was also linked with the Mackworths.[23] Botterell was doubtless well known to Thomas Mackworth, the former Ludlow M.P.

Shropshire's representation had been scheduled for reduction to six, seven, or eight M.P.s, more proportionately to its population, in three abortive schemes of 1648–50. To the first and second Protectorate Parliaments, elected in 1654 and 1656, it sent eight M.P.s: four for the county, two for Shrewsbury, one each for Bridgnorth and Ludlow.[24] The Mackworths commanded three of these seats in 1654. The elder Humphrey sat for the shire, with Gen. Mytton, Col. Robert Corbet of Stanwardine,[25] and Corbet's son-in-law Philip Yonge of Caynton, whose ancestors had sat occasionally for the shire in the later Middle Ages.[26] Shrewsbury returned the younger Humphrey Mackworth and a draper, Alderman Richard Cheshire.[27] Col. William Crowne, who married the elder Mackworth's sister, was returned for Bridgnorth. The new Ludlow

[11] Underdown, op. cit. 95, 97, 104–5; B. Worden, *The Rump Parl. 1648–1653* (1974), 179–80.
[12] He was voted out by the Rump 24 Jan. 1651: Underdown, op. cit. 289.
[13] Ibid. App. A.
[14] Ibid. 30.
[15] Ibid. 37, 39–40.
[16] *T.S.A.S.* iv. 156–8; 2nd ser. vi. 19–20; above, p. 112.
[17] *T.S.A.S.* 2nd ser. vii. 37.
[18] D. Underdown, *Royalist Conspiracy in Eng.*; *T.S.A.S.* 3rd ser. x. 87–168.
[19] Hist. MSS. Com. 29, *14th Rep. II, Portland*, iii, p. 187.
[20] *D.N.B.*; *T.S.A.S.* liv. 190–2, 212.
[21] Fam. discussed in *T.S.A.S.* 3rd ser. x. 136–7. See also ibid. 2nd ser. i. 384, 390 sqq.
[22] See pp. 112–13.
[23] R. Gough, *Antiquities and Memoirs of Parish of Myddle* (1875), 98.
[24] V. F. Snow, 'Parliamentary Reapportionment Proposals in the Puritan Revolution', *E.H.R.* lxxiv. 440 (tabulated in Worden, *Rump Parl.* 397). Details of boro. representation in the Rump's 1650 scheme are unknown.
[25] Gough, *Antiquities of Myddle*, 46.
[26] *T.S.A.S.* 4th ser. x. 189; xi. 25–6.
[27] *T.S.A.S.* liv. 169.

M.P., John Aston, had been leading the opposition to the royalists there since 1640.[28] There is no sign that any 1654 return was contested.

The 1656 elections, which it was the duty of the new major-generals to conduct,[29] seem to reflect the continuing influence of the Mackworths, who had promptly suppressed the 1655 royalist rising,[30] as well as the congruent newer influence of James Berry, the major-general, with headquarters in Shrewsbury.[31] The county was represented by Thomas Mackworth, Philip Yonge, Andrew Lloyd, and Samuel More of Linley, an active army officer and son of the M.P. for Bishop's Castle 1640–3. Mytton, not in the new Parliament, was probably sick: he died in November. Thomas Mackworth's brother Humphrey sat for Shrewsbury, of which he was governor and town clerk, together with another Shrewsbury merchant, the rich Samuel Jones of Berwick. John Aston sat again for Ludlow, which Berry had found an 'unruly town' in November 1655.[32] At Bridgnorth, however, there was a new M.P. in Maj. Edmund Waring, an Anabaptist, captain of the county militia troop under Berry, and shortly to be made sheriff;[33] he was presumably the major-general's nominee. The presence of new, and the absence of familiar, names were even more striking in 1656 than in 1654. Lloyd was excluded from taking his seat in the new Parliament.

The 1659 elections were held in the old constituencies and on the old franchise. The shire and Shrewsbury each sent up a Mackworth, but three southern boroughs slipped back into the hands of the local gentry, and some of the old parliamentary families returned to the Commons. The new knights of the shire were two of the four returned in 1656: Thomas Mackworth and Philip Yonge. Mackworth's brother Humphrey sat for a third time for Shrewsbury; his new colleague William Jones had been recorder of the borough since 1645. Samuel More lost any opportunity to remain a knight of the shire, and sat for Bishop's Castle with William Oakeley, also the son of a former M.P. At Much Wenlock Francis Lawley belonged to a family which had provided many M.P.s, but Thomas Whitmore of Ludstone probably owed his new place to his position as the borough's recorder and perhaps to kinship with the Whitmores of Apley and other families.[34] At Ludlow Job Charlton was a newcomer, but Samuel Baldwyn was the son of the M.P. disabled in 1644. At Bridgnorth, however, the new county establishment was still in control, for the borough returned Waring again and another army officer, John Humphrey. Throughout the troubles Bridgnorth was the only Shropshire borough never represented either by one of its own townsmen or by gentlemen of the immediate neighbourhood. Its M.P.s 1646–60 were five military men, of whom only the first two, Clive and Charlton, came from families of standing in the county. The fact that Shrewsbury returned one townsman in 1645 and others (as the Mackworths' colleagues) in the 1650s may indicate some exercise of independent choice in that borough. In the county generally, the elections of 1645–6, 1653, 1654, and 1656 suggest a total dominance by the new rulers of the county, a dominance partly broken in 1659 by the return of at least five M.P.s who were to support the king's restoration.

[28] Ibid. lvi. 290–1.
[29] D. W. Rannie, 'Cromwell's Major-Generals', E.H.R. x. 498–500; J. Berry and S. G. Lee, A Cromwellian Major-General (1938), 149.
[30] T.S.A.S. 3rd ser. x. 139 sqq.; Underdown, Royalist Conspiracy, 146–8.
[31] Berry and Lee, Cromwellian Maj.-Gen. 134–5.
[32] Ibid. 130. Early in 1656 Berry had been ready to set up his headquarters in Ludlow: ibid. 157, 173.
[33] Ibid. 153, 289; T.S.A.S. 3rd ser. x. 148. Thos. Hunt was still sheriff 18 July 1656 (S.R.O. 215/68) and presumably during the elections, but Waring succ. later that yr. (above, pp. 110, 114).
[34] T.S.A.S. liv. 192–3.

1660-1832

Shropshire, p. 256. Shrewsbury, p. 264. Bridgnorth, p. 275. Ludlow, p. 283. Much Wenlock, p. 291. Bishop's Castle, p. 297.

THE dominant interest in Shropshire after the Restoration was that of the Newports of High Ercall.[35] Between 1660 and 1734 members of the family sat not only for the county but also for Bishop's Castle, Much Wenlock, and Ludlow as convenient. In the 1660s and earlier 1670s they were Court supporters, but thereafter they led the Shropshire Whigs. The 1st baron, who had bought his dignity from Charles I in 1642, died in exile in 1651.[36] His son Francis was a pillar of the Cavalier cause in Shropshire after 1660 when he was made lieutenant: in 1668 he became comptroller, and in 1672 treasurer, of the Household, and he was still sufficiently in favour at Court to be made a viscount in March 1675. In 1679, however, he was left out of the re-modelled Privy Council. Connected through his mother with the Levesons and through his wife with the Russells, he became a Whig, and in 1687 James II deprived him of the treasurership and the lieutenancy. At the Revolution he recovered both posts, and in 1694 William III made him earl of Bradford.[37] His son Richard, an opponent of the Court earlier than his father, became lieutenant in 1704 and succeeded as 2nd earl in 1708. Throughout the bitter contests of the time he continued his support of the Whigs. The Tories deprived him of the lieutenancy in 1712, though the new regime restored it to him two years later.[38] Richard's son Henry succeeded as 3rd earl in 1723 and was made lieutenant in 1724. He was an equally firm Whig. He died in 1734, however, without legitimate issue and was succeeded by an imbecile brother (d. 1762).[39]

The sister of the last Newport earls of Bradford married Orlando Bridgeman in 1719. Their son Henry (d. 1800) inherited Weston Park (Staffs.) after his uncle's death in 1762 and was created Baron Bradford in 1794. His son Orlando was created earl of Bradford in 1815.[40] The Bridgemans had Lancashire property which served to further their parliamentary ambitions there,[41] but in Shropshire their interest in no way matched that which the Newports had wielded. Those Bridgemans who obtained Shropshire seats secured them by patronage in the boroughs; not until 1842 did a Bridgeman sit for the county. The reason was that the Bridgemans, though owning estates round Knockin and Ness since the 1670s,[42] acquired only part of the Newports' lands, the bulk of which passed away from the legitimate heirs: the 3rd earl of Bradford left them to his bastard John Harrison (later Newport) with remainder to Harrison's mother Anne Smyth.[43] John Newport died in 1783,[44] having been a lunatic for over forty years. His mother had died in 1742 leaving the reversion of the estates to her former lover, the miserly and unscrupulous William Pulteney, earl of Bath.[45] The Pulteney interest, however, was little regarded, even in Shrewsbury, before the 1770s. Bath died in 1764, his brother and heir Gen. Harry Pulteney three years later. Their property then passed to their cousin's daughter, William Johnstone's

[35] Hist. Parl., Commons, 1715-54, i. 308; ii. 294.
[36] D.N.B.
[37] Ibid.
[38] See p. 359.
[39] Hist. Parl., Commons, 1715-54, ii. 294.
[40] Complete Peerage, ii. 275-6; V.C.H. Staffs. iv. 173.
[41] V.C.H. Lancs. ii. 232, 358; v. 35, 184-5, 238 n. 25, 247-8, 259; Hist. Parl., Commons, 1754-90, i. 321-2; ii. 117-8.
[42] T.S.A.S. 3rd ser. ii. 1, 21.
[43] Prob. 11/669 ff. 25v.-28v. (P.C.C. 4 Ducie); Harrison Change of Name Act, 1736, 9 Geo. II, c. 1 (Private, not printed).
[44] Gent. Mag. liii. 452.
[45] Ibid. xii. 602-3; Prob. 11/722 (P.C.C. 337 Trenley); Sir L. Namier, Structure of Politics at the Accession of Geo. III (1961), 258, 262; Hist. Parl., Commons, 1715-54, ii. 294, 376. A few weeks before Mrs. Smyth's death Phillips Gybbon, a political ally (ibid. 93) of Pulteney (who was to be John Newport's trustee), and Ben. Bathurst procured the passage of the Marriages of Lunatics Act, 1742, 15 Geo. II, c. 30, forbidding lunatics to marry: C.J. xxiv. 262, 268, 278, 280-1, 288, 334.

wife.[46] Johnstone took the name Pulteney and, by promoting the cause of the Shrewsbury freemen against the Whig corporation, became M.P. for the borough in 1775 and sat for thirty years. He had no appreciable interest in the county. He died in 1805, and soon after the death of his daughter Lady Bath (1808), the estates were split up, some passing to the earl of Darlington.[47]

The 3rd earl of Bradford was succeeded as lieutenant, and eventually as the county's most influential peer, by H. A. Herbert of Oakly Park near Ludlow. Herbert was related to the Barons Herbert of Chirbury whose title, having become extinct in 1691 and again (after a second creation) in 1738, was re-created for him in 1743.[48] In Montgomeryshire another Herbert line had held Red (later Powis) Castle and Powisland since 1587. The barons, earls, and marquesses of Powis of that line had been royalist, Cavalier, and then Jacobite until the 2nd marquess was restored to his estates in 1722. In 1748 the 3rd marquess died, leaving his estates to his distant kinsman Lord Herbert, who was created earl of Powis two months later and married his benefactor's niece in 1751.[49] Powis never wielded a decisive influence in county elections; though he frustrated the hopes of a Whig candidate for the county in 1766, he was able to do so only in alliance with the Tory squires. Nevertheless Powis was as firm a Whig as the earls of Bradford had been and in George II's last years was the recognized leader of those independent men, 'the Shropshire Whigs', in their dealings with the Whig ministries of the day.[50] His leading position was not without challenge or interruption by richer peers or those with greater ministerial connexions; from 1761 to 1764 he lost the lieutenancy to Lord Bath, who had been promised it by Bute,[51] and at much the same time two possessors of a new kind of wealth returned enriched by service in India.

Of the two nabobs who made a place for themselves in Shropshire politics only Robert Clive founded a lasting and widespread political interest in the county.[52] Sir George Pigot, who bought Patshull (Staffs.) in 1765, contented himself with his mistresses and with a seat at Bridgnorth. The convenient dignity of an Irish peerage (1766) allowed Pigot (like Clive) to remain in the Commons: he and his brother sat for the borough successively from 1768 to 1784, but the Pigots' interest, though felt in Stafford,[53] extended nowhere in Shropshire beyond Bridgnorth. A later Pigot sat for Bridgnorth 1832-52,[54] but the Pigots' interest ended when Patshull was sold in 1848.[55]

The Clives of Styche were country gentlemen of long pedigree[56] but modest income: the proconsul's father Richard, great-grandson of the Parliamentarian soldier Robert Clive, practised law in London.[57] On his first return from India (1753-5) Robert Clive made no attempt to establish a political position in Shropshire, though he spent much money on a Cornish borough for which he was unseated.[58] By the time he left India for the second time, in 1760, he had accumulated a fortune of almost £300,000. Besides that he had acquired a *jagir* of £27,000 a year in 1759, the emolument of a sinecure granted him by the Mogul emperor.[59] He was in England again from July 1760 to June 1764, and Lord Powis introduced him to the corporation of Shrewsbury. He

[46] *Complete Peerage*, ii. 23–4.
[47] Ibid. 27–8; S.R.O. 1045/358, 500–4; Loton Hall MSS., Sir B. Leighton's diary, 24 Oct. 1848.
[48] *Complete Peerage*, vi. 443–4; below, p. 359.
[49] *Complete Peerage*, x. 643–51; Namier, *Politics at Accession of Geo. III*, 279.
[50] Namier, op. cit. 235–6, 248–54. Their independence is well illustrated by an important vote in which the only Salop. M.P. to support the (Whig) ministry was a Tory, the 8 Whigs present voting with the opposition: Linda J. Colley, 'The Mitchell Election Division, 24 Mar. 1755', *Bull. Inst. Hist. Res.* xlix. 94.

[51] Namier, op. cit. 237, 261, 280–2.
[52] Ibid. 238, 244–5.
[53] *Hist. Parl., Commons, 1754–90*, iii. 279–81; *D.N.B.*; *S.H.C.* 1920 and 1922, 294.
[54] See pp. 331–4.   [55] *V.C.H. Staffs.* xvii. 20.
[56] *Visit. Salop. 1623*, i. 121–5; S.R.O. 1635/1–2.
[57] *Hist. Parl., Commons, 1754–90*, ii. 224; above, p. 251.
[58] *Hist. Parl., Commons, 1754–90*, i. 234; ii. 225; Lucy S. Sutherland, *E. India Co. in Eighteenth-Cent. Politics* (1952), 85; *Bull. Inst. Hist. Res.* xlix. 80–107.
[59] *Hist. Parl., Commons, 1754–90*, ii. 225; Namier, *Politics at Accession of Geo. III*, 289–90, 292–4.

rented Condover Hall near by and sat for Shrewsbury from 1760 until his death. Clive's purchase of Walcot and other near-by estates in the 1760s gave him two seats at Bishop's Castle,[60] while his purchase of Oakly Park from Powis about 1769 brought him an interest in Ludlow, where the Herberts and Clives continued to co-operate.[61] Clive had ambitions for the county too, and in 1766 the ageing Powis saw him as the successor to his position in Shropshire.[62] The two interests did in the end coalesce, though only after the deaths of Powis (1772) and Clive (1774). In 1784 the 2nd Lord Clive married the 2nd earl of Powis's only sister. Powis died unmarried in 1801 and his estates passed into the family of his brother-in-law, for whom the earldom of Powis was re-created in 1804.[63] The political leadership in Shropshire built up by the 1st earl of Powis thus survived virtually intact, undisturbed by these dynastic events. In Shrewsbury, it is true, there was a successful challenge from William Pulteney, and Powis's successors failed to maintain the Whig corporation ascendancy over which he had presided as recorder. Nevertheless the Herberts and Clives monopolized the lieutenancy from 1764 to 1839[64] and the subjection of Ludlow and Bishop's Castle continued almost uninterruptedly until the end of the period.

Shropshire

The county was represented by two Cavaliers in 1660 and 1661. Within twenty years, however, divisions among the gentry were apparent, and between 1695 and 1727 there were at least eight polls, the usual result being a division of the seats between Whig and Tory. In their years of country-wide success, however, the parties were able to take both seats: the Whigs did so in 1679 (twice), 1681, 1708, and 1715, the Tories in 1685 and 1710. From 1722 the Tories monopolized both seats for over eighty years, an achievement facilitated by the collapse of the Newport interest in 1734. The gentry families acquired fixed hereditary attitudes, and no single aristocratic interest replaced that of the Newports. From 1749 the Whigs left both county seats to the Tories. The compromise was convenient, and a Whig who threatened it by canvassing in 1766 obtained no support from the leading Whig peers. The two Whig candidates in 1831 polled badly.

Sir Henry Vernon and Sir William Whitmore, the members in the Convention, and Sir Francis Lawley (Whitmore's brother-in-law) and Sir Richard Ottley, the knights of the shire returned to the Cavalier Parliament, were all zealous young royalists. In 1660 the M.P.s happened to represent the north and south of the county; Whitmore was the only member of his family to sit for the county, Vernon the third and last of his.[65] Ottley died in 1670 and at the by-election a Newport candidate emerged. Lord Newport's son Richard, a minor in 1661, began a representation of the county which endured for the rest of that Parliament (1670-9) and six of the seven ensuing ones (1679-81, 1689-98).[66] By 1677 he had become a firm Country M.P., though his father was still counted a Court supporter. In his change of politics Richard Newport was the forerunner of his family, who soon afterwards took up the leadership of the Shropshire Whigs.[67]

The county moved in the same political direction, for at both general elections of 1679 and again in 1681 it chose two Whigs. Sir Francis Lawley, a placeman and a

---

[60] Namier, op. cit. 290–1, 294.
[61] See p. 288.
[62] India Office Libr., MS. Eur. G. 37/40, Powis to Clive, – May 1766.
[63] Burke, *Peerage* (1949), 1631.
[64] See pp. 359–60.
[65] *T.S.A.S.* 4th ser. xi. 38–9, 184; xii. 1–2; above, p. 239. Vernon lived at Hodnet, Whitmore at Apley Pk.
[66] *T.S.A.S.* 4th ser. xii. 2–3, 6. From 1694, when his father was cr. earl of Bradford, he was known as Ld. Newport.
[67] K. H. D. Haley, 'Shaftesbury's Lists of the Lay Peers and Members of the Commons, 1677–8', *Bull. Inst. Hist. Res.* xliii. 94, 100; above, p. 254.

strong Court M.P., did not stand for the county after the dissolution of the Cavalier Parliament, seeking a seat at Much Wenlock instead.[68] Newport was returned with Sir Vincent Corbet of Moreton[69] at both 1679 elections,[70] though on the second occasion they were not in coalition.[71] Corbet's death in 1681,[72] shortly before the election, opened the way for William Leveson-Gower, Newport's second cousin. Leveson-Gower was a recent, and temporary, convert to Whiggism and in 1683 was to become one of Monmouth's sureties.[73] There was 'a private election amongst the gentlemen of the county' who chose Newport and Leveson-Gower, but Sir John Corbet and a Mr. Leighton of Wattlesborough thought 'to set their votes together to oppose Mr. Gower' and Leighton canvassed around Westbury; in the end, however, finding themselves too weak, they desisted.[74] The prior meeting of the county gentlemen, a procedure invariably followed for two centuries thereafter,[75] is the earliest of its kind known in the county, as is the canvass by Corbet and Leighton. Charles II called no more Parliaments, and the Court's triumph after 1681 led Sir Uvedale Corbett and others to form a club for the maintenance of Whig principles in 1684; it met quarterly and, still known as Sir Uvedale Corbett's Club, ceased to exist soon after its centenary meeting on 2 August 1784.[76]

In 1685 the Newport control was broken, though for one Parliament only. Two Tories, Edward Kynaston of Oteley and John Walcot of Walcot, were returned. Both, as deputy lieutenants, had hounded the Whig suspects of 1683, among them William Leveson-Gower.[77] Kynaston was later a Jacobite,[78] but in 1688 Walcot earned his contemporaries' regard by his conscientious refusal to support James II and Jeffreys in their attempts to repeal the penal laws and the tests.[79]

Throughout William III's reign the county returned one Whig and one Tory. A county meeting as early as September 1688 had expected Newport's return to sit with Kynaston,[80] as indeed happened in January 1689 and at the next two general elections (1690 and 1695). The earliest county poll in Shropshire of which record has been found took place in 1695,[81] and that election was also notable for a first attempt by the Herbert interest to influence the representation of the county. Francis Herbert of Oakly Park, who had sat for Ludlow in the 1689 Convention, was at law with his uncle's widow Lady Herbert; she was Newport's sister, and Herbert's family dispute 'stirred him up to oppose Lord Newport's being made knight of the shire'. He won the support of several gentlemen for his 'faction' but a 'composition' was made and before the end of October Herbert withdrew.[82] Nevertheless on 7 November there was a poll, for a second Whig appeared in Sir Edward Leighton, who had failed to get in for Shrewsbury.[83] The poll was oddly low: 281 votes for Newport, 157 for Kynaston, and 147 for Leighton. Leading gentlemen split their votes between Newport and Kynaston, and it was votes from lower down the social scale which brought Leighton so near to success. All but 8 of the 56 plumpers supported Newport and Kynaston in roughly equal numbers.[84]

[68] *Bull. Inst. Hist. Res.* xliii. 100; below, p. 291.
[69] J. R. Jones, 'Shaftesbury's "Worthy Men": a Whig View of the Parl. of 1679', *Bull. Inst. Hist. Res.* xxx. 239.
[70] *T.S.A.S.* 4th ser. xii. 3.
[71] Suggested by Longleat MSS., Thynne Papers, xx, f. 376. Refs. to these papers were supplied by Mr. J. B. Lawson of Shrews. Sch.
[72] S.R.O. 2960/1/1.
[73] *T.S.A.S.* 4th ser. xii. 3-4; *S.H.C.* 1920 and 1922, 127-8, 135, 247-8; *Bull. Inst. Hist. Res.* xliii. 101.
[74] Longleat MSS., Thynne Papers, xxi, f. 219.
[75] See p. 323.
[76] Owen and Blakeway, *Hist. Shrews.* i. 584.
[77] *Cal. S.P. Dom.* July-Sept. 1683, 18, 105.

[78] *T.S.A.S.* 4th ser. xii. 4-5.
[79] Ibid. 5-6, *xvi*; J. R. Burton, *Some Collections Towards Hist. of Fam. of Walcot of Walcot* (Shrews. priv. print. 1930), 58-60.
[80] P.R.O. 30/53/8 f. 123.
[81] *T.S.A.S.* 4th ser. xii. 6. Cf. above, pp. 234, 251.
[82] Surr. R.O., Acc. 775. A3, Somers MSS., Rob. Harley to Sir John Somers, 29 Oct. 1695; B.L. Add. MS. 29578, ff. 529, 531; *Complete Peerage*, vi. 443.
[83] See p. 266.
[84] *T.S.A.S.* 4th ser. xii. 6; Bodl. MS. Blakeway 1, ff. 202-203v.; Loton Hall MSS., 'A Poll of the Freeholders for the Co. of Salop. . . . 7th day of Nov. 1695 . . .'. All give slightly different figs.

The division between Whig and Tory continued. In 1698 Leighton succeeded New-port and in 1699 the dead Kynaston was replaced by another Tory, Robert Lloyd of Aston. Finally in January 1701 Leighton retired and was replaced by another Whig, Sir Humphrey Briggs. Battle was fully joined only in December 1701 when there appeared two Tories, Robert Lloyd and Richard Owen, and three Whigs, Richard Corbet of Moreton, Sir Humphrey Briggs, and the Hon. Gervase Pierrepont. Corbet headed the poll and Lloyd came second, though Pierrepont's 255 votes may have robbed the Whigs of the second seat.[85] As it was the first county contest with more than three candidates, the question of coalitions between candidates became a thorny issue. It caused great concern to one Whig, John Bridgeman, for Corbet and Lloyd had married his sisters. Bridgeman, who had given all his interest to Lloyd at the two previous elections, now determined to divide it between Lloyd and Corbet; Lloyd, however, was seeking votes for Owen as well as himself. Corbet, who had stood only at very short notice and at Lord Newport's instance, did not coalesce with Briggs but Newport sought votes for them both. Bridgeman wrote: 'If asked for my interest for Mr. Owen I am not yet resolved as to that point, for I am but little acquainted with him and I am for hearing the sentiments of the gentlemen of him before I give an answer'. He could see the factions already forming and feared to be asked at this election for his interest for either set of coalesced candidates at the next.[86] That did not happen, for in 1702, at the first general election of Anne's reign, the contest, as in 1695, was three-cornered. Again one of each party was elected: the Tory Roger Owen of Condover at the head of the poll and the Whig Richard Corbet. Lloyd was defeated.[87]

The 1705 election was compromised, and Robert Lloyd returned to sit with a staunch Whig, Sir Robert Corbet of Adderley.[88] Three years later Lord Newport's son Henry replaced Lloyd, so that for the first time since 1681 the county returned two Whigs; both voted against Dr. Sacheverell.[89] The 1710 election saw the largest poll yet for the county. Two Tories declared themselves in July:[90] John Kynaston of Hordley, M.P. for Shrewsbury in seven Parliaments (1695-1709),[91] and Robert Lloyd of Aston, Sacheverell's patron and former pupil, who had just succeeded to his father's estates at the age of 22. For the Whigs Henry, Lord Newport,[92] stood again with Richard Corbet; he had in fact begun making interest even earlier than the two Tories, though receiving 'very cold answers from some of his old friends'.[93] The Newport interest exerted itself to the utmost, but the influence of Sacheverell's visit and the activities of Richard Cresswell of Bridgnorth, especially in sending circulars to the clergy,[94] prevailed. Kynaston and Lloyd were elected; Corbet, who had headed the poll in December 1701, came bottom in 1710.[95] The county election was held after all the borough elections, and in the last few days the energies of many gentlemen were concentrated on it. Charles Baldwyn of Aqualate (Staffs.) wrote gleefully that 'there went above 50 clergymen together in a body into the field who all voted for Kynaston and Lloyd; 'twas a very fine sight'. The bringing in of freeholders was organized by areas. The Baldwyn brothers brought in those from Newport, among whom the Tories had a majority.[96]

Lloyd retired in 1713. Kynaston joined with a second Tory candidate, Sir John

[85] *T.S.A.S.* 4th ser. xii. 6-7; N.L.W., Aston Hall 4402.
[86] Weston Hall, Sir John Bridgeman's letter bks., no. 8.
[87] *T.S.A.S.* 4th ser. xii. 8; N.L.W., Aston Hall 4403-4.
[88] For this para. see *T.S.A.S.* 4th ser. xii. 9-11.
[89] See sources referred to below, p. 277, n. 92.
[90] Lincs. R.O., Monson MSS. 7/13/124; N.L.W., Ottley Papers 2567.

[91] See p. 266.
[92] So known since his grandfather's death in 1708: Weston Hall, Sir J. Bridgeman's letter bks., no. 4, f. 26.
[93] N.L.W., Ottley Papers 2567.
[94] Lincs. R.O., Monson MSS. 7/13/124.
[95] N.L.W., Aston Hall 4405.
[96] *T.S.A.S.* 4th ser. xii. 7, 10; N.L.W., Ottley Papers 2581, 2584.

Astley who had acquired an interest in the Prince family's estates by his marriage to Mary Prince in 1709. The Whigs put up only Lord Newport[97] who failed to persuade Sir John Bridgeman to join him.[98] Newport thought it necessary to deny Tory allegations that in 1710 he had said he would give money to build a bawdy house but none to build a church.[99] It was perhaps that denial which Bridgeman ordered his bailiffs of Knockin and Ness to show to the freeholders in their bailiwicks, adding: 'tell them that I desire they will read it and assure them that I believe the truth of it'.[1] In a slightly lower poll than in 1710 Newport and Kynaston were elected, narrowly defeating Astley.[2]

Within three weeks of Queen Anne's death Newport again asked Bridgeman to stand with him. Instead Bridgeman tried to compromise the county's 'unhappy differences' by asking his Tory nephew Robert Lloyd to join Newport and thus avoid a contest. Lloyd refused, but did agree to stand 'on his own bottom' and not join Kynaston. Bridgeman hoped that a general meeting of gentlemen proposed by Newport would compromise the election,[3] but party feeling was too strong. In the end Kynaston stood alone for the Tories, but was beaten by Newport and a second Whig, Sir Robert Corbet. The poll was slightly lower than in 1713. The pattern for the rest of the century was set by the 1722 election when John Kynaston and Robert Lloyd were returned, beating the sitting Whigs. The poll was the highest known before 1832. Newport himself came bottom, and next year he succeeded as 3rd earl of Bradford.[4]

The 1727 poll was the last before 1831, but no record of the numbers is known. A new generation of Tories had arisen, and the candidates were William Lacon Childe of Kinlet and John Walcot of Walcot, grandson of a Tory knight of the shire (1685-7) and already burdened with debt. The earliest known extant printed handbill for a Shropshire county election, dated 13 July 1727, shows the Whigs in some indecision. A caucus of eighteen gentlemen including Sir John Bridgeman, H. A. Herbert, William Forester, Bromwich Pope, George Weld, and Richard Whitmore, sought support again for Sir Robert Corbet and 'such other gentleman as the majority of our friends shall agree to set up'. Even so the Tories did not spare their efforts. Walcot and Childe canvassed for six weeks and were said to have made 'personal application' to every freeholder in the county. They were returned, and a petition alleging malpractice in the delivery of the election writ failed to unseat them.[5]

At the next general election Walcot and Childe refused to stand. In March 1734, before the dissolution, they told their friends at the Shropshire Club in London of their decision; at the same time they proposed to the club that Sir John Astley, beaten in 1713, and Corbet Kynaston of Hordley were 'proper persons to succeed'.[6] Kynaston, a strong Jacobite and former Shrewsbury M.P., was the eldest son of the Tory knight of the shire 1710-15 and 1722-7; on his father's death a few months earlier he had succeeded to some £8,000 a year.[7] A general meeting of the county gentlemen was necessary to confirm the new Tory candidates.[8] The Whigs, as in 1727, were uncertain about contesting more than one seat. Newcastle was told that the Shropshire Whigs

[97] *T.S.A.S.* 4th ser. viii. 95, 122; xii. 12, 14; Owen and Blakeway, *Hist. Shrews.* ii. 140.
[98] Staffs. R.O., D.1287/10/4a, Newport to Bridgeman, 3 Dec. 1712; Weston Hall, Sir J. Bridgeman's letter bks., no. 4, f. 65.
[99] *Declarations of Ld. Newport and other Gentlemen in Answer to a Scandalous Report* . . . ([1713]; copy in Staffs. R.O., D.1287/10/4a).
[1] Weston Hall, Sir J. Bridgeman's letter bks., no. 4, f. 72.
[2] *T.S.A.S.* 4th ser. xii. 12; S.R.O. 177/1, p. 50; *True Copy of Poll of Co. of Salop begun Sept. 17th, 1713* (1714;

copy in S.P.L., accession 407).
[3] Weston Hall, Sir J. Bridgeman's letter bks., no. 4, ff. 81–3.
[4] *T.S.A.S.* 4th ser. xii. 9, 12.
[5] Ibid. 12–13; 3rd ser. viii. 136; Bodl. MS. Eng. Misc. e. 344, f. 82; N.L.W., Ottley Papers 2750.
[6] N.L.W., Ottley Papers 2354.
[7] *T.S.A.S.* 2nd ser. vi. 217–19, 336–9; 4th ser. xii. 14–15.
[8] N.L.W., Ottley Papers 2354. It was held 26 Mar., during the assizes.

hoped to find one candidate, and Sir Humphrey Briggs hoped that two Whigs might be returned if Lord Bradford could be persuaded to help; it was said that Bradford's mother had offered 'to be at £3,000 expense on the Whig side'.[9] The Tories, however, were unopposed.[10]

Kynaston died burdened with debt in 1740 and the family interest was split up.[11] His death enabled Shropshire to be represented for the next 25 years by as fine a pair of Tory squires as ever adorned the representation of an English county, for Astley's new colleague was Richard Lyster of Rowton. Like Kynaston, Lyster had sat for Shrewsbury, and both had suffered from the 1723 decision of a Whig House of Commons on the Shrewsbury election petition.[12] Neither Astley nor Lyster was replaced during his lifetime.

The Shropshire Whigs were in disarray by the middle of the century. The 3rd earl of Bradford had died soon after the 1734 election, his mother in 1737.[13] H. A. Herbert, created Lord Herbert of Chirbury in 1743 and earl of Powis in 1748, never enjoyed any influence in county elections comparable to that of the earls of Bradford.[14] In 1749 a compromise left the county seats to the Tory squires and the Shrewsbury seats to the Whigs.[15]

In January 1766 Richard Lyster was rumoured to be dying.[16] Sir Henry Bridgeman, nephew of the last two earls of Bradford and M.P. for Ludlow on the Powis interest, resolved to attempt the county for the Old Whigs.[17] He and his agents, of whom the eminent Shrewsbury attorneys Robert Pemberton[18] and John Ashby[19] were the chief, went to great lengths to canvass the county.[20] The chief landowners, the magistrates,[21] and others with interest[22] were listed, and two hundred or more letters were written, some to persons who claimed very little interest.[23] 'Circulating letters' were prepared for individual freeholders and meetings were held in propitious places.[24] Support for Bridgeman was by no means negligible, one list showing 58 landowners in his favour; notable among his supporters were Brooke ('the Stag') Forester and his son George. At the general meeting in Shrewsbury on 25 April, four days after Lyster's burial, eighty or more gentlemen attended to support Bridgeman,[25] but Charles Baldwyn of Aqualate, a leading magistrate and son-in-law of William Lacon Childe, knight of the shire 1727–34, had been equally active in canvassing,[26] though there are hints of his meanness with money. No general comparison of strengths is possible, but it is clear that most of the gentry supported Baldwyn. At the meeting Brooke Forester had to admit that Bridgeman did not have a majority,[27] and Ashby concluded that Bridgeman had no option but a 'well concerted retreat upon full notice to the county gentlemen' and a declaration to stand for the county at the next general election.[28] The result of so much hard work had been 802, possibly 848, promises for Bridgeman,

9 B.L. Add. MS. 32688, f. 187v.
10 T.S.A.S. 4th ser. xii. 14.
11 Ibid. 15.
12 Ibid. 16–17; Namier, Politics at Accession of Geo. III, 239–40.
13 Complete Peerage, ii. 274–5.
14 Namier, Politics at Accession of Geo. III, 235–6, 238–9, 279.
15 Camd. Misc. xxiii (Camd. 4th ser. vii), 150; below, p. 268.
16 India Office Libr., MS. Eur. G. 37/40, Ld. Powis to Ld. Clive, May 1766.
17 India Office Libr., MS. Eur. G. 37/39, Sir Hen. Bridgeman to Ric. Clive, 13 Apr. 1766. For the Old Whigs see below and n. 45.
18 Blakeway, Sheriffs, 192; R. C. B. Pemberton, Pemberton Pedigrees (Bedford, 1923), chart 16. His elder bro. and elder son were chmn. of q. sess. 1785–97 and 1822–30 respectively: below, p. 360.
19 T.S.A.S. lix. 53–62.

20 For this and the next two paras. see Staffs. R.O., D.1287/10/4b.
21 Numbering 247 without the privy councillors, etc.
22 e.g. over 500 land-tax commissioners, 53 officers and supervisors of the excise.
23 See e.g. ibid., Rob. More (19 Mar. 1766), Ed. Moreton (28 Mar. 1766), and Ld. Stamford (28 Apr. 1766) to Sir H. Bridgeman.
24 Inns in Oswestry, Llanymynech, Worthen, and Broseley.
25 Ibid., Thos. Hill to [Sir H. Bridgeman], 27 Apr. 1766; ibid., bk. of signatures of Bridgeman's supporters; S.P.R. Heref. vii. 447.
26 Staffs. R.O., D.(W.)1788, P. 45, B. 11, list of freeholders canvassed; above, pp. 118–19, 259.
27 Staffs. R.O., D.1287/10/4b, draft letter beginning 'Distribute the enclosed as soon as possible . . .', n.d.
28 Ibid., Ashby to John Heaton, 29 Apr. 1766.

rather unevenly distributed through the county, though with concentrations in the north-west,[29] in Shrewsbury,[30] and around Wellington and Much Wenlock.[31] Bridgeman, however, who had remained in London throughout,[32] knew the much higher numbers of votes in some earlier polls and could see that his forces were inadequate. He was in fact nominated at the general meeting[33] but was under pressure from Lord Powis to resign his Ludlow seat[34] and on 1 May he withdrew from the county contest.[35] Baldwyn was returned unopposed to display in the Commons for the next fourteen years the talents of a 'puzzle-headed' Tory country gentleman.[36]

The sources of Bridgeman's weakness had been many. He did not dispose of the old Newport interest, though he seems to have contemplated an attempt to set aside the 3rd earl of Bradford's will on the ground that he was 'as mad as a March hare' when he made it.[37] He had almost no lords among his supporters. Only an Irish peer (Pigot) and a Welsh bishop (St. Asaph) were for him.[38] Lord Craven, as a Tory,[39] was naturally against him.[40] The Whig peers deserted to Baldwyn,[41] the most influential among them belonging to groups strongly opposed to the Rockingham Whigs on whose behalf Bridgeman had stood. Lord Gower, his brother-in-law the duke of Bridgwater, and Lord Weymouth were Bedford Whigs,[42] and Lord Lyttelton, a Grenvillite, also had family ties with the Bedford group.[43] Worse still for Bridgeman's prospects Powis and Lord Clive had separated themselves in Westminster politics from Newcastle[44] and the Rockingham Whigs,[45] a group with little or no influence in Shropshire politics thereafter.[46]

Powis found the whole affair deeply painful and was able to ruin any chance Bridgeman might have had.[47] According to Powis, Bridgeman had first sought his interest towards the end of 1764 but had never sought either his consent to the resignation of his Ludlow seat or his 'approbation' for an attempt on the county. Of their frigid interviews in London Powis complained that Bridgeman 'paid me no compliment of consultation or deference, and acted upon his own bottom, as a person detached and separated from me'. Powis had some grounds of complaint; he had, after all, given Bridgeman a seat at Ludlow and secured him a place worth £1,000 a year. Moreover the compromise with the Tories arranged in 1749 and approved by Powis seemed to be threatened by the response of the Whig gentlemen[48] to Bridgeman's applications.

Lyster's death came very inconveniently for Lord Clive who was in India 1764–6.[49] As his adviser John Walsh wrote to him, 'The mischief of this matter is that whoever

[29] Besides his own influence that of the Lloyds of Aston and the Myddeltons of Chirk (see also N.L.W., Chirk Castle C.56) was important to Bridgeman.
[30] Promises from 46 gentlemen and 93 tradesmen.
[31] Where the Foresters, Thos. Eyton, Edw. Cludde, Edw. Pemberton, and John Smitheman were active. There were promises of 'ten workmen in the Dale [who] will be directed by Mr. Reynolds'.
[32] Staffs. R.O., D.1287/10/4b, Ashby to Heaton, 29 Apr. 1766.
[33] Ibid., letter cited above, n. 27.
[34] Ibid., Powis to Bridgeman, 29 Apr. 1766.
[35] Circular letter in N.L.W., Chirk Castle C.56.
[36] Hist. Parl., Commons, 1754–90, ii. 44.
[37] Staffs. R.O., D.1287/10/4b, memoranda relating to execution of will of Hen., earl of Bradford, 27 Apr. 1766.
[38] Ibid., List of persons promising their Interest, Mar. 1766.
[39] Hist. Parl., Commons, 1754–90, ii. 275.
[40] Craven owned Stokesay, then tenanted by Baldwyn: J. F. A. Mason, Stokesay Castle [Derby, 1963].
[41] India Office Libr., MS. Eur. G. 37/40, ff. 16–17.
[42] Hist. Parl., Commons, 1754–90, iii. 39, 351; D.N.B.

sub Egerton, Fra., duke of Bridgewater; Staffs. R.O., D.1287/10/4b, S. J. Haynes to Bridgeman, 17 Apr. 1766.
[43] R. J. S. Hoffman, The Marquis: A Study of Ld. Rockingham, 1730–1782 (1973), 141, 144; Complete Peerage, viii. 310 note h. His bro. Sir Ric. had married Bedford's sis. and was thus Bridgwater's stepfather: ibid. ii. 313–14.
[44] Powis in 1762, Clive in 1763: Namier, Politics at Accession of Geo. III, 283–6, 293–8.
[45] For their connexion with Newcastle and the Old Whigs see F. O'Gorman, Rise of Party in Eng.: the Rockingham Whigs, 1760–82 (1975), 55–7, 113–17; Hoffman, The Marquis, 36 sqq.
[46] Brooke Forester e.g. was contemptuous of them as early as Mar. 1765: Lucy S. Sutherland, 'Edm. Burke and the First Rockingham Ministry', E.H.R. xlvii. 53 n. 4.
[47] For this para. see India Office Libr., MS. Eur. G. 37/40; above, p. 260; below, p. 288.
[48] Personally very displeasing to Powis in the cases of Forester and Whitmore: India Office Libr., MS. Eur. G. 37/40, Powis to Clive, — May 1766.
[49] D.N.B.

is elected will be a bar to your coming in for the county at the general election should you be so inclined'.[50] Clive's trustees were in a difficulty and, divided among themselves, determined on neutrality.[51] Clive's father explained to Bridgeman that his son's attorney had been instructed to join Lord Powis, Forester, and Whitmore 'in the Whig interest'; Powis, however, had been 'first named' and for that reason and because of the great friendship between Powis and the Clives, Richard Clive[52] thought his son's intention best fulfilled by support of Powis.[53]

Bridgeman was rumoured to be considering an attempt on the county in 1768, but in the event he found a safer seat at Much Wenlock.[54] In 1772, after Astley's death, Bridgeman again thought of seeking a county seat at a by-election. On that occasion, however, Brooke Forester was unwilling to back him,[55] and a county meeting chaired by Sir Rowland Hill chose Sir Watkin Williams Wynn. At the meeting there was an impassioned diatribe by Robert Pigott of Chetwynd, against an outsider[56] with 'a long list of lords' behind him. Pigott and Henry Powys, supporters of Bridgeman in 1766, tried to put forward Pigott's brother-in-law John Mytton of Halston. Eventually, however, Mytton agreed not to stand.[57] Bridgeman announced that he might stand at the general election, and got from Brooke Forester the wise advice to 'go as far as you can before you trust my Lord Powis'.[58] Sir Thomas Whitmore showed even more mistrust of Powis: 'Experience has shown that he can infuse a supineness into some Whigs which should be guarded against by gaining promises of support from those who might otherwise sleep on his pillow, and I fear active service can't be expected from him'. Whitmore also believed that experience showed the need for 'more than fair words' before 'the united interest of Bridgwater and Gower' could be relied on, and the Bridgwater interest would, he feared, 'come in but lame to the Whig side'.[59] For Bridgeman the 1772 by-election must have been particularly galling, for Sir Watkin was supported by William Pulteney who wielded the old Newport interest.[60]

The criticism of Sir Watkin's intrusion into Shropshire politics did not have to be repeated, for in 1774, at the first general election after he came of age, he was unopposed in Denbighshire where his family possessed the dominant interest.[61] The 1774 election opened a century during which, with intervals, the Hills controlled one of the county seats and vacancies were normally filled without dispute. Bridgeman took Brooke Forester's advice to 'stick to old Wenlock' and gave up all thoughts of the county.[62] The Foresters, Bridgeman, and other Whigs transferred their support to Noel Hill of Attingham, the retiring M.P. for Shrewsbury,[63] and Hill and Baldwyn were nominated unanimously.[64] Mytton refused to stand.[65] When, in 1780, increasing pressure of debt forced Baldwyn to retire, the Hills held both seats for one Parliament (1780–4), Noel Hill being joined by his second cousin Richard Hill who succeeded to Hawkstone and his father's baronetcy in 1783. The latter became one of the leading independent M.P.s; he was not only the traditional country gentleman in politics, but also the first prominent Evangelical to sit in the Commons, where he spoke with

[50] Hist. Parl., Commons, 1754–90, i. 361.
[51] Ibid.; India Office Libr., MS. Eur. G. 37/39, Clive trustees to Thos. Wingfield, 17 Apr. 1766.
[52] M.P. for Montgomery on the Powis interest.
[53] MS. Eur. G. 37/39, Ric. Clive to [Sir H. Bridgeman], 14 Apr. 1766.
[54] Hist. Parl., Commons, 1754–90, ii. 117; below, p. 295.
[55] Staffs. R.O., D.1287/10/4a, the Revd. John Jones (4 Feb. 1772) and Brooke Forester (8 Feb. 1772), to Sir H. Bridgeman.
[56] But see below, pp. 294, 295 sqq.
[57] Staffs. R.O., D.1287/10/4a, Jones (13 Feb. 1772) and Brooke Forester (21 Feb. 1772) to Bridgeman.
[58] Ibid., Sir H. Bridgeman to Brooke Forester, 29 Feb. 1772 (enclosing copy of advertisement); Forester to Bridgeman, 4 Mar. 1772.
[59] Ibid., Whitmore to Bridgeman, 9 Mar. 1772.
[60] Bodl. MS. Top. Salop. c. 3, f. 50.
[61] Hist. Parl., Commons, 1754–90, i. 463; iii. 671–2.
[62] Staffs. R.O., D.1287/10/4a, Forester to Bridgeman, 2 Mar. 1774.
[63] Ibid., Brooke Forester to Sir H. Bridgeman (3 Apr. 1774) and Bridgeman's reply (5 Apr.), Geo. Forester to —, 22 Apr. 1774; S.R.O. 112, N. Hill's letter bk. 1774; below, p. 269.
[64] Shrews. Chron. 3 and 10 Sept. 1774.
[65] Ibid. 6 Aug. 1774.

some frequency but little success. Both Hills were firm Pittites. Noel Hill retired in 1784 on the promise of a peerage, his creation as Lord Berwick giving some offence to Sir Richard.[66]

During the remaining fifty years before 1832 changes were few. Hill and another Tory, John Kynaston (later Kynaston Powell) of Hardwick, sat together from 1784 to 1806 when Hill retired. Kynaston Powell (cr. bt. 1818) and John Cotes[67] of Woodcote sat from 1806 to 1821. The young Rowland Hill (who succeeded his grandfather as 4th baronet in 1824) and John Cressett Pelham of Cound succeeded Cotes and Kynaston Powell on their respective deaths in 1821 and 1822.[68] But such stability was not achieved without alarms. Kynaston Powell put forward a claim to the barony of Grey of Powis in 1800; had it been successful, the claim would have vacated his seat, for which Sir Corbet Corbet of Adderley and Richard Lyster of Rowton were potential candidates.[69] In 1806 Sir Richard Hill hoped to be succeeded by his nephew Col. John Hill, but his interest was sought by Cotes who claimed to have the support of Lord Bradford and others. Hill therefore gave his interest to Cotes to preserve 'the peace of the county'.[70] Corbet challenged Cotes for the succession and began to canvass, but Cotes had a preponderance of interest and Corbet retired at the county meeting after securing Cotes's assent to face-saving remarks.[71] Bradford's tenants around Knockin all showed 'the greatest readiness' to meet their landlord's wishes at the election and many who were independent of him 'showed equal readiness'.[72] Bradford's influence at the time was enhanced by his militia colonelcy.[73] In 1821 Rowland Hill seems to have replaced Cotes without difficulty[74] but a year later, on Kynaston Powell's death, three candidates emerged: William Lloyd of Aston, who was regarded as a Whig and had been laying plans since the previous November;[75] William Lacon Childe, then M.P. for Much Wenlock and regarded as an Ultra; and John Cressett Pelham, a less extreme Tory.[76] John Mytton offered Lloyd the goodwill he had gained on the hunting field but warned that it would cost £20,000 to contest the county.[77] In the end Lloyd and Childe withdrew.[78]

Thus the peace was endangered only at by-elections, when one seat was at issue. Not since 1727 had two sitting M.P.s been challenged at a general election. In 1831, however, during the excitement over the Reform Bill, there was at last a poll. At the end of 1830 John Watton, owner of the *Shrewsbury Chronicle*, had wanted a county meeting to demand Reform,[79] and next summer William Lloyd of Aston put in a late candidacy as a Whig.[80] Unfortunately for him John Mytton also stood as a Whig, and the notoriety of that sportsman's life[81] prevented Lloyd from coalescing with him.[82] The freeholders around Bridgnorth announced their support for Lloyd 'and any other respectable candidate advocating the measure of Reform',[83] and one supporter's wife wrote to Lloyd concerning Mytton that 'a *private reform* must be affected, ere I

[66] *Hist. Parl.*, *Commons*, 1754–90, i. 361; ii. 44–5, 623–5; *T.S.A.S.* lviii. 167–77.
[67] Sometimes referred to as a Whig (*T.S.A.S.* 4th ser. xii. 21) but he was too lukewarm and inactive to count as a party man: *Shrews. Chron.* 7 Sept. 1821; ex inf. Hist. of Parl.
[68] *T.S.A.S.* 4th ser. xii. 19–21.
[69] Ibid. 11, 20–1; *Complete Peerage*, vi. 142 note h, 697–701; S.R.O. 567, box 47, Rob. Corbett to —, [1800].
[70] Staffs. R.O., D.1287/10/4a, Sir Ric. Hill to Bradford, 27 Oct. 1806.
[71] Ibid., Hen. Wrottesley (28 Oct. 1806), John Simpson (5 Nov. 1806), and Thos. Eyton (9 Nov. 1806) to Bradford; *Corresp. of Geo.*, *Prince of Wales*, ed. A. Aspinall, vi (1969), 36.
[72] Staffs. R.O., D.1287/10/4a, Hen. Bowman to Bradford, 18 Nov. 1806.

[73] S.R.O. 190/25.
[74] *T.S.A.S.* 4th ser. xii. 21. Cf. *Shrews. Chron.* 19 Oct. 1821.
[75] N.L.W., Aston Hall corresp. 296, 460–1.
[76] Staffs. R.O., D.1287/10/4a, Ld. Forester to Wm. Lacon Childe, [? 29 Oct.] 1822; *T.S.A.S.* 4th ser. xii. 21–3; below, pp. 296–7.
[77] N.L.W., Aston Hall corresp. 991.
[78] Ibid. 527.
[79] Ibid. 1097.
[80] Ibid. 186.
[81] 'Nimrod' [C. J. Apperley], *The Life of John Mytton, Esq. of Halston* (1893 edn.), 77 sqq., 93–7; Sir B. Burke, *A Second Series of Vicissitudes of Families* (1860), 112–25.
[82] N.L.W., Aston Hall corresp. 5327.
[83] Printed handbill, 6 May 1831: scrapbk. *penes* the late H. L. Cunnington of Bridgnorth.

could think him capable of assisting in a public one'.[84] Lloyd had the support of Wol-ryche Whitmore of Dudmaston, through whom the Reform Fund sent £600 to assist the cause in Shropshire.[85] Unjustifiably sanguine as his campaign progressed, Lloyd forced Hill and Cressett Pelham to canvass hard,[86] but with sad results for himself. He expected to beat Cressett Pelham and indeed did so on the show; to his dis-appointment, however, he found Hill helping Cressett Pelham while Mytton was a mere hindrance to himself.[87] Hill clearly had much greater appeal than Cressett Pelham and polled many more plumpers, but 1,268 votes for Hill and Cressett Pelham were more than sufficient to put Lloyd badly into third place; only in Oswestry hundred and Bradford South did Lloyd poll better than Cressett Pelham.[88]

Shrewsbury

Shrewsbury was bitterly contested from 1677 by families which were also concerned with county politics. Some of its M.P.s went on to sit for the county, a promotion hardly ever accorded to M.P.s for the other boroughs. The political character of the borough's M.P.s came to depend on rival interpretations of the qualification for the franchise. A Whig House of Commons narrowed it in 1709, a Tory one widened it five years later. It was narrowed again by a Whig House in 1723 when the franchise, previously in the burgesses without limitation, was restricted to resident burgesses paying scot and lot. As a result the numbers voting fell from about 1,900 in 1722 to 400–500 in 1727 and 1734 and to even fewer in 1747, 1768, and 1774. A 1774 court decision, however, reversed the position, in effect extending the franchise to all burgesses assessed to the local rates. Numbers voting rose again and in 1826 and 1830 were over 1,000. The 1723 decision soon produced, as it was intended to do, a change in the representation; since 1679 the M.P.s had usually been Tories, but by 1749 there was a Whig majority among the electors.

Shrewsbury was notably less loyalist than the rest of the county in 1660, for the men it returned to the Convention were Samuel Jones of Berwick, a merchant who had sat in the 1656 Parliament, and his cousin Thomas Jones of Sandford, the town clerk.[89] Neither was a convinced royalist, and Thomas Jones was unacceptable to the new regime. Despite the corporation's decision in July 1660 to restore those of its members who had been excluded in 1645, the Presbyterians remained strong, and at first the Crown had little power to oppose to them; Thomas Jones was re-elected to Parliament in 1661, though with a royalist colleague, and he remained town clerk for two years after the Restoration despite the king's express wish to the contrary. Jones's influence during those years encouraged 'factious ministers', who rejected the Prayer Book, to preach 'boldly and seditiously'. It is clear too that he was an active opponent of the Crown. He tried to have one of the king's enemies made postmaster of Shrewsbury, an office with ample opportunity for espionage, and early in 1661 he was encouraging Maj. Edmund Waring, the former governor of Shrewsbury, to disregard his house arrest. At the end of 1661 Jones tried, with the help of the mayor, a fellow Presbyterian, to prevent the Corporation Act[90] from being enforced; he planned to fill vacancies among the aldermen and common councilmen with new men who could not have been purged under the Act, a design which was promptly thwarted by the deputy lieutenants.

[84] N.L.W., Aston Hall corresp. 1248.
[85] Ibid. 998.
[86] Ibid. 5326–8.   [87] Ibid. 5329.
[88] *Correct Alphab. List of Freeholders who voted . . . at Electn. for Co. of Salop. . . . May 9th, 1831, and following*

Days (Shrews. n.d.; copy in S.R.O. 310/8).
[89] For this para. and the next see *T.S.A.S.* 4th ser. xii. 215–17; Owen and Blakeway, *Hist. Shrews.* i. 479–84, 487, 534, 543–4; S.R.O. 3365/2713.
[90] 13 Chas. II, Stat. II, c. 1.

Shrewsbury provided ample occupation for the Corporation Act commissioners. In August and September 1662, headed by the lieutenant Lord Newport, they excluded 9 aldermen (including the deposed mayor) and 12 councilmen and arranged the appointment of 24 new aldermen and 48 new councilmen. Five officers were replaced and, after two attempts, Adam Ottley, brother of the chief deputy lieutenant, was made town clerk in Jones's place. The many vacancies eased the commissioners' work; the deputy lieutenants' action against Jones and the corporation in 1661 left the council barely at half strength. The government's determination to strengthen its Shrewsbury supporters remained clear: thirty burgesses were removed in October 1662 and March 1663, and in 1664 a new charter was prepared whose main object was to name the aldermen, councilmen, recorder, steward, and town clerk.

The purges of the 1660s must have contributed to the borough's predominantly Tory complexion after the beginning of parliamentary contests there in 1676. By then Jones was reconciled to the government; knighted in 1671, he was made a justice of King's Bench in April 1676.[91] The colleague elected with him in 1661, Robert Leighton of Wattlesborough, a royalist and once an intended knight of the Royal Oak, had moved in the opposite political direction and was a 'Country' M.P. by 1677.[92] Manoeuvrings to succeed Jones began on his promotion, though the by-election was not held until March 1677. According to Sir Richard Corbett the borough declared for him first, whereas Edward Kynaston of Hordley, who had a house at Albrightlee within the borough liberties, only declared a fortnight later and consequently could hope to make headway only 'by expense'.[93] The long-delayed poll lasted three days and about 1,600 voted.[94] A shrewd observer had thought that Kynaston, 'sure of the rabble party that wants money', would win unless Corbett could 'outwit the drinking party and prevail with the mayor to make a return'.[95] Corbett was elected; the mayor[96] had helped but Corbett's success in mobilizing new burgesses, including non-residents, had also counted for much. Each side was said to have spent at least £1,000,[97] though the contest had been personal rather than political. Kynaston was to become a Tory[98] and it was already clear that Corbett was a Court supporter too.[99]

Shrewsbury seems to have been uncontested in 1679 and 1681. Leighton stood aside and Corbett and Kynaston, the rivals of 1677, were returned on all three occasions.[1] The Newport interest was exerted on Corbett's behalf in 1679.[2] Corbett was an old opponent of the Country Party or Whigs but Kynaston's similar attitude was slower to emerge.[3]

Shrewsbury continued Tory for thirty years more. There remained, it is true, some disaffection. In 1683 George Weld wrote darkly to Secretary Jenkins that conventicles were 'winked at, if not countenanced'.[4] Nevertheless another royal reform of the corporation produced submissiveness and the return of two Tories to James II's only Parliament. The borough had surrendered its charter in 1684 and negotiated with Sir Thomas Jones, the former M.P., about a new one. It was in fact James II who issued the new one in March 1685. It fixed the aldermen and councilmen at 12 and 24, but its main purpose was to name the mayor, aldermen, and councilmen, a new recorder (the earl of Shrewsbury) and steward, and the town clerk (Thomas Edwardes),

[91] D.N.B.
[92] T.S.A.S. 4th ser. xii. 217; Bull. Inst. Hist. Res. xliii. 100.
[93] Cal. S.P. Dom. 1678, 34-6.
[94] S.P.L., MS. 286.
[95] Herbert Corresp. ed. W. J. Smith (1968), 227.
[96] A client of Corbett's uncle Ld. Newport: Owen and Blakeway, Hist. Shrews. i. 481, 485, 534.
[97] Cal. S.P. Dom. 1678, 34-6; C.J. ix. 482, 530; S.P.L.,

MS. 286. Parl. was dissolved before Kynaston's petition was heard.
[98] See below.
[99] Like Ld. Newport: Bull. Inst. Hist. Res. xliii. 94, 100.
[1] T.S.A.S. 4th ser. xii. 217-19.
[2] Longleat MSS., Thynne Papers, xx, f. 376.
[3] Bull. Inst. Hist. Res. xxx. 239.
[4] Cal. S.P. Dom. July-Sept. 1683, 301. Jenkins had lived in Salop. during the Interregnum: D.N.B.

and to empower the Crown to remove any of them or their successors. The aldermen named first were Edward Kynaston of Hordley and Sir Francis Edwardes, M.P.s for the borough in the 1685 Parliament[5] which was so favourable to the king. Edwardes was elected mayor at Michaelmas.

Shrewsbury spared no expense when James II visited it in August 1687 but, as elsewhere, the king's policies alienated even his supporters. In January 1688 James had to replace the recorder and steward, 5 of the aldermen, and 9 of the councilmen named less than three years earlier.[6] Six months later the government proposed Rowland Hunt of Boreatton, Edward Gosnell of Rossall (mayor 1682-3), and George Clive of Walford as suitable to represent the borough in Parliament;[7] all were of insignificant local standing. Sir Francis Edwardes and another Tory, Lord Newport's brother Andrew, were ready to stand in a September election, though in the event James never summoned another Parliament. Instead Edwardes and Newport were returned to the Convention early in 1689, apparently unopposed.

Of the next eleven elections before the Septennial Act[8] at least six were contested, often bitterly. There was a 'great poll' in 1690[9] when Andrew Newport and Richard Mytton of Halston won. John Kynaston, son of Edward Kynaston of Hordley and leader of the Shropshire Tories, came forward in 1695 and was returned with Newport; the Whig Sir Edward Leighton came forward late and was beaten.[10] John Kynaston and another Tory, Richard Mytton, son of the M.P. elected in 1690, were returned at the next six elections. In 1702 they were opposed by two Whigs, Thomas Jones of Carreghofa and William Prince; the former was Sir Edward Leighton's son-in-law and grandson of the M.P. from 1660 to 1676. In 1708 Sir Edward Leighton himself stood again, though he was ready to give way to Richard Corbet or to stand jointly with him.[11] What the Whig voters of Shrewsbury could not do was then achieved by a Whig House of Commons, for Leighton petitioned against Kynaston and Mytton on the grounds of 'bribery, menaces and other ill practices' by them and their agents and of the mayor's partiality.[12] He also alleged that the right of election was in the resident burgesses. In 1709 the Commons decided, despite evidence to the contrary, that the franchise was vested in the burgesses inhabiting the borough and suburbs, paying scot and lot and not in receipt of charity, though the borough and suburbs were not defined. Leighton was awarded one seat.[13] The other was filled in January 1710 at a by-election in which the Kynaston interest supported Edward Cressett of Cound, who was nevertheless beaten by Thomas Jones, the 1702 candidate, by 179 to 128.[14]

On 31 March 1710 and during the assizes there were demonstrations in the town in favour of Dr. Sacheverell,[15] who visited Shrewsbury in July and was received in triumph by the Tory candidates,[16] Cressett and Mytton, already in the field against two Whigs, Jones and Leighton. All were reported 'very busy', but it was thought that Leighton would 'give out'.[17] In October the Tories naturally won, even on the smaller electorate, and the Whigs did not even petition.[18]

Still the battle went on. In 1713 Mytton retired and two Tories, Cressett and the young Corbet Kynaston, stood against Thomas Jones. Cressett and Jones were

[5] Owen and Blakeway, *Hist. Shrews.* i. 492-4, 535; *T.S.A.S.* 4th ser. xii. 219. Thos. Edwardes had been town clk. since 1681: Owen and Blakeway, op. cit. i. 544; N.L.W., Castle Hill 13, 2175.

[6] Owen and Blakeway, op. cit. i. 497-8.

[7] G. Duckett, *Penal Laws and Test Act*, ii (1883), 185.

[8] 1 Geo. I, Stat. II, c. 38.

[9] N.L.W., MS. 11449E, no. 26.

[10] B.L. Loan 29/301.

[11] Weston Hall, Sir John Bridgeman's letter bks., no. 4.

[12] *C.J.* xvi. 14, 212.

[13] Ibid. 247-8.

[14] Weston Hall, Sir J. Bridgeman's letter bks., no. 4, f. 32.

[15] *A Letter to the . . . earl of Bradford* (published 6 May 1710; copy at Cornell Univ.).

[16] G. Holmes, *Trial of Dr. Sacheverell* (1973), 244, 245 n., 247.

[17] N.L.W., Ottley Papers 2567.

[18] *Case of the Sitting Members . . .* (1723).

returned, Jones's being the first Whig success at Shrewsbury in a general election. Both sides petitioned. Kynaston produced evidence of 21 returns by the burgesses at large since 1478; Jones maintained that the franchise lay in the resident burgesses paying scot and lot but could adduce only three returns in support of his case. A Tory House of Commons vested the franchise in the burgesses without limitation in May 1714; it also increased Kynaston's poll by over 90 out-burgesses' rejected votes and seated Kynaston in Jones's place. A separate petition against Cressett was dismissed.[19]

In 1715, the year in which the mob demolished the Shrewsbury Presbyterian meeting-house,[20] the election was compromised[21] after much 'foul play',[22] and Kynaston and Jones were returned. Jones soon died and was succeeded by Andrew Corbet of Moreton, who did not, however, take part in the great contest of 1722 but stood down in favour of his cousin Orlando Bridgeman, who was Lord Bradford's son-in-law. On the wider franchise the electors returned Corbet Kynaston and another Tory, Richard Lyster of Rowton, with 1,144 and 1,119 votes against 744 and 725 for two Whigs, Bridgeman and Sir Richard Corbett of Longnor.[23] The Whigs petitioned on the grounds of bribery and corruption. The Whigs themselves, however, had had the corporation's support and, according to the Tories, the mayor had admitted 138 burgesses, mostly foreigners and tenants of Lord Bradford, in the Whig interest and had held the election at the time of the assizes in hopes of a tumult which would justify the closure of the poll.[24] The Whig majority in the Commons restated the Whig decision of 1709 on the franchise but the parliamentary borough was reduced by the exclusion of the liberties and most of the suburbs. After an unusually complicated computation of the poll the two Whigs were seated in place of the Tories.[25] Perhaps it was to reduce the resultant unrest that dragoons were quartered in Shrewsbury for two years while Bridgeman and Corbett represented the borough.[26]

It seems extraordinary that after all these Whig endeavours all three candidates in 1727 should have been Tories. Orlando Bridgeman had intended to stand and a suggestion that he offer the mayor 'any sum he will accept of' to make enough burgesses to ensure success[27] shows the Whigs' dependence on corporation support. Bridgeman, however, gave up[28] and at the poll Corbet Kynaston was defeated by Lyster and Sir John Astley.[29]

Despite the Tory success in 1727 Shrewsbury passed thereafter wholly into the hands of the Whigs. The Whigs were considering candidates as early as October 1732.[30] William Kynaston of Ruyton-XI-Towns, a master in Chancery, and Sir Richard Corbett, M.P. 1723-7, had come forward by August 1733 when Newcastle's agent forecast their victory, 'the persons who brought mandamuses when admitted freemen being non-suited the last assizes';[31] some non-resident burgesses had evidently been denied the vote. Next year Corbett and Kynaston defeated Richard Lyster and John Mytton; eight companies of foot were stationed in the suburbs to support the corporation and overawe the Tories.[32] Lyster and Mytton petitioned, alleging partisan acceptance and refusal of votes by the mayor and that Kynaston's estate was insufficient to qualify him for membership of the Commons; nevertheless the petition was soon

[19] C.J. xvii. 479.
[20] Owen and Blakeway, Hist. Shrews. i. 504.
[21] Staffs. R.O., D.1287/10/4a, canvass in Maesbrook, etc. (Bridgeman country), yielding 30 promises for Jones, 2 for Jones and Kynaston.
[22] N.L.W., Ottley Papers 1631.
[23] Hist. Parl., Commons, 1715-54, i. 311-12, 487, 577; i. 183.
[24] T.S.A.S. xi. 204; Case of the Sitting Members ... (1723).
[25] C.J. xx. 190-4.

[26] S.R.O. 567, box 14, petition of Shrews. innkeepers to Corbett and Bridgeman, n.d.
[27] Staffs. R.O., D.1287/18/8, J. Hollings to O. Bridgeman, 23 July 1727.
[28] Ibid., D.1287/10/4a, John Bridgeman to Mrs. Williams, 30 Aug. 1727.
[29] T.S.A.S. 4th ser. xii. 12, 231.
[30] N.L.W., Ottley Papers 2375.
[31] B.L. Add. MS. 32688, f. 187v.
[32] T.S.A.S. 4th ser. iv. 66; S.P.L., Deeds 46.

dropped[33] and Lyster had to wait for a county seat. Kynaston and Corbett were unopposed in 1741 and beat Robert Pigott of Chetwynd and R. P. Astley, the 21-years-old son of the knight of the shire, in 1747; it was the last four-cornered contest for nearly ninety years. About 290 voted, 200 fewer than in 1727; only 7 split their votes. The second Whig was only 9 votes ahead of the first Tory. The growth of religious dissent in the town was one cause of the Whig successes, and a list was printed labelling many Whig voters as dissenters. According to their opponents the defeated candidates adopted 'notorious' practices to persuade many to vote 'against their old friends and principles' and many against 'promises just before made'.[34] Astley and Pigott petitioned, adding to the customary charges a new allegation, that the mayor had accepted the votes of paupers and of others in receipt of charity. The petition, however, was withdrawn.[35]

This situation clearly called for action and compromise. The Whig corporation set about ensuring a majority by striking out burgesses who could not prove freedom by descent and by manipulating parish assessments. Faced by the probability of vacancies for the borough, the party leaders agreed to leave Shrewsbury to the Whigs and the county to the Tories. On Kynaston's death (1749) Thomas Hill was put up by the corporation and the gentlemen of both parties. It was a course greatly to the satisfaction of the town's Presbyterians, and it eventually had the support of both Astley and Lord Powis.[36] Powis's dominance in Shrewsbury, of which he was recorder, was thus confirmed.[37]

The Hills held one seat for all but ten of the next 65 years; briefly (1805–6) they held both. Their position, however, was not at first secure. In 1753 a Shrewsbury attorney tried to organize an opposition at the next election on behalf of 'some few capital merchants of commanding interest' who wished to put up a candidate.[38] Some country gentlemen supported the attempt and the parallel efforts to qualify a few poor burgesses to vote.[39] Hill told his Tory nephew Edward Kynaston that, following the 1749 compact, Powis would retaliate by opposing the Tories in the county if the Tories opposed Hill in Shrewsbury.[40] Robert More, a former M.P. for Bishop's Castle and a Whig 'of the primitive stamp', came forward in Corbett's place at the invitation of the Shrewsbury dissenters in October 1753.[41] Even after that Lyster persuaded the Tory gentlemen to adhere to the 1749 compact, and he and Astley went so far as to attend in support of Hill and More at the April election.[42] The opposition's candidate had been a stranger.[43]

More's decision in 1759 to retire at the end of the Parliament produced a struggle between an old interest and a new one, for the two candidates for the succession were both well able to indulge the venal habits of many Shrewsbury electors. One was Lord Pulteney, only son of the rich Lord Bath[44] who disposed of the old Newport interest; the other was Robert Clive who in July 1760, newly home from India, was introduced by Powis to the 'principal friends to the corporation interest'.[45]

More had sought Bath's interest in 1754, but in 1759, when Bath in turn sought

[33] C.J. xxii. 346, 503, 741; N.L.W., Wynnstay, box L, no. 1222 (petition).

[34] C 109/71/2/16; S.P.L., Deeds 19163; T.S.A.S. iii. 221–38.

[35] C.J. xxv. 426, 476.

[36] Hist. Parl., Commons, 1715–54, i. 309, 312; T.S.A.S. 4th ser. iv. 67.

[37] Camd. Misc. xxiii (Camd. 4th ser. vii), 150.

[38] S.R.O. 112, Thos. Hill's letter bk. 1753–9, Hill to Ld. Powis, 23 July 1753.

[39] The progress of the opposition from July 1753 can be traced ibid., passim.

[40] Ibid., Hill to Kynaston, 30 Aug. 1753.

[41] Hist. Parl., Commons, 1754–90, iii. 164.

[42] S.R.O. 112, T. Hill's letter bk. 1753–9, Hill to Powis, 16 Apr. 1754.

[43] Ld. Bathurst's son Hen.: ibid., Hill to Rob. More (16 Feb. 1754) and Rog. Kynaston (2 Mar. 1754). Hist. Parl., Commons, 1754–90, ii. 66, wrongly attributes the opposition to Hen.'s uncle, Ben. Bathurst.

[44] Bath had declined to support Bathurst's opposition in 1754: S.R.O. 112, T. Hill's letter bk. 1753–9, Hill to Rob. More, 16 Feb., 2 Mar. 1754.

[45] C 109/74/2/233.

More's assistance for Lord Pulteney, he received an insulting, and widely circulated, reply.[46] George II's death brought matters to a head, but Powis's sang-froid in the face of anxious pleas for a compromise from Newcastle[47] proved justified. Pulteney sought Astley's support and spent lavishly,[48] but found little welcome and withdrew. Hill and Clive were accordingly unopposed. Over £600 judicious charity was laid out just before the election.[49] Clive's position at Shrewsbury during the next thirteen years, especially during his absences and illnesses, owed much to the exertions made on his behalf by his kinsmen, friends, and servants, and above all to those of the Shrewsbury attorney, John Ashby.[50] Clive's residence in the county was at first at Condover, close to Shrewsbury, but in 1763 he moved away to Walcot.[51]

By the end of 1767 Hill, who now seldom voted, had determined to pass his seat on to his son Noel.[52] In October Clive took the sensible step of having Thomas Wingfield made mayor for 1767–8, election year, by accelerated promotion.[53] In December there were misgivings in the Clive camp as a result of the attempted formation of an Independent Club 'of the lower sort of burgesses' in opposition to the corporation's 'friends'. Lord Powis thought the club 'a set of inconsiderable people' wanting themselves noticed 'in order to get a little money dispersed among them'; to his mind, there had always been 50 or 60 such at Shrewsbury elections. This time Powis's confidence was misplaced: the reduction in the burgesses' numbers effected by the corporation since 1747[54] ensured that fifty electors could have considerable weight. Moreover a third candidate was now available, for William Pulteney, the rich new wielder of the Newport interest and an opponent of Clive at India House,[55] was ready to come out against him at Shrewsbury; Clive thought he had engineered the new club.[56] For the next seven years Pulteney was to be the moving spirit behind the events which ended the old Whig corporation control of Shrewsbury and the political influence which Powis and Clive derived from it.

Pulteney had limited success in 1768. His supporters' club was reputed 70-strong in February and the poll suggests that some Hill support was detached from Clive. Clive, however, though criticized for his slowness in declaring and canvassing, persuaded the Hills to coalesce with him and had the support of the gentry, the dissenters, most Whigs, and many Tories. A lavish distribution of 'highly seasonable' charity in January and a March canvass by George Clive put Clive 52 votes ahead of Pulteney, though Hill easily topped the poll. In all Clive spent £1,050.[57]

Petitions against Clive's return failed, but Pulteney went to work to undermine the corporation influence so unduly used, as the petitions claimed, on Clive's behalf.[58] While Clive started a club of his own[59] and nursed the borough in the usual ways,[60] Pulteney gave financial support to the popular party in the long and complicated mandamus case whose object was to strengthen that element among the electors most open to his influence.[61] The case arose out of the selectiveness with which the mayors admitted those qualified for the freedom of the borough by apprenticeship or birth.

[46] Namier, *Politics at Accession of Geo. III*, 257–9.
[47] B.L. Add. MS. 32912, ff. 106–7.
[48] Staffs. R.O., D.1287/18/8, J. Corbet to [Sir H. Bridgeman], 13 Aug. 1760.
[49] India Office Libr., MS. Eur. G. 37/50.
[50] *Hist. Parl.*, *Commons*, 1754–90, ii. 225–6; *T.S.A.S.* lix. 53–62.
[51] See pp. 255–6, 303.
[52] India Office Libr., MS. Eur. G. 37/50.
[53] C 109/74/2/74.
[54] India Office Libr., MS. Eur. G. 37/50–1. Wingfield estimated the decrease at 100.
[55] Lucy S. Sutherland, *E. India Co. in Eighteenth-Cent. Politics* (1952), 139–40.

[56] India Office Libr., MS. Eur. G. 37/51. Clive himself was elected to the existing (Whig) Loyal Club.
[57] Ibid. 50–2, 83; C 109/72/5, seven copies of poll list.
[58] *C.J.* xxxii. 48; C 109/71/1/11; C 109/74/2/30, 70, 72.
[59] The Soc. of Free Burgesses, est. 1769 with 46 members: C 109/72/7/187.
[60] e.g. by helping the Eng. Bridge trustees and Shrews. waterworks proprietors and by contributing to a loan to the mayor: C 109/71/4/30; C 109/74/2/430; India Office Libr., MS. Eur. G. 37/63 (9 Feb., 4 Mar. 1772).
[61] T. H. B. Oldfield, *Hist. of Boros. of Gt. Brit.* (1792), ii. 405–12; idem, *Representative Hist. of Gt. Brit. and Irel.* (1816), iv. 383–8; India Office Libr., MS. Eur. G. 37/52.

The votes of a few such would-be burgesses had been rejected in 1768 and one Richard Baxter secured a mandamus requiring cause to be shown for refusal of the freedom; he claimed, as the corporation denied, that automatic admission was immemorial. In December 1771 Baxter won his case thanks at the end to Serjeant Dunning's oratory,[62] and 'strange mad work' followed in Shrewsbury when the news was known.[63] The corporation refused to comply with the court ruling but all the justices in King's Bench refused a motion for re-trial. The death nine months later of that great manager Lord Powis dealt the corporation another blow[64] and more were to follow. In 1774 the Powis interest was deeply involved in the Montgomeryshire contest,[65] and at Shrewsbury Hill's replacement[66] by Charlton Leighton of Wattlesborough weakened the connexion between Clive and the second man.[67] When St. Chad's parish assessments were revised that summer, Pulteney's success in introducing non-residents gave them 'an occasional contrivance to vote'[68] and produced vigorous canvassing on both sides,[69] the usual stratagems,[70] and heavy expense.[71] The poll which opened on 11 October presented an extraordinary scene.[72] Pulteney proposed to his opponents and to the mayor, John Ashby, that freemen be admitted to poll in accordance with the 1771 King's Bench ruling. Needless to say they were not, and instead the voters were brought up in fives, the qualifications of each one being tested by the candidates' and the mayor's learned counsel. Ashby rejected 225 'mandamus men' whose votes would have put Pulteney at the head of the poll with 341 votes to Clive's 309 and Leighton's 238.[73] On the 14th the declared poll gave Clive 210, Leighton 178,[74] and Pulteney 171 (68 plumpers),[75] but five weeks later, on 19 November, the final verdict in the mandamus suit was given against the corporation and Pulteney's chances of success by petition[76] were improved. Three days later Clive killed himself and Shrewsbury politics were thrown into confusion.

The new Lord Clive was under age, a fact which had almost prevented his return for Ludlow and would have been fatal in the early by-election expected in Shrewsbury. The Clives considered running George Clive, and Richard Morhall of Onslow saw himself as warming the seat for the new Lord Clive. Within five days of the suicide Robert Pigott of Chetwynd and John Mytton of Halston had been thought of and had retired, and Leighton's brother-in-law, John Corbet of Sundorne, had come forward. On 28 November a public meeting revealed the divisions in the town, Morhall declared himself, and Corbet canvassed, supported by 'the whole Pultonian interest', which would otherwise have gone to Pigott or Mytton.[77] The town was in turmoil, and by the 30th the mayor, Thomas Loxdale, beset by requests to swear in burgesses, was longing for 'more peaceable times'.[78]

[62] Hist. MSS. Com. 35, *14th Rep. IV, Kenyon*, pp. 502–3; *Shrews. Burgess Roll*, ed. H. E. Forrest (Shrews. 1924), pp. viii–x, xiv–xv.

[63] C 109/72/7/245.

[64] He had been recorder 1749–71: Owen and Blakeway, *Hist. Shrews.* i. 539.

[65] P. D. G. Thomas, 'The Montgomeryshire Electn. of 1774', *Montg. Coll.* lix. 116–29.

[66] He moved on to be kt. of the shire (p. 262), thus achieving what Clive could not.

[67] Attingham supported Leighton and dissuaded him from supporting the mandamus plaintiffs: C 109/71/4/28; C 109/74/2/18.

[68] C 109/71/3; C 109/71/4/27. Geo. Clive had canvassed in Apr. using the 1773 assessments: C 109/71/1/1, etc.

[69] C 109/71/2/1; C 109/74/2/18.

[70] Clive's agent gave dinners (ibid.) and engaged all the Shrews. chaises and their horses for a fortnight (C 109/71/4/15). It was feared that Pulteney might try to separate Clive and Leighton, not as united as Clive and Hill: C 109/71/4/1, 7.

[71] The electn. cost Clive £1,243: C 109/74/2/62–3. Succinct contemporary acct. of the electn. in *S.P.R. St. Asaph*, ii(1), 490; acct. (with some errors) in T. Auden, *Shrews.* (1905), 218–23; collection of addresses, etc., *The Shrews. Jubilee* (Shrews. [1775]); Ashby's lists, etc., in C 109/72/5.

[72] For the rest of this para. see S.P.L., MS. 2526; plate facing p. 97, above.

[73] C 109/71/1/20.

[74] Ashby had credited him with c. 170 in July: C 109/74/2/18.

[75] Rejected votes would have put Pulteney 12 ahead of Leighton: C 109/72/7/49.

[76] *Shrews. Chron.* 26 Nov. 1774; S.P.L., Deeds 19167, Dr. Cheney Hart to Wm. Cheney Hart, 23 Nov. 1774; *C.J.* xxxv. 20, 49.

[77] *Shrews. Chron.* 3 Dec. 1774; C 109/71/4/6; C 109/72/7/238; C 109/74/2/337.

[78] C 109/71/4/8.

Pulteney had the upper hand and used his opportunities well. He rejected the easy way of withdrawing his petition to secure his own unopposed return in Clive's place. This delayed the new election[79] and in January Serjeant Dunning sued out a peremptory mandamus for the admission of burgesses.[80] On 6 March Pulteney at last withdrew his petition, a day before it was to be heard.[81] Next day another petition in his interest was heard and, the two court rulings having been noted, Pulteney was seated in Leighton's place. Appropriate rejoicings followed; next week Pulteney came to Shrewsbury in triumph and the town was canvassed for John Corbet. Morhall withdrew, and Corbet was returned in Clive's place. The 'steady corporation people' were 'all aghast and know not what to say or do'.[82] Pulteney had carried both seats and had put an end to the corporation's control of the franchise and to the Clive interest. He was to sit for Shrewsbury for thirty years, unopposed at five general elections, and a Pulteney legend grew up to which candidates could still appeal years after Sir William's death.[83] Pulteney, however, had too much sense to parade his influence, and he and his colleagues always issued separate addresses.

There were no contests for 21 years after Pulteney's victory. Corbet retired in 1780[84] to be succeeded by Sir Charlton Leighton. In 1784 the borough, regaled with the now conventional 'very elegant entertainments' backed its M.P.s' support of Pitt, and Fox was burnt in effigy.[85] Leighton died five months after the election and Robert Corbett of Longnor came forward claiming that he had refrained from offering himself on a previous occasion[86] from attachment to Leighton; nevertheless he withdrew to preserve 'the peace of the town' and in face of a 'most powerful combination' which backed the knight of the shire's brother John Hill,[87] who sat with Pulteney until 1796.

The great contest of 1796[88] was rightly dubbed 'a family contest . . . sprung from a pique'.[89] It was fought to decide whether an Attingham or a Hawkstone Hill should hold the second seat; Pulteney remained neutral.[90] John Hill of Hawkstone had enjoyed Attingham support but in 1795 Lord Berwick wrote to Sir Richard Hill to announce his intention of maintaining the Attingham interest. The candidate was to be his brother William who had come of age in 1794 but whose success implied John Hill's retirement or defeat. A family conference at Attingham in November failed to produce a compromise[91] and next month John Hill issued an address.[92] Argument, pamphleteering,[93] canvassing, and 'entertainment' began, and by the end of 1795 the town was 'in confusion'.[94]

It was claimed for William Hill, 'the Attingham Lad', that as long ago as 1785 Sir Richard had told an Attingham supporter that his brother would eventually make way at Shrewsbury for a son of Lord Berwick (d. 1789). Of course Hawkstone denied a story which implied contempt for the borough's independence.[95] Memories were long.

[79] Shrews. Chron. 17 Dec. 1774; C 109/71/4/7, 8.
[80] C 109/71/4/22.
[81] C.J. xxxv. 174.
[82] Ibid. 175, 183; Shrews. Chron. 11 and 18 Mar. 1775; S.P.L., Deeds 19167, Hart to Hart, 6, 7, 15, and 21 Mar. 1775.
[83] See p. 274, n. 45.
[84] Shrews. Chron. 9 Sept. 1780. There was talk of a contest though nothing came of it: Hist. Parl., Commons, 1754–90, iii. 364.
[85] Shrews. Chron. 21 Feb., 3 Apr. 1784.
[86] Presumably 1780.
[87] Shrews. Chron. 11 and 18 Sept. 1784. Corbet proposed Hill.
[88] For this and the next two paras. see P. R. L. Brown, 'That a Contested Electn. is a remaining Proof of the Existence of Original Sin' ([1952]; TS. penes Prof. Brown); A. P. Jenkins, 'Boro. Politics in Shrews.: the General Electn. of 1796' (Oxford Univ. B.A. dissertation [1972]; copy in S.R.O. 3396); idem, 'Two Salop. Electns. of the Late 18th and Early 19th Cents.', Trans. Caradoc & Severn Valley Field Club, xvi. 124–6.
[89] S.R.O. 549/20; Bodl. MS. Top. Salop. c. 3, f. 177.
[90] Though probably with a preference for John Hill: S.R.O. 549/7.
[91] Ibid. /34. Cf. Bodl. MS. Top. Salop. c. 3, f. 161; Shrews. Chron. 3 June 1796.
[92] Shrews. Chron. 4 Dec. 1795.
[93] There are collections in S.R.O. 549/1–35; Shrews. Sch. Libr.; Bodl. MS. Top. Salop. c. 3. See also S.P.L., MS. 6760. The Shrews. Chron. (15 Apr. 1796) refused to print 'squibs' but accepted 'advertisements'. Sir R. Hill's biblical interests were often satirized.
[94] S.R.O. 840, box 151, Rob. Jeffreys to Thos. Jones, 29 Dec. 1795.
[95] S.R.O. 549/3.

Noel Hill's opposition to Pulteney in the mandamus case was remembered against his son,[96] and the country gentry supporting William Hill[97] were said to be those who had supported Noel Hill earlier; they were now accused of supporting Attingham with a view to the imposition of their own nominee on the borough after Pulteney's death.[98]

The candidates spilt 'a shower of gold'.[99] A later estimate of £100,000[1] is too high: mainly in the two months April–June Attingham spent something over £15,414, of which £6,384 went to 36 innkeepers for food, drink,[2] and lodging; £2,382 went on burgesses' lodgings which, because of the uncertainty about the election date, had to be taken for a year in order to provide accommodation and also perhaps to satisfy the requirement of 'occasional residence' expected of burgesses.[3] Between December 1795 and May 1796 1,659 new burgesses were traced and sworn,[4] 'non-resident collected from all quarters, tag, rag, and bob-tail fresh imported on this occasion, far fetched and dear bought indeed if they turn out mere ciphers'.[5] Ciphers indeed they were to be. It was thought important to have the new burgesses put in the 1796 parochial assessments, and in April the election of Attingham churchwardens in three town parishes was toasted as the prelude to victory;[6] in the poll, however, during which disorder was only narrowly averted, William Hill took only 963 votes to John Hill's 1,007 and Pulteney's 1,884. In the event William Hill owed his victory to the mayor's rejection, on counsel's advice, of over 1,500 votes on the ground that they were not in the 1795 assessments. From 'burgesses assessed' Pulteney polled 370, William Hill 242, John Hill 153. Nearly all the new burgesses gave one vote to Pulteney; only seven men voted for both Hills.[7]

William Hill urged that to challenge his return would be 'something worse than insanity'[8] but John Hill petitioned, alleging bribery and corruption and partisan admission or rejection of votes by the mayor.[9] The petition was eventually dropped[10] on the understanding that at the next vacancy John Hill would be returned without opposition from Attingham.[11] Pulteney and William Hill (also a Pittite) were unopposed in 1802. Pulteney died in 1805[12] and John Hill duly succeeded. Richard Lyster and the Hon. H. G. Bennet came forward but withdrew in the interest of peace. Lyster actually proposed John Hill whose seconder solemnly denied that there was any agreement between Attingham and Hawkstone; Bennet equally solemnly protested against the family combination and warned of a severe contest to come.[13] For over a year the rivals of 1796 held both seats.

Bennet was a leading figure in Shrewsbury politics for the next twenty years. He represented the former Astley interest, being a grandson of the 3rd earl of Tankerville by a co-heir of the Tory Sir John Astley. A well connected and radical Whig of some note, Bennet was a member of 'the Mountain', the associate of other advanced politicians in London, and a would-be humanitarian reformer.[14] His chance came in 1806

[96] S.R.O. 549/7, 13.
[97] Incl. the Corbetts of Longnor and the Myttons: *Shrews. Chron.* 3 June 1796.
[98] S.R.O. 549/10.
[99] *Heber Letters, 1783–1832,* ed. R. H. Cholmondeley (1950), 94.
[1] Oldfield, *Rep. Hist. of Gt. Brit. and Irel.* (1816), iv. 388.
[2] Hard drinking is also supposed to have taken place at Attingham.
[3] Calculations and analysis in Brown, op. cit. Hawkstone, further from Shrews., probably spent to less effect.
[4] Admissions *penes* chief executive, Boro. of Shrews. and Atcham (1977).
[5] *Heber Letters, 1783–1832,* 97.
[6] *Shrews. Chron.* 15 Apr. 1796.
[7] Ibid. 10 June 1796; *Heber Letters,* 96–7; *Correct*

Alphab. List of Burgesses who voted at Electn. for Shrews., May 30, 1796, and following days (Shrews. 1796; copy in Shrews. Sch. Libr.).
[8] *Shrews. Chron.* 10 June 1796.
[9] *C.J.* lii. 40.
[10] Announcement by John Hill, 3 Nov. 1796: S.R.O. 549/35. The petition, however, remained before the Commons until 9 Nov. 1797: *C.J.* liii. 38.
[11] See below.
[12] *Shrews. Chron.* 7 June 1805.
[13] Ibid. 14 June 1805.
[14] G. Wallas, *Life of Fra. Place* (1925), 178; *Creevey Papers,* ed. Sir H. Maxwell (1905), 36, 210, 215–16; *Creevey's Life and Times,* ed. J. Gore (1934), 64, 81, 106, 116–17, 129–30; J. L. and Barbara Hammond, *The Town Labourer, 1760–1832* (1925), 78–80, 187–92; Owen and Blakeway, *Hist. Shrews.* ii. 141–2.

when John Hill, then aged 66, retired.[15] Hill had profited little from the expenditure of 1796; his eldest son Col. John Hill was considered by Hawkstone for Shrewsbury as well as for the county, but in the event did not come forward.[16] Supported by Attingham, Hawkstone, and other leading county families, William Hill was sure of the first seat. The second, however, was contested between Bennet and Thomas Jones of Stanley Park, a Tory who came forward under the banner of 'Jones and Independence' and posed as the true successor of Pulteney, on whose interest he had earlier sat for Weymouth.[17] Bennet coalesced with Hill but sought votes as an 'Independent Man' and denounced Jones's vote for the slave trade.[18] Lord Bradford as commander of the militia found himself entreated by the candidates to allow electors in the militia to travel from East Anglia; he supported William Hill and Bennet as soon as he was assured that his 'old friend' John Hill had retired.[19] The election was violent and expensive, and much printed matter was again produced. The town was soon in 'a very unpleasant state of heat and confusion',[20] and Kynaston Powell estimated the cost to each candidate of a single day's polling at £100 or more 'exclusive of a little bribery which now begins to appear'. Polling lasted twelve days and Hill's and Bennet's advantage in militia voters helped to put the latter into second place.[21] Jones's spirited final speech attacked 'a most monstrous coalition of candidates', 'a most unexampled combination of the surrounding nobility, gentry and clergy', and 'altered assessments, sham succession, false inhabitants, swapped voters, resurrection men, paper eaters, and a monopoly of agents'. Jones reminded his hearers that Rowland Hunt, the advocate of last-minute compromise on the hustings in 1796, had recommended the choice of one member from the aristocracy and one who was a commoner.[22] The Whig Bennet, however, like William Hill, was a peer's son.

For some months agitation was almost continuous; the 'Friends of Independence' met on behalf of Jones and the 'Friends of the Real Independence' of Shrewsbury on behalf of Bennet.[23] A petition against Bennet's election had been upheld and a new writ issued when the 1807 general election supervened. Bennet's election had been voided on a purely technical ground, for he had neglected to qualify himself before the poll.[24]

The admission of the votes of non-resident assessed burgesses had decided the 1806 election; their rejection was to decide that of 1807, when both Bennet and Jones claimed the support of the town tradesmen. Just as in 1806 Bennet had denounced Jones's vote against abolition of the slave trade, so in 1807 Jones apparently made capital out of Bennet's vote for Roman Catholic relief.[25] Again the poll lasted twelve days, but Jones, with 138 plumpers, beat Bennet into third place by over 20.[26] Both elections had seen much intimidation and revenge,[27] and Bennet was said to have spent twenty or thirty thousand pounds.[28] A local lady blessed with a short memory thought the 1807 contest had 'made more quarrels and discord in private families than I suppose any election ever did before'.[29] Bennet complained bitterly that the mayor had arbitrarily departed from the century-old practice of the borough and ignored the decisions of a Commons committee in accepting or rejecting votes[30] and

---

[15] *Shrews. Chron.* 24 Oct. 1806.
[16] Staffs. R.O., D.1287/10/4a, Sir Ric. Hill to —, 27 Oct. 1806.
[17] Ex inf. Dr. R. Thorne, of the Hist. of Parliament.
[18] *Shrews. Chron.* 31 Oct., 7 Nov., 12 Dec. 1806.
[19] Staffs. R.O., D.1287/10/4a, Bradford to —, 30 Oct. 1806.
[20] Ibid., Thos. Eyton to —, 9 Nov. 1806.
[21] Ibid., J. Kynaston Powell to —, 8 Nov. 1806.
[22] *Shrews. Chron.* 21 Nov. 1806. Cf. ibid. 3 June 1796.

[23] Ibid. 12 Dec. 1806; 24 Apr., 1 May 1807.
[24] *C.J.* lxii. 38–9, 99, 360; S.R.O. 665/1/5995.
[25] *Shrews. Chron.* 1, 8 and 15 May 1807.
[26] *Correct Alphab. List of Burgesses who voted at Electn. for Shrews., 7th May, 1807, and eleven following Days* (Shrews. n.d.; copy in Shrews. Sch. Libr.).
[27] *Shrews. Chron.* 22 May 1807.
[28] Ibid. 19 June 1807.
[29] N.L.W., Aston Hall corresp. 4134.
[30] *Shrews. Chron.* 22 May 1807.

lodged a petition, which he ultimately withdrew.[31] Jones (cr. bt. 1808) made little use of his victory. Though active in earlier Parliaments, he spoke only once as M.P. for Shrewsbury. He died in 1811 and Bennet faced a new rival for the traders' votes, but this time one who was himself a Shrewsbury manufacturer with many employees of his own, for Benjamin Benyon,[32] who had supported Bennet in 1806 and 1807 and shared his Whig views, came forward against him in 1811. In the end Benyon preferred not to stand a poll until the next general election;[33] by then, however, his chances were poor.

William Hill had been absent when Pulteney was replaced. He had been a diplomat since 1805, and in 1807 his appointment to the court of Sardinia was thought 'a little bit of a job', engineered by Lady Hester Stanhope, with whom his name was then linked.[34] He retained the ability to charm the ladies noted by some in 1796,[35] but his 'lisping mumbling manner of speaking, which often gives more appearance of humour to what he says than it deserves' was now little heard in the Commons,[36] from which he retired in 1812. He was replaced by John Hill's second son, Gen. Sir Rowland Hill, though some would have preferred the general's elder brother John. It was Bennet's turn to claim Pulteney's mantle and head the poll.[37] He gleefully wrote to Brougham: 'Who would have thought that the Mountain could have lifted so high its head?'.[38] Gen. Hill was in Spain and, if the war continued, was unlikely to take his seat. Benyon offered himself as 'a friend, a fellow townsman and a tradesman' but retired before a 'combination of influence' when the general was only six votes behind (330 to 336)[39] with more votes in reserve among the 372 electors still unpolled.[40] Hill never sat. He was ennobled in 1814, and Benyon contested the succession with Richard Lyster of Rowton, proposed by Lord Hill's father.[41] The traders were probably in a fractious and anxious mood as a result of the long war and the speeches on the hustings in 1812 suggest the growth of an opposition to interference by the gentry in the choice of one M.P.;[42] this element was again strong in 1814[43] when the ironmaster William Hazledine was one of its leaders,[44] and Lyster too tried to claim the trading vote.[45] Any euphoria responsible for Hill's election was past; Hill himself had been a 'non-representative'. On the fifth day of the poll, however, Benyon was crushed.[46] He was the last townsman to contest the borough for some decades, and in 1818 Shrewsbury was uncontested for the first time since 1802, though Benyon's seconder of four years before now voiced a demand for a second Whig candidate.[47]

Within a year Lyster was dead, but no Whig sought to replace him. The Hawkstone interest and other gentlemen put forward the notorious John Mytton, 22-years-old son-in-law of Bennet's former rival Sir Thomas Jones. He was opposed by another young Tory, Archdeacon Corbett's son Panton. Though both families had supported William Hill in 1796,[48] Corbett came forward in 1819 with the corporation's support[49] while behind Mytton 'the pride of the aristocracy' united with 'the lowest of the people' to keep out the candidate of the trading interest.[50] Corbett's respectability did

[31] C.J. lxii. 638; T.S.A.S. 4th ser. xii. 245.
[32] T.S.A.S. lvi. 49–68.
[33] Shrews. Chron. 6 Dec. 1811.
[34] Ld. Granville Leveson Gower (First Earl Granville): Private Corresp. 1781 to 1821, ed. Castalia, Ctss. Granville (1916), ii. 312.
[35] Heber Letters, 1783–1832, 94; Granville Corresp. 1781 to 1821, i. 494.
[36] Granville Corresp. 1781 to 1821, ii. 552.
[37] Shrews. Chron. 9 Oct. 1812.
[38] Univ. Coll. London, Brougham MSS., no. 32131.
[39] Shrews. Chron. 9 and 16 Oct. 1812.
[40] Univ. Coll. London, Brougham MSS., no. 32131.
[41] Shrews. Chron. 27 May 1814.

[42] Ibid. 9 Oct. 1812.
[43] Ibid. 27 May, 10 June 1814.
[44] Ibid. 6 May 1814. It was perhaps this opposition group which wished Panton Corbett to stand: S.R.O. 1066/118, 5 May 1819.
[45] Shrews. Chron. 27 May, 10 June 1814. The Lysters' connexion with Pulteney was also recalled.
[46] Ibid. 27 May 1814; Salopian Jnl. 1 June 1814.
[47] Shrews. Chron. 19 June 1818. Cf. The Late Elections . . . (1818), 276–7. Benyon was returned for Stafford: S.H.C. 1933(1), 43–4; ibid. 1950–1, 281–2, 284, 286.
[48] See p. 272, n. 97.   [49] S.R.O. 840 uncat.
[50] S.R.O. 1066/118–19 (5 May–28 June 1819). Benyon strongly urged Corbett's candidacy.

not avail against Mytton's optimistic promise to abandon 'the follies of my youth'.[51] Towards the end of the eight days' poll, marked by violence,[52] Mytton drew ahead and he won by 384 to 287.[53] He had respectable supporters, including the town's historian Blakeway. According to the Corbetts, however, Mytton resorted to large-scale bribery,[54] as indeed his proposer, John Cressett Pelham, had broadly hinted that he would.[55] An attempt had been made in 1814 to reduce the cost of elections by omitting the public dinners which had followed their close;[56] but the dinners given separately at various inns in 1819 and the grand balls given by both sides[57] must also have been expensive.[58]

Mytton, the tenth and last of his family to sit for Shrewsbury, did not sit long. He quit the Commons even more swiftly than Westminster and Harrow schools, for in 1820, the year before he fled abroad from his creditors,[59] he did not stand, and Bennet and Corbett were unopposed. The last three elections before 1832 returned one Tory and one Whig. Bennet's retirement in 1826 brought forward R. A. Slaney of Walford, an active Whig. As in 1812, the surviving M.P. easily headed the poll: Corbett had 627 votes, Slaney 387, and a second Tory, Thomas Boycott of Rudge, withdrew after four days with 283.[60] Four years later the 1830 election demonstrated 'the omnipotency of gold'. The poll was headed by Richard Jenkins, a native of Cruckton who had recently returned home after holding high office in India for over twenty years — 'a proper nabob for our independent voters'.[61] Jenkins had 754 votes, Slaney 563. Corbett came third with 445, reputedly through failure to apply 'gold spurs' to the electorate. In 1831 there promised, for the first time since 1747, to be a four-cornered contest. Jenkins's running-mate was Thomas Boycott, while Slaney's Whig colleague was Richard Potter, later M.P. for Wigan. By arrangement Boycott and Potter withdrew after one day's polling. Potter was fourth;[62] a second Whig candidate at Shrewsbury apparently still had less chance than a second Tory. The electorate was now well over a thousand, and the constituency had regularly shown a disposition for venality and violence. Already local gentlemen were failing to come forward with their former alacrity.

Bridgnorth

Throughout the period and beyond it Bridgnorth elections were dominated by six generations of the Whitmores of Apley, and by the late 18th century their success had given a proverb to the English language: 'All on one side like a Bridgnorth election'.[63] The family interest returned at least one member at every election of the period except that of 1710, and Bridgnorth politics were usually about the second seat. The Actons of Aldenham had claims to it until the 1750s and later the Pigots of Patshull (Staffs.) used a nabob fortune to acquire it, but it was normally in the Whitmores' gift. Their position, however, depended on constant expenditure to secure domination of the borough government. The electorate increased rapidly from 1663; by 1741 at 1,400 or more it was one of the largest in the kingdom.[64] An increasing proportion of voters, well over half by the 1820s, was non-resident.

[51] *Shrews. Chron.* 21 May 1819. [52] Ibid. 28 May 1819.
[53] *Correct Alphab. Lists of Burgesses who Voted, . . . at Electn. for Shrews. 17th May, 1819, and following Days* (Shrews. 1819; copy in S.P.L., Morris-Eyton Coll. no. 51).
[54] *Shrews. Chron.* 4 June 1819; S.R.O. 1066/118–19 (5 May–28 June 1819).
[55] *Shrews. Chron.* 21 May 1819.
[56] Ibid. 3 June 1814.
[57] Ibid. 4, 11 and 18 June 1819.
[58] Corbett, who did not bribe, spent £2,000: S.R.O. 1066/119 (28 June 1819).

[59] *D.N.B.*
[60] *Shrews. Chron.* 16 June 1826.
[61] F. A. Hagar, 'Ric. Jenkins and the Residency at Nagpur, 1807–1826' (Univ. of California Ph.D. thesis, 1960; copy in S.R.O. 1071); S.R.O. 840, box 159, Wm. Jeffreys to Sir Tyrwhitt Jones, 7 July 1830 (speculating also about the attitude of Ld. Tankerville).
[62] *T.S.A.S.* 4th ser. xii. 251–3.
[63] J. F. A. Mason, *Boro. of Bridgnorth 1157–1957* (Bridgnorth, 1957), 31.
[64] Namier, *Politics at Accession of Geo. III*, 242.

Sir William Whitmore, a zealous royalist churchman, sat for the county in the 1660 Convention.[65] In April Monck wrote to the bailiffs requesting a seat for Secretary Thurloe. Thurloe approached the influential Thomas Gilbert, rector of Edgmond,[66] who told him, however, that the 'sevenfold greater part' of Bridgnorth was committed to 'an high Cavalier choice' of both burgesses, the electors being under the 'over-powerful sway of their great landlords, meeting together'. A canvass showed that not even Monck himself could have been elected without an unequivocal declaration for the king.[67] Many royalist gentlemen were made freemen[68] and John Bennett, Whitmore's brother-in-law, was returned with Sir Walter Acton.[69]

Acton stood down in 1661 and Whitmore took up the family seat. When Bennett died in 1663 the second seat was filled by Whitmore's brother Sir Thomas.[70] There was, however, a severe contest and 182 new burgesses were admitted in six weeks.[71] The brothers were returned at the three elections 1679-81; by then Sir William was a Shaftesburian and Sir Thomas a Court supporter.[72] They were opposed only at the second 1679 election, when John Wolryche of Dudmaston seems to have been the first to try to defeat the Whitmores by polling non-resident voters. As many as 227 new burgesses were admitted: 129 in the Whitmores' interest and 98 in Wolryche's. The defeated Wolryche petitioned[73] but the result is not known.

Sir Thomas died in 1683 and was succeeded in 1685 by a kinsman, Roger Pope of Woolstaston.[74] Pope was James II's choice as prospective member in September 1688.[75] By then, however, local feeling against the king ran high,[76] and Whitmore was ready to support the prince of Orange in arms.[77] Nevertheless in 1689 Sir Edward Acton, 'Jacobite' son of the 1660 M.P., was returned unopposed with Sir William.[78] Both later voted as Tories,[79] and were unopposed until 1698. That year many new burgesses were again admitted,[80] and the third man was Roger Pope. The corporation was divided, but in the electorate at large the Whitmore–Acton coalition had 521 and 407 votes respectively against Pope's 162.[81]

When Sir William Whitmore died in 1699 his heir was his cousin's son William Whitmore of Lower Slaughter (Glos.), a minor.[82] Sir William was succeeded as M.P. by Roger Pope the younger, son of the 1698 candidate. The division of seats between Apley and Aldenham continued for three more elections[83] but at the second, in November 1701, there was a poll. Opposition came from a local gentleman, John Beech of Oldbury. This time the corporation was more united.[84] The electorate was again increased by new admissions, as also happened before the 1702 election.[85] In 1702, if a third candidate appeared, he did not stand a poll. Pope retired and the Apley interest returned a zealous Whig, Sir Humphrey Briggs of Haughton.[86]

From 1689 to 1705 the Whitmores and Actons had amicably divided the seats and twice repelled a third man. The coalition, however, broke down permanently in 1705. William Whitmore, then of age, claimed the family seat, and Whitmore Acton, son of

[65] See p. 256.
[66] See p. 113.
[67] *State Papers of John Thurloe*, ed. T. Birch (1742), vii, pp. 888, 895.
[68] Bridgnorth boro. rec., leet bk. 3, pp. 761–3.
[69] *T.S.A.S.* 4th ser. v. 16, 62.
[70] Ibid. 16, 62–3.
[71] Bridgnorth boro. rec., leet bk. 3, pp. 804–15.
[72] *Bull. Inst. Hist. Res.* xxx. 239.
[73] *T.S.A.S.* 4th ser. v. 16; Bridgnorth boro. rec., leet bk. 3, pp. 900–11; 'A Note of the Burgesses of Bridgnorth from Oct. 1637' (MS. at Aldenham Pk. in the 1950s); *C.J.* ix. 578.
[74] *T.S.A.S.* 4th ser. v. 17, 63–4.
[75] S.P. 44/56 p. 438.
[76] Mason, *Bridgnorth*, 26–7.
[77] Ibid. 28.

[78] *T.S.A.S.* 4th ser. v. 17, 64. For Acton see K. Feiling, *Hist. of Tory Party, 1640–1714*, 497.
[79] I. F. Burton, P. W. J. Riley, and E. Rowlands, *Political Parties in Reigns of Wm. III and Anne* (*Bull. Inst. Hist. Res.* Special Suppl. no. 7), 47, 58.
[80] Bridgnorth boro. rec., 10 (burgess rolls)/2/1–94.
[81] Bridgnorth boro. rec., 43/1 (bailiffs' election bk.), ff. 87, 88; S.R.O. 1093, box 159, poll bk.
[82] Namier, *Politics at Accession of Geo. III*, 243; *V.C.H. Glos.* vi. 130.
[83] *T.S.A.S.* 4th ser. v. 17, 64.
[84] S.R.O. 1093, box 31, poll bk. (Pope 319, Acton 249, Beech 94); Bridgnorth boro. rec., 43/1, ff. 90, 94.
[85] Bridgnorth boro. rec., 10/4/1–134.
[86] *T.S.A.S.* 4th ser. v. 17, 64–5; 4th ser. xii. 7.

Sir Edward, came forward for the other. Briggs, however, stood again,[87] apparently with Whitmore's approval.[88] There was a strenuous contest; the aldermen were again split, and again there was a great increase in the electorate. Briggs and Whitmore received 528 and 449 votes respectively, Acton only 333.[89] The two Whigs were returned without alarms in 1708.[90]

In 1710 the Sacheverell affair allowed a zealous Tory to inflict on Whitmore the only defeat sustained by his family at Bridgnorth,[91] and that despite the fact that Whitmore had not even voted on the Sacheverell issue.[92] Two Tories, young Richard Cresswell of Sidbury and Whitmore Acton,[93] were in the field as early as June, but the former took the lead. Sacheverell came to Bridgnorth in July and was met by Cresswell and Acton amid public rejoicing;[94] nevertheless the Tory triumph three months later was due also to Cresswell's energetic organization. Between the 1705 poll and May 1710 87 burgesses had been admitted, but in the next six weeks over 230 were made.[95] Cresswell and Acton, with 520 and 511 votes, defeated Whitmore and Briggs (501 and 474).[96] Cresswell had only a little property in Bridgnorth,[97] but his success in influencing the existing out-voters and in securing the admission of 45 new ones[98] overcame that handicap. He devoted special attention to the London out-voters.[99] Long before the end of August he had engaged all the Bridgnorth burgesses in London and more in Southwark.[1] Whitmore, mourning the loss of a first-born son, did not take Cresswell's challenge seriously until too late, and in July Briggs was still at Bath.[2] Later Whitmore impaired his chances by too much endeavour to help Briggs.[3] Lord Newport had visited the town,[4] but to no avail. Whitmore did not petition; Briggs did[5] though naturally without success.

Cresswell's career as M.P. for Bridgnorth was stormy. In 1711 he was arrested for drinking the Pretender's health,[6] though that would probably not have caused him any unpopularity in Bridgnorth.[7] In 1713, however, Cresswell was returned for the Tory borough of Wootton Bassett (Wilts.)[8] and the parliamentary careers of his descendants were unconnected with Shropshire.[9]

William Whitmore regained his seat without a contest in 1713 and sat until his death. His colleague in 1713, 1715, and 1722 was John Weaver of Morville,[10] whose extensive property in Bridgnorth had descended from the Smythes, M.P.s under Edward VI and James I.[11] Whitmore died in 1725. His sons were under age and for some years the family interest was operated by their mother. St. John Charlton of Apley Castle, a friend of the 3rd earl of Bradford, succeeded Whitmore unopposed.[12]

In the fourteen years following George I's death not only was the Whitmore interest opposed at three general elections by the local Tories, but Whitmore candidates for the corporation were also opposed. The lead in this was taken first by the Actons, later assisted by a Lawley and finally replaced by a Lee.

[87] Ibid. 4th ser. v. 17, 65.
[88] S.R.O. 1224, box 174, Eliz., Lady Wolryche, to Geo. Weld, 5 Apr. 1705.
[89] S.R.O. 1093, box 159, poll bk.; Bridgnorth boro. rec., 10/6/1–124; 43/1, ff. 98, 100.
[90] T.S.A.S. 4th ser. v. 17.
[91] But see p. 335.
[92] Sources marshalled by R. R. Walcott, 'Division-lists of Ho. of Commons, 1689–1715', Bull. Inst. Hist. Res. xiv. 33–5.
[93] T.S.A.S. 4th ser. v. 65–6.
[94] Post Boy, 14–17 Oct. 1710; Lincs. R.O., Monson MSS., 7/13/123–4; above, p. 258.
[95] Bridgnorth boro. rec., 10/6–15; S.R.O. 1093, box 159, list of burgesses made 1705–10.
[96] S.R.O. 1093, box 159, poll bk.; N.L.W., Ottley Papers 2580.

[97] Papers penes Mr. John Reed, Sidbury Hall.
[98] S.R.O. 1093, box 159, list of burgesses made 1705–10 and poll bk.
[99] Bridgnorth boro. rec., 10/8/139–47.
[1] S.R.O. 1224/21/41.
[2] N.L.W., Ottley Papers 2567.   [3] Ibid. 2580.
[4] Post Boy, 14–17 Oct. 1710.   [5] C.J. xvi. 416.
[6] B.L. Add. MS. 17677, ff. 367–8.
[7] Mason, Bridgnorth, 27; Bodl. MS. Eng. misc. e. 344, ff. 25b, 27b.
[8] T.S.A.S. 4th ser. v. 66; V.C.H. Wilts. v. 226; ix. 198; Hist. Parl., Commons, 1715–54, i. 353.
[9] Hist. Parl., Commons, 1754–90, ii. 276.
[10] T.S.A.S. 4th ser. v. 17–18, 66.
[11] Ibid. liv. 197–8; Mason, Bridgnorth, 28.
[12] Hist. Parl., Commons, 1715–54, i. 310, 543–4; ii. 535–6.

In July 1727 Sir Whitmore Acton, M.P. 1710-13, came forward singly for the Tories against Weaver and Charlton, in whose joint favour the full weight of the Apley interest was exerted. Later Acton's brother Edward joined him, and a fifth candidate appeared in Edward Bridgen.[13] Bridgen's grandfather, a cooper, had come to the town before 1622 and had founded a successful and prolific family;[14] the 1727 candidate was a London wine merchant[15] and his candidacy probably reflected the City's hostility to Walpole.[16] The Bridgens were Acton supporters,[17] but Edward Bridgen's candidacy naturally took votes from Edward Acton. The election appears to have cost Apley over £2,800, most of which went on drink. Nevertheless £441, possibly more, was spent in payments to voters; altogether 305 burgesses received payment and the interest got value for its money; 275 voted for their friends. In all 1,102 voted. There were only 18 plumpers, though as many as 87 split votes; 597 gave double Whig votes, and 400 double Tory votes, of whom 94 threw away their second vote on Bridgen. Charlton and Weaver won by over 100 votes.[18]

The high feeling caused by the 1727 election was shown a few months later. In January of each alternate year the resident burgesses elected two bridgemasters who after two years automatically became chamberlains and, after two more years, aldermen. The two bailiffs, returning officers, were chosen from the aldermen.[19] The key to the borough's government thus lay in the January elections and promotions. In January 1728 Richard Bridgen, one of the bailiffs and an Acton supporter, refused to admit the bridgemasters, two Whitmore supporters, as chamberlains and two other Whitmore supporters as new bridgemasters. A suit was brought against the bailiffs, costing Apley £389. Judgement, however, was for the defendants, and the four Apley supporters had to wait a year for two favourable bailiffs to admit them to office.[20]

William Whitmore's son Thomas came of age in 1732 and became a candidate for the family seat; his partner was Grey James Grove of Pool Hall, Alveley, a relative of Lord Stamford. On the Tory side Sir Whitmore Acton was dead; his son, Sir Richard, had a new partner in Sir Robert Lawley of Spoonhill, the Lawleys' former prospects at Much Wenlock having been greatly reduced. Whitmore and Acton were under 30.[21] At the bridgemasters' election of January 1733 about 320 voted, and two Tories were elected[22] in spite of 'all the efforts of a very powerful opposite faction'.[23] The rate of admission of new burgesses thereupon quickened.[24] The tension between the parties erupted in August when a dispute over precedence between the high bailiff and a new bailiff elected by direct suffrage resulted in a riot at a meeting of the common hall.[25] The election of bailiffs on 21 September turned into a test of endurance. The evenly divided electoral jury was locked in the Burgesses' Hall without food, fire, or candle for 65 hours before it would compromise by electing one bailiff of each persuasion; a Tory mob besieged the hall during the election.[26] Next year the parliamentary election gave Whitmore and Grove a majority of just over 200 in a poll of 1,219 over four days. Acton and Lawley, who had together spent over £1,030 since July 1733,

[13] Bodl. MS. Eng. misc. e. 344, f. 82; *T.S.A.S.* 4th ser. v. 18; N.L.W., Ottley Papers 2754, 2766.

[14] Bridgnorth boro. rec., leet bk. 3, p. 373; S.P.L., MS. 4646, p. 125.

[15] *Obituary Prior to 1800 . . . compiled by Sir Wm. Musgrave,* i (Harl. Soc. xliv), 255.

[16] J. H. Plumb, *Sir Rob. Walpole, the King's Minister* (1960), 170–1, 179–82.

[17] S.R.O. 1093, box 159, poll bk. (indexed).

[18] *T.S.A.S.* 4th ser. v. 18; Apley Estate Office, Bridgnorth, poll bk.; S.R.O. 1093, box 159, poll bks.

[19] Mason, *Bridgnorth*, 20.

[20] Apley Estate Office, vol. 147, money disbursed on acct. of lawsuit concerning the chamberlains and bridge-master, 1728; S.R.O. 1093, box 57, covenant to subscribe to defence costs of bailiffs and others, 24 Apr. 1728; Bridgnorth boro. rec., bridgemasters' electn. papers; ibid., common hall order bk. 2, ff. 71–4.

[21] *Hist. Parl., Commons,* 1715–54, ii. 88, 535; G.E.C. *Baronetage,* ii. 217; S.P.L., MS. 2793, p. 257; S. Shaw, *Hist. . . . of Staffs.* ii (1801), *21; below, p. 294.

[22] Bridgnorth boro. rec., bridgemasters' electn. papers.

[23] B.L. Add. MS. 32326, f. 20.

[24] Bridgnorth boro. rec., 10/36–9.

[25] Bridgnorth boro. rec., bailiffs' electn. papers.

[26] *London Evening Post,* 20–23 Oct. 1733; Bridgnorth boro. rec., 43/1, f. 117v.

petitioned in vain.[27] No Lawley ever stood again at Bridgnorth and no Acton for well over a century.

Party feeling nevertheless survived. The 1735 election of bridgemasters was contested[28] and party passions were manifest at the bailiffs' election in 1739. Again an evenly divided jury was locked up for 70 hours; it compromised only when a Whig juror suffered a severe attack of gout which 'reduced his associates to a necessity of relaxing from their pretensions'.[29] In the 1741 general election, for the first time since 1705, there were only three candidates. Acton did not stand[30] and Lancelot Lee of Coton stood alone for the Tories. The Whigs were therefore optimistic and Thomas Whitmore and his brother William (of Lower Slaughter) came forward.[31] The poll of over 1,300 was the highest ever recorded but Lee was soundly beaten, 326 votes behind Thomas Whitmore and 277 behind William. There were few split votes, or plumpers for Whitmore.[32] Until 1790 polling took place in St. Mary's church. That gave the Whitmores an advantage, as the Green, a public house on their estate, adjoined the church; voters were fed into the church from the Green ten at a time. In 1741 a stranger was at the Green in the evening of the last day of the poll when a Tory mob arrived; he was killed in the ensuing stone-throwing. As a result charges of murder, riot, and assault were heard at the assizes. The presence and active encouragement of one or more of the gentry was a feature of all such disturbances, and Lancelot Lee's brother was prominent in the mob on this occasion.[33]

Between 1741 and 1784 there was no threat of a poll at Bridgnorth, though there was certainly not complete peace. The increased majorities of the Whitmore interest in 1734 and 1741 gave their opponents no prospect of success, and the Tory gentlemen subsided into inactivity. Sir Richard Acton became a Roman Catholic in the 1750s,[34] thus disabling himself from membership of the Commons. At the three general elections after 1741 the Whitmores were able to dispose of the second seat as they wished. In 1747 William Whitmore retired and his brother Sir Thomas (knighted 1744) was joined by Arthur Weaver of Morville; their fathers had sat together 1713–25. Weaver retired in 1754 and his interest, in the hands of absentees, did not again contest the borough until the 1830s.[35] Sir Thomas Whitmore also retired in 1754, and his brother William (who became a general in 1758) was returned with the Hon. John Grey, son of the Whig Lord Stamford, seated near by at Enville (Staffs.).[36] In 1754 Stamford gave the town 100 guineas and the M.P.s provided new maces.[37] The Whitmores' choice of colleagues from 1747 may have helped to preserve the peace, for the Weavers were connected with the Actons[38] and Grey was Sir Richard Acton's brother-in-law.[39]

In 1749–50 Lord Egmont observed that 'by dint of vast expense [Sir Thomas] Whitmore commands this borough'.[40] In 1766, however, an interest appeared which could spend even more lavishly than the Whitmores, for Bridgnorth, like Shrewsbury, caught the eye of a famous nabob.[41] In August 1765 Sir George Pigot, M.P. for the

[27] *London Evening Post*, 4–7 May 1734; Bridgnorth boro. rec., common hall order bk. 3, pp. 17–18; S.R.O. 1093, box 31A, Edw. Bickerton's disbursement on acct. of Sir Ric. Acton and Sir Rob. Lawley; *C.J.* xxii. 339–40.

[28] Bridgnorth boro. rec., bridgemasters' electn. papers.

[29] Bridgnorth boro. rec., 43/1, f. 129v.; B.L. Add. MS. 32326, f. 13v.

[30] *T.S.A.S.* 4th ser. v. 18. He nevertheless polled 30 votes.

[31] *Hist. Parl., Commons, 1715–54*, ii. 535–6; *V.C.H. Glos.* vi. 130.

[32] Apley Estate Office, MS. poll bk. 1741; Bridgnorth

boro. rec., common hall order bk. 3, pp. 87–9; N.L.W., Ottley Papers 3653.

[33] Bridgnorth boro. rec., papers *re* death of an unknown man during 1741 election.

[34] D. Mathew, *Acton: the Formative Years* (1946), 15.

[35] *T.S.A.S.* 4th ser. v. 18, 67–8; ibid. liv. 198; *Montg. Coll.* xxii. 79, 89–92, 94 sqq.; below, p. 331.

[36] *Hist. Parl., Commons, 1754–90*, ii. 553; iii. 632.

[37] Mason, *Bridgnorth*, 21, 46.

[38] *T.S.A.S.* liv. 198.

[39] Burke, *Peerage* (1949), 18, 1892.

[40] *Camd. Misc.* xxiii (Camd. 4th ser. vii), 151.

[41] See pp. 255–6, 268–70.

notoriously corrupt borough of Wallingford (Berks.), bought Patshull for £80,000.[42] Like Lord Clive, Pigot had no hope of a county seat. Accordingly in February 1766, newly ennobled with an Irish peerage,[43] he made overtures to the bailiffs and others, who then waited on Sir Thomas Whitmore to propose Lord Pigot as Lt.-Gen. Whitmore's colleague. The general drafted an apoplectic memorial to Pigot, stressing that Pigot's new friends were by no means sufficient 'to disturb the repose of a borough which has long been in Sir T. Whitmore's family'.[44] Admissions of burgesses, however, increased considerably in 1766 and 1767;[45] probably Pigot's largesse was at work. The Whitmores agreed to divide the representation and in 1768 the general and Pigot were returned unopposed.[46]

Quiet seemed to descend again during a period when the Whitmores' estates were at their greatest extent. The general died in 1771 and his seat passed to Major Thomas Whitmore, Sir Thomas's heir. Sir Thomas died in 1773, leaving the major a patrimony increased to some 11,700 a.[47] The Wolryche estate at Dudmaston passed to the Whitmores in 1774[48] bringing the family property up to some 14,800 a.[49] In 1774 Major Whitmore canvassed jointly with Lord Pigot, and in 1780 with Vice-Admiral Hugh Pigot, who had succeeded to the other seat on his brother's death in 1777.[50]

Bridgnorth was the only Shropshire constituency contested in 1784. Admiral Pigot was a gambling companion of Fox and had been a supporter of the Fox–North coalition (1783),[51] and Pitt's friends took an interest in his electoral prospects.[52] The rumour of a dissolution reached Bridgnorth on 26 January 1784. Next day a meeting of resident burgesses put forward Thomas Whitmore and Isaac Hawkins Browne.[53] Browne had bought Badger Hall[54] and was already involved in the town's affairs.[55] Browne's and Pigot's supporters began to canvass at once, while Whitmore's agent urged him to make greater efforts. For the next two months Browne and Pigot conducted a prolonged poster and newspaper battle. At the same time there was a contest in charity.[56] The merits of Fox and Pitt did not figure in these exchanges.

At the election Pigot had the aid of a local poetess, Miss Henrietta Rhodes, who 'shone with animated zeal for her naval friend'.[57] He was not, however, helped by Whitmore despite the near identity of their political views. Before the poll Whitmore announced that he was neutral between Browne and Pigot.[58] Pigot, the loser, however, condemned the 'dark and insidious' practices of 'pretended friends';[59] at some stage Whitmore had turned his influence against the admiral.[60]

The assertion that Bridgnorth voters 'gave proof of their independence' by displacing Pigot in 1784[61] is thus not wholly correct; Pigot's defeat was a triumph for Apley. Browne, however, was put into first place by plumpers from the industrial Midlands.[62]

[42] Yarlington Lodge (Som.), papers *penes* (1968) Sir Rob. Pigot; *Hist. Parl., Commons.* 1754–90, iii. 280.

[43] *Complete Peerage*, x. 520.

[44] Glos. R.O., D 45/X2 17 (32 b–c).

[45] Bridgnorth boro. rec., common hall order bk. 3, *passim*.

[46] *Hist. Parl., Commons*, 1754–90, i. 362.

[47] *T.S.A.S.* 4th ser. v. 69; *V.C.H. Salop.* viii. 101, 152, 173; B.L. Add. MS. 38458, ff. 83, 85; 38469, ff. 290, 320, 329; S.R.O. 3628; Apley Estate Office, vol. of misc. letters, wills, accts., etc., f. 196.

[48] G.E.C. *Baronetage*, ii. 124, note b.

[49] B.L. Add. MS. 38469, f. 284v.

[50] Bridgnorth boro. rec., candidates' draft circular letter, 5 Oct. 1774; *Shrews. Chron.* 9 and 16 Sept. 1780; *T.S.A.S.* 4th ser. v. 19, 68–9; *D.N.B.*

[51] Hist. MSS. Com. 42, *15th Rep. VI, Carlisle*, pp. 410, 484, 487, 490–1, 497, 544, 548.

[52] *Parl. Papers of J. Robinson* (Camd. 3rd ser. xxxiii), 75.

[53] *Shrews. Chron.* 31 Jan., 7 Feb. 1784.

[54] Blakeway, *Sheriffs*, 211.

[55] As chmn. of the initial meeting of subscribers to the New Road, 1782: Bridgnorth boro. rec., New Road Trust papers.

[56] *Shrews. Chron.* 14 Feb.–27 Mar. 1784; Bridgnorth boro. rec., poster.

[57] Bodl. MS. Top. Salop. c. 1, f. 605.

[58] *Shrews. Chron.* 3 Apr. 1784.

[59] Ibid. 17 Apr. 1784.

[60] Apley Estate Office, joint electn. expense accts. of Whitmore and Browne (totalling £3,847); Whitmore spent more besides. Electors living in Worcs. who were canvassed for Whitmore voted for Whitmore and Browne: Apley Estate Office, vol. of misc. letters, wills, accts., etc., f. 116; Bridgnorth boro. rec., poll bk. 1784. The operations of the Apley interest from this time are amply illustrated in S.R.O. 1104, letter bks. of Thos. Barnfield.

[61] Oldfield, *Hist. of Boros.* (1792), ii. 418.

[62] Bridgnorth boro. rec., poll bk. 1784.

After 43 years without a contest it had been necessary to make 380 new burgesses in seven days, the highest number made for any Bridgnorth election.[63] Only about two fifths of the electorate of some 1,500 were resident[64] and thenceforth until 1832 the out-voters were in a majority.[65]

In the forty years after 1784 the electoral peace of Bridgnorth was disturbed only once. The Pigots, however, did not give up immediately, and their supporters continued to contend for borough offices.[66] In 1789 it was believed that the admiral or another Pigot would stand again[67] but Whitmore and Browne, standing jointly in 1790, were unopposed.[68] Early in 1795 there were still those who hoped to persuade Whitmore to substitute a member of the Pigot family for Browne.[69] Thereafter, however, the Pigots dropped out of Bridgnorth politics for a generation. So too did the former Weaver interest when, in the same year, the absentee Arthur Blayney, who had inherited it, died.[70] Whitmore died by accident in April 1795.[71] To the end he had voted with the Foxite rump in the Commons,[72] but his cousin and successor John Whitmore was a director of the Bank of England and a Pittite and had the enthusiastic support of Browne.[73] Browne sat on, proud of his independence, until 1812.[74] Serious[75] about his parliamentary duties, he made some forty speeches in 28 years,[76] and from time to time he sent Pitt courteous and well considered advice.[77] Among Browne's friends was the Birmingham manufacturer,[78] Matthew Boulton, whose support he eagerly sought when Boulton became a Bridgnorth burgess in 1788.[79]

A disturbance of the electoral peace occurred in 1802 when a contest was 'begun vindictively and terminated wantonly'. Browne and John Whitmore were oppposed by the young George Knudson, said to be a West Indian,[80] who came forward on the day before the election, at the solicitation of an alderman and a few burgesses.[81] The election shows the importance of the Birmingham manufacturers. Matthew Boulton and his colleagues appealed for help for two candidates who had, in Boulton's view, 'so zealously attended to the wishes and prosperity of the trade and town of Birmingham'. Boulton thought that Browne, as an owner of iron and coal, and Whitmore, as a director of the Bank of England, had overwhelming claims. Browne in particular had transacted the Birmingham manufacturers' business in three of four Parliaments, and had ever been ready to give advice.[82] In the event there was no need to bring in the Birmingham out-voters; only 80 or so new burgesses were made, out-voters were not polled in any numbers, and Knudson's ignominious defeat[83] merely emphasized the firm grip of local interests when only resident voters were polled.

In 1804 there were unfounded rumours that Browne was to be ennobled, and the Radical duke of Norfolk seems to have been invited by a party in the borough to suggest a replacement.[84] Two years later Thomas Whitmore of Apley, the major's son,

[63] Ibid., common hall order bk. 4, pp. 106–37.
[64] Ibid., poll bk. 1784. [65] Mason, *Bridgnorth*, 32.
[66] Bridgnorth boro. rec., papers in *Rex v. Downes*, 1785–6; ibid., burgesses' admission papers; ibid., common hall order bk. 4, p. 154; ibid., papers in *Rex v. Smith and Dallewy*; ibid., licensing papers, 1786; *European Mag.* viii (1785), 317 (wrongly dates bailiffs' election).
[67] Dudmaston Hall, MSS. of Lady Labouchere, Mrs. Frances Barbara Whitmore to Wm. Whitmore, June or July 178[9].
[68] *Shrews. Chron.* 18 and 25 June 1790.
[69] Yarlington Lodge, papers *penes* (1968) Sir Rob. Pigot, Thos. Mytton to Geo. Pigot, 23 Feb. 1795.
[70] *T.S.A.S.* liv. 198. [71] Ibid. 4th ser. v. 69.
[72] L. G. Mitchell, *Chas. Jas. Fox and the Disintegration of the Whig Party 1782–1794* (1971), 298.
[73] P.R.O. 30/8/116, Browne to Pitt, 19 Apr. 1795.

[74] *Shrews. Chron.* 9 Oct. 1812.
[75] Earlier his life had not been without ludicrous moments: *Works of the Rev. Sydney Smith* (1859), ii. 147.
[76] *Parl. Hist. of Eng.* xxiv–xxxvi; 1–23 *Parl. Deb.* 1st ser.
[77] P.R.O. 30/8/116, 249, 264. [78] *D.N.B.*
[79] Birm. Ref. Libr., Assay Office Boulton Papers, B. 5/142.
[80] But his father came from Calcutta: J. Foster, *Alumni Oxonienses . . . 1715–1886*, ii. 806.
[81] Birm. Ref. Libr., Assay Office Boulton Papers, B. 2/68–71, 75; S.R.O. 1104, letter bks. of Thos. Barnfield, sen., no. 3, Barnfield to Revd. Dr. [Geo.] Whitmore, 5 July 1802.
[82] Birm. Ref. Libr., Assay Office Boulton Papers, B. 2/71–2.
[83] Ibid. B. 2/67, 74; Bridgnorth boro. rec., common hall order bk. 5, pp. 136–44; *Shrews. Chron.* 9 July 1802.
[84] *T.S.A.S.* xlvii. 188; *D.N.B.*

took up his seat,[85] to exemplify during almost 25 years the qualities of a staunch[86] and silent[87] Tory. Before his retirement in 1812 Browne offered his support to the Hon. Charles Cecil Cope Jenkinson of Pitchford, Lord Liverpool's half-brother.[88] Jenkinson addressed nearly a hundred influential gentlemen, had not a single refusal, and was thus able to refuse an invitation to stand for Sussex.[89] Six years later Jenkinson stood for East Grinstead (Suss.).[90] His equally Tory and equally silent[91] successor, Sir Thomas John Tyrwhitt Jones of Stanley Hall,[92] professed extreme satisfaction at having secured the approval of Browne[93] who died that year.[94] The changed character of the electorate was apparent when in 1818 the out-voters in Birmingham were persuaded that Birmingham's interests were 'materially connected with the proper representation of the borough of Bridgnorth'.[95] Tyrwhitt Jones thought it prudent to make a list of the London burgesses, of whom there were 42.[96]

In 1820 Thomas Whitmore was faced by a dilemma. The second seat was sought by his cousin William Wolryche Whitmore of Dudmaston who was as convinced and loquacious a Whig reformer as Thomas was a staunch and silent Tory. Nevertheless for ten years the elder cousin supported his Whig kinsman. In 1820 a Tory squire, Ralph Benson of Lutwyche, canvassed the electors,[97] but there was no serious test of strength and Benson withdrew,[98] having charged the Whitmores with subverting the electors' rights.[99]

Unlike any other Whitmore, Wolryche Whitmore actually spoke in the Commons. Allegedly prolix and soporiferous,[1] he spoke on slavery, emigration, India, and the currency,[2] and in 1821 seconded the motion for parliamentary reform put by his wife's cousin,[3] Lord John Russell.[4] Above all he advocated freer trade and changes in the corn laws,[5] views that were anathema to the landed interest in the constituency but appealed to the manufacturing element among the out-voters,[6] and he had much support from resident middle-class voters,[7] some of them dissenters.[8] Local Tories easily rallied opposition to him, but had no local candidate.

In 1826 Wolryche Whitmore was opposed by Ebenezer Ludlow, town clerk of Bristol[9] and a notably eloquent lawyer;[10] his chief supporters were John Clare, a Wolverhampton parson, and W. L. Lampet, a rich Bridgnorth resident of Oxfordshire descent.[11] There had been no poll since 1802, and 307 new burgesses were made.[12] There were meetings and open houses in the west midland towns. After five days' polling Ludlow abandoned the contest, just over 100 votes behind Wolryche Whitmore. Thomas Whitmore was easily top. In Bridgnorth itself 291 voted and, although many were ready to vote for both Whitmores, Ludlow was only 64 votes behind his Whig

[85] *T.S.A.S.* 4th ser. v. 70.
[86] B.L. Add. MS. 40407, f. 131.
[87] 6–41 *Parl. Deb.* 1st ser.; 1–25 *Parl. Deb.* 2nd ser.; 1–8 *Parl. Deb.* 3rd ser.
[88] *Complete Peerage*, viii. 89.
[89] B.L. Add. MS. 38328, ff. 45v.–6; 38739, f. 74v.; N.L.W., Pitchford Hall, Jenkinson's letter bk., Jenkinson to Ld. Sheffield (4 Oct. 1812), Ld. Liverpool (5 Oct. 1812), and Ctss. of Aboyne (11 Oct. 1812). S. R. Glynne had evidently considered standing (Bodl. John Johnson collection, Gitton MSS., poster dated at Farmcott 29 Sept.), but did not persevere.
[90] Henry S. Smith, *Parliaments of Eng. from 1715 to 1847*, ed. F. W. S. Craig (1973), 552.
[91] 37–41 *Parl. Deb.* 1st ser.; 1–3 *Parl. Deb.* 2nd ser.
[92] *T.S.A.S.* 4th ser. v. 71.
[93] *Salopian Jnl.* 10 June 1818; *The Late Elections . . .* (London, 1818), 21–2.
[94] *T.S.A.S.* 4th ser. v. 70.
[95] *Shrews. Chron.* 5 June 1818.
[96] S.R.O. 840, box 164, copy list of Bridgnorth voters resident in London.
[97] *Shrews. Chron.* 18 and 25 Feb. 1820.
[98] Ibid. 3 Mar. 1820.
[99] *Bridgnorth Jnl.* 1 June 1951.
[1] Hughes, *Sheriffs*, 21–2.
[2] 1–25 *Parl. Deb.* 2nd ser.; 1–6 *Parl. Deb.* 3rd ser.
[3] Burke, *Land. Gent.* (1952), 2707; Burke, *Peerage* (1949), 164–5, 246.
[4] 5 *Parl. Deb.* 2nd ser. 622.   [5] Hughes, *Sheriffs*, 21–2.
[6] Bridgnorth boro. rec., MS. poll bk. 1830; Bowen & Sons, of Dudley, to John Pritchard, 15 July 1830 (transcript supplied by Mr. J. D. Nichol of Shrews.).
[7] Dudmaston Hall, MSS. of Lady Labouchere, list of W. W. Whitmore's electn. cttee. June 1826.
[8] e.g. the McMichaels and the Sings: *S.P.R. Nonconformist Registers*, ii. 183–5.
[9] F. Boase, *Modern Eng. Biog.* ii (1897), 527.
[10] *Gent. Mag.* cxxviii(1), 666–7.
[11] *Bridgnorth Jnl.* 25 May 1951.
[12] Bridgnorth boro. rec., common hall order bk. 6, pp. 146–86.

rival in town votes. Ludlow and his agents canvassed hard among the out-voters, of whom no fewer than 555 voted, but the Whitmores' efforts were just as thorough and Ludlow could not overtake Wolryche Whitmore. The Whitmores' joint bill for the election came to £3,854, of which £1,213 went to the town publicans and £327 on bringing in out-voters.[13]

By 1830 Wolryche Whitmore had displeased not only the local Tories by his vote for Roman Catholic emancipation,[14] but also interests outside. In 1830 the Tories tried the efficacy of wealth. The new third man was Richard Arkwright,[15] grandson of the inventor,[16] who probably had the support of the East India Company[17] and perhaps that of Wellington's ministry, both of which resented Wolryche Whitmore's opposition to the impending renewal of the company's charter.[18] The contest was said to be one on which 'the eyes of the commercial inhabitants of this country have been intensely fixed'. Virulence against the 'family compact' was more bitter than ever.[19] Immense efforts produced another 227 new burgesses.[20]

Arkwright was proposed by Clare and seconded by another parson. Clare nevertheless acknowledged that Thomas Whitmore could return 'whom he likes' for the borough.[21] No more residents could be polled than in 1826, but many more out-voters were brought in. The proportion, and perhaps the absolute number, of out-voters polled was higher than at any previous election.[22] For the Whitmores, London out-voters were managed by the London firm of Whitmore & Co., the principals of which were the candidates' second cousins; Worcester voters were managed by Wolryche Whitmore's brother-in-law, Elias Isaac. Wolryche Whitmore produced one voter from as far away as Chichester. The Whitmores spent almost £7,700 between them,[23] and Arkwright's expenses were reportedly £10,000.[24] Arkwright retired after three days' polling, over 300 votes behind Wolryche Whitmore, with Thomas Whitmore again top.[25]

Recurring expenditure on the 1830 scale could not be contemplated at Apley; the 1832 Reform Act,[26] which abolished out-voters, may have come just in time for Thomas Whitmore. Impressed perhaps by local feeling in favour of parliamentary reform,[27] he retired, and in 1831 allowed his cousin to take one seat, and James Foster of Coton Hall, a Stourbridge ironmaster who had seconded Wolryche Whitmore in 1830,[28] the other. Both were Whigs, but the Bridgnorth Tories did not oppose them,[29] and the borough cast two votes for the 1832 Reform Bill.[30]

Ludlow

The Restoration did not restore the influence of the Council in the Marches in Ludlow elections, though that influence was exercised under James II. From 1660 to 1727 there was no single dominant interest, and Ludlow was contested by local families; the Charltons of Ludford, the Baldwyns of Stokesay, and the Walcots of

[13] Dudmaston Hall, poll bk. *penes* (1951) Capt. G. C. Wolryche-Whitmore; *Bridgnorth Jnl.* 22 June 1951; Orsett Hall (Ess.), papers *penes* (in 1950s) Sir Fra. Whitmore, electn. acct. of T. Whitmore and W. W. Whitmore, June 1826.

[14] Printed handbill, 8 Nov. 1828: scrapbk. *penes* the late H. L. Cunnington, of Bridgnorth; *Shrews. Chron.* 5 Aug. 1830.

[15] *T.S.A.S.* 4th ser. v. 20.

[16] *D.N.B.*

[17] *Shrews. Chron.* 5 Aug. 1830. Arkwright denied it.

[18] Ibid. 23 July 1830.

[19] Ibid. 5 Aug. 1830.

[20] Bridgnorth boro. rec., common hall order bk. 6,

pp. 329–77.

[21] *Shrews. Chron.* 5 Aug. 1830.

[22] Bridgnorth boro. rec., MS. poll bk. 1830.

[23] Dudmaston Hall, MSS. of Lady Labouchere, 'Acct. of Expenses attending Messrs. Whitmores' electn. . . . Aug. 1830'; Burke, *Land. Gent.* (1952), 2706–7.

[24] *Bridgnorth Jnl.* 24 Aug. 1951.

[25] *T.S.A.S.* 4th ser. v. 20.

[26] Representation of the People Act, 1832, 2 Wm. IV, c. 45.

[27] *Shrews. Chron.* 18 Mar., 22 Apr. 1831.

[28] Ibid. 5 Aug. 1830.

[29] *T.S.A.S.* 4th ser. v. 20.

[30] 11 *Parl. Deb.* 3rd ser. 781–2.

Walcot and Bitterley were at first the most active. The Charltons were Tory; the Baldwyns, at first Whig, and Walcots, at first Tory, later changed parties. In 1689 a Herbert of Oakly Park first sat for the borough, and his descendants controlled it from 1727, sitting almost continuously until its parliamentary status was abolished in 1885 and representing the Ludlow county division 1922–45. After 1727 there were only two contests before the 1832 Reform Act, only one of which was carried to a real poll.[31]

From 1661 to 1698 a borough by-law limited the Ludlow franchise to resident burgesses, about a hundred in number. During that period the by-law and the promotions and deaths of M.P.s gave the candidates, who were often lawyers, many opportunities to petition. For most of the 18th century out-voters were far more numerous than resident voters. In the early 19th century the franchise was restricted by deliberate management to well under a hundred electors.

In 1660 the Twelve and the Twenty-Five at Ludlow ordered that, as before, the election of M.P.s was confined to themselves, and on the same day they elected two Cavaliers, Job Charlton, M.P. in 1659, and Timothy Littleton, the recorder. By the same order those M.P.s were to be elected by the Twelve and the Twenty-Five 'or others as they in their wisdom shall think fit'. Job Charlton, a lawyer and son of a Whitton man who had prospered in London, bought Ludford in 1667. Littleton was the brother of Charles I's lord keeper.[32] The corporation ruling of 1660 was reversed in 1661; Samuel Baldwyn, Charlton's colleague in 1659, came forward on the narrow franchise against the sitting member and Charlton and Baldwyn were elected by 25 and 21 votes respectively to Littleton's 14; but when the common burgesses were polled the figures became Charlton 45, Littleton 40, and Baldwyn 34.[33] Baldwyn petitioned against Littleton's return but the Commons committee, chaired by Charlton, reported in favour of the Twelve and Twenty-Five and the resident common burgesses.[34] Except in 1685 the common burgesses were not thereafter excluded from the Ludlow franchise.

The narrowness of that franchise made the enforcement of the Corporation Act[35] particularly important. The commissioners under the Act removed 3 aldermen, 2 common councilmen, and 15 burgesses; they appointed 3 aldermen, 4 common councilmen, and 10 burgesses. The corporation was packed with Cavaliers; of the commissioners Charles Baldwyn and William Bowdler were made aldermen, Thomas Crump became a common councilman, and 5 others became burgesses.[36]

For some time the Ludlow M.P.s supported the Court. In 1664 both were Court dependants.[37] Littleton, on becoming a baron of the Exchequer in 1670, was succeeded by Col. Somerset Foxe of Caynham, a royalist whose great-grandfather had sat for Ludlow.[38] Charlton was nominated by the Court as speaker in 1673, but withdrew after a fortnight owing to ill health.[39] In 1677 Shaftesbury listed Foxe and Charlton as 'very vile',[40] and the Whigs got no satisfaction at Ludlow from the 1679 elections.

In February 1679 Sir Job Charlton, recorder since 1675, was succeeded by his son Francis. In September Foxe did not stand. Francis Charlton and Thomas Walcot, serjeant at law, stood. Both were courtiers. Walcot was opposed by a Shaftesburian Charles Baldwyn, son of Samuel. The franchise was still an issue, for the candidates had to undertake to abide solely by the votes of the common councillors and other

[31] At uncontested Ludlow electns. formal polls were nevertheless held: S.R.O. 356, boxes 301–2, poll bks. 1734–1806.

[32] S.R.O. 356/2/2, f. 171; T.S.A.S. 2nd ser. vii. 30–1; 2nd ser. xi. 307.

[33] T.S.A.S. 2nd ser. vii. 31; Staffs. R.O., D.(W.) 1788, P.46, B.6, 'Mr. Baldwyn's Breviatt'.

[34] C.J. viii. 14.

[35] 13 Chas. II, Stat. II, c. 1.

[36] S.R.O. 356/2/2, ff. 208–10.

[37] J. R. Jones, 'Ct. Dependents in 1664', Bull. Inst. Hist. Res. xxxiv. 85.

[38] T.S.A.S. 2nd ser. vii. 32–3.

[39] D.N.B.

[40] Bull. Inst. Hist. Res. xliii. 100.

sworn burgesses. Charlton and Walcot were returned. According to Baldwyn, however, Charlton had 50 votes, Baldwyn 48, and Walcot 43. Baldwyn contended that the town clerk, Charlton's brother William, had refused to accept the votes of three further burgesses because they were reputed 'fanatics' or nonconformists, and because one of them was thought to have been turned out by the Corporation Act and ought therefore not to vote.[41] In 1680 the Whigs dismissed William Charlton from the town clerkship,[42] and at the 1681 election the tables were turned, for the Whig Baldwyn received 55 votes, Charlton 46, and Walcot 16; four other candidates received 17 votes between them.[43] Charlton and Walcot had received 34 joint votes in 1679, but in 1680 Charlton and Baldwyn received 37.

The outgoing bailiffs surrendered the borough charter in October 1684, and five months later James II issued a new one naming Francis, Sir Job, and William Charlton, and Somerset Foxe to the corporation and William Charlton as town clerk and steward. This charter vested the parliamentary franchise in the Twelve and Twenty-Five. The lord president of the Council in the Marches was empowered to replace officers at the king's direction,[44] and under James II Ludlow duly returned two firm supporters of the king. In 1685 two lawyers were elected unanimously: Sir Edward Herbert, a younger son of the 2nd Lord Herbert of Chirbury, Jeffreys's successor as chief justice of Chester and later a Jacobite, and William Charlton, the town clerk.[45] Charlton's death three days later was followed by the unopposed election of a rich London merchant, Sir Josiah Child. Child's daughter had married the lord president's eldest son.[46] Before the year was out Herbert's promotion to lord chief justice was followed by the unopposed return of Sir Edward Lutwyche of Lutwyche, a king's serjeant.[47] In 1688 the choice of M.P.s was left to the lord president, who recommended Humphrey Cornewall of Burford and Charles Molloy, a lawyer.[48] In December James dissolved the corporation, an act that was to create disputed claims to the franchise.[49] In 1689 two Williamite M.P.s, Francis Herbert and Charles Baldwyn, were returned.[50] Herbert was the son of Richard Herbert of Oakly Park and nephew of the 4th Lord Herbert of Chirbury (d. 1691). Francis was the ancestor of many Ludlow M.P.s; Baldwyn had sat for Ludlow in 1681.[51] The following year, 1690, ushered in an agitated period in Ludlow politics; an enlargement of the electorate resulted, though one less marked than at Bridgnorth and Much Wenlock.

Eleven of the thirteen general elections between 1690 and 1727 were contested at Ludlow. In 1690 Francis Charlton, claiming to act as mayor under the 1685 charter, secured the election writ and returned Thomas Hanmer, his brother-in-law, and William Gower of Monkland (Herefs.), a turbulent lawyer, after an election by 'new corporation men' and 28 burgesses all qualified under that charter. The rival candidates were the Hon. Fitton Gerard, son of Lord Macclesfield (the last lord president), and Francis Lloyd of Crickadarn (Brec.). Gerard and Lloyd claimed that on the same day they had been unanimously elected by those qualified under Edward IV's charter and that the sheriff had torn up the bailiffs' indenture returning them;[52] they petitioned.[53] The charter under which Charlton claimed to act excluded the burgesses whom he had allowed to vote. The Commons committee held that Hanmer and Gower had a majority of burgesses old and new, but ordered a new election.[54] That

[41] Staffs. R.O., D.(W.) 1788, P.18, B.1; ibid. P.46, B.6; T.S.A.S. 2nd ser. vii. 33–4; 2nd ser. xi. 307.
[42] T.S.A.S. 2nd ser. vii. 34.
[43] Staffs. R.O., D.(W.) 1788, P.46, B.6.
[44] C.J. x. 352–3, 521–2.
[45] T.S.A.S. 2nd ser. vii. 34.
[46] Ibid. 35; D.N.B. sub Child, Sir Josiah; Complete Peerage, ii. 52–3.
[47] T.S.A.S. 2nd ser. vii. 35.
[48] G. Duckett, Penal Laws and Test Acts, ii (1883), 185; ex inf. Hist. of Parl.
[49] C.J. x. 353.
[50] Ibid. 522.
[51] T.S.A.S. 2nd ser. vii. 35–6.
[52] Ibid. 36; C.J. x. 353; Caroline A. J. Skeel, Council in the Marches of Wales (1904), 178–9, 287.
[53] C.J. x. 428.
[54] Ibid. 521–2.

too was contested, for Lloyd and a new partner, Col. Silius Titus, opposed Hanmer and Gower. On 14 January 1691 the two former were returned with 57 and 49 votes respectively against 41 for Gower and 39 for Hanmer. The losers petitioned, maintaining that their opponents' majority depended on over 20 votes of burgesses improperly created. Burgesses made under the 1685 charter had ceased to be an issue. The claims of non-residents, however, were put forward for the first time. Lloyd and Titus maintained that only residents could vote, Hanmer and Gower that non-residents were eligible. The Commons decided for Titus and Lloyd.[55]

A powerful interest appeared on the scene when, in August 1695, it was rumoured that the Crown had granted temporary custody of Ludlow castle to Lord Bradford in order to further the candidacy of his son Thomas Newport.[56] In October the 2nd earl of Macclesfield set up Lloyd, by then recorder, and a Col. Mathews,[57] and a week later 'very great expense' by Newport, Lloyd, and Charles Baldwyn was reported.[58] Mathews appears to have withdrawn, and Newport and Baldwyn were returned. Lloyd submitted a petition but then withdrew it.[59]

Three years later there was again a contest. Francis Herbert and William Gower, standing together, were returned, and Newport was defeated. His petition against the return of Gower, and a petition by Newport's supporters against the refusal of their votes, had important results. Charles Baldwyn, a former M.P., maintained to the Commons committee that the sons and sons-in-law of burgesses did not become burgesses as of right, and that the chamber need admit only those whom it chose. The committee ruled that the men in question had a right to be admitted. Supporting the committee, the Commons resolved that no formal petition was necessary to secure admission as a burgess, despite a by-law of 1663. The Commons made no reservation as to residents and thus opened the way to out-voters at Ludlow. The voters in 1698 had been polled 'as they stood in their places, in the hall', a practice that increased numbers soon made impossible, but Newport maintained that the bailiffs had not admitted 34 qualified men with whose votes he would have beaten Gower. In fact the high bailiff was against Newport and the low bailiff for him. The committee found for Gower but the Commons reversed the decision by a small majority and declared Newport elected.[60]

In January 1701 Gower was again returned, with the Tory Sir Thomas Powys of Henley, who was a kinsman of the Littletons and as attorney general had led the prosecution of the Seven Bishops. In December 1701, however, there was yet another three-cornered contest; Gower was defeated and Powys returned with Francis Herbert. Gower petitioned against Herbert's return on the grounds of bribery and corruption, but no decision was given.[61] In 1702 Gower was prevailed upon to stand aside; Powys was elected both for Ludlow and (on the Boscawen interest) for Truro. Robert Harley expected 'great endeavours' to persuade Powys to sit for Truro and allow Gower to sit one last time for Ludlow; Powys would thereby make his future position at Ludlow secure, 'Gower giving assurance never more to appear, who otherwise will always find him trouble enough by his friends and by his activity'.[62] Powys, however, sat for Ludlow and in 1705 Gower came forward again, to be defeated by Powys and Acton Baldwyn, son of the 1695 M.P. The electorate, a mere 90 in 1679,[63] now numbered over 300 and non-residents had been admitted to the franchise. Powys and Baldwyn

[55] Ibid. 575–6; *T.S.A.S.* 2nd ser. vii. 36–7.
[56] B.L. Loan 29/188, f. 28.
[57] Ibid. 29/301, And. Newport to Rob. Harley, 22 Oct. 1695.
[58] Surr. R.O., Acc. 775. A3, Somers MSS., Rob. Harley to Sir John Somers, 29 Oct. 1695.
[59] *C.J.* xi. 338, 394.
[60] *C.J.* xii. 536–9. The ruling as to individual petitions is wrongly reported by Oldfield, *Hist of Boros.* (1792), ii. 425, and *Rep. Hist. of Gt. Brit. and Irel.* (1816), iv. 397.
[61] *C.J.* xiii. 651.
[62] B.L. Add. MS. 28055, ff. 3v., 4.
[63] Staffs. R.O., D.(W.) 1788, P.18, B.1.

were returned in 1708 and 1710, but on both occasions only after much activity. In 1708 the defeated candidate was Humphrey Cornewall.[64]

In July 1710 Dr. Sacheverell visited Ludlow where, as elsewhere, his visit stirred up feeling. Both sitting M.P.s had voted against Sacheverell's impeachment, but Baldwyn would not declare himself until August; he had 'very much wanted an honest gentleman to appear'.[65] In July Powys wrote to a supporter that he knew not 'who and who are together', as none would declare.[66] By September there were four in the field, Baldwyn and Powys on the Tory side, and Francis Herbert and the Baldwyns' cousin Humphrey Walcot of Bitterley on the other. Baldwyn wrote: 'Mr. Herbert is a thorough paced Whig, Walcot behaves himself like a villain, Sir Thomas Powys behaves himself very friendly towards me, but we are none of us joined and I believe shall stand upon our own legs'. Walcot, having bought several votes for over £20 each, had spent over £1,000, Powys £400, and Baldwyn £200, though he expected to have to spend another £100.[67] Herbert throughout tried to persuade Baldwyn to join Walcot, but at the end was outmanœuvred. On 2 October Walcot met Powys by appointment and, without telling Herbert, agreed to stand down; he did so apparently at the order of the Court signified through his kinsman and patron James Brydges, the paymaster general. When Herbert heard the news a report spread that he would stand, whereupon Powys fetched in at least fifty more burgesses. The election was held on 6 October. A poll was in fact demanded on Walcot's behalf, in which he received 9 votes to over 200 each for Powys and Baldwyn.[68] It was the most spectacular of the Tory triumphs in Shropshire in 1710.

Within twenty years, however, the Whigs obtained a firm hold on Ludlow. In 1713 Powys became a justice of Queen's Bench, and his colleague Baldwyn was confronted by Walcot and Herbert. Baldwyn and Walcot were returned. Two years later Herbert and Walcot easily defeated Baldwyn, a Hanoverian Tory in 1714.[69] Walcot had the support of Brydges,[70] earl of Carnarvon (the future duke of Chandos), who was negotiating the purchase of an estate at Bishop's Castle.[71] Baldwyn petitioned against both victors on the ground of bribery, but withdrew.[72] In 1719 Herbert died, after four short spells as M.P. for Ludlow. His eldest son was only sixteen, and the vacancy was filled by a stranger, Sir Robert Raymond, a barrister. Raymond had been elected at Bishop's Castle on the Harley interest in 1710, but in 1717 the Whig ministry was trying to win him over.[73] His election in 1719 was on Chandos's recommendation[74] and presumably on the Herbert interest; in 1720 he was made attorney general. Two years later Baldwyn made his last effort. In November 1721 Chandos was recommending Raymond for re-election, confident that Walcot would be top and that Raymond would defeat the new candidate Abel Ketelby,[75] a local Tory barrister. Chandos, however, soon feared Walcot's defeat and found Raymond a seat at Helston (Cornw.).[76] Over 500 voted, and Ketelby and Baldwyn, thought a potential Jacobite in 1721,[77] easily beat Walcot, who had thought himself so secure that he tried, through Chandos, to stop burgesses being brought down to Ludlow; forty, however, set out on foot, confident of reward.[78]

Baldwyn died early in 1727 and the long ascendancy of the Oakly Park interest began immediately. Henry Arthur Herbert, Francis Herbert's eldest son, had become M.P.

[64] Ibid.
[65] N.L.W., Ottley Papers 2578.
[66] S.R.O. 3385/2/32.
[67] N.L.W., Ottley Papers 2578.
[68] Ibid. 2587.
[69] Ibid. 1631.
[70] Huntington Libr., ST 57/10, pp. 247–9; 57/11, p. 125.
[71] See p. 300.
[72] C.J. xviii. 29, 366.
[73] B.L. Stowe MS. 750, f. 181.
[74] Hist. Parl., Commons, 1715–54, ii. 379.
[75] Northants. R.O., Temple (Stowe) coll., Chandos letter bk. 20, p. 3.
[76] Ibid., pp. 27, 44.
[77] Hist. Parl., Commons, 1715–54, i. 311, 430.
[78] Chandos letter bk. 20, pp. 165–6.

for Bletchingley (Surr.) on coming of age in 1724, and it was his next brother Richard who succeeded to Baldwyn's seat in 1727. At the general election later that year the brothers stood jointly and, after a five days' poll in which 710 votes were cast, defeated William Pearce Hall of Downton and Edmund Pytts of Kyre (Worcs.) in what proved to be the last poll at Ludlow for 99 years. To Chandos's annoyance the Walcots supported Hall, and the duke divided his interest between the elder Herbert and Hall.[79]

Chandos's wishes ceased to matter. Between the 1727 and 1734 general elections no fewer than 158 burgesses were admitted, considerably more than during the previous quarter of a century; most were non-resident gentry and lawyers,[80] presumably Whigs, and they provided the basis of the Herberts' power in Ludlow. From 1727 the Oakly Park interest, held by the Herberts and Clives, nominated to both seats and always provided one M.P., sometimes both. The Herbert brothers sat until 1741 when the younger was replaced by Sir William Corbet of Adderley, who had sat for Montgomeryshire on the Herbert interest (1727-41). Two years later Richard returned to the Commons when his brother was created Lord Herbert of Chirbury.[81] In 1748 Corbet died, and the earl of Powis (formerly Lord Herbert)[82] 'without the least solicitation' offered the seat to Sir Henry Bridgeman, Lord Bradford's nephew.[83] The situation at Ludlow had changed since 1727; according to Bridgeman the election was carried on peaceably, for Powis had a great personal interest there exclusive of his great estate, 'without which great estates are of little consequence'.[84] Egmont described Ludlow as 'totally in Lord Powis', on whom he added: 'I think this a much more artful man than he appears — and for aught I know may keep fair on both sides. But there is not a man in England in whom Pelham places more confidence'.[85]

In 1754 Richard Herbert died, and Powis brought in a kinsman who had settled in England that year as his agent, Edward Herbert of Muckross (co. Kerry). A visitor to Ludlow in 1756, alluding to Milton's *Comus*, wrote: 'The god is now vanquished: but, at the revolution of every seven years, his rout does not fail to keep up orgies . . . as Lord Powis knows to his cost, for he has spent twenty or thirty thousand pounds in entertaining them'.[86] The fear of unnecessary 'orgies' was not altogether extinct. In 1766 Bridgeman offended Powis by his ambitions for a county seat;[87] had they occasioned a by-election at Ludlow, opposition might have been mounted there, for W. P. Hall began to distribute money among the electors,[88] and was also engaging county electors for Charles Baldwyn,[89] Bridgeman's Tory rival for the county.[90] In 1768 Bridgeman had to find another seat, which was provided by the Foresters at Much Wenlock. At Ludlow Powis brought in his nephew William Fellowes.[91] The other borough seat was occupied 1768-74 by Herberts, Edward (d. 1770) and his son Thomas. Powis's son succeeded to the earldom in 1772 when under age and so never sat in the Commons. His father had sold Oakly Park about 1769 to Lord Clive, but the families co-operated and the new earl continued to control Ludlow. In 1774 he put forward Clive's young son Edward and Lord Villiers. The Clive interest was uneasy, for £473 was spent.[92] Circulars were sent out,[93] and Clive thought his agent's personal attendance

[79] Huntington Libr., ST 57/30, pp. 75, 119, 121.
[80] S.R.O. 356, box 283, list of copy entries of burgesses' admissions 1690-1773. Cf. S.R.O. 356/2/5, f. 308. Comparatively few townsmen were admitted during these yrs.
[81] *T.S.A.S.* 2nd ser. vii. 41-2.
[82] *Complete Peerage*, x. 651.
[83] Staffs. R.O., D.1287/10/4a, Hen. Bridgeman to Mrs. Bridgeman, 2 Jan. 1748/9.
[84] Ibid.
[85] *Camd. Misc.* xxiii (Camd. 4th ser. vii), 151.
[86] *Works of Geo., Ld. Lyttelton*, ed. G. E. Ayscough

(1774), iii. 738; S.R.O. 356, box 295, corresp. between Powis and town clk. of Ludlow.
[87] See p. 261.
[88] India Office Libr., MS. Eur. G. 37/39; Staffs. R.O., D.1287/10/4b, memo. by N. Tonkes *re* canvass for Bridgeman, 19 Apr. 1766.
[89] Staffs. R.O., D.(W.) 1788, P.45, B.11, list of freeholders canvassed.
[90] See p. 260.
[91] *T.S.A.S.* 2nd ser. vii. 43.
[92] C 109/72/6.
[93] C 109/6/3, 34.

'absolutely necessary'.[94] There had been rumours of an opposition to Villiers, though W. P. Hall denied any such intention. Such opposition would ultimately have made it impossible for the Hon. Edward Clive to stand, for he was not of age until March 1775.[95] The need for a stop-gap candidate was considered,[96] and Edward Clive canvassed on his own behalf or, should the need arise, his father's.[97] Edward Clive and Villiers were returned unopposed in October 1774.

The bailiffs were apparently uneasy under the Powis yoke in 1776, when Hall assured them that he still wished to see the burgesses 'triumph in their independence'.[98] In 1780 Thomas Beale of the Heath, Leintwardine, actually challenged the Powis candidates. Powis's letters signifying his choice of his cousin Frederick Cornewall, previously M.P. for Leominster, as Lord Clive's colleague were delayed. Unaware of Powis's choice,[99] Beale had been brought forward by the 'patriots and discontents' of Ludlow at a public meeting held as early as 20 June, in order to help the burgesses to recover the borough's 'independence',[1] and found himself committed too far to withdraw. Clive and Cornewall set to work; the latter thought the threat 'serious' and called on North's ministry for help.[2] Powis was later said to have offered the borough to Richard Payne Knight,[3] whose ironmaster grandfather had bought the Downton Castle estate; he certainly persuaded him to support Cornewall.[4] Powis was publicly criticized by Beale for his 'open and avowed interposition' in favour of his candidates and was attacked anonymously for printing circulars 'directing' their election.[5] His candidates were criticized for voting against Dunning's resolution,[6] and Cornewall was singled out as too deaf to be a useful M.P.[7]

Presumably none of this worried Powis. During the contest only 33 new burgesses were admitted. Even more than at Bridgnorth the balance of the constituency had changed, for there were now as many as 226 out-voters, forming some nine tenths of the electorate.[8] Coaches were engaged to bring voters from London.[9] Beale canvassed from June to early September in many places; among the burgesses, however, he had only 31 promises to Clive's 113 and Cornewall's 117,[10] and four days before election day he withdrew.[11] His explanation ('a little inattention to the engagements of some of my well-wishers')[12] suggests that Powis had found means to remind them of their primary obligations.

On Cornewall's death in 1783 Powis put forward Somerset Davies, son of a Ludlow associate of Clive's late agent. Davies was attacked as a 'novus homo' who lacked the support of any country gentleman apart from Richard Payne Knight, who was hardly 'independent'.[13] There was no opposition, but by the end of the year Powis withdrew support from Davies and put forward Knight,[14] then M.P. for Leominster. Classical scholar and connoisseur, Knight was well known as an exponent of the extreme picturesque school of landscape gardening and architecture, and designed and built his seat, Downton Castle.[15] There was an attempt to find a third candidate before the

[94] C 109/71/4/20.
[95] C 109/71/4/19.
[96] C 109/72/3, H. Strachey to J. Ashby, 'Tues. night' [?4 Oct. 1774].
[97] C 109/71/4/19.
[98] S.R.O. 356, box 294, W. P. Hall to burgesses of Ludlow, 3 June 1776.
[99] B.L. Add. MS. 38458, f. 118.
[1] Shrews. Chron. 24 June 1780.
[2] Ibid. 9 Sept. 1780; B.L. Add. MS. 38458, ff. 116, 125–7; 38578, ff. 54, 58.
[3] Shrews. Chron. 10 May 1783.
[4] Ibid. 5 and 26 Aug. 1780; Hist. Parl., Commons, 1754–90, iii. 13.
[5] Shrews. Chron. 9 Sept. 1780.

[6] Ibid. 1 July 1780. Cf. D.N.B. sub Dunning, John.
[7] Shrews. Chron. 5 Aug. 1780.
[8] S.R.O. 356/2/6, pp. 256–9.
[9] B.L. Add. MS. 38458, f. 126.
[10] S.R.O. 356, box 282, canvass bk.; ibid., box 302, Beale's canvassing acct.
[11] Shrews. Chron. 16 Sept. 1780.
[12] Ibid. 23 Sept. 1780.
[13] Ibid. 10 May 1783.
[14] S.R.O. 356, box 294, S. Davies to —, 20 Dec. 1783. The statement (Oldfield, Hist. of Boros. (1792), ii. 421) that Knight 'originally became a candidate on the independent interest of the Town' is incorrect.
[15] D.N.B.; E. Hyams, Capability Brown and Humphry Repton (1971), 143.

1784 election, but T. R. Salwey of the Lodge, Overton, could not face the expense of making out-burgesses on the necessary scale,[16] and Nicholas Lechmere of Hanley Castle (Worcs.), nephew and heir of the last Charlton of Ludford, was deterred by likely expenses of £2,000.[17] Lechmere's brother Edmund was anxious for him to persevere, but their uncle hesitated because of the cost and a prior commitment to Lord Clive.[18] In the end no opposition was mounted.

For the next forty years Ludlow politics were almost uniformly peaceful. Powis continued to dispose of parliamentary interest there until his death in 1801. His sister had married Lord Clive in 1784, and under their marriage settlement Oakly Park and much of the Clive property, and so the control of Ludlow, passed to their younger son, the Hon. Robert Henry Clive.

Lord Clive was a Portland Whig, Knight a Foxite Whig and a supporter of parliamentary reform. There was an optimistic attempt in 1789 to interest Pitt in a plan to turn at least one of them out,[19] but they sat together until Clive received a peerage of Great Britain in 1794. He was succeeded at Ludlow by his brother Capt. the Hon. Robert Clive. Neither brother spoke in the Commons. In 1802 Lord Clive was absent in India and John Nicholls, M.P. for Tregony (Cornw.), was rumoured to intend trouble at Ludlow, but nothing came of this.[20] Knight wrote a monody on the death of his hero Fox, but then lost interest in Parliament and retired; three years later he moved to London where for long he ate and talked prodigiously at the table of Holland House.[21]

From 1806 to 1832 both M.P.s were Clives. The Hon. Robert Clive sat for one year with his young nephew Viscount Clive, heir to the earldom of Powis re-created in 1804 for the 2nd Lord Clive; Viscount Clive sat with a barrister kinsman, Henry Clive, from 1807 until 1818, and thereafter until 1832 with his own brother the Hon. R. H. Clive. After 1806 the borough provided two loyal and usually silent Tory votes. Henry Clive was later, as M.P. for Montgomery, an undistinguished under-secretary of state at the Home Office; Viscount Clive waited six years to make his maiden speech, and was silent from 1819 to 1826.

In 1816 it was stated that Ludlow 'submits implicitly to the nomination of its patron',[22] Powis. In 1826, however, occurred the first poll for 99 years. Edmund Lechmere Charlton opposed the now close corporation of Ludlow and the sons of the man whom his father Nicholas Lechmere had reluctantly declined to oppose in 1784. The number of burgesses had declined to about sixty, and Lechmere Charlton received 3 votes against 14 each for the Clives; votes tendered but rejected, however, would have returned Lechmere Charlton and the Hon. R. H. Clive with 15 each.[23] Lechmere Charlton petitioned; he argued that the last determination by the Commons was that of 1661, but the Commons committee ruled in favour of that of 1698.[24] He remained at the centre of opposition to the Clives for years. In 1827 rival meetings in Ludlow voiced criticism and praise of the Clives, whose latest expression of munificence was in the recent industrial distress and in their expenditure of £800 on a burial ground. The most contentious issue was the Ludlow charter.[25]

In 1829 Viscount Clive found unsought prominence. Peel, then Home Secretary,

[16] S.R.O. 356, box 294, T. R. Salwey to Jas. Kinnersley, 9 Jan. 1794.
[17] T.S.A.S. 2nd ser. vii. 45; S.R.O. 356, box 294,— to [Edm. Lechmere, 1784].
[18] S.R.O. 356, box 302, Edm. Lechmere to Jas. Kinnersley, 27 Mar. [1784].
[19] Hist. Parl., Commons, 1754–90, i. 363; ii. 223; iii. 13.
[20] N.L.W., Powis Castle corresp. 5247, 5249.
[21] Jnl. of the Hon. H. E. Fox, ed. earl of Ilchester (1923), 37, 57.
[22] Oldfield, Rep. Hist. of Gt. Brit. and Irel. (1816), iv. 397.
[23] S.R.O. 356, box 302, poll bk. 1826.
[24] C.J. lxxxii. 81, 439, 456.
[25] S.R.O. 356, box 295, copy address from burgesses and inh. of Ludlow to recorder and M.P.s, 11 Nov. 1827.

requested him to move the Address after the King's Speech foreshadowing concessions to Roman Catholics. Clive had done the duty before, but on this occasion it was with reluctance; his 'Protestant' views were the cause both of the invitation and of his reservations.[26] Next year Clive, though 'deaf as a post and not very bright', was entrusted by Wellington with a negotiation to bring Palmerston back to the Government side.[27]

Lechmere Charlton came forward in 1830 but was persuaded to withdraw by Charles Greville and C. W. Williams Wynn. He also agreed to withdraw from a corporation contest, while Clive agreed to pay him £1,125 towards his costs and not to oppose a petition to settle the disputed franchise.[28] Lechmere Charlton was destined nevertheless to sit for Ludlow.[29]

Much Wenlock

For almost the whole period and beyond it Much Wenlock was dominated by the Forester family. After 1679 ten Foresters sat for the borough.[30] Until the borough's disfranchisement in 1885 the Foresters controlled at least one seat except in 1685 and, except in special circumstances, a member of the family or a relation by marriage always sat; they filled both seats from 1738 to 1744 and from 1758 to 1761. At first, however, other local families represented the borough.

In 1660 Much Wenlock was the only Shropshire borough to return the same M.P.s as in 1659, Sir Francis Lawley and Thomas Whitmore.[31] As at Bridgnorth royalism was in the ascendant, and Sir John Weld the younger, bailiff 1660-1, admitted 14 gentlemen among a total of 29 new burgesses.[32] In 1661 Lawley's standing was perhaps too high[33] and Whitmore's probably too insignificant to represent the borough. Sir Thomas Littleton, M.P. 1640-6, was returned again, with the bailiff's brother George,[34] the first of five Welds to sit for the borough in the next half-century. The Welds, a prominent City family, had bought Willey from the Lacons before the Civil Wars; they were connected by marriage with the Whitmores of Apley Park, also a City family but with local roots.[35] In 1677-8 Littleton was thought moderate and inclined towards the 'country', Weld a violent 'courtier'.[36]

February 1679 saw a four-cornered contest at Much Wenlock, the first in Shropshire. Littleton stood again. Lawley, a courtier,[37] stood for Much Wenlock again rather than for the county. Both, however, were defeated by William Forester of Dothill and Sir John Weld of Willey.[38] Weld had been knighted by Charles I in 1642[39] and had married the daughter of Sir George Whitmore,[40] the royalist London alderman.[41] Forester, created a burgess immediately before the election,[42] was then just over 23 and a leading, perhaps a treasonous, Whig.[43] There was much cross-voting among the 276 polled: 61 voted for Littleton and Forester, 67 for Lawley and Weld, and 50 for Weld and Forester. Since the bailiffs voted for Weld and Forester, and the courtier

[26] B.L. Add. MS. 40398, ff. 101-3. Cf. N. Gash, *Mr. Secretary Peel* (1961), 551.

[27] Gash, op. cit. 643; *Jnl. of Mrs. Arbuthnot 1820-1832*, ed. F. Bamford and duke of Wellington (1950), ii. 389.

[28] *T.S.A.S.* 2nd ser. vii. 48.

[29] See p. 336.

[30] Namier, *Politics at Accession of Geo. III*, 244.

[31] *T.S.A.S.* 3rd ser. ii. 331; 4th ser. v. 62; xii. 215. At Bp.'s Cas. and Ludlow one of the 1659 M.P.s was returned: above, p. 284, and below, p. 297.

[32] S.R.O. 1224, box 335, bk. of extracts from M. Wenlock boro. rec. 1660-1810, p. [2].

[33] He moved on to sit for the co.: see p. 256.

[34] *T.S.A.S.* 3rd ser. ii. 333.

[35] M. D. G. Wanklyn, 'John Weld of Willey 1585-1665', *W. Midlands Studs*. iii. 88-9.

[36] *Bull. Inst. Hist. Res*. xliii. 100; A. Browning, *Thos. Osborne, Earl of Danby*, iii (1951), 39, 70, 90, 95, 114. This Geo. Weld (d. 1696) is to be distinguished from his nephew Geo. Weld, M.P. (d. 1701): above, p. 97 n. 85.

[37] *T.S.A.S.* 3rd ser. ii. 331.

[38] S.R.O. 1224/21/29.

[39] *T.S.A.S.* 4th ser. ii. 224.

[40] Ibid. 3rd ser. ii. 333.

[41] *D.N.B.*

[42] S.R.O. 1224, box 335, extracts bk., p. [64].

[43] *T.S.A.S.* 2nd ser. iii. 169-70; 3rd ser. ii. 333-4.

Sir Thomas Whitmore[44] for Weld and Lawley (his brother-in-law),[45] it may be deduced that Weld and Forester, although on opposite sides in the Exclusion controversy,[46] represented the dominant interests in the borough and liberties.

There were again four candidates in August 1679. Littleton had given up and found a seat at East Grinstead (Suss.).[47] The new candidate was John Wolryche of Dudmaston whose family still owned the land that had enabled his father to represent the borough.[48] Forester and Wolryche, in coalition, were returned, probably with Weld third and Lawley bottom.[49] The winners spent £124.[50] It was a gain for the Exclusionists. There was probably much less cross-voting than in February. A comparison of votes promised in August and those cast in February shows a hardening of party lines. The Country vote seems to have held up slightly better than the Court vote. Nevertheless the biggest change was in those who had split their votes in February; in August far fewer of them intended to do so.[51]

Not many burgesses were made for the 1679 elections.[52] On 21 October 1679, however, the bailiff admitted 66[53] in the interest of Forester and Wolryche. They were apparently unopposed in 1681 and were gratefully entertained for their 'good service'.[54] Preparations for future contests nevertheless continued. In 1683–4 169 burgesses were made, 144 of them in January and February 1684, perhaps in expectation of a general election that was never called; 34 of the 70 admitted on 8 January were in the Weld interest, the other 36 perhaps in that of William Forester,[55] who had been implicated in plots against the regime in 1683.[56] The number of burgesses rose to 610 by February 1684: 350 within the liberty, including 80 in Much Wenlock itself, and 260 without, including 25 in or near Shrewsbury and 81 in or near Bridgnorth. The total included many Shropshire gentlemen.[57]

In 1685 George Weld (d. 1701), a partisan of James II,[58] was returned with Thomas Lawley, son of Sir Francis[59] and the last Lawley to represent the borough until 1826. In the early months of James II's reign Forester knew better than to stand against Weld, who had been active as a deputy lieutenant in 1683;[60] Wolryche may have been ill.[61] At the Revolution, however, Forester came into his own. In 1710 he thought that what he had then done had not been forgotten by some of his friends nor forgiven by his enemies.[62]

From 1689 to 1708 Much Wenlock politics were outwardly stable. In January 1689 Forester (knighted the following August)[63] returned to sit with Weld in that and the next four Parliaments, then with Weld's son George (d. 1748) in the next three Parliaments, and finally with another son of Weld's, Thomas, in 1708.[64] Soon after the Revolution Forester, at the Board of the Green Cloth, was defending the new Court against a new Country party.[65] George Weld (d. 1701) voted as a 'Jacobite' in 1689[66] but his sons were Whigs[67] and his family was supported by two locally prominent Whig families, the Wolryches and the Whitmores. His daughter Elizabeth married Sir Thomas Wolryche in 1689[68] and the Whitmore connexion was of long standing.[69]

[44] T.S.A.S. 4th ser. iv. 276–7; Bull. Inst. Hist. Res. xliii. 100.
[45] S.R.O. 1224/21/29.
[46] For Weld's views (1677) see Bull. Inst. Hist. Res. xliii. 100.
[47] T.S.A.S. 3rd ser. ii. 328.
[48] Ibid. 4th ser. iv. 139, 144.
[49] S.R.O. 1224/21/2.
[50] S.R.O. 1224/21/26.
[51] S.R.O. 1224/21/2, 29.
[52] S.R.O. 1224, box 335, extracts bk.
[53] Ibid. pp. [66–7].
[54] Ibid. p. [68].
[55] Ibid. pp. [74–5].
[56] T.S.A.S. 3rd ser. ii. 333–4.
[57] S.R.O. 1224/21/28.
[58] Browning, Thos. Osborne, iii. 169, 206.
[59] T.S.A.S. 3rd ser. ii. 335.
[60] Ibid. 3rd ser. iv. 176–7.
[61] He d. in June in his late 40s: ibid. 4th ser. iv. 116.
[62] S.R.O. 1224/21/39.
[63] T.S.A.S. 3rd ser. ii. 333.
[64] Ibid. 336.
[65] J. A. Downie, 'The Commission of Public Accts. and the formation of the Country Party', E.H.R. xci. 45–6.
[66] Browning, Thos. Osborne, iii. 169.
[67] W. A. Speck, 'The Choice of a Speaker in 1705', Bull. Inst. Hist. Res. xxxvii. 43; S.R.O. 1224/21/30, 32.
[68] T.S.A.S. 4th ser. iv. 116–17.
[69] Burke, Land. Gent. (1952), 2706; above, p. 291.

There was nevertheless some excitement in the twenty years after William III's accession. In 1695 Forester and George Weld (d. 1701) beat Sir Francis Lawley.[70] That was perhaps the occasion when Lawley, unable to persuade his fellow Tory, Weld, to coalesce against Forester, applied to Forester for 70 or 80 second votes to defeat Weld.[71] The Lawleys remained quiet after 1695. That may have been partly due to the fact that the bailiff 1696-7 supported Forester[72] and admitted 238 burgesses on behalf of Sir Thomas Wolryche and Sir William Whitmore.[73] In 1704 a potential outside influence (that of the Berties) was neutralized when the borough's electoral procedure was changed; the lord of the manor's privilege of nominating a 'sixman' to choose the next bailiff was abrogated by the bailiff, the justice, and the bailiff's peers, and the bailiff and bailiff's peers assumed the right of electing the next bailiff.[74]

In 1709 relations between Forester and George Weld (d. 1748) were not good. Forester thought that Weld and his father had long neglected their interest in the constituency,[75] and in that year a contest for bailiff temporarily divided the two men.[76] They came together in 1710 to face a Tory attack. Despite ill-health Forester had to stand because his son William was under age, but was not prepared to do so with Thomas Weld, who was replaced by his brother George.[77] After Dr. Sacheverell's visit to Much Wenlock[78] the pace quickened; there were rumours that Whitmore Acton of Aldenham was standing for the Tories in order to make Forester spend money, though treating was not customary there, and that Sir Thomas Lawley and a Lutwyche were standing jointly.[79] In the end Lawley stood with his brother Richard.[80]

The number of burgesses had increased. Forester and Weld secured the admission of those who would not only vote for them in 1710 but 'make our elections of bailiffs safer and easier hereafter';[81] 122 were made on 16 August[82] and a few more later. In October 790 were listed;[83] among those recently admitted were three Whigs who were to be defeated elsewhere in the county. The support of Wolryche, Lord Bradford, and William Whitmore of Apley for Forester and Weld proved more successful than that of Wolryche, Bradford, and other Whigs for Whitmore at Bridgnorth.[84] Sir Thomas Lawley's object at Much Wenlock was probably a compromise with Weld, whereby either Lawley would give Weld his interest for the 1710 election or Lawley would stand in 1710 and Weld or Wolryche at the next election. Forester, however, saw no point, for Lawley, if he once got in, 'would soon find means of strengthening his interest and pretending to it ever after'.[85] Forester and Weld were easy winners and polled especially well at Little Wenlock and Wellington, where Forester's property lay.[86] Petitions were quickly prepared.[87] Lawley could win only by establishing the disqualification of all voters resident outside Much Wenlock itself; his petition and that of several burgesses alleged that he had a majority of those resident inside.[88] For the sitting members it was argued that the 1468 charter had restricted the suffrage only during the period in which Much Wenlock had returned one M.P.[89] The petitions were soon dropped.[90]

George Weld, the last of his family to sit for Much Wenlock, retired in 1713. Sir William Forester (d. 1718) and his son William presented the second seat in rapid succession to prominent Shropshire Whigs: William Whitmore in 1713, the Hon.

[70] S.R.O. 1224/21/37, probably refers back to 1695.
[71] S.R.O. 1224/21/36.
[72] S.R.O. 1224/21/32.
[73] S.R.O. 1224/21/36; S.R.O. 1224, box 335, extracts bk., pp. [111-13].
[74] S.R.O. 1224, box 335, extracts bk., p. [128].
[75] S.R.O. 1224/21/31.
[76] S.R.O. 1224/21/32-3.
[77] S.R.O. 1224/21/32; T.S.A.S. 3rd ser. ii. 337.
[78] G. Holmes, Trial of Dr. Sacheverell (1973), 244.

[79] S.R.O. 1224/21/34.
[80] C.J. xvi. 417.
[81] S.R.O. 1224/21/39.
[82] S.R.O. 1224, box 335, extracts bk., pp. [144-5].
[83] S.R.O. 1093, box 31A, burgess list 1710.
[84] See p. 277.
[85] S.R.O. 1224/21/37.
[86] S.R.O. 1224/21/45-7.
[87] S.R.O. 1224/21/49.
[88] S.R.O. 1224/21/50-1; C.J. xvi. 417.
[89] S.R.O. 1224/21/52.
[90] S.R.O. 1224/21/50.

Richard Newport in 1714,[91] the Hon Thomas Newport (later Lord Torrington) in 1715,[92] and Sir Humphrey Briggs in 1716.[93] The younger William Forester replaced his father as M.P. in 1715;[94] 81 new burgesses were admitted before the election, no doubt in the Foresters' interest.[95] In 1722, to oblige Lord Bradford, William Forester stood down, putting forward a placeman, Samuel Edwards of Frodesley and West Coppice, with the sitting member, Briggs.[96] Sir Thomas Lawley and Edward Cressett opposed them unsuccessfully in the last contest for almost a century. Lawley and Cressett petitioned fruitlessly, arguing as in 1710 for the limitation of the suffrage.[97]

After 1722 the Foresters controlled both seats peacefully for over sixty years, and with intermittent alarms for a further forty. William Forester the younger married the rich Catherine Brooke in 1714,[98] and in 1734 their son married the heiress of the last George Weld of Willey.[99] The Foresters' position near the town was thus improved. The Lawleys moved to Staffordshire[1] and the unexploited Bertie interest continued in absentee hands when, in 1714, the property was bought by Sir John Wynn of Watstay (later Wynnstay);[2] in 1736 Watkin Williams Wynn held 185 of the town's 279 messuages.[3]

In 1727 William Forester returned his brother-in-law John Sambrooke, a Turkey merchant, with Samuel Edwards.[4] Sambrooke, though a staunch Whig, frequently voted against the ministry on the ground that the ministers acted 'contrary to the interest of their country and Whig principles'.[5] Lord Bradford considered him a Tory and in 1733 opposed his re-election, preferring his own brother-in-law Orlando Bridgeman. Lord Gower and Watkin Williams Wynn, two extreme Tories with property in the constituency, were ready to support Sambrooke and Forester jointly[6] even though Forester was supporting Walpole throughout the Excise crisis.[7] Sambrooke pleaded with Forester to persuade Bradford to change his mind, claiming that other Whigs (including Orlando Bridgeman) had voting records similar to his own. The quarrel, however, was so public that Bradford could not retreat. Sambrooke had to withdraw[8] and Forester and Edwards were returned.[9] Sambrooke died a few weeks later,[10] Edwards in 1738.[11] Forester, according to his mother, had disliked Edwards, who would not have had a single vote without Forester's support.[12] Forester then returned his son Brooke ('the Stag') as his own colleague. From 1741 Brooke Forester sat with his brother-in-law Sir Brian Broughton-Delves[13] and from 1744 to 1754 with Isaac Hawkins Browne, F.R.S., who owned some property in the franchise.[14] In 1749 Much Wenlock was said to be 'in Forester'.[15] In 1754 William Forester returned to sit with his son Brooke, and when the father died in 1758 Brooke Forester was joined, albeit reluctantly because of the expense,[16] by his own son George. From 1761 to 1768 Brooke Forester sat with his brother Cecil.

George Forester replaced his father in 1768. For over forty years, between his amours and his hunting, George Forester dominated the borough's politics, though

[91] T.S.A.S. 3rd ser. ii. 337. Newport was Wm. Forester's 2nd cos.: ibid. 2nd ser. iii. 166-8.
[92] Ric. Newport's uncle: ibid. 3rd ser. ii. 338.
[93] The 1646 M.P.'s grandson: Hist. Parl., Commons, 1715-54, i. 487.
[94] Ibid. ii. 45.
[95] S.R.O. 1224, box 335, extracts bk., p. [156].
[96] Hist. Parl., Commons, 1715-54, ii. 5; T.S.A.S. 3rd ser. ii. 339; S.R.O. 1224, box 335, Lady Mary Forester to Wm. Forester, 26 Feb. 1733/4.
[97] C.J. xx. 28.
[98] T.S.A.S. 3rd ser. ii. 338.
[99] Hist. Parl., Commons, 1715-54, ii. 45.
[1] T.S.A.S. lviii. 223.
[2] C.P. 25(2)/960/13 Anne East. [no. 6].

[3] N.L.W., Wynnstay M 2530.
[4] Hist. Parl., Commons, 1715-54, ii. 405.
[5] S.R.O. 1224, box 335, Sambrooke to Wm. Forester, 16 Sept. 1733.
[6] Hist. Parl., Commons, 1715-54, ii. 405.
[7] Ibid. 45.
[8] Ibid. 405-6.
[9] Ibid. i. 312.
[10] Ibid. ii. 406.
[11] Ibid. 5.
[12] S.R.O. 1224, box 335, Lady Mary Forester to Wm. Forester, 26 Feb. 1733/4.
[13] Hist. Parl., Commons, 1715-54, i. 312, 495.
[14] Ibid. 312, 496.
[15] Camd. Misc. xxiii (Camd. 4th ser. vii), 151.
[16] S.R.O. 1224, box 336, Geo. Forester to Wm. Forester, 26 Feb. 1758.

he gave his seat to his young cousin and heir Cecil in 1790.[17] He was active in Parliament on behalf of Much Wenlock, and particularly of its ironmasters.[18] From 1768 to 1820 George and Cecil Forester returned members of the Bridgeman family for the second seat.[19] In 1768 Sir Henry Bridgeman, unable to stand for Ludlow since his breach with Lord Powis,[20] found refuge at Much Wenlock, whose patron had supported his attempt on the county in 1766.[21] Bridgeman sat until his ennoblement in 1794.[22] Forester twice, in 1780 and 1784, retired from contesting his seat, but each time was returned unopposed at a subsequent by-election.[23] In 1780 the seat was vacated when Thomas Whitmore, returned for Bridgnorth as well as Much Wenlock, chose the former;[24] in 1785 John Simpson (formerly Bridgeman), Sir Henry's son, gave back Forester's seat as he had privately undertaken to do at the general election.[25] Nevertheless the Foresters' control was occasionally difficult, often expensive, and eventually reduced. The manœuvres of 1780 and 1784–5 arose from growing resistance to the Foresters' domination.

In 1780 Sir Watkin Williams Wynn began to ponder the limits of the parliamentary borough and the rights of the out-voters.[26] He had sat for Shropshire 1772–4 and thereafter for Denbighshire. He had begun to assert his influence in Merionethshire and Montgomeryshire,[27] and would probably never need to seek an English county seat. In Much Wenlock, however, his interest might be of use. The Foresters' control of one seat was unshakeable, and Sir Watkin's object was to secure the second seat, occupied by Sir Henry Bridgeman. In 1782 there were rumours that Bridgeman was to be ennobled, and a public meeting was called to consider a successor who should either reside or have property in the franchise, to reprove the sitting M.P.s for non-attendance in Parliament, to defend the borough from threatened disfranchisement, and to open a subscription for the election of 'independent men'. Forester had reputedly offered the second seat to Robert Corbett of Longnor who, in reply, had styled Forester 'his Polar Star'.[28] No peerage, however, was granted. Nevertheless, in 1784 apparently, George Forester called a meeting of gentlemen of the franchise, which agreed that he should name one M.P. and the gentlemen the other. The two Bridgemans were chosen, the younger being intended to be succeeded by Forester at a by-election in 1785.[29] A few months later Sir Watkin sought the support of two landlords, Sir Robert Lawley, an absentee, and Sir Richard Acton, a Roman Catholic.[30] The 1785 by-election was nevertheless uncontested.[31]

Sir Watkin died prematurely in 1789 and his son of the same name came of age in 1793.[32] In 1794 Sir Henry Bridgeman at last received his peerage, becoming Baron Bradford.[33] Under the 1784 agreement Forester could not nominate a candidate to the vacant second seat. Nevertheless he promised his interest for the Hon. John Simpson provided that 'the burgesses in Common Hall assembled' would allow him to come forward. Forester thought the only possible rival was Thomas Harries of Benthall, but he was under age and his family interest had been neglected. Forester's advice was to secure Sir Watkin immediately,[34] and the new Sir Watkin promised every support.[35] Bridgeman and Forester then saw the young Sir Robert Lawley,[36]

[17] *Hist. Parl., Commons*, 1754–90, i. 364; ii. 449–51.
[18] *T.S.A.S.* lviii. 221. [19] Ibid. 222.
[20] See p. 288. [21] See p. 260.
[22] *T.S.A.S.* lviii. 222.
[23] *Hist. Parl., Commons*, 1754–90, i. 364; ii. 451; *Shrews. Chron.* 16 Dec. 1780.
[24] See p. 280.
[25] *Hist. Parl., Commons*, 1754–90, i. 364; ii. 117; *T.S.A.S.* lviii. 228.
[26] *T.S.A.S.* lviii. 227.
[27] *Hist. Parl., Commons*, 1754–90, iii. 671–2.

[28] *T.S.A.S.* lviii. 227–8; N.L.W., Wynnstay, box 56/107.
[29] *T.S.A.S.* lviii. 228. [30] Ibid. 223, 228.
[31] *Hist. Parl., Commons*, 1754–90, ii. 451.
[32] *Dict. Welsh Biog.* 1100.
[33] *T.S.A.S.* lviii. 228.
[34] Staffs. R.O., D.1287/18/8, Forester to Bridgeman, 27 July 1794.
[35] Ibid., Williams Wynn to Bridgeman, [early Aug. 1794].
[36] Ibid., Forester to Bridgeman, 7 Aug. 1794.

after which Forester advised communication with Harries.[37] After these precautions Simpson was returned in September.[38] Had Sir Watkin insisted, however, Forester would for the sake of peace have accepted Lawley for the second seat.[39]

By the following May Sir Watkin was considering putting forward his brother Charles. Forester was ready to agree, but said that if Sir Watkin should try to bring forward Robert Lawley neither he 'nor the country shall swallow that dose as a composing draft' to Simpson's detriment. Forester took comfort in the thought that Sir Watkin 'frequently causes disputes in haste, and repents at leisure for his misconduct'.[40] He need not have worried; the next Parliament was elected before Sir Watkin's brother came of age.[41] In 1806 Sir Watkin raised an opposition but did not take it to the poll; thenceforth the Foresters and Bridgemans determined to oppose the Williams Wynns. Cecil Forester and Simpson sat together as supporters of Administration until 1820 without a contest[42] but the Foresters could not relax. Both sides used local attorneys in their intrigues. Sir Watkin, Lawley, and the Actons used Collins & Hinton of Much Wenlock, but the Foresters and Bridgemans kept the firm's head Richard Collins sweet by annual payments until 1813 and by securing the town clerkship for him in 1809,[43] thus fulfilling a promise made fourteen years earlier.[44] The Foresters used Marshall & Lewis, of Bridgnorth, until 1794 when they took their business to the successful firm founded by Marshall & Lewis's clerk, John Pritchard, by then situated at Broseley. Pritchard attended to the admission of burgesses in the Forester interest and to entertainment at elections.[45] The average cost to the Foresters and Bridgemans of the eight general elections and two by-elections, all 'uncontested', between 1784 and 1818 was £650. The most expensive cost £1,000.[46] That of 1806, when a poll was threatened, cost £834, £725 of which went to local innkeepers;[47] in Much Wenlock over a thousand dinners were given to burgesses or even to future burgesses, 322 dinners in Broseley and Benthall, 302 in Little Wenlock, 64 in Madeley Wood, and 31 in Wellington.[48] In 1807, when no poll was threatened, only £400 was spent.[49] Moreover, nursing the constituency cost Forester and Simpson between them £255 a year from 1804 to 1810.[50] Such sums, however, were well within the Foresters' means; in 1811 Cecil Forester estimated his annual income from land as £17,000.[51]

Cecil Forester retired in 1820, ostensibly because of gout but no doubt also in expectation of the peerage he was to receive in the coronation honours of his friend George IV.[52] He put forward his brother Francis but there was no Bridgeman candidate. Forester and Simpson wanted Simpson's nephew Lord Newport to stand at both Much Wenlock and Wigan, but expense deterred the Bridgemans. Newport stood for Wigan only, and neither of his brothers was put forward for Much Wenlock.[53] Forester then gave his support to an eloquent Ultra, William Lacon Childe of Kinlet who was the local gentlemen's candidate.[54] Sir Watkin, piqued at not being consulted, put forward a Whig Reformer, Paul Beilby Lawley,[55] brother of the man whom George Forester

[37] Staffs. R.O., D.1287/18/8, same to same, 11 Aug. 1794.
[38] T.S.A.S. 3rd ser. ii. 349.
[39] Staffs. R.O., D.1287/18/8, Forester to Bridgeman, 7 Aug. 1794.
[40] Ibid., Forester to Ld. Bradford, 20 May 1795.
[41] T.S.A.S. 3rd ser. ii. 349; Burke, Peerage (1967), 2716.
[42] T.S.A.S. lviii. 224–5, 230.
[43] Ibid. 229.
[44] S.R.O. 1224, box 336, Collins to Geo. Forester, 14 Sept. 1809.
[45] T.S.A.S. lviii. 224.
[46] Ibid. 234.
[47] S.R.O. 1224, box 336, election acct. Nov. 1806.

[48] Staffs. R.O., D.1287/10/4a, election accts. 1806.
[49] Ibid. election accts. 1807; S.R.O. 1224, box 336, election acct. May 1807.
[50] T.S.A.S. lviii. 234.
[51] N.L.W., H. Williams Wynn MSS. 2791.
[52] T.S.A.S. 3rd ser. ii. 349; Complete Peerage, ii. 654; v. 553. He gave ill-health as his reason for retiring: T.S.A.S. lviii. 230; Shrews. Chron. 25 Feb. 1820.
[53] T.S.A.S. lviii. 230; Staffs. R.O., D.1287/10/4a, Lady Bradford to Newport, [24 Feb. 1820].
[54] T.S.A.S. 3rd ser. ii. 350; T.S.A.S. lviii. 230–1; and see above, p. 263.
[55] T.S.A.S. 3rd ser. ii. 352; T.S.A.S. lviii. 231.

would not have accepted in 1795. A Harries was considered but did not go forward.[56] In the first poll for nearly a century Forester and Childe, in coalition and with the Darbys' support,[57] beat Lawley fairly easily.[58]

In 1820 Sir Robert Lawley asserted to his brother that the vote was in the resident burgesses only; 'if so the borough is Sir W.'s and mine and Forester has no right in it'. His brother, he thought, should have tried to poll the greatest number of residents, and have been prepared to petition accordingly.[59] In 1822 Sir Watkin revived the question of the parliamentary borough's limits, arguing that they were more or less those of the town. At last the Williams Wynn interest forced a compromise; rather than face a legal battle Lord Forester decided to divide the representation. Lord Clive and Cecil Jenkinson, both Tories, were the intermediaries.[60] In 1826 Forester put forward his eldest son the Hon. J. G. W. Weld-Forester, and the second seat was filled by the loser of 1820, who had changed his name to Thompson. Thompson was the last Lawley to sit for the borough. Weld-Forester succeeded to the barony in 1828 and was followed as M.P. by his next brother the Hon. G. C. W. Weld-Forester, who had just come of age. Weld-Forester and Thompson were returned unopposed at the last three elections before 1832.[61]

Bishop's Castle

From 1660 to 1695 Bishop's Castle was represented by squires with estates in and around the town. Most supported the Court, though Richard More of Linley was a strong Whig. At first there was no sign of the disputes and corruption that were to mark the years between 1695 and 1765. From 1768 the borough was dominated by the Clives and its peace little disturbed.[62] A native of Bishop's Castle was returned in 1681 and another stood unsuccessfully in 1754. In the 18th century the Morrises of Bishop's Castle exerted an influence on election politics in the interests of the Whig ministries and of Corbyn Morris's education and official career.[63] Generally, however, the resident burgesses played little independent part in politics, and the electors simply sold their votes. Most of the borough's M.P.s were strangers; some were men of distinction,[64] but all were able, either personally or through a political patron, to indulge the electors' venality.

Two Cavaliers were returned in 1660, 1661, and February 1679: William Oakeley of Oakeley, the 1659 M.P. and a prospective knight of the Royal Oak, and his brother-in-law Edmund Waring of Owlbury.[65] In September 1679 Oakeley was succeeded by another Court supporter, Richard Scriven of Frodesley. At the election of the third Exclusion Parliament, however, in February 1681, two new M.P.s were returned. Sir Richard Mason of Sutton (Surr.)[66] was a courtier; Richard More of Linley, son of the 1659 M.P., was a Whig. Mason was a native of Bishop's Castle and his family's wealth was to dominate elections there for most of the next fifty years. In 1685 Bishop's Castle, like the other Shropshire boroughs, returned two supporters of James II: Edmund Waring and Francis Charlton, the son of Waring's brother-in-law Sir Job. Charlton had inherited property in and near the town, including Blunden Hall near

[56] *T.S.A.S.* lviii. 224.
[57] S.R.O. 1224, box 337, J. Clayton to G. Pritchard, 7 Mar. 1820.
[58] *T.S.A.S.* 3rd ser. ii. 350.
[59] Hull Univ., Brynmor Jones Libr., DDFA/39/45, Sir Rob. Lawley to P. B. Lawley, 1 Apr. [1820].
[60] *T.S.A.S.* lviii. 231.
[61] Ibid. 3rd ser. ii. 351–3.
[62] Namier, *Politics at Accession of Geo. III*, 162.

[63] *Essays in Eighteenth-Cent. Hist.* arr. Rosalind Mitchison (1966), 216–17; and see below. Much material cited below for Morris's interest and career was made available by Mr. J. B. Lawson, to whom thanks are due.
[64] *T.S.A.S.* 2nd ser. x. 34. Eleven M.P.s for the boro. 1701–1832 are in *D.N.B.*
[65] For this para. see *T.S.A.S.* 2nd ser. x. 50–2; *Bull. Inst. Hist. Res.* xliii. 100.
[66] *V.C.H. Surr.* iv. 200, 244–5.

the church, from his mother, daughter and heir of William Blunden, M.P. 1625–6.

The members continued to change with rapidity. The Whig Richard More was returned again to the 1689 Convention when his colleague was Walter Waring who had inherited Owlbury in 1687 on the death of his father, the former M.P. In 1690 there may have been a poll. The M.P.s were the veteran William Oakeley, returned at the four general elections between 1659 and February 1679, and Richard Mason, Sir Richard Mason's nephew.[67] Their deaths during the 1690–5 Parliament marked the end of a generation during which the choice of M.P.s may, as in 1681, 1685, and 1689, have been a response to basic political sentiments; Oakeley's death also marked the beginning of a longer period in which all was determined by cash.

Both by-elections were contested. Mason died in 1690 and Walter Waring succeeded him.[68] Richard More had come forward but desisted at Waring's request, only to find when he stood again in 1695 on Oakeley's death that those who had promised him 'all their interest the next time' now solicited against him on behalf of a violent opponent.[69] This was Oakeley's nephew Henry Newton of Heightley, a leading county magistrate.[70] More found the contest both 'troublesome and chargeable'. The bailiff, who was against him,[71] made a double return, but Parliament was dissolved before More's petition was heard.[72]

Nine of the eleven general elections between 1695 and 1722 were contested at Bishop's Castle, though not always to a poll. In 1695 Newton withdrew after 'great expense'[73] and two Whigs were returned, More and Charles Mason of Rockley, Richard Mason's younger brother.[74] During the next thirty years the unprincipled[75] Mason was to be returned for the borough eight times, suffering defeat twice during the Tory successes of Anne's last years and on a third and final occasion in 1727; he was twice unseated for bribery before, in 1726, he himself succeeded in unseating a rival for bribery even more blatant than his own.

Richard More died just before the 1698 general election, and for some years Bishop's Castle politics were influenced by the matrimonial affairs of Sir Richard Mason's younger daughter Anne. The manor of Bishop's Castle had been settled on her in 1683 when, aged fifteen, she had married Lord Brandon who had become 2nd earl of Macclesfield in 1694. The couple had separated in 1685. They were divorced, and Anne's children were bastardized, in April 1698 when Anne recovered most of the property inherited from her father.[76] In the 1698 election the former countess, known as Lady Mason, and the earl sponsored rival candidates, her brother-in-law Sir William Brownlow and the earl's cousin Sir Gilbert Gerard. Charles Mason and, for the first time since 1589, one of the Walcots also stood. Mason was Lady Mason's cousin, but he was allied with Gerard and there was much cross-voting. Mason headed the poll. Brownlow was second with 37 votes, only one ahead of Gerard who petitioned against Brownlow's return. The Commons committee agreed that the franchise was in the bailiff and resident burgesses, though there was argument about the requirements for residence. The committee then heard evidence of a kind which the borough was often to provide in the years to come. Macclesfield and his ex-wife

[67] *T.S.A.S.* 2nd ser. x. 52; S.P.L., MS. 2288, *sub* Mason of Bp.'s Cas. (the source used hereafter for the Masons' relationships).

[68] *T.S.A.S.* 2nd ser. x. 52.

[69] B.L. Loan 29/151, Ric. More to Rob. Harley, 1 Mar. 1694/5.

[70] E. F. Oakeley, *The Oakeley Pedigree* (priv. print. 1934), 16, 57, 61, 72; *Hist. Parl., Commons, 1715–54,* i. 570–1; above, p. 97. Newton is wrongly identified with a contemporary of the same name in *T.S.A.S.* 2nd ser. x. 52–3.

[71] B.L. Loan 29/151, More to Harley, 1 Mar. 1694/5.

[72] *C.J.* xi. 296–7, 319.

[73] Surr. R.O., Acc. 775. A3, Somers MSS., Rob. Harley to Sir John Somers, 29 Oct. 1695.

[74] *T.S.A.S.* 2nd ser. x. 53.

[75] *Cal. Treas. Papers, 1697–1702,* 424; 1720–8, 417; *Cal. Treas. Bks.* 1700–1, 7, 135–6; 1710(2), 51, 54; *Cal. Treas. Bks. & Papers, 1729–30,* 411.

[76] S.R.O. 552/17/595; *Complete Peerage,* viii. 331; *Boswell's Life of Johnson,* ed. G. B. Hill and L. F. Powell, i (1934), 169–74.

had bribed, treated, and threatened the electors, and there were already signs of that besetting temptation in small venal boroughs, refusal to promise until the poll was imminent. The price of a vote increased to £40 or even £50. One elector alleged that Gerard and Mason had visited him on the eve of the election, when Brownlow and Gerard presumably had 36 promises each, and had offered any sum necessary for a vote for Gerard. Nevertheless there was no petition against Mason. In February 1700 the committee voted to seat Gerard in Brownlow's place but the Commons declared the burgesses notoriously guilty of bribery and ordered that Brownlow's seat remain unfilled that session.[77]

Both 1701 elections were contested and bribery continued. Both elections produced petitions, and there were petitions against Mason on both occasions. In January the four 1698 candidates stood again. The bailiff was Mason's father Thomas. George Walcot apparently headed the poll, Mason was declared second with 38, followed by Brownlow with 34. Brownlow petitioned successfully against Mason, though he died before the Commons' committee gave its ruling. Gerard petitioned unsuccessfully against Walcot. Again there was evidence of Mason's visits to electors on the eve of the poll. Mason was found guilty of notorious bribery and ordered to be taken into the custody of the serjeant at arms. The writ for a new election was withheld for the session.[78] On 5 November 1701, six days before the dissolution of Parliament, Macclesfield died.[79] At the election a fortnight later his cousin did not stand, and the candidates were Mason, Walcot, and the former countess's second husband Lt.-Col. Henry Brett,[80] a Gloucestershire squire who had aided Brownlow in January.[81] Brett headed the poll with 70 votes and Mason was returned with a narrow majority over Walcot.[82] It was Walcot's turn to petition against Mason. Mason and his relatives were charged with bribery, and Mason's uncle, the bailiff Betton, was accused of arbitrary refusal of votes for Walcot. With such assistance Mason had not needed to appear until the day before the poll, and again there was evidence of bribery on the eve of a poll which might be swung either way; 5 guineas was the usual sum, and rent-free properties were (as in 1698) an inducement. At the poll a separate list of votes was apparently made for each candidate. Charles Mason's, kept by Robert Mason, gave Mason 42 votes and Walcot 39; Walcot's list, partly by omitting Betton's vote for Mason, gave Walcot 41 votes, Mason 40. One man's vote was claimed by both rivals; as he went up to vote he had reportedly said that he was to have £5 whichever way he voted. Mason and Walcot were both declared not duly elected, the latter after a Commons division. The new writ was again withheld, though after the demise of the Crown.[83]

Eight of the ten general elections between 1698 and 1722 occasioned petitions at Bishop's Castle, but in the first half of Anne's reign local political rivalries seem to have achieved some sort of balance. The 1702 and 1708 general elections were apparently uncontested, as was a 1706 by-election; petitions after the 1705 general election were withdrawn. In 1702 Mason and Brett were returned.[84] After another four-cornered contest they were returned a third time in 1705, but Richard Harnage and Charles Walcot, George's elder brother, petitioned, accusing their rivals of bribery and the bailiff, Maurice Pugh, of partisan refusal and acceptance of votes.[85] Mason, however, who had property in Montgomeryshire,[86] had also been elected for Montgomery.

[77] T.S.A.S. 2nd ser. x. 53–4; C.J. xii. 353; xiii. 169–72; Burke, Ext. & Dorm. Baronetcies (1844), 217–18; J. R. Burton, Some Collections Towards Hist. of Fam. of Walcot of Walcot (Shrews. priv. print. 1930), 77–8.
[78] C.J. xiii. 329, 334, 536–8. Brownlow's wife had d. Mar. 1700: O. Manning and W. Bray, Hist. and Antiquities of Surr. ii (1809), 483.
[79] Complete Peerage, viii. 332; C.J. xiii. 644. [80] D.N.B.
[81] C.J. xiii. 537. [82] T.S.A.S. 2nd ser. x. 54.
[83] C.J. xiii. 649, 831–3, 835.
[84] T.S.A.S. 2nd ser. x. 55.
[85] C.J. xv. 11, 16. For Walcot see Burton, op. cit. 70–6.
[86] S.R.O. 1011, box 176, abstr. of title to £43,000 secured on late Chas. Mason's estate.

Early in 1706, after the failure of a petition against his return for that borough, Harnage and Walcot withdrew their petitions against his return for Bishop's Castle and Mason chose to sit for Montgomery.[87] At the subsequent by-election another Whig, Lord Bradford's grandson the Hon. Henry Newport, was unopposed. Harnage may have withdrawn his petition in return for promised interest at the next election, for in 1708 Newport moved on to sit for the county, Brett did not stand, and Harnage and Mason were unopposed.[88] Harnage, a government clothing contractor and army agent, had recently inherited property near Bishop's Castle[89] and it seems likely that a marriage between his niece and Mason was contemplated.[90]

In October 1710 Harnage and Mason stood again, but the Tory minister Robert Harley of Brampton Bryan, used his influence[91] to return Robert Raymond, whom he had made solicitor general.[92] The poll is not known but Mason was defeated and his political harmony with Harnage was broken.[93] Mason petitioned against Harnage[94] but no determination is known. Three years later Mason stood aside and Harnage and Sir Robert Raymond were returned after a three-cornered contest. The new opposition candidate was Sir Charles Lloyd of Moel-y-garth whose family traditions and marital connexions were soundly Whig.[95] Lloyd petitioned against both sitting M.P.s,[96] but the queen's death ended the matter.

The Harleys had soon to find another candidate, for Raymond was removed from office on George I's accession.[97] In September 1714 that successful war profiteer James Brydges, with the wealth of a recent paymaster general at his disposal,[98] thought of standing, but next month he inherited his father's peerage and was created earl of Carnarvon. By December, anxious to further his negotiations with Edward Harley for the purchase of his estate at Bishop's Castle, he was urging his kinsman and business associate, Humphrey Walcot, to assist Lord Harley's candidacy, though as a Whig Carnarvon was naturally anxious that his request to one Tory to help another should be kept secret.[99] After five years out of Parliament Charles Mason again came forward at the last moment; though his debts were reported to be greater than his estate, he was 'furnished with money' and secured a majority after the poll had opened: 'bank bills and money fled about', and bribes amounted to £10 a head, and sometimes to £40 or £50. On 31 January 1715 Harnage topped the poll and Mason beat Harley by 3 or 4 votes. Harley's disappointed family castigated the 'villainous roguery' of the 'profligate wretches' of Bishop's Castle in the harshest terms, and the electors' 'baseness and perfidy' decided Edward Harley to sell his Bishop's Castle estate, so that his son might not be tempted 'into a great expense upon such mercenary rascals'.[1] Harley petitioned, but in that Whig House of Commons the petition was not proceeded with.[2]

[87] C.J. xv. 14–15, 91, 94–5, 126, 163–4.
[88] T.S.A.S. 2nd ser. x. 55–6.
[89] Hist. Parl., Commons, 1715–54, ii. 112; C.J. xi. 769, 785–6.
[90] Mason had been made a trustee for the pmnt. of her and her sisters' marr. portions in 1697: S.P.L., MS. 6, pp. 62–3. Cf. ibid., MS. 4078, pp. 658–9. In a 1708 will he named her his sole executrix: ibid., MS. 2288, sub Mason of Bp.'s Cas. Doubtless marriage was contemplated. See, however, below, n. 93.
[91] Hist. MSS. Com. 29, Portland, vii, p. 22.
[92] D.N.B. Said to have been a Tory or mild Whig in Anne's reign, Raymond joined the Whigs in 1717: Hist. Parl., Commons, 1715–54, ii. 379; Holmes, Trial of Dr. Sacheverell, 105–8.
[93] Private harmony may have ended too. Mason had probably deceived Mary Harnage with a prospect of marriage. In 1739 he left a widow Alice (and issue by her) his executrix and sole legatee, but Mary Harnage or Mason also claimed to be his widow, devisee, and executrix: Prob.

11/699 (P.C.C. 264 Henchman); S.R.O. 1011, box 176, abstr. of title to £43,000 secured on late Chas. Mason's estate, p. 20; above, n. 90. Hist. Parl., Commons, 1715–54, ii. 245, states that Mary Harnage was Mason's wife; S.P.L., MS. 2288, sub Mason of Bp.'s Cas., states that she was his 2nd wife. But they probably did not marry.
[94] T.S.A.S. 2nd ser. x. 56; C.J. xvi. 422.
[95] T.S.A.S. 2nd ser. x. 56; Dict. Welsh Biog. 572; Owen and Blakeway, Hist. Shrews. i. 505 n. 2.
[96] C.J. xvii. 486.
[97] D.N.B.
[98] C. H. Collins Baker and Muriel I. Baker, Life and Circumstances of Jas. Brydges, First Duke of Chandos (1949), 44–62.
[99] Huntington Libr., ST 57/10, pp. 256–7; ST 57/11, pp. 191–3, 216, 221, 245–6; Complete Peerage, iii. 129–30. For Walcot see Baker, op. cit. 360 and n., 428 and n.; Burton, Fam. of Walcot, 78; above, p. 287.
[1] Hist. Parl., Commons, 1715–54, i. 309; Hist. MSS. Com. 29, Portland, v, pp. 505–6, 663.
[2] C.J. xviii. 39–40, 493, 652.

In 1718 Carnarvon, soon to be created duke of Chandos, bought Harley's estate[3] in haste and repented at leisure. In his efforts to control one[4] seat he kept in regular touch with his local agents, paid proper attention to filling vacancies in the corporation,[5] and wrote with due deference to those thought to have influence, notably Edmund Morris.[6] Nevertheless the expense began to tell. Chandos's nominee on Harnage's death in 1719 was an old friend and agent, Sir Matthew Decker, a rich merchant and banker. There was no opposition. Mason was 'very civil' to Chandos over the vacancy, but the duke unwisely went to considerable expense 'purely to oblige the town' and appetites were whetted. By the end of 1721 Decker had 'had enough' of Parliament[7] and Chandos, after prolonged secrecy, put forward his legal adviser, W. P. Williams, a rich Jacobite who never visited the borough. The duke naively hoped that a lesser sum than in 1719 would prevent any opposition, especially as he was ready to pay for the paving of the town's streets.[8] Nevertheless a third candidate appeared. Bowater Vernon of Hanbury (Worcs.), a ministerialist, raised the level of corruption to new heights, announcing that he had 'brought down money to carry the election if that would do it'.[9] By early March 'prodigious spending' was reported.[10] Chandos was allowed only one member; Vernon, 'the South Sea man', was determined to outbid him for the other. Chandos foresaw difficulties for Mason who was 'not much prepared with *unum necessarium*'. The candidates stood independently, Chandos wishing Mason well but judging a coalition with him might damage his own man. Mason brought in non-resident burgesses but the bailiff, who was in the duke's interest, refused to poll them. Williams and Vernon were returned, the latter having 52 votes and Mason 16. The duke was soon borrowing from Williams and offering to sell him his Radnorshire and Bishop's Castle estates; many of his Bishop's Castle tenants were electors, and Chandos claimed that the property would give 'the command of a borough', though adding disingenuously 'I cannot say without some expense attending each election'.[11] Williams sensibly bought another property from the duke.[12]

Mason's petition against Vernon, alleging bribery and corruption and the refusal of qualified voters,[13] was finally heard in 1726. Mason showed that all but one of Vernon's 52 voters, some of whom were Mason's tenants, had been bribed; the usual sum was £12 to a voter and a guinea to his wife, a total of nearly £600. The Commons committee gave Vernon's seat to Mason.[14] Chandos had spent nearly £700,[15] and would presumably have been equally vulnerable to charges of bribery.

After nine expensive years Chandos sold his Bishop's Castle estate to his nephew John Walcot of Walcot.[16] That was shortly before the 1727 election, when the first candidates in the field were Brig.-Gen. William Newton of Hampton and the Whig Robert More of Linley.[17] Newton, younger brother of the 1695 M.P.,[18] withdrew. More was John Walcot's cousin and three generations of his family had already sat

[3] S.R.O. 552/17/595; *Complete Peerage*, iii. 130.
[4] See e.g. Huntington Libr., ST 57/30, pp. 101-2, 125.
[5] Ibid. ST 57 *passim*; Northants R.O., Temple (Stowe) coll., Chandos letter bk. 20 (esp. pp. 19-21, 24, 238-41).
[6] A lessee of Charlton property in the boro., whose son, Corbyn, Chandos maintained at the Charterhouse: S.R.O. 11/610-12, 666; S.R.O. 552/17/156; S.R.O. 665/2/box 61, leases of 1710, 1732, and 1736; Chandos letter bk. 20, pp. 111, 239; Baker, *Duke of Chandos*, 92 n. 2.
[7] Chandos letter bk. 20, pp. 49-50, 143; *Hist. Parl., Commons, 1715-54*, i. 608.
[8] Chandos letter bk. 20, pp. 24, 49-50, 52-3, 121-2, 125-7, 134-5, 144-5; *Hist. Parl., Commons, 1715-54*, ii. 545-6.
[9] *Hist. Parl., Commons, 1715-54*, ii. 496. An earlier

third man had withdrawn: Chandos letter bk. 20, p. 105.
[10] Hist. MSS. Com. 29, *Portland*, vii, p. 314.
[11] Chandos letter bk. 20, pp. 136-7, 168-9, 178-9, 197, 213, 246.
[12] *V.C.H. Mdx.* iv. 114.
[13] *C.J.* xx. 30, 242, 335, 547-8.
[14] Ibid. 681-2. The arithmetic in *T.S.A.S.* 2nd ser. x. 57-8, is not correct. Oldfield, *Rep. Hist. of Gt. Brit. and Irel.* (1816), iv. 403-4, gives other figs.
[15] Chandos letter bk. 20, pp. 183-4.
[16] S.R.O. 151, box 12, Chandos to J. Walcot, 3 Apr. 1727. Cf. S.R.O. 112/1/1881, 1886, 1888-9.
[17] Huntington Libr., ST 57/30, pp. 88, 91; S.P.L., MS. 2792, pp. 130-1; MS. 4360, p. 321.
[18] Huntington Libr., ST 57/30, p. 135; above, p. 298.

for the borough.[19] Chandos's expenses were by no means over. Walcot was standing for the county and put his interest at the disposal of the duke's son Lord Henry Brydges, a minor.[20] Mason stood again and, despite his poverty, the price of votes was bid up.[21] Eventually, however, the duke withdrew Carnarvon (as Lord Henry had become). He learnt that his friend John Plumptre, the placeman, was being put forward for Bishop's Castle by the duke of Newcastle in order to facilitate a compromise elsewhere. More and Plumptre were returned with 61 and 46 votes, Richard Oakeley polling 23. Charles Mason, in his last appearance, polled a derisory 6: *unum necessarium* had again been wanting. A year later Mason was 'in miserable circumstances'.[22]

Chandos did not intervene in 1734, though he tried to persuade Walcot to support their kinsman William Leigh of Adlestrop (Glos.).[23] More, no longer sure of his cousin Walcot's neutrality, had become dependent on Edmund Morris's aid;[24] in October 1733 More had feared he might 'sink under Mr. Walcot's opposition' and in February 1734 he reported that three of Walcot's servants had paraded round the borough with a drunken mob crying 'down with the roundheads, damn More, down with him'. More also reported that three leading Shropshire Tories were influencing Walcot against him.[25] Despite the unsubtle allusions to the politics of More's family,[26] however, Walcot in the end put forward only one candidate, his fellow Tory Edward Kynaston of Hardwick, younger son of a former knight of the shire. Kynaston had inherited most of his father's personal wealth and had married Sir Charles Lloyd's daughter; as yet he wished to be thought a Jacobite.[27]

Five years later, in 1739, Chandos again secured Walcot's interest for Lord Carnarvon. The duke knew that the burgesses would expect 'satisfaction',[28] and in fact there was a contest. More had retired. Walcot's candidates were Carnarvon, now an opponent of Walpole, and Andrew Hill, a Tory neighbour of the Walcots. Two ministerialists, aided by Corbyn Morris, opposed them but were beaten in an expensive contest.[29] Carnarvon sat only three years, for his father died in 1744. Five years after the election the new duke, still unable to pay his election bills, lamented to Walcot that he wished he had never seen Bishop's Castle. His father, who had never visited the borough, had contributed a mere £70, and Carnarvon had had to borrow at exorbitant interest to meet the rest.[30]

In 1744 the ministry obtained Carnarvon's seat for Lord Trentham[31] whose father Lord Gower had just gone over to it.[32] John Walcot evidently considered an intervention[33] but nothing came of it. Trentham was the only member of his family to sit for a Shropshire seat after 1685,[34] and his return was perhaps secured by the local efforts of H. A. Herbert (cr. Lord Herbert of Chirbury 1743) and Corbyn Morris. After the 1741 election Herbert and Morris had continued to nurse the borough,[35] evidently in co-operation. Soon after the by-election Morris seems to have obtained the prospect of official promotion.[36]

[19] Most recently his uncles Ric. More (d. 1698) and Wm. Oakeley (d. 1695): S.P.L., MS. 4079, pp. 1155–6; Burton, *Fam. of Walcot*, 81.
[20] Huntington Libr., ST 57/30, pp. 88, 98, 151, 173.
[21] Ibid., pp. 98–9, 130–1, 135, 148, 152, 163, 173.
[22] Ibid., pp. 182, 271; *Hist. Parl., Commons*, 1715–54, i. 309; ii. 245, 358.
[23] Huntington Libr., ST 57/43, pp. 214, 280, 298–9; *V.C.H. Glos.* vi. 10–11.
[24] Cambridge Univ. Libr., Cholmondeley (Houghton) Corr., 1505a, 1830, 2003, 2355, 3294. Over several yrs. More, in letters to Walpole, had promoted Corbyn Morris's career.
[25] *Hist. Parl., Commons*, 1715–54, ii. 274.
[26] See pp. 92, 250–1, 253.
[27] *Hist. Parl., Commons*, 1715–54, ii. 194–5; *T.S.A.S.* 2nd ser. vi. 216–20; 2nd ser. x. 59; above, p. 259.

[28] *T.S.A.S.* 3rd ser. ix. 261.
[29] *Hist. Parl., Commons*, 1715–54, i. 309–10; Cambridge Univ. Libr., Cholmondeley (Houghton) Corr., 3079. Walpole also solicited H. A. Herbert's aid for the ministerialists.
[30] *T.S.A.S.* 3rd ser. ix. 262–4, 266; *Complete Peerage*, iii. 130–1.
[31] *T.S.A.S.* 2nd ser. x. 59–60.
[32] *S.H.C.* 4th ser. vi. 115.
[33] S.R.O. 5/1/102. [34] See pp. 257, 321.
[35] Herbert was evidently interesting himself in the rebuilding of the guildhall: S.R.O. 552/14/box 465, plan, elevation & estimate for building Bp.'s Cas. guildhall, Nov. 1745. For Morris see S.R.O. 151, box 12, Morris to boro. bailiff, 14 and 17 Nov. 1741.
[36] Cambridge Univ. Libr., Cholmondeley (Houghton) Corr., 3191; B.L. Add. MS. 32705, ff. 39–41.

For a few more years the Walcots, though ever more heavily in debt, continued to control Bishop's Castle.[37] In 1747 John Walcot returned two Tories: his banker (and creditor for £8,500), Samuel Child, and a stranger who had recently married money, J. R. Lytton of Knebworth (Herts.). Child died in 1752 and in 1753 Walcot replaced him with his own brother-in-law John Dashwood King.[38] The bills, however, remained outstanding and when they were paid it was often only after deductions had been made;[39] the burgesses' consequent resentment encouraged Corbyn Morris, who had not interfered in the by-election, to organize a ministerialist opposition to the Walcot interest.[40] Commodore Temple West's seat at Buckingham was earmarked for one of his Grenville cousins at the general election due in 1754. He therefore considered Bishop's Castle and was told that a seat there was '£1,000 risk, £2,000 sure'. Morris, hoping no doubt for the advancement of his career by the powerful Grenville clan, offered to manage West's election, and there was a vigorous contest.[41] As late as March 1754 Newcastle expected West's return.[42] West's cousin, however, the Hon. George Grenville, a Treasury lord, had advised withdrawal[43] and the event proved him right for West did not stand the poll. Opposition to the Walcot candidates at the poll came instead from Jeremiah Brown, a native of Bishop's Castle who had managed Vernon's bribery in 1722,[44] and from Robert de Cornwall of Berrington (Herefs.). It failed; Dashwood King and Samuel Child's Tory nephew, Barnaby Backwell, were returned by a large majority. Backwell died the same year and the Tory Walter Waring of Owlbury replaced him in 1755.[45] The Grenvilles' interest in the borough had nevertheless been roused. Four years later, when Waring needed money, he raised it by agreeing with George Grenville, by then Pitt's brother-in-law and treasurer of the navy in the Pitt–Newcastle ministry, to vacate his seat in favour of Grenville's brother Henry. Amid much carousing Grenville was returned unopposed, Waring's interest and Pitt's popularity being 'quite invincible'.[46]

The 1761 election was the last before the demise of the Walcots' interest, and Samuel Child's son Francis was returned unopposed with Peregrine Cust. Both were associated with opposition; Child was a Tory like his father while Cust's brother, Sir John, was a Leicester House associate of John Walcot's brother-in-law Sir Francis Dashwood,[47] a leading independent M.P. of twenty years' standing.[48] Cust, a City businessman, was well able to afford votes at Bishop's Castle and through his mother had connexions with the borough: Lady Cust's father, Sir William Brownlow, had sat for it 1698–1700 and her grandfather, Sir Richard Mason, had represented it in the 1681 Parliament. It was to her that Cust dutifully ascribed his election 'not only without opposition but with the united hearts of the whole town'.[49] The 'united hearts' cost him £1,200.[50]

John Walcot's debts were over £48,000 by 1761. He hid from his creditors, and in 1763 his son Charles sold the Walcot estate, with a promise of all his interest in the borough, to Lord Clive for a greatly inflated price.[51] On 23 September 1763, just before

[37] *Camd. Misc.* xxiii (Camd. 4th ser. vii), 151.

[38] *Hist. Parl., Commons,* 1715–54, i. 309–10, 549–50, 605–6; ii. 235, 504–5.

[39] The bills printed in *T.S.A.S.* 3rd ser. ix. 264–5, have endorsements of receipt showing deductions (unprinted): see originals in S.R.O. 151, box 12 (containing also unpublished unreceipted accts.).

[40] Nottingham Univ. Libr., Newcastle (Clumber) MSS., letters to Morris from B. Bright (21 Feb. 1753), S. Griffiths (27 Feb. 1753), and S. Longueville (17 Mar. 1753) (refs. supplied by Mr. J. B. Lawson).

[41] L. M. Wiggin, *The Faction of Cousins: A Political Acct. of the Grenvilles, 1733–1763* (1958), 154–5.

[42] B.L. Add. MS. 32995, ff. 66v., 113, 138v.

[43] Wiggin, op. cit. 155.   [44] *C.J.* xx. 682.

[45] *Hist. Parl., Commons,* 1715–54, i. 581; 1754–90, i. 361; ii. 34–5, 302; iii. 606–7. Cornwall's petition was soon withdrawn: *C.J.* xxvii. 34, 76.

[46] Namier, *Politics at Accession of Geo. III,* 246–7.

[47] *Hist. Parl., Commons,* 1754–90, ii. 212, 291–2.

[48] Betty Kemp, *Sir Fra. Dashwood* (1967), chap. 2.

[49] Namier, op. cit. 247–8.

[50] S.R.O. 599/3. The expense of £2,400 was shared by Child and Cust.

[51] *Hist. Parl., Commons,* 1715–54, ii. 505; 1754–90, iii. 591.

Clive took possession of the estate, Francis Child died, 'rather sooner than I could have wished', as Clive confessed, for he felt 'almost an utter stranger to the borough'. Walter Waring, the former M.P., who had had express news of Child's death, had begun an immediate canvass and gained 24 hours on the Clives.[52] He also gained the support of Grenville's ministry and of Cust, and the government was anxious to enlist Corbyn Morris's influence on his behalf. Cust warned Charles Walcot that 'all' his family, in effect his uncle Lord Le Despencer (as Sir Francis Dashwood had just become), would disapprove of any support he might give to Clive's cousin George Clive, 'a professed enemy to Administration'. Such support, Cust alleged, might injure Despencer's prospects of office under Grenville,[53] and in fact Despencer lent his name in support of Waring.[54] Walcot, however, honoured his commitment to Lord Clive and obtained in return Clive's promise of a seat at the next general election.[55] Indeed Walcot, who had been on the spot when Waring's canvass began, had at once ridden with the news to his old home, Clive's new seat. A few votes had been lost during his absence, for some electors, thinking there would be no contest, had promised to Waring. Nevertheless the combined interest of the Clives and Walcots assured a majority for George Clive. Lord Clive was determined to spend the 'utmost farthing' and urged Newcastle and Pitt to persuade Waring to desist and so avoid 'utter ruin', his fortune being insufficient for success.[56] During the campaign Lord Clive, through Lord Powis's mediation,[57] was covertly dissociating himself from Newcastle's opposition group and it was through Secretary Sandwich, who was working the local excisemen in Waring's favour, that Waring received Clive's offer of £1,000 for his withdrawal. The offer was rejected, but George Clive won by 80 votes to 53.[58] The subsequent petitions were not taken seriously.[59]

Within three weeks of the poll Lord Clive, having definitely broken with Newcastle, had offered his 'poor services' to Grenville,[60] and so Despencer's prospects were not affected by any taint of opposition to Grenville on his nephew's part.[61] Cust too was quickly reassured by Grenville that he would not be prejudiced by his activity against George Clive, but in 1768 he was again on the opposite side to Clive and had to seek a seat elsewhere.[62]

The 1763 contest was the last for nearly forty years, though Clive had to lay out still more money to achieve full control. Waring caused trouble in 1765[63] and renewed his candidacy in 1767. At the end of that year, however, Clive bought his Shropshire estates and secured a promise of his 'entire interest' at Bishop's Castle and of his free support there.[64] In 1770, Clive rounded off his properties by buying Corbyn Morris's leaseholds[65] and by the acquisition from Lord Catherlough of Charles Mason's former estates and the mortgages on them.[66] Thereafter the borough remained in the control of Lord Clive and his son Edward until the latter's absence in India gave his opponents a chance in 1802.[67]

As he had promised in 1763, Clive offered Charles Walcot the nomination to one of the seats in 1768. At first Walcot, who had tried to keep up an independent interest,[68]

[52] Namier, op. cit. 291.
[53] Ibid. 293; *Additional Grenville Papers, 1763-1765*, ed. J. R. G. Tomlinson (1962), 41, 44-5, 54-5, 63-4; Burton, *Fam. of Walcot*, 89.
[54] Kemp, *Dashwood*, 64.
[55] *Hist. Parl., Commons*, 1754-90, iii. 591. Walcot had succ. to his uncle Despencer's seat at Weymouth in Apr.
[56] Namier, op. cit. 291.
[57] Tomlinson, *Add. Grenville Papers*, 69-71; India Office Libr., MS. Eur. G 546/III-VII, ff. 92-3.
[58] Namier, op. cit. 292-3.
[59] *C.J.* xxix. 702, 784; Tomlinson, *Add. Grenville Papers*, 72.
[60] Namier, op. cit. 294.
[61] Kemp, *Dashwood*, chap. 3.
[62] *Hist. Parl., Commons*, 1754-90, ii. 292; Tomlinson, *Add. Grenville Papers*, 71.
[63] *Hist. Parl., Commons*, 1754-90, iii. 607.
[64] Namier, op. cit. 294.
[65] S.R.O. 552/17/591.
[66] S.R.O. 1011, box 176, abstr. of title to £43,000 secured on late Chas. Mason's estate.
[67] *Hist. Parl., Commons*, 1754-90, i. 362; Namier, op. cit. 294.
[68] India Office Libr., MS. Eur. G 37/48, G. Clive to Ld. Clive, 6 Oct. 1767. Walcot was soon humbly asking favours: ibid. 37/49, Walcot to Ld. Clive, 4 Nov. 1767.

wanted to put forward his brother John, but he would have had to bear half the expense and wisely accepted Clive's offer of £1,000 to be released from his promise;[69] John Walcot was accommodated by a place in the Post Office found by his uncle Despencer,[70] joint postmaster general since 1766.[71] Clive was thus free to return his cousin George again and with him his own brother William,[72] though at a cost of £1,200.[73]

Bishop's Castle was quiet under the Clives' sway by 1768,[74] and for over thirty years its M.P.s were changed to suit the Clives' convenience. George Clive sat until his death in 1779 when his seat was given to William Clive who sat for almost 41 years, eventually becoming Father of the House of Commons. During the Parliaments of 1768-74 and 1774-80 the other seat was occupied alternately by Alexander Wedderburn,[75] an ambitious lawyer ally of Lord Clive, and Henry Strachey,[76] Clive's secretary; frequent by-elections were necessary as Wedderburn rose up the legal hierarchy and Strachey acquired places. Strachey and Clive were unopposed in the last four elections of the 18th century.

The Clives' estimate for Bishop's Castle in 1774 was £3,028, more than the combined estimates for Shrewsbury, Ludlow, and Okehampton (Devon).[77] Corruption did not cease with contests and the price of a general election vote was £20;[78] by-election votes cost less[79] but general treating was a feature of all elections.[80] Nevertheless, though expensive, the borough was reliable,[81] and the Clives and Strachey (cr. bt. 1801) became complacent.[82] Some electors came to feel they were not receiving their deserts and their chance came in 1802, when Bishop's Castle was one of the Clive boroughs where the family's opponents took advantage of the 2nd Lord Clive's prolonged absence (1798-1803) in India[83] to mount an attack.

According to the Clives the local leaders' objectives were 25 guineas a head rather than the customary 20 and the ousting of Sir Henry Strachey. J. C. Kinchant of Park Hall, Whittington, to whom Strachey had given great offence, was also involved; he had inherited Blunden Hall and other property in the borough from the Charltons. The opposition's first candidate was Thomas Clarke of Peplow, a newcomer to county society with an 'immense fortune' gained from the Liverpool slave trade. Between March and May Clarke's canvassing and treating created 'dreadful confusion' and secured Strachey's withdrawal. Strachey acknowledged that only a relative of Lord Clive could hold the second seat and was replaced by Col. John Robinson, Clive's brother-in-law. Clarke, realizing that he could not outspend the Clives, withdrew, thereby enabling the Clives to secure a majority. He was replaced at a late stage by R. B. Robson, a Foxite who had had to give up a family seat at Okehampton and was associated with opponents of Clive's Indian policy. Kinchant joined Robson 'merely to take the second votes'. The Clives won, though not overwhelmingly and only at a high

[69] Hist. Parl., Commons, 1754-90, i. 362; iii. 591.
[70] Burton, Fam. of Walcot, 90, 94-5. Humph. Walcot (1753-1807), the bros.' 2nd cos., also held a Post Office appointment: ibid. 80.
[71] Kemp, Dashwood, 87-90.
[72] T.S.A.S. 2nd ser. x. 62; Namier, op. cit. 295.
[73] India Office Libr., MS. Eur. G 37/83, trial balances for house steward's bks. for 30 Sept. 1768.
[74] Ibid. 37/51, Thos. Wingfield to John Walsh, 8 Feb. 1768; 37/52, G. Clive to Ld. Clive, 29 Mar. 1768. Cf. India Office Libr., Sutton Ct. MSS., Ld. Clive to H. Strachey, 22 Apr. 1768. For the rest of this para. see T.S.A.S. 2nd ser. x. 62-4; Hist. Parl., Commons, 1754-90, i. 239-40, 256; ii. 227, 229; iii. 487-9, 618-20.
[75] See also D.N.B.
[76] See also ibid. In 1770 he marr. Lady Clive's cos.
[77] C 109/74/2/62-3. A threatened opposition soon flickered out: T.S.A.S. lix. 58. Care was taken to satisfy

supporters after the electn.: C 109/71/4/5 (endorsed 'Mr. G. Clive on the subject of bribing the B. Castle electors ex post facto'), 22.
[78] India Office Libr., MS. Eur. G 37/53, Thos. Home to G. Clive, 8 July 1768. It was 20 gns. by 1802-3: see ibid. 37/71, R. W[ilding] to Ld. Clive, 17 May 1803; and next para.
[79] C 109/74, loose papers, no. 119 (Ashby's bill for 1770, specifying 104 pmnts. of 3 gns.).
[80] C 109/72/3/41 (Ld. Clive to Ashby, 13 Jan. 1771); Shrews. Chron. 7 Feb. 1784; 25 June 1790.
[81] Oldfield, Hist. of Boros. (1792), ii. 428.
[82] Cf. Wm. Clive's refs. to Strachey in Feb. 1801 and June 1802: N.L.W., Clive Corresp. 2nd ser. 2180, 2283. In Apr. 1802 Strachey attributed the opposition's success to the slackness of Ld. Clive's agents: ibid. 561.
[83] D.N.B.

cost.[84] With good reason they were greatly relieved when Kinchant's petition was ruled vexatious and frivolous.[85]

The opposition survived. Some of its voters, rejected in 1802, subsequently qualified themselves as electors,[86] and the Kinchant interest stimulated Whig concern with the borough in the 1806[87] and 1807[88] general elections. The Clives' opponents also gave some trouble over the borough charters in 1807.[89] In 1816 the borough was considered 'entirely' under the direction of the head of the Clive family (cr. earl of Powis 1804),[90] but there soon began a succession of three contests within the space of 21 months in which some of the leading Radicals from the city of Westminster took advantage of the persistent local opposition to the Clives.

The first contest began at the end of 1817,[91] and in 1818 Sir Francis Burdett proposed his friend and fellow member of the 'Rota', the Hon. Douglas Kinnaird, to the burgesses. A line from an election song reveals the continuity of opposition: 'the lads of old Clarke, can yet strike the blow'.[92] Kinnaird also had Kinchant support[93] and was confident of success.[94] He brought in Joseph Hume as his second man,[95] but Hume named a replacement and withdrew shortly before the poll,[96] and in the event Clive and Robinson did better than they had in 1802.[97] After the poll the vanquished threatened to petition, and their forecast that the borough would no longer be 'enrolled in the list of the usurped possessions of a borough-mongering family'[98] temporarily came true. Kinnaird stood again at the 1819 by-election following Lt.-Gen. Robinson's death. Lord Valentia, whose family owned an estate just over the county boundary in Staffordshire,[99] was the Clive candidate, and was beaten by 87 votes to 83.[1] He petitioned[2] but Parliament was dissolved before his case was heard.

Some explanation of Valentia's defeat is to be found in a report of William Holmes during the 1820 general election campaign. William Clive retired and the family went outside its own ranks for both candidates. Edward Rogers was a barrister. His father, a Ludlow alderman, had prospered in London and had bought Stanage Park (Radnors.); the senior line of the family had long been settled near the borough.[3] Holmes, a stranger, was the Tory chief whip.[4] Kinnaird visited the borough on 14 February,[5] Holmes on 21 February. Holmes's report was gloomy. 'Through the most unaccountable neglect and apathy on the part of the Clives', he wrote, 'Kinnaird has taken up a position that would require a duke of Wellington in electioneering tactics to dislodge him from'. He thought both seats might be won if only the Clives would exert their influence 'boldly and manfully'; at the same time he confessed that he had 'scarcely a hope' of being elected.[6] Mr. King, Sir William Eliott,[7] and Robert Knight were all

[84] S.R.O. 552/23/57; N.L.W., Clive Corresp. 2nd ser. 556, 561–3, 643, 2147, 2282–3, 2286–7; Bp.'s Cas. boro. rec., poll. For Kinchant see S.R.O. 552/17/147; *T.S.A.S.* 2nd ser. vii. 104, 116. For Clarke see above, p. 133.

[85] *C.J.* lviii. 41–2, 409; India Office Libr., MS. Eur. G 37/71, R. W[ilding] to Ld. Clive, 17 May 1803.

[86] India Office Libr., MS. Eur. G 37/71, R. W[ilding] to Ld. Clive, 17 May 1803.

[87] N.L.W., Powis Castle Corresp. 5627.

[88] Grenville MSS., Lady Grizelda Tekell to Ld. Grenville and Grenville's reply, 26–7 Apr. [1807].

[89] N.L.W., Clive Corresp. 2nd ser. 365; S.R.O. 552/23/54, 90–109. A case dragged on for some yrs.

[90] Oldfield, *Rep. Hist. of Gt. Brit. and Irel.* (1816), iv. 405.

[91] S.R.O. 552/22/31.

[92] Bp.'s Cas. boro. rec., printed notices, etc., of meetings and resolutions, Jan. 1818; ibid., copy of electn. song. For Kinnaird, who also stood at Westminster in 1818, see *D.N.B.*; *The Late Elections . . .* (London, 1818), 355, 368.

[93] From J. C. Kinchant's bro. Fra.: Bp.'s Cas. boro. rec., printed addresses 27 Jan., 9 Feb. 1818; see also B.L. Add. MS. 36457, ff. 44–7. For Fra. Kinchant see Burke, *Land. Gent.* (1914), 1083.

[94] B.L. Add. MS. 51565, f. 131.

[95] Bp.'s Cas. boro. rec., printed address, n.d.

[96] Ibid. 13 June 1818. The new man was the Radical Sir Wm. Eliott.

[97] *Shrews. Chron.* 26 June 1818.

[98] *The Late Elections*, 14. [99] *V.C.H. Worcs.* iii. 6.

[1] *Salopian Jnl.* 7 and 14 July 1819.

[2] Copy of petition in Bp.'s Cas. boro. rec.; ref. in *C.J.* lxxv. 181.

[3] *T.S.A.S.* 2nd ser. x. 66. [4] Ibid.; *D.N.B.*

[5] *Shrews. Chron.* 18 Feb. 1820.

[6] T 64/261, 'Dog-Shock' [Holmes] to Chas. Arbuthnot, 21 Feb. 1820.

[7] The 1818 candidate (above, n. 96) whose 1818 drink bills were causing him trouble with his agent: Bp.'s Cas. boro. rec., corresp. between Eliott and John Griffiths, solicitor, 1820–1.

mentioned as possible partners for Kinnaird[8] but it was Knight, a Warwickshire squire, who stood. He and Kinnaird were proposed by Richard Griffiths, the Kinchant agent who had opposed the Clives in 1802.[9] At the poll 174 voted,[10] more than ever before;[11] there were no split votes. The bailiff's vote for Holmes and Rogers closed the poll and produced a tie: 87 votes for all four candidates.[12] Both sides petitioned. The Commons committee ruled that the franchise was in the resident and non-resident capital burgesses, thus allowing the Clives the votes of absentee aldermen, and in the burgesses resident for a year and a day with a legal settlement in the borough. The scrutiny gave Kinnaird and Knight a majority of one, but following an investigation of bribery Kinnaird and Knight were held to have been defeated by one vote.[13]

At the last three elections before Reform the Clives retained control without difficulty.[14] Holmes and Rogers were unopposed in 1826. In 1830 Holmes, accommodated elsewhere, was replaced by Lady Powis's kinsman, F. H. Cornewall of Diddlebury, whose father, then bishop of Bristol, had helped to manage the Clive interest in 1802. Next year Cornewall was succeeded by J. L. Knight, a rich and successful barrister whose opinion Lord Powis had taken from time to time. Knight, with Rogers and others, making what play they could with Whig bribery, defended the borough in the debates on reform but they spoke its funeral oration: in Lord John Russell's deliberately offensive phrase, merely the 'pomp of mourning eloquence' to deck the borough's 'obsequies'.[15] For Bishop's Castle reform meant disfranchisement.

Bishop's Castle has been classed with those boroughs which 'to some extent retrieved their character'. Long notorious for open venality, it is alleged to have led 'a much better regulated existence' after 1768.[16] In fact the borough, though less disturbed, remained hardly less corrupt than before. Bishop's Castle has also been described as so 'safe and cheap' after 1768 that its M.P.s could be changed 'with ease and frequency',[17] but it was certainly not cheap; nor, from 1802 to 1820, was it safe. For nearly a century and a half, both before the advent of the Clives and under their sway, the politics of Bishop's Castle were dominated by *unum necessarium*.

Shropshire members made little contribution to the debates on the first Reform Bill of 1830–1: Cressett Pelham spoke against it,[18] Cornewall made a minor intervention,[19] Slaney welcomed it,[20] but the rest said nothing about it. When the Bill received its second reading only Slaney, Thompson, and Wolryche Whitmore were in the majority.[21] In the division on Gascoyne's amendment, which wrecked the Bill in April, Cressett Pelham cast a rogue vote with Slaney, Thompson, and Wolryche Whitmore against the amendment.[22]

After the 1831 general election Cressett Pelham spoke persistently against the second Bill,[23] correctly perceiving its long-term consequences.[24] Slaney spoke three times for it,[25] but Wolryche Whitmore, Lord John Russell's cousin, again said nothing. What preoccupied Shropshire at this stage of the second Bill was the fate of Bishop's Castle. Having fewer than 2,000 inhabitants, the borough was to be disfranchised

[8] *Shrews. Chron.* 3 Mar. 1820.
[9] Ibid. 10 Mar. 1820; *V.C.H. Warws.* iii. 214. For Knight's father, Ld. Catherlough, see above, p. 304. For Griffiths see S.R.O. 552/22/16, p. 3; 552/23/57.
[10] S.R.O. 552/22/49. Another 9 votes were rejected.
[11] There is an undated list of 194 burgesses in Bp.'s Cas. boro. rec.
[12] *Shrews. Chron.* 17 Mar. 1820.
[13] Ibid. 9, 16, and 23 June 1820; *C.J.* lxxv. 181–2, 316.
[14] For this para. see *T.S.A.S.* 2nd ser. x. 67. For the Cornewalls see ibid. 4th ser. iii. 291–301; S.P.L., MS. 2791, pp. 53–4, 372; sources cited above, p. 306. For

Knight see *D.N.B.* sub Bruce, Sir Jas. Lewis Knight-; S.R.O. 552/17/596–7; 552/23/59.
[15] 5 *Parl. Deb.* 3rd ser. 98–108.
[16] Namier, *Politics at Accession of Geo. III*, 162.
[17] *Hist. Parl., Commons*, 1754–90, i. 362.
[18] 3 *Parl. Deb.* 3rd ser. 1604.
[19] Ibid. 1723.
[20] Ibid. 674.
[21] Ibid. 805–16.
[22] Ibid. 1690–9.
[23] 4 *Parl. Deb.* 3rd ser. 966 sqq.
[24] Ibid. 1158; 6 *Parl. Deb.* 3rd ser. 149.
[25] 4 *Parl. Deb.* 3rd ser. 278, 654; 5 *Parl. Deb.* 3rd ser. 631.

under the Bill's Schedule A which had caused so much incredulity and derision when first read out; the borough's M.P.s courted the same reaction by their exaggerated praise of Bishop's Castle in the long committee debate on the schedule. Knight claimed that the electors were 'as free from improper bias' as any in the kingdom and that the only influence acknowledged by the burgesses was that of 'kindness'.[26] Rogers made a lame defence of the borough against the charge of bribery;[27] Cressett Pelham too denied that Bishop's Castle was influenced by corruption.[28] Such statements evoked highly sceptical reactions from Russell and Althorp,[29] and nothing more was heard of Knight's threat to move the deletion of Bishop's Castle from Schedule A either by union with some other borough or by other means. On third reading the Shropshire M.P.s divided 8 to 4 against the Bill, Foster joining the 3 other Whigs in voting for it.[30]

The changes introduced into the third Reform Bill in December led Lord Clive to break his silence and welcome the alterations, for he had by then come to admit the need for some reform. He soon modified his position, but at the time it was a notable concession by a well connected diehard.[31] In the debates Knight made some sound points on drafting and procedure[32] and Slaney spoke, as before, to attack 'virtual representation'.[33] Cressett Pelham was again loquacious, but he stressed more than before his position as an 'independent member' unswayed by influence and aware of real distress in the country which the Bill would do nothing to alleviate.[34] The rest were silent. On third reading, in March 1832, the twelve M.P.s divided exactly as they had done six months before. The knights of the shire and the members for Ludlow and Bishop's Castle voted against reform, the members for Shrewsbury and Much Wenlock divided their votes, and, thanks to Thomas Whitmore's complaisance at the 1831 general election, Bridgnorth gave two votes for reform.[35]

In the Lords, Bradford, Powis, and Forester had all voted against the second reading of the second Bill in October 1831.[36] Bradford had switched to support the second reading of the third Bill in the crucial division of April 1832[37] and, though he rejoined his two colleagues to defeat the government early in May,[38] a month later only Powis voted in the small minority of 22 against the Bill's third reading.[39]

1832-85

Southern Division, p. 314. Northern Division, p. 318. Shrewsbury, p. 323. Bridgnorth, p. 330. Ludlow, p. 336. Much Wenlock, p. 339.

FROM 1832 to 1868 Shropshire continued to send twelve members to Parliament. The 1832 Reform Act[40] disfranchised Bishop's Castle but split the county into Northern and Southern divisions with two M.P.s each. At the beginning of the period the two divisions contained some 173,700 inhabitants and 7,473 electors, the Northern being the smaller, more populous, and less agricultural. Parliamentary Shropshire gained Farlow (Herefs.) and yielded the Shropshire parts of Halesowen to a Worcestershire

[26] 5 *Parl. Deb.* 3rd ser. 98.
[27] Ibid. 99.
[28] Ibid.
[29] Ibid. 101, 105.
[30] 7 *Parl. Deb.* 3rd ser. 466–76.
[31] 9 *Parl. Deb.* 3rd ser. 193, 200; M. G. Brock, *Gt. Reform Act* (1974), 266.
[32] 9 *Parl. Deb.* 3rd ser. 758 sqq.
[33] Ibid. 472.
[34] Ibid. 673; 11 *Parl. Deb.* 3rd ser. 651.

[35] 11 *Parl. Deb.* 3rd ser. 780–6.
[36] 8 *Parl. Deb.* 3rd ser. 339–44.
[37] 12 *Parl. Deb.* 3rd ser. 453–60.
[38] Ibid. 723–8.
[39] 13 *Parl. Deb.* 3rd ser. 374.
[40] For this para. see Representation of the People Act, 1832, 2 & 3 Wm. IV, cc. 45, 64; Lewis, *Topog. Dict. Eng.* (1835), v, index to plans (pp. 1, 3–5) and plates LXXI–LXXIII; below, pp. 314, 318–19. For this section see also below, p. 319 n. 70.

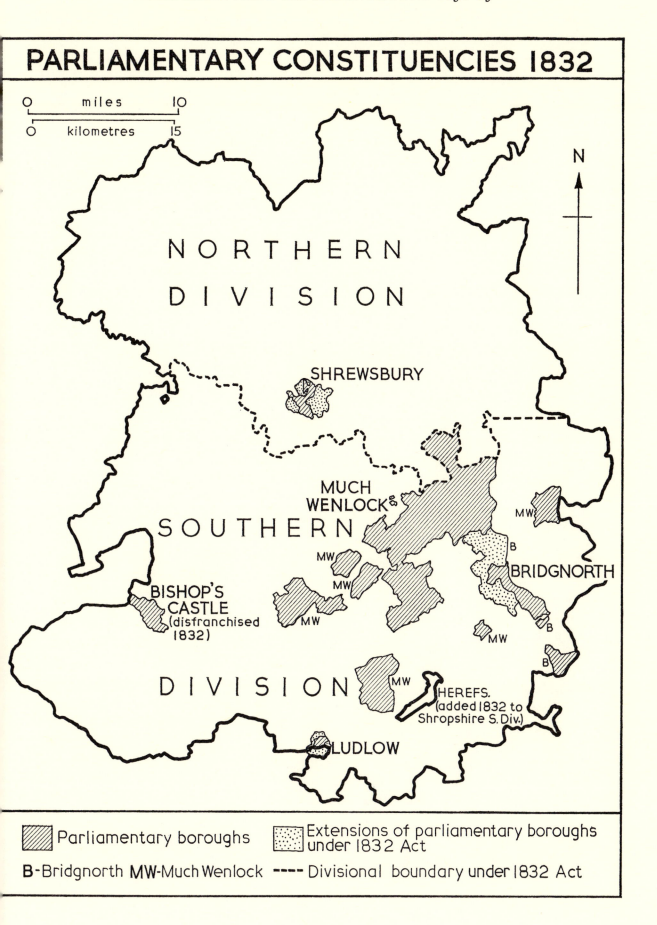

PARLIAMENTARY CONSTITUENCIES 1832

O miles 10
O kilometres 15

N

NORTHERN DIVISION

SHREWSBURY

MUCH WENLOCK

SOUTHERN

BISHOP'S CASTLE (disfranchised 1832)

MW

MW

MW

BRIDGNORTH
B

B
MW
B

DIVISION

MW

HEREFS. (added 1832 to Shropshire S. Div.)

LUDLOW

▨ Parliamentary boroughs   ⋮ Extensions of parliamentary boroughs under 1832 Act

B-Bridgnorth MW-Much Wenlock ---- Divisional boundary under 1832 Act

parliamentary division. The boundaries of all but one of the four remaining parliamentary boroughs were changed; Much Wenlock remained unaltered and anomalous, more like a county division than a borough.[41] Bridgnorth[42] and, to a lesser extent, Ludlow were given something of the same mixed character by the inclusion within their parliamentary boundaries of adjacent rural areas, Ludlow taking in the Herefordshire township of Ludford. The four parliamentary boroughs contained some 46,900 inhabitants and 3,510 electors.

Shropshire electors were over-represented. In the 1850s in the Northern and Southern divisions each M.P. represented 2,113 and 1,591 electors respectively, the average in county divisions being 3,186; against a national average of 1,202 borough electors to each M.P. Shrewsbury had 808, Much Wenlock 435, Bridgnorth 339, and Ludlow 203.[43] Bridgnorth and Ludlow each lost a member under the 1867 Reform Act,[44] but no constituency boundary was altered until 1885.

The 1832 Act enhanced the political dominance of the landed interest in Shropshire. Instead of two there were four county seats for the more zealous and affluent local magnates. The two seats at Bishop's Castle, less honorific than county seats, disappeared, the former M.P.s ending their connexion with Shropshire. Black Country and Birmingham industrialists no longer needed to influence the representation of Shropshire boroughs, and the balance between peers and commoners and Whigs and Tories among the county's landowners thus became more important. In Bridgnorth, Ludlow, and Much Wenlock the family interests dominant before 1832 retained all or much of their control. Bridgnorth and Ludlow were nevertheless frequently contested, and at Ludlow the increase in electorate and area reduced, but did not destroy, the control exercised by Lord Powis's family.

The statistics of landowning collected in 1873[45] illuminate the half-century up to 1885. About three-eighths of the county were owned by some two dozen peers and nearly a fifth was in the hands of seven peers with over 10,000 a. each. Three dynasties of absentees owned much land outside the county also: the dowager Lady Bridgwater and her successors from 1853 the Earls Brownlow,[46] the dukes of Cleveland, and above all the dukes of Sutherland. Although he did not live in the county, the 2nd duke of Sutherland's 17,000 a. round Lilleshall were sufficient for him to be made lord lieutenant by Melbourne in 1839,[47] the only Whig to hold the office in 19th-century Shropshire. Sutherland's family, however, had largely withdrawn from local politics before the period began, and the 3rd duke's failure to exert himself for the Liberals in the 1860s,[48] though a disappointment, can hardly have surprised local Liberals. The earls of Powis and Bradford, though seated in Montgomeryshire and Staffordshire, can hardly be considered absentees. In 1873 Powis owned more land in Shropshire (26,986 a.) than anyone else, but his family's public and political activities seem to have been concentrated in Wales, where he owned more.[49] Bradford owned 10,883 a. in Shropshire

[41] *T.S.A.S.* 3rd ser. ii. 300.

[42] *Sel. Cttee. on Bridgnorth Election Petition*, H.C. 203, p. 153 (1852–3), viii.

[43] Hughenden Manor, Disraeli MSS., B/XI/C/4(i). In 1852 a proposed £10 county franchise would have added over 6,000 electors in the 2 divisions: ibid. B/XI/A/8. Acknowledgment is due to the National Trust for permission to study and quote from these papers.

[44] Representation of the People Act, 1867, 30 & 31 Vic. c. 102. The need for at least partial disfranchisement of such boros. had been clear for some yrs.: Disraeli MSS., B/XI/B/18b.

[45] *Ret. of Owners of Land*, H.C. 38–II, Salop. (1874), lxxii(2); J. Bateman, *Gt. Landowners of Gt. Brit. and Ireland* (1883).

[46] *Complete Peerage*, ii. 315–16, 349.

[47] See p. 360.

[48] E. Richards, 'Social and Electoral Influence of the Trentham Interest, 1800–1860', *Midland Hist.* iii. 117–48; below, pp. 316, 321.

[49] For the 2nd earl see *D.N.B.*, but for his notable success as a Salop. D.L. during the 1842 disturbances see S.R.O., q. sess. Constabulary Cttee. rep. bk. 1839–53, pp. 202–4, 223, 225, 236–7, 240; B. S. Trinder, *Indust. Revolution in Shropshire* (1973), 389–93; E. W. Gladstone, *Shropshire Yeomanry, 1795–1945* (1953), 44. For the 3rd earl see *Dict. Welsh Biog.* 780; above, p. 161 n. 57. Nevertheless (at first as Ld. Clive) he regularly attended Salop. q. sess. from 1843: *Orders of Q. Sess.* iv. 26 sqq.

and as much again in other counties. The two other peers with large Shropshire estates were more exclusively Shropshire figures: Lord Hill had 16,554 a. in the county and none elsewhere, Lord Forester owned 14,891 a. in the county and 724 a. outside. Powis, Bradford, Hill, and Forester and their successors were Tories in and after 1832,[50] and holders of three of those titles held the lieutenancy for over a century after Sutherland's resignation.[51] Other peers owned smaller Shropshire estates; some, like those of Lords Combermere, Tankerville, Kilmorey, and Wenlock, were appendages to greater estates elsewhere. Wenlock was the prime mover in an attempted Liberal revival in the county in 1865.[52]

Rather more than a quarter of the county was owned by the country gentlemen, three of whom became peers during the period.[53] Best endowed was the Hon. R. H. Clive (d. 1854), who inherited the Oakly Park estate in 1801;[54] his grandson, who became Lord Windsor in 1869 and was created earl of Plymouth in 1905,[55] owned over 11,000 a. Four other families owned over 8,000 a.[56] and five more had 6,000–8,000 a.[57] To those ten families should probably be added the Williams Wynns and Ormsby-Gores. Both owned less than 4,000 a. in Shropshire but both had estates elsewhere which increased their political weight in the county. Sir Watkin Williams Wynn's great estates in Wales gave him a political base there, and in Shropshire he was content to exercise his influence at Much Wenlock in the early years of the period. The Ormsby-Gores, newcomers to Shropshire politics, lacked political security in Ireland or Wales but their estates in those countries made them rich enough to share the Northern division of Shropshire with Lord Hill. Many from these well endowed ranks could aspire to represent a county division or borough. More typical of the Shropshire landed gentry, however, were the 33 owners of estates extending over 3,000–6,000 a. in the county.[58] Few of them found an independent way[59] into Parliament for a Shropshire seat during the first half of the period, R. A. Slaney and, for briefer spells, John Cotes and Lechmere Charlton being perhaps the only exceptions.[60] In the second half of the period, however, the squires began to elbow their way into Parliament. Three Conservative Leightons and, with aristocratic help, the Liberal, Jasper More, all won county divisions, Sir Baldwin Leighton's efforts in 1859 against the aristocrats and richer landowners of his own party opening the way for other Conservative squires.[61]

Among those forty-five or so families only the heads of the Dalberg-Acton, Cotes, More, Lloyd, Slaney, and Whitmore (of Dudmaston) families were of strongly Whig or Liberal tendency in 1832, and of these William Lloyd was a Conservative within five years[62] while the Wolryche-Whitmores of Dudmaston were Conservative after 1858.[63] The paucity of Liberal Shropshire squires explains the Liberal hopes pinned on A. P. Lonsdale (later Heywood-Lonsdale), a newcomer to the county in 1868.[64]

Shropshire always returned a majority of Conservative M.P.s during the period, and

[50] *Complete Peerage*, ii. 276; v. 553; vi. 520–2; x. 652–4.
[51] See p. 360.
[52] See p. 316.
[53] Lds. Acton, Windsor, and Harlech. Ld. Rowton (cr. 1880) hardly counts as a Salop. landowner before 1889: see p. 323 n. 17.
[54] *T.S.A.S.* 4th ser. xii. 33; *Montg. Coll.* viii. 17.
[55] *Complete Peerage*, xii(2), 801–2.
[56] (Baldwyn-)Childe of Kinlet, Corbet of Adderley, Corbet of Sundorne, and Whitmore of Apley Pk. whose estate was bought by W. O. Foster in 1867.
[57] Botfield, Corbet of Acton Reynald, Dalberg-Acton (peers from 1869), Lyster, and Thursby(-Pelham).
[58] Allcroft (from 1869), Benson, Borough, Charlton (later Meyrick) of Apley Cas., Cholmondeley (heirs of Owen), Corbett of Longnor, Cotes, Eyton (co-heirs of Slaney), Heywood (from the 1860s; Heywood-Lonsdale

from 1877), Howard of Corby Cas. (Cumb.) and Middleton Priors, Hulton-Harrop, Hunt, Kynaston, Leighton, Lloyd of Aston, LLoyd, Mainwaring, More, Childe(-Pemberton), Plowden, Pritchard, Rouse-Boughton, Severne, Sitwell, Smythe, Sparrow of Ch. Preen (from 1848), Stanier (from 1873), Tayleur, Tyrwhitt, Warter (from the 1860s), Wingfield, Wolryche-Whitmore, and Woodward of Hopton Ct.
[59] Dod's seat was not really an independent one (p. 320). He died in 1863 and his est. was bought by J. P. Heywood.
[60] Gaskell (when first elected) and Pritchard perhaps hardly count as Salop. landed squires. Both eventually became Libs.
[61] i.e. Col. E. Corbett, J. E. Severne, and Leighton's own two sons.
[62] See p. 320.
[63] When Whitmore died.
[64] See p. 322.

political solidarity was perhaps reinforced by ecclesiastical allegiance, for in 1851 Shropshire was the tenth most Anglican county in England.[65] Nine Tories and three Whigs were elected in 1832, in the aftermath of reform, but it was the high-water of Whig success for the next 25 years. In 1835 12 Tories were returned, and a similar band, the 'Twelve Apostles', was elected in 1841.[66] Repeal of the corn laws caused some Tory disarray, 2 Liberals and a Peelite being returned in 1847.[67] Eleven Conservatives, however, were returned in 1852, though one of them was replaced by a Liberal–Conservative after petition.[68] Thereafter matters went less well for local Conservatives. Nine Conservatives, two Liberals, and a Liberal–Conservative were returned in 1857 and 1859. The Liberal–Conservative was again elected in 1865, when four other seats were won by Liberals, one of which was later lost on petition. Only 2 Liberals were returned in 1868, but they won 4 seats in 1874 and 3 in 1880. The fluctuations were mainly due to changes of allegiance among borough electors, especially those of Shrewsbury.

Fifty-five men sat for Shropshire constituencies between 1832 and 1885 and they came from thirty-nine different families. The Clives and Herberts supplied seven, the Leightons three, and the families of Hill, Ormsby-Gore, Cust, Bridgeman, Vane, Cotes, Whitmore, and Weld-Forester two each. Thirty-nine of the members, including one who later changed his allegiance, were first elected as Tories, and the average tenure of a seat was almost eleven years. Eight, or at most nine, of the fifty-five could be described as strangers to the county, all of them borough M.P.s.[69] Twenty of the fifty-five were close relatives of peers or themselves became peers after they had sat. Three country squires sat for the Northern division and five for the Southern, but the four county seats were normally safe for connexions of the peerage.

The dominance of Tory peers and gentry in the county was to some extent offset by the press. For much of the period the *Shrewsbury Chronicle*, the leading county paper, was Radical in tone. John Watton (d. 1850) became its sole owner in 1813 and from the 1820s his paper wholeheartedly supported Reform. After 1832 the *Chronicle* supported the Whigs and Liberals for forty years, and Watton's son, another John (d. 1895),[70] proposed W. J. Clement's nomination for the Shrewsbury Liberals in 1865.[71] By 1872, however, the *Chronicle* had lost sympathy with Gladstonian Liberalism.[72] Though reserving praise for 'moderate' Liberals, later for Liberal Unionists, the paper became steadily more anti-Radical and Conservative during Victoria's last thirty years.

No other paper matched the *Chronicle*'s circulation[73] or its proprietorial continuity of over eighty years;[74] indeed no other even survived the half century after 1832. Nevertheless by the beginning of the period the *Salopian Journal* was strongly Conservative and provided some political balance to the *Chronicle*. From 1806 the *Journal*'s owners, the Eddowes family, employed Joseph Morris, at first as an apprentice but later as the manager of their business and editor of their paper for upwards of twenty years. When he left in 1841, on a change of ownership,[75] Morris was one of the most prominent ultra-Tories in Shrewsbury.[76] In 1843 the paper was sold out of John Eddowes's hands, only

[65] A. Everitt, *The Pattern of Rural Dissent: the Nineteenth Cent.* (Leicester Univ. Dept. of Eng. Local Hist., Occ. Papers, 2nd ser. iv), 69.

[66] The phrase had been used of the 1835 victors, but with much less jubilation than in 1841.

[67] See pp. 315, 328, 338.

[68] See p. 334.

[69] Hanmer, Disraeli, Figgins, and Straight for Shrews., Gaskell (when first elected) and Brown for M. Wenlock, and Romilly, Alcock, and Fraser for Ludlow.

[70] Unless otherwise stated this and the next four paras. are based on *Through Nine Reigns: 200 Years of the Shrews.*

Chron. 1772–1972 (Bi-Centenary Souvenir, 23 Nov. 1972), 50–5; The Times, *Tercentenary Handlist of Newspapers* (1920).

[71] *Shrews. Chron.* 14 July 1865.

[72] See e.g. ibid. 2 and 6 Feb. 1872.

[73] See e.g. *Shropshire Conservative*, 15 Apr., 17 June 1843.

[74] Cf. *Shrews. Jnl.* 21 Mar. 1883; *Shrews. Chron.* 8 Jan. 1892.

[75] *Salopian Jnl.* 10 Nov. 1841; *T.S.A.S.* 3rd ser. i. 1–3.

[76] *Shrews. Chron.* 20 Apr. 1860; *Eddowes's Jnl.* 25 Apr. 1860 (obits.).

to cease a few weeks later.[77] Meanwhile the Eddowes family had brought out *Eddowes's Shrewsbury Journal* (1843–91), which maintained its Conservative allegiance[78] long after the family ceased to own it in 1853.[79] In 1884, however, after another change of ownership, it ceased to be a Conservative paper.[80]

At least in the earlier 1840s there was a degree of political balance between county papers with smaller circulations. The *Shrewsbury News and Cambrian Reporter* (1838–44) was Liberal[81] and the scandal-mongering *Salopian Telegraph and Border Review* (1841–4) was violently anti-Conservative.[82] The *Shropshire Conservative* (1840–61) was edited by T. J. Ouseley,[83] a strong supporter of Disraeli and of the protectionist cause in the 1840s. Ouseley had previously edited the *Shropshire Mercury* (1839–40) but had been dismissed for his rancorous conduct of that paper.[84] The *Salopian Telegraph* subjected Ouseley to attacks of extreme scurrility[85] while, from the beginning, Ouseley's paper was bitterly hostile to the owner of the *Chronicle*, whom it lampooned as a liar, 'Ananias' Watton.[86] The *Conservative* outlived both the *News* and the *Telegraph*, and in 1843, when the *Salopian Journal* ceased, it jubilantly proclaimed itself the county's senior Conservative paper.[87] Nevertheless towards the end of its life the *Conservative* probably had no great influence: in 1857 one prominent Conservative, albeit one who had little reason to favour the paper,[88] considered it 'a very obscure print read by few'.[89]

In the latter part of the period the Liberals founded new papers which balanced the *Chronicle*'s defection. The *Shrewsbury Free Press* appeared in 1865 and by 1875 it claimed to be the county's leading Liberal organ. In 1881 it was replaced by the *Shropshire Guardian*[90] brought out by a newly formed company of rich Shropshire Liberals.[91] The company bought the *Shrewsbury Journal* in 1884 and turned it into a professedly non-political paper,[92] though it soon began to provide considerable coverage of Liberal politics.[93] By purchasing the *Journal* the company also acquired the *Shropshire Evening News*, founded a year previously[94] and apparently modelled on the chain of Radical papers set up about that time by Andrew Carnegie, the American steel magnate, and his Wolverhampton associate Thomas Graham.[95]

Local newspapers, founded from the 1850s on, tended to be Conservative, as were those at Bridgnorth,[96] Wellington,[97] Ludlow,[98] and Whitchurch.[99] At Oswestry[1] and Newport,[2] however, there were papers which supported the Liberals.

Political excitement never again sank to the low level of the late 18th and early 19th centuries, but Shropshire was politically quieter than most counties during this half-

[77] *Shropshire Conservative*, 28 Jan., 4 Feb., 15 Apr. 1843.
[78] *Eddowes's Jnl.* 1 Feb. 1843.
[79] Ibid. 30 Mar., 6 Apr. 1853; *Shrews. Jnl.* 21 Mar. 1883.
[80] *Eddowes's Jnl.* 29 Oct., 5 Nov. 1884.
[81] The *Shropshire Conservative* characterized it as 'Chartist' and 'Radical': 19 Sept., 28 Nov. 1840.
[82] Successor to the *Salopian Budget and Border Sentinel* (2–30 Oct. 1841) which the Conservative 'Knot' in Shrews. (below, p. 325) had suppressed by reporting it for evasion of stamp duty: *Salopian Telegraph and Border Review*, 6 Nov. 1841.
[83] He apparently became the paper's owner 1847 × 1851: S.R.O., q. sess. Finance Cttee. rep. bk. 1843–50, pp. 120, 185; S. Bagshaw, *Dir. Salop.* (1851), 108.
[84] *Ten Towns Messenger*, 31 Jan. 1840; *Shropshire Mercury*, 1 Feb., 27 June 1840; *Shropshire Conservative*, 29 Nov. 1845.
[85] Commonly referring to him as 'Judas O'Sly'.
[86] *Shropshire Conservative*, 5–19 Dec. 1840; 16 Jan., 17 Apr. 1841; 11 Mar. 1843. Cf. Acts 5: 1–11.
[87] *Shropshire Conservative*, 15 Apr. 1843.
[88] Sir B. Leighton: see p. 155.
[89] Loton Hall MSS., Sir B. Leighton's diary, 21 Mar.

1857.
[90] *Shrews. Free Press*, 11 June 1865; 6 Mar. 1875; *Shropshire Guardian*, 19 Aug. 1881.
[91] B.T. 31/2847/15660.
[92] *Eddowes's Jnl.* 29 Oct., 5 Nov. 1884.
[93] Cf. reporting of the 1885 'Liberal Demonstration' in Shrews. in *Eddowes's Jnl.* 4 Nov. 1885, and *Shrews. Chron.* 6 Nov. 1885.
[94] *Wellington Jnl.* 2 Jan. 1892.
[95] *Through Nine Reigns*, 54. Cf. B. J. Hendrick, *Life of And. Carnegie* (1933), 226–34, 237.
[96] *Bridgnorth Beacon* (1852–4); *Bridgnorth Jnl.* (founded 1854).
[97] *Wellington Jnl.* (founded 1854). In 1874 it absorbed the *Shropshire News* (formerly the *Wellington Adv.*, formerly the *Rlwy. Messenger*, founded 1849).
[98] *Ludlow Standard* (1840); *Ludlow Adv.* (founded 1855).
[99] *Whitchurch Herald* (founded 1869).
[1] *Oswestry Adv.* (founded 1849). See jubilee (4 Jan. 1899) and centenary (5 Jan. 1949) suppls.
[2] *Newport Adv.* (founded 1855 and published as the *Newport and Mkt. Drayton Adv.* from 1869). See *Life of Chas. Silvester Horne*, ed. W. B. Selbie [1920], 3–5.

century. Lectures on the corn laws in the Wellington area in 1842 did not disturb the peace.[3] Later that year there was widespread unrest in the area but it was industrial rather than political in character,[4] and Shropshire remained relatively peaceful.[5] Generally the outlets provided by election rowdyism, often organized in the interests of rival candidates, seem to have sufficed for the fiercer spirits among the lower classes of the towns.[6] Not until 1885, however, were all Shropshire seats contested at one election. Excitement was highest in 1832 when there were four serious polls, a formal poll in the Southern division, and a Whig withdrawal after a serious canvass at Bridgnorth. Neither county division was contested at a general election between 1832 and 1865 nor was Much Wenlock between 1835 and 1874. The new registration procedure made for accurate forecasting,[7] with the result that there were 4 Shropshire polls in 1835, 3 in 1837, 1841, 1847, and 1852, only 1 in 1857, none at all in 1859, and only 3 in 1865. In 1868, as after the previous Reform Act, there was greater excitement; 5 polls were held, the only unopposed return being at Much Wenlock. There were 3 polls in 1874 and 5 in 1880.[8]

The issue which most preoccupied the landowners was the repeal of the corn laws. Wolryche Whitmore agitated in favour of repeal,[9] and a few other squires agreed with him. Most landowners and farmers, however, were strongly opposed to repeal, and for the most part their M.P.s concurred. Ormsby-Gore, for example, condemned repeal as harmful to agriculture in Ireland, and Gaskell also spoke against it, dismissing Wolryche Whitmore's prediction of its effects.[10] M.P.s, however, were probably more divided than their electors. In the crisis of 1846 three of the Twelve Apostles voted for repeal: the Hon. R. H. Clive, George Tomline, and Beriah Botfield.[11] T. C. Whitmore finally avoided a vote but was nevertheless classed as one of the 'Four Traitors' by local protectionists.[12] Tomline never returned to his Conservative allegiance, though the others did. There was a move to censure Clive publicly for his vote, but it was thwarted by Sir Baldwin Leighton and others.[13] Though several gentlemen refused to propose Clive at the 1847 election,[14] the controversy over the corn laws had little lasting effect on political relations in the county outside Shrewsbury.

Southern Division

The Southern division contained some 75,300 inhabitants; 51 per cent of its 15,632 families were chiefly employed in agriculture, 26 per cent chiefly in trade, manufactures, and handicraft. Nearly two thirds of the farmers were employing labour outside their own families.[15] Shifnal was the most populous parish in the division; Bishop's Castle, Clun, Cleobury Mortimer, Church Stretton, and Albrighton (near Shifnal) were the only other places of any size, though there were scattered mining settlements in Pontesbury and Westbury parishes and around the Titterstone Clee.[16] The divisional electors included freeholders in the parliamentary boroughs of Bridgnorth, Ludlow, and Much Wenlock, and those towns were important places of assembly and disorder

[3] S.R.O., q. sess. Constabulary Cttee. rep. bk. 1839–53, p. 196.
[4] Sources cited in n. 49, above.
[5] Cf. F. C. Mather, 'The General Strike of 1842', *Popular Protest and Public Order . . . 1790–1920*, ed. R. Quinault and J. Stevenson (1974), 115–40.
[6] See pp. 316–17, 328, 332.
[7] J. A. Thomas, 'The System of Registration and the Development of Party Organization, 1832–1870', *History*, N.S. xxxv. 81–98.
[8] The absence of a poll does not of course mean that there was no contest.
[9] See p. 282.
[10] 86 *Parl. Deb.* 3rd ser. 139–40, 340–4.
[11] Ibid. 721–6.
[12] Ibid. 726; *Shropshire Conservative*, 7 Mar. 1846. Cf. ibid. 4 July 1846.
[13] B. Leighton, 'Short Acct. of Life of Sir B. Leighton, Bt.' (TS. in S.R.O. 783, parcel 194), p. 77.
[14] Loton Hall MSS., diary of Sir B. Leighton, 4 Aug. 1847.
[15] *Census*, 1831.
[16] *V.C.H. Salop.* i. 450–2; ii. 15, 219–29; viii. 253–4, 279–81, 306, 308, 322–4.

in the few contested elections. The place of nomination and declaration, however, was fixed at Church Stretton,[17] perhaps because of its nearness to Shrewsbury whence the forces of law and order could be summoned in case of disturbances. In 1852 influence in the division was held to be 'much divided' being 'chiefly possessed' by Lords Powis and Bradford, the duke of Cleveland, and others.[18]

The Conservatives held both seats without a contest until 1865, but at 3 of the last 4 general elections before 1885 the peace was disturbed, once successfully, by the Liberal squire R. J. More. The division's representation was dominated by the Clives and Bridgemans; a Clive or a Herbert[19] sat 1832-59 and 1865-76, Lord Newport 1842-65. Nevertheless the Southern division does not present so unchanging a picture of monopoly by two families as the Northern.

In 1832 neither former knight of the shire stood for the Southern division, the intention being that Lord Darlington and Thomas Whitmore should represent it with the essential support of Powis's brother the Hon. R. H. Clive of Oakly Park. Darlington, Lord Cleveland's son, had been a Whig until about 1829,[20] Whitmore, a Bridgnorth M.P. for twenty-five years, was a lifelong Tory.[21] Conservative plans, however, were disrupted when Clive, who had already pledged support for Darlington and Whitmore, was unexpectedly defeated at Ludlow on 14 December. He was promptly brought forward for the division, and on 17 December, after the nominations, Whitmore withdrew in his favour. A poll was required as Whitmore had been nominated, but it was a mere formality. Fewer than a quarter of the 2,791 electors voted, and Whitmore received only 20 votes to 642 for Clive and 573 for Darlington. Clive had never canvassed a single elector,[22] and the influence of Oakly obviously outweighed that of Apley. The aristocratic influence which was to dominate the division for over thirty years was thus publicly demonstrated and the parliamentary career of a leading squire was brought to an end.

Darlington succeeded as 2nd duke of Cleveland in 1842, being replaced by Lord Newport despite his absence abroad at the time.[23] Newport combined minor office under Derby, and later, in the Lords, under Disraeli and Salisbury,[24] with a zealous devotion to the turf.[25] Clive, a firm supporter of Peel, voted against the corn laws.[26] At his death in 1854 his seat went to his son Robert Windsor-Clive, Newport's brother-in-law.[27] Only on Windsor-Clive's premature death in August 1859 did the Conservative leaders in the division make way for a local squire. At the general election earlier that year Sir Baldwin Leighton had tried to come forward as a Conservative for the Northern division, but he had been kept out by the leading Conservative landowners. Having learnt the need for haste, he moved quickly in August, securing the approval of Lords Powis and Boyne and the duke of Cleveland within a week of Windsor-Clive's death. His efforts were rewarded. At the election he was unopposed, few being present except some of his tenants and their families.

Col. Percy Herbert, the 2nd Lord Powis's son, replaced Newport in 1865 after his succession as earl of Bradford.[28] At the general election three months later the young

[17] 2 & 3 Wm. IV, c. 64, s. 17.
[18] C. R. Dod, *Electoral Facts from 1832 to 1853*, ed. H. J. Hanham (1972), 275.
[19] In 1807 Ld. Clive (2nd Ld. Powis from 1839) changed his surname from Clive to Herbert: *Complete Peerage*, x. 653.
[20] Ibid. iii. 285, listing his previous parl. seats.
[21] *T.S.A.S.* 4th ser. xii. 32-3; see above, pp. 281-2.
[22] *Salopian Jnl.* 19 and 26 Dec. 1832.
[23] His uncle, C. O. Bridgeman, issued his addresses, etc.: Staffs. R.O., D.1287/10/4a.
[24] Vice-chamberlain of the Household Feb.-Dec. 1852

and 1858-9, ld. chamberlain of the Household 1866-8, master of the horse 1874-80 and 1885-6: *Complete Peerage*, ii. 276.
[25] *T.S.A.S.* 4th ser. xii. 35.
[26] B. Leighton, 'Short Acct. of Life of Sir Baldwin Leighton, Bt.' (TS. in S.R.O. 783, parcel 194), p. 77; see p. 314.
[27] Burke, *Peerage* (1949), 246, 1597. For the rest of the para. see Loton Hall MSS., Sir B. Leighton's diary, 4 Aug.-14 Sept. 1859; below, pp. 320-1.
[28] *D.N.B.* sub Herbert, Sir Percy Egerton; *Complete Peerage*, ii. 276.

Robert Jasper More, the heir of Linley, stood for the Liberals against Leighton and Herbert, and the energies suppressed for a generation were released in a fierce campaign.

The 1865 attack on the division was mounted by a small group of leading Shropshire Liberals.[29] At the centre were Lord Wenlock and his new Shropshire agent C. S. Bigge. No candidate could be found among the connexions of the peerage and late in June, after a month of preparations, R. J. More's candidacy became known. More's father believed that he could regard the seat as only a 'temporary honour', and More himself had not expected to be a candidate; he had, however, seen something of politics and was a good speaker. His vigorous and intelligent campaign, directed largely by himself, was supported by Lords Granville and Wenlock and two other Liberal peers,[30] and the rich ironmaster W. O. Foster[31] was helpful around Bridgnorth. More had support from professional men, and Dr. W. J. Clement, then the county's most energetic Liberal, was active around Shrewsbury and wrote to all members of the medical profession. Only some half a dozen squires, however, supported him,[32] and one of them[33] was, like Foster, preoccupied by the Bridgnorth contest. Lack of gentry support was the great Liberal weakness and produced financial difficulty. Wenlock offered half of the campaign expense with central party help, if Sutherland would provide the other half, but the duke refused. Management was easier than finance. Bigge gave More great assistance and Wenlock engaged a Bridgnorth solicitor as More's agent; in Ludlow three of the leading solicitors were retained.

The contest soon became a highly personal one between More and Leighton. Ten years earlier Leighton had prosecuted his gamekeeper for taking two rabbits, thus depriving a family of its livelihood. The incident[34] was raked up and Leighton was bombarded with rabbit skins when speaking at Bridgnorth and elsewhere.[35] Thomas Brassey's navvies working on the Wellington and Market Drayton line were given a day off and went to a turbulent meeting taking all the rabbits' heads they could collect.[36] The Poaching Prevention Act of 1862[37] also assisted Leighton's undoing[38] and his poor-law activities were held up to scorn.[39] It was asserted later that he was further damaged by the unpopularity of Lord Powis's family in the Clun area.[40] From the start More urged the abolition of the malt tax, and was increasingly able to appear as the tenant farmers' candidate. On the hustings he advocated a division of the two seats between a landlords' and a farmers' candidate, a more radical view than his father's, that the 'princely estates' of Lord Wenlock and the duke of Cleveland entitled them to claim one seat from Lord Powis and the Conservatives. The nomination was attended by 300 roughs brought for the Conservatives. Some were paid agitators led by a prize-fighter; at least 100, however, were Leighton's tenants and neighbours. More, aware of Conservative plans, had an equal force of miners. Only with great difficulty did Leighton get a hearing, but More, whom even Leighton acknowledged a good speaker, spoke effectively, converting even the prize-fighter's men who afterwards volunteered him their services at half price.

Four days before the poll the Conservative agents were sure that More was beaten by

[29] For this and the next two paras. see Univ. of Hull, Brynmor Jones Libr., DDFA/39/52; S.R.O. 2836/1; Loton Hall MSS., Sir B. Leighton's diary, 17 June–28 July 1865; *T.S.A.S.* lix. 142, 165–7.

[30] Lds. Craven and Stafford, around Craven Arms and Shifnal respectively.

[31] Liberal M.P. for S. Staffs. 1857–68.

[32] Sir Edw. Blount, Sir C. F. Smythe, John Cotes, T. H. Hope-Edwardes, the Revd. Art. Oakeley, and John Pritchard, the last named hardly counting as a squire.

[33] Sir J. Dalberg-Acton.

[34] Which had not gone unnoticed in the N. div. in 1859:

Eddowes's Jnl. 4 May 1859.

[35] J. A. Bridges, *Reminiscences of a Country Politician* (1906), 7–8.

[36] J. Beard, *My Shropshire Days on Common Ways* [1948], 61–2; *Eddowes's Jnl.* 19 July 1865.   [37] 25 & 26 Vic. c. 114.

[38] Leighton, 'Life of Leighton' (S.R.O. 783, parcel 194), pp. 78–80; *Extracts from Letters & Speeches, &c., of Sir Baldwin Leighton, Bt.*, ed. Frances C. Childe (Shrews. priv. print. 1875), 61–3.

[39] *T.S.A.S.* 4th ser. xii. 36; above, pp. 171–2.

[40] Staffs. R.O., D.1287/10/4a, the Revd. E. G. Childe to Ld. Newport, 22 Oct. 1868.

almost 600. In fact he headed the poll with 1,837 votes (1,298 plumpers) to Herbert's 1,678 and Leighton's 1,399.[41] The Conservative canvassers had been thoroughly deceived, doubtless by tenant farmers. More had spent £6,456, Herbert and Leighton together over £6,300[42] for the return of Herbert alone. Powis had long exercised the greatest influence in the division, but he had had to deal with a Ludlow contest. Such distraction had been part of the Liberals' strategy from the beginning, though they had not managed to start a contest in Much Wenlock.[43] Conservatives in Bridgnorth, however, had had a contest while those in the Northern division had been briefly threatened with one.

The 1868 election illustrates the workings of party finance.[44] Powis and the other Conservative magnates hoped to avoid an expensive contest to regain the lost seat. Powis, fearing that his brother might be ousted, would have preferred no contest. A few zealous Conservative squires, however, wished to promote the return of Col. Edward Corbett of Longnor instead of Jasper More. Corbett was well qualified as commander of the militia, a former master of hounds, and son of a former Shrewsbury M.P.[45] While eager to come forward, however, Corbett required a guarantee of £5,000, and Herbert had no money either. Three weeks before the election their local backers appealed to Disraeli through his secretary Montagu Lowry-Corry[46] for aid towards the £5,500 thought necessary to secure their return. They thought that Lord Boyne, whose son was in their view the obvious choice for Conservative candidate, should put up £2,000 and that they themselves could find £1,000; the rest, however, they wanted from central party funds. Corbett came forward as soon as Lowry-Corry and the Conservative chief whip had collected enough promises to allow the latter to guarantee the balance. The duke of Sutherland refused to contribute to Liberal expenses. More had not paid all his bills for the 1865 contest and would not, by himself, meet the cost of another serious contest, and the Liberal chief whip and Lord Granville could not match the funds available to the Conservatives. According to the Liberal chief whip the county and the Carlton Club found £9,000 for More's opponents[47] whose expenses were later reported as £9,189.[48]

More could already point to his distinguished position in the Central Chamber of Agriculture which he had helped to found in 1866 and of which he was elected president in 1868. His continued cry for the abolition of the malt tax moreover was a matter in which he was genuinely interested,[49] though it was less effective than in 1865.[50] Corbett had been a popular master of the Shropshire Hounds. At the nominations Herbert and Corbett were attended by a body of Black Country roughs. More, the 'farmers' member', was attended, as his 17th-century ancestors at Bishop's Castle might have been, by yokels clad in red, a colour in the family arms. The scene was impressive and memorable.[51] Corbett aroused much derision by drawing attention to his services at the lunatic asylum but then chanced to mention his years as master; that, in a county devoted to field sports, was accepted as ample proof of capacity for political affairs, and Corbett's further remarks were loudly applauded.[52] At the poll

[41] Poll Bk. of S. Salop. Election: 18th July 1865 (Shrews. [1865]; copy in S.R.O. 310/9).

[42] Eddowes's Jnl. 11 and 18 Oct. 1865.

[43] Hull Univ., Brynmor Jones Libr., DDFA/39/52, T. Hardwicke to C. S. Bigge, 15 May 1865. Cf. S.R.O. 2836/1.

[44] For this para. see H. J. Hanham, Electns. and Party Management: Politics in the time of Disraeli and Gladstone (1959), 381-2; Staffs. R.O., D.1287/10/4a, Childe to Newport, 22 and 26 Oct. 1868.

[45] For Corbett see T.S.A.S. 4th ser. xii. 41; V.C.H. Salop. ii. 170; viii. 110; above, pp. 139, 142, 164.

[46] See pp. 322-3.

[47] Hanham, Elections and Party Management, 381-2.

[48] Shrews. Chron. 29 Jan. 1869.

[49] A. H. H. Matthews, Fifty Years of Agricultural Politics . . . 1865-1915 (1915), 257, 416; F. J. Ingleson, Shropshire Chamber of Agriculture, 1866-1966: a Century of Service (Shropshire Chamber of Agric. [1966]), 3-4.

[50] Disraeli MSS., B/IX/G/35.

[51] Shrews. Chron. 18 Apr. 1913 (speech by G. Butler Lloyd).

[52] Bridges, Reminiscences, 10-12. For Conservative posters issued during the contest see S.R.O. 2095/39-41.

More gained even more plumpers than in 1865 but the joint votes for the two Conservatives rose to 2,274 (from 1,181 in 1865). The final figures were: Herbert 2,703, Corbett 2,514, and More 2,161 (1,677 plumpers). More did well in the west and around Much Wenlock but badly around Pontesbury and in the south and south-east.[53] Much of the money raised for Herbert and Corbett was doubtless spent on the roughs and the extra 1,100 Conservative voters.

More had to wait seventeen years to re-enter Parliament. He did not oppose Sir Percy Herbert and Corbett in 1874, or their Conservative successors. J. E. Severne of Wallop was unopposed after Herbert's death in 1876 during More's absence in Bulgaria,[54] and Sir Baldwyn Leighton was unopposed in 1877 when Corbett retired. In the Commons Leighton joined his brother Stanley, whose election for the Northern division the previous year had been a victory for the farmers over the gentlemen.[55] Stanley's triumph may indeed have helped his brother. Corbett's retirement had been very sudden, and it was at first 'arranged' that Lord Bradford's second son, Capt. F. C. Bridgeman, should succeed him. At a meeting in Shrewsbury, however, there was a move in favour of Leighton among the farmers; some of them sent him an 'urgent request' to attend, and he did so 'with the intention of being guided by the meeting'. Two or three other names were mentioned but when Leighton's was brought forward 'the whole room held up their hands' and he accepted nomination.[56]

From 1877 to 1885 a Leighton brother sat for each division. Both were able men and a well informed contemporary described Sir Baldwyn as 'a gentleman of whom any legislative assembly might be proud': 'Statistics are his *forte*, omniscience his foible . . . local taxation is written in the firm lines about his mouth, and terminable annuities sparkle in his eye. His speech, . . . owing to the immense pressure of thought, . . . projects miscellaneous information without that orderly arrangement which is a necessity to the more commonplace mind'.[57] Those qualities did not prevent the divisional electors from putting Leighton at the top of the poll in 1880. At last More came forward again, the Conservatives asserting that he had done so only at the last moment when Liberal success throughout the country was becoming apparent.[58] He was joined by J. W. Handley Davenport, who had recently sold his Cheshire estates[59] and aspired to earn, by 'untiring exertions in the interests of land', an equal right to the title More had borne so long, 'the Farmer's Friend'.[60] Both, however, were beaten. Leighton took 2,491 votes against 2,216 for Severne, 2,140 for More, and 1,634 for Davenport. Conservative success owed something to the exertions of Lt.-Col. W. S. Kenyon-Slaney of Hatton Grange, who made a successful first foray into electioneering and began to be aware of his own considerable political gifts. On polling day he spent over eight hours 'working hard' at Shifnal polling booth and so securing 'several doubtfuls'. It was an impressive result for the Conservatives for a quantity of Conservative votes was thought to have gone to More.[61]

Northern Division

The Northern division contained some 98,400 inhabitants; 39·8 per cent of its 20,107

[53] *Poll Bk. of S. Salop. Election: 23rd Nov. 1868* (Shrews. n.d.; copy in S.R.O. 310/9).
[54] R. J. More, *Under the Balkans* (1877).
[55] See p. 323.
[56] Loton Hall MSS., 'Some Intimate Details Concerning Several Salop. Families by Sir Baldwin Leighton & His Daughter', loose extract from diary of Sir Baldwin Leighton, Aug. 1877. Leighton's unopposed return cost him c. £700.

[57] H. W. Lucy, *Diary of Two Parliaments* (1885), 406. Lucy ('Toby, M.P.' of *Punch*) had served his journalistic apprenticeship in Shrews. in the 1860s: *D.N.B.* 1922–30.
[58] *Eddowes's Jnl.* 14 Apr. 1880.
[59] At Bramhall: G. Ormerod, *Hist. of Co. . . . of Chester* (1882), iii. 828.
[60] *Eddowes's Jnl.* 7 Apr. 1880; S.R.O. 508/12–13, 18–19.
[61] *Memoir of . . . Wm. Kenyon-Slaney*, ed. W. Durnford (1909), 42–3.

families were engaged chiefly in agriculture, 40·1 per cent chiefly in trade, manufactures, and handicraft. As in the Southern division nearly two thirds of the farmers employed labour outside their own families. Industry predominated in Wellington and the coalfield parishes and townships to the east.[62] Elsewhere there were more and larger towns than in the Southern division: Market Drayton, Ellesmere, Newport, Oswestry, Wem, and Whitchurch. The divisional electors included freeholders in the parliamentary borough of Shrewsbury, where nominations and declarations took place.[63] In 1852 influence was held to be 'chiefly possessed' by Lord Hill and Sir Vincent Corbet; on the whole, however, it was 'not much centred in individuals', the duke of Sutherland, William Ormsby-Gore, Lord Kilmorey, and 'many others' sharing it.[64] The Bridgwater property was also of great importance, but was then the subject of litigation.[65] When Lord Hill went bankrupt in 1894 one local paper blamed the 'electoral extravagances of past generations',[66] but the explanation seems hardly adequate; the division was rarely contested during the years of the Hills' dominance[67] and the Southern division was probably a greater expense to its representatives than the Northern.[68]

The disharmony of 1831 was repeated in the division in 1832. Two candidates of long-established local families entered the field: the Tory Sir Rowland Hill, knight of the shire in the last Parliament, and the moderate Whig John Cotes of Woodcote, son of a former county member. John Cressett Pelham, Hill's Tory junior colleague in the last Parliament, had decided to contest Shrewsbury, and a new Tory came forward. William Ormsby-Gore owned estates in Ireland and Wales but lacked a safe seat there. Having married the heiress of Brogyntyn in 1815, he therefore turned his attention to Shropshire. His Whig opponents lampooned him as an Irishman. Hill was neutral between Cotes and Ormsby-Gore, but agents retained for Hill were also retained for Ormsby-Gore and for some months before the election Hill had repeatedly to deny the existence of a coalition between himself and Ormsby-Gore, which their agents' actions suggested.[69]

Political excitement was high; 4,296 of the 4,682 electors voted, putting Hill at the head of the poll.[70] Despite a poetic appeal to the 'manly Shropshire Yeoman' to stand by King and Church and vote for Hill and Ormsby-Gore,[71] Cotes, though handicapped by gout,[72] was held to be 'backed by secret service money and the wild cry of reform',[73] and he beat Ormsby-Gore by 72 votes, to become the only Whig ever returned for the division. Despite William Lloyd's zealous assistance in the Oswestry area[74] Cotes did worst there. Wellington was the area of greatest Whig strength; Cotes was easily in front there and received 439 plumpers. Hill headed the poll at Shrewsbury and Whitchurch, Ormsby-Gore at Oswestry.

As late as December 1834 William Lloyd still hoped that Cotes would stand again,[75] but Hill and Ormsby-Gore were unopposed in January 1835. Ormsby-Gore described himself in his election address[76] as 'independent . . . of any man, and unshackled by any

[62] Dawley, Hadley, Ketley, Lilleshall, Wombridge, and Wrockwardine Wood: *V.C.H. Salop.* i. 32–3, and map facing p. 1; Trinder, *Indust. Revolution in Salop.*, esp. pp. 7, 231–66, 376–95.

[63] *Census*, 1831; *V.C.H. Salop.* ii. 219–29; 2 & 3 Wm. IV, c. 64, s. 17.

[64] Dod, *Electoral Facts*, 274–5.

[65] *Complete Peerage*, ii. 315 note a.

[66] *Shrews. Chron.* 28 Sept. 1894 (editorial).

[67] A threatened contest or even no contest, however, could be expensive: see p. 321; S.R.O. 365/2–3.

[68] Loton Hall MSS., Sir B. Leighton's diary, 23 Mar. 1852.

[69] *T.S.A.S.* 4th ser. xii. 25–7; S.P.L., Morris-Eyton Collection, 285; N.L.W., Aston Hall 5332.

[70] *McCalmont's Parliamentary Poll Bk. . . . 1832–1918*, ed. J. Vincent and M. Stenton (1971), 263. Except where otherwise stated, the rest of the section covering the yrs. 1832–85 is based on this source.

[71] For the rest of this para. see *T.S.A.S.* 4th ser. xii. 25–6; S.P.L., Morris-Eyton Collection, 285; *Salop. Election: N. Div. Lists of Electors who voted . . . Dec. 18th and 19th, 1832* (Shrews. 1833; copy in S.R.O. 2095/37).

[72] N.L.W., Aston Hall 5332.

[73] Ibid. 326.

[74] Ibid. 2225.

[75] Ibid. 381.

[76] *Salopian Jnl.* 7 Jan. 1835.

political ties', though he also expressed his agreement with Peel's Tamworth Manifesto.

The next poll did not take place until 1868, for the Conservatives were strong, their opponents weak. The North Shropshire Conservative Association was set up in 1836 at a meeting in Shrewsbury chaired by the influential J. A. LLoyd; Lord Bradford became its first president. The association's rules provided that it would work with a sub-committee of Shrewsbury Conservatives on the 'necessary operations' in the borough.[77] The Whigs were in less good case. In July 1834 William Lloyd and the duke of Sutherland discussed the formation of a committee to watch the list of electors; Sutherland consulted the other Whig duke, Cleveland, and they agreed that as peers they could not take a lead in such business. A little later Sutherland also refused to subscribe towards Cotes's return.[78] Between the 1835 and 1837 elections Lloyd himself became an avowed Conservative, giving his assent to the Tamworth Manifesto.[79]

For much of the fifty years after 1835 the Hills and Ormsby-Gores monopolized the division.[80] Sir Rowland Hill sat 1832–42, his eldest son 1857–65; William Ormsby-Gore sat 1835–57, his eldest son 1859–76. Sir Rowland Hill, secure as master of the North Shropshire Hounds (1834–8),[81] sat until his succession as 2nd Lord Hill in December 1842. Lord Dungannon then thought of coming forward[82] but his estates on the border gave him a poor claim compared with the other aspirant, Lord Clive, who sat 1843–8 and was followed by J. W. Dod of Cloverley (1848–59). When Ormsby-Gore retired in 1857 the Hills provided his successor in the Hon. R. C. Hill. There was considerable dissatisfaction at Hawkstone's return of both M.P.s, for Dod had evidently been regarded as Hill's 'warming pan'.[83]

After twenty-four years of such amicable arrangements the peace was disturbed in 1859. The inactive Dod was perhaps already succumbing to the debts which forced him to leave his house shortly before his death four years later.[84] Whatever the cause, he resigned, and he did so to make way for J. R. Ormsby-Gore.[85]

Dod's intention became generally known towards the end of March but he gave Ormsby-Gore and Lord Hill at least three weeks' prior notice. Sir Baldwin Leighton, anxious to get into Parliament, considered Dod's conduct 'most unfair'[86] and decided to challenge the Hills' and Ormsby-Gores' monopoly of the division. He canvassed for almost a month, convinced that a majority of the 'country squires' were for him; at first he thought they could carry the election. He was soon undeceived. Among the peers Leighton was assisted only by Powis, whose influence was mainly in the Southern division, and Bradford. Ormsby-Gore's supporters, however, included 'everyone connected with the Hills', the duke of Cleveland, Lords Forester, Kenyon, and Combermere, and Lord Brownlow's trustees. Besides a preponderance among the great landowners Ormsby-Gore had the most active agents. On 2 April Leighton found J. J. Peele of Shrewsbury already retained by his opponent; on 4 April he retained R. D. Newill of Wellington but found that Peele had used his lead to retain every attorney in Whitchurch and all but one in Wem.

Ormsby-Gore's weightiest supporters, Lord Brownlow's trustees and Lord Hill, allowed Leighton's agents to waste time canvassing their tenants, while everywhere 'the screw was put on'. Hill professed neutrality, but in many places his son's agents were

77 N.L.W., Aston Hall 643; S.R.O. 665/3/33.
78 N.L.W., Aston Hall 381.
79 Ibid. 237, 525, 643.
80 For this para., unless otherwise stated, see *T.S.A.S.* 4th ser. xii. 26–9.
81 *V.C.H. Salop.* ii. 170.
82 N.L.W., Aston Hall 1142. His seat was Brynkinalt Hall (in Chirk, Denb.).

83 Loton Hall MSS., Sir B. Leighton's diary, 21 Mar. 1857.
84 Ibid. 11 June 1863.
85 For the next three paras. see ibid. 27 Mar.–Apr. 1859. At Loton there are vols. of letters, speeches, etc., for the 3 occasions on which Leighton came forward (1859, 1865).
86 Leighton had withdrawn in 1848 when Dod was first elected and had later proposed him on the hustings: diary 27 Mar. 1859.

also retained for Ormsby-Gore and elsewhere their agents canvassed together; as in 1832, Ormsby-Gore's supporters thus 'drew the Hawkstone interest more towards them' despite Leighton's protests. There were about 4,000 electors and it was reckoned that 2,600–3,000 would vote. Leighton received 1,640 promises. It was not enough, for as the election drew on Ormsby-Gore's agents persuaded electors who had promised to Hill and Leighton to plump for Hill because his seat was in danger; electors who had agreed to plump for Hill, however, were told by his agents and Ormsby-Gore's that Hill was safe and they might give their second vote to Ormsby-Gore.

Leighton thought such sharp practice gave him little chance of a majority. He tried for an arbitration of claims. Lord Hill, he thought, was annoyed by the unexpected contest and its expense but, though 'anxious' to compromise, had not the tact to effect it. In fact Hill's interest had been taken over by 'old Gore', who was determined that his son '*coûte que coûte* should continue the contest'. Leighton decided to withdraw on 21 April: the contest, not being political, could not go on 'without danger of breaking up many friendships and leading to much animosity'.[87] Privately Leighton recorded the slight sensation caused by Mrs. Ormsby-Gore's campaigning. Both wives had written letters for their husbands,[88] but Mrs. Ormsby-Gore had canvassed in Oswestry, pressing electors too hard and not leaving shops without 'a promise or an insult'. At Shrewsbury she canvassed farmers in Market Square and 'observations were made upon her which it is to be hoped did not reach her ears'. The contest probably cost Ormsby-Gore about £3,000, Leighton some £1,640, and Hill some £1,430.[89]

By 1865 the Liberals were determined to contest a division and their choice, falling at first on the Northern, produced a change of Conservative candidate. Hill was 'disgusted with Parliament'[90] and the expense of a contest was 'not convenient' to his father, who may also have felt that his influence had waned since 1859. Consequently Lord Hill, though much annoyed, was obliged to retire his son. He was no loss to the Commons or his constituents; he seldom attended and took no part in the business.[91] Lord Hill arranged for his son's seat to go to Earl Brownlow's uncle, Maj. C. H. Cust; it was generally supposed that he would warm the seat for his younger nephew Adelbert,[92] a keen young Conservative politician.[93] After his defeat by Ormsby-Gore in 1859 Leighton had felt that a Liberal in the division next time would have 'a very good chance of success',[94] but in 1865 he was shocked when the Liberals chose a 22-years-old army officer 'perfectly unfitted' to be a county member. The candidate was Lord Albert Sutherland-Leveson-Gower, a brother of the new duke of Sutherland.[95] Palmerston sought the duke's support for him, but the duke referred him to the dowager duchess and even Palmerston's normally unfailing charm failed.[96] After a week's work by his agents and a reputed expenditure of about £1,400 Lord Albert retired, acknowledging that 'the place would not suit him'.[97] One Liberal attorney thought that John Cotes of Woodcote should then have come forward, for 'all the machinery was in working order'.[98] Nevertheless the Conservatives, though put to considerable expense,[99] were unopposed. In 1866 Cust made way for his nephew who, however, succeeded as

[87] S.R.O. 1466, uncat., draft letter to agents as to cause of Leighton's retirement, 5 May 1859. Cf. *Eddowes's Jnl.* 11 May 1859.

[88] N.L.W., Aston Hall 2357–9, 4222.

[89] Leighton's estimates, exceeding, in his own case and Ormsby-Gore's, the figs. published under the Corrupt Practices Prevention Act, 1854, 17 & 18 Vic. c. 102, s. 28.

[90] Univ. of Hull, Brynmor Jones Libr., DDFA/39/52, R. J. More to C. S. Bigge, 19 May [1865].

[91] According to Leighton, who also recorded that Hill 'detests Parliament', adding: 'these sort of members . . . are a great injury to the landed interest and we have too

many of the class on both sides the House': Loton Hall MSS., Sir B. Leighton's diary, 3 June 1865. [92] Ibid.

[93] R. J. Olney, *Lincs. Politics, 1832–1885* (1973), 70, 168–9, 171.

[94] Leighton's diary, Apr. 1859. [95] Ibid. 3 June 1865.

[96] Ld. R. Gower, *My Reminiscences* (1895), 142–3.

[97] S.R.O. 2836/1; Loton Hall MSS., Sir B. Leighton's diary, 3 June 1865.

[98] Univ. of Hull, Brynmor Jones Libr., DDFA/39/52, T. Hardwicke to C. S. Bigge, 21 June 1865.

[99] Loton Hall MSS., Sir B. Leighton's diary, 28 July 1865 (press cutting), giving their expenses as £1,822 each.

3rd Earl Brownlow in 1867. His place was taken by another heir to a peerage, the 22-years-old Lord Newport who, despite his residence at Castle Bromwich,[1] could claim much deeper roots in Shropshire than the Custs.

In 1868 there was at last a poll; like the last, thirty-six years earlier, it followed a Reform Act. In June Jasper More suggested a newcomer to the county, A. P. Lonsdale, as a Liberal candidate, on the grounds that he was 'clever, popular, and rich' and that his uncle, J. P. Heywood, a millionaire banker, had recently bought the Cloverley Hall estate.[2] Neither then, however, nor later did Heywood-Lonsdale (as he became) rise to the Liberals' expectations[3] and in mid August the Liberal chief whip was still 'beating about' for a candidate.[4] Eventually R. G. Jebb of the Lyth, Ellesmere, stood, asserting that he would not have done so had More been unopposed in the Southern division.[5] Jebb got some days' start by concealing his intention of standing. He claimed to know Ireland well[6] and fought on behalf of the proposed disestablishment of the Church of Ireland, the main issue in the general election. 'Protestant Electors' on the other side were consequently urged to remember 1688, William of Orange, and 'the Protestant Cause!' and to vote for Ormsby-Gore and Newport, 'the Opponents of Rome! And the Supporters of an Orthodox and Tolerant Church!!' The squires were solid for Ormsby-Gore and Newport[7] and the Conservative victory was greater than expected: Ormsby-Gore polled 3,602 votes, Newport 3,403, Jebb 2,412. Jebb came last in five of the eight polling districts, including the Ellesmere district where he lived; he came second in the Newport and Whitchurch districts, but only in the industrial Wellington district did he manage, like Cotes in 1832, to head the poll.[8] The formidable Mrs. Ormsby-Gore had thought Wellington, Newport, and Dawley 'very bad' for the two dukes' agents were 'doing their best', and she had asked Lord Hill to persuade Sutherland to allow Conservative canvassing of his tenants.[9] In fact the two Liberal dukes had afforded their party little active support. Cleveland claimed always to have belonged to 'the old Whig party' but had deplored the emergence of a Liberal candidate and declined to put any 'undue pressure' on his tenants.[10] Sutherland had again refused any financial support of his party's candidate.[11] Ormsby-Gore and Newport spent £8,028 between them, Jebb £3,196.[12]

Ormsby-Gore and Newport were unopposed in 1874. Ormsby-Gore's services to his constituents were slight[13] but in January 1876 Disraeli had him created Lord Harlech.[14] Six weeks earlier Ormsby-Gore had assured his chief that his seat was 'perfectly safe' for he and his colleagues had always attended to, and paid for, the registration themselves instead of leaving it to a society. He promised to consult the division's most influential gentlemen about a successor, adding that he wanted 'a little conversation' on that subject with 'your secretary Monty Corry as a Shropshire man'.[15] Lowry-Corry was clearly offered the seat but, perhaps wisely, declined it;[16] despite Ormsby-Gore's

[1] *T.S.A.S.* 4th ser. xii. 30–1; *V.C.H. Warws.* iv. 45.

[2] *T.S.A.S.* 4th ser. xii. 28; S.R.O. 1093, corresp., no. 502; W. D. Rubinstein, 'Brit. Millionaires, 1809–1949', *Bull. Inst. Hist. Res.* xlvii. 208; H. D. Harrod, *Muniments of Shavington* (Shrews. 1891), 11, 132.

[3] *T.S.A.S.* lix. 174; *Eddowes's Jnl.* 31 Mar. 1880.

[4] B.L. Add. MS. 44194, f. 97.

[5] *Eddowes's Jnl.* 11 Nov. 1868.

[6] Perhaps with some justification: Francesca M. Wilson, *Rebel Dau. of a Country House: the Life of Eglantyne Jebb* (1967), 23 sqq.

[7] *Eddowes's Jnl.* 11 and 25 Nov. 1868; S.P.L., scrapbk. (accession 3043), pp. 1–12, 16, 20–2.

[8] *Eddowes's Jnl.* 25 Nov. 1868.

[9] Disraeli MSS., B/IX/G/52.

[10] Staffs. R.O., D.1287/10/4a, duke of Cleveland to Ld. Bradford, 14 Nov. 1868, deploring also the Cons. opposition to More in the S. div.

[11] Hanham, *Elections and Party Management*, 26.

[12] *Eddowes's Jnl.* 3 Feb. 1869.

[13] H. W. Lucy, *Diary of Two Parls.* i (*The Disraeli Parl. 1874–1880*) (1885), 99–100. Cf. S.R.O. 298/9.

[14] *Complete Peerage*, vi. 322; R. Blake, *Disraeli* (1966), 687–8.

[15] Disraeli MSS., C/I/B/46a.

[16] In 1880 Beaconsfield, anxious to get Lowry-Corry a peerage, described to the queen (11 Apr.) how he had once 'refused the uncontested representation of his own county', as a member's duties were inconsistent with those of a P.M.'s private sec.: W. F. Monypenny and G. E. Buckle, *Life of B. Disraeli, Earl of Beaconsfield* (1910–20), vi. 529. The 1876 vacancy must be meant. The letter, however, is not completely veracious (Blake, op. cit. 715), and may have exaggerated Lowry-Corry's prospects.

tactful description he was not yet really 'a Shropshire man'.[17] The other names which Ormsby-Gore had mentioned to Disraeli in December 1875 had more chance of local acceptance. They included S. K. Mainwaring of Oteley and Stanley Leighton[18] whose father had settled Sweeney on him in 1869 and who had married a Williams Wynn in 1873.[19] Leighton promptly offered himself as candidate on 30 December 1875.[20] C. S. LLoyd, however, called a private meeting of about forty gentlemen who put forward Mainwaring on 3 January.[21] The division then saw that unusual phenomenon, a contested by-election for a county seat.

A sharp fight ensued between 'Muscle' (Mainwaring) and 'Brains' (Leighton). Mainwaring ('a silent bucolical Thing')[22] was not a good speaker. Leighton, however, spoke fluently and well, and got off to a good start at a large meeting of agriculturists in Shrewsbury,[23] his knowledge of agricultural issues appearing superior to Mainwaring's. Two thirds of Leighton's central election committee were listed as 'Mr.' rather than 'Esquire', and the chairman was a farmer, J. Bowen Jones of Ensdon. It was the first election in the division after the 1872 Ballot Act,[24] and Leighton's propaganda insisted that the landlords could no longer put the screw on; the farmers were urged to use the ballot to defeat, if necessary by deceiving, their landlords. Leighton's political principles were not in doubt[25] but his opposition to others of his class brought him Liberal support. In the prevailing atmosphere Mainwaring was discredited among the farmers by LLoyd's meeting. Mainwaring's agent published the names of some 400 farmers who were said to support Mainwaring, but Bowen Jones discredited it as a 'phantom list'. An electorate of some 7,600 returned Leighton by the very narrow margin of 2,737 to 2,700; he could not have won without some of the division's many potential Liberal votes. The landlords had been beaten by one who naturally presented himself, with some justice, as the 'Farmers' Friend' and the 'Tenant Farmers' Candidate'. In the words of one broadsheet, it was proved that 'the Ballot's stronger than the Squire', but the proof cost £11,953.[26] Mainwaring's expenses were almost as great[27] and his committee decided not to petition.[28] Leighton soon made himself acceptable to most of his erstwhile opponents; by Christmas Lord Bradford was singing his praises to Beaconsfield.[29] Leighton and Newport were unopposed in 1880, and Leighton continued in Parliament until his death in 1901.[30]

Shrewsbury

Shrewsbury remained the most turbulent, frequently contested Shropshire borough after the 1832 boundary changes.[31] The electorate in 1832 numbered 1,714, about half of whom were burgesses; it fell fairly rapidly, reaching 1,538 in 1843. The number of burgesses fell but the electorate increased and was some 1,703 in 1851; by 1860, however, it had fallen to 1,565.[32] After the 1867 Reform Act[33] it rose to 3,381 and had

[17] He acquired a vested interest in the Rowton estate (to which he succ. in 1889) only in 1880: Complete Peerage, xi. 214 note b. This modifies the acct. in V.C.H. Salop. viii. 201.
[18] Disraeli MSS., C/I/B/46a.
[19] Loton Hall MSS., Sir B. Leighton's diary, 11 Aug. 1869; Burke, Peerage (1949), 1199.
[20] Eddowes's Jnl. 5 Jan. 1876.
[21] Ibid. 5 and 12 Jan. 1876; S.R.O. 298/9, 11–13.
[22] S.R.O. 298/4. For this para. see T.S.A.S. lix. 170–80; Eddowes's Jnl. 12, 19 and 26 Jan., 9 Feb. 1876; S.R.O. 298/1–13; S.R.O. 394/5–8; D.N.B. 1901–11.
[23] As More had done in 1865: S.R.O. 2836/1.
[24] 35 & 36 Vic. c. 33.
[25] Those of Disraelian Conservatism. Cf. T.S.A.S. lix.

172; F. M. L. Thompson, Eng. Landed Soc. in the Nineteenth Cent. (1963), 4.
[26] The published fig. was slightly different: Eddowes's Jnl. 12 Apr. 1876.
[27] Published as £10,688: ibid. 26 Apr. 1876.
[28] Disraeli MSS., B/XXI/B/849.
[29] Ibid. 823.
[30] See pp. 350–1.
[31] 2 & 3 Wm. IV, c. 64, sched. (O), no. 29; S. Lewis, Topog. Dict. Eng. (1835), v, plate LXXII.
[32] Ret. Electors Registered, H.C. 189, p. 194 (1833), xxvii; Ret. Electors, H.C. 11, p. 9 (1844), xxxviii; Ret. Electors, H.C. 8, p. 10 (1852), xlii; Ret. Electors, &c. (Cities and Boros.), H.C. 129, p. 4 (1860), lv.
[33] 30 & 31 Vic. c. 102.

reached 3,779 by 1884.[34] In 1852 little or no 'personal' influence prevailed and less money was being spent than formerly.[35] Nevertheless the power of drink[36] and money was undiminished, and Shrewsbury remained one of the notoriously corrupt boroughs of 19th-century England.[37]

The borough was contested at 10 of the period's 12 general elections and 2 of the 3 by-elections. Five times it returned two Whigs or Liberals, five times one Whig or Liberal and one Tory. Only in 1835 and 1841, however, years of Tory triumph in Shropshire, did it return two Tories. When one of each party was returned the Tory headed the poll three times out of five. The borough was predominantly Tory in the decade after 1832 but then became increasingly Liberal. Conservatives did not stand at the two general elections after their 1857 defeat, but they returned one M.P. in 1868 and another at an 1870 by-election. In 1874 and 1880 the Liberals won easily, though their opponents did at least field two candidates, a step which they took only six times during the period.[38]

Although Shrewsbury saw so much Whig or Liberal success, fewer Whigs or Liberals were elected for it than Tories. That was due to R. A. Slaney's predominance for much of the thirty years after 1832. Slaney, M.P. since 1826, contested 6 of the 8 elections between 1832 and 1859, was unopposed at the last of them, and won 4 of the 5 at which he was opposed; his only defeat was in 1835. In 1841 and 1852 he withdrew, though in 1841 he might have done well.[39] Slaney was a noted advocate of reform[40] and his publications included pamphlets on current issues and some of his Commons speeches.[41] Probably more important for his local standing were his sporting interests;[42] above all his long-standing connexion with Shrewsbury races.[43] His Conservative opponents thought him their most dangerous foe, not only because of his readiness to spend,[44] but also because of his ability to garner non-Whig votes.[45]

The most prominent Conservative was not an M.P. but an organizer, the barber John Frail, of Mardol, who was the mainspring of his party's cause in Shrewsbury from the late 1830s until his death in 1879 just after he had at last achieved the mayoralty. He did not always exert an emollient influence.[46] Like several Shropshire M.P.s he had the essential connexion with the turf, being clerk of the Shrewsbury course.[47] Other members of the Conservative 'Knot' around Frail were Edward Haycock, the county surveyor,[48] and John Eddowes, owner of the *Salopian Journal*. Other important Conservatives were the antiquaries Joseph and George Morris.[49] On the Liberal side the chief organizer was the Shrewsbury surgeon Dr. W. J. Clement (d. 1870).[50]

In 1832 and 1835 Shrewsbury was contested by two Tories and a Whig. Slaney's Tory colleague of the last Parliament, Sir Richard Jenkins, withdrew on the ground of ill health[51] and the new Tory challengers were the ageing John Cressett Pelham[52] and Sir John Hanmer of Bettisfield Park, a Flintshire landowner with colliery interests. Hanmer was to be ennobled by Gladstone forty years later, but in 1832, like his friend

[34] *Ret. Electors in Cities and Boros.* H.C. 419, p. 3 (1868–9), 1; *Ret. Parl. Constituencies (No. of Electors),* H.C. 11, p. 4 (1884), lxii.
[35] Dod, *Electoral Facts,* 283.
[36] B. Harrison, *Drink and the Victorians* (1971), 343.
[37] H. M. Pelling, *Social Geog. of Brit. Elections* (1967), 429; *T.S.A.S.* 4th ser. xii. 115 sqq.
[38] i.e. in 1832, 1837, 1841, 1857, 1874, and 1880.
[39] See p. 327.
[40] *D.N.B.*
[41] B.M. *Gen. Cat. of Printed Books . . . to 1955* (photo-lithographic edn. 1959–66), cciii, cols. 565–6.
[42] *V.C.H. Salop.* ii. 184, 194–6.
[43] Ibid. 179, 182.
[44] Even between elections: Loton Hall MSS., Sir B.

Leighton's diary, 19 May 1862.
[45] See p. 327.
[46] J. L. Hobbs, 'John Frail, Election Agent', *Trans. Caradoc and Severn Valley Field Club,* xv. 133–40.
[47] And of many others: *V.C.H. Salop.* ii. 179. Cf. S.R.O. 140/4–5.
[48] *Shropshire Mag.* Feb. 1960, 18.
[49] S.P.L., Shropshire Miscellanea, viii (accession 2760), pp. 2–11; above, p. 312.
[50] *Salopian Telegraph and Border Review,* 30 Apr. 1842; above, p. 316.
[51] S.R.O. 2304/2. Perhaps expense was the real reason: Loton Hall MSS., Sir B. Leighton's diary, 30 Dec. 1853.
[52] See pp. 263–4.

Gladstone, he was a sound Tory of 23 just down from Christ Church.[53] Hanmer's agent spent £2,074. Armed with a copy of Jenkins's 1830 expenses, Hanmer achieved several economies.[54] A Whig broadsheet song depicted Cressett Pelham as a decrepit parliamentary beggar soliciting votes and promising crowns where Hanmer promised shillings,[55] but if he did distribute largesse Cressett Pelham benefited little thereby. Hanmer polled 808 votes, Slaney 797 (378 plumpers), Cressett Pelham 634, figures which suggest a considerable personal following for Slaney.[56] In 1835, however, Hanmer polled 761, Cressett Pelham 629, and Slaney 578 (337 plumpers); nearly half the voters voted for Hanmer and Cressett Pelham. One observer thought that Slaney would just have headed the poll through the elimination of split votes, had a second Whig stood. Slaney polled fewer than a quarter of the burgesses' votes but had a narrow lead in those cast by newly enfranchised voters.[57] As the number of burgesses declined the Whigs were to fare better, but not for some years yet. After 1835, however, for as long as the borough returned two M.P.s, the Whigs or Liberals always ran two candidates at general elections.

In 1837 Hanmer 'departed much lighter in purse'[58] to find a seat elsewhere.[59] Jenkins returned to stand with Cressett Pelham, and Slaney stood with the radical Francis Dashwood. Jenkins and Slaney polled 700 and 697 votes against 655 for Cressett Pelham and 537 for Dashwood.[60] Whatever the borough's character, 3 of its 4 M.P.s in the first 3 Parliaments after 1832 were men of some past or future distinction;[61] 3 were local men, and the fourth, Hanmer, lived just over the county boundary. Only one stranger, Dashwood, had so far contested the borough. In and after 1841, however, strangers appeared in some numbers.

The 1839 registration had gone extremely well for the Shrewsbury Conservatives,[62] but Cressett Pelham had died in 1838[63] and in 1839 Jenkins had become chairman of the East India Company.[64] The new candidates were Benjamin Disraeli and George Tomline.[65] For Disraeli Shrewsbury represented a secure haven at a crucial period of his career. He had broken with his constituency of Maidstone[66] and was considering Leicester as his next seat when, in December 1839, his old friend, Lord Forester, forwarded a letter from Rice Wynne, a Shrewsbury solicitor.[67] Years afterwards Disraeli wrote that Forester was his earliest supporter 'and never changed or faltered'; admittedly the words were written to Forester's sister, Lady Bradford,[68] but Disraeli believed in gratitude.[69]

It had been rumoured that Lord Clive, who had come of age in 1839, might stand,[70] but he decided to wait for a county seat.[71] William Lloyd of Aston was apparently also a possible candidate.[72] Wynne reported a very favourable registration[73] and calculated a gain of 189 Conservative votes on the 1837 figures.[74] Disraeli's two great concerns were

[53] Complete Peerage, vi. 291 note c. T.S.A.S. 4th ser. xii. 253–4, and D.N.B. wrongly imply that he was a Whig in the 1830s.

[54] N.L.W., Bettisfield Park 785 (endorsed by Hanmer 'Caveat Emptor'). He had paid his bill by Apr. 1833.

[55] S.R.O. 549/47 (parody of a sentimental poem 'The Beggar': S. Shaw, Hist. . . . of Staffs. ii (1801), 237–8).

[56] Correct Alphab. List of Electors who voted at Electn. . . . for Shrews., 13th and 14th Dec. 1832 (Shrews. 1833; copy in S.R.O. 665/3/28); E. Edwards, Parl. Elections of Boro. of Shrews. from 1283 to 1859 (Shrews. 1859), 31.

[57] Corr. Alphab. List of Electors who voted at Electn. . . . for Shrews., 8th and 9th Jan. 1835 (Shrews. 1835; copy in S.R.O. 665/3/32); and see MS. note in Bodl. copy.

[58] S.R.O. 2763, uncat., A New Song, for Shrews. Boro' Election, 1837. According to A Patriotic Carol, for Shrews. Boro' Election, 1837 (ibid.), 'Sir John no more boasts ample store . . .'.

[59] V.C.H. Yorks. E.R. i. 243.

[60] T.S.A.S. 4th ser. xii. 255; Corr. Alphab. List of Electors who voted at Electn. . . . for Shrews., 26th July, 1837 (Shrews. 1837; copy in S.R.O. 665/3/34).

[61] For Slaney, Jenkins, and Hanmer see D.N.B., for Cressett Pelham Gent. Mag. new ser. xi(1), 661.

[62] Disraeli MSS., B/I/B/4.

[63] V.C.H. Salop. viii. 64.

[64] D.N.B.

[65] T.S.A.S. 4th ser. xii. 255.

[66] Monypenny and Buckle, Disraeli, ii. 113.

[67] Disraeli MSS., B/I/B/1, 3.

[68] Marquess of Zetland, Letters of Disraeli to Lady Bradford and Lady Chesterfield (1929), i. 75.

[69] Blake, Disraeli, 684–6, 714–16.

[70] Disraeli MSS., B/I/B/4.

[71] See p. 320.

[72] N.L.W., Aston Hall 1137.

[73] Disraeli MSS., B/I/B/4.

[74] Ibid. 2d.

that his success should be absolutely certain and that his expenses should be as low as possible.[75] Negotiations on this delicate subject were conducted with William Holmes,[76] once M.P. for Bishop's Castle and formerly Tory chief whip. Forester and Lord Powis stressed to Wynne that the lawyers' expenses would have to be greatly reduced and treating and the opening of public houses 'entirely done away with'. On 11 May 1841 Forester wrote to tell Disraeli what instructions Wynne had been given but he had to add that 'if Slaney and Marshall stand there is no doubt but that they will spend money'. There was, too, the 'great difficulty' of finding Disraeli a colleague connected with the county. It was presumably Forester and Powis who produced Tomline. His paternal estates lay in eastern England[77] but he owned property, formerly his mother's, in Ford and Winnington.[78]

Disraeli kept his intentions secret. On 26 May an intermediary in Leicester was still asking him if he intended to move there.[79] Next day, however, Disraeli wrote to accept the requisition from over 700 Shrewsbury electors to himself and Tomline, provided that an 'open and avowed coalition' and a 'simple and single' management were agreed upon. He agreed that Tomline's name should appear first, on the understanding that if the party could return only one M.P., the choice would fall on him.[80] Tomline's assistance, however, was essential to Disraeli who a few days later had to write urgently to him pointing out that his withdrawal would render Disraeli's presence in the next Parliament 'very doubtful': the time when he might have arranged 'one & one' with Slaney had gone and he could not fight two Whigs single-handed.[81] Tomline stuck to Shrewsbury and, to the Tories' joy, Slaney withdrew early in June. Wynne thought he would have polled fifty more votes than any other opponent.[82] The Whigs who eventually fought the election[83] were as much strangers as Disraeli and came into the contest very late.

Mrs. Disraeli made an impressive and successful appearance in the campaign, and her engaging irrationality won her 'immense popularity' with the electors.[84] The opposition thought her husband's debts might impress them too, and Disraeli had to denounce as 'utterly false' the allegation that judgement had been entered against him for debts of £22,000,[85] a denial which did not give an accurate view of his financial position.[86] Nevertheless, in Disraeli's own triumphant words to his sister, the contest though 'sharp' was 'never for a moment doubtful'.[87] In fact he had had to endure the most scurrilous anti-Semitic abuse.[88] Early in March Joseph Morris had forecast a Conservative majority of 'near if not quite 200 for any two Conservative candidates'.[89] He was proved correct; much as expected, Tomline and Disraeli won with 793 and 785 votes against 605 and 578 for the Whigs. Voting was along party lines with few split votes or plumpers, and each pair of candidates ran under party, rather than individual, colours.[90]

On the night of his victory Disraeli dined at Loton, Sir Baldwin Leighton's seat. There he received a hurried note from the staunch[91] Joseph Morris warning of an

[75] For the rest of this para. see ibid. 5.
[76] See pp. 306–7.
[77] Burke, *Land. Gent.* (18th edn.), i (1965), 585.
[78] *V.C.H. Salop.* viii. 208, 232.
[79] Disraeli MSS., B/I/B/6.
[80] Ibid. 8ab (two drafts of Disraeli's letter of acceptance with conditions). Ld. Rowton gave the signed requisition to the Beaconsfield Club, Shrews., in 1887; it later found its way back to the Disraeli MSS. (B/I/B, no ref.).
[81] Suff. R.O., HA 119: 503/13, Disraeli to Tomline, 31 May [1841]. Cf. R. J. Olney, *Lincs. Politics, 1832–1885* (1973), 110.
[82] Disraeli MSS., B/I/B/12; S.P.L., Morris-Eyton Collection, 293.
[83] *T.S.A.S.* 4th ser. xii. 256. Cf. *Dict. Welsh Biog.* 730;

D.N.B. sub Parry, Sir Love.
[84] Monypenny and Buckle, *Disraeli*, ii. 113; Sotheby Parke Bernet & Co. *Cat. of Autograph Letters: Sale 12–13 Dec. 1977*, 152.
[85] Monypenny and Buckle, op cit. ii. 116; Disraeli MSS., B/I/B/29.
[86] Blake, *Disraeli*, 163.
[87] Monypenny and Buckle, *Disraeli*, ii. 114.
[88] Ibid.; Sir W. A. Fraser, *Disraeli and his Day* (1891), 473–4.
[89] N.L.W., Aston Hall 984.
[90] *Corr. Alphab. List of Electors who voted at Electn. . . . for Shrews., 29th June, 1841* (Shrews. 1841; copy in S.R.O. 665/3/36); *T.S.A.S.* 4th ser. xii. 255.
[91] Disraeli MSS., B/I/B/17.

'immense mob' of 'opposition blackguards' assembled in Frankwell to attack him on his return. Disraeli took Morris's advice not to leave Loton that night[92] and stayed several days to be charmed by the house and its family.[93] Leighton thought his guest clever and very ambitious but 'devoid of principle except that of getting himself on in the world'.[94]

For nine months Disraeli was uncertain whether he would in fact retain his seat, for there was a petition against the Tories' return on grounds of bribery. It was, however, dropped in April 1842 in return for the dropping of a Tory petition against the Whig M.P.s for Gloucester.[95]

Disraeli seems to have had better relations with Shrewsbury than with Maidstone. His opposition to the new Poor Law won him some approval,[96] his speeches were faithfully reported in the local Conservative press, and he even visited the borough in 1843 and 1844 and made some notable speeches there.[97] Repeal of the corn laws, however, wrought more havoc among the Shrewsbury Conservatives than elsewhere in Shropshire, for Tomline supported repeal. T. J. Ouseley,[98] one of Disraeli's Shrewsbury correspondents, bitterly described the confusion and Frail's behaviour at the 1846 registration. Frail was 'paid in Mr. Tomline's interest' and had objected to Ouseley and to Dryden Corbet of Sundorne who, as a protectionist, would have plumped for Disraeli. Ouseley expected clerical support for Disraeli in view of his position on the Maynooth grant and advised him to attend in person. 'Money alone', he added, could return Tomline who was out of favour with both parties owing to his 'apostasy'.[99] The maltster Richard Taylor told Disraeli prophetically at the end of May 1846 that he had never seen the Conservatives so divided and that many of them would not vote for Tomline. Should Tomline succeed, he said, it would have cost him 'a very large sum', for Frail would not work 'without being well paid, some way or other'.[1]

Disraeli could probably have been returned again for Shrewsbury had he wished, but Frail's activities may have made the seat less attractive to him[2] and in August 1847 he secured the county seat that he desired when he was returned for Buckinghamshire. In May C. L. Butler, a son of Lord Dunboyne, had begun poorly as protectionist candidate by employing an inadequate agent.[3] At the end of June Disraeli, doubtless without authority, had offered the candidacy to Lord Salisbury's son-in-law, J. M. Balfour, who refused it.[4] E. H. Baldock, however, a stranger who replaced Butler, did very well. He had Disraeli's endorsement[5] and in a close contest headed the poll with 768 votes. Slaney polled 743, only 3 more than the Liberal–Conservative Tomline.[6]

The country gentlemen still exerted some influence in Shrewsbury elections. Robert Burton of Longner, Dryden Corbet of Sundorne, Col. R. F. Hill of Kingsland (Lord Hill's brother), and J. T. Smitheman Edwardes were thought to have great weight,[7] though their territorial interest was negligible. Later Robert Burton became the Tory leader in the town, and William Butler Lloyd was also influential.[8] After 1847, however, few local country gentlemen came forward as candidates.[9] Their place

[92] Disraeli MSS., B/I/B/28.
[93] Monypenny and Buckle, Disraeli, ii. 114.
[94] Loton Hall MSS., Sir B. Leighton's diary, 28 June 1841.
[95] Monypenny and Buckle, Disraeli, ii. 134–5; Suff. R.O., HA 119: 503/13, expenses of Tomline and Disraeli, Sept. 1841–Apr. 1842.
[96] Disraeli MSS., B/I/B/16.
[97] Monypenny and Buckle, Disraeli, ii. 143, 231, 244.
[98] See p. 313.
[99] Disraeli MSS., B/I/B/20.   [1] Ibid. 22a.
[2] Edwards, Parl. Electns. of Shrews. to 1859, 39, attributes Disraeli's move to 'some secret meddling mismanagement' of the local Conservative agents.

[3] Disraeli MSS., B/I/B/22a.
[4] Ibid. 25.   [5] Ibid. 26.
[6] Corr. Alphab. List of Electors who voted at Electn. for Shrews., 29th July 1847 (Shrews. 1847; copy in S.R.O. 58/4/2).
[7] Disraeli MSS., B/I/B/26. For Smitheman Edwardes see Loton Hall MSS., Sir B. Leighton's diary, 29 Oct. 1851; V.C.H. Salop. viii. 65.
[8] Hughes, Sheriffs, 45; Eddowes's Jnl. 17 Oct. 1855 (editorial); Trans. Caradoc and Severn Valley Field Club, xv. 138–9.
[9] Apart from R. A. Slaney and C. C. Cotes. For most of the period 1885–1918, however, Shrews. was represented by local landowners or their relations: see pp. 352–3.

was taken by professional men, usually lawyers and often rich. Frail, whose services to Shrewsbury Conservatism may have been exaggerated, seems to have played a deep, disruptive game at the 1847 election, in the end making the seat safe for Tomline, who became a Liberal.

In June 1852 Slaney withdrew, but Tomline and Baldock were both in the field,[10] though Tomline may at first have been hoping to find a safer or less expensive seat elsewhere.[11] A second Conservative appeared but withdrew, and the final third candidate was another Liberal, a London barrister. Tomline polled a remarkable 1,153 votes; Baldock, who next month married the daughter of Sir Andrew Corbet of Acton Reynald, easily came second with 736.

The 1857 election began a period of almost continuous Conservative eclipse at Shrewsbury. Tomline and Slaney polled 706 and 695 (652 joint votes); the two defeated Conservatives, both strangers, were well behind with 548 and 484 (477 joint votes). There were few plumpers or split votes.[12] Two years later, during the furore over a further reform of the parliamentary franchise after the rejection of Derby's Reform Bill,[13] Tomline and Slaney stood again. First one of the defeated Tories of 1857, and then R. B. Oakeley of Oswaldkirk (Yorks. N.R.), came forward for the Conservatives, only to withdraw in turn. The Liberals were unopposed.[14] Frail assured Disraeli that Slaney would 'never again trouble us' and that Tomline too would have 'no chance' in the future since he had refused to pay.[15] His words say little for his judgement. Tomline had another unopposed return before him and was to sit for the borough for over nine more years.

Slaney died in May 1862[16] and Oakeley returned to fight the consequent by-election, though against the wishes of many Conservatives.[17] Oakeley had been consoled for his 1859 failure, and had been given reason to make a second attempt on the borough, by his marriage later that year to William Field's daughter.[18] A prominent Shrewsbury merchant since at least the 1850s[19] Field was also a lessee, with his brother-in-law Thomas Brassey, of the Shrewsbury & Hereford Railway whose locomotive works at Coleham employed much labour in the borough.[20] In 1862 Oakeley had his father-in-law's support, though not, apparently, Brassey's,[21] whose sympathies were probably Liberal[22] but who seems to have stayed neutral for family reasons.[23] The Liberals ran Henry Robertson, a shrewd choice against a candidate who might have been expected to have the support of Field and Brassey. Robertson was a Scots civil engineer of great competence and wide achievement; as the promoter and builder of railways to Shrewsbury and as builder of the Kingsland bridge (opened 1883)[24] he probably had more influence on the town's daily life than any other of its M.P.s. Oakeley benefited little from his father-in-law's support and was damaged by his withdrawal in 1859[25] and by a

[10] For this para. see Edwards, *Parl. Electns. of Shrews. to 1859*, 41–3; *T.S.A.S.* 4th ser. xii. 260; *Alphab. List of Electors who voted at Electn. of Reps. for Shrews.*, *7th July*, *1852* (Shrews. n.d.; copy in S.P.L., accession 293).

[11] *A Victorian M.P. and his Constituents: the Corresp. of H. W. Tancred, 1841-1859* (Banbury Hist. Soc. viii), p. xxxvi.

[12] Shrews. Sch. Libr., records of poll printed by local press.

[13] Ll. Woodward, *The Age of Reform, 1815-1870* (1962), 171–2; *Eng. Hist. Doc. 1833-1874*, ed. G. M. Young and W. D. Handcock (1956), 148–55.

[14] Edwards, *Parl. Elections of Shrews. to 1859*, 47–9.

[15] Disraeli MSS., B/XXI/T/151–6 (catalogued under 'Trail').

[16] *Eddowes's Jnl.* 21 May 1862; *Shrews. Chron.* 23 May 1862.

[17] Loton Hall MSS., Sir B. Leighton's diary, 19 May

1862.

[18] S.R.O. 1048/51, p. 108.

[19] *P.O. Dir. Salop.* (1856). Field's Mercantile Co. Ltd. was est. 1864: *Kelly's Dir. Salop.* (1891).

[20] *Eddowes's Jnl.* 12 Oct. 1859; *Route of Shrews. & Heref. Rlwy., Described and Illustrated* . . . (Leominster, 1860), dedication and p. vi.

[21] *Shrews. Chron.* 6 June 1862.

[22] J. Beard, *My Shropshire Days on Common Ways* [1948], 61.

[23] He had publicly to disapprove of a suggestion that his son, Thos. (later a Lib. politician and 1st Earl Brassey), oppose Oakeley for the Libs.: *Eddowes's Jnl.* 21 May 1862.

[24] *T.S.A.S.* 4th ser. xii. 261–2; *Shrews. Chron.* 30 May 1862; E. T. MacDermot, *Hist. of G.W.R.* ed. C. R. Clinker (1964), i. 177–9, 211, 227; *Kelly's Dir. Salop.* (1885), 937.

[25] *Eddowes's Jnl.* 28 May 1862; *Shrews. Chron.* 30 May 1862.

widely reported legal action which brought his name into some disrepute. Many Conservatives abstained[26] and Robertson won by 671 to 361.[27] Strangely enough, however, Robertson was not brought forward again in 1865 when the Conservatives did not oppose Tomline and a new Liberal, the well known Dr. W. J. Clement, long prominent in borough politics.[28]

There was a sudden short-lived Conservative revival after the 1867 Reform Act.[29] At Newmarket Frail promised Disraeli's secretary, Lowry-Corry, to put forward two Conservatives[30] and eventually two were found: a London typefounder and city alderman, James Figgins, and a young London barrister, Douglas Straight.[31] The Liberal chief whip thought they were the sort 'who can only win by bribery'.[32] Clement and Tomline stood again for the Liberals,[33] but it became clear that Tomline was merely keeping his options open at Shrewsbury while trying to secure the seat at Grimsby. After his late withdrawal the supporters of Clement and Figgins came to an 'honourable compromise'. Straight withdrew, and Clement and Figgins would have been unopposed but for a late intrusion by a little-known Liberal. The voters gave the compromise overwhelming support. Clement polled 1,840, Figgins 1,751, with 1,047 votes split between them. The second Liberal polled only 685.

Straight made a good impression and was invited back after Clement's death in 1870. His Liberal opponent was C. C. Cotes of Woodcote, the first local country gentleman, apart from Slaney, to stand at Shrewsbury since 1837. Straight won by only 1,291 to 1,253 votes.[34] It was considered the 'purest election ever known in the borough' but one shrewd observer thought that the 'whole truth', had it emerged, would have voided the election. There was a petition, eventually very expensive to Cotes, on the grounds of undue influence and bribery and treating by Straight's agents. A well disposed judge, however, found for Straight,[35] and Shrewsbury thus had two Conservative M.P.s 1870–4.

The circumstances in which Figgins and Straight had won, however, had been largely fortuitous, produced by Tomline's desertion in 1868 and Clement's death in 1870. Even after several years in which the Conservatives' electoral prospects had improved nationally by an increase in borough electorates,[36] the seats could not be held against two good local Liberals in more normal circumstances. Accordingly the two Conservative seats gained in years of general Liberal triumph were lost in 1874 when the Conservatives were returned to power at Westminster. Cotes and Robertson beat the sitting M.P.s in 1874, and in 1880 they beat A. R. Scoble, another barrister, and Lord Newry, Lord Kilmorey's heir. In Shrewsbury at the end of the period the Liberals were thus dominant in parliamentary, though not in local, elections.

Bridgnorth

The 1832 Reform Act strengthened the hold of the Whitmores of Apley Park on one

[26] Loton Hall MSS., Sir B. Leighton's diary, 19 May–2 June 1862.

[27] *Eddowes's Jnl.* 11 June 1862. An independent polled 10 votes: ibid.; *Shrews. Chron.* 30 May 1862; S.R.O. 394/4.

[28] *T.S.A.S.* 4th ser. xii. 262; *Eddowes's Jnl.* 31 Aug. 1870; *Shrews. Chron.* 2 Sept. 1870 (obits.).

[29] 30 & 31 Vic. c. 102. [30] Disraeli MSS., B/IX/G/36.

[31] *Eddowes's Jnl.* 4 Nov. 1868.

[32] B.L. Add. MS. 44347, f. 232v.

[33] For the rest of this para. see Olney, *Lincs. Politics, 1832–1885*, 5, 166–7; *Eddowes's Jnl.* 4, 11 and 18 Nov. 1868; *T.S.A.S.* 4th ser. xii. 263; *Shrews. Boro. Electn., Nov. 17th, 1868: Poll Bk.* (Shrews. 1868; copy in S.R.O. 140/2).

[34] *Shrews. Chron.* 23 Sept. 1870; *T.S.A.S.* 4th ser. xii.

263–4; *Shrews. Boro. Electn., Sept. 21st, 1870* (Shrews. n.d.; copy in S.R.O. 310/10).

[35] *Shrews. Chron.* 9 Dec. 1870; Loton Hall MSS., Sir B. Leighton's diary, 6 Dec. 1870; M. Williams, *Leaves of a Life* (1890), i. 270–9; E. L. O'Malley and H. Hardcastle, *Reps. of Decisions of Judges for Trial of Electn. Pets., pursuant to Parl. Electns. Act, 1868*, ii (1875), 36–7. H. W. Lucy, *Men and Manner in Parliament* (1919), 254, vividly attributes a bumptious parliamentary style to Straight.

[36] Under the Poor Rate Assessment and Collection Act, 1869, 32 & 33 Vic. c. 41, s. 19: Blake, *Disraeli*, 536. The Shrews. electorate had increased less than the average to only 3,620 (1873): *Ret. relating to Electoral Statistics*, H.C. 381, p. 6 (1874), liii; cf. above, pp. 323, 325. For the rest of this para. see *T.S.A.S.* 4th ser. xii. 264–5.

of the two Bridgnorth seats and twenty years later theirs was still the only influence worthy of mention.[37] From 1832 the parliamentary borough comprised the townships of Quatford, Quatt Jarvis, and Romsley within the municipal liberties and Eardington township and the parishes of Astley Abbots, Oldbury, and Tasley in Stottesdon hundred.[38] Astley Abbots was partly Whitmore property[39] and the number of electors likely to defer to their interest was increased by the Act, a change symbolized by the extension of the parliamentary borough into the prospect from Thomas Whitmore's drawing room.

Reform came just in time for the Whitmores; the loss of out-voters made elections much cheaper despite the continuance of treating for a decade. As early as June 1832 Wolryche Whitmore accurately assessed the Reform Act's effect on the constituency as 'giving a greatly increased weight to local interests, and imparting to it a character of a more decidely agricultural description'.[40] The industrialists of towns like Wolverhampton, Stourbridge, and Kidderminster, at last having local seats open to their influence, ceased to need virtual representation through a Bridgnorth M.P. From 1832 to 1835 Wolryche Whitmore himself sat for Wolverhampton where his political opinions were more acceptable.[41] His Apley kinsmen were never again inclined to reserve the second seat for their own family but, after one stumble in the first decade after 1832, their ability to deliver it to a fellow Conservative was for a time enhanced. Bridgnorth was nevertheless contested at all general elections except three (1832, 1857, and 1859) in its last half century as a parliamentary borough.

In 1832 Thomas Whitmore hoped to sit for the Southern division of the county.[42] His seat at Bridgnorth was taken by his eldest son T. C. Whitmore, who sat until 1852. During those twenty years T. C. Whitmore's colleague, save for an interval in 1837-8, was Robert (from 1837 Sir Robert) Pigot of Patshull, great-nephew of the nabob whom the Whitmores had had to accept some sixty years earlier.[43] Until his death in 1858 Wolryche Whitmore, though no longer prominent on the national scene after 1835, was one of those who led attempts to substitute a succession of Whig candidates for Pigot in the second seat. For some years after 1835 the borough council was predominantly Liberal, and the Liberal leaders in the town were the Baptist tanner Joshua Sing and the successful architect John Smalman of Quatford Castle, both of whom became mayor,[44] and the three leading carpet manufacturers, the McMichaels, the Griersons, and the Southwells.[45] Nevertheless only one Whig parliamentary candidate in the twenty years after 1832 was from a local family.[46] Most local landowners were Tories, notably E. L. Gatacre of Gatacre, T. P. Purton of Faintree, and T. W. Wylde Browne of Glazeley, a kinsman of the Whitmores.[47] George Bellett, rector of St. Leonard's 1835-71, was a leading supporter of the Whitmores among the clergy.[48]

The interest held a century earlier by John and Arthur Weaver had passed to their Whig heirs, the Hanbury-Tracys.[49] Charles Hanbury-Tracy (cr. Lord Sudeley 1838) canvassed Bridgnorth in 1832 but was elected for Tewkesbury (Glos.).[50] His second son Henry was decisively beaten in 1835 with 353 votes to Whitmore's 490 and Pigot's

[37] Dod, *Electoral Facts*, 32.
[38] 2 & 3 Wm. IV, c. 64, sched. (O), no. 29; Lewis, *Topog. Dict. Eng.* (1835), v, plate LXXIII; *V.C.H. Salop.* ii. 210-11.
[39] S.R.O. 3628, plate III.
[40] Electn. handbill, 12 June 1832: scrapbk. *penes* the late H. L. Cunnington.
[41] G. P. Mander and N. W. Tildesley, *Hist. of Wolverhampton* (Wolverhampton, 1960), 168.
[42] See p. 315.
[43] See p. 280.
[44] H. M. Colvin, *Biog. Dict. Eng. Architects, 1660-1840* (1954), 544; J. F. A. Mason, *Boro. of Bridgnorth 1157-1957*

(Bridgnorth, 1957), 35, 40-1.
[45] Mason, *Bridgnorth*, 42-3; *Bridgnorth Election Petition*, H.C. 203, pp. 70-1, 107, 134 (1852-3), viii; *Shropshire Conservative*, 29 May 1841 (advt. of T. Elcock).
[46] Sir J. Easthope: see p. 333.
[47] For the relationship see S.P.L., accession 2326, f. 184; *Bridgnorth Election Petition*, 154-8.
[48] *Memoir of the Rev. Geo. Bellett, M.A.* (priv. print. 1889; copy in S.P.L.), pp. xvi, 120.
[49] F. Leach, *County Seats of Salop.* (Shrews. 1891), 328; above, p. 279.
[50] *T.S.A.S.* 4th ser. v. 20; *Complete Peerage*, xii(1), 422.

423. In 1837, however, Henry defeated Pigot by four votes, and the exact course of events at the election was still hotly disputed by three surviving bystanders as late as 1903.[51] It was apparently common knowledge that some of Pigot's voters would be detained in Shrewsbury as jurors or witnesses at the assizes (24–5 July), and Mayor Shipley, a Liberal, refused to postpone the poll. The Conservatives evidently resorted to stratagem. They organized a riot which destroyed the polling booth in East Castle Street (Hanbury-Tracy territory)[52] to compel the mayor to adjourn the poll on its first day (25 July). The Liberals countered by destroying another booth and the violence enabled Shipley to close the poll. Next day he declared that he had no power to re-open it and that consequently Whitmore and Hanbury-Tracy were elected with 429 and 371 votes to Pigot's 367. Hanbury-Tracy had a slight lead among the 526 burgesses' votes, Pigot an even slighter one among the 201 occupiers'. Hanbury-Tracy had been supported by the three carpet manufacturers; they were all on the borough council, whose members gave Hanbury-Tracy 13 votes, Whitmore 4, and Pigot 1.[53] Hanbury-Tracy's flag had flown from two carpet factories and from the town hall, in all of which polling booths had been set up. Pigot petitioned against Hanbury-Tracy's return, two of Hanbury-Tracy's voters against Whitmore's return.

Individuals on both sides suffered after the election.[54] In November three Whig borough magistrates contrived the dismissal of their clerk J. J. Smith on the ground of incompetent advice leading to the irregular appointment of 170 special constables for the election. Smith, who was also town clerk, alleged in turn that the anger of the rate-payers, who were faced with a special rate to pay for these partisan constables recruited by the Whigs in Wellington and Broseley, had caused the Whig magistrates to make him their scapegoat. Later James Ranoe, the town clerk's man, was imprisoned for debt at Lord Sudeley's suit. Shipley found it advisable to quit the town.

Both parties had begun to look to their numbers. In October 1837 a Conservative club was founded by the Whitmores and others.[55] On the other side there was a futile attempt by Wolryche Whitmore to create 42 Whig burgesses by manufacturing tenancies at the town mills; the would-be faggot voters, rejected at the registration, were naturally known to the Conservatives as 'the Forty Thieves'.[56] On 30 January 1838 the registration went well for the Conservatives and led to Hanbury-Tracy's withdrawal. In February, before the Commons select committee sat, he proposed that both petitions be withdrawn and announced that he would resign his seat, the electorate having been 'essentially altered' and 'numbers of my friends . . . disqualified by the last registration'.[57] Pigot was promptly returned unopposed in Hanbury-Tracy's place, the Conservatives triumphing with fireworks, cannon, bells, and processions. Reinforced by the Conservative Association, the Whitmores' control had been enhanced.[58]

The Hanbury-Tracy interest took no further part in Bridgnorth politics. In 1841 the Whig challenge was taken up by the Acton interest, then in the hands of Sir John Dalberg-Acton's mother and stepfather, Lord and Lady Leveson;[59] Leveson (2nd Earl Granville 1846), then a young Whig grandee, was to be a prop of the Shropshire Liberals for fifty years. F. J. Howard, former M.P. for Youghal (co. Cork) was put

[51] *Bridgnorth Jnl.* 25 July, 1, 8, 15, and 22 Aug. 1903. For the rest of this para., unless otherwise stated, see *C.J.* xciii. 24–6, 123–4; S.R.O. 2763 uncat.

[52] S.R.O. 511/3; *T.S.A.S.* lii. 163.

[53] *Poll for Electn. of Members for Bridgnorth, July 25th, 1837* (Ironbridge, n.d.; copy in S.P.L.).

[54] For this para. see S.R.O. 2664 uncat., papers *re* compensation for J. J. Smith after dismissal as clk. to Bridgnorth magistrates, 1837–8; Bridgnorth boro. rec., subscription for maintenance of Ranoe's wife and fam.

[55] *Shrews. Chron.* 13 Oct. 1837.

[56] *Wolverhampton Chron.* 27 Oct. 1841; *Shropshire Conservative*, 25 Sept., 23 Oct. 1841.

[57] S.R.O. 2763 uncat., Hanbury-Tracy's printed address to the electors of Bridgnorth, 14 Feb. 1838; *C.J.* xciii. 163, 268.

[58] Chastleton Ho. (Oxon.), papers *penes* the late A. Clutton-Brock, letter of Mrs. Mary Anne Sparkes to Mrs. Dolly Whitmore-Jones, 23 Feb. 1838.

[59] D. Mathew's *Acton: the Formative Years* (1946) and *Ld. Acton and His Times* (1968) describe the relationship between step-father and stepson.

forward. He came from the Whig aristrocracy; his mother was a Lambton, his wife a Cavendish, and as a grandson of the 5th earl of Carlisle he could claim kinship with the Leveson-Gowers. Amid protests a Radical, Nicholas Throckmorton, came forward an hour or so before the poll closed.[60] Howard did extremely badly despite the support of Wolryche Whitmore, who proposed him, Lady Leveson, and the Bridgnorth carpet manufacturers.[61] The majority for Whitmore and Pigot exceeded expectations; they polled 496 and 475 (450 joint votes) to 225 for Howard and 66 for Throckmorton.[62] The victory was a prelude to considerable Conservative success at the municipal registration in October[63] and to a Conservative victory in the borough elections in November when, after some years of Radical success, three Tories and one Radical were elected.[64] Further successes produced a Conservative majority on the council in 1843;[65] thereafter Bridgnorth municipal elections were often uncontested and seldom reflected national politics.[66]

The 1847 election was 'considerably shorn' of its 'usual concomitants'; bands of music and flags were the only entertainment afforded,[67] for T. C. Whitmore refused to continue treating after his father's death in 1846.[68] Whitmore stood as a Liberal–Conservative, neutral between the other two candidates; having paired at the division on the repeal of the corn laws,[69] he naturally had Wolryche Whitmore's support. Pigot was thus deprived of the 'friendly auspices' he had hitherto received from Apley.[70] The third man was Sir John Easthope, a rich businessman and owner of the *Morning Chronicle*. Though a native of Tewkesbury, he came of a Bridgnorth family and was a burgess.[71] He was thus one of only two members of Bridgnorth families to contest the borough in modern times,[72] and with 368 votes (only 20 fewer than Pigot) he did much better than the aristocratic stranger in 1841. Whitmore easily topped the poll with 611 votes, the highest total polled by a Whitmore after 1832. The second votes of those who voted for him were more equally divided than usual: 334 for Pigot, 263 for Easthope. Whitmore shared votes with Easthope which would normally have gone to the latter alone.[73]

In 1852 T. C. Whitmore made way for his brother Henry, the last Whitmore to sit for Bridgnorth and reputedly the ugliest man in the Commons.[74] The Peelite flirtation was over and Henry stood as a Conservative, though his marriage earlier in the year to Adelaide Darby[75] may have gained him some Liberal support. Undeterred by the 1841 result Granville put forward another aristocratic stranger, the Hon. F. W. Cadogan, for the Liberals. According to Whitmore's proposer, T. W. Wylde Browne, there was but one issue, Popery versus Protestantism.[76] Whitmore polled 442 votes, Pigot 360; Cadogan ended 77 votes behind Pigot. Pigot's agent, however, had gone too far. Three of Cadogan's voters petitioned against Pigot and Whitmore on the grounds of bribery, corruption, and treating. Whitmore was exonerated and awarded costs, but Pigot was

[60] *Wolverhampton Chron.* 5 and 26 June 1841; Burke, *Peerage* (1949), 18, 353, 1943, 1986–7. S.R.O. 2763 uncat., draft protest against Throckmorton, 2 July 1841. Throckmorton was presumably Nic. John (d. 1848), bro. of Dalberg-Acton's uncle.

[61] *Wolverhampton Chron.* 3 July 1841.

[62] Hen. S. Smith, *Reg. Parl. Contested Electns.* (1842), 17.

[63] *Wolverhampton Chron.* 9 Oct. 1841; S.R.O. 2763 uncat., Bridgnorth Municipal Revising, 11–13 Oct. 1841.

[64] The Radical only by the mayor's casting vote: *Wolverhampton Chron.* 6 Nov. 1841.

[65] Electn. handbills: scrapbk. *penes* the late H. L. Cunnington.

[66] e.g. the 1858 mun. elections concerned the town's old and new markets: Mason, *Bridgnorth*, 49.

[67] *Wolverhampton Chron.* 4 Aug. 1847.

[68] *Bridgnorth Election Petition*, pp. 165–6.

[69] See p. 314.

[70] *Wolverhampton Chron.* 4 Aug. 1847. They were not renewed in 1852: *Bridgnorth Election Petition*, 140.

[71] *D.N.B.*; F. Boase, *Modern Eng. Biog.* i. 953; S.R.O. 840, box 124, copy list of Bridgnorth voters resident in London [1812].

[72] Edw. Bridgen was the other, in 1727: see p. 278.

[73] *Poll Bk. for . . . Bridgnorth, July 29, 1847* (Bridgnorth n.d.; copy in S.R.O. 2095/34).

[74] Inf. from Sir Fra. Whitmore (d. 1962), who, however, was not 4 years old when Hen. Whitmore (his great-uncle) died. Cf. S.R.O. 2095/20.

[75] Burke, *Peerage* (1967), 2649.

[76] *Wolverhampton Chron.* 14 July 1852.

unseated for bribery by his agents.[77] The Whitmores had no private doubt of Pigot's guilt,[78] though only one of the twenty-five charges of bribery was proved.[79] It was widely suspected that Cadogan had contested the election simply to trap Pigot; the petition had been planned long before, and Liberal efforts seem to have stopped half way through the poll.[80]

A procession of seedy witnesses testified to the Commons select committee, which learned the special significance in Bridgnorth of the phrase 'I will see you again', used when canvassing electors.[81] The committee was also regaled with election verses put about by Henry Whitmore. They began:[82]

> Bridgnorth can't remember
> No Whitmore for Member.

The lines enshrined all that a Bridgnorth voter needed, or in many cases wished, to know. Cobden asserted that a fair enquiry would reveal a degree of corruption that would put even Salisbury and St. Albans in the shade. Nevertheless, despite a petition by 79 electors including the only two manufacturing capitalists of Bridgnorth, the usual move for the postponement of a new writ was defeated. T. C. Whitmore's evidence on his orders against treating in 1847 was stressed by the chairman of the select committee and evidently carried much weight.[83]

Cadogan refused to stand again in 1853 when the Whitmores declined to divide the borough with the Liberals.[84] Nevertheless Pigot's unseating deprived Apley of its remaining influence over the second seat. The Conservatives sent down G. W. Hope, a former M.P. for Southampton, to be introduced to the electors by T. C. Whitmore[85] but he withdrew after a discouraging canvass. In the Commons Disraeli used Hope's rejection as proof that the Whitmore interest was less powerful than had been alleged.[86] In fact, though Disraeli seems not to have known it, Whitmore was engaged in a fierce conflict with the borough over the proposed line of the Severn Valley Railway, which he thought would run too close to his house,[87] and his influence was accordingly weakened. Hope's place was taken by the Broseley banker, John Pritchard, a former Conservative calling himself a Liberal–Conservative. Pritchard, who favoured the proposed railway line, was returned unopposed as a 'perfectly independent man totally unconnected with all family influence'.[88]

Pritchard and Henry Whitmore were unopposed in 1857 and 1859, Pritchard maintaining his hybrid politics while Whitmore became a Tory whip, viewing askance Pritchard's growing influence.[89] From 1854 the Conservative cause was strengthened locally by the *Bridgnorth Journal* owned by Clement Edkins.

In 1865 Sir John Dalberg-Acton of Aldenham contested Bridgnorth after six years' undistinguished representation of Carlow (co. Carlow).[90] It was the first time for over 130 years that an Acton had fought a Whitmore for a Bridgnorth seat. In 1734 the Actons had been Tory, the Whitmores Whig. In the 1865 contest the politics were

[77] *C.J.* cviii. 14, 67, 292.
[78] Dudmaston Hall, MSS. of Lady Labouchere, Mrs. Hen. Whitmore's diary, 17 Oct. 1852, 20 Feb. 1853.
[79] 125 *Parl. Deb.* 3rd ser. 244.
[80] *Bridgnorth Election Petition*, 22–3, 136–9, 155, 158, 165.
[81] Ibid. 27, 139–40, 160, 167, 170. Cf. *The Times*, 24 Feb. 1853.
[82] *Bridgnorth Election Petition*, 105, 163.
[83] 124 *Parl. Deb.* 3rd ser. 734, 875–84, 1287–8; 125 *Parl. Deb.* 3rd ser. 233–46; *C.J.* cviii. 339–40.
[84] *Bridgnorth Election Petition*, 225–8.
[85] 125 *Parl. Deb.* 3rd ser. 243. For Hope see Burke, *Land. Gent.* (1886), 918.

[86] 125 *Parl Deb.* 3rd ser. 242–4.
[87] Mason, *Bridgnorth*, 30, 50; S.R.O. 511/2. Whitmore's interests were eventually protected by ss. 20–2 of the Severn Valley Railway Act, 1853, 16 & 17 Vic. c. 227 (Local and Personal).
[88] *Bridgnorth Beacon*, 1 Apr. 1853. In due course Pritchard's own house, Stanmore Grove, was threatened by the proposed (though not constructed) Wolverhampton–Bridgnorth line: Bridgnorth boro. rec., Wolverhampton Rlwy. papers; *Eddowes's Jnl.* 28 Feb., 7 Mar. 1866; Mason, *Bridgnorth*, 50–1.
[89] Disraeli MSS., B/XXI/W/325.
[90] Mathew, *Ld. Acton and His Times*, 19, 27, 106–9, 117, 125.

reversed. Sir John, then engaged in establishing his scholarly reputation, was a Roman Catholic.[91] The Tories were hampered by the fact that the Apley interest was in some disarray, for T. C. Whitmore had died earlier in the year. There was some turbulence and one observer, well qualified to judge, described an incident during the contest as 'by far the liveliest election fight I ever witnessed'.[92] Nevertheless fewer voted than in the previous contest thirteen years before, and many split their votes. Pritchard, by then a Liberal, headed the poll with 299; Dalberg-Acton had 289, Whitmore 288. Whitmore polled fewer votes from burgesses (119) than Pritchard (131) and Dalberg-Acton (151) but led in occupiers' votes; he had a clear lead of 35 to 12 over Dalberg-Acton in Astley Abbots and of 7 to nil among Anglican clergymen.[93] Dalberg-Acton was unseated after a petition which cost Whitmore over £1,000;[94] one of his voters was found to be ineligible and his agent had bribed another with £4 'travelling expenses'.[95]

In 1868 Jasper More wanted Dalberg-Acton and Pritchard to settle which of them should stand for Bridgnorth and which for Wenlock. He regarded both as Liberal 'certainties'.[96] Pritchard, however, announced his retirement,[97] and the field was clear for Dalberg-Acton at Bridgnorth[98] where there were solid grounds for More's optimism. The Liberal Lord Sudeley, it is true, had sold his property in 1865,[99] but that was more than balanced by the sale of Apley two years later. In 1867 the estate was bought by W. O. Foster, a Stourbridge ironmaster and nephew of Wolryche Whitmore's 1831 colleague.[1] Foster was a Liberal, and it might have been expected that the enlargement of the electorate, in pre-ballot conditions, would have denied Henry Whitmore any chance of success when Dalberg-Acton fought him for the single seat. For the first time the carpet manufacturers, whose mill hands were 'all Radically inclined',[2] and the owner of Apley were on the same side. Foster had publicly to deny that he had put the screw on his tenants though he also announced his personal support for Dalberg-Acton.[3] Over a thousand voted and Whitmore won by 548 to 497.[4] Whether or not it may be regarded as a free vote on 210 years of Whitmore rule, there was certainly much appeal to anti-Popish sentiment.[5] One poster may have had some deterrent effect: 'Vote for Sir John! who will stop those wicked Bridgnorth Races'.[6]

At the beginning of 1870 Whitmore resigned. He had been a Tory whip since 1855 and a founder of the Junior Carlton Club in 1864. While temporarily out of the House, however, he had been passed over in the whip's office for his junior, the Hon. Gerard Noel. His supersession had rankled[7] and in December 1869, he wrote a reproachful letter to Disraeli expressing the disappointment of a loyal country gentleman.[8] He was the last of his family to sit for the borough and was commemorated at Bridgnorth with unconscious irony by a drinking fountain.[9]

W. H. Foster, son of the new owner of Apley,[10] took Whitmore's seat, having

[91] Ibid. *passim*; above, pp. 278-9.
[92] J. A. Bridges, *Reminiscences of a Country Politician* (1906), 18-20.
[93] *Poll Bk. for . . . Bridgnorth, July 12th, 1865* (Bridgnorth n.d.; copy in S.R.O. 2095/35).
[94] Disraeli MSS., B/XXI/W/333.
[95] 182 *Parl. Deb.* 3rd ser. 729-30. After the 1865 Cons. débâcle Derby's managers thought that too many boro. candidates had been too confident and that the Libs. had bribed heavily: Derby Papers, box 104, letters from M. Spofforth (2 Aug. 1865) and Col. T. E. Taylor (6 Dec. 1865).
[96] S.R.O. 1093, corresp., no. 502.
[97] S.R.O. 2095/10 (dated 8 July 1868).
[98] His address to the electors (ibid. /9) was dated 8 July 1868 at Herrnsheim on the Rhine.
[99] S.R.O. 511/3; 2471/2; *Complete Peerage*, xii(1), 423.
[1] *T.S.A.S.* lix. 145; above, p. 283.

[2] Bridges, *Reminiscences*, 21.
[3] S.R.O. 2095/13, 14, 57.
[4] *Poll Bk. for . . . Bridgnorth, 18th Nov. 1868* (Bridgnorth n.d.; copy in S.R.O. 2095/36).
[5] S.R.O. 2095/19, 21, 30. Ibid. 16 probably also relates to the 1868 election.
[6] S.R.O. 2095/11.
[7] Disraeli MSS., B/XXI/W/333, 335, 340. Possibly Whitmore was scapegoat for the 1864 Cons. revolt led by Sir B. Leighton, which saved Palmerston's ministry: J. E. Denison, Vct. Ossington, *Notes from my Jnl. when Speaker of the Ho. of Commons* (1900), 168-70; *T.S.A.S.* lix. 127, 164.
[8] Disraeli MSS., B/XXI/W/337. In Mar. 1868 Whitmore refused an appointment abroad: ibid. 334.
[9] S.R.O. 924/241; 1931/35; 2763 uncat., photo. of fountain; *Kelly's Dir. Salop.* (1885).
[10] Burke, *Land. Gent.* (1898), i. 542.

promised an 'independent support' to Gladstone. T. M. Southwell, the carpet manufacturer who proposed him, observed that nowhere was feeling in favour of a 'local member' stronger than in Bridgnorth. Foster, apparently invited to stand by the local leaders of both parties, was unopposed.[11] Still a Liberal in 1874, he beat a Conservative by over 400 votes. By 1880, however, he was a Conservative and in a rowdy election beat a Liberal by a rather smaller majority. Neither in 1874 nor in 1880 was he opposed by a local man.

The Apley interest had easily survived the changes in its politics since 1831, and for the final fifteen years of the parliamentary borough's existence the town estate, which since 1311 had returned Palmers, Hordes, and the Olympian Whitmores, sent up at last the son of a Stourbridge ironmaster.

Ludlow

In Ludlow Lord Powis's interest was 'much disturbed by the Reform Act'[12] but survived with somewhat reduced control of the borough's representation. Contests, however, were frequent. Formerly the small number of burgesses was an obvious convenience for the Herberts and Clives. The new electorate, consisting almost entirely of £10 householders, posed new problems, and the family's answer, to judge from the 1839 by-election, was mass corruption.

The change was immediately obvious in 1832 when the Clive brothers, M.P.s together for Ludlow since 1818,[13] fought two Whigs. On 13 December Lord Clive (198 votes) was returned at the head of a poll of 339 voters, but the Hon. R. H. Clive (169) was beaten into third place by the Whig Edward Romilly (185). Romilly had property in Glamorgan but his father, the celebrated law reformer, had married Anne Garbett of Knill Court (Herefs.) near Presteigne[14] and their son had taken a prominent part in Radnorshire politics as a Reformer in 1831;[15] the second Whig, a stranger, took only 115 votes. In a savage farewell R. H. Clive described the contest as 'remarkable for unexampled deceit and treachery' and promised never to stand for Ludlow again.[16] A few days later he was elected for the county's Southern division.[17] After this rebuff the Clives never again tried to run family candidates for both seats. Nevertheless, except between 1839 and 1847, a member of the family held one seat as long as the parliamentary borough existed.[18] The Clives were not always able to deliver the second seat to another Conservative before 1852, but the Whigs normally had no hope of more than one seat.

The Tories temporarily recovered the second seat in 1835, though their victory cannot be ascribed to the Clive interest. In the absence of a second Whig Lord Clive headed the poll with 234 votes, and 159 votes for Edmund Lechmere Charlton were enough to beat Romilly into third place by five. As a bitter opponent of the Clives, Lechmere Charlton had disturbed Ludlow's electoral peace in the previous decade, and in 1835 he denied being a Clive protégé, claiming rather to stand as the corporation's nominee and an opponent of municipal reform.[19] Romilly's cousin thought he must 'certainly' have bribed.[20] The Whigs expected him to gain at Ludlow by the registration later in 1835[21] and in 1837, when two Whigs stood, Lechmere Charlton should have

[11] *Bridgnorth Jnl.* 15 Jan., 12 and 19 Feb. 1870.
[12] Dod, *Electoral Facts*, 197. [13] See p. 290.
[14] *T.S.A.S.* 2nd ser. vii. 47–8; *D.N.B. sub* Romilly, Sir Sam. Edw. Romilly's bro. John (later Ld. Romilly: *D.N.B.*) was recorder of Ludlow 1836–8: *T.S.A.S.* 2nd ser. xi. 308, 328–9.
[15] D. R. Ll. Adams, 'The Parl. Representation of Radnors. 1536–1832' (Univ. of Wales M.A. thesis, 1970), 484, 487.

[16] *Salopian Jnl.* 19 Dec. 1832.   [17] See p. 315.
[18] Sir L. Namier, *Structure of Politics at Accession of Geo. III* (1961), 242, and table facing p. 245.
[19] *T.S.A.S.* 2nd ser. vii. 48–9; above, pp. 290–1.
[20] *Romilly's Cambridge Diary 1832–1842*, ed. J. P. T. Bury (1967), 67.
[21] Lambton Estate Office, Chester-le-Street, Lambton Papers, Jos. Parkes to Ld. Durham, 23 Oct. 1835.

been the second Tory. To his supporters' anger, however, he withdrew at the last moment,[22] presenting the second seat to a Whig, Lt.-Col. Henry Salwey of Runnymede Park (Surr.), a younger son of a local landowner and the son-in-law of another. Lord Clive (193 votes) and Salwey (188) easily beat the Whig stranger Thomas Alcock (158).[23] A Whig organizer thought Lechmere Charlton a 'madman and rogue' but welcomed his help in both parliamentary and municipal elections.[24] Lechmere Charlton (d. 1845) did not stand again; the obscure scandals of his private life and parliamentary career,[25] his late withdrawal in 1837, the railing fifty-page pamphlet which he had issued to justify it,[26] his support of Whigs in 1837 and 1839 and of the Tory Botfield in 1840,[27] and his failure to settle the question of his encroachments on Whitcliffe common[28] can have left him with neither credit nor credibility as a Tory candidate.

The Powis interest received another rebuff at the 1839 by-election after Lord Clive's succession as 2nd earl of Powis. Thomas Alcock, the Whig loser of 1837, beat Henry Clive by 186 votes to 182, and Ludlow was therefore briefly (1839-40) represented by two Whigs. Alcock was supported by the Tory Lechmere Charlton, whom he rescued from financial embarrassment when he acquired the mortgages on the Ludford Park estate. The Tories petitioned. The case was heard in 1840. Alcock declined to defend his seat, but certain electors had petitioned in his stead.[29]

The select committee heard from the landlord of the Golden Lion, where Alcock had spent three weeks, an arresting definition of Ludlow politics: 'We have no Tories or Radicals; the politics of Ludlow are whether we are to choose a member for ourselves, or have one family dictate to us, and we are called Clivites and Reformers.'[30] He over-simplified. Even Ludlow politics could not be isolated altogether from national politics, and in fact a very prominent member of each party had come down to help the candidates. William Holmes[31] had the 'whole management' of Clive's campaign,[32] and the acute James Coppock, the notable Whig agent and former secretary of the Reform Club, managed Alcock's.[33] The prominent Shrewsbury Conservative John Frail also came to Ludlow with Edward Haycock, the county surveyor, to manage 'the dirty work'.[34] When the Whigs were said to be importing 'foreign blackguards', roughs from Shrewsbury, Frail wrote to the owner of the *Salopian Journal*, well known for his readiness to organize similar assistance for Tories, and he sent a Bridgnorth pugilist who had assisted the Whitmores' efforts there.[35]

There was indiscriminate open treating, men being kept inside partisan public houses all night by alarmist tales of the arrival of roughs from outside the town.[36] Rodney Anderson, a young Ludlow attorney and secretary of Alcock's committee, deposed that all electors in Alcock's interest were members of his 80- or 90-strong committee 'as a means of securing their votes'; committee members could drink free.[37] A Clivite committee at Dinham House managed the election, another at the Blue Boar bringing up voters. Vital transactions, however, took place at the Feathers where Frail

[22] *Salopian Jnl.* 2 Aug. 1837.
[23] *T.S.A.S.* 2nd ser. vii. 49; Burke, *Land. Gent.* (1952), 2238. Clive's voting figures (quoted here) differed slightly from Salwey's claims.
[24] MSS. *penes* Mrs. Jebb, Kingsland (Suss.), Jos. Parkes to E. J. Stanley, Treas. sec., [2 Nov. 1837].
[25] *T.S.A.S.* xlix. 232-3; S.P.L., accession 4659; J. Grant, *Random Recollections of the Ho. of Commons* (1836), 373-4, 378; *Salopian Jnl.* 10 June 1835.
[26] *To The . . . Electors of . . . Ludlow* (Ludlow, 1837; copy in S.P.L., accession 2556).
[27] As early as 1836 he was having to justify the contradictions of his political career: letter to *Salopian Jnl.* 26 Oct. 1836.
[28] E. Jones, *Pen Sketches of Old Ludlow* (2nd ser., Ludlow,

1913; copy in S.P.L., accession 1424), 'Whitcliff Common'.
[29] *T.S.A.S.* 2nd ser. vii. 49-50; *C.J.* xciv. 374-5, 415, 424, 534; xcv. 58, 74, 121-2, 127, 222, 228, 234, 277; 52 *Parl. Deb.* 3rd ser. 770-4, 809-21.
[30] *Mins. of Evid. before Sel. Cttee. on Ludlow Electn. Petitions*, H.C. 229, p. 8 (1840), ix.
[31] *D.N.B.*; above, pp. 306-7.
[32] *Evid. bef. Cttee. on Ludlow Electn. Pets.* 115.
[33] Ibid. 98.
[34] Ibid. 127-8; above, p. 325.
[35] *Evid. bef. Cttee. on Ludlow Electn. Pets.* 131; *Eddowes's Jnl.* 8 Apr. 1840.
[36] *Eddowes's Jnl.* 8 Apr. 1840.
[37] *Evid. bef. Cttee. on Ludlow Electn. Pets.* 29-31. Anderson had proposed Salwey in 1837: *Salopian Jnl.* 2 Aug. 1837.

had a private room 'to see the voters'. One Clive voter received as much as £300.[38] On the other side Coppock too was ready to offer three-figure sums for votes.[39]

The select committee saw a number of remarkably shifty witnesses, the most noteworthy being a Clivite renegade. John Brookes Revis had lived in Ludlow from 1835 to 1838, had written in west midland newspapers in the Conservative interest, and had helped to found a Ludlow 'Conservative institution' in 1836. He too was brought from Shrewsbury in 1839 and also disbursed money.[40] He alleged that Holmes told him to bribe, with £500 if need be, during the poll's last stages; that particular sum was an exaggeration, but one of Clive's solicitors told Revis that 'if money is to win it, we are to win it'.[41] All Revis's knowledge was turned against Clive, for Holmes had unwisely refused to pay him. Consequently, about the beginning of March 1840, Revis, intent on revenge, told Coppock in London of the 'base' treatment he had received from 'the Tory aristocracy of Shropshire'.[42] Coppock advanced him £150 to enable him to go to Ludlow in search of information.[43] Radicals in the Commons later made much play with Revis's evidence,[44] though the members of the select committee discounted it.[45]

Clive and Alcock were both found guilty of bribery by their agents. Even allowing for exaggeration or falsehood in the evidence, the conclusion was clearly just. Alcock was unseated and the election voided.[46] Coppock was proved to have handed a publican a £30 bribe for a specific elector, though he eventually emerged unscathed.[47]

The borough might have come near disfranchisement as a result of Clive's petition. After numerous Commons divisions, however, Radical moves for an inquiry into bribery, treating, and intimidation at Ludlow were defeated;[48] the existence of a Whig government doubtless moderated Radical demands. The Powis interest too seems to have acted prudently in not running another Clive until 1847. At the 1840 by-election to fill Alcock's seat Beriah Botfield, of Norton (Northants.) and Decker Hill (in Shifnal),[49] stood as a Conservative; like Alcock he had Lechmere Charlton's support. An enthusiastic antiquary[50] whose great wealth drawn from the local iron industry[51] made him 'by far the richest commoner in Shropshire',[52] Botfield beat a Whig stranger[53] by 194 votes to 160.[54] In the 1841 general election Botfield and a new Conservative, James Ackers of Heath House, easily beat Salwey by 222 and 219 votes to 156.[55]

Henry Bayley Clive of Styche, a kinsman of Lord Powis, was brought forward in 1847, and thereafter a Clive or a Herbert sat for Ludlow until 1885. In 1847 Clive and Salwey almost tied with 207 and 206 votes, and Botfield was 23 behind Salwey. Salwey was beaten in 1852 by Robert Clive, son of the Hon. R. H. Clive, and by a Liberal–Conservative, Lord William Powlett (later 3rd duke of Cleveland), who polled 250 and 214 votes to Salwey's 157. In 1854 Clive was succeeded by his cousin Col. Percy Herbert, Lord Powis's brother, who was in turn replaced in 1860 by the Hon. G. H. W.

[38] Evid. bef. Cttee. on Ludlow Electn. Pets. 113, 118, 126, 128.
[39] Ibid. 57.
[40] Ibid. 112 sqq. S.P.L., Watton press cuttings, iii. 203 sqq. contains inf. about Revis.
[41] Evid. bef. Cttee. on Ludlow Electn. Pets. 121, 123.
[42] Ibid. 133–4.
[43] Ibid. 135 sqq.
[44] 53 Parl. Deb. 3rd ser. 1370–1408; 54 Parl. Deb. 3rd ser. 49–68, 76–111.
[45] 53 Parl. Deb. 3rd ser. 1023–6, 1394–5.
[46] C.J. xcv. 277.
[47] For details see N. Gash, Politics in the Age of Peel (1953), 425–6; Annual Register, 1840, 65–6.
[48] 53 Parl. Deb. 3rd ser. 1367–1408; 54 Parl. Deb. 3rd ser. 49–68, 76–111.

[49] D.N.B. Under his uncle's will Sotfield had to live at Decker Hill (which he detested) for 6 months a year: Hatfield Ho., MSS. of 3rd marquess of Salisbury, Ld. Powis to Salisbury, 22 Dec. 1879. Thanks are due to Ld. Salisbury for permission to use and quote from these papers.
[50] D.N.B.
[51] Trinder, Indust. Revolution in Salop., 73–4, 241, 396; V.C.H. Salop. i. 451, 464–5, 476.
[52] Loton Hall MSS., Sir B. Leighton's diary, 8 Aug. 1858.
[53] G. G. de H. Larpent: D.N.B.
[54] T.S.A.S. 2nd ser. vii. 50. There was a Lib. petition alleging corrupt and illegal practices: C.J. xcv. 410, 437, 512.
[55] T.S.A.S. 2nd ser. vii. 50–1.

Windsor-Clive, brother of Robert Clive, M.P. 1852–4.[56] Each moved in turn from Ludlow to the Southern division,[57] following the precedent set in different circumstances by the Hon. R. H. Clive in 1832. The division was clearly regarded as a more dignified constituency; for Herbert it certainly proved a more expensive one.[58]

There was no contest at Ludlow between 1852 and 1865, and Lord Powis evidently regarded the family seat there as entirely safe. Late in 1858 Lord Derby, anxious to get a protégé into the Commons, had evidently heard that Powis was willing for his brother to vacate Ludlow and 'could and would return a member for us'. Derby's ministry, however, fell and Powis was not required to act on his forthright 18th-century undertaking.[59] The last Conservatives to sit with the Powis nominee were Beriah Botfield (d. 1863), Sir W. A. Fraser, a stranger, and J. E. Severne of Wallop, elected in 1857, 1863, and 1865 respectively. The seat was an expensive one costing Botfield £300 or £400 a year as well as nearly £1,000 towards the restoration of St. Lawrence's in 1859–60. Fraser too had had to pay £450 a year besides £500 for his unopposed return in 1863. The contest at the 1865 general election was intended to distract Conservative energies from the Southern division. Fraser angrily decided to retire, asserting in the Carlton Club that the opposition was 'all owing to the lawyers . . . on both sides' who wanted a contest. The Liberal, Sir William Yardley, was easily beaten, polling only 137 votes to Windsor-Clive's 236 and Severne's 209.[60]

The highest number of Ludlow voters polled under the first Reform Act was 621 in 1852. The 1867 Act considerably increased the electorate and abolished one of the seats,[61] but Windsor-Clive easily retained the surviving seat until 1885. In 1868,[62] at the last election before the 1872 Ballot Act, he had 72 per cent of the poll, beating Yardley by 428 to 170. He was equally successful in Ludlow itself, in Stanton Lacy and Ludford, and among the burgesses; all four lodgers on the register voted for him.[63] He was unopposed in 1874, and in 1880 he had 60 per cent of the poll, beating L. E. Glyn, a London barrister, by 525 to 343.[64]

Altogether five members of the Clive or Herbert family sat for Ludlow between 1832 and 1885; five of the other eight M.P.s were local men, the Whigs Romilly and Alcock and the Tory Fraser being the exceptions. By and large disturbance of interests by the Reform Acts was greater than at Bridgnorth, but the Clives and Herberts found compensation in the county's Southern division.[65]

Much Wenlock

Much Wenlock, with boundaries unaltered by the 1832 Reform Act,[66] was one of the most extensive parliamentary boroughs. It included 17 parishes,[67] many of them rural in character, and covered some 71 square miles.[68] It was, moreover, very far from being typical of the small parliamentary boroughs of the day, agricultural in character and centred on a small town.[69] North and east of the town there was much industry:

[56] Ibid. 51–2; Namier, *Politics at Accession of Geo. III*, 242, 245, and table facing p. 245.

[57] Disraeli later strongly disliked this practice: marquess of Zetland, *Letters of Disraeli to Lady Bradford and Lady Chesterfield* (1929), ii. 162.

[58] See pp. 315, 317–18, 336.

[59] MSS. of 14th earl of Derby (*penes* Ld. Blake, the Queen's Coll., Oxf.), 184/1, pp. 344–5, Derby to Gen. Hill. Derby wrote to Powis on the eve of the ministry's fall: ibid. 187/1.

[60] *T.S.A.S.* 2nd ser. vii. 52–3; Loton Hall MSS., Sir B. Leighton's diary, 22 June 1865; S.R.O. 2881/2/52–7; 3036/2/29; above, p. 317.

[61] Rep. of the People Act, 1867, 30 & 31 Vic. c. 102.

[62] For a Radical survey of the constituency see Bishopsgate Foundation (Bishopsgate Inst., London), Howell collection, rep. on Ludlow boro. 27 Aug. 1868.

[63] *Alphab. List of Poll . . . for . . . Ludlow . . . 17th Nov. 1868* (Ludlow, n.d.; copy in S.P.L., accession 1726).

[64] *T.S.A.S.* 2nd ser. vii. 53; *Eddowes's Jnl.* 3 Mar. 1880.

[65] See pp. 315, 330–1.   [66] See p. 310.

[67] *V.C.H. Salop.* ii. 211. It also included Posenhall extra-parochial place.

[68] *Census*, 1831.

[69] With which it is classed by Hanham, *Electns. and Party Management*, 39 and n. 1.

potteries at Benthall, mines and foundries at Broseley, ironworks at Coalbrookdale, and coalpits and porcelain works in Madeley.[70] There were 17,435 inhabitants; over 41 per cent of the families were chiefly engaged in trade, manufactures, and handicraft, less than 18 per cent chiefly in agriculture.[71]

The 1832 Act more than trebled the electorate; 489 householders were added to 202 burgesses.[72] By 1836–7 there were 223 burgesses and 683 householders.[73] The 1867 Reform Act[74] enlarged the electorate still further, but neither Act affected the position of the Weld-Foresters, who held one of the seats without great difficulty until the borough was disfranchised in 1885. Indeed Wenlock politics, municipal[75] as well as parliamentary, continued remarkably stable after 1832. Only four men sat for the borough between 1832 and 1885 and there were only five contests: in 1832, 1835, 1874 (the general election and a by-election), and 1880. In 1852 influence was said to be 'chiefly possessed' by Lords Forester and Bradford (brothers-in-law),[76] though some was in the hands of Sir Watkin Williams Wynn.[77] After 1832 Bradford was content to support the Weld-Forester candidate.

Col. G. C. W. Weld-Forester, who had sat since 1828,[78] continued as M.P. until 1874, by which time he had become Father of the House of Commons.[79] His Whig colleague in the last unreformed Parliament, P. B. Thompson (cr. Lord Wenlock 1839), owned great estates in Yorkshire and, with the trebling of Yorkshire county seats, was able to find a seat for the East Riding in 1832.[80] Thompson's move enabled the interest of his wife's cousin, Sir Watkin Williams Wynn,[81] to come into its own at last; Sir Watkin's tenants in Wenlock itself (on the Abbey estate) and his ten or more inns in the town supplied occupiers' votes.[82] In the autumn of 1832 Sir Watkin (5th baronet) offered his support for the second seat to Sir Richard Acton, who was then abroad. On 1 November, however, after waiting until the last possible moment for Acton's reply, he brought forward the 22-years-old J. M. Gaskell[83] who had recently married his niece Mary,[84] daughter of the Grenvillite politician C. W. Williams Wynn.[85]

Gaskell was one of a small coterie of ardent young Tories at Christ Church four of whom sat in the first reformed Parliament.[86] Though offered candidacies in Yorkshire, Essex, and Ireland,[87] Gaskell chose Wenlock. It was an arduous constituency to fight after 1832, taking at least three weeks to canvass.[88] The Tories' opponents included Quakers, Methodists, and radicals 'who infest parts of the franchise in great numbers';[89] in 1832, led by the Darbys of Coalbrookdale, they ran Matthew Bridges, a Bristol ironmaster and a radical pledged to support vote by ballot, triennial Parliaments, and complete repeal of the corn laws.[90] Gaskell canvassed in a carriage and four with 8 or 10 outriders, Bridges in a gig with Joseph Reynolds, lord of the manor of Madeley, a parson named Bartlett, and 'two Quakers named Darby'[91] of whose eminence Gaskell was clearly unaware. Gaskell and Weld-Forester did not coalesce and represented different kinds of Toryism, Gaskell being an ardent admirer of Peel.[92] Bridges fought a

[70] Dod, *Electoral Facts*, 331.
[71] *Census*, 1831.
[72] *Ret. Electors Registered*, H.C. 189, p. 215 (1833), xxvii.
[73] *Ret. Electors Registered 1836 and 1837*, H.C. 329, p. 96 (1837–8), xliv.
[74] 30 & 31 Vic. c. 102.
[75] A contest in Madeley ward, Apr. 1866, was the first for over 20 yrs. Less than 30 per cent of the electorate voted: *Ret. of Electors*, H.C. 11, p. 73 (1867), lvi.
[76] Burke, *Peerage* (1949), 247, 782.
[77] Dod, *Electoral Facts*, 331.
[78] See p. 297.
[79] *T.S.A.S.* 3rd ser. ii. 352.
[80] *Complete Peerage*, xii(2), 486; 2 Wm. IV, c. 45, s. 12.
[81] L. G. Pine, *New Extinct Peerage, 1884–1971* (1972), 43, 291; Burke, *Peerage* (1967), 320, 2716–17.
[82] N.L.W., Wynnstay box E, no. 93 (valuation, 1835).
[83] S.R.O. 1093, corresp., nos. 248–9; B.L. Add. MS. 44161, f. 85.
[84] Burke, *Peerage* (1949), 2183.
[85] *D.N.B.*
[86] They included Sir J. Hanmer (above, pp. 325–6). See refs. to Gaskell and Hanmer in *Gladstone Diaries*, i–ii, ed. M. R. D. Foot (1968).
[87] B.L. Add. MS. 44161, ff. 73–7, 83–4.
[88] Ibid., ff. 85, 88, 90, 123.
[89] Ibid., f. 85.
[90] Ibid.; S.R.O. 1093, corresp., no. 249 (letter wrongly ascribed to Sir Watkin in *T.S.A.S.* lviii. 232; it was written by his bro. C. W. Williams Wynn).
[91] B.L. Add. MS. 44161, f. 87.
[92] Ibid., f. 73v.

vituperative campaign[93] and ran Gaskell closer than he expected. The electorate was 691. Weld-Forester headed the poll (448 votes), and Gaskell (330) put Bridges into third place by only 22.[94]

In the autumn of 1833 the opposition, directed mainly against Weld-Forester rather than Gaskell, entered over two hundred objections at the registration, but with little success.[95] At the 1834 registration the Tories gained twelve.[96] The 1835 election caught the Wenlock Radicals without a candidate; in 1834 six names had been mentioned, including that of W. Wolryche Whitmore who had just ceased to sit for Wolverhampton.[97] Sir William Somerville, the Radical Irish baronet,[98] came forward very late and was soundly beaten. Weld-Forester, though he had expected defeat, headed the poll with 519; Gaskell polled 422 and Somerville, who had many plumpers, 323.[99]

In 1838 an observer thought that Gaskell had 'very considerable powers of elocution' and 'a strength and sincerity' in his devotion to Conservative principles which, if he chose, 'could not fail to make him a man of some importance'.[1] He did not, however, live up to his early promise.[2] In due course he was given minor office in Peel's second ministry,[3] until he resigned in opposition to the repeal of the corn laws.[4] Like Gaskell, Weld-Forester was a protectionist,[5] but his elder brother (and predecessor as M.P.), Lord Forester, who also held minor office under Peel,[6] actually voted for repeal.[7]

Weld-Forester and Gaskell sat together until 1868 without further opposition. The explanation of the long peace seems to be that, while they represented distinct interests[8] in the borough which were independently strengthened during their long incumbencies, the two M.P.s diverged in politics. Lord Forester, 'living . . . much below his income', greatly extended the Willey estate by purchase,[9] and in the 1850s the Weld-Foresters no doubt drew strength from their support of the Severn Valley Railway project, so beneficial to the local brick and tile trade.[10] Gaskell's interest became more independent in 1857 when he bought the Wenlock Abbey estate from Sir Watkin Williams Wynn.[11] By that time Gaskell's politics had changed too. Weld-Forester was given minor office by Derby,[12] under whom, however, Gaskell refused to serve. Like Gladstone he followed Palmerston, becoming a moderate Liberal in the latter part of his parliamentary career.[13] Gaskell's changed politics, his acquisition of the Williams Wynn property, and his wife's connexion with Lord Wenlock[14] must have dampened Liberal efforts in the constituency. For a time Abraham Darby and his brother-in-law, Henry Dickinson, interested themselves in the registration on behalf of the Liberals,[15] but they ceased to do so after 1853. In 1865 the Liberals considered at least two possible Wenlock candidates to distract Conservative energies from Jasper More's campaign in the Southern division, but nothing came of it.[16]

The 1867 Reform Act affected Wenlock more than any other Shropshire constituency, for by it the electorate was again trebled. In 1851-2 it had been exactly one less than in 1836-7 (905 against 906). During the intervening years the number of burgesses had

[93] Ibid., ff. 85, 88, 89v.
[94] *T.S.A.S.* 3rd ser. ii. 353. B.L. Add. MS. 44161, f. 95, gives similar figs., increasing each candidate's poll by *c.* 20-30 votes.
[95] B.L. Add. MS. 44161, ff. 99v.-100.   [96] Ibid., f. 121.
[97] Ibid., f. 123.   [98] *D.N.B.*
[99] B.L. Add. MS. 44161, ff. 126v.-7; N.L.W., Aston Hall 326; *T.S.A.S.* 3rd ser. ii. 354; J. Randall, *Broseley and Its Surroundings* (Madeley, 1879), 243.
[1] J. Grant, *Brit. Senate in 1838* (1838), ii. 92-6.
[2] *T.S.A.S.* 3rd ser. ii. 353-4 (Gladstone's judgement).
[3] A Treasury ld. 1841-6: ibid.
[4] See p. 314. Randall, *Broseley*, 244, is unreliable on Gaskell's earlier career.
[5] Dod, *Electoral Facts*, 331.
[6] Capt. of the Corps of Gentlemen-at-Arms 1841-6: *Complete Peerage*, v. 553.
[7] 86 *Parl. Deb.* 3rd ser. 1406.
[8] Randall, *Broseley*, 244, seems wrong to imply that Gaskell depended on the Willey interest.
[9] *T.S.A.S.* lix. 145-6.
[10] Ibid. 3rd ser. ii. 351; Randall, *Broseley*, 152.
[11] *T.S.A.S.* 3rd ser. ii. 354.
[12] Comptroller of the Household 1852-3, 1858-9; *Complete Peerage*, v. 553.
[13] *Eddowes's Jnl.* 12 Feb. 1873; *Shrews. Chron.* 14 Feb. 1873 (obits.); B.L. Add. MS. 44161, f. 136.
[14] She was his 2nd cos.: Pine, *Ext. Peerage, 1884-1971*, 291; Burke, *Peerage* (1949), 249, 2183.
[15] B.L. Add. MS. 44161, ff. 99v.-100, 123.   [16] See p. 317.

dropped from 223 to 135, that of householders had risen from 683 to 770.[17] A year before the 1867 Act there had been 961 electors.[18] In 1868, however, the electorate soared to 3,445,[19] giving local Liberals new confidence. On the suggestion of W. H. Darby the retiring Bridgnorth Liberal M.P., John Pritchard, was asked to stand, but he declined, advising the impossibility of success. At Darby's further suggestion a requisition was made on A. H. Brown, a grandson of Sir William Brown, the Liverpool merchant banker; it was widely supported.[20] Gaskell retired,[21] leaving Weld-Forester and Brown unopposed. Brown's Liberal politics and place of origin, Beilby Grange (Yorks. W.R.),[22] suggest a connexion with the Lawleys[23] and may have deterred the Conservatives from running a second man, for the industrial nature of the north-eastern part of the constituency meant that only two well-established local landed candidates could hope to hold both seats for the Conservatives.

The changing nature of the constituency was reflected in the 1874 general election, when the borough was contested by one Conservative and two Liberals. Weld-Forester and Brown stood again, and the second Liberal was C. G. M. Gaskell, son of the former M.P. (d. 1873). Gaskell fared badly, polling only 846 votes to Weld-Forester's 1,708 and Brown's 1,575. The contest cost Weld-Forester £1,595, Gaskell £1,251, but Brown only £734.[24] It was the first contest for 39 years and the Conservatives began to feel the need to defend their position in the constituency. Lord Forester was old and childless, and his death would unseat his brother. In the summer of 1874 Lord Bradford agreed to undertake the 'disagreeable duty' of presenting the prizes and speaking at the National Olympian Association's meeting at Much Wenlock. He did so for political reasons 'rather than from any great fondness for National Olympian Festivals'; chiefly in fact to help defeat the chances of 'young Gaskell, young Lawley, or Jasper More' at a possible election and to help to undermine the position of Brown, the sitting Liberal.[25] Later that year 'young Lawley' did indeed try to capture the second seat for the Liberals.[26] Gen. Weld-Forester succeeded to his brother's peerage in October,[27] and his nephew C. T. Weld-Forester stood for the Conservatives only to be opposed by Lord Wenlock's son and heir, Beilby Lawley. A by-election which had been dubbed 'Homeric' saw Weld-Forester the winner by 1,720 to 1,401.[28] Disraeli had been very nervous and Gerard Noel, the Conservative whip, had thought the contest hopeless, but Weld-Forester's uncle, Lord Bradford, had been confident and thought the Lawleys had shown 'great arrogance' in fighting at all.[29] The Conservatives thought a Liberal petition possible,[30] but none was presented. In 1880, despite the existence of a Liberal association in the borough affiliated to the new National Liberal Federation,[31] the Liberals fared worse than in 1874. C. T. Weld-Forester headed the poll with over 2,000 votes. Brown beat a local Tory squire, R. A. Benson of Lutwyche, into third place, but by less than half of his lead over the Liberal third man in 1874.[32]

[17] *Ret. Electors*, H.C. 329, p. 96 (1838), xliv; *Ret. Electors*, H.C. 8, p. 9 (1852), xlii.

[18] *Ret. relative to Parl. Boros.* H.C. 121, p. 5 (1867), lvi.

[19] *Ret. relating to Parl. Constituencies (Population, &c)*, H.C. 432, p. 9 (1877), lxviii.

[20] Randall, *Broseley*, 244. For the Browns see Burke, *Peerage* (1967), 356; A. Ellis, *Heir of Adventure: the story of Brown, Shipley & Co.* (1960); *Who Was Who, 1916–1928*, 132.

[21] His wife's (d. 1869) poor health being the 'main cause': B.L. Add. MS. 44161, f. 135v.

[22] *T.S.A.S.* 3rd ser. ii. 355.

[23] Seated at Escrick Pk. (Yorks. E.R.), which they had inherited from Beilby Thompson's dau.: Pine, *Ext. Peerage, 1884–1971*, 291.

[24] *Eddowes's Jnl.* 11 Feb. 1874; *Ret. of Charges made to Candidates at the late Electns. . . .*, H.C. 358, p. 31 (1874), liii.

[25] Disraeli MSS., B/XXI/B/799. In the end Mrs. Forester, not Bradford, presented the prizes.

[26] Thus the compact at Wenlock alleged by Hanham (*Electns. and Party Management*, 57 n. 1) did not last until 1880.

[27] *Complete Peerage*, v. 553.

[28] *T.S.A.S.* 3rd ser. ii. 302, 356; S.R.O. 2076/2–8.

[29] Zetland, *Letters of Disraeli to Lady Bradford and Lady Chesterfield*, i. 170–1.

[30] S.R.O. 1224, box 333, telegram Spofforth to Potts, 10 Dec. 1874.

[31] B. McGill, 'Fra. Schnadhorst and Lib. Party Organization', *Jnl. Modern Hist.* xxxiv. 21.

[32] *T.S.A.S.* 3rd ser. ii. 357.

Liberal efforts to win both seats continued until, in 1884, it became clear that the borough was to be disfranchised. Granville's nephew George Leveson-Gower appeared briefly as a second Liberal in 1883-4. He was adopted primarily on account of his uncle's and his father's 'preponderating interest' in the Lilleshall Co., though the extensive Lilleshall estate belonging to the head of his family the duke of Sutherland, still 'nominally' a Liberal, also counted and Leveson-Gower also had C. G. M. Gaskell's support.[33]

The Weld-Foresters' achievement in retaining their borough seat until 1885 is even more remarkable than those of the Whitmores at Bridgnorth and the Clives and Herberts at Ludlow. The Whitmores ceased to represent Bridgnorth before the 1872 Ballot Act, although Henry Whitmore's victory in 1868, after the sale of his family's estates and in pre-ballot conditions, was a notable one. The Clives did win a contest at Ludlow after the Ballot Act, and represented the Ludlow division of the county well into the 20th century;[34] nevertheless they were returned by a more agricultural, and probably more deferential, electorate than that which returned the Weld-Foresters for Wenlock until 1885. By the 1870s a majority of Wenlock electors had links with industry, not the land, but in 1874 and 1880 a Weld-Forester still headed the poll, and the only Liberal who had sought to oust him was a Lawley, the representative of a landed interest as ancient as the Weld-Foresters' own.

1885-1918

Wellington (or Mid-Shropshire) Division, p. 345. Ludlow (or Southern) Division, p. 346. Newport (or Northern) Division, p. 348. Oswestry (or Western) Division, p. 350. Shrewsbury, p. 352.

THE 1885 redistribution created five single-member constituencies in Shropshire, halving its representation. Shrewsbury remained a parliamentary borough though losing a member. The three other boroughs lost their parliamentary status, and four county divisions were created in place of the former two. The more obvious anomalies were corrected. The excess of borough over county members was ended; the too generous representation of south Shropshire was reduced in favour of the north; and all the main industrial area, formerly divided between constituencies, was included in the new Mid (or Wellington) division.[35]

In 1881 the county's male population was 124,157, of whom 3,444 were professional men, 3,594 were in domestic occupations (mainly servants), and 4,329 in commerce; agriculture employed 28,241, industry 42,459, including 7,201 general labourers, 4,032 coal miners, and over 3,000 ironworkers; of the remaining 50,925 unoccupied males about a third were children under five. Agriculture was less important than it had been fifty years before, though many men classified as industrial workers in fact depended on agriculture.[36] The county was less hard hit by the agricultural depression than areas more exclusively dependent on arable farming;[37] in 1881 there were 428,110 a. under permanent pasture and only 152,596 a. under corn crops.[38]

There were eight general elections during the period but only in 1885, 1906, and

[33] Sir G. Leveson Gower, *Years of Content, 1858–1886* (1940), 211–13.
[34] See pp. 335, 339.
[35] Redistrib. of Seats Act, 1885, 48 & 49 Vic. c. 23; *Stanford's Parl. . . . Atlas of Eng. and Wales* (1885), 199–204, and map; map on p. 344.
[36] *Census*, 1881. The figs. relate to the 'registration

county' (for which see above, pp. 169, 171, and map on p. 170) and their total (132,992) is thus greater than the male pop. of Salop.
[37] *Rep. R. Com. on Poor Laws, App. XVII* [Cd. 4690], p. 207, H.C. (1909), xliii.
[38] *Stanford's Parl. Atlas*, 204.

January 1910 were all Shropshire seats contested.[39] Shrewsbury and Wellington were contested six times, Newport and Oswestry five, Ludlow four. In 1885 Shrewsbury, like many other boroughs, went Conservative, but three of the four county divisions went Liberal as the rural labourers expressed their gratitude for the vote.[40] The county thus returned three Liberal and two Conservative members on the only occasion in its history when the Conservative share of the vote (48·1 per cent) was exceeded by another party's, the Liberals' 51·9 per cent.

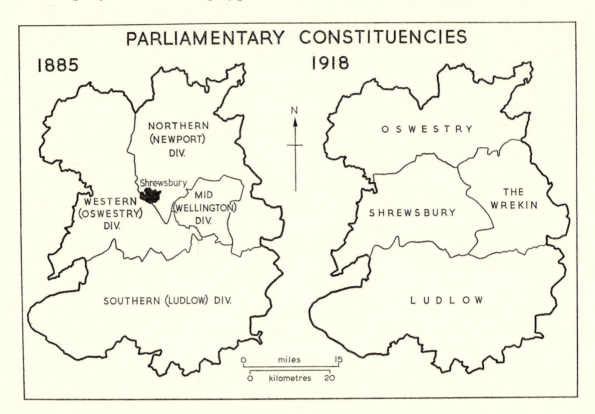

The period of so-called adult male suffrage[41] thus began with a considerable reverse for the Conservatives, justifying their earlier misgivings. Lord Powis, commenting on the Liberals' proposed electoral reforms in 1884, had hoped to see borough freeholders, 'presumably not very open to corruption', voting in their boroughs as a 'makeweight' and relieving county divisions of voters whose interests were 'bricks and mortar' not 'turnips and barley'.[42] The subsequent borough disfranchisements were also opposed by Powis[43] and others.[44] Nevertheless at the next four general elections all five members were Conservatives or Conservative allies; in 1895 and 1900 only one seat was contested against them, both times unsuccessfully. In 1906, the nadir of Conservative fortunes, and at both 1910 elections four Conservatives and one Liberal were returned. Even in 1906, when the Conservative majorities were narrow and the Liberal one was large, the Conservatives had a slight majority of the total vote, and they widened the gap in January 1910. In and after 1886 the Conservatives thus resumed their wonted dominance, the message 'We are five in Shropshire', sent to Lord Salisbury in 1892, obviously echoing the triumph of 1841.[45]

[39] Details of elections and candidates 1885–1918 are based, unless otherwise stated, on *McCalmont's Parl. Poll Bk. . . . 1832–1918*, ed. J. Vincent and M. Stenton (1971).
[40] Conferred by the Rep. of the People Act, 1884, 48 Vic. c. 3.
[41] Cf. H. M. Pelling, *Social Geog. of Brit. Elections* (1967), 6–8.

[42] Hatfield Ho., MSS. of 3rd marquess of Salisbury, Powis to Salisbury, 1 Feb. 1884.
[43] Ibid., Powis to Salisbury, 27 Nov. 1884.
[44] *Shrews. Chron.* 16 Jan. 1885 (editorial); *Bridgnorth Jnl.* 14 and 21 Nov. 1903 (speech by R. J. More, as corrected).
[45] *Bridgnorth Jnl.* 23 July 1892; see p. 312.

The reason for continued Conservative dominance, unforeseeable in 1885, was the Liberal split over Irish home rule in 1886. The members for Ludlow and Wellington stayed in Parliament as Liberal Unionists, the former eventually being succeeded by a Conservative. The member for Newport expressed his new Unionist principles by retirement and made a Conservative victory possible. The Gladstonian Liberals also lost their local press support. The Shropshire Guardian and Shrewsbury Herald Newspaper Co. Ltd. did not survive the Liberal split. It was wound up in 1886, its leading shareholder, A. P. Heywood-Lonsdale, taking over its assets and liabilities.[46] He kept the company's three papers afloat for four or five years but the *Evening News* ceased in 1890, *Eddowes's Shrewsbury Journal* and the *Shropshire Guardian* at the end of the following year.[47] The *Guardian* at least, like Heywood-Lonsdale himself,[48] had become Liberal Unionist in sympathy during its last years.[49] In 1891 Lord Granville died;[50] he was president of the Shropshire Central Liberal Council and of the Newport Division Liberal Association and had supported the Liberal cause in the county for fifty years. For some years Liberal organization in Shropshire was torpid, though new Liberal associations had been set up promptly in all the new divisions except Ludlow.[51]

After the collapse of Liberal opposition in 1895 and 1900, however, a Liberal revival was almost inevitable. Its mainspring was a newcomer to the county. Alfred Billson, born in Leicester in 1839, had settled in Liverpool where he had become a successful solicitor, a newspaper proprietor and director, and a prominent Liberal politician.[52] He took a lease of Rowton Castle and, according to W. C. Bridgeman who had good reason to know, was responsible for the selection of Liberal candidates for all the Shropshire divisions and for a sustained platform attack on landlords and the system of land tenure.[53] Liberal candidates contested all three Shropshire by-elections of the 1900-6 Parliament and there was a short-lived Liberal gain at Oswestry in 1904. All five seats were fought at the 1906 general election, and the Wellington division returned a Liberal. Billson seems to have given more cohesion to the modern Liberal cause in Shropshire than anyone else, but the impetus did not survive the first election of 1910, and Billson was by then dead.[54] The leading Shropshire Conservative during the period of Billson's activity was Edward Corbett of Longnor, son of the late M.P. for South Shropshire. Though not a professional politician like Billson, Corbett was a worthy and energetic opponent.[55]

Wellington (or Mid-Shropshire) Division

The compact new Wellington division, the most Liberal in Shropshire, included some agricultural villages, but within it were concentrated not only the urban and industrial parishes of the old parliamentary borough of Much Wenlock (Broseley and Madeley) but also Wellington, Dawley, Lilleshall, and Oakengates, the industrial parts of the old Northern division. The market town of Wellington was the principal centre of population and had a significant number of Conservative middle-class electors.[56] Elsewhere there were firms employing several hundred men each,[57] and at

[46] B.T. 31/2847/15660.
[47] The Times, *Tercentenary Handlist of Newspapers* (1920); *Wellington Jnl.* 2 Jan. 1892.
[48] *Shrews. Chron.* 26 Feb. 1897 (obit.).
[49] See e.g. its comments on Lib. by-electn. disasters in 1891 and (19 Dec. 1891) an anti-Gladstone leader.
[50] *Shropshire Guardian*, 4 Apr. 1891.
[51] *Lib. Yr. Bk. 1887*, 287, 303-4; ibid. *1888*, 272, 295; *1889*, 220, 245.
[52] *The Times*, 10 July 1907; *Who Was Who, 1897-1916*, 63; B.L. Add. MS. 46105.
[53] *Memoir of . . . Wm. Kenyon-Slaney*, ed. W. Durnford (1909), 58-60.
[54] *The Times*, 10 July 1907.
[55] *Shrews. Chron.* 13 Sept. 1918 (obit.).
[56] Pelling, *Social Geog. of Brit. Elections*, 188, 193; *Bridgnorth Jnl.* 29 Jan. 1910.
[57] Notably the Coalbrookdale, Lilleshall, and Madeley Wood cos., C. & W. Walker, various tileries, brickworks, etc., of the Severn Gorge: *Kelly's Dir. Salop.* (1885); *V.C.H. Salop.* i. 442-4, 456, 467-8, 470-2, 477, 479.

Madeley there were over a thousand ironworkers and miners who were strong Liberal supporters.[58] By 1888 there were clubs at Broseley and St. George's affiliated to the Working Men's Club and Institute Union.[59] The division had a smaller population than the other three, and its electorate remained a smaller proportion of the population than in the others, never quite reaching 9,000. There was an abnormally low number of electors on a property qualification; they only once exceeded 400 whereas in each of the other three divisions there were over a thousand. The number of lodgers entitled to vote was at first low, but in time became the largest in the county.[60]

Nonconformity was strong in the urban areas, and in 1885 any Liberal candidate would have fared well. The candidate was A. H. Brown who had already sat for Much Wenlock for 17 years,[61] and his success was assured. Naturally no sitting Conservative member would take on such a hopeless seat, and it was thus in Wellington that Lt.-Col. W. S. Kenyon-Slaney, a landowner from the Newport division, fought his first election. He made a considerable impression but was beaten by nearly two to one.[62] In 1886 Brown became a Liberal Unionist and was unopposed. In 1892, as a supporter of Disestablishment,[63] he could not secure the full Conservative vote but seems to have kept a large proportion of the Liberal vote, winning by a fair margin in a small poll against a Gladstonian. There was a slight swing against Brown on a yet lower poll in 1900, but again he beat another Liberal by over a thousand votes.

Brown retired in 1906 after 38 years in the Commons, where latterly he was an influential member.[64] C. S. Henry, a Liberal from Australia,[65] came forward and beat Hildebrand Harmsworth, fifth of the celebrated brothers,[66] standing for the Conservatives. Both were strangers, though Henry had been renting a house in Wellington since at least 1905.[67] Henry kept his seat at the next three elections, on the last occasion, December 1910, beating Capt. the Hon. G. C. B. Weld-Forester. That was a notable result. The Conservatives may have erred in changing their candidate so often. Nevertheless, even allowing for the brevity of Weld-Forester's campaign, the fact that the son and heir of the last M.P. for Wenlock[68] actually achieved a slightly lower proportion of the vote than a stranger had done in January was a sign of changed times. Whatever was the case elsewhere in Shropshire, in the Wellington division the influence of even the greatest landed family was of little account by 1910. The Conservative share of the vote was higher than in the black year 1885, but the division had become a Liberal island in a Conservative sea. It was moreover ready to move further left; the Wellington Socialist Society had been formed in 1897.[69]

Ludlow (or Southern) Division

Ludlow was the most extensive Shropshire division and had the second largest electorate. It stretched from Clun Forest thirty miles eastwards to the Severn–Trent watershed near Wolverhampton. Electors on a property qualification numbered about 900 in an electorate of rather more than 10,000. In 1903 the largest groups of such electors were in Ludlow, Bridgnorth, Much Wenlock, Stokesay and Craven Arms, and Church Stretton, and the agricultural vote was then estimated at about two thirds

[58] Kelly's Dir. Salop. (1885; 1891); Pelling, op. cit. 193.
[59] Lib. and Radical Yr. Bk. 1888, 468.
[60] Ret. showing . . . Electors on Reg. . . . Pop. and Inh. Houses in each Constituency, H.C. 116 (1900), lxvii; H.C. 69 (1911), lxii; and intervening rets.
[61] Pelling, op. cit. 193; above, p. 342.
[62] Durnford, Kenyon-Slaney, 51–4.
[63] Pelling, op. cit. 193.
[64] A. Ellis, Heir of Adventure: the Story of Brown, Shipley & Co. (1960), 121, 144; Sir H. Clay, Ld. Norman

(1957), 52.
[65] W. Mate & Sons Ltd., Shropshire: Historical, Descriptive, Biographical (1906), pt. 2, p. 21.
[66] Burke, Peerage (1949), 954.
[67] i.e. the Brooklands, from the Instone fam. He was still renting it in 1917. See S.R.O. 1681, box 50, lease of 18 Jan. 1907; Kelly's Dir. Salop. (1905; 1917).
[68] Burke, Peerage (1949), 783.
[69] J. Beard, My Shropshire Days on Common Ways [1948], 67.

of the whole; until 1905 not more than ten lodgers were qualified as electors. Liberal support came from four particular groups: the quarrymen of the Clee Hills, the railwaymen of Craven Arms and other places, the Highley miners, and the Bridgnorth carpet weavers.[70] The last-named, like the rural labourers formerly in Much Wenlock parliamentary borough,[71] were not newly enfranchised, though neither group had voted in the old Southern division.

The 1885 redistribution ended the parliamentary careers of all but one of the M.P.s for Wenlock, Ludlow, and Bridgnorth. The two candidates in 1885,[72] Sir Baldwyn Leighton and R. J. More, had fought each other in 1880 for the old Southern division. Leighton now had the active support of some 80 members of the Bridgnorth Habitation of the Primrose League, formed in November 1885. T. M. Southwell, the leading Bridgnorth carpet manufacturer, campaigned strongly for More, and, mindful of the events of 1880, the mayor had the town hall barricaded, 53 Staffordshire police being kept on hand. In Ludlow the leading Liberal was Maj. Rodney Anderson, a relic of the 1840 borough election. Liberal emissaries were active in the villages, and More was returned by a majority of nearly 600 in a poll of under 9,000.

More became a Liberal Unionist in 1886 and was unopposed by the Conservatives for the rest of his life. In Bridgnorth the most notable convert to Unionism was T. M. Southwell, whose son W. L. Southwell subjected More's Gladstonian opponent to forceful questioning in 1892. More then had a runaway victory over a stranger. Locally the main issue in 1892 seems to have been Ireland.[73]

More's great success as an agricultural member can be judged from reports of his activity in the last year of his life. In February and April 1903 he held meetings to test farmers' reactions to R. W. Hanbury's proposal for local agricultural advisory committees,[74] after Hanbury's death laying Lord Onslow's proposal for local agricultural correspondents[75] before his constituents. In the autumn he tried hard to devote time to all parts of the division, dining with farmers' clubs[76] and, in the last month of his life, attending the Bridgnorth municipal banquet, spending some days among the Highley miners, and speaking at Craven Arms.[77] The *Bridgnorth Journal* found More's epitaph in words he had used at his first political meeting nearly forty years before: 'At the close of my career I could wish it to be said of me that I was not a bad kind of fellow, that I made a very good neighbour, and that I was a good farmer and a good farmer's friend'.[78] Those words help to explain why he kept his seat; to the tenant farmers' solid support were added More's county connexions, his national position in the Central Chamber of Agriculture since its inception nearly forty years before,[79] his fluent speaking style, and his readiness with the pen. The combination was irresistible.

The succession to More caused a problem, the only one of its kind in Shropshire produced by the Liberal split. Earlier in 1903, More having decided to retire, the divisional Conservative association, which supported him, and a member of the Liberal Unionist central organization had agreed that the national compact of 1886 still covered Ludlow. The candidate then selected was neither a Conservative nor a local man and after More's death he quickly withdrew. A prominent Liberal Unionist suggested that a Conservative should be run as a Liberal Unionist, and Rowland Hunt

[70] Sources cited in n. 60, above; Pelling, op. cit. 198–9; *The Times*, 16 and 18 Dec. 1903.

[71] Sir G. Leveson Gower, *Years of Content, 1858–1886* (1940), 211–12.

[72] For this para. see *Bridgnorth Jnl.* 14 and 21 Nov., 5 Dec. 1885; above, pp. 318, 337.

[73] *Bridgnorth Jnl.* 2 July 1892.

[74] Ibid. 21 Feb., 18 Apr. 1903.

[75] For Onslow's proposal see *The Times*, 17 July 1903.

[76] *Bridgnorth Jnl.* 19 Sept., 31 Oct., 7 Nov. 1903.

[77] Ibid. 14, 21, and 28 Nov. 1903.

[78] Ibid. 28 Nov. 1903. When More first spoke the words the *Jnl.* was his fierce opponent.

[79] A. H. H. Matthews, *Fifty Years of Agric. Politics . . . 1865–1915* (1915), pp. vii, 246, 257, 318, 352–3. He was its 2nd chmn. (1868–9): ibid. 416. Salop. sent 3 deputies to the Chamber; only 4 of the affiliated bodies sent more: ibid. 418–20.

of Boreatton agreed to stand, though he did not use the offending description in his election address. He was a former master of the Wheatland.[80] This was the period of Billson's Liberal revival and a Liberal candidate was already in the field in the person of Fred Horne, of Hinnington. As a tenant farmer[81] and member of the Chamber of Agriculture[82] he was a shrewd choice as candidate in succession to More. His brother Silvester, a leading Congregational minister in London,[83] helped in the campaign.[84] Hunt's selection does not seem to have offended local Liberal Unionists, but it angered a leading Conservative. Hunt was a Roman Catholic and the Evangelical Lord Forester refused his support, though his son agreed to lend his.[85] Apart from its sectarian overtones, the campaign was complicated by the Liberal Unionist split over tariff reform. It brought Horne unexpected support from J. Bowen-Jones, widely respected by the farmers, from the duke of Devonshire, Chamberlain's free-trader antagonist, and, too late to be of use, from the Liberal, free-trader Bishop Percival of Hereford.[86] T. M. Southwell asserted grandiloquently that the 'whole world' had watched the contest, 'the first . . . in which a rural constituency had given a vote on Mr. Chamberlain's views' which Hunt supported.[87] Farmers and labourers alike seem to have been unimpressed by free trade[88] and Horne was beaten by 970 votes.

In 1906 Hunt stood as a Conservative, beating Horne again, though by a slightly reduced majority. In Bridgnorth Hunt's main supporter was the leading Conservative and churchman, W. L. Southwell.[89] In January 1910 Hunt easily beat a new challenger who, like his agent, was a stranger. Church concern over Disestablishment and education was evident, and Hunt thought that Roman Catholic priests worked very hard for the Unionists throughout the county. Liberal enthusiasm, on the other hand, was considered much lower than in 1903 or 1906, especially among local nonconformists, and the Liberal candidate probably appealed too much to class dissensions.[90] Hunt was not opposed again. The 1903 by-election was one of the earliest in the country in which motor-cars were used to take voters to the poll,[91] and it was something of an innovation that peers from outside the county were brought in to speak in 1906 and 1910.[92]

Newport (or Northern) Division

The sprawling Newport constituency included the small towns of Whitchurch, Market Drayton, Wem, Newport, and Shifnal. It was largely agricultural, including good stock-rearing and dairying country in the north, but there was also a little industry on the fringe of the Wellington division. The division had the largest electorate in Shropshire, a high proportion of electors on a property qualification, and a small number of lodgers with the vote. Shrewsbury borough freeholders voted in the division and were doubtless largely Conservative.[93] On the other hand nonconformity and Radical politics went hand in hand among the rural labourers, notably in the heathlands around High Ercall.[94]

[80] *The Times*, 28 Dec. 1903 (letter of H. D. Greene, M.P. for Shrews.). For Hunt see obits. in *Shrews. Chron.* 3 Dec. 1943 and *Bridgnorth Jnl.* 4 Dec. 1943; *V.C.H. Salop.* ii. 170; *The Times*, 24 Dec. 1903 (for his mastership of the Wheatland).

[81] On Col. Kenyon-Slaney's estate: Durnford, *Kenyon-Slaney*, 58–65.

[82] *The Times*, 30 Nov. 1903.

[83] *Life of Chas. Silvester Horne*, ed. W. B. Selbie [1920]; *Who Was Who, 1897–1916*, 352. He conducted Billson's funeral: *The Times*, 15 July 1907.

[84] Selbie, op. cit. 177, 185–7 (stressing the issues raised by the 1902 Educ. Act).

[85] *Shrews. Chron.* 10 Dec. 1903. Ld. Forester's refusal

was welcomed by Horne: *The Times*, 19 Dec. 1903.

[86] *The Times*, 17–19 Dec. 1903; W. Temple, *Life of Bp. Percival* (1921), 235–41.

[87] *Bridgnorth Jnl.* 26 Dec. 1903.

[88] *The Times*, 18 and 22 Dec. 1903.

[89] *Bridgnorth Jnl.* 13 Jan. 1906.

[90] Ibid. 1 and 15 Jan. 1910; W. Suss. R.O., Leo Maxse papers, 461.

[91] *Bridgnorth Jnl.* 26 Dec. 1903.

[92] Ld. Beauchamp for Horne in 1906, Ld. Willoughby de Broke for Hunt in 1910: ibid. 13 Jan. 1906; 1 Jan. 1910.

[93] Pelling, op. cit. 198, 200; sources cited above, p. 346 n. 60.

[94] Beard, *My Shropshire Days*.

In 1885 it naturally fell to Lord Newport, the former Conservative M.P. for the old Northern division, to contest the constituency. The Liberals mounted a sustained attack which, to Lord Bradford's surprise,[95] succeeded. Robert Bickersteth won by some 350 votes. Newport, who thought his opponent 'very formidable from his moderation', believed that 'a very strong set' for his seat was made from Birmingham and that Bickersteth had Lord Granville's firm support.[96] Liberal enthusiasm was 'infectious', with men 'tramping through dark lanes' to Conservative meetings to 'stick up for Gladstone'. There was a serious riot at Market Drayton, and at Stanton upon Hine Heath intense feeling was aroused when the Radical vicar declared for the Conservatives because Bickersteth declined to support anti-ritualistic legislation.[97] Newport decided not to stand again and vainly hoped to be called up to the Lords in his father's lifetime.[98]

The Liberal split, however, was fatal to the party's newly won hold on the division. Bickersteth became a Liberal Unionist and did not stand in 1886. In March 1886 the Conservatives brought forward a formidable candidate, Lt.-Col. W. S. Kenyon-Slaney of Hatton Grange, a pillar of the Albrighton Hunt and soon to become Newport's brother-in-law.[99] Kenyon-Slaney had first realized his political gifts in 1880 and had fought a good campaign in the Wellington division in 1885. His record as an excellent landlord was questioned only at the height of party warfare, and in 1886 he crushed his opponent, a stranger. In 1892 he defeated, though by a smaller majority, a more dangerous local opponent, W. H. Lander of Tibberton, who fought in the tenant farmers' interest.[1] It seems that most of the farmers voted against Lander and many also influenced their labourers to do so; one of the arguments against him was that he had broken 'all the political traditions of his family'.[2]

Kenyon-Slaney was unopposed in 1895 and 1900. His military rank conceals a varied ancestry and connexion; he was by no means the bluff colonel who had unwittingly strayed into politics. His great-grandfather, Lord Kenyon, was lord chief justice 1788–1802.[3] His grandfather and uncle had chaired Shropshire quarter sessions for many years,[4] the uncle (J. R. Kenyon) being also Vinerian Professor of English Law at Oxford 1843–80;[5] his maternal grandfather was R. A. Slaney, a notable advocate of reform and Liberal M.P. for Shrewsbury.[6] Kenyon-Slaney himself was one of the best platform orators in England, endowed with a voice of 'astounding' power.[7] In the Commons he spoke frequently, but on subjects he knew. He sponsored a Pure Beer Bill[8] and moved the Kenyon-Slaney clause in the 1902 Education Act,[9] being perhaps the only Shropshire member to have a clause thus distinguished by his name.[10]

The Kenyon-Slaney clause may have lost him some local support, and in 1906 the many calls on his services as a speaker also contributed to the smallness of his majority (176).[11] Francis Neilson, however, was probably an abler opponent than Kenyon-Slaney had yet fought. A distant connexion of Gladstone[12] and doubtless another

[95] Hatfield Ho., MSS. of 3rd marquess of Salisbury, Bradford to Salisbury, 3 Nov. 1885.

[96] Ibid., Newport to Salisbury, 28 Dec. 1885.

[97] Beard, op. cit. 29, 98–100; *Shrews. Chron.* 4 Dec. 1885; 8 Jan. 1886. Bickersteth's father, bp. of Ripon, had been a noted Evangelical preacher: *D.N.B. sub* Bickersteth, Rob. (1816–84).

[98] Hatfield Ho., MSS. of 3rd marquess of Salisbury, Newport to Salisbury, 3 Nov. 1885.

[99] Durnford, *Kenyon-Slaney*, 39, 48–9, 54–5, 127–9, 138–9.

[1] Ibid. 41–3, 55–65; above, p. 346.

[2] Beard, op. cit. 80.

[3] *D.N.B.*

[4] See p. 360.

[5] J. Foster, *Alumni Oxonienses . . . 1715–1886*, ii. 789;

Hist. Reg. Univ. of Oxf. (1900), 64.

[6] See p. 325.

[7] Durnford, op. cit. 66–7, 77; H. W. Lucy, *Diary of the Unionist Parl.* (1900), 128, 173.

[8] Durnford, op. cit. 76–7; 39 *Parl. Deb.* 4th ser. 99–105, 130. For the agricultural significance of such a measure see *S.C.C. Mins.* Joint Cttee. of S.C.C. and Salop. Chamber of Agric. rep. 28 July 1894, 67–8.

[9] 2 Edw. VII, c. 42, s. 7(6).

[10] The clause corresponded to his views (Durnford, op. cit. 56), but was presumably moved at govt. request: A. S. T. Griffith-Boscawen, *Fourteen Yrs. in Parl.* (1907), 246.

[11] Durnford, op. cit. 58–9, 65–6, 83.

[12] F. Neilson, *My Life in Two Worlds* (Appleton, Wis.), i(1952), 16, 243–4.

product of Billson's energy,[13] he had been candidate for Newport since 1902 and knew the division well from his schooldays.[14] An able speaker on subjects which interested him,[15] he was, like Kenyon-Slaney, adept at dealing with hecklers.[16]

Kenyon-Slaney immediately set about a reorganization of his constituency party. A permanent organizing secretary was appointed and addressed over 70 village meetings in the winter of 1907–8 and circulated a monthly magazine to the electors.[17] Those efforts were rewarded when Kenyon-Slaney died in 1908, for Neilson had continued to nurse the division.[18] Kenyon-Slaney's successor was Beville Stanier of Peplow Hall, new owner of the *Shrewsbury Chronicle* and an experienced farmer later to become active in the Central Chamber of Agriculture.[19] During the campaign many party workers on both sides came into the division after an important Wolverhampton by-election, and the Liberals held up to thirty meetings a night. Neilson was credited with the nonconformist vote and was thought to have a majority in the villages, but the suffragettes opposed him and the Licensing Bill probably did him great harm. Stanier won by 951 votes. Neilson complained that 'apart from the personalities' Shrewsbury had been 'a millstone' round his neck. Stanier owed his victory to the Shrewsbury freeholders and to the voters in Market Drayton, Newport, Wem, and Whitchurch, especially the last named which had been 'a great Radical stronghold' in 1906. Conservative majorities among the Shrewsbury freeholders and the electors of the small towns thus sufficed to offset a Liberal majority in the villages and among the miners and ironworkers of Priorslee, canvassed for Neilson by various Labour M.P.s.[20]

Stanier increased his majority against a fresh Liberal candidate in January 1910 and was unopposed in December. The division was thus always Conservative except in its first year of existence.

Oswestry (or Western) Division

The Oswestry division between 1885 and 1918 was curiously shaped, extending from the Flintshire border round the outskirts of Shrewsbury almost to Much Wenlock. Oswestry, with over 2,000 electors, and Ellesmere were its only towns. The division was predominantly agricultural, though there were miners at Oswestry and Snailbeach and Cambrian Railway men at Oswestry. The electorate was slightly smaller than those of the Newport and Ludlow divisions. Between 1900 and 1910 the number of electors on a property qualification varied from 1,316 to 1,494, or about 12 per cent of the total of 10,000 or more. Until 1906 the division had more lodgers on the roll than the other three divisions combined, and their number doubled between 1904 and 1905, perhaps owing to Billson's activities.[21] It was the one English division, apart from Monmouthshire, with a sizeable Welsh-speaking population,[22] concentrated near Oswestry itself. The nonconformist Welshmen, with the miners and railwaymen, provided the nucleus of Liberal support in the division. Except between 1904 and 1906, however, it was represented by Conservatives.

Stanley Leighton, M.P. for the old Northern division, naturally fought the new division in 1885, though the president of the divisional Conservative association, the 2nd Lord Harlech, was not on good terms with him[23] until 1896.[24] Leighton, though he

[13] Neilson, op. cit. i. 242–3, 278.
[14] Ibid. 1, 5–14, 17–19, 234, 272–4.
[15] Free trade and land-value taxation: ibid. 239–42, 244–8.
[16] Ibid. 275–9.   [17] *The Times*, 11–12 May 1908.
[18] Neilson, op. cit. i. 275, 284.
[19] Mate, *Shropshire*, pt. 2, p. 58; *Through Nine Reigns, 200 Years of The Shrews. Chron.* (Bi-Centenary Souvenir, 23 Nov. 1972), 52; Matthews, *Fifty Years of Agric.*

Politics, 65, 367.
[20] *The Times*, 5–8 and 11–16 May 1908; Neilson, op. cit. i. 247–8, 259, 274, 284.
[21] Sources cited above, p. 346 n. 60.
[22] Pelling, op. cit. 199.
[23] Owing, no doubt, to the events of 1876: see p. 323.
[24] Reconciliation noted in Leighton's obit.: *Shrews. Chron.* 10 May 1901.

did not endear himself to Radical Welshmen, took a constant and genuine interest in the affairs of Wales[25] and was chairman of the Clergy Defence Committee during the 1887–9 Welsh tithe riots.[26] In 1885 Leighton fought largely on one of the two dominant national questions, Disestablishment.[27] The issue could hardly have been exploited to the same extent in any other English constituency. In one with a Welsh nonconformist element, however, there were clearly extra votes to be garnered from Anglicans, and in that gloomy year for Shropshire Conservatives Leighton won by almost a thousand.

In 1887, after eleven years in Parliament, Leighton sought a colonial governorship from Salisbury[28] but in vain. Opposed only in 1895, he stayed in the Commons until his death in 1901, taking part less frequently in debates[29] and exercising a 'curious gift' of 'looking as if he were saying something pointed'.[30] Through 'honest animosity' to Gladstone he developed a habit of interrupting him and became known as 'the man from Shropshire'.[31]

When Leighton died A. H. Bright, an advanced Liberal, was quickly chosen as candidate, having been active in the constituency some months. Bright, a remote connexion of Gladstone, came like Billson from Liverpool, where he had business interests.[32] In 1901 he had a house near Oswestry.[33] The Conservatives chose Lord Harlech's heir, the Hon. G. R. C. Ormsby-Gore; the tenant farmers had expected to be consulted but were mollified by the news that their man would not stand.[34] Ormsby-Gore, aided by Kenyon-Slaney, won easily in a short, strenuous campaign. Bright's chances in an area strongly represented in the K.S.L.I. in South Africa had not been improved by a visit to Oswestry of Lloyd George, then strongly anti-war.[35] By coincidence[36] the yeomanry were training in Harlech's park, but they were kept in camp and there were no incidents; voters only were allowed out, in mufti.[37]

Bright nursed the constituency assiduously, and three years later Ormsby-Gore succeeded as 3rd Lord Harlech. W. C. Bridgeman, of Leigh Manor, became the Conservative candidate,[38] and the Liberals had a second chance under Billson's reorganization. The 1904 by-election[39] saw 'almost unparalleled activity' on both sides. Both parties held forty to fifty meetings in one week towards the end of the campaign, and each strove to bring in numerous outside speakers such as Henry Chaplin and Winston Churchill. Conservative M.P.s and Liberal candidates for other Shropshire divisions appeared regularly. Feelings ran high and amid 'wild disorder' at Oswestry market Conservative farmers broke up a Free Trade Union meeting; it was only one of several violent incidents. Personalities were sharp; Bridgeman was angered by a denial that he was a Shropshire man, Bright by an accusation that he employed lascars on his ships.

Bridgeman was a protectionist, Bright a free-trader, and the food issue brought in the national pressure groups. Nevertheless local bodies, such as the Oswestry Trades and Labour Council which was unanimous for Bright, perhaps had more effect. The

[25] K. O. Morgan, *Wales in Brit. Politics, 1868–1922* (1970), 89, 96, 100, 131, 176.

[26] Pelling, op. cit. 199, n. 5; S.R.O. 1060/318–448.

[27] Pelling, op. cit. 199.

[28] Hatfield Ho., MSS. of 3rd marquess of Salisbury, Leighton to Salisbury, 4 Feb., 11 Dec. 1887.

[29] *Shrews. Chron.* 10 May 1901.

[30] H. W. Lucy, *Diary of Home Rule Parl.* (1896), 267.

[31] In allusion to Gridley the Chancery suitor's conduct in *Bleak House* (ch. 1): *Shrews. Chron.* 10 May 1901. The sobriquet was variously attributed to Ld. E. FitzMaurice and Sir G. Trevelyan: Lucy, *Diary of the Salisbury Parl.* (1892), 80; idem, *Home Rule Parl.* 266.

[32] *The Times,* 9 and 13 May 1901; 28 July 1904.

[33] Ibid. 13 May 1901.

[34] Ibid. 11 and 18 May 1901. The farmers' man was J. Bowen-Jones.

[35] Ibid. 13–15, 17–18, 20–25, and 27 May 1901; Durnford, *Kenyon-Slaney,* 59.

[36] In the 18th cent. it would have been welcomed or contrived.

[37] E. W. Gladstone, *Shropshire Yeomanry, 1795–1945* (1953), 169, 172–3. Ormsby-Gore was a yeomanry officer.

[38] *The Times,* 27 June, 1–2 July 1904. Bridgeman had been mentioned, with Ld. Newport, as a possible candidate in 1901: ibid. 9 May 1901.

[39] Ibid. 2–28 July 1904.

Liberals were thought to benefit from a miners' strike at Hanwood and from a split among the 400 innkeepers of the division when the Shropshire Free Licence-holders Association came out for Bright in opposition to the 'brewers' Bill' sponsored by Balfour's government. Liberal organization was good; the party's preparations had been far advanced and they 'flooded' the constituency with 'special organizers'.

Voters in Oswestry itself were thought to be fairly evenly divided. Both candidates devoted much time to the south of the division where the Liberals had been weak, and Bridgeman had taken care to be seconded by a supporter representing that end of the division. On polling day there was another sign of good Liberal organization; Bright had twenty motor cars, slightly more than Bridgeman, though Bridgeman had more carriages. To general surprise the Liberals, armed with 'pictures of Chinese slaves in chains and the big and little loaf',[40] won by 385 votes, taking a Shropshire agricultural seat for the only time since 1885.

Bridgeman, cousin to Lord Bradford and a remoter kinsman of the 3rd earl of Powis,[41] was thus connected with the two families which had dominated the two county divisions before 1885. He was re-adopted a week after his defeat,[42] and improvements to divisional party organization were begun before the end of the year.[43] In 1906 he turned the tables on Bright, beating him by 503 votes. He won both 1910 elections, when the National Conservative League was strong in the constituency.[44]

Shrewsbury

Shrewsbury was the only Shropshire seat held by the Conservatives throughout the period. Extension of the franchise in 1884 made little difference to the size and composition of the borough electorate which included a large and powerful middle-class element. There were 4,000–4,800 electors, about 90 per cent qualified on the occupation franchise, very few as lodgers or freemen.[45]

There was a reversal of fortune at Shrewsbury in 1885. In 1880 only 45·5 per cent of the vote had gone to the Conservatives; in 1885, however, they polled 59·8 per cent, the gap between the parties being wider than at any other election of the period. Parnell had directed Irish voters to support the Conservatives,[46] but there were probably few in Shrewsbury, where most Irish lived 'by the most precarious means'.[47] The reversal may have been partly due to a change of Liberal candidate; of the two former M.P.s, Cotes retired from Parliament and Robertson was elected for Merionethshire.[48] The new Liberal candidate, Charles Waring,[49] was beaten by James Watson, a Birmingham businessman who had bought Lord Denbigh's Berwick estate in 1875.[50] Watson was returned again next year by a slightly smaller majority in an oddly low poll.

Probably as a result of those two defeats the Shrewsbury Liberal Association was said to be 'practically *non est*' in 1887, though there was a ward association in Ditherington. Associations were revived or formed in the next two years,[51] but such moves met with no parliamentary success. In 1892 'for once' the borough 'made an attempt at electoral purity'[52] and, perhaps in consequence,[53] there was a low poll. The Conservative winner

[40] Durnford, op. cit. 60.
[41] Relationships obliquely referred to in Pelling, op. cit. 199–200. Cf. Burke, *Peerage* (1949), 246–7, 254, 1630–1.
[42] *The Times*, 5 Aug. 1904.
[43] See the first issue (1904) of *The Oswestry and W. Shropshire Conservative*, a monthly mag. edited by the local agent: S.R.O. 3029/3.
[44] *The Times*, 26 Jan. 1910; Pelling, op. cit. 200. See also S.R.O. 1930/3–16, 18–21, 23–4.
[45] Sources cited above, p. 346 n. 60; Pelling, op. cit. 188, 191.
[46] *Shrews. Chron.* 27 Nov. 1885.
[47] J. Denvir, *Irish in Brit.* (1892), 411.
[48] *T.S.A.S.* 4th ser. xii. 262, 265.
[49] F. Boase, *Modern Eng. Biog.* iii. 1201; Burke, *Land. Gent.* (1898), 1545.
[50] *T.S.A.S.* 4th ser. xii. 265–6; S.R.O. 450/31/3 (withdrawn); S.R.O. 643/1; *Shrews. Chron.* 16 Oct. 1885; *Eddowes's Jnl.* 19 Jan. 1876; 25 Nov., 2 Dec. 1885; 28 Apr. 1886.
[51] *Lib. and Radical Yr. Bk.* 1887–8. [52] Pelling, op. cit. 191.
[53] Beard, *My Shropshire Days*, 6–7.

was H. D. Greene, the new recorder of Ludlow; he was unopposed in 1895 and 1900.[54]

The election of Greene's Conservative successor in 1906 cannot be understood without reference to the endemic[55] corruption of Shrewsbury politics. E. G. Hemmerde, a young barrister,[56] became Liberal candidate for Shrewsbury during Billson's re-organization. A Liverpool man and a not too scrupulous opportunist,[57] Hemmerde was a bird of passage much after the fashion of the Tory barristers who had stood for Shrewsbury half a century earlier. In 1903 he had appeared in Shrewsbury as counsel for Liberal petitioners against a result in the 1902 municipal elections. The petition's success, however, rebounded on him and his party. The public revelation of extensive corruption by both parties, and perhaps too the prospect of losing an established system of bribery, had been resented in the town. Accordingly the electors kept Hemmerde out in 1906; when the Liberals did so well elsewhere,[58] the Conservative share of the vote in Shrewsbury fell by a mere 0·6 per cent from that obtained in 1892. If Billson had been behind the petition, he had evidently made a mistake. It should also be noted, however, that Hemmerde's Conservative opponent, Sir Clement Lloyd Hill, who had made a successful career in the diplomatic service,[59] was well connected locally. Nephew of the 2nd Lord Hill (d. 1875), he came of a family historically linked with Shrewsbury politics; more significantly perhaps, he was cousin to Kenyon-Slaney, the Newport M.P.[60]

Hill held his seat easily at both 1910 elections. In December his last-minute opponent was Thomas Pace, a Shrewsbury builder and a Lib.-Lab. candidate,[61] the first to stand for Labour in Shropshire politics. G. Butler Lloyd of Shelton Hall, who was brought forward by the Shrewsbury Conservatives on Hill's death in 1913,[62] also had local roots; a Shrewsbury alderman and former mayor, he was a native of Monkmoor and in 1880 had married the grand-daughter of Sir Richard Jenkins, M.P. for Shrewsbury 1837–41.[63] His victory over J. R. Morris saw the Conservative share of the vote grow to 58·3 per cent. Thus on the eve of the First World War victory for a Conservative candidate with really local roots was as predictable as it had been unexpected in 1885.

In 1904, speaking at Oswestry, A. H. Bright described the county as 'sick unto death of the domination of the Tory squires'.[64] He spoke too soon. Obvious characteristics of the generation after 1885 were the continued domination of the three more agricultural divisions by well established county families, and the stable and traditional political habits of the county after the short-lived upset of 1885.

The decrease in the number of Shropshire members sent up to Westminster produced no decline in the quality of the county's representation in Parliament. It is possible that Shropshire had never been so well represented as in the years when the Oswestry, Newport, and Ludlow divisions returned local squires, the varying abilities, however idiosyncratic, of R. J. More,[65] Stanley Leighton,[66] W. S. Kenyon-Slaney,[67] and W. C. Bridgeman[68] bearing comparison with those of any of their predecessors.

[54] T.S.A.S. 4th ser. xii. 266.
[55] Rep. R. Com. on Poor Laws, App. XVII [Cd. 4690], pp. 195, 200, H.C. (1909), xliii.
[56] Who Was Who, 1941–50, 527.
[57] Neilson, My Life in Two Worlds, i. 304–8.
[58] Shrews. Mun. Election Petition [Cd. 1541], H.C. (1903), lv; Pelling, op. cit. 191 (omitting mention of Lib. bribery), 225, 429; Shrews. Chron. 23 Jan.–6 Feb. 1903.
[59] T.S.A.S. 4th ser. xii. 267.
[60] Burke, Peerage (1949), 1011, 1114. In 1889 Hill had marr. the widow of Chas. Waring, the 1885 Lib. candidate: The Times, 10 Apr. 1913 (obit.).
[61] See Shrews. Chron. 7 Apr. 1933 (obit.).
[62] Ibid. 18 Apr. 1913.
[63] T.S.A.S. 4th ser. xii. 268; Shrews. Chron. 4 Apr. 1930 (obit.). For his county connexions see above, p. 145, n. 87.
[64] The Times, 28 July 1904.   [65] Ibid. 27 Nov. 1903.
[66] Ibid. 6 May 1901; D.N.B. 1901–11; Montg. Coll. xxxii. 151–4; S.P.R. Heref. vi, pp. vii–x and frontispiece (obits. and photos.).
[67] The Times, 25 Apr. 1908; Shrews. Chron. 1 May 1908.
[68] The Times, 15 Aug. 1935.

1918-74

IN 1918 the five Shropshire constituencies were reduced to four, and for the first time the county was represented in the Commons proportionately to its population.[69] Shrewsbury borough constituency was replaced by a new county division of the same name and the Newport division disappeared. Other changes gathered the industrial area of Shropshire more than before into one parliamentary division. On the other hand rural parishes which had not previously voted with Shrewsbury borough were included in the Shrewsbury division, and more rural parishes than the Wellington division had contained were added to the Wrekin.[70] In each case a partly middle-class and partly industrial constituency was diluted with a fairly small rural electorate.

The electorates of the new constituencies were by no means equal in size. Before the Second World War the Wrekin and Oswestry divisions had markedly larger electorates than the Shrewsbury and Ludlow divisions, although the discrepancy between the Shrewsbury and Oswestry divisions had become much smaller by 1945. By then the Ludlow electorate was much the smallest in the county, the Wrekin much the largest.[71] That imbalance was corrected in 1948[72] when Much Wenlock borough was transferred to Ludlow county constituency. The borough included Madeley and Broseley, and the industrial population of Ludlow constituency was thus slightly increased at the expense of the Wrekin's, though without altering markedly the different social and political characteristics of the two constituencies. The 1948 redistribution left Oswestry the most populous Shropshire constituency, but in the early 1960s it was overtaken by the Wrekin.

Changes made in 1970 left Shropshire still with four county constituencies, a more generous representation than its population then warranted. The boundaries of all four were altered.[73] With one exception the changes were of little consequence, designed only to bring constituency boundaries into line with alterations to the county boundary (1965)[74] and to the urban and rural districts and civil parishes (1966). Paradoxically the effect of the most important change was to reduce the electorate of the smallest constituency, Ludlow, by increasing that of the largest, the Wrekin. Besides Little Wenlock, Ludlow lost to the Wrekin a populous area of old industry and new development which had been absorbed by Dawley U.D. in 1966: Coalbrookdale, Ironbridge, and Madeley, with the facing south bank of the Severn taken from Benthall and Broseley. Ludlow gained Stockton and Sutton Maddock from the Wrekin,[75] but the changes represented a net loss to Ludlow and a net gain to the Wrekin of some 8,700 electors on the 1971–2 register.[76]

At the 1918 general election Rowland Hunt retired from Parliament. His seat at Ludlow went to Sir Beville Stanier, newly created a baronet, who had lost his seat at Newport by the redistribution. The other three members were returned for their old seats. The Coalition 'coupon' carried all four seats and only G. Butler Lloyd at Shrewsbury and W. C. Bridgeman at Oswestry were opposed, both by Labour candidates. In the Wrekin division, where Labour's main strength in the county was to

[69] Except where otherwise stated the rest of this section, completed 1974–5, is based on F. W. S. Craig, *Brit. Parl. Election Results, 1918–1949* (1969); Craig, *Brit. Parl. Election Results, 1950–70* (1971); *The Times Guide to the Ho. of Commons Feb. 1974*; *The Times Guide to the Ho. of Commons Oct. 1974*.

[70] Rep. of the People Act, 1918, 8 & 9 Geo. V, c. 64; map on p. 344, above.

[71] 35,990 and 55,158 respectively. Shrews. was 46,854, Oswestry 48,719.

[72] Rep. of the People Act, 1948, 11 & 12 Geo. VI, c. 65.

[73] *Boundary Com. Eng.: 2nd Periodical Rep.* [Cmnd. 4084], pp. 28, 55, 113–14, H.C. (1968–9), xxvi; *Parl. Constituencies (Eng.) Order, 1970* (Stat. Instr. 1970, no. 1674); S.R.O. 2320, 2497.

[74] *V.C.H. Salop.* ii. 204; S.R.O. 3267/16.

[75] *V.C.H. Salop.* ii. 235–7; S.R.O. 1751/1–2; S.R.O. 2981, parcel 6.

[76] S.R.O. 2497/2, pp. 415D, 461–518; 3, pp. 536–41.

lie, Sir Charles Henry (cr. bt. 1911), the Coalition Liberal and a strong partisan of Lloyd George,[77] was unopposed.

During the next half century, in good years for their party, the Shropshire Conservatives took all four seats. The Liberals, who ran candidates intermittently, were successful only once, in 1923. In good years for their party Labour members were returned for the Wrekin, though the seat did not always go to the party of the incoming government at a general election.[78]

Labour first contested the Wrekin at a by-election in 1920 caused by Henry's death, but their candidate was defeated by Charles Palmer, an Independent who died just over eight months later. In November 1920 Labour put up the same candidate again[79] but again he was defeated by another Independent, the distinguished soldier, Maj.-Gen. Sir Charles Townshend.[80] The Conservatives won a Ludlow by-election early in 1922, and their local organization was better prepared than those of the two other parties for the general election later that year. Labour ran two candidates and the Liberals three, but the Conservatives won all four seats. In 1923, however, the Conservatives lost two seats, suffering their heaviest defeat in Shropshire since 1885. Despite differences between the president of its Liberal association, Lord Acton, and the Liberal candidate, Joseph Sunlight,[81] the Shrewsbury division returned Sunlight, a Manchester architect of Russian Jewish extraction,[82] as the county's last Liberal M.P. The Wrekin returned Henry Nixon as the county's first Labour member; there the sitting Conservative, H. S. Button, had withdrawn through disagreement with Baldwin over Protection[83] and been replaced by a local colliery owner.[84] In three-cornered fights the Conservatives might have held both seats, but the Liberals had been dissuaded from running a candidate in the Wrekin by Labour threats to run a candidate in Shrewsbury.[85] The Conservatives regained both seats in 1924 when their candidate for the Wrekin was a working man with local connexions.[86]

From 1929 Shropshire tended to vote in accordance with national trends at general elections, and there is no need to continue a chronological account. The Conservatives remained the dominant Shropshire party, especially in the 1930s and 1950s, decades of Liberal eclipse. Only the Conservatives contested every seat throughout the period, winning all four at the general elections of 1931, 1935, 1955, 1959, 1964, and 1970. In 1931, four times in the 1950s, and in 1970 they took over half the county's votes, securing their highest share, 59·3 per cent, in 1955 against Labour candidates only. The Liberals' efforts after 1918 were spasmodic; the 1929 general election was the only occasion before that of 1964 when they contested all Shropshire seats. Their challenge was most consistent in Oswestry and Shrewsbury, where, before and after the Second World War, Labour fared worst. Labour did best in the Wrekin, contested by the Liberals at only one by-election and one general election between Henry's death in 1919 and 1964. The Wrekin was the only Shropshire seat ever held by the Labour party, which won it at seven general elections between 1929 and 1974. In 1930–1 the Wrekin Divisional Labour Party helped to form the Federation of Shropshire Labour Parties, partly to concentrate on county-council representation.[87] The federation, however,

[77] R. Douglas, 'Classification of M.P.s elected in 1918', *Bull. Inst. Hist. Res.* xlvii. 92; T. Wilson, *Downfall of Lib. Party, 1914–1935* (1966), 86, 104, 114.

[78] e.g. 1951 and 1964.

[79] C. Duncan. See *Who Was Who, 1929–40*, 391.

[80] Heir presumptive (1889–1916) to the 6th Marquess Townshend: *D.N.B.* 1922–30.

[81] *Shrews. Chron.* 9 Feb., Oct.–Nov. 1923; cf. S.R.O. 1093, corresp. nos. 859, 874, 909. Acton was evidently more disposed than Sunlight to co-operation with Lab.:

ibid. nos. 906, 917, 919, 921.

[82] *Shrews. Chron.* 3 and 10 Nov. 1922; *Through Nine Reigns, 200 Years of The Shrews. Chron.* (Bi-Centenary Souvenir, 23 Nov. 1972), 53; *Who's Who, 1976*, 2306.

[83] *The Times*, 21–2 Nov. 1923.

[84] A. N. Fielden. See *V.C.H. Salop.* viii. 280.

[85] *The Times*, 22 Nov. 1923. Cf. above, n. 81.

[86] T. Oakley: see p. 357.

[87] S.R.O. 3251/1, pp. 28, 43, 47–8, 74.

soon lapsed[88] and Labour remained weak in the rest of the county, a conference of the four parties seeming 'not all that important' to one national Labour leader in 1967.[89]

Between the wars Labour's consistent performance in the Wrekin seems to have owed more to the loyalty of Labour voters than to party organization. From 1928, it is true, the divisional party was able to afford a paid organizing secretary, but only because Edith Picton-Turbervill (candidate 1925–9 and 1931–4, M.P. 1929–31)[90] could subsidize its administrative expenses. After the 1931 general election registered membership of the divisional party, always low, dropped below 500 approaching half of its 1925 level, and the secretary had to be paid off when the candidate's annual subsidy ceased later that year.[91] The divisional party could make only a small contribution to election expenses,[92] and Edith Picton-Turbervill and G. T. Garratt (candidate 1934–6)[93] had to bear most of those expenses themselves.[94]

By 1931, relatively late, Labour had displaced the Liberals as the main opposition party in the county. Figures from the four general elections[95] contested by the three national parties throughout Shropshire (Table IV) suggest that Liberal decline

TABLE IV

Percentages of Shropshire Votes cast at four General Elections

	1929	1964	Feb. 1974	Oct. 1974
Conservative	46·3	47·9	43·1	43·0
Labour	25·3	34·1	31·1	33·2
Liberal	28·4	18·0	25·8	23·8

slightly strengthened Conservative dominance. At general elections after 1931 no Liberal candidate came second in any Shropshire constituency until February 1974. In that election, however, the Liberal candidate came second everywhere but the Wrekin, an achievement foreshadowed in Shropshire, as elsewhere,[96] by by-election results in the 1960s.[97] In October 1974 the Liberals again came second in Ludlow[98] and Shrewsbury and almost succeeded in doing so in Oswestry. In Shropshire, Liberal revival then seemed to be leading to a more equal division of votes between all three national parties.

After almost half a century of universal adult suffrage[99] it might be questioned whether Shropshire still had a separately identifiable political life. In most of the county, however, there remained an unusually strong preference for local candidates, though the minority parties in each constituency did not always bear that in mind in their selections. First in Wellington and then in the Wrekin the possession or lack of local roots seemed to make little or no discernible difference to candidates of any party after 1906. Henry, the last Liberal to represent the division (1906–19), had no local

[88] Efforts to revive it were made in 1932 and 1935: ibid., pp. 132, 151, 304, 309.
[89] R. H. S. Crossman, *Diaries of a Cabinet Minister*, ii (1976), 415. Cf. *Shropshire Star*, 10–11 July 1967.
[90] S.R.O. 3251/1, pp. 281–2; *Express & Star*, 7 May 1934.
[91] S.R.O. 3251/1, pp. 92–5, 111 (ann. rep. for 1931), 168 (ann. rep. for 1932), 228 (ann. rep. for 1933). The 1925 membership (800) was said in 1934 to be the 'highest point ever before reached'.
[92] Ibid., pp. 86, 323.
[93] Ibid., pp. 250, 265, 270–1, 338. Garratt was a retired

Indian civil servant from Teignmouth (Devon).
[94] Ibid., pp. 83, 86, 109–10, 125, 135, 238–40, 323.
[95] All returned Lab. to something short of real national power.
[96] *By-Elections in Brit. Politics*, ed. C. Cooke and J. Ramsden (1973), 198–221.
[97] Libs. came second at Ludlow in 1960 and Oswestry in 1961, the only Salop. by-elections since 1941.
[98] Where their share of the vote increased, against the national trend.
[99] Since the passing of the Rep. of the People (Equal Franchise) Act, 1928, 18 & 19 Geo. V, c. 12.

connexions,[1] nor did the two Independents who followed him, Palmer (1920) and Townshend (1920-2). Palmer indeed, like Henry nine years before,[2] beat a seemingly strong local candidate: John Bayley, who stood for the Coalition, was a personal friend of Lloyd George and had forty years of public service in the county to his credit.[3] Palmer and Townshend were put up for the seat by the notorious demagogue and swindler, Horatio Bottomley, whose Independent Parliamentary Group they joined. Palmer was Bottomley's assistant editor of *John Bull*.[4] In 1922, when Bottomley's ruin was about to be accomplished as a result of a sensational Shrewsbury trial,[5] Townshend hinted to Lord Forester, president of the local Conservative association, that he would be 'proud' to continue to represent the division, in future as a Conservative.[6] No invitation, however, was made. In the half century after 1922 the Wrekin was represented by six Conservative and four Labour members. All but one of the Conservatives were business or professional men without local connexions.[7] The exception, Thomas Oakley (1924-9), was a London railwayman who had been born at Prees[8] and was one of the three working men to have represented the constituency. The other two were Labour. Henry Nixon (1923-4) was a trade-union leader from the north-east of England[9] and I. O. Thomas (1945-55), from south Wales, was an official of the National Union of Railwaymen.[10] The two other Labour members were Edith Picton-Turbervill (1929-31),[11] the only woman to have represented a Shropshire constituency, and G. T. Fowler (1966-70, re-elected twice in 1974), a university don. Edith Picton-Turbervill is credited with having been the first woman M.P. to be entirely responsible for introducing and securing the passing of an Act of Parliament.[12] Fowler was the first Shropshire Labour member to be appointed to a ministerial post,[13] and he involved himself in local as well as parliamentary politics.[14]

The principle of Shropshire men for Shropshire seats was seldom forgotten in the three other constituencies. In 1922 a local paper noted that both the Conservative and the Liberal candidates for Shrewsbury had to overcome the obstacle of not being local men. For Lord Sandon, the Conservative candidate, however, things were doubly difficult, for some local Conservatives resented the way in which the former member, G. Butler Lloyd, had been 'jettisoned'.[15] Nevertheless the members for Shrewsbury were usually strangers[16] until 1945 when the division returned Lt.-Cdr. J. A. Langford Holt (knighted 1962), born and educated in Shrewsbury and grandson of a former mayor of the borough.[17] The Conservatives of the other two constituencies showed a continued aversion from carpet-baggers. W. C. Bridgeman[18] sat for Oswestry from 1906 to 1929, finishing his career as Home Secretary under Bonar Law and Baldwin

[1] See p. 346.

[2] See p. 346.

[3] *The Times*, 23 Jan., 7 and 21 Feb. 1920; *V.C.H. Salop.* ii. 163; above, p. 186.

[4] J. Symons, *Horatio Bottomley* (1955), 220-1. The 1941 Wrekin by-election may have revived memories of Bottomley. His friend N. Pemberton Billing, another First World War demagogue, broke the party truce, as he had in 1916, to urge all-out bombing of Germany: ibid. 187, 217; Cooke and Ramsden, *By-Elections in Brit. Politics*, 166, 171-2. He won more votes in the Wrekin than in his other contests in 1941.

[5] That of Reuben Bigland at Salop. assizes for incitement to blackmail: *Shrews. Chron.* 24 Feb. 1922.

[6] Ibid. 17 Feb. 1922.

[7] H. S. Button (1922-3), Col. J. Baldwin-Webb (1931-40), W. A. Colegate (1941-5), Capt. W. Yates (1955-66), and Dr. J. A. P. Trafford (1970-4). See *Who Was Who, 1929-40*, 56; *1941-50*, 174; *1951-60*, 228-9; *Who's Who, 1974*, 3293-4, 3621; Burke, *Land. Gent.* (1952), 489.

[8] *Who Was Who, 1929-40*, 1014.

[9] Ibid. 1005.

[10] *Who's Who, 1974*, 3238-9.

[11] Formerly Picton-Warlow. See *Who Was Who, 1951-60*, 875; Burke, *Land. Gent.* (1952), 2564.

[12] The Sentence of Death (Expectant Mothers) Act, 1931, 21 & 22 Geo. V, c. 24: S.R.O. 3251/1, pp. 32, 36-7, 282; Edith Picton-Turbervill, *Life is Good* (1939), 202-9.

[13] *Who's Who, 1975*, 1096; Crossman, *Diaries of a Cabinet Minister*, ii. 436.

[14] As leader of Wrekin Dist. Council.

[15] *Shrews. Chron.* 17 Nov. 1922.

[16] Ld. Sandon (1922-3, 1924-9) was heir apparent to the earldom of Harrowby and landed estates in Staffs. and Glos., G. A. V. Duckworth (1929-45) a West Country man. See Burke, *Peerage* (1967), 1189; Burke, *Land Gent.* (1952), 699. For Sunlight (1923-4) see above, p. 355.

[17] *Shrews. Chron.* 25 May, 1 June 1945. His grandfather founded a Shrews. business c. 1870 and was mayor 1890-1: *Industries of Shropshire (and District) Business Review* [1891], pp. 5, 17 (copy in S.P.L.).

[18] See pp. 351-2.

(1922–4) and First Lord of the Admiralty under Baldwin (1924–9). He was made a viscount in 1929,[19] and for the next sixteen years the member for Oswestry was Maj. B. E. P. Leighton of Sweeney Hall, whose father had sat for the Northern and Oswestry divisions 1876–1901.[20] In 1935 Leighton was the last Shropshire Conservative to be given an unopposed return. His successor, Col. O. B. S. Poole (1945–50), was a stranger to the division,[21] but from 1950 to 1961 the member was the Hon. W. D. Ormsby-Gore, grandson of the member for Oswestry division 1901–4.[22] In 1961, after five successful years as a junior Foreign Office minister, Ormsby-Gore, a connexion by marriage of the British prime minister and of the American president,[23] was appointed ambassador to the United States of America.[24] His successor as member for Oswestry was W. J. Biffen, an economist and businessman[25] and eventually a leading right-wing Conservative;[26] he made his home in the constituency.[27]

Fidelity to ancient ties was even more marked in the Ludlow division which for over twenty years after Stanier's death, was represented by Clives: Lord Windsor (1922–3) and his father's cousin George Windsor-Clive (1923–45).[28] The next member, Lt.-Col. Uvedale Corbett of Stableford, was the first since 1885 to come from the Bridgnorth side of the division. The senior branch of his family, seated at Longnor, had already produced three leading Shropshire politicians.[29] Corbett's successor in 1951, C. J. Holland-Martin, a prominent banker and member of a Worcestershire family,[30] was a stranger to the county. Despite his distinguished Conservative connexions,[31] his selection caused some discontent. One local newspaper of normally Conservative views expressed real regret that there had not been time to bring forward a local Conservative candidate.[32] Holland-Martin's vote diminished by 0·3 per cent against a local railwayman representing Labour[33] at an election in which the national Conservative vote increased by 4·5 per cent.[34] Holland-Martin died in 1960, and the credentials of his successor, Jasper More of Linley,[35] included ancestors who had sat for the county, Ludlow, and Bishop's Castle in the 17th century, for Shrewsbury and Bishop's Castle in the 18th century, for the Southern division from 1865 to 1868, and for the Ludlow division from 1885 to 1903.

It cannot be said that local connexions assured a seat to any Shropshire Conservative candidate who would have lost it without them, but local Conservative associations seldom saw fit to adopt those without such connexions. Even in the mid 20th century many constituency workers apparently still wished to echo the words of one of their number in 1892: 'We have had one common cause at heart and that has been to return Shropshire men to Parliament'.[36]

[19] *Who Was Who, 1929–40*, 160. Characterized as the only 'old-fashioned country landowner' in Baldwin's first cabinet: A. J. P. Taylor, *Eng. Hist. 1914–1945* (1965), 236.

[20] Burke, *Peerage* (1949), 1199; above, pp. 323, 350–1.

[21] Later influential in the Conservative party, he was cr. Ld. Poole in 1958: Burke, *Peerage* (1967), 2011.

[22] Ibid. 1181.

[23] Ld. Hartington, Ormsby-Gore's cos. and M. H. Macmillan's neph., had married Kathleen Kennedy, sis. of the future president; Ormsby-Gore's sis. was Macmillan's dau.-in-law: ibid. (1949), 594, 597, 952, 1776; *Daily Express*, 23 Sept., 23 Oct. 1961.

[24] *The Times*, 1 June 1961.

[25] A. Roth and Janice Kerbey, *Business Background of M.P.s* (1972), 38.

[26] See e.g. *Sunday Times*, 27 Oct. 1974.

[27] At Kinton, which was, however, transferred to the Shrews. constituency in 1970: S.R.O. 2320/2, p. 249; S.R.O. 2497/1, p. 438; above, p. 354.

[28] Sir L. Namier, *Structure of Politics at Accession of Geo. III* (1961), table facing p. 245.

[29] See pp. 139, 274–5, 317–18, 345; Burke, *Land. Gent.* (1952), 526–8; *V.C.H. Salop.* viii. 110.

[30] *Who Was Who, 1951–1960*, 533; Burke, *Land. Gent.* (18th edn.), i (1965), 493; *V.C.H. Worcs.* iii. 470. His banking interests provided brief parliamentary embarrassment: *The Times*, 13, 19, 26, and 28 July, 26–28 Oct., 2 Nov. 1955.

[31] He was Joint Hon. Treasurer of the Conservative party 1947–60, his colleague 1952–5 being O. B. S. Poole (D. Butler and Jennie Freeman, *Brit. Political Facts, 1900–1967* (1968), 100), and bro.-in-law to the 10th duke of Devonshire and M. H. Macmillan (Burke, *Peerage* (1967), 751).

[32] *Bridgnorth Jnl.* 28 Sept. 1951.

[33] R. J. Barker.

[34] Butler and Freeman, op. cit. 143.

[35] J. More, *A Tale of Two Houses* (Shrews. 1978), 108–10.

[36] *Bridgnorth Jnl.* 23 July 1892.

OFFICERS, SEALS, AND ARMS

LORD-LIEUTENANTS

George, earl of Shrewsbury, aptd. 1586, probably held office until 1587.[1]

Henry, earl of Pembroke, aptd. 1587,[2] d. 1601.

Edward, Baron Zouche, aptd. 1602, held office until 1607.

Ralph, Baron Eure, aptd. 1607, held office until 1617.

Thomas, Baron Gerard, aptd. Mar. 1617, held office until Nov. 1617.

William, Baron Compton (cr. earl of Northampton 1618), aptd. 1617, d. 1630.

John, earl of Bridgwater, aptd. 1631, held office until 1642[3] or 1643.[4]

Edward, Baron Lyttelton, aptd. by Parliament Mar. 1642,[5] dismissed Sept. 1642.[6]

Robert, earl of Essex (d. 1646), aptd. by Parliament 1642.[7] Under Essex, general of the Parliamentarian army 1642–5,[8] military command in Shropshire and adjacent counties devolved on Sir William Waller 1643,[9] the earl of Denbigh 1643–4,[10] and Col. Thomas Mytton 1643–5.[11] Thereafter military operations were conducted by the county committee.[12]

The Crown aptd. no successor to Bridgwater, though Lord Capel[13] seems to have exercised vestiges of the pre-war lieutenants' responsibilities in Shropshire in 1643.[14] The apt. of Prince Rupert as 'president of Wales' was under consideration Dec. 1643 × Apr. 1644 and would have included the lieutenancy of Shropshire.[15] In January 1644, however, Rupert (cr. duke of Cumberland) was aptd. lieutenant-general of North Wales, Lancashire, Cheshire, Shropshire, and Worcestershire.[16] Rupert acquired a degree of civil authority,[17] and military command in the county devolved on his lieutenant, Lord Byron, 1643–4.[18] Rupert's authority in the Marches passed to his brother Prince Maurice 1644–5.[19]

Francis, Baron Newport (cr. Viscount Newport 1675), aptd. 1660, dismissed 1687.[20]

George, Baron Jeffreys of Wem, aptd. 1687, committed to the Tower 1688.[21]

Francis, Viscount Newport (cr. earl of Bradford 1694), re-aptd. 1689, held office until 1704.[22]

Richard, Viscount Newport (succ. as earl of Bradford 1708), aptd. 1704, held office until 1712.[23]

Charles, duke of Shrewsbury, K.G., aptd. 1712, held office until 1714.[24]

Richard, earl of Bradford, re-aptd. 1714, died 1723.[25]

Henry, earl of Bradford, aptd. 1724, died 1734.[26]

Henry Arthur Herbert (cr. Baron Herbert of Chirbury 1743, earl of Powis 1748) aptd. 1735, held office until 1760.[27]

William, earl of Bath, aptd. 1761, d. 1764.[28]

Henry Arthur, earl of Powis, re-aptd. 1764, d. 1772.[29]

Robert, Baron Clive of Plassey, K.B., aptd. 1772, d. 1774.[30]

---

[1] See p. 84. Shrews. was presumably the first lieut. aptd. after the office was conceived as permanent: ibid. For earlier, temporary, lieutenancies over Salop. see ibid. and sources there cited.

[2] This and the 5 following apts. are listed in J. C. Sainty, *Lieutenants of Counties, 1585–1642* (*Bull. Inst. Hist. Res.* Special Suppl. viii), 37–8.

[3] *T.S.A.S.* 3rd ser. iii. 343; Caroline A. J. Skeel, *Council in the Marches of Wales* (1904), 150–1; below, n. 5.

[4] J. F. Rees, *Studies in Welsh Hist.* (Cardiff [1947]), 162.

[5] Nominated by Ho. of Commons 11 Feb. 1642 (*C.J.* ii. 427); predecessor's commission annulled by Parl. 5 Mar. 1642 (Sainty, *Lieuts.* 10 n.).

[6] *C.J.* ii. 756.

[7] *T.S.A.S.* 3rd ser. iii. 343–4.

[8] *D.N.B.*

[9] Serjeant-major-general of Glos., Wilts., Som., Salop., and Bristol, he was to have the assistance of the dep. lieuts. of those cos.: *D.N.B.*; *L.J.* v. 602.

[10] Commander-in-chief of Parl. forces in Warws. (incl. Coventry), Worcs., Staffs. (incl. Lichfield), and Salop.: *D.N.B.*

[11] See above, p. 112; *Dict. Welsh Biog.* 679. Mytton was sheriff 1644–6 (Blakeway, *Sheriffs*, 22) but from May 1645 his military command was exercised in N. Wales.

[12] See e.g. Owen and Blakeway, *Hist. Shrews.* i. 448 n. 3; above, pp. 112–14. Cf. D. W. Rannie, 'Cromwell's Major-Generals', *E.H.R.* x. 474, 482–3. Ludlow, the last royalist garrison in Salop., was besieged by the cttee., though it actually surrendered (May 1646) to the governor of Heref.: W. J. Farrow, *Great Civil War in Salop.* (*1642–49*) (Shrews. 1926), 94–5.

[13] Aptd. lt.-gen. of Salop., Ches., and N. Wales *c.* Mar. 1643: S.R.O. 3365/2570; *D.N.B.*; Clarendon, *Hist. of the Rebellion*, ed. W. D. Macray (1888), vi. 172 (refs. owed to Mr. H. Beaumont).

[14] i.e. the apt. of what were in effect dep. lieuts., to raise the militia: Bridgnorth boro. rec., common hall order bk. i, f. 34 (Capel's apt. of Wolryche, May 1643). In Nov. 1643 Capel was described as lt.-gen. 'under the prince' (Bodl. MS. Carte, vii, f. 637), i.e. the prince of Wales (see below, n. 16; Owen and Blakeway, *Hist. Shrews.* i. 435).

[15] Rees, *Studies in Welsh Hist.* 162–7; above, pp. 84, 107. The apt. was evidently opposed by Lds. Digby and Herbert.

[16] Rees, op. cit. 164–5; Bodl. MS. Carte, viii, ff. 528, 546; *D.N.B.* In theory Rupert was doubtless subordinate to the prince of Wales, captain-general of Wales and the Marches.

[17] e.g. the power to apt. tax commissioners: *D.N.B.* Cf. Owen and Blakeway, *Hist. Shrews.* i. 439–40, 443.

[18] Described as field marshal of Ches., Salop., and N. Wales, he was in theory subordinate to Capel: Bodl. MS. Carte, vii, f. 637. Capel, however, withdrew *c.* Dec. 1643 (Hist. MSS. Com. 27, *12th Rep. IX, Beaufort,* p. 41), and his commission was superseded (Bodl. MS. Carte, viii, f. 112). Early in 1644 Byron was said to be Rupert's lieut.: *D.N.B.* These refs. were supplied by Mr. Beaumont.

[19] *D.N.B.*; Owen and Blakeway, *Hist. Shrews.* i. 447. Rupert had been made royal commander-in-chief. Sir Wm. Vaughan was 'general' of Salop. and adjoining cos. 1644–5: *T.S.A.S.* 2nd ser. vii. 135–41; *D.N.B.*

[20] *T.S.A.S.* 3rd ser. iv. 141, 182.

[21] Ibid. 275; *D.N.B.*

[22] *T.S.A.S.* 3rd ser. iv. 278.

[23] Ibid. 284. He was the son of his predecessor in office.

[24] Ibid.

[25] Ibid. 285.

[26] Ibid. He was the son of his predecessor in office.

[27] Ibid.

[28] Ibid. 286.

[29] Ibid. 286–7.

[30] Ibid. 287–8; C 66/3739 mm. 9–10.

359

Edward, Baron Clive of Plassey, aptd. 1775, held office until 1798.[31]

George Edward Henry Arthur, earl of Powis, aptd. 1798, d. 1801.[32]

Lieutenancy in commission, 1801–4.[33]

Edward, earl of Powis, re-aptd. 1804, d. 1839.[34]

George Granville, duke of Sutherland, K.G., aptd. 1839, res. 1845.[35]

Rowland, Viscount Hill, aptd. 1845, d. 1875.[36]

Orlando George Charles, earl of Bradford, aptd. 1875, res. 1896.[37]

George Charles, earl of Powis, aptd. 1896,[38] res. 1951.[39]

Robert Clive, Viscount Bridgeman, K.B.E., C.B., D.S.O., M.C., aptd. 1951,[40] res. 1970.[41]

Lt.-Col. Arthur Heywood-Lonsdale, C.B.E., M.C., aptd. 1970,[42] res. 1974.[43]

John Robert Stratford Dugdale, aptd. 1975.[44]

CHAIRMEN OF QUARTER SESSIONS FROM 1773

Charles Baldwyn, el. 1773,[45] ceased to attend sessions 1779.[46]

Edward Pemberton, el. 1785,[47] res. 1797.[48]

Sir Corbet Corbet, Bt., el. 1798,[49] res. 1822.[50]

Thomas Pemberton, el. 1822,[51] res. 1830.[52]

The Hon. Thomas Kenyon, el. 1830,[53] res. 1850.[54]

Panton Corbett, el. 1850,[55] res. 1855.[56]

Sir Baldwin Leighton, Bt., el. 1855,[57] d. 1871.[58]

John Robert Kenyon, Q.C., el. 1871,[59] d. 1880.[60]

William Layton Lowndes, el. 1880,[61] res. 1882.[62]

Alfred Salwey, el. 1883,[63] res. 1889.[64]

Sir Offley Wakeman, Bt., el. 1889,[65] res. 1914.[66]

Robert Lloyd Kenyon, el. 1914,[67] res. 1927.[68]

The Hon. Sir William Francis Kyffin Taylor, G.B.E., K.C., el. 1927,[69] res. 1947.[70]

The Rt. Hon. Sir Wintringham Norton Stable, P.C., M.C., el. to take office in 1948,[71] res. 1967.[72]

Richard Michael Arthur Chetwynd-Talbot, el. 1967;[73] office abolished 1971.[74]

CHAIRMEN OF THE COUNTY COUNCIL

Alfred Salwey, el. 1889, res. 1893.[75]

Salusbury Kynaston Mainwaring, el. 1893, d. 1895.[76]

John Bowen Bowen-Jones (cr. bt. 1911), el. 1895, res. 1920.[77]

Lt.-Col. Henry Heywood Heywood-Lonsdale, D.S.O., T.D., el. 1920, d. 1930.[78]

Thomas Ward Green, el. 1931, res. 1943.[79]

Capt. Sir Offley Wakeman, Bt. C.B.E., el. 1943, res. 1963.[80]

William Merrill Walton Fell, el. 1963, held office until 1966.[81]

Lt.-Col. Arthur Heywood-Lonsdale, C.B.E., M.C., el. 1966, held office until 1969.[82]

---

[31] *T.S.A.S.* 3rd ser. iv. 288. He was the son of his predecessor in office and the bro.-in-law of his successor: Burke, *Peerage* (1949), 1631.

[32] *T.S.A.S.* 3rd ser. iv. 288–9.

[33] During the 2nd Ld. Clive's absence in India: above, p. 131.

[34] *T.S.A.S.* 3rd ser. iv. 289. The former Ld. Clive (lieut. 1775–98), who was cr. earl of Powis 14 May 1804, three weeks before his re-apt. as lieut.: *Complete Peerage*, x. 652–3.

[35] *T.S.A.S.* 3rd ser. iv. 290.

[36] Ibid. 291; B.L. Add. MS. 40576, ff. 183–6, 227–36 (ref. owed to Dr. J. F. A. Mason). Peel had earlier approached the duke of Cleveland.

[37] *T.S.A.S.* 3rd ser. iv. 294; S.R.O., q. sess. min. bk. 17, Mids. 1896. His wife was Disraeli's close friend: R. Blake, *Disraeli* (1966), 531–2.

[38] S.R.O. 752/4; 1665/23. Ld. Boyne (some 8,000 a.) had been considered but was thought 'hardly big enough': Hatfield Ho., MSS. of 3rd marquess of Salisbury, docket by S. K. McDonnell on letter of duke of Devonshire, 2 July 1896 (ref. owed to Dr. Mason).

[39] S.R.O. 1665/18–22, 24–28, 30, 34.

[40] S.R.O. 411/1; 1665/34.

[41] *Lond. Gaz.* 26 Mar. 1970 (p. 3524).

[42] S.R.O. 2340/1. Aptd., like his two predecessors, under the Militia Act, 1882, 45 & 46 Vic. c. 49, s. 29.

[43] S.R.O. 3231/1.

[44] S.R.O. 3405/1. Aptd. under the Local Govt. Act, 1972, c. 70, s. 218 (giving statutory recognition to the title 'lord-lieutenant').

[45] *Orders of Q. Sess.* ii. 233. Baldwyn was the first permanent chmn. For earlier chmn. see above, pp. 98, 118.

[46] *Orders of Q. Sess.* ii, preface to orders 1772–82, p. iv.

[47] Ibid. iii. 10–11.

[48] Ibid. 88. See below, n. 52.

[49] *Orders of Q. Sess.* ii, preface to orders 1772–82, p. iv; iii. 88.

[50] Ibid. iii. 229.

[51] Ibid. 228–9.

[52] Ibid. 282–3. He was neph. to Edw. Pemberton: Blakeway, *Sheriffs*, 191–2; R. C. B. Pemberton, *Pemberton Pedigrees* (Bedford, 1923), chart 16, nos. 77, 94.

[53] *Orders of Q. Sess.* iii. 283.

[54] Ibid. iv. 80. See below, n. 59.

[55] *Orders of Q. Sess.* iv. 80. Dep. chmn. 1848–9 and 1850: ibid. 68, 74, 77. Previously vice-chmn. Mont. q. sess. (res. 1845): Loton Hall MSS., Sir B. Leighton's diary, Oct. 1845.

[56] *Orders of Q. Sess.* iv. 107.

[57] Ibid. Previously acting chmn. of Mont. q. sess.

(1844–7) under C. W. Williams Wynn, and vice-chmn. (1845–7) and chmn. (1847–55) of Mont. q. sess.: Loton Hall MSS., Sir B. Leighton's diary, 4 Jan. 1844, Oct. 1845, 8 Apr. 1847, 4 Jan. 1855. Dep. chmn. Salop. q. sess. 1849–50, 1850–5: *Orders of Q. Sess.* iv. 74, 77, 80.

[58] *Orders of Q. Sess.* iv. 196.

[59] Ibid. He was the eldest son of the Hon. Thos. Kenyon: Burke, *Peerage* (1949), 1113. See also below, n. 67.

[60] *Orders of Q. Sess.* iv. 245.

[61] Ibid.

[62] Ibid. 258.

[63] Ibid.

[64] S.R.O., q. sess. min. bk. 17, 2 July 1889.

[65] Ibid.

[66] Ibid. min. bk. 19, pp. 123–4.

[67] Ibid. He was the eldest son of J. R. Kenyon: Burke, *Peerage* (1949), 1113.

[68] S.R.O., q. sess. min. bk. 20, pp. 101–2.

[69] Ibid.

[70] Ibid. min. bk. 21, pp. 253–4; S.R.O. 2696/19, pp. 1–2. Made K.B.E. 1918, G.B.E. 1929, he was cr. Ld. Maenan 1948: Burke, *Peerage* (1949), Addendum, p. 19. He d. 1951: S.R.O. 2696/19, p. 88.

[71] S.R.O., q. sess. min. bk. 21, p. 254; S.R.O. 2696/19, p. 9.

[72] S.R.O. 2696/20, p. 125. He was made a P.C. 1965: S.R.O. 1476/1. See *The Times*, 24 Nov. 1977 (obit.).

[73] S.R.O. 2696/20, p. 125. Dep. chmn. since 1950: S.R.O. 331/1.

[74] Under the Courts Act, 1971, c. 23.

[75] S.R.O. 113/1, pp. 5–6, 469. He was chmn. of q. sess. 1883–9 and d. 1902: see above; Burke, *Land. Gent.* (1952), 2238–9.

[76] *S.C.C. Mins.* 28 Oct. 1893, 4; ibid. 1895–6, 132–3; Burke, *Land. Gent.* (18th edn.), ii (1969), 421.

[77] *S.C.C. Mins.* 1895–6, 133; 1920–1, 46, 120; Burke, *Peerage* (1923), 1266. He was vice-chmn. 1889–95: S.R.O. 113/1, p. 6.

[78] *S.C.C. Mins.* 1920–1, 35; 1930–1, 302–3, 427; Burke, *Land. Gent.* (18th edn.), i (1965), 458. His father, A. P. Heywood-Lonsdale, was vice-chmn. 1895–7: *S.C.C. Mins.* 1895–6, 160; 1897–8, 478, 518.

[79] *S.C.C. Mins.* 1931–2, 2. He was vice-chmn. 1927–31, 1943–6: ibid. 1927–8, 73; 1943–4, 2; 1945–6, 345.

[80] Ibid. 1943–4, 2; 1963–4, 1–2. He was vice-chmn. 1931–43 and was made C.B.E. 1957: ibid. 1931–2, 3; Debrett, *Peerage* (1972–3), 2062.

[81] *S.C.C. Mins.* 1963–4, 1–2; 1966–7, 2.

[82] Ibid. 1966–7, 1; 1969–70, 2. He was vice-chmn. 1963–6 and was made C.B.E. 1968 and lieut. 1970: *Kelly's Handbk. to Titled, Landed and Official Classes* (1971), 967; see above.

Sir Leonard Schroeder Swinnerton Dyer, Bt., el. 1969, held office until 1972.[83]
Lt.-Col. Arthur Patrick Sykes, M.B.E., el. 1972, held office until 1974.[84]
Lt.-Col. Robert Charles Gilfrid Morris-Eyton, el. 1974,[85] held office until 1977.
Eric Charles John Whittingham, el. 1977.

CLERKS OF THE PEACE AND OF THE COUNTY COUNCIL
The clerks have been fully listed elsewhere.[86]

COUNTY TREASURERS (LATER BANKERS)
Richard Davis, aptd. 1739,[87] d. 1748.[88]
Isaac Pritchard, aptd. 1748,[89] d. 1764.[90]
John Flint (Corbett from 1804), el. 1764,[91] d. 1806.[92]
Joshua Peele, el. 1807,[93] res. 1829.[94]
Joshua John Peele, aptd. 1829,[95] d. 1873.[96]
Edmund Cresswell Peele, aptd. 1873,[97] res. 1886.[98]
George Moultrie Salt, aptd. 1886,[99] res. 1906.[1]
Arthur Gill, aptd. 1906,[2] d. 1923.[3]

In 1923 the treasurership was granted to Barclays Bank Ltd., Shrewsbury.[4] In 1946, after the renewal of the banking contract with Barclays Bank Ltd., the bank's apt. as treasurer was ended and the title of treasurer was conferred on the county accountant.[5]

COUNTY TREASURERS (FORMERLY COUNTY ACCOUNTANT, FORMERLY COUNTY FINANCIAL CLERK)
William Baxter, aptd. county financial clerk 1889,[6] retired 1925.[7]
Percy John Crawley, aptd. county accountant 1925,[8] named county treasurer 1946,[9] retired 1950.[10]
Leonard Copplestone, aptd. 1950,[11] retired 1974.[12]
Ronald Richard Renville, aptd. to take office in 1974.[13]

COUNTY SURVEYORS
Thomas Telford, aptd. 1788,[14] d. 1834.[15]
Edward Haycock, aptd. 1834, res. 1866.[16]
Thomas Groves, aptd. 1866, d. 1886.[17]
William Norman Swettenham, aptd. 1887,[18] apt. terminated 1889.[19]
Alfred Thomas Davis, aptd. 1889, res. 1923.[20]
William Henry Butler, aptd. to take office in 1924, retired 1948.[21]
George Cyril Cowie, aptd. 1948, retired 1964.[22]
Raymond John Mare, M.C., aptd. 1964.[23]

COUNTY SEAL
In 1824 quarter sessions ordered the striking of a seal bearing the words 'County of Salop'[24] for purposes specified in the Gaols Act, 1824.[25] It is probably to be identified with a circular die,[26] 1¼ in. in diameter, displaying a royal crown over an escutcheon of arms of three leopards' faces all within the words 'Clerk of the Peace's Office'; outside a border of dots is the legend, sans-serif: THE SEAL OF THE COUNTY OF SALOP.

SALOP COUNTY COUNCIL: SEALS
In 1889 the county council resolved to have a common seal displaying the coats of arms of the Shropshire boroughs set round the 'county arms' in the centre.[27] The circular die,[28] 2½ in. in diameter, displays centrally on a diapered background over the enscrolled word 'Salop' an escutcheon of arms of three leopards' faces; above, surmounting the enscrolled word 'Shrewsbury', is a smaller escutcheon of the same arms followed clockwise around the central escutcheon by others charged with the arms of the boroughs of Ludlow, Wenlock, Bishop's Castle, Oswestry, and Bridgnorth, an intertwining scroll naming each borough beneath its escutcheon. Outside an embattled border is the legend, sans-serif: SIGILLUM COMMUNE CONCILII COMITATUS SALOPIENSIS.

In 1896 a new seal was struck.[29] The circular die,[30]

[83] S.C.C. Mins. 1969-70, 1; 1972-3, 2. He was vice-chmn. 1966-9: ibid. 1966-7, 2.
[84] Ibid. 1972-3, 1; 1973-4, 1. He was vice-chmn. 1969-72: ibid. 1969-70, 3.
[85] Ibid. 1974-5, 2. He was chmn. (1973-4) of the provisional co. council est. 12 Apr. 1973 and established under the Local Govt. Act, 1972, c. 70, s. 18: Co. Council of Salop Mins. 1973-4, 69.
[86] Sir E. Stephens, Clerks of the Counties, 1360-1960 (1961), 151-3; idem, Clerks of the Counties: a Suppl. 1960-74, ed. P. McCall (n.d.), sub Salop.
[87] Orders of Q. Sess. ii. 99. He was aptd. under the provisions of the Co. Rates Act, 1738, 12 Geo. II, c. 29.
[88] S.P.R. Lich. xvi. 1114.
[89] Orders of Q. Sess. ii. 125.
[90] Ibid. 192.   [91] Ibid.
[92] Ibid. iii, pp. viii, 135.
[93] Ibid. He was the grandson of his predecessor in office.
[94] Ibid. pp. viii, 277.
[95] Ibid. He was the son of his predecessor in office: S.P.L., MS. 2794, p. 489.
[96] Orders of Q. Sess. iii, p. viii.
[97] Ibid. iv. 212. He was the son of his predecessor in office (S.P.L., MS. 2794, p. 489) and previously dep. co. treasurer (e.g. Eddowes's Jnl. 16 Oct. 1872).
[98] Orders of Q. Sess. iv. 274.
[99] Ibid. 275. He was cos. to his predecessor in office, their mothers (nées Moultrie) being sis.: S.P.L., MS. 2794, pp. 489, 620-1; S.P.R. Heref. ix. 270, 272.
[1] S.C.C. Mins. 1906-7, 77.
[2] Ibid. 78, 86-7. He was branch manager of a bank eventually merged in Barclays Bank Ltd.: Kelly's Dir. Salop. (1905; 1909; 1917); Shrews. Chron. 3 Aug. 1923.
[3] Then ld. of the man. of Ford: Shrews. Chron. 3 Aug. 1923; V.C.H. Salop. viii. 230.
[4] S.C.C. Mins. 1923-4, 215, 286.
[5] Ibid. 1946-7, 79.
[6] S.C.C. Mins. Finance and Gen. Purposes Cttee. rep. 10 Aug. 1889.
[7] Shrews. Chron. 13 Feb., 8 May 1925.
[8] S.C.C. Mins. 1925-6, 148, 154.
[9] Ibid. 1946-7, 79.
[10] Ibid. 1949-50, 350.
[11] Ibid.
[12] Ibid. 1973-4, 391.
[13] Co. Council of Salop Mins. 1973-4, 75, 89.
[14] See p. 127.
[15] Sir A. Gibb, Story of Telford (1935), 23, 289.
[16] Orders of Q. Sess. iii. 301; iv. 173.
[17] Ibid. iv. 173, 279.
[18] Ibid. 279.
[19] S.C.C. Mins. Officers &c. Cttee. rep. 23 Mar. 1889; S.R.O. 113/1, p. 21.
[20] S.R.O. 113/1, pp. 32-3; S.C.C. Mins. 1923-4, 135, 190, 209.
[21] S.C.C. Mins. 1923-4, 210, 221; 1947-8, 392.
[22] Ibid. 1947-8, 392; 1948-9, 2, 8; 1963-4, 430.
[23] Ibid. 1964-5, 51.
[24] S.R.O., q. sess. Auditing Cttee. and Finance Cttee. rep. bk. 1824-37, pp. 9-10.
[25] i.e. for authenticating the passes of discharged prisoners: 5 Geo. IV, c. 85, s. 23.
[26] S.R.O. 2696/35.
[27] Shrews. Chron. 5 Apr. 1889.
[28] S.R.O. 950/1. For a description and for heraldic and aesthetic objections to the design see A. C. Fox-Davies's remarks in T.S.A.S. 2nd ser. viii. 15, 19-20.
[29] Shrews. Chron. 31 July 1896. It was to be used from the council meeting of 7 Nov. 1896.
[30] S.R.O. 950/2. Illustrated in T.S.A.S. 2nd ser. xii. 45.

2½ in. in diameter, displays an escutcheon of the newly granted arms of the council over the enscrolled motto 'Floreat Salopia'. Legend, Roman, within a border of roundles: SIGILLUM COMMUNE CONCILII COMITATUS SALOPIENSIS. The die was defaced in 1959.[31]

A third seal, struck to replace that described above, is circular, 2¼ in. in diameter;[32] it shows the council's arms encircled by the legend, Roman: SIGILLVM COMMVNE CONCILII COMITATVS SALOPIENSIS.

SALOP COUNTY COUNCIL: ARMS

In 1896, after criticism of the county council's assumption that the arms of the borough of Shrewsbury constituted also the 'county arms',[33] the council applied for,[34] and was granted,[35] a coat of arms. The grant owed much to the energy and generosity of Sir Offley Wakeman, a county councillor and chairman of quarter sessions. The council was the second county council to obtain such a grant.[36]

SALOP COUNTY COUNCIL: INSIGNIA

In 1950 a chairman's badge of office was presented to the county council by its vice-chairman and one of the county's leading farmers, Alderman T. C. Ward of Lubstree Park. The badge, worked in 9 ct. and 18 ct. gold, displays the arms of the county council in enamel over the motto 'Floreat Salopia'; surrounding the arms are the words 'Chairman' and 'Salop County Council' embellished with wheat ears and oak leaves symbolic of the farms and woodlands of Shropshire; over all is a mural crown flanked by two flowers. The badge, suspended on a blue ribbon, has been worn by the chairman when presiding at council meetings or attending civic functions, and on other ceremonial occasions.[37]

OTHER SEALS

Ludlow was *caput* of the earldom of March (abolished 1490) and permanent headquarters of the Council in the Marches of Wales (abolished 1689), both of which had official seals.[38] At Shrewsbury in 1473, after Edward IV's conference with the marcher lords about peace-keeping in the marches, the earldom 'Seal of the Marches' was put to indentures of agreement which had been concluded between the king and the lords.[39] The seal of the Council in the Marches of Wales was kept by one of the council's oldest-established officers, the clerk of the signet.[40] An impression of Charles II's reign[41] is circular, 1⅞ in. in diameter, showing the royal arms encircled by the Garter inscribed with the order's motto; below, on a scroll, are the words 'Concilium Marchiar:'; above between the initials C and R, are the royal crown and the ostrich feathers of the prince of Wales; around all and within a carved border are the enscrolled name and abbreviated titles of Charles II. The silver, ivory-handled matrix was acquired for Ludlow Museum in 1970.[42]

The sheriffs of Shropshire do not seem to have had an official seal, each sheriff using his private, armorial seal instead.[43]

SALOP COUNTY COUNCIL. *Erminois three piles azure, two issuant from the chief and one in base, each charged with a leopard's head or*

[31] S.R.O. 1403/1, 19 Mar. 1959 (p. 9).
[32] Brought into use on 26 Feb. 1959 (ibid.), it was still in use in 1977 (inf. from S.C.C.). Designed by the co. architect, the seal was executed by Shaw & Sons: S.R.O. 1403/1, 9 Oct. 1958 (p. 8).
[33] See above, and above, n. 28.
[34] *Shrews. Chron.* 8 May 1896.
[35] *T.S.A.S.* 2nd ser. xii. 45–7; S.R.O. 752/5. In 1974 the arms were confirmed to the new co. council (ibid., endorsement of 20 June 1975) in accordance with the Local Govt. Act, 1972, c. 70, s. 247.
[36] *Genealogical Mag.* ii. 33; *Shrews. Chron.* 8 May 1896.
[37] S.C.C. Co. Secretary's Dept., file GP 710; *Shrews. Chron.* 3 Mar. 1950. Designed by C. J. Shiner of Edgbaston, in association with C. W. McIntosh, dep. co. architect, the badge was executed by Dodd & Walters of Birm.
[38] See pp. 44 n. 58, 80.

[39] R. A. Griffiths, 'Wales and the Marches', *Fifteenth-cent. Eng. 1399–1509*, ed. S. B. Chrimes *et al.* (1974), 160.
[40] Penry Williams, *Council in the Marches of Wales under Eliz. I* (Cardiff, 1958), 14, 149, 159. In the early 17th cent. the seal does not seem to have itinerated with the ld. president: ibid. 302.
[41] B.L. seals, D.C., A 144; illustrated in R. H. C[live], *Documents connected with the Hist. of Ludlow, and the Lds. Marchers* (1841), 189. Cf. W. de G. Birch, *Cat. of Seals in B.M.* ii. 226.
[42] It had belonged to the Charltons of Ludford (descendants of a ch. justice of Chester *temp.* Chas. II) and the Leightons of Sweeney. See *Ludlow Adv.* 20 Aug. 1970. *T.S.A.S.* 2nd ser. vii. 30; G. Ormerod, *Hist. of Co. of Chester* (1882), i. 65–6) and the Leightons of Sweeney. See *Ludlow Adv.* 20 Aug. 1970.
[43] H. Jenkinson, *Guide to Seals in P.R.O.* (1968), 51–2; Blakeway, *Sheriffs*, 236 and n. 1.

INDEX

NOTE. The following abbreviations used in the index, sometimes with the addition of the letter *s* to form the plural, may require elucidation: Alf., Alfred; agric., agricultural, agriculture; Alex., Alexander; And., Andrew; Ant., Anthony; apt., appointed; Art., Arthur; archbp., archbishop; archd., archdeacon; assoc., association; b., born; Bart., Bartholomew; Benj., Benjamin; boro., borough; bp., bishop; bro., brother; bur., buried; *c., circa*; capt., captain; cast., castle; cath., cathedral, catholic(-ism); ch., chief, church; Chas., Charles; chmn., chairman; Chris., Christopher; clk., clerk; co., company, county; coll., college; com., commission; const., constable; ct., court; ctss., countess; cttee., committee; d., died; dau., daughter; dchss., duchess; dioc., diocese; dist., district; divn., division; Edm., Edmund; educ., education; Edw., Edward; electn., election; Eliz., Elizabeth; Eng., England, English; fam., family; fl., flourished; Fra., Francis; Fred., Frederick; Geo., George; Geof., Geoffrey; Gilb., Gilbert; govt., government; gt., great; Hen., Henry; Herb., Herbert; Heref., Hereford; ho., house; hosp., hospital; Humph., Humphrey; hund., hundred; ind., industry; insp., inspection, inspector; Irel., Ireland; J.P., justice of the peace; Jas., James; Jos., Joseph; ld., lord; lib., liberty; Lichf., Lichfield; lieut., lieutenant; m., married; M.P., member of Parliament; Mat., Matthew; mchnss., marchioness; Mic., Michael; mkt., market; *n*, note; Nic., Nicholas; nonconf., nonconformist, nonconformity; par., parish; parl., parliament(-arian, -ary); Phil., Philip; Pk., Park; prot., protestant; q.sess., quarter sessions; Revd., Reverend; Ric., Richard; rlwy., railway; Rob., Robert; Rog., Roger; Rom., Roman; s., son; S.C.C., Salop County Council; Sam., Samuel; sch., school; sess., sessions; Sim., Simon; sis., sister; sjt., serjeant; Steph., Stephen; supt., superintendent; Thos., Thomas; Tim., Timothy; univ., university; vct., viscount; Wal., Walter; Wm., William; w., wife.

A page number in italics denotes an illustration; a dagger (†) with a page number indicates a plate facing that page.

CORRIGENDA TO VOLUMES I AND II

Earlier corrigenda to Volume I were published in Volume II, pp. 315–20. In references to pages printed in more than one column 'a', 'b', and 'c' following a page number denote the first, second, and third column.

Vol. I, page 276, line 57, *for* 'viii, 266' *read* 'vii, 5'
,, ,, 276, line 59, *for* '96' *read* '93'
,, ,, 405, line 28, *for* 'of the' *read* 'of a supposed'
,, ,, 423b, line 17, *for* 'Bridgnorth' *read* 'Shrewsbury'
,, ,, 424a, line 21, *before* 'now' *add* 'formerly at Vaughan's Mansion and', *and for* 'school of art' *read* 'technical school'
,, ,, 424a, line 23, *delete* 'at Vaughan's Mansion,'
Vol. II, page xx, line 26 and *passim, for* 'Salop. Peace Roll, 1404–14' *read* 'Salop. Peace Roll, 1400–14'
,, ,, xx, line 26, *for* 'Shropshire Peace Roll, 1404–14' *read* 'Shropshire Peace Roll, 1400–14'
,, ,, 24, *delete* Salop deanery boundary where Whitchurch ancient parish enters Cheshire
,, ,, 24, *move* Newport deanery boundary to include Eyton upon the Weald Moors and Preston upon the Weald Moors
,, ,, 46b, line 30, *for* 'died' *read* 'dead by'
,, ,, 48b, line 15, *for* 'Richard' *read* 'Roger'
,, ,, 52, note 34, *for* 'vii' *read* 'viii'
,, ,, 62b, line 34, *for* 'son' *read* 'stepson'
,, ,, 65a, line 18, *for* '1350' *read* '1354'
,, ,, 67a, line 31, *for* '1354' *read* '1355'
,, ,, 73, note 52, *for* '94, 128' *read* '84, 94'
,, ,, 74, note 81, line 1, *for* '70–70v.' *read* '97–97v.'
,, ,, 74, note 81, line 2, *for* 'just' *read* 'shortly'
,, ,, 77b, lines 9–10, *for* '1523 to Robert Watson, the last abbot,' *read* '1518 to Abbot Cockerell'
,, ,, 78, note 56, line 2, *for* 'v' *read* 'vi'
,, ,, 79b, line 41, *for* 'resigned 1499' *read* 'resigned by 1499'
,, ,, 79b, line 42, *for* 'Beyton, elected 1499' *read* 'Berton, elected by 1499'
,, ,, 79, note 4, *delete* '169.'
,, ,, 84b, line 45, *after* '1491' *add* 'or 1492'
,, ,, 106, note 16, *for* '74' *read* '174'
,, ,, 123b, line 15, *for* 'that' *read* 'than'
,, ,, 125b, line 11, *for* '1291' *read* '1290'
,, ,, 142a, line 24, *for* 'then' *read* 'a former'
,, ,, 152, note 13, *for* '106' *read* '156'
,, ,, 164a, line 39, *for* '1744' *read* '1746'
,, ,, 170a, line 43, *for* 'Bailey' *read* 'Bayley'
,, ,, 170b, line 10, *for* 'C.T.' *read* 'C.J.'
,, ,, 170, note 32, *for* 'Eddowes's' *read* 'Salop.'
,, ,, 170, note 38, *for* 'C.T.' *read* 'C.J.'
,, ,, 172a, line 33, *for* 'Smyth' *read* 'Smythe'
,, ,, 192a, last line, *after* 'Agricultural' *add* 'Reading'
,, ,, 192b, line 35, *for* '1859' *read* '1858'
,, ,, 194, note 1, *for* 'Thorneycroft' *read* 'Thornycroft'
,, ,, 204, lines 32–3, *for* 'in 1831' *read* 'and the divisions of hundreds, as they appear in the 1831 *Census Report*,'
,, ,, 205, line 25, *for* 'Oswestry, and Wenlock' *read* 'and Oswestry'
,, ,, 205, line 26, *for* 'and Shrewsbury' *read* ', Shrewsbury, and Wenlock'
,, ,, 207, *s.v.* 'Bradford South', col. 1, *delete* 'Longdon upon Tern'
,, ,, 207, *s.v.* 'Bradford South', col. 1, *before entry* 'Sheriffhales' *add new entry* 'Preston upon the Weald Moors'
,, ,, 207, *s.v.* 'Bradford South', col. 2, *for* 'Preston upon the Weald Moors' *read* 'Longdon upon Tern'
,, ,, 207, *for last sentence read* 'Preston upon the Weald Moors and Longdon upon Tern are shown in their correct divisions (as above) in the 1841 *Census Report*.'
,, ,, 209, line 17, *before* 'Shipton' *add* 'the greater part of'
,, ,, 209, line 20, *before* 'Shipton' *add* 'the greater part of'
,, ,, 209, *s.v.* 'Oswestry', *before entry* 'Felton, West' *add new entry* 'Ellesmere (part of) [32a]'
,, ,, 209, *after note 32 add new note* '[32a] i.e. Dudleston chapelry. Remainder in Pimhill Hundred and Flintshire.'
,, ,, 209, note 38, *after* 'in' *add* 'Oswestry Hundred and'
,, ,, 209, note 41, *delete* ', Leaton, and Wollascott'
,, ,, 210, line 18, *for* 'The' *read* 'Purslow'
,, ,, 210, line 18, *delete* 'Clun Hundred and'
,, ,, 211, note 62, *delete* ', Leaton, and Wollascott'
,, ,, 215, line 3, *for* 'was' *read* ',' *and for* 'until it' *read* ','
,, ,, 220, *s.v.* 'Bishop's Castle bor.', *for* '2,805' *in the 1871 column read* '1,805'
,, ,, 229, note d, *for* 'Whitchurch U.S.D.' *read* 'The district', *and delete* 'until 1895'
,, ,, 230, line 12, *for* 'West' *read* 'North'
,, ,, 230, line 14, *after* 'Bradford,' *add* 'Chirbury,'
,, ,, 238, col. 2, *s.v.* 'Algar', *delete* 'Earl,' *and* ', 348–9'
,, ,, 238b, *after entry* 'Algar' *add new entry* 'Algar, Earl, T.R.E., 348–9'
,, ,, 238c, *after entry* 'Astley' *add new entry* 'Aston (*Estune*) in Church Stoke (Mont.), 318'
,, ,, 238c, *s.v.* 'Benthall', *for* 'Much Wenlock' *read* 'Alberbury'
,, ,, 239a, *after* 'Burertone' *add new entry* 'Burford (*Bureford*), 344'
,, ,, 240a, *s.v.* 'Edernion', *for* 'Edernion' *read* 'Edeyrnion'
,, ,, 240b, *s.v.* 'Estone', *for* 'Bottereu' *read* 'Botterell'
,, ,, 240b, *delete entry* 'Estune (unidentified)'
,, ,, 240c, *after entry* 'Forton' *add new entry* 'Fouswardine (*Fuloordie*) in Sidbury, 318'
,, ,, 240c, *s.v.* 'Fuloordie', *for* '(unidentified), 324' *read* 'see Fouswardine'
,, ,, 240c, *s.v.* 'Gislord', *for* 'Gislord' *read* 'Gislold'
,, ,, 240c, *after entry* 'Goisfrid' *add new entries* 'Golding (*Goldene*) in Cound, 320' *and* '*Goseford* (unidentified), 318'
,, ,, 241a, *after entry* 'Hopesay' *add new entry* 'Hopton (*Hoptune*) in Church Stoke (Mont.), 318'

CORRIGENDA TO VOLUMES I AND II

Vol. II, page 241*a, s.v.* 'Hoptune', *for* '(unidentified), 318' *read* ', *see* Hopton'
   „   „   241*b, s.v.* 'Lawley', *for* '*Lanelei*' *read* '*Lauelei*'
   „   „   241*c, s.v.* 'Leintwardine', *after* '336' *add* ', 345'
   „   „   242*b, s.v.* 'Newtone', *for* '*Newtone*' *read* '*Newetone*'
   „   „   243*c, s.v.* 'Steele', *for* 'Press' *read* 'Prees'
   „   „   248*c, s.v.* 'Aston, in Wellington', *delete sub-entry* 'Overley Hill'
   „   „   251*a, after entry* 'Berth' *add new entry* 'Berton, Geof., Abbot of Lilleshall, ii. 79'
   „   „   251*b, delete entry* 'Beyton'
   „   „   252*a, s.v.* 'Blackfordby, Swarteclyve', *for* '11' *read* 'ii'
   „   „   254*c, s.v.* 'Brockton (formerly Staffs.)', *for* 'formerly Staffs.' *read* 'Staffs.; Salop. 1895–1965'
   „   „   258*c, s.v.* 'Chirbury Hundred', *after* '221' *add* ', 230'
   „   „   259*c, s.v.* 'Clive, Hen. Bailey', *for* 'Bailey' *read* 'Bayley'
   „   „   264*c, s.v.* 'Dudleston, chap.', *after* '5 *n*,' *add* '209 *n*,'
   „   „   266*a, s.v.* 'Ellesmere, town hall', *after* 'i.' *add* '198,'
   „   „   267*a, s.v.* 'Eyton' (*surname*), *delete sub-entry* 'Ric., son of Mat. of', *and before sub-entry* 'Thos. (fl. 1538)' *add*
                 new sub-entry 'Rog., son of Mat. of, *see* Roger *clericus*'
   „   „   272*b, s.v.* 'Haygate', *for* '*see* Wellington' *read* 'in Wellington and Wrockwardine, i. 268'
   „   „   273*a, after entry* 'High Rocks' *add new entry* 'Higher Kempley, *see* Kempley, Higher'
   „   „   274*a, after entry* 'Hopton Castle' *add new entry* 'Hopton Gate, *see* Downton, in Stanton Lacy'
   „   „   278*a, s.v.* 'Leaton, in St. Mary's', *for* ', ii. 209 *n*, 211 *n*' *read* ','
   „   „   279*b, s.v.* 'Lilleshall Abbey, muniments, treasurer's rolls', *after* '20' *add* ', 76'
   „   „   281*a, after entry* 'Longslow' *add new entry* 'Longville, Cheney, *see* Cheney Longville'
   „   „   283*a, s.v.* 'Madeley, man.', *after* '466' *add* ', 467'
   „   „   286*a, s.v.* 'Morris', *for* 'C.T.' *read* 'C.J.'
   „   „   288*b, after entry* 'North Molton' *add new entry* 'North Regiment of Shropshire Local Militia, ii. 230'
   „   „   288*c, after entry* 'Oak Hill Castle Ring' *add new entry* 'Oakeley, *see* Lea and Oakeley'
   „   „   290*a, s.v.* 'Overley Hill', *for* '*see* Aston, in Wellington' *read* 'in Wellington and Wrockwardine, i. 268'
   „   „   293*b, s.v.* 'Puleston, Sir Ric. (d. 1840)', *for* '11' *read* 'ii'
   „   „   294*b, delete entry* 'Richard *clericus*'
   „   „   295*a, before entry* 'Roger Fitz Corbet' *add new entry* 'Roger *clericus* (son of Mat. of Eyton), ii. 48'
   „   „   298*a, s.v.* 'Sheriffhales', *delete* 'formerly'
   „   „   299*c, s.v.* 'Shrewsbury' (*town*), *after sub-entry* 'Technical Coll.' *add new sub-entry* 'Technical Sch., i. 424'
   „   „   301*c, s.v.* 'Shropshire Militia', *after* 'and see' *add* 'North Regiment of Shropshire Local Militia;', *and at end*
                 delete '; West Regiment'
   „   „   301*c, after entry* 'Shropshire Wanderers' *add new entry* 'Shuffnall, *see* Shifnal'
   „   „   301*c, delete entry* 'Shuttnol'
   „   „   302*b, s.v.* 'Smith-Stanier', *add sub-entry* 'and see Stanier'
   „   „   303*a, s.v.* 'Stanier', *add sub-entry* 'and see Smith, Hubert'
   „   „   308*c, s.v.* 'Wellington', *delete sub-entry* 'Haygate'
   „   „   309*a, s.v.* 'Wellington, and see', *after* 'Hadley, New;' *add* 'Haygate;' *and after* 'Newdale;' *add* 'Overley Hill;'
   „   „   309*c, s.vv.* 'Wenlock Agricultural Society' *and* 'Wenlock Olympian Society', *after* 'Agricultural' *add*
                 'Reading'
   „   „   310*a, delete entry* 'West Regiment (militia)'
   „   „   310*c, s.v.* 'Whitchurch, hosp.', *after* 'hosp.' *add* '(supposed)'
   „   „   312*b, s.v.* 'Wollascott', *for* ', ii. 209 *n*, 211 *n*' *read* ':'
   „   „   313*c, s.v.* 'Wrockwardine, and see', *after* 'Cluddley;' *add* 'Haygate;' *and after* 'Orleton;' *add* 'Overley Hill;'